Relentless Reformer

Politics and Society in Twentieth-Century America

SERIES EDITORS
WILLIAM CHAFE, GARY GERSTLE, LINDA GORDON, AND JULIAN ZELIZER

RECENT BOOKS IN THE SERIES

Relentless Reformer

JOSEPHINE ROCHE AND PROGRESSIVISM
in Twentieth-Century America

ROBYN MUNCY

PRINCETON UNIVERSITY PRESS
PRINCETON & OXFORD

press.princeton.edu

Cover photograph by Chase LTD., Photography, the George Meany Memorial AFL-CIO
Archives, Special Collections & University Archives, University of Maryland Libraries.
Photograph © AFL-CIO, used with permission.

ISBN 978–0-691–12273–1

Library of Congress Control Number: 2014935546

British Library Cataloging-in-Publication Data is available

This book has been composed in Sabon LT Std, Folio Std, and Egyptienne Becker

Printed on acid-free paper. ∞

Printed in the United States of America

10 9 8 7 6 5 4 3 2 1

FOR MOM, DAD, AND MER

CONTENTS

PART III

SECOND BURST OF PROGRESSIVE REFORM: HEIGHT OF ROCHE'S RENOWN, 1933–1948

PART IV

SECOND TEMPORARY REVERSAL OF PROGRESSIVE REFORM: ROCHE BUILDS A PRIVATE WELFARE SYSTEM IN THE COALFIELDS, 1948–1963

PART V

THIRD BURST OF PROGRESSIVE REFORM: ROCHE RECLAIMS THE FULL PROGRESSIVE AGENDA, 1960–1976

ACKNOWLEDGMENTS

I could write nearly as long a story of my adventures researching Josephine Roche's life as I wrote about her life itself. Susan Ware was the first person who encouraged me to pursue a full biography of Roche. She set me on the path by contracting an entry on Roche for *Notable American Women* (Belknap Press, 2004). Susan has since read proposals and conference papers about Roche and at every point offered sound advice and effective encouragement. Thank you, Susan. I also want to thank here a particular labor historian, who, when I informed him I might write a book on Josephine Roche, referred to her as a "toady" of John L. Lewis. That description was so at odds with everything I had learned about Roche to that point that it gave me extra incentive to take the plunge into biography.

As every historian does, I have depended on many archivists and librarians. Special thanks to Walter Bowman at the State of Kentucky Archives; Larry DeWitt at the Social Security Administration Archives in Baltimore; Michael Hussey at the National Archives in College Park; Barry Kernfeld in the Labor History Collection at the Pennsylvania State University Libraries; Carol Leadenham and Ron Bulatoff at the Hoover Institution; William LeFevre at Wayne State University's Walter P. Reuther Library and Archives; Halyna Myroniuk at the University of Minnesota's Immigration History Research Center; Gayle Richardson in the Manuscripts Division of the Huntington Library; Michael Ridderbusch at the University of West Virginia Libraries; Cynthia Rand in the Denver Public Library's Western History Collection; Angie Reinecke in the Archives at the University of Wisconsin, Platteville; Dean Rogers at Vassar College's Special Collections; Ellen Shea at Radcliffe's Schlesinger Library; Frank Tapp at the Auraria Library in Denver; Eileen Witte in the Vassar College Alumnae Office; and all the wonderful archivists at the Franklin D.

Roosevelt Presidential Library in Hyde Park, New York, especially Bob Clark. The biggest shout-out goes to David Hays at the University of Colorado at Boulder for years and years of help with Roche's own papers and other collections in the Archives of the Norlin Library.

For special efforts in providing photographs, thank you to Jennifer Sanchez of the University of Colorado Libraries, Coi E. Drummond-Gehrig of the Denver Public Library, Melissa VanOtterloo of the Stephen H. Hart Library and Research Center in Denver, and John G. Lewis.

Dr. George Strassler of Neligh, Nebraska, deserves a chapter of thanks. On behalf of the Antelope County Historical Society, he responded to a query I sent in June 2007, and we have been corresponding ever since. George provided photographs of nineteenth-century Neligh and dug up information on Roche's family that I never could have located myself. He spent hours mining newspapers and public records in Neligh as well as Omaha. Collaborating with him has been one of the unexpected delights of this project, and I thank him profoundly for the material aid as well as his enthusiasm for the biography.

For sharing her own work on Josephine Roche, thanks to Rachel Greenfield, and for eagerness to have the book in her hand, the same to Sally Greenberg, executive director of the National Consumers' League.

Thanks, too, for financial support from several institutions. The University of Maryland at College Park supported two semester-long sabbaticals and the University's Graduate Research Board a semester's research leave. The Franklin D. Roosevelt Presidential Library offered a travel grant, and the Woodrow Wilson International Center for Scholars a fellowship in 2007–2008. I began writing the biography at the Center, which invited me back as a Public Policy Scholar in summer 2009. The Center was the best imaginable place to write and connected me with Angela Cavalucci and Kristen Kelley, who were superb research assistants.

Many people have read chapters, conference papers, and articles that were part of this project. For their help, thanks to Edward Berkowitz, Miriam Cohen, Thomas Dublin, Maureen Flanagan, Gary Gerstle, Paul Gibson, Marie Gottschalk, Jacquelyn Dowd Hall, Edward Linenthal, Clare Lyons, Laura Mayhall, Sonya Michel, Sidney Milkis, Becky Muncy, Bob Muncy, Meredith Muncy, Elisabeth Perry, Tess Speranza, Tony Speranza, Landon Storrs, Leslie Woodcock Tentler, and Susan Ware. A special thanks to Richard Mulcahy, who knows more about the United Mine Workers of America Welfare and Retirement Fund than anyone else on earth and read more than one draft of my thinking about the fund. Joyous thanks to my draft reading group from the Wilson Center for monthly food and fellowship since 2007. This devoted group of scholars, activists, and friends has read drafts of many chapters: Marie-Therese "MT" Connolly, Mary Ellen Curtin, Matthew Dallek, Deirdre Moloney,

Philippa Strum, Patricia Sullivan, Wendy Williams, and Salim Yaqub. For reading the entire manuscript when it was much longer than the book version, thanks beyond words to Linda Gordon, Chuck Myers, and an anonymous reader for Princeton University Press. You dramatically improved the final product. Thank you, too, to anyone I have inadvertently omitted from the list.

I so appreciate the help and support of Princeton University Press. Brigitta van Rheinberg first signed the project when it was only a glimmer in my eye; Chuck Myers took a full draft to the Board of Editors; and Eric Crahan has brought it the last mile with crucial technical and administrative help from the remarkable Eric Henney and Ellen Foos and copy editor Jennifer Harris. Many, many thanks to each of you. I am thrilled to place Roche's biography in the Politics and Society in Twentieth-Century America Series at Princeton. Thanks especially to series editors Linda Gordon and Gary Gerstle for their support of the project since its inception.

In the course of researching Roche's life, I have had the pleasure of talking to or corresponding with several people who knew her or who could direct me to people who did. For those conversations, thanks especially to Gerald R. Armstrong, Mary Beth Corrigan, Earl Dotter, Daniel Edelman, Clarice Feldman, and William E. Owens. Mary Beth put me in touch with Earl Dotter, a photojournalist and former VISTA volunteer who photographed Roche in the 1970s and allowed me not only to see and use his beautiful photographs but also to sit in his home and peruse his collection of union newspapers.

The most amazing research story connected to this biography began in a conversation with Daniel Edelman, who met Roche toward the end of her career, when she was under fire from miners dissatisfied with her administration of the United Mine Workers of America Welfare and Retirement Fund. He suggested I contact Gerald Armstrong, who in the late twentieth century served as president of Roche's former coal company, Rocky Mountain Fuel, and who knew Roche well in her last years. In a telephone conversation, Gerry then revealed that he suspected there might be valuable materials related to Roche among the papers of Read Lewis, who had been Roche's friend from the 1910s until her death in the 1970s. Gerry helped me figure out a way to locate members of Read Lewis's family. The first person I reached was David Johnson, Read Lewis's grand-nephew, who confirmed that his uncle, Harmon Lewis, held Read's papers at his home in New Hampshire. On David's recommendation, Harmon agreed to let me look through the papers just in case they might contain anything from or about Josephine Roche. In fall 2009, David accompanied me to Harmon's home, where we all three went to the attic and, as rain pattered down on the roof above us, opened box after box of Read's papers. In the course of that magical afternoon, we discovered over 300 letters between Josephine Roche and Read Lewis. Since Roche had purged personal information from her own manuscript collection, this set of letters took me closer to Roche's heart and soul than any other source. Thank you so very, very much to Harmon and David for a thrilling research adventure as well as access to such a rich source on Josephine Roche. Thanks, too, to John G. Lewis, Harmon's son, who has since that revelatory afternoon devoted much time and care to making sure I had everything I needed from the Read Lewis Papers.

There is no way adequately to thank my family and closest friends for putting up with this project for a decade. Fran Dolan, thank you for weekly conversations about Roche and the writing process and everything else in life. You helped me hang in when the joy of discovery disappeared into the drudgery of revision. To Tony Speranza and Tess Speranza, thank you for ten years of nearly daily conversations about Josephine Roche, for taking on extra domestic burdens during my research trips, and for reading chapters. I regret that I could not incorporate all of your suggestions in the final manuscript, especially the ones that would have made it juicier and more interactive. I loved every one of your ideas and will be forever grateful for your encouragement and engagement with the project. My parents, Bob and Becky Muncy, and my sister, Meredith Muncy, have also read chapters, talked with me endlessly about Roche, visited with their own friends about Roche, and assumed I really would finish the book when I was not so sure. I dedicate this biography to the three of them, utterly insufficient compensation for a lifetime of confidence, spirit, and love.

Relentless Reformer

INTRODUCTION

In the 1930s, Josephine Roche was a progressive celebrity. First Lady Eleanor Roosevelt hailed her as "one of the friends and acquaintances who have been and are an inspiration to me."[1] The *Literary Digest* suggested Roche as a presidential candidate.[2] In a poll conducted by Bamberger and Co., Josephine Roche bested Elizabeth Arden as "the most prominent woman business executive in the country."[3] *American Women: The Official Who's Who among the Women of the Nation* named Roche one of the republic's ten most outstanding women.[4] Radio stations broadcast dramatic reenactments of episodes from Roche's life, and schools in Colorado displayed her photo next to those of Franklin D. Roosevelt and Charles Lindbergh.[5] At New York City's posh Cosmopolitan Club, Roche received a National Achievement Award for her contributions to the "culture of the world," and an official at the founding convention of the Congress of Industrial Organizations, a new militant labor federation, introduced her as "the greatest outstanding liberal in our country" and "the greatest woman of our time."[6] Two historians confirmed the judgment in 1939, dubbing Roche "one of the most distinguished women in American public life."[7]

Gray-eyed, square-jawed, and sparking with energy, the middle-aged Josephine Roche was celebrated in the 1930s because she was the second-highest-ranking woman in Franklin Roosevelt's New Deal government and the only American woman to run a coal company. Remarkably, she operated the company as an experiment in progressive labor relations: workers and owners alike weighed in on virtually every aspect of company policy. Roche had been a committed progressive reformer since her graduation from Vassar College in 1908, after which she stumped for women's suffrage, opposed jail time for juvenile crime, and sought to incorporate immigrants more fully into American life. Her activism took its

1

extraordinary turn in 1927, when she inherited her father's shares in the Rocky Mountain Fuel Company (RMF), an expansive coal mining enterprise in Colorado. Instead of simply living off her inheritance, she amassed enough shares to become the majority stockholder of RMF, ousted its anti-labor management, and invited the United Mine Workers of America (UMW) to unionize the company's miners. She signed a historic contract with the workers in August 1928 and, as head of RMF, fought doggedly to protect her progressive industrial enterprise from both the ravages of the Great Depression and the efforts of competitors to drive her out of business.

Roche's version of industrial management won widespread acclaim and admitted her to a national political elite. Shortly after Franklin Roosevelt was inaugurated as president in 1933, Roche ran for governor of Colorado on the slogan "Roosevelt, Roche, and Recovery," and when her whirlwind primary bid failed, Roosevelt appointed her assistant secretary of the treasury. From that position, Roche helped to hammer out the founding legislation of the U.S. welfare state—the Social Security Act—supervised a massive expansion of the U.S. Public Health Service, directed the National Youth Administration (NYA), and oversaw the development of a national health plan that would be enacted piecemeal over the decades after World War II. Indeed, when Medicare passed in 1965, it was identified on the floor of Congress by Oregon's Senator Wayne Morse "as a reality made possible in no small part by the historic struggle of one of this country's most illustrious citizens, Josephine Roche."[8]

This biography seeks to explain first how Josephine Roche moved from a small town on the Great Plains, where she was born in 1886, to the nation's capital, where she joined Roosevelt's administration in 1934. Especially significant in explaining her achievements were her education at Vassar, mentoring by a progressive reform community in Denver, and the meaning she made of the momentous coal strike in Colorado that culminated in the Ludlow Massacre of 1914. After witnessing the injustices perpetrated by coal mine owners against their workers in that conflagration, Roche spent much of the rest of her life trying, in her words, to "right the wrong of Ludlow."[9]

This biography also explains how, having achieved renown in the 1930s, Roche largely disappeared from history and memory, a disappearing act made all the more mysterious by Roche's stunning post–New Deal resume. In the late 1940s, after turning sixty, Roche undertook an entirely new challenge: she relinquished her shares in RMF and became director of the United Mine Workers of America Welfare and Retirement Fund, which she built into one of the largest and most influential private health and pension programs in the United States. In her work at the fund, Roche aimed not only to improve the living standards of coal miners but also to support organized labor and to restructure American medicine in such a way as to make it more accessible to Americans of modest means. She built a pathbreaking hospital chain and promoted the development of managed care in medicine. In other words, Roche continued to build institutions with which Americans live in the twenty-first century. She did not leave the fund until 1971, when she was driven out at age eighty-four in the midst of a murderous contest for control of the mine workers' union. How could such a woman disappear from history?

The explanation has many layers, and the narrative ahead emphasizes two of them. The first was the anti-communist crusade of the 1940s and 1950s, which convinced Roche to dodge the public spotlight for a decade, thereby surrendering the name recognition she achieved in the 1930s.[10] This self-effacement then allowed widespread assumptions about old women—especially that they lacked initiative and authority in public life—to shape popular representations of Roche in the 1970s and after. These representations attributed the bulk of her achievements in the postwar decades to her partner at the fund, John L. Lewis. To the extent that Roche was remembered at all after 1971, she was considered nothing more than a rubberstamp to Lewis, a gross misrepresentation that this biography will correct.[11]

John L. Lewis was, of course, a titan of organized labor, and he was an intimate friend and ally of Roche over many decades. She admired him tremendously. But in their operation of the mine workers' Welfare and Retirement Fund, Roche was more often in the driver's seat than Lewis. Setting the record straight on this point is vital not only to Roche's memory but also to our larger understanding of women's roles in shaping American life and the processes by which those contributions have so often been obscured. Sorting out the partnership between Roche and Lewis is a contribution to gender justice.

The restoration to history of an important and fascinating woman does not, however, constitute the full meaning of Roche's life story. Because she remained active from the Progressive Era (1890s to early 1920s) through the New Deal and the Great Society, her biography also offers a new way of conceptualizing the trajectory of progressive reform in twentieth-century America.[12] Progressivism was a major strain within American political culture that emerged in the late nineteenth century among activists anxious to secure their country's signature institutions—political democracy and the rough social equality on which they believed democracy depended—in the face of challenges posed by a new corporate and industrialized economy. Rapid urbanization and massive immigration were among those challenges. Over the course of the early twentieth century, progressives created new institutions, within both government and civil society, aimed to make democracy viable in their increasingly impersonal society riven by differences of class, nationality, gender, and race.

In a field-shaping book on reform movements in the early twentieth century, historian Richard Hofstadter famously identified the period from 1890 to World War II as the Age of (Progressive) Reform.[13] The 1920s, he argued, represented only a "temporary reversal" in the fortunes of reformers and so should not deter us from understanding the entire period as one dominated by reforming ideals. When viewed through the life of Josephine Roche, Hofstadter's "Age of Reform" appears not to have ended in the 1940s but to have continued into the 1970s. What Hofstadter could not have known as he penned *The Age of Reform* in the 1950s was that he was writing in yet another of progressivism's "temporary reversals." The embers of progressivism were smoldering through the immediate postwar decade just as they did in the 1920s, and they would flame up once more in the 1960s. This book, in the process of narrating Roche's life story, makes the case for an Age of Progressive Reform that reached from the late nineteenth century into the 1970s.

The progressivism of the 1960s and 1970s was, of course, hardly identical to that of the early twentieth century or the New Deal. Changes in context as well as creed differentiated the twentieth century's three progressive episodes. Roche's life brings some of those differences into sharp focus. But of even more interest here are the ways that ideals forged during the Progressive Era not only survived to shape the policies and institutions of the New Deal in the 1930s, as many other historians have argued, but also endured the shocks of the late 1940s—especially the Cold War and an emboldened anti-communist campaign at home—to reemerge in public policy and social movements in the 1960s.[14] Roche's life story cannot bear out the whole of the continuities and changes in the progressive tradition from the Progressive Era through the Great Society, but it does provide a remarkable vantage point from which to capture significant aspects of that whole.

Indeed, Roche was positioned within the progressive reform movements of the twentieth century in such a way as to make her life unusually revelatory of a multifaceted, decades-long progressive history shared by women and men alike. Roche was formed equally by progressive communities in the East, where as a young woman she witnessed the struggles of new immigrants crowded into urban neighborhoods, and in the West, where discriminatory railroad rates and drought were greater concerns. She operated not only in reform networks dominated by women but also in those dominated by men. She absorbed the tenets of social science progressivism, a strain that emphasized public policy as the solution to social problems, as well as those of labor progressivism, which envisioned the self-organization of workers as the crucial component for promoting social justice.[15] She carried those ideals through the tempering processes of economic depression in the 1930s, global war in the 1940s, and unprecedented prosperity in the 1950s, bringing them to bear in the explosive 1960s. As a result, Roche's life refracts multiple strains within the progressive tradition as they shot through the first three-quarters of the twentieth century.

In fact, Roche's life responds to many of the most important questions raised by historians about progressive reform. How, for instance, could the same reform movement encompass both moral reformers and labor progressives, the former seeming determined to *constrain* workers through campaigns against alcohol, prostitution, and gambling and the latter seeking explicitly to *empower* workers? Did World War I, with its attempt at economic planning and promise of national self-determination, enthrone progressive ideals, or, as it suppressed dissent and tolerated attacks on diversity in the United States, entomb them? Is the New Deal better understood as the culmination of progressive reform or the generator of modern liberalism? Were Cold War liberals the heirs to or betrayers of their progressive forbears? If, as many historians argue, robust health and welfare benefits in the private sector stymied the development of a comprehensive welfare state in the postwar United States, why were coal miners, who had one of the best private health programs in the country, clamoring in the 1960s for federal aid? Given the emergence of racial justice as the premier concern of reform campaigns in the 1960s, did that era represent a decisive break from the past, or did it express values consistent with earlier progressive episodes when class justice dominated the agenda? In sum, how are we to conceptualize the history of progressive reform in twentieth-century America?

As they unfurl in the chapters ahead, answers to these questions depend in part on how we identify the central concern of early twentieth-century progressivism. Without question, Josephine Roche's primary concern was inequality. Over the years, she filled her files with reports on the concentration of wealth within a tiny elite, and she continually insisted that the threat to all things American came from "economic inequality, intolerance, human denial."[16] Economic inequalities, however, were not the whole of Roche's concern. She aimed to diminish inequalities of power, too. Wealth and power were (and are) intimately related, of course, but they were not identical and were sometimes treated independently. When Roche pressed for women's suffrage, workers' participation in managerial decisions, or racial minorities' leadership in devising policies for eradicating racial injustice, she was seeking to equalize relations of power. When she sought minimum wage laws, progressive taxation, or unemployment insurance, she directly addressed inequalities of wealth. When she hoped "to see all the workers of America organized in unions," she hoped for the diminution of inequalities in both arenas.[17]

Diminishing inequalities of wealth and power was for many reformers the center of the progressive impulse. Although this desire did not motivate them all, it did inspire millions of reformers, and it crossed multiple categories of reform.[18] The concern with inequality also connected reformers in the early twentieth century with those of the New Deal and the Great Society eras. Unlike more radical activists, progressives rarely expected perfect equality ever to reign, but they passionately believed the current degree of inequality in their society was intolerable and must be reduced if human beings were to lead worthy lives and America were to deliver on its democratic promise. Progressive methods for decreasing inequalities included public policies aimed at ensuring individual economic security and regulating corporate power as well as the promotion of a more inclusive and vigorous democracy. For Roche, the most significant engine of what she called a "dynamic democracy" was an aroused and organized citizenry, especially a thriving labor movement.[19]

By setting inequality at the heart of progressivism, Josephine Roche's life story suggests that the period from the late nineteenth century into the 1970s constituted an age of progressive reform, broken by two brief reversals. The reversals were periods when, at the level of national politics and government, progressivism did not dominate. The first temporary reversal occurred in the 1920s, when conservatives won the White House and reformers scrambled to fashion responses to such innovations as welfare capitalism, the Bolshevik experiment, and a newly organized and defined U.S. patriotism. Another reversal occurred in the long 1950s, when the Cold War's anti-communist crusade together with a growing economy destroyed many progressive organizations, ostensibly melted workers and employers into the same "middle class," eroded commitment to democratic decision making, and built a nearly unbreachable wall between reformers and their former allies on the left. These changes were significant enough to require a new label for those who continued to press for some items on the earlier progressive agenda. Like so many others, Roche temporarily ceased to be a progressive and became a Cold War liberal.[20] But progressivism lived on in smoldering bits and pieces within postwar liberal politics as well as in private sector experiments and emergent social movements in the 1950s. As Roche's story shows, those embers helped to produce the century's final episode of progressive reform in the 1960s and 1970s. The Great Society embodied a new progressivism produced by cross-fertilization between a new left and postwar liberalism.[21]

Although this book is not specifically about women's progressivism or female reform, it does contribute to U.S. women's history.[22] Most obviously, Josephine Roche expands our notion of what it meant to be a woman in the first six decades of the twentieth century. She did things that our current histories would not lead us to expect women to do—like becoming a coal magnate on the eve of the Great Depression.[23] But her story also helps to explain why so many of Roche's female firsts remained *sui generis*. Her experience reveals the kinds of cultural and political moves that dulled the potential for broader change that her gender breakthroughs might otherwise have carried. Despite her astonishing success in the coal industry in the early 1930s, for example, Roche was often represented more as a "humanitarian" than as a businesswoman, making her achievement in industry more about the allegedly female characteristic of charity than about the ability of women to achieve a healthy bottom line.[24] Similarly, when Roche was exercising power over thousands of men in the New Deal government, she was simultaneously subordinated to some of those same men by serving tea at administration functions. Perhaps most sobering, Roche's biography shows how a woman of such accomplishment and significance was written out of memory and history altogether, robbing subsequent generations of the capacious expectations for women that her example might have created. In sum, this life story helps to explain how American women's prospects could improve so dramatically across the twentieth century and yet remain unequal to men's.

Roche's biography speaks in other powerful ways to our own time as well. Her story resonates especially with our current experience of increasing economic inequality, a trend that resumed in the late twentieth century after several decades of diminution and continues unabated in the twenty-first. In part because of the gradual abandonment of innovations pioneered by progressives in the early and mid-twentieth century, income inequality began to reincrease significantly in the 1970s. The result is that, in 2012, the top 10 percent of income earners in the United States claimed 50.4 percent of the country's annual income, a percentage higher than at any time since 1917. As for recent trends, between 2009 and 2012, the incomes of the highest-earning 1 percent increased by 31.4 percent, while the incomes of the remaining 99 percent grew by only 0.4 percent.[25] Wealth inequality is even greater than income inequality, having reached levels unmatched since before the Great Depression. Between 1983 and 2010, the top 5 percent of Americans scored 74.2 percent of the nation's increase in wealth, while the bottom 60 percent of Americans suffered a decline.[26] In 2005, the top 1 percent of Americans owned over 30 percent of the nation's wealth; the top 20 percent owned over 80 percent.[27] For those who worry that these levels of inequality are constricting individual lives, eroding national community, and depriving the world of contributions from those hampered only by lack of resources rather than deficiencies of ability or desire, Roche's life reveals a deep vein of historical precedent from which to draw insight and inspiration. It offers a potent political heritage that insisted private property carried public obligations, corporations had responsibilities to workers and consumers as well as to stockholders, economic security was a prerequisite for the exercise of genuine liberty, and the self-organization of workers was the *sine qua non* for social justice. Progressivism rejected the inevitability of inequality and devised effective ways to diminish it. As a result, by the 1950s, Americans achieved the highest level of economic equality in all of U.S. history.

As the foregoing would suggest, this biography is overwhelmingly a political biography. Roche was, to the everlasting consternation of reporters, an extremely private person. But she left enough evidence of her personality and interior life for us to know her as a woman of energy, conviction, and, to use one of her favorite words, guts. Her godson reported long after her death that Roche disdained people with no "guts," and she was given to chiding anyone she perceived as gutless. When one member of Franklin Roosevelt's New Deal cabinet suggested that Roche would give the administration much needed "charm," she retorted, "What this administration needs is guts."[28] At a meeting of mine operators where Roche was urged to the speaker's rostrum because the proceedings reportedly needed "some beauty," she responded, "What this meeting needs is guts."[29]

Roche was proud of her own mettle. Throughout her life, she sought new challenges that would both promote the cause of social justice as she defined it and move her into realms previously barred to women. Although her stint as Denver's first policewoman in 1912–1913 ended in abysmal failure, for instance, she always included it in her life story, gleefully narrating tales of her late-night prowls in the city's dicey saloon district.[30] Those tales confirmed her courage and demonstrated her gender innovation; they painted her as the gutsy person she wanted to be. In her mid-twenties, she brilliantly articulated this aspect of her personality after riding a "half-broken" horse. "I've had some wild gallops on a horse that isn't quite broken yet," she reported to a friend, "a few men have been on him, but no woman, so the hours spent with him have been most exhilarating exercise."[31]

While Roche was a woman of intense conviction, her love of risk, of creating something from nothing, of being "in the thick of it," as she sometimes put it, led her to some unsavory choices.[32] In fact, whenever Roche was faced with the choice of either remaining true to her full set of moral and political commitments or being fully effective on behalf of only a few, she always chose effectiveness. It was a trait that explained many of her decisions, some of which were frankly corrupt. In the 1930s, she accepted secret loans from the United Mine Workers of America to keep her coal company out of bankruptcy, and in 1940 she refused to campaign for Franklin Roosevelt unless he found public money to keep her coal company afloat. Most spectacularly, her career ended in an explosion of accusations that she had violated her fiduciary responsibility to beneficiaries of the coal miners' welfare fund by colluding with the miners' union.

Josephine Roche was no saint. Part of what makes her so interesting is precisely her willingness to get down in the muck of economic and political life. She had no interest in polishing a pristine moral reputation. She was interested in exercising power on behalf of her most cherished values. Sometimes, she felt she had to choose some of those values over others, and she was willing to fight dirty to defend them if she thought she had to. Her shady dealings never enriched her personally; they were aimed at preserving what she saw as progressive institutions built to improve the lives of workers. Even when her choices were not admirable, they were understandable. They remind us that our imperfect world does not offer any of us perfect options and that compromise is often at the center of an effective life.

As a child, Josephine Roche rode a stagecoach into the Rocky Mountains for family vacations, and she lived to see a man on the moon. Her longevity as a participant in American life makes her individual story peculiarly revealing of the continuities and changes in the progressive reform tradition in twentieth-century America. The verve with which Roche led that long life was captured in an interview when she was eighty-five and campaigning for democracy within the coal miners' union. A reporter asked if she planned to retire soon and write her memoirs. She snapped back, "Oh no, I'm going to do things now. I only have 10 minutes left, and I'm afraid I didn't fight hard enough."[33] That progressive fight and the woman who made it are the subjects of this book.

PART I

FIRST BURST OF PROGRESSIVE REFORM: ROCHE'S APPRENTICESHIP, 1886–1918

Josephine Roche's birth coincided with the opening of the Age of Reform. During her childhood and adolescence, progressivism emerged as a critique of the vast inequalities created by the new corporate, industrial economy coming to dominate American life. When Roche entered adulthood, her life all but merged with the progressive movement. The prime concern of both was to improve the material lives of workers and consumers and empower them within the new corporate order. By the close of the first burst of progressive reform—shortly after World War I—Roche had completed her apprenticeship as a reformer and was prepared to initiate progressive ventures of her own.

CHAPTER 1

CHILDHOOD IN THE WEST, EDUCATION IN THE EAST, 1886–1908

E xplaining Josephine Roche's extraordinary life begins with her ambitious family, the cultural and political context of her Western childhood, and her formal education in the East.

Josephine Aspinwall Roche was born on December 2, 1886, in the small town of Neligh, Nebraska.[1] Neligh perched on the 98th meridian, the longitudinal line that, according to one eminent historian, divided the civilization of the eastern United States from that of the West. In making the transition from the timbered, wet climate of the East to the treeless, semi-arid climate of the Plains, he argued, American institutions—from methods of farming to law and literature—changed.[2] Rooted in the boundary between East and West, Neligh was the perfect birthplace for a woman who would be formed equally by those two distinct regions and who would over the course of her life constantly cross boundaries, not only between East and West but also between women and men, social scientists and union organizers, workers and employers. In retrospect, her birth on a boundary seemed to mark Josephine Roche for life.

So did the high hopes of her parents, John J. Roche and Ella Aspinwall Roche, who migrated to Neligh after early careers in education. Originally from Maine, the willowy Ella C. Aspinwall graduated from Wisconsin State Normal School in 1873 and, demonstrating considerable independence and ambition, returned five years later to serve on the faculty.[3] John Roche also attended the Normal School and taught while studying for the bar, which he passed in 1877. The next year, he was elected District Attorney in Wisconsin's LaFayette County.[4] Even that elective position, however, did not fulfill John Roche's highest aspirations. In 1880, he set his sights on real estate in Neligh, a mill town in Nebraska's Antelope County.[5]

John Roche's timing was exquisite. He arrived in Neligh the very year the Fremont, Elkhorn, and Missouri Valley Railroad dramatically transformed the hamlet's economic prospects by connecting it to eastern markets. Property values soared, encouraging him to found the First National Bank of Neligh, an institution that, through loans for land, facilitated other men's purchase of property at skyrocketing prices.[6] When the town incorporated in 1881, Roche was elected one of its trustees. The next year, he married his Wisconsin sweetheart and represented Antelope County in the state legislature for the first of two terms.[7] A decade after Roche opened the bank, Neligh hosted a U.S. land office, milled flour and lumber, and exported agricultural surpluses.[8] The Roches' future looked bright.

Josephine's singular position in this striving family gave her unique opportunities. In 1884, John and Ella Roche celebrated the birth of a son, Joseph Aspinwall Roche, who died only four months later.[9] In 1886, the couple transferred the name of their deceased son to their newborn daughter, Josephine Aspinwall Roche (figure 1). With the name, they seem to have transferred all their ambitions for a son to their daughter as well. When Josephine was born, one local newspaper warned readers not to expect to find her father behind the counter at the bank but instead to search him out at home, where "you will probably find him looking contentedly at the girl baby which arrived at his home yesterday."[10] Family friends later spoke of the "intelligent devotion" that the couple lavished on their daughter, and her mother eventually wrote to Josephine of "your mother's ambition for you," an ambition she believed that Josephine knew "full well—only too well."[11] Josephine's life would surely have been different had Joseph survived to claim the attention and resources of a first-born male child. As it was, Josephine drew every hope and asset that John and Ella Roche had to invest in their heirs.

Some aspects of her inheritance Josephine would ultimately reject, however—chief among them, her father's political views. John Roche was a pro-business Republican who believed in the unlimited prerogatives of property. He opposed organized labor, saw government exclusively as the protector of property rights, and devoted his life to the exploitation of natural and human resources his daughter would strive to conserve.[12] Josephine's opposing political views explicitly formed after she left home, but the cultural and political context of her early childhood also encouraged rebellion.

The cultural context was captured in stories spun by the men and women who first settled Antelope County and identified themselves as the area's pioneer generation. These early settlers painted themselves as a heroic group apart from that of Josephine's father, who came to Nebraska only after the railroad eased life so much that even the climate reportedly improved.[13] During Josephine's early childhood, Antelope County's pioneers began publishing tales of their valiant efforts to coax crops from the area's unfriendly soil and their victory over grasshoppers and prairie fires that plagued the county in the 1870s.[14] They bragged about outlasting "Doc" Middleton, a notorious cattle thief, who was in 1879 finally brought down by U.S. marshals and a cavalry unit.[15] Such stories, vividly contrasting the adventurous heroism of Neligh's pioneers to the tamer triumphs of approving mortgages, resonated powerfully in Josephine Roche's later life. By encouraging sympathy for the literally groundbreaking group that preceded her banker-father to the Plains, they produced a critical distance from her father himself. Moreover, as an adult, Josephine voiced the spirit of pioneer struggle when she enthused, "I've had a wonderful life myself because I've always been in the middle of a fight."[16] In her own tales, corrupt political machines and greedy corporate magnates stood in for the likes of Doc Middleton, but Josephine Roche often understood herself to be taking down bad guys. Stories told by the founders of Antelope County during her childhood echoed in Josephine's persistent delight in battle, penchant for drama, and disdain for the profit-seeking life of her father.

Politics in Nebraska fed that disdain. As Josephine grew from toddler to child, a dissident political movement in the state cast bankers and railroad executives among the archest of villains. Conditions in Roche's own Antelope County explained why. In the 1870s, when migrants from the Midwest were first beginning to break the soil in Antelope County, the Burlington and Missouri Railroad owned over 90,000 acres of the county's best agricultural land. Much of that tract was a grant from the U.S. government intended to encourage railroad service to the state. Pioneer farmers grumbled that this federal giveaway to a giant corporation might have provided several hundred struggling farm families with 160 acres each under the Homestead Act. It hardly seemed fair that their own government lavished such benefits on wealthy corporations while hardworking families risked body and soul trying to cultivate wild, dry ground. Making matters worse, the Burlington and Missouri never provided rail service to the county, and it refused to pay taxes on the prime land.[17] When the railroad was finally forced to put the land up for sale, it did so at prices that forced buyers into debt—even though the railroad had itself paid nothing for the land. In the late 1880s and early 1890s, disastrous weather made mortgage payments impossible for many who bought the railroad's high-priced parcels. At that point, foreclosing bankers looked as villainous as the railroads, profiting as they did from the labor of those who improved the land and were then left with nothing to show for it.[18]

This same situation pertained through much of the Great Plains and helped to produce the populist movement of the 1890s. Whether that movement directly shaped the young Josephine Roche or affected her thinking later through the staying power of its issues and ideals, the democratic insurgency of the 1890s lived on in her activism. Josephine was about to turn four when farmers and wage-earners in Nebraska formed the People's Independent Party as a protest against the inordinate power that big businesses seemed to wield in the state's political and economic life.[19] Demanding regulation of railroads and the elimination of other monopolistic corporations, the insurgent party shocked the state's Republican political establishment in 1890 by winning the majority of seats in Nebraska's state legislature as well as two of the state's three congressional seats.[20] In 1892, an alliance of small business owners, dissident farmers, and industrial workers formed a national third party and convened their presidential nominating convention in Nebraska's own Omaha. Josephine was five years old. Reducing the economic inequality created by the emergence of vast corporations and ending corporate control of government were the goals of the new Populist Party. In imagining how to wrest government from bankers and railroad executives and achieve some semblance of economic equality among Americans, the Populists devised a political agenda that undergirded reform movements for decades to come. They also transformed Josephine Roche's home state just as she reached an age with potential for political consciousness.[21] Populists and their Democratic Party allies took over Nebraska's state legislature in 1896, as Josephine turned ten, and passed the first initiative and referendum laws in the country while also regulating the state's stockyards and telephone companies.[22] Politically, Josephine Roche proved more a child of Nebraska's Populists than of her biological father.

Although little direct evidence of Josephine's childhood remains, several of its elements are clear. For one thing, her childhood accustomed her to movement. In 1894, not long after Josephine started school, her family left Neligh.[23] The motive is unclear, but a faltering economy probably convinced John Roche that continuing opportunity lay elsewhere.[24] The family bounced around for a while, living briefly in Sioux City, Iowa, and then in Sault Ste. Marie, a town on the Upper Peninsula of Michigan.[25] At some point in the 1890s, the peripatetic family returned to Nebraska, where John Roche again took up work in the financial industry, this time in the bustling city of Omaha.[26]

There, the Roches' ambitions for their daughter took discernible form. Although they had limited power over the laws and expectations that excluded most American women from the ballot box and political office, Josephine Roche's parents did not enforce Victorian expectations of feminine passivity. Family friends described Josephine as a tomboy who preferred bloomers to dressy clothes.[27] She loved to ride horses and to climb; she enjoyed family vacations in Estes Park, Colorado, which the family reached by harrowing stagecoach rides. Even as a teenager, she slid down haystacks with cousins back in Wisconsin.[28] In addition, John and Ella Roche aimed to give their daughter the finest education they could manage.

Indeed, Josephine received the best education the Plains had to offer. In 1901, she enrolled at Brownell Hall, a prestigious Episcopal girls' school in Omaha. The fussy parlors of the school suggested stifling Victorian domesticity, but when Josephine matriculated, the new head of school, Euphan Macrae, was applying for accreditation by all the women's colleges in the country as well as the University of Chicago and the University of Nebraska. Representing the first generation of college-educated women, Macrae hired her teaching staff from the nation's finest schools and devoted Brownell Hall to the cause of higher education for women. Roche's course of study included Greek and Latin, English and French, algebra and both American and English history. By the time of Josephine's graduation in 1904 (figure 2), Macrae had won the accreditations she sought. As a result, the bloomer-loving banker's daughter was a member of the first Brownell class to symbolize its scholarly accomplishments by wearing caps and gowns at graduation.[29]

Josephine Roche used her Brownell certificate to attend Vassar College in Poughkeepsie, New York, an institution opened in 1865 and intended by its founder to be for its all-female student body "what Yale and Harvard are to young men."[30] Vassar was located in the Hudson River Valley about 80 miles north of New York City and was part of a very successful late nineteenth-century push for women's higher education. By the time Josephine Roche registered in 1904, nearly 40 percent of all undergraduates in the United States were women. Still, since higher education remained a province of the privileged—fewer than 5 percent of college-aged Americans actually attended in 1900—the second generation of college women did not take their education for granted. They knew they were lucky.[31]

Vassar College powerfully influenced the eager, chubby-cheeked Nebraskan who traveled 1,000 miles by train to enroll. With her long, dark hair arranged in a Gibson-girl pompadour, Roche fit in perfectly with Vassar's student body.[32] Like Brownell Hall, Vassar attracted girls who were overwhelmingly Protestant, white, and middle class.[33] The school also promoted frenetic activity that required dressing for dinner each evening, mandatory chapels, occasional high teas, and seasonal trips up the Hudson River. A frenzied pace suited Roche, who was described in her senior yearbook as "Cheerful and happy in the prospect of having more to do that day than she could possibly accomplish."[34] Vassar's emphasis on sports rewarded Roche's tomboy tendencies, and in a western teen exposed to the populist revolt, Vassar's insistence on democratic social relations gained easy traction. Although Vassar's students were generally middle class, their financial resources ranged broadly, and the college insisted that all students receive equal treatment regardless of wealth. The administration demonstrated its dedication to equality even in such matters as assigning girls to dormitories: rooms varied in size and amenities, but Vassar charged the same rate for every room so that students were not segregated by wealth. The practice distinguished Roche's alma mater from many other women's colleges.[35] Indeed, so central was equal treatment to the school's identity that some students condemned the formation of cliques or any special circle of friends as "undemocratic" and therefore contrary to the school's values.[36]

Roche's courses at Vassar both shaped her and revealed much about who she already was. One of her intellectual passions was ancient European languages. The totally absorbing process of translation apparently enthralled Roche, who took four years of Greek and four years of Latin in addition to Latin composition.[37] Love of ancient languages suggested Roche's joy in sustained concentration and attention to detail. It also unexpectedly nourished the embryonic feminism latent in Roche's tomboy tendencies and desire for higher education. Legendary chair of the Classics Department Abby Leach encouraged her students to lead an independent and active public life.[38] During the years when Roche was among her students, Leach bemoaned the constraints confining too many women's lives. "We have not freed ourselves," she lamented, "from the conventional view that a woman exists merely to please, to minister to the wants of the family, to live softly and idly if the family exchequer allows it." Leach worried that only a narrow range of motives was generally permitted to women, which she summed up lyrically as "all for love and nothing for logic." These motives were insufficient, Leach thought, to a present day that called "for clear vision, bravery in facing facts, and unerring judgment."[39] She might have said, "What this era needs is guts," so closely did Leach's spirit resound in Roche's future statements. As sponsor of Vassar's Hellenic Society, which Roche joined every year, Leach had opportunities outside the classroom as well as in it to model for Roche a fully realized, independent womanhood and to nurture Roche toward her own independent life.[40]

Vassar College shaped Roche's self-presentation as well as her ideas about gender. Although women with a variety of views attended Vassar, and most would eventually marry and rear children, many of Roche's classmates shared Leach's belief in women's individuality. An editorial in the student newspaper during Roche's senior year argued that the characteristics so often associated with women were not natural but created by (limited) experience. "If women could once throw aside the idea that the qualities attributed to them are innate and inevitable, or even acquire courage to avoid doing what is expected of them, those cloying phrases 'a woman's reason,' 'women's mental privilege,' 'the eternal feminine' (as applied to sophistry) might fade into the dimness of the past when women were not allowed to train their minds."[41] In describing the spirit of Vassar College, another writer insisted that it subsisted in "cordially acknowledging the merits [that each woman's] individuality has won them."[42] An editorial in the student newspaper insisted that the best type of college woman was "a beautiful woman who has the qualities of an honorable man."[43] As an adult, Roche was often described as a mix of feminine and masculine traits, and she herself rejected the notion that any traits *were* masculine or feminine.[44]

Fittingly, many Vassar students, including Roche, avidly supported women's suffrage and did so despite the surprising opposition of their college president. James Monroe Taylor, who permitted campus lectures on socialism and discouraged classroom lectures in favor of participatory discussions, refused to allow students to form a chapter of the Collegiate Equal Suffrage Association or to invite suffragists to declaim on campus.[45] These rules drove suffrage activism underground. Clandestine support for the cause resulted in a deliciously defiant act the last semester of Roche's senior year. In May 1908, student suffragists arranged for a Vassar alumna to address the campus's secret suffrage club. In the face of President Taylor's unyielding refusal to allow the event on campus, forty students reportedly scaled the campus walls under cover of darkness and applauded several suffrage speakers in a neighboring graveyard.[46]

Although Roche may not have participated in this particular off-campus event, its spirit of derring-do would have suited her. In choosing extracurricular activities, Roche gravitated toward those that allowed her to compete openly, to try out behavior generally marked unfeminine, and to make common cause with a team. In her senior year, Roche competed on her class's track team, and in her junior and senior years, played guard on her class's basketball team.[47] The latter was quite an achievement because basketball was all the rage in women's colleges, and Vassar was no exception.[48] Only seven players made the varsity squad for each class, and their fans took up their cause with great spirit.[49] Yellow was the color of Roche's team, and members of her class often turned out for games wearing sunflower costumes and carrying yellow parasols.[50] Roche also won a place in the campus dramatic society every year.[51] Historian Helen Lefkowitz Horowitz has argued that in campus dramatics as well as sports, women students learned to play male roles, to wield power, and to act aggressively.[52] In those ways, drama, too, helped to fit the scholar from Nebraska for her unorthodox future.

These same characteristics held true for the only office that Roche ever held at Vassar, which was clerk of her debating team, Qui Vive. An activity reserved to men at many coeducational universities, debate offered Roche pleasures that combined those of sports, dramatics, and the study of ancient languages: it required studious attention to detail, a flare for performance, and a competitive spirit.[53] It proceeded according to the ruthless logic that Abby Leach believed was often forbidden to women, and it required qualities that Leach insisted the world needed most: clear vision and bravery in facing facts. According to one of Roche's teammates in Qui Vive, "a many-sided consideration gives each girl a chance to form her own opinion" of one subject at a time.[54] While Roche was clerk, Qui Vive debated hot political issues, including the prohibition of Japanese immigration, workmen's compensation programs, and federal regulation of industry.[55] In earlier years, the group debated whether a tariff might bring in enough revenue to "maintain and advance the best interests of the United States."[56] The alternative was the progressive income tax proposed in the 1890s by the Populist Party. In 1905, an intersociety debate focused on the value of the union shop for the working classes, and an intrasociety debate asked whether President Theodore Roosevelt was right to recommend that the Interstate Commerce Commission (ICC) be empowered to fix railroad rates.[57] If Roche did not arrive at Vassar fully informed of the significant political issues of her day, Qui Vive brought her up to speed.

So did her participation in the College Settlement Association.[58] One of the new opportunities that the first generation of college-educated women launched for the second was life in a social settlement, a building or set of buildings in a working-class neighborhood where more privileged people went to live, hoping to act as a bridge between the middle and working classes. The first such undertaking appeared on the East Side of London, where in 1884 a group of university men took up residence in hopes of sharing the benefits of their educations with the neighborhood's working-class families. Many of America's college women subsequently visited that experimental establishment and saw in it a model both for responding to the class cleavages created by industrialization in the United States and for spawning a new set of life opportunities for educated women. At the same time, then, that western farmers organized against the inequalities created by railroads and banks on the Great Plains, college-educated women founded institutions to diminish inequalities created by similar corporations in urban areas. By the time Roche attended Vassar, New York City alone counted forty-five settlements. Soon, hundreds of them flourished in cities across the United States.[59]

Among other things, Roche's membership in the College Settlement Association introduced her to new ways of imagining adult women's lives. When settlement resident Mary White Ovington came to campus during Roche's first semester, she embodied new possibilities for being female. She was unmarried and lived in New York City's Greenwich House, a brick edifice snuggled into the warren of narrow streets that ran through Greenwich Village. Greenwich House had both male and female residents, many of them university students or professors, all of whom aimed to make common cause with the neighborhood's working-class families. In the process, Greenwich House was remaking middle-class manhood and womanhood. It provided new ways for women to lead lives independent of family and for women and men to work together as equals in public projects.[60]

In their attempts to close class and gender divides, social settlements became generators of progressive reform. Class divisions seemed especially threatening in the late nineteenth century because the emergence of national corporations, which by 1900 catapulted the United States to world leadership in industrial production, seemed to produce a class of permanent wage-earners hopeless ever of owning a farm or business. Lacking such mobility, the new workers perceived their interests as sharply different from those of their employers, and violent conflict was often the result. Moreover, as centers of the country's burgeoning corporate enterprises, American cities were magnets for a new foreign immigration that totaled 24 million between 1880 and 1920. The result was an increasingly heterogeneous working class, often unconscionably exploited by employers and suffering the failure of urban infrastructures to meet workers' needs for housing, transportation, education, and health care.[61] Settlement activists joined their working-class neighbors in trying to improve these conditions and give new workers a voice in public life.

In Roche's senior year, settlement resident Michael Davis explained to Vassar's settlement association, "The most important function of the settlement worker to society in general is to break down class lines, to bear the message between class and class."[62] As college graduates set up their social settlements in working-class neighborhoods, they crossed the boundary separating social classes, explored the conditions of wage-earners' lives, and set out to decrease material and political inequalities. They attempted the latter through a variety of programs, including day nurseries, health clinics, citizenship instruction, and English classes. To the same ends, many settlements eventually lobbied state governments for policies to increase the wages, reduce the hours, and improve the safety of wage earners. They approached municipal councils for better sanitation systems, more stringent building codes, and streetlights. They advocated compulsory education laws; an end to child labor; public playgrounds and recreational programs. Settlement workers were, in short, both creating new civil society initiatives and urging the expansion of government to promote greater equality among Americans. Such innovations came to be called progressivism.[63]

To figure out what other sorts of undertakings might serve their purposes, settlement residents relied on social science research. In her lecture to Roche's settlement association, Ovington laid out this commitment. In order to address problems of poverty, she explained, reformers needed "carefully compiled statistics" documenting the cost of living for working families. With this sort of information, settlement workers believed they could determine good public policy and design social services for improving workers' lives.[64] In Roche's junior year, Mary van Kleeck, another New York progressive, shared her enthusiasm for social science research as she presented her own findings on the exploitive hours worked by wage-earning women.[65]

Exposed to these methods through her membership in the Settlement Association, Roche explored them further in economics courses. In her junior year, she enrolled in one of the most popular courses at Vassar: Dr. Herbert Mills' year-long introduction to economics.[66] Especially interested in class divisions, Mills encouraged his students to commit themselves to righting the wrongs committed by what he saw as an all-too-powerful corporate elite. Mills spearheaded at Vassar a culture of social mission that gave the school a reputation for producing a large group of progressive social activists throughout the early twentieth century.[67]

Encouraged by Mills, Roche volunteered in a Denver juvenile court the summer following her junior year. By then, her parents had moved from Omaha to the Mile-High City, where her father became an officer in the Rocky Mountain Fuel Company (RMF), a coal-mining concern in Colorado. Having learned from Mills about newfangled courts organized specifically to serve children, Roche was thrilled to discover that one of the leading lights of the juvenile court movement worked in her parents' new home city. When she made contact with the famous "kids' judge," Benjamin Lindsey, he arranged for her to do probation work at his court during her summer vacation.[68]

Ben Lindsey was a formative influence on Josephine Roche. A migrant from the South, Lindsey practiced law in Denver during the 1890s. In 1901, he was appointed a county judge, an office he used to craft new ways of responding to juvenile crime. Lindsey wished to separate children from adult criminals and instead of punishing youth for unlawful behavior guide them toward respect for the law. The juvenile court was imagined by Lindsey and other progressives as an institution for reforming wayward children if they were at fault and for reforming the world if it were the guiltier party.[69] Lindsey rarely found children genuinely culpable. He fingered instead corporations, landlords, and corrupt politicians that exploited working-class families. Firm in the conviction that economic conditions were ultimately responsible for most juvenile crime, Lindsey and other judges in the emerging juvenile courts devised legislation to change those conditions, conditions that bred poverty and powerlessness among too many Americans. For children already mired in the legal system, Lindsey and judges of his ilk pioneered the practice of probation rather than incarceration.[70]

Roche's summer work inspired her desire to join Lindsey on a more permanent basis, but before she could do so, she had to complete college. In her senior year, she volunteered at a fledgling juvenile court in Poughkeepsie and enrolled in several economics courses taught by James Williams, a recent Ph.D. from Columbia University.[71] Infusing those courses were the ideas of scholars like Henry Rogers Seager, professor of economics at Columbia, who lectured at Vassar while Roche was there. In his talk, Seager made the case that Roche was encountering in all her social science courses: social research was the foundation for solutions to the myriad social problems created by the emergence of corporate capitalism, and those solutions involved not only the good offices of voluntary associations but also the more powerful and comprehensive influence of government action.[72]

The idea that government should be involved in regulating economic relations in the interest of workers and consumers had, during Roche's adolescence, trickled up from settlements, local political insurgencies, and universities to the highest reaches of the U.S. government. As a result, since 1901, when the assassination of President William McKinley promoted Vice President Theodore Roosevelt to the White House, the federal government had demonstrated new reach and purpose. In 1902, the nation's first progressive president intervened in a strike of coal miners, forcing the mine owners into arbitration that raised wages and reduced hours. In 1906, Roosevelt cheered when Congress passed the Hepburn Act, which increased the power of the ICC to review railroad rates and enforce its regulatory decisions. Also in 1906, federal lawmakers passed the Pure Food and Drug Act and the Meat Inspection Act, both intended to protect consumers from contaminated food and ineffective drugs. Progressivism, originating in a movement of ordinary people opposed to the inequalities produced by unregulated corporate power, had thus arrived in Washington, DC.[73]

It had also arrived in the heart and soul of Josephine Roche. In her senior year, Roche published "Reclaiming the Western Lands" in Vassar's student newspaper. The article introduced readers, most of them from the wet and timbered East, to the problem of aridity in yet unsettled areas of the American West. Those areas, the senior classics scholar argued, offered enormous benefits to the country as a whole, which included "the opportunity they offer to persons capable and eager for self-support, . . . the outlet they furnish for the surplus energy of the country, and finally the chances they afford the great numbers of unemployed in times of depression of earning a comfortable living and adding to the nation's wealth instead of being a drain on its resources." With this sort of promise, Roche insisted, "there can be no doubt that the problem of making the enormous tracts of these arid public lands fit for settlement, or in short, the problem of irrigation, is one of the most vital and far reaching of the time." The question was, she explained, who should do the irrigating: private companies or the federal government. In her view, "these problems are to be successfully coped with only by the government of the nation."[74] Young Josephine Roche was in 1908 envisioning for the U.S. government an economic development project akin to but larger even than the future Tennessee Valley Authority (TVA). "Reclaiming the Western Lands" was Roche's first written proclamation of commitment to progressive values. It confirmed what her membership in the Settlement Association, work in juvenile courts, and ongoing enrollment in economics courses suggested: by the time she completed her undergraduate education, Roche had rejected her father's preference for unregulated private enterprise. She had signed on instead to the progressive hope for government interventions in economic life that aimed to distribute the benefits of America's enormous productive capacity more equally than private markets would do.

"Reclaiming the Western Lands" also indicated a new stage in Roche's development of a public voice. For all her activity at Vassar, Roche did not generally put herself forward as a leader. She did not hold class offices, edit the school newspaper, or organize clubs. "While in college," a reporter later observed, "Miss Roche was not a conspicuous member of her class though she was much liked and admired by a small group of friends."[75] An intimate later said that Roche "did not distinguish herself by brilliancy" at Vassar "but teachers and students soon found out 'you could always depend on Josephine Roche.' "[76] Through the frenzied activity of Roche's college years, she was, it would appear, just in the process of finding her leadership feet. Only in her senior year did she finally achieve enough stability to put herself forward as a public authority, which she did in "Reclaiming the Western Lands."

Vassar College set Josephine Roche directly on her life path. It encouraged her to lead an independent life and provided models for doing so. It imbued her with democratic ideals and the progressive desire to diminish inequalities of wealth and power. Vassar convinced Roche that social science research was the foundation for progressive public policies and steeped her in a feminism that dismissed innate differences between women and men. Although she could not have known it at the time, she had even met some of the people with whom she would later make common cause. Mary van Kleeck would be an ally in Roche's campaign to democratize the coal industry; Michael Davis would join her movement for a national health plan. She had much more to learn before taking a leadership role in the progressive movement, but her childhood on the Plains and education at Vassar had pried her loose from the political and economic perspectives of her parents and readied her to accept the lessons that lay ahead.

CHAPTER 2

ASPIRING FEMINIST AND SOCIAL SCIENCE PROGRESSIVE, 1908–1912

Shortly after graduating from Vassar, Josephine Roche pursued graduate study at Columbia University in New York City. Her courses and life experiences in New York built directly on the foundation laid by her undergraduate education. Her studies deepened her understanding of the social sciences and gave her feminism more specific shape as she sought explanations for prostitution and what scholars would later call the "gender wage gap." Through all of these experiences, Roche embedded herself securely in eastern reform communities.

Even during her years in New York, however, the West remained vivid to Roche—and exciting. Its special allure was created by a year she spent in Denver after graduating from Vassar. Living with her increasingly wealthy parents at the Hotel Metropole, Roche worked in 1908–1909 at Ben Lindsey's juvenile court.[1] Her main duty was supervising girls on probation; through Lindsey, Roche also connected with other reformers and helped to build a remarkable community of progressives, who would constitute perhaps the most significant element in explaining her unusual life path. The influential group at first included progressive lawyer Edward Costigan and his activist wife, Mabel, as well as the editor of Denver's *Rocky Mountain News*, Edward Keating. These three had joined Lindsey in fighting political corruption in Denver for years before Roche joined them.[2] Soon after she arrived, the group took in muckraking journalists Harvey O'Higgins and George Creel as well as O'Higgins's wife, Anna. The witty and urbane Harvey O'Higgins arrived on assignment from *Everybody's Magazine* in spring 1909 to expose corruption in Colorado's politics.[3] George Creel, a volatile and self-righteous newspaperman from Kansas City, moved to Denver in 1909 to write for the *Denver*

Post.[4] Other activists came and went over the years, but this inner circle especially shaped Josephine Roche's future. During her first year in Denver, the group took her in with such warmth that they created an affectionate nickname for her, Sojo, and often included her much more conservative parents in their socializing. Just as parents might, they teased her about the slang she adopted and fretted over her health and overwork. Josephine was for them a sort of protégé—young, smart, enthusiastic, ready to take on the world. They had much to teach her, and she eagerly accepted their tutelage.[5]

Belonging to this "gang," as they called themselves, Roche participated not only in the nascent juvenile justice movement but also in battles against "The Beast," Lindsey's histrionic term for corporate control of American government and politics. Like progressives across the country, Lindsey had by 1908 "discovered" that corporate interests exercised excessive power in his local government.[6] In Denver, these interests included public utilities like the Denver Gas and Electric Company and coal concerns like John D. Rockefeller's Colorado Fuel and Iron. In the eyes of progressive reformers, the inordinate influence of these companies undermined democracy, and it motivated them to mount anti-corruption campaigns aimed at diminishing the political power of business and empowering ordinary voters. In the process of conducting such campaigns himself, Lindsey had made so many enemies that despite wide public support for his work at the juvenile court neither the Republican nor the Democratic Party would nominate him in 1908 for the judgeship he had held since 1901. In the face of warnings that an independent candidate could never win an election in Denver, Lindsey tried it in 1908.

This was Josephine Roche's first election, and her opinions mattered materially because women enjoyed full voting rights in Colorado. In that regard, Colorado's women were extremely unusual: by 1908, only four states had fully enfranchised their female citizens, all of them in the West.[7] Roche loved being in the suffrage vanguard, and in the fall elections of 1908, her association with Lindsey made that election an especially thrilling baptism in the electoral process. After weeks of teaching voters how to "scratch" their ballots for an independent candidate and canvassing potentially supportive precincts, Lindsey's female supporters stood sentinel at every polling place on Election Day, wearing long white streamers emblazoned "Vote for Lindsey." To the astonishment of all, Lindsey won by over 10,000 votes.[8] Josephine Roche's first foray into electoral politics was a rousing success and ignited in her a fiery enthusiasm for electoral politics.

However exciting her first election, though, Roche was determined to continue her education in the East. In fall 1909, Roche set off for graduate work in political science at Columbia University. Harvey and Anna

O'Higgins, returning to New York themselves that autumn, accompanied her on the long train trip.

While Denver offered Roche full political participation, New York City introduced her to a new set of social problems. New York's population was more than 20 times that of Denver's. That larger population slightly favored women; Denver's favored men. The majority of Denver's population was native-born and of native parentage, while the vast majority of New Yorkers was either foreign-born or of foreign parentage. Denverites who were foreign-born tended to be from northern and western Europe, but in New York immigrants were more likely to be from Italy or Russia than any other single country.[9] Ethnic diversity, the dilemmas of immigrants, and the peculiar difficulties of women workers were as a result more obviously on display in New York than in Denver.

Roche contracted for anything but the ivory tower when she decided to pursue graduate work in this huge and heterogeneous eastern metropolis. From the beginning, she paired classroom study of social problems with on-the-ground experiences in city courts, on picket lines, and in immigrant homes. While working at Columbia with Edward Devine, whose textbook on the relief of poverty she had plowed through at Vassar, and Samuel McCune Lindsay, a reformer deeply interested in social legislation, she also sought out work in voluntary associations. Shortly after her arrival in the city, she reported excitedly to Ben Lindsey: "I am going to do a good deal of active work, in the settlements and particularly under the Probation Commission. I had a long interview with Miss Miner, who is on the Commission, this morning . . . she is going to put me to work at once." Roche continued, "I plan to give a day and a half or perhaps two days a week to the Probation work, and hope to arrange for some time in the settlements." She concluded, "Sometimes I feel as though I could not get enough to do."[10] Roche remained very much the Vassar grad who was delighted by having more to do in a day than she could possibly accomplish.

The coursework that Roche squeezed into her frenetic New York life focused on social economics, political economy, and history taught by a who's who of progressive thinkers. In addition to Devine and Lindsay, these luminaries included the renowned historian James Harvey Robinson, German-trained economist Vladimir Simkhovitch, and famed sociologist Franklin Giddings. Robinson's former student Charles Beard was also among them, as was the economist Henry Rogers Seager. These men deepened Roche's education in social science progressivism, infusing her with ideas she carried through her long life.

One of those ideas was skepticism toward tradition, an attitude most effectively cultivated perhaps by Robinson. "The history of thought is one of the most potent means of dissolving the bonds of prejudice and the restraints of routine," he insisted. "It not only enables us to reach a clear perception of our duties and responsibilities by explaining the manner in which existing problems have arisen, but it promotes that intellectual liberty upon which progress fundamentally depends."[11] Roche had not been particularly interested in history at Vassar, but she took three courses from Robinson while at Columbia, and she remained in touch with him and his family for decades thereafter.[12] Her speeches later in life echoed his teachings, which Roche first encountered in Robinson's famous intellectual history course, a year-long survey of European thought "popularly known as 'the Downfall of Christianity.' "[13]

In place of religious faith, Robinson promoted faith in constant progress toward a more perfect secular world. In his course on the French Revolution, Roche heard him insist that progressive reform, interpreted as an inclination toward more egalitarian social relations, was the very essence of history.[14] This conviction took root in Robinson's belief that the world was always in flux and that since change was the central fact of life, conservatives, who sought refuge in the authority of the past and in arguments that human nature set distinct limits on possibilities for change, were patently wrong. The study of history demonstrated, Robinson proclaimed, the "extraordinary variety" of human habits, institutions, and feelings across time and space, and thus demolished the conservative's appeal to human nature as a bulwark against change. Human "nature" changed constantly. Moreover, human beings had the power, according to Robinson, to "cooperate with and direct" the "innate force of change" that operated at the heart of reality. That being so, Robinson had the audacity to preach that "the abolition of poverty and disease and war, and the promotion of happy and rational lives" were not beyond human reach. Indeed, given the leap already made from "ape-like animal" to "ingenious flint-chipping artist," anything was possible.[15]

The belief in constant change led social science progressives to insist on the partiality, open-endedness, and contextuality of all knowledge. In Robinson's plain-speaking, "truth is relative."[16] They believed in learning by doing, indeed that experience and experiment were the only reliable bases for knowledge. To be worth anything, social scientific theories required study of the actual lives of flesh-and-blood human beings. Because the world perpetually changed and knowledge was inevitably limited, though, "no scientific prognosis of our future is possible."[17] This conviction sank so deep into Roche's consciousness that she would thirty years later rail against the fraudulence of actuarial science because it presumed to predict the future.

In his analyses of history, Robinson drove home another tenet of social science progressivism by which Roche lived her life: that social and economic conditions explained historical events. Unlike historians of an earlier generation, Robinson was interested in "conditions and institutions" of everyday life rather than dramatic political events directed by an elite.[18] Like other progressives, he saw material conditions as a fundamental dimension of what he called the "appalling" complexity of historical causation.[19] In graduate school and throughout her life, Roche insisted that everything from crime through sexual relations to strikes resulted from "conditions," and if Americans wished to improve sexual relations, reduce crime, or prevent strikes, they had to change the conditions that produced them.

Roche's coursework at Columbia also helps to explain her openness over many decades to political ideas and allies farther left on the political spectrum than she and demonstrates that her alliances with the Left were part and parcel of progressivism itself. Although Roche's professors were not Marxists, they recognized their debt to Karl Marx's economic interpretation of history. Vladimir Simkhovitch, with whom Roche studied socialism, nihilism, and anarchism, contended that while no serious thinker accepted Marx's deterministic claim that economic structures produced all other aspects of human endeavor, the primacy of economic conditions to historical causation was irrefutable.[20] He went on to argue that although Marx had made a signal contribution to socialist thought, the trends that he believed must inevitably lead to the dictatorship of the proletariat—the disappearance of the middle class, for instance, and the increasing immiseration of the working class—had not continued as Marx predicted. As a result, according to Marx's own theory, socialist revolution was now impossible.[21]

Given that impossibility, socialists had, according to Simkhovitch, revised Marx to the point that they were now mostly gradualists pushing for incremental change toward a more just world through democratic means. And that was just what progressive reformers were.[22] Most socialists and progressives, he averred, agreed that class struggle now occurred through speech, the press, and the ballot and that basic industry would eventually be controlled by government either through regulation or outright ownership.[23] Thus did socialism and progressivism, in Simkhovitch's view, converge. These arguments represented only one of many ways of thinking about the relationship between socialism and progressivism in the early twentieth century, but Simkhovitch's particular vision shaped Roche, and his example illustrated the inclination of many early twentieth-century progressives to reach out to—even to identify with—those farther left on the political spectrum. Drawing sharp distinctions between their own politics and that of activists farther left was simply not their interest.[24]

As if to shine a bright light on some of the very social and economic conditions that Roche studied in her graduate courses, a great labor uprising rocked New York during her first semester at Columbia. In November 1909, between 20,000 and 30,000 garment workers in New York City—mostly teenaged immigrant women—went on strike against their employers. Strikers wanted union recognition, higher wages, shorter hours, and safer working conditions. It was the largest strike by women workers to that point in U.S. history.[25]

Roche may have first become acquainted with the strike through her work with the New York Probation and Protective Commission (PPC). The PPC was in 1909 a private initiative that intervened in the legal process on behalf of arrested girls. By providing a girls-only detention home, the PPC kept the girls out of jail while they awaited trial. If a girl was convicted, the commission pressed for probation rather than incarceration and, if that plea was successful, supervised the probation. Roche's job for the commission stationed her by turns in the city's night court, a new institution set up specifically to arraign prostitutes, and the older magistrates' courts. In each place, she interviewed and advised girls who had run-ins with the law.[26] As the strike developed, some of her interviewees were striking seamstresses, who were arrested by the hundreds and dragged through the courts. Strikers were often enraged by the violence of police efforts to break up their picket lines, and they surely regaled Roche with grievances from their workplaces, anxieties about their families, and the excitement of taking matters into their own hands. The justice of their cause persuaded Roche, and many other middle-class women, to take to the streets with them.[27] In fact, Roche became so devoted to the picket line that Harvey O'Higgins teased her about being "down in the slums organizing anarchy instead of attending to your studies."[28]

As enthusiastically as Roche participated in the Uprising, however, the fight to unionize workers did not at this point become the focus of her reforming attention. The results of the strike may have been one reason. Although hundreds of employers raised wages and recognized the International Ladies Garment Workers Union (ILGWU), others refused to negotiate with any workers' organization, and the strikers' concern about safety on the shop floor was ignored entirely. One result was the horrific Triangle Shirtwaist Factory Fire in March 1911, which killed 146 workers, many of them teenaged immigrant girls. Roche witnessed the aftermath of that devastating tragedy.[29]

But there was another reason for Roche's relative lack of interest in unionization. Striking girls provided evidence for Roche's research, and she took their points of view very seriously, but they did not weigh heavily enough in her interpretive community to rivet her attention to labor organizing.[30] The group with whom Roche more seriously analyzed events in 1909 was her academic community, and that group did not construe unionization as a major aspect of the solution to turn-of-the-century social problems. With regard to diminishing economic and social inequality, the emphases of her curriculum at Columbia (and Vassar) leaned unambiguously in the direction of state action rather than toward the organization of workers.

In fact, the social scientists' lack of attention to labor unions was nearly total. In courses on social economics, where Roche studied what one professor named the "misery" of the working class—overcrowded living conditions, child labor, preventable illnesses, "exploitation of employees and consumers"—unionization as a possible solution to these problems never came up. Another of Roche's courses focused on the causes of poverty and another on the relation between poverty and crime; again, labor unions made no appearance.[31] Within the curriculum organized by Devine and Lindsay, social legislation supplemented by the efforts of civic associations offered the only imaginable response to social injustice.[32] Roche's courses in political economy also downplayed labor organization. Among the courses that Roche took during her three and a half years at Columbia, only one explicitly studied the labor movement. That was Henry Rogers Seager's course on "the labor problem." Even there, however, students spent only half of the term studying labor organizations. The other half analyzed social legislation.[33]

The social scientists' predilections were understandable. Labor unions at the time organized only a small portion of American workers, and most were bent on privileging a few skilled workers over the larger group considered unskilled. Add to that the disapproval of the labor movement among the university administrators to whom professors were beholden, and you have a solid explanation for progressive academics' wariness of the labor movement.[34] The crucial point is, however, that the version of progressivism that Roche absorbed through her academic life was social science progressivism, a strain of reform thinking that emphasized public policy as the prime method for diminishing inequalities of wealth and power and that showed little faith in the independent organization of workers. Roche's commitment to organized labor would come later and from sources other than her formal education.

Roche did fully internalize social science progressivism during her stint at Columbia. That much was clear in the master's thesis she wrote during her first year of graduate study. Titled "Economic Conditions in Relation to the Delinquency of Girls," her thesis explored the relationship between female delinquency, especially prostitution, and the material conditions of girls' lives. It did so on the theory that delinquent girls were neither sinful nor disposed by heredity to delinquency but were nudged toward destructive behavior by the social and economic particulars of daily life. Roche's research was on the cutting edge of work on female delinquency, an emerging specialty among women reformers and social scientists concerned with the welfare of the growing population of adolescent girls who worked for wages in American cities.[35] The new kinds of independence these girls won from paid labor, the anonymity of urban life, and the availability of commercial amusements allowed them to establish their own standards of behavior, which seemed to many middle-class Americans as well as working-class parents dangerous in the extreme. Most obvious and alarming, working-class girls were pioneering moral codes that allowed much greater leeway in sexual matters than most middle-class reformers thought healthy or wise. Since virtually any sexual experience outside marriage was believed by Roche and her colleagues to set a girl on the slippery slope toward prostitution, they initially defined much of what was becoming accepted social conduct among working-class girls as female delinquency.[36]

By taking on female delinquency, Roche joined a growing national campaign against vice, the targets of which were prostitution, gambling, and drunkenness. A wide range of motives moved reformers to study and oppose these practices, some of them progressive and some of them not, and Roche's mature perspective on vice developed after her graduate study.[37] But through her M.A. research, Roche came to an understanding of one aspect of that larger set of issues, which was prostitution.[38]

Roche viewed prostitution as the product of capitalist social relations shaped by a gender system that subordinated women to men.[39] As a progressive, Roche looked first to economic explanations of social phenomena, and she found a significant contributor to female delinquency in the peculiarly low wages of women and girls. She did not, however, attribute those low wages to economic laws or rationality but to gender discrimination.[40] She argued emphatically that the particularly low wages of female workers were not attributable to girls' own choice of low-wage employment or productive inefficiency.[41] Rather, a crucial contributing factor to the paltry wages of women and girls was what Roche called employers' "instinctive tendency to discriminate" against women and girls.[42] "Ingrained in people's minds so deeply that it may not consciously guide their reasoning and action," she elaborated, "is the traditional conception of woman as a dependent, engaged in the home in activities for which she receives shelter, food and care, but never monetary recompense." Despite overwhelming evidence to the contrary, employers continued to believe every girl has "somebody to keep her from having to live entirely on the wage she earns." This "time-worn opinion," according to Roche, largely explained the wage gap between women and men.[43]

Roche thus developed an understanding of women's wages that took to heart Vladimir Simkhovitch's insistence that, despite the primacy of economics in historical explanation, cultural systems operated independently of the economic base and in fact shaped that base.[44] One of those cultural systems was, to Roche's feminist way of thinking, what scholars now call "gender," a set of ideas about and practices of manhood and womanhood that has changed over time and varied among communities at any one time. Roche's M.A. thesis presented women's economic dependence, and by extension womanhood itself, as historical rather than natural. Women were not, according to Roche, inevitably dependent. Where female dependency existed, it was created by the exigencies of particular historical moments, and it was subject to change.

Indeed, history had already undermined women's economic dependence on men, rendering it by 1910 what Roche called "an antiquated condition."[45] Her research demonstrated for women workers in New York what was true for women workers in industry more generally: a significant percentage were the sole breadwinners for their families and many more contributed to the family budget over and above what was necessary to support themselves.[46] Moreover, a considerable number—about 35 percent—lived on their own. If working women had ever been economic dependents, they certainly were not in 1910.[47]

Even despite their economic responsibilities and wages inadequate to meet them, however, most working girls did not capitulate to prostitution. Roche maintained that low wages could not, therefore, be the sole cause of female delinquency. This recognition was extremely important to women workers, most of whom were badly paid and indignant at the suggestion that they were teetering on the brink of streetwalking.[48] Roche argued that while low wages alone were not "the cause" of delinquency, "it is the girl on this margin of economic competency and reward who feels especially keenly the opportunity for supplementing her wage that is always open to women and girls. . . . She has always the sex commodity to increase her income—and it sells well."[49]

In Roche's analysis, a spectrum of conditions—all of them rooted in either economic conditions or what we would later call "sexism"—colluded with low wages to induce girls to prostitution. These conditions ranged from sexual harassment at work to immersion in a consumer culture that created desire for goods that working girls could rarely afford. Exhaustion from excessive hours of work, loneliness, and violent home conditions—all played a role in causing prostitution. Overcrowded living conditions that afforded girls "no privacy of body or soul" drove some low-wage earners to the streets. The fatigue of parents, so tired they could offer no sympathy or even rest to their children after a hard day's work, sometimes contributed. So did dull work. One girl, considered "wild" by her family, was not so much wild, Roche thought, as bored to death by her work and out late at night to compensate for it.[50] The dehumanizing grind that industrialization so often made of waged work was part of Roche's explanation for female sexual delinquency.

So was the sexual double standard. At some length, Roche pointed out the central role that male consumers of all classes played in creating and sustaining prostitution. "As long as their generous investments continue to be ignored, covered up and condoned," Roche argued, prostitution would thrive.[51] Referring to the organization of consumer power among women reformers eager to improve the conditions of workers, Roche remarked, "In every other branch of the economic world we are holding the consumer responsible for the supply that is created by his demand. Why not this one?"[52] Roche was angry that men were not held to the same standard of sexual restraint as women and girls, and, rather than loosen restrictions on women—a telling choice—she preferred to tighten the restrictions on men.

Roche believed that sex was a potentially beautiful aspect of human experience but that it belonged ideally within the safe haven of marriage.[53] She did not at this point see significant distinctions among the nonmarital sexual experiences of working-class girls, and if she did recognize circumstances in which sex expressed a girl's own passionate desire and resulted in her genuine delight, Roche did not write about it. Although she circulated in Greenwich Village among artists and activists eager to break the restraints on women's sexuality, she does not seem to have shared their zeal for women's sexual freedom. Both sex radicals and more cautious reformers like Roche rejected some aspects of the dominant gender system, which insisted that men had greater sexual need than women. But while radicals rejected the dominant view of women and thus promoted greater freedom for women, Roche and progressives like her rejected the view of men and thus urged greater restrictions on men. Either way, the goal was to equalize the prerogatives of women and men.[54]

As for amelioration of female sexual delinquency, Roche argued that only a multipronged program, some of it economic, some of it cultural, could be effective. In this, she was precisely in line with other progressives who were writing on the subject or about to do so.[55] Progressive public policies that guaranteed a minimum wage to women were one part of her solution (union organizing did not appear in her recommendations).[56] Ending the sexual double standard was another prerequisite for ending girls' delinquency. To that end, children needed early sex instruction so that they would put health above all other considerations in their sexual decisions and insist that men be held to the same standard of sexual conduct as women. Good juvenile courts to sympathize with and counsel young people were another part of her solution, as Roche believed courts like Ben Lindsey's could help girls find constructive ways out of oppressive conditions that might otherwise drive them to prostitution. She also recommended greater recreational opportunities for young women and, of course, more research.[57]

Some of Roche's solutions to the problem of prostitution illuminated the sort of feminist she was becoming. Her support for minimum wage and maximum hours laws for women were one example. Progressives like Roche preferred protective labor legislation for all workers, male and female, but early twentieth-century courts blocked such policies for men. Just two years before Roche completed her master's thesis, the Supreme Court ruled, however, that women workers were so different from men that they could be granted special protections under the law. Citing women's peculiar weaknesses in the labor market and their biological value to the nation as actual or potential mothers, the Supreme Court allowed states to offer protections to women that they could not offer men. Thus, for instance, states could enact blanket maximum hours laws for women workers that the courts would not allow for men.[58]

The court's emphasis on the weaknesses and dependency of women rankled many feminists, but reformers like Roche put forward other arguments—feminist arguments—on behalf of such policies. Roche understood the unregulated labor market as an institution that subordinated women to men especially by paying women lower wages for comparable work. If that labor market were ever to promote women's independence rather than enforce their subordination, it had to be reformed. Minimum wage laws and maximum hours laws for women provided a method for that reformation; they might ameliorate the wage discrimination already operating against women workers. Roche thus argued for the special treatment of women workers not because women were naturally weak or dependent but because the labor market discriminated against them in a way it did not discriminate against men.[59]

Activists who explicitly called themselves feminists in the early twentieth century generally opposed sex-specific labor laws. They argued that such laws did not so much protect women workers as make it harder for them to find employment because employers faced special burdens when hiring women. Because these advocates claimed the name "feminist," reformers who supported protective labor legislation for women did not generally identify as feminists.[60]

Roche was among the reformers who did not self-identify as feminists, but she qualifies according to current standards. The most important commitment of feminism is opposition to women's subordination to men, and Roche certainly fulfilled that requirement. She also believed that women and men were more alike than different, that most apparent differences were created by history and not nature, and that those socially constructed differences were unjust to women. She resisted arguments that women were more nurturing, pacific, or cooperative than men and fought in many an arena to equalize the opportunities and conditions of women and men. Indeed, she saw minimum wage laws for women workers as a method for promoting women's equality in the labor market, not for hardening women's inferior economic opportunities.

Not all protective labor legislation had the same ramifications, however, and probing Roche's thinking about night work for women shows how easily class-sensitive analyses could produce discriminatory policies. Many progressives advocated the legal prohibition of night work for women workers. Roche herself argued, "Any kind of night work is undesirable for a girl, not only because it means she must be alone on the streets at a time when she is more liable to be endangered, but also in her place of work the number of liberties taken with her seem to increase with the very fact of its being night." She gave examples of the degrading insults and sexual harassment to which women were subject even in workplaces that would have seemed unusually safe.[61]

As Roche typed this evidence into her thesis, however, she enjoyed the freedom of being out on the city streets in the wee hours of the morning. While in graduate school, she sat up late in New York City's night court, waiting to interview accused criminals, and in Denver just a few years later she would take delight in nocturnal prowling through saloon districts as a vice cop. Roche did not want anyone restricting her work to the daylight hours, and she would soon howl with outrage when one of her mentors in Denver insulted her independence "by fretting and protesting against my doing night work."[62]

Roche's support for restricting working-class women's access to night work while exercising complete freedom herself was not simple hypocrisy, but it did result in class and gender discrimination. It was not simple hypocrisy because Roche knew that her class position granted certain kinds of protections on the streets that working-class girls did not enjoy. Like any woman, Roche took risks by being out alone at night, but in her workplaces and even on the street, potential harassers knew that a woman of her class had resources for punishing insult that working-class girls more than likely did not. To bear this out, Roche had to look no further than the utterly divergent experiences of working-class and middle-class women on the picket lines during the garment workers' Uprising. While policemen and judges thought nothing of breaking the ribs and tearing the clothes of working-class pickets, they were mortified when they unintentionally arrested pickets from higher classes.[63] Roche was right to think her class position protected her from some forms of violence and offense that working-class women and girls routinely faced. In recognizing this material reality, her anxiety about night work for working-class women was class-sensitive.

Roche's solution to the problem, however, was to restrict the opportunities of working-class women rather than to restrain men. Early twentieth-century progressives—even those desperate to advance women's prospects—had not yet imagined the means by which to restrain men from sexual harassment and violence. The infinitely easier solution to women's peculiar vulnerabilities was to restrict women themselves. Taking that easier route, Roche advocated a narrowing of working-class women's prerogatives that she utterly rejected for herself, and she does not seem to have recognized the inequity in that position. She did not notice that in advocating the prohibition of night work for wage-earning women, she was redefining the terms of working-class women's subordination rather than equalizing women and men. In this case, her class-sensitive analysis led her to support a discriminatory policy.[64]

Roche had plenty of opportunities to continue thinking about class and gender inequalities as her research within working-class communities continued after she completed her M.A. degree in 1910. The Russell Sage Foundation granted her a fellowship for investigating "foreign girls in industry," which funded her first year of doctoral work. The next year, she worked for the Public Education Association of New York, inquiring into the vocational opportunities available to children leaving the public school system.[65] These studies, based largely on door-to-door interviews, took Roche into tenement houses that sheltered thousands upon thousands of New York's immigrant workers.[66] The interviews represented Roche's conviction that statistics collected from government agencies, employers, and civic associations, even though they might document low wages, long hours, high unemployment, and ill-health among immigrant workers, were never sufficient for understanding social problems. "Records give facts, and are the basis of thorough work," she insisted, "but a fact plucked from all its human surroundings and set down in black and white, while it is the truth, is not enlightenment." For that, "one must know the human elements." These human elements could be ascertained only by actually getting to know those whose lives one wished to understand.[67] Roche had internalized her professors' commitment to the contextual nature of knowledge. And to the extent that Roche believed she must strive to understand the point of view of her research subjects, her approach to creating social science expertise required establishing personal relationships with those she studied.[68]

Consequently, in her second and third years of graduate school, Roche entered one immigrant apartment after another to gather data, and, as she did so, built personal relationships with working-class families. She sat in dark and crowded rooms, held babies on her lap, and discovered conditions well beyond the particular focus of her research.[69] Part of her goal was "comprehending sympathetically" the point of view and values of the communities she studied.[70] She wanted to see the world from their perspective. To some degree, she succeeded. "The most important result," of getting to know the subjects of her research personally was "the revelation of [moral] standards as sincere as they were different from our own."[71]

As Roche probed those standards, she came to believe that some immigrant groups nurtured values far superior to those of old-stock Americans. The contrast between what she beheld in Italian immigrant families, for instance, and knew of native-born Americans prompted a bitter condemnation of what she saw as the competitive, grasping values of American life. "Every field of our life is cultivated," she said, "according to the 'survival of the fittest.'" Regrettably, the "fittest under our conditions is the weed that can choke out most of its neighbors and spread itself over the social wheat."[72] The "social wheat," in this case, were Italian immigrants whose values she thought more humane than those dominant in the United States. She said of Italian families, "They wanted a life with music in it, and love and benevolence." They expected to marry young, to have large families, to dance and play music, to support others in times of crisis without giving it a thought.[73] So far as Roche could see, these were values that America needed, dominated as it was instead by "a race that married late and raised few children, that schemed and saved, and invested shrewdly, denying themselves everything but the joy of overreaching their neighbors until they had enough money to buy the labor" of Italian families "at the price of starvation."[74]

Although Roche accepted for her own life the modern disciplines that encouraged later marriage, fewer children, and careful budgeting, she allowed her encounters with immigrants to open her eyes to the losses in those choices. Her cross-class relationships revealed to her the damage done to generosity and community by the rationalized life required of many who would succeed in America on American terms. She was willing to question the values of her class and culture in light of alternatives her research subjects offered, and she seemed equally to mourn the restrictions that Italian families set on their daughters' lives and what she saw as the inevitable lifting of those restrictions as Italian girls Americanized.[75] Through her research, Roche also entered into relationships of mutual responsibility with some of the families she met. She sometimes sought jobs or health care for family members of those she interviewed, and the families invited her to weddings and christenings.[76] The objects of Roche's research were also subjects who, in some measure, transformed her perspectives.

While gathering data for her investigations, Roche enhanced her opportunities for cross-class acquaintances by moving into Greenwich House, the social settlement that had sent so many speakers to Vassar in her undergraduate days. One of Roche's professors, Vladimir Simkhovitch, and his wife, Mary Kingsbury Simkhovitch, ran the settlement, which was situated in the western part of Greenwich Village.[77] Inhabited by immigrants from nearly two dozen different countries, including especially Italians and Germans, the neighborhood also housed second-generation Irish and a significant number of African Americans.[78] Mary Simkhovitch claimed that she and the other founders of Greenwich House did not move into the neighborhood to tell its inhabitants how to improve their lives but rather to join the existing life of the community: "To feel together, to have the sense of comradeship, of fellowship" with their neighbors and then out of their common experience to develop joint projects.[79] It was no doubt this sentiment to which Roche referred when, as an older woman, she wrote to Vladimir Simkhovitch, "I have always cherished the priceless experience, the opening up of rare opportunities, and most of all the stimulus to fundamental thinking which you two gave me."[80]

That fundamental thinking was in evidence during the summer of 1911, when Roche wrestled mightily with how she might push harder toward more democratic personal relationships with working-class New Yorkers. While visiting her parents back in Denver, Roche confided to fellow settlement resident Read Lewis that she longed for "more democratic relations" with many of the girls in the neighborhood club she directed at the settlement and that she was considering moving out of Greenwich House to gain an "opportunity for experiments I'd love to try in the way of mixing people." If she had her own place, she could then have friends from Columbia and some of the boys and older girls served by the settlement "in for an evening." She wished for cross-class community outside the formal structures of the settlement or research.[81] However short she may have fallen from her own ideals, Roche strove in the 1910s to create more equal personal relations in her own life as well as to support policies that would reduce the economic inequalities between women and men, workers and employers.

Capturing those ideals in 1911, Roche and Read Lewis drew up what she later called their "Code," a set of values to which they committed their lives. The earnest young settlement workers actually wrote down this profession of faith on a moonlit night, sitting on the banks of the Hudson River. The Code demonstrated that the progressivism of Roche's professors had really taken hold and that her highest hope was to promote democratic decision making as well as egalitarian social and economic relations. In addition to the "scientific attitude of mind," which insisted that "the only source of knowledge is the observation of phenomena through our senses," the two affirmed their belief in the "potential progress of mankind . . . through their own efforts" and in "the ideals of democracy." They believed that "all mankind is united by bonds of common origin and heritage," that "our civilization is a social inheritance in which each has the right fully to share." Economic production, they insisted, "is a social process whose fruits all, being interdependent, should abundantly enjoy."[82] This Code identified goals to which Josephine Roche aspired the rest of her life.

In greater flux were the methods for reaching those goals. While Roche believed her research a genuine contribution to the process, in 1911 she was even more intrigued by the possibilities of politics. During a summer visit to Denver, she wrote back to New York, "I've had a few interesting talks with some of the 'Insurgents' here," referring to her Denver friends and their plans for a third-party effort in an upcoming election. "After an evening with the Costigans, I'm perfectly wild to be here & in the thick of it."[83]

The longing to be part of the rough and tumble of electoral politics perhaps gave greater urgency to Roche's work for women's suffrage back in New York. On behalf of the cause, she made speeches on street corners, marched in parades, and organized debates at Greenwich House.[84] In spring 1912, she asked Lindsey to tell Ed Costigan, "the suffrage parade is a week from Saturday and that we want him here as he was last year!"[85] Harvey and Anna O'Higgins did march in that parade and reported, "Josephine made a dandy soap-box speech."[86] That summer, Roche joined several other members of the Woman Suffrage Party of New York in proselytizing at Forty-first Street and Tenth Avenue. The speeches were, however, "interrupted by rocks, deluges of water, stale vegetables and a crowd of roughs." Undeterred, the intrepid activists returned to the site the very next week, riding in an open-air car. With police to protect them this time, they spoke to a crowd estimated at 200 to 300.[87] Despite frequent absences from the city between 1912 and the final victory of women's suffrage in New York in 1917, Roche never cut herself off from the campaign there. Political citizenship for women of all classes was an integral part of her progressive agenda.

Josephine Roche's soapbox speeches represented another step on her path toward public leadership. Although she did not yet direct a reform campaign, she was an increasingly vocal and visible advocate for progressive causes. Indeed, while in New York, she had fully absorbed the tenets of feminist social science progressivism and was ripe for the exciting possibilities back in Denver that would soon end her graduate studies and propel her to new heights of public authority.

CHAPTER 3

EMERGENCE AS A PUBLIC LEADER, 1912–1913

T he specific opportunity that drew Josephine Roche out of graduate school in 1912 was the chance to serve as Denver's first policewoman. She was thrilled to go back west. "I find a certain quality of life here that I hungered for in vain all the time I worked in New York," she explained, "I think perhaps I can express it by saying I feel more master of myself here."[1] By "mastery" of herself, Roche did not refer to personal freedom, which New York offered in greater degree than Denver, but to something she craved even more than freedom. That something was power. Only months after taking the police position, Roche transformed it into a command post in the campaign against Denver's notorious political machine. As a policewoman, Josephine Roche emerged as a controversial public figure with a stomach for battle.

Roche's permanent return to Denver was facilitated by political upheaval in Denver and the nation. In May 1912, while Roche was wrapping up another year of graduate work in New York, her friends in Denver won a remarkable local victory. Joined by other progressives, they formed an organization called the Citizens' Party, the purpose of which was to elect a mayor and city council free of allegiance to the corporate interests that controlled the state's Democratic and Republican parties.[2] To the great surprise of all, the Citizens' Party swept the election.[3] The victorious mayoral candidate, Henry Arnold, then appointed George Creel, stalwart of Roche's political "gang," as police commissioner.[4] The unlikely appointment would soon redirect Roche's life.

Meanwhile, other members of Roche's "gang," Benjamin Lindsey and Edward Costigan, were helping to organize one of the most important national third-party experiments in American history. The Progressive

Party, which would also shape Roche's future, initially sprouted from dissatisfactions among progressive Republicans, who expected their favorite candidate to win the Republican Party's presidential nomination in June 1912. When he did not, the disappointed activists formed a new party, intending to nominate former president Theodore Roosevelt to carry their banner in the presidential race. Rumored as a possible vice-presidential candidate, Lindsey devoted considerable energies to organizing a branch of the Progressive Party in Colorado, and most of Roche's political circle went right along with him.[5] Costigan chaired the party's State Central Committee and was by acclamation nominated its candidate for governor.[6] Even though Roche was living in New York at the time, Lindsey and Costigan wangled her designation as an official delegate from Colorado to the party's national convention. "I was the only woman incidentally in the Colorado crowd of twenty," she reported to a friend, adding, "I can't say I was at all disturbed by my oneness."[7]

The character of the Progressive Party's national convention helps to explain why Roche would subsequently view politics as potentially a "fine, just thing."[8] Held in the cavernous Coliseum of Chicago between August 5 and 7, 1912, the convention was likened at the time to a religious revival, attended by thousands of women and men who held the highest ideals and were bursting with hope for making American politics serve those lofty goals. Participants believed they were reinvigorating democracy and that, in their hands, party politics could transcend the petty ambitions of crass politicians and become a method for improving the lives of countless Americans disadvantaged by the new corporate order.[9]

One of several hundred official delegates, Roche belonged to a female elite. Even though the press wrote obsessively about the unusual numbers of women attending the Progressive Party convention, probably fewer than twenty served as official delegates.[10] The venerable reformer, Jane Addams, acted as their chief. According to Roche, Addams "had the women delegates to breakfast Tuesday and Wednesday mornings, where there was worked out the plan for sending out a call to the women of all states and for their organization with men on state and county committees."[11] That plan pleased Roche. She wanted women and men working together, not separately, in politics.

Fittingly then, for all her participation in women's caucuses during the convention, Roche was more deeply intrigued by the glimpses of power provided by her male mentors. She confided, "I'll have to confess, however, that the most interesting part of it all to me has been the interviews Ed [Costigan] and the Judge [Lindsey] have included me in with Roosevelt." Those interviews focused on a situation in Colorado that tested the presidential candidate's loyalties. After Costigan's nomination for governor by Colorado's Progressive Party, an old friend of Roosevelt's had started angling for the Republican nomination there. Costigan desperately needed Roosevelt to make a public commitment to the state's Progressive Party ticket. Otherwise, the fledgling party had no chance of taking flight. Roche was fascinated by the negotiations. She observed of Roosevelt, "He has been a most interesting person to watch and listen to during the proceedings." After a final midnight conference, "a public statement has been secured," she reported with relief, "and the fall campaign will be the most thrilling yet out there."[12] Roosevelt supported Costigan.

Roche's experience with her male mentors at the convention was formative. By drawing Roche into politics not only as one of the few official women delegates at the convention but also as a participant in cloaked deal-cutting sessions, the men in Denver provided her a proximity to power rare among women of her generation and assured her that women's place was at the center of power.[13] The experience also helps to explain her future comfort with backroom deals. Because of it—or similar experiences—Roche discerned an intimate relationship between covert deal making and the fulfillment of principle. If convincing Roosevelt to endorse Costigan's gubernatorial bid increased the possibility of winning egalitarian public policies, then hidden pacts on behalf of power-seekers sometimes served the highest ideals and had to be one of the arrows in a reformer's quiver.

The Progressive Party platform was chock full of high ideals. Roche thought it so forward-looking that she had trouble believing it a product of "this century & not the next." No wonder, then, that this platform laid out nearly the whole of Roche's political commitments for the next sixty years.[14] In fact, she repeated phrases directly from the platform into her old age.

Outlining a new meaning for American government and expanding the scope of American politics, the preface to the platform asserted, "the people must use their sovereign powers to establish and maintain equal opportunity and industrial justice." To do so, they must, according to the platform, "dissolve the unholy alliance between corrupt business and corrupt politics," which acted as "an invisible government owing no allegiance and acknowledging no responsibility to the people." To resecure "government by a self-controlled democracy," the party pledged its support for much of the populists' old platform: direct primaries for nomination of state and national offices; the direct election of senators; and the initiative, referendum, and recall of elected officials. It even supported the recall of some state-level judicial decisions. To Roche and her Colorado crowd, recalling judicial decisions by popular vote seemed a reasonable way to lodge more power in a larger public, diminishing the undue authority of a judicial elite.[15]

In relation to the economy, the Progressive Party also followed the populists in advocating the subordination of private enterprise to the public interest. Specifically, the platform proposed "a strong National regulation of inter-State corporations," which must make their transactions public and justify their profit through genuine service to the citizenry. The platform insisted further that all land and other natural resources currently under state or federal control should remain in public hands.

Beyond this program of political and economic democracy, the Progressive Party platform promoted a dramatic expansion of governmental responsibility for the welfare of individual citizens. Proclaiming that the "supreme duty of the Nation is the conservation of human resources," the Progressive Party supported a broad range of labor and social welfare measures that demonstrated progressives' intention to diminish class and gender inequalities.[16] Redistributive measures like an inheritance tax and a progressive income tax as well as social insurance for the ill, aged, and unemployed addressed class inequities. Support for unionization and the prohibition of injunctions in labor disputes did the same. Promotion of women's suffrage and minimum wage laws for women workers took aim at gender inequality.[17]

Racial inequalities proved more problematic. Roche, like many of her white progressive colleagues, barely noticed racial inequality until the 1930s, and others soft-pedaled opposition to racial injustice in hopes of winning the white South to the new party. As a result, the platform did not explicitly condemn racial discrimination or even racial violence.[18] Although the party did oppose convict labor, a practice especially oppressive to African Americans, the convention seated lily-white delegations from three southern states despite vociferous protests. The committee in charge of this decision argued along with Roosevelt that only when the Progressive Party was established as a national organization could it work effectively for social and economic justice for black Americans below the Mason-Dixon Line.[19]

Some members of the Progressive Party nevertheless stood firm for an immediate commitment to racial justice. Thirteen northern and border states sent interracial delegations to the convention; many white as well as black delegates protested the all-white contingents from the South.[20] Even after the party seated the all-white delegations, most black delegates remained at the convention and, in recognition of the party's potential benefit to all marginalized people, a contingent within the Women's Convention of the Black Baptist Church soon endorsed Roosevelt's candidacy.[21] Racial justice was thus a compelling issue for some progressives, both black and white. For Roche and many others, however, it was at this point a much lower priority than class and gender justice.

With the platform decided and representation uneasily sorted out, delegates nominated their candidates for office and dispersed to campaign. In the end, Ben Lindsey did not run as Roosevelt's vice-presidential candidate. California's Hiram Johnson won that honor. But, committed to the party's national platform and even more enthusiastic about the Colorado party's candidates and ballot measures, Roche spent the rest of August campaigning for the Progressive Party in Denver.[22] To her dismay, Roosevelt would not win the presidency, but he gave the Democratic victor, Woodrow Wilson, a genuine run for his money.

Given her excitement about the election, Roche may have been torn about returning to New York in September 1912.[23] But return she did, expecting to complete her Ph.D.[24] No sooner had she settled into her classes, however, than she received an urgent message from Denver: the Commissioner of Police wanted her to become Denver's first policewoman.[25]

Throughout the campaign season, George Creel had been enjoying the prerogatives of his appointment to Denver's Fire and Police Board. Among other things, they granted him substantial power in hiring two inspectors of public amusements, positions created by Denver's reforming city council to enforce new rules regulating the city's dance halls, skating rinks, and movie theaters. The novel regulations aimed especially to protect Denver's youth from exploitation by purveyors of alcohol and sex.[26] One new regulation prohibited boys and girls under eighteen from attending public dances after 10:00 pm unless accompanied by a parent, another required that everyone under twenty-one register in a ledger on entering a dance hall, and yet another forbade anyone under eighteen to be in a dance hall that sold liquor.[27] When the city council specified that one of the new inspectors of public amusements should be a woman, Creel could think of no one better qualified than his gang's protégé, Josephine Roche.[28]

Roche jumped at the chance to return to Denver even though it meant sacrificing whole dimensions of her rich life. She would live in a much smaller town and at home with her parents; she would miss New York's opera, theater, and museums. She would have to give up Sunday "tramps" in the Hudson River Valley with her friend Read Lewis and their discussions of art, novels, and the meaning of life. In her own words, leaving New York required "the giving up of such countless things of value—all the intellectual stimulus, the great variety of interests and friends, the many beautiful things, the personal liberty, and freedom of expression."[29] At the same time, Roche was just not satisfied with the life of a student and researcher. She was ready to try her hand at changing the world more directly, to "be of it all," in her words.[30] She wanted direct public power.

To a reporter in Denver, she explained, "I am so delighted to get back home where the social questions are connected with government."[31]

Although New York State had begun passing a raft of social legislation in 1912, thereby connecting the social question to government there as well, Roche did have reason for thinking Denver ahead in the progressive race. Not only had reformers swept local elections in May and state offices in November, but by significant margins, Colorado's voters had approved many progressive referenda in the recent election. As a result, the state now provided public stipends for poor widows with dependent children, mandated the eight-hour day for women workers and miners, and allowed voters to recall some judicial decisions as well as elected officials.[32] Roche hoped to support implementation of the Mothers' Compensation Act and the Eight-Hour Law for women workers in addition to pursuing her police work because she saw them all as interrelated aspects of changing the conditions that disadvantaged working-class families.[33] Moreover, of course, she wanted to be in a place where women voted, and she was delighted by the prospect of working with Lindsey and Creel.[34]

Roche was able to extricate herself from New York just before Thanksgiving. She hopped a train to Chicago, and then caught another on to Denver. During the last leg of her journey, she crossed from the East into the West and was mesmerized by the awesome beauty of the Plains, visible through her train window. "The sage, buffalo grass & tumbleweeds are almost as lovely & golden a brown as the hills on the Hudson last Sunday," she wrote. "It is so good to see just as far as you can see. On all sides." And then, as she continued to watch out the train's window at sunset, not too far outside Denver, she witnessed "the wildest bunch of horses galloping madly away from us." She wistfully observed, "They look as if they could go forever." It was hard to believe, she thought, "that forty eight hours ago I was on Broadway in a taxi!"[35] Josephine Roche loved both horses and taxis, but western landscapes exerted a special pull on her. They touched her in a way no eastern vista ever did.

Although her parents opposed her taking the police job—perhaps because of its physical dangers; perhaps because it too dramatically violated gender norms—Roche was sworn in as one of Denver's inspectors of amusements on November 20, 1912.[36] She refused to carry a weapon and, in fact, heartily endorsed Creel's decision that police should not carry even night sticks. But Roche proudly wore her silver police badge (and later a deputy sheriff's badge) as she patrolled Denver's dance halls, movie theaters, and skating rinks.[37] Decades later, when she was preparing her papers for deposit in the University of Colorado Archives, Roche carefully preserved those badges (figure 3).[38] Her stint as a law enforcement officer meant a lot to her.

The silver badges of law enforcement represented one of Roche's many chances to expand the meaning of womanhood. They identified her with the rugged and edgy masculinity of lawmen in the Wild West. Such heroes had figured in the stories that Roche heard as a child in Nebraska, and, well beyond the West, sheriffs like Bat Masterson and Wyatt Earp assumed legendary status for their steely courage and lethal skill with a six-shooter. Most interesting, those famous sheriffs had often spent time on the wrong side of the law themselves. They were men who could defeat the wiliest and most vicious criminals because they were themselves cunning and cruel. An active member of Roche's progressive circle in Denver, muckraking journalist William MacLeod Raine was a prolific producer of sentimental Westerns, a new genre of fiction featuring such western heroes.[39] There can be little question, then, that Roche was aware of the violent and individualistic masculinity widely associated with western lawmen, and she toyed with that association when she took her new job. Just as she had pushed the gender envelope in college by playing sports and debating, just as she relished being the only woman in her delegation at the Progressive Party convention, so did she thrill at breaking the bonds of femininity by pinning to her chest the badge of a western lawman.[40]

The badge was not Roche's only masculine prop. She looked the part of a western lawman in other ways, too. In the early 1910s, her public self-presentation was fearsome (figure 4). She favored long-skirted suits, no jewelry, and broad-brimmed hats. Given her still somewhat chubby face and round glasses, she exuded the spirit of a woman who took no guff. In private, the matter seems to have been entirely different, as friends described her as "strong, gentle, maternal." But public photographs between 1912 and 1913 show Roche to be a supremely self-confident woman aiming to project authority in no uncertain terms.[41]

Even as Roche infused womanhood with masculine traits, she simultaneously attempted to imbue the law with feminine qualities. In particular, she hoped to transform law enforcement by associating it with persuasion and cooperation rather than raw force. After only five weeks in the police department, she was troubled to have "found the people's attitude toward the law and toward women here. It seems almost beyond belief that to the big majority, government—law does mean force—physical, brute force." She came to this conclusion by watching the response of thousands of Denverites to the police in the city's large dance halls late at night, when fights routinely broke out and police intervened. To many, she explained, the police "meant simply something that bullied them, struck them, and got the best of them—usually—but a something they could evade at times & fool, and when this hated something is represented in a woman—oh then there's contempt." This vision of both law and women appalled her but also increased her commitment to her work: "If I never do anything else I'm going to make some of them anyway, realize that law and government are not the things of animal force they think them—and that no one is more concerned in or fit for carrying that out than women."[42]

To this end, she ridiculed the suggestion that she pack a weapon and avoided wholesale arrests. She opted instead for reason and counsel. Roche never took children into custody; she just took them home when they were out too late, imbibing alcohol, or flirting with trouble in other ways. At first, she found businessmen generally cooperative as she explained the city's new rules and urged compliance.[43] Just after Christmas, Roche tested her unarmed legal authority during an investigation of a summer resort situated on the outskirts of Denver. As it was winter, the resort was mostly deserted, but the manager tried to keep his skating rink open. Because the rink had no proper license, authorities had recently shut it down, "but intuition told" Roche that the enterprise might be operating on the sly. About 10:00 pm on a cold night, she approached the jumble of dark and mostly abandoned buildings, where the rink gave off the "only bit of light on endless stretches of black planes." She went inside. Fingers metaphorically crossed, she walked up to the manager and "after explaining who I was . . . politely (oh <u>very</u> politely) ordered the place closed at once." She held her breath because she feared the manager would not actually do as she ordered. To her surprise: "He went straight over and rang the gong, and in fifteen minutes the place was empty!"[44] She was deeply relieved that the authority of her badge seemed to carry the day. It was a victory for the moral rather than "animal force" of law. The episode also demonstrated Roche's considerable courage.

Roche's new work demanded every ounce of that courage. Only three days after she returned to Denver, George Creel and Ben Lindsey left town to attend George's nuptials to actress Blanche Bates. Roche was anxious about their leaving for even a few weeks because it became clear very quickly that the reform mayor elected in May had, to use her understated phrase, "not made good." In her view, "He's meant well but is weak." In particular, he failed to stand up to the remnants of Denver's political machine who still dominated the city's Fire and Police Board. Moreover, unbeknownst to her but very soon apparent, "George . . . had a terrific fight to get me appointed. . . . Not only those in the administration were opposed, but the women politicians were much angered that one of their number were not to get the job as a reward for campaign services."[45]

As soon as Lindsey and Creel were out of town, conservative forces in the city moved against various progressive achievements. For instance, they attempted to gut the new Mothers' Compensation Act. Mothers' compensation had nothing officially to do with Roche's police job, but she was very committed to the measure because it sought, in her eyes, to supplant charity with justice. Her understanding of the act was "to get away from charity" by devoting public monies to stipends for widows with young children so that these single mothers would not have to work for wages. Using taxpayer dollars for the purpose recognized mother-hood as a valuable and honorable public service. But Mayor Arnold re-fused to include an appropriation in the city budget to fund the compen-sation program and insisted that money for the program should come instead from the city's Charity Board. Roche was outraged at that be-trayal of the bill's intent and helped to rouse Denver's citizens against Arnold's threat.[46]

Roche led that effort on top of her fourteen-hour days on a police beat. Her midnight rounds of the city's commercial amusements left her six hours to sleep at night—when she was lucky. What she witnessed on the streets of Denver in the wee hours shocked her at first, but she quickly got "over blushing with shame," even though she freely admitted that her "first week was a series of mortifications." Although she had fraternized with girls arrested for sexual offenses in New York, she had apparently not been so close to the actual sale of sex there as she was in Denver, and the experience made her want to "stand on a street corner . . . and tell people what their young men were doing, and just make them wake up." Despite the hardships, she found the work "indescribably delightful" and now saw her work in New York as a "dilettante existence." "Frankly, I am just crazy about everything here—the hard parts included. It's stirring and fascinating."[47]

Stirring indeed. Since reformers held all positions in city government that had been elected in May, and the old guard retained many other positions, some city agencies were pretty much at war. When Roche de-scribed Denver as in "an extraordinary state of upheaval," she was not exaggerating. Instead of driving Roche crazy, however, the upheaval "cheered" her because she saw the topsy-turviness as a sign that democ-racy was having its way. "We've had ten years of a perfectly running and oiled city machine and I think the present friction indicative of a rather wholesome change." She exclaimed, "Let 'em row and talk it out! There never was a time before when any but the chosen few could express themselves."[48]

As late as December, most of the conflict did not touch Roche's police work. As long as she focused on the amusements that catered mainly to adolescents, she maintained general support for her work. But Roche re-stricted her work to the juvenile ordinances only briefly. Early in 1913, she joined George Creel in a crusade to rid the city of prostitution, ex-panded her purview to investigate a wider range of businesses, and participated in a special election to change Denver's form of government. These entangled issues plunged Roche into a spectacular controversy that ended George Creel's career as police commissioner, demonstrated progressives' potential for violating the rights of people they aimed to support, and culminated in a very public showdown between Roche and the political machine in Denver. In the process, Roche emerged as a progressive leader in her own right.

When Denver's reforming city council decided to regulate dance halls and skating rinks, it built on an older set of restrictions against gambling, prostitution, and alcohol. Earlier municipal ordinances prohibited the sale of liquor to minors, ordered restaurants and cafés to sell liquor to adults only with food, and stopped the sale of liquor at any establishment after midnight. Saloons, which paid a higher licensing fee than restaurants or cafés, could sell liquor without food but were still subject to the other restrictions.[49] Gambling and prostitution were altogether illegal.[50] These older restrictions had long been observed more in the breach than in earnest thanks to close connections between Denver's commercial interests and municipal government. In some saloons, gambling brought in a brisk business for which proprietors occasionally paid small fines that they treated as a sort of extra licensing fee. Paying off the police kept the number of raids to a minimum.[51] Cooperative elected officials also helped. When in power, Denver's machine politicians made sure the police overlooked saloonkeepers' violations of the gambling and liquor laws in exchange for votes that the barkeeps controlled on election days. The mayor's power to review liquor licenses each year gave him another kind of hold on the political loyalty of businessmen in the saloon district.[52] These entanglements between city government and local businesses were one target of the Citizens' Party, whose members knew that an attack on gambling was an attack on the political machine, and to weaken the political machine was a threat to the profits that saloonkeepers accrued through gambling.

Prostitution was another element in this mix of politics and commerce. As in other cities around the country and especially those in the West, prostitution was closely associated with the central city's saloons and gambling houses.[53] Denver's well-known red-light district was in the heart of the saloon neighborhood.[54] In addition to larger brothels, or "parlor houses," the district featured a stretch of stalls open to the street like latter-day suburban car garages, each stall, or "crib," enclosable with a corrugated door. When the door was open, the interior of each crib was fully on display, featuring a woman, a bed, a chair, and a washstand. When a customer entered, the door was unceremoniously pulled down. A few minutes later, it reopened, and the woman awaited her next customer. Because prostitution improved business in the saloon district, it

was another illicit enterprise protected by Denver's political machine; because adolescent boys and girls joined adult men in packing the crib district every night, Josephine Roche saw prostitution as a legitimate concern of her police work.[55]

She was not the first Denverite worried about prostitution. As was true
elsewhere, the sex trade in Denver drew the attention of a wide spectrum
of reformers, not all of them progressives.[56] Before Roche's return to the
city, a group of ministers, for instance, had urged George Creel to initiate
a campaign against prostitution, not because it exploited women, as
Roche believed, but because prostitutes were immoral. Another contingent worried about "white slavery," a phrase used to conjure the image of
innocent girls lured into sex by deception or drugs and then held in captivity to satisfy the sexual desires of unscrupulous customers.[57] Along
with Roche, Creel rejected these interpretations of the trade. He did not
see prostitutes as sinners in need of salvation, criminals in need of jail
time, or innocents ruined by depraved men. As a progressive, he saw
them as poor women with few alternative means of support. Most prostitutes, he insisted, were "helpless victims of economic and industrial injustices."[58] He also came to agree with Roche that prostitution represented acquiescence in the sexual double standard, especially the
assumption that men had to have more sex than most women desired
and so must have sex available on the open market. To use his own
words, Creel rejected the "physiological necessity of the male" as justification for prostitution.[59]

Because he believed prostitution a danger to prostitutes themselves,
Creel moved as police commissioner to undermine the institution through
indirect measures. He shut down massage parlors and other fronts for the
trade. He closed the red-light district to minors and forbade the sale of
alcohol there.[60] By December 1912, he estimated that only 250 of an
original 700 prostitutes continued to ply their trade in Denver, and all
without arresting a single woman.[61] He proudly proclaimed, "I will not
hound the individual prostitute."[62] Many saloonkeepers and their political allies did not share Creel's satisfaction with this diminution of the
trade, which they perceived as a threat to their incomes and political
power.

Late in 1912, Roche, Creel, and other members of the Citizens' Party
opened a new front against that same political-business alliance. They
began circulating petitions for a special election to change the governing
structure of Denver.[63] The reformers believed they might further weaken
the local political machine if they replaced the strong mayor and city
council with an elected commission. Each commissioner would be elected
at large, and each would oversee a particular area of municipal governance. One commissioner would supervise public safety; another, taxa-

tion; someone else, social welfare; and so on. The commissioners would constitute the legislative body of the city and also act as executives, leaving the mayor only to preside over commission meetings and municipal ceremonies.

Commission government, though it did not assure representation from every urban ward, was not an undemocratic form of municipal self-rule. Commissioners were after all elected, and in places like Denver, the goal of reformers was to create a governing system that dispersed executive power across the several commissioners in hopes that business interests— ranging from saloonkeepers to power companies and railroads—would be less able to control them than they could a single mayor. In this hope, progressives would be disappointed, but in Denver their goal was to undercut the power of politically corrupt businesses rather than the working-class or immigrant voters that reformers in some cities may have targeted.[64] Confirming the reformers' analysis, business interests in Denver fought their drive for commission government, and even won over the reforming mayor, Henry Arnold, who became a bitter enemy of Roche and her progressive circle as a result. Roche and her cronies nonetheless collected enough signatures to force a special election on municipal government, which was scheduled for February 14, 1913.[65]

As that campaign heated up, Creel's battle with his fellow commissioners on the Fire and Police Board intensified. They reversed his decision to prohibit alcohol in the red-light district, which weakened his campaign against prostitution and the political alliances built on protecting the trade.[66] At the same time, Creel started receiving what he perceived as "appalling statistics, furnished by the hospital authorities, free dispensaries and the medical profession," reporting the rampant "spread of venereal disease" in Denver.[67] In response, Creel reignited his anti-prostitution campaign by acting as though the red-light district was the source of rampant VD. In doing so, Creel represented the progressive zeitgeist. Even as he was merging the issues of venereal disease and prostitution, a national coalition of doctors, feminists, moralists, and progressives was forming the American Social Hygiene Association, a political coalition devoted to, among other things, the eradication of prostitution because of its association with disease.[68]

Roche was well prepared to help Creel meet mounting public concern about venereal disease and to do so in a way they both imagined might free some women from prostitution. While Roche was in New York, the state had passed a law requiring all convicted prostitutes to submit to an examination for venereal disease. Those who tested positive could be detained for up to a year while they were treated.[69] Maude Miner, founder of the detention facility where Roche worked during her first year of graduate school, had instituted a similar procedure for "delinquent" girls in her care and become a major advocate of these procedures across the country.[70]

No doubt with New York's model in mind, Roche and Creel decided early in 1913 to take Denver's prostitutes into custody, test them for venereal disease, and treat those who tested positive. "Any other course," Creel explained, "meant scattering the plague over city and state."[71] Creel and Roche insisted that their roundup not only protected public health but also served prostitutes themselves. The staggeringly high rate of disease among those arraigned provided some evidence for the claim: of the first 144 women arrested, 95 tested positive for venereal disease.[72] With that information, Roche went to the crib district and convinced some women to submit voluntarily to testing.[73] Both Roche and Creel hoped they might help women find alternatives to prostitution while they awaited test results, a hope that, however sincere, proved vain.[74]

Ironically, Roche's and Creel's motive to protect public health and save prostitutes from their profession rather than simply punish individual women for breaking the law resulted in egregious violations of prostitutes' civil rights. If the duo had aimed only to punish crimes, each accused woman would have been arrested, fined, and released. As it was, each was forcibly tested for syphilis and gonorrhea and held for ten days until test results were conclusive. Any who were disease-free were then released; any who tested positive were held for treatment, a ghastly regimen of Salvarsan injections followed by multiple doses of mercury, a known poison.[75] Detentions for both testing and treatment were strictly *in*voluntary.

In this campaign, Roche and Creel vividly demonstrated the potential for progressive intentions to produce anti-progressive results. Both reformers genuinely yearned to improve the lives of women they saw as exploited because of their womanhood and poverty. But they could not imagine a way to rein in the exploiters rather than the exploited. And, given the very inequalities they opposed, as policymakers they had less power to restrict the exploiters than to adjust the exploited in some way. The result was that Roche and Creel never suggested arresting customers or pimps, examining their bodies, and then holding them for test results or treatment. Students at the local high schools, where venereal disease was known to be spreading, were not detained and forced to undergo physical examinations. In the name of ameliorating class and gender exploitation, Roche and Creel violated the civil rights of only working-class women. Gender and class privilege continued to protect men and better-off women from similar violations. Race, too, was implicated. The one shred of evidence on the issue reveals that on one night of Creel's round-ups, 22 women were arrested in the red-light district, 20 of whom were black.[76] Even if these 20 were the only black women among the 144 initially arrested, black women would have been disproportionately represented among the detained because black people accounted for less than 3 percent of Denver's total population and black women would have accounted for over 13 percent of those arrested.[77]

For a social science progressive like Roche, the detentions provided an irresistible research opportunity. She was eager to interview those in custody to establish their reasons for entering "the life." When her interviews revealed that half entered prostitution from dire economic need, she published the data in local newspapers and bombarded local women's groups with her findings, hoping to deflect moral condemnation away from prostitutes and onto a sexist labor market. Indeed, Roche spoke all over town at women's clubs and many other civic organizations to convince the public both that the "physiological necessity of the male" was a sham and that women went into prostitution not from immorality but from economic desperation. In the process, she made her progressive feminist analysis of prostitution front-page news.[78]

Roche's anti-vice crusade cautions against construing campaigns against prostitution, alcohol, and gambling exclusively as attempts to impose middle-class morality on workers.[79] Progressives like Roche mounted anti-vice campaigns because they recognized an exploitive labor and gender relationship in prostitution and a potentially exploitive consumer relationship in saloons and gambling houses. Moreover, because businesses specializing in vice routinely established corrupt liaisons with local governments, and they were, in Colorado at least, politically allied with larger corporate interests, they posed a threat to democratic governance. "Moral reform" was, for Roche and others like her, motivated by desires to reinvigorate democracy and rein in corporate power, not by a desire to discipline a rowdy working class.[80]

Roche explicitly rejected personal morality as the issue in her anti-vice work. Although she was willing to make common cause with religious opponents of prostitution, for instance, she loathed doing so. She deeply resented their "making the whole great civic, political and economic problem a religious one." Roche believed not only that the religious or moral analysis of prostitution was erroneous but also that the pious stand against it was politically ineffective. For one thing, the churchgoers often "made themselves and their 'moral question' so prominent that of course it antagonized the few intelligent voters" who might vote against machine politicians if the issue were properly construed. (Roche's implicit equation of "religious" with "unintelligent" is a stark illustration of the arrogance with which she at times expressed herself and a reason for the vehemence of the backlash against progressivism among religious conservatives later in the century.) Second, Roche had a skeptical view of the priority the pious gave to their allegedly "moral" commitments on Election Day. Of "the dear church people" she said: "So many of them own property around the red light district" that "on a secret ballot they can vote their property interests with the feeling of duty done in having told their neighbor to be good."[81] Here again, Roche construed prostitution not as a moral issue but as an economic issue: prostitution profited the propertied.

Despite Roche's ceaseless public relations work, the reaction against shuttering the red-light district was swift and firm. Denverites protested the expense of detaining and treating prostitutes, and they believed the detentions exceeded Creel's legitimate powers. But most of all, businessmen in and around the red-light district raised a ruckus against their loss of income. In the midst of what Roche called a "volcanic existence of charges and answer," the mayor suspended Creel from the Fire and Police Board, ostensibly for calling the fire commissioner names but really for his attack on the saloon and red-light districts. The suspension came shortly before the special election on commission government, which was correctly perceived as another attack on the same political and economic interests as Creel's anti-vice work.[82] As the referendum on commission government neared, Creel's and Roche's opponents pulled out all the stops against it, revealing themselves to be, in Roche's view, the "old style double standard 'woman's place is in the home' types."[83] One angrily proclaimed that Roche had no business "doing a <u>man's</u> work," to which she exploded, "it was because it [police work] <u>had</u> been a man's work through the centuries that we had our conditions today."[84]

Although progressives won their bid for commission government by a huge margin, Creel was not reinstated as head of the police department. He consequently returned to New York City, where his wife resumed her stage career, and he returned to writing.[85] The former progressive Mayor Arnold then allied himself squarely with the older machine and the remaining Fire and Police Board against Creel's anti-vice campaign. Inspector Roche was left in a precarious position. Indeed, she later described her situation as "a hopeless job."[86] It was made the more so by the fact that her other closest ally, Judge Lindsey, suffered what Roche termed a "dreadful nervous breakdown" shortly after the February election.[87] His collapse sent him to bed for a month and not long after to a sanitarium in Battle Creek, Michigan.[88] With Lindsey and Creel out of the picture, Roche occupied the spotlight alone as an indignant opponent of the political corruption that depended on illicit commerce. "Since the Judge left it's been worse," she sighed," With him and George gone and Ed overwhelmed with [other] work . . . there's been no one to turn to."[89]

Roche sincerely missed her allies, but their absence allowed her to come into her own as a public leader. By investing her with public authority and then abandoning her, Roche's Denver mentors left her in sole command of the anti-corruption campaign. As a result, there remained no sign of the ordinary student struggling to find her leadership feet at Vassar College. Roche instead became the constant focus of giant headlines, some of which she wrote herself. Hoping against hope that local elections in May might change prospects for progressive measures in the city, Roche remained fully on the offensive against Denver's political machine.[90]

It was a bitter battle. Just as her opponents hired a detective to shadow her, hoping "to get something on" her, she set out to destroy the president of the Fire and Police Board, A. A. Blakely. She informed her friends in New York, "I'm collecting the dope on Blakely."[91] In mid-March, she went public with her reconnaissance: she reported to the press that Blakely had promised legal protection to dance halls that sold liquor after midnight.[92] In a series of articles, she then exposed extensive violations of the city's liquor laws, a series of which, to put it lightly, the "mayor did not approve" and about which "the members of the fire and police board were in no way enthusiastic."[93] In fact, Roche knew that from that moment on, the mayor and the Fire and Police Board were doing everything in their power to get rid of her.[94]

Rather than back off, Roche intensified her undercover research. She spent the next month working as an investigator for Denver's vice commission, an increasingly common device of reformers eager to break corporate power in their cities by attacking gambling, drunkenness, and prostitution.[95] Roche's investigation focused on restaurants and cafés in Denver, which she visited in the wee hours of the morning during the first three weeks of April. In minute detail, she recorded in one establishment after another the selling of liquor without food, open solicitation by prostitutes, serving of liquor after midnight and to minors, as well as the routine appearance of policemen who ignored these violations of city ordinances. She usually visited the cafés and restaurants with an escort, and they were sometimes ushered into a private room, where they were served martinis or beer after hours and where the waiter suggestively "knocked each time before entering."[96]

Only days after Roche concluded this research, she was fired as inspector of public amusements. She found out through a local newspaper. "On Thursday," she wrote, "I picked up a paper and saw in big headlines that I'd been fired—my first notification!"[97] The mayor circumspectly explained the discharge as a matter of cost-cutting. A. A. Blakely was not so restrained. He skewered Roche and her reforming colleagues for gender bending and intruding into family life: "I do not favor long-haired men and short-haired women who step into the limelight and direct fathers and mothers how they should bring up their children."[98]

Roche's dismissal, as the local press reported, "started a wave of indignant protest and resentment which spread like wildfire over the city."[99] Denver's organized women denounced the mayor and Blakely for this "infamous outrage," which they insisted was payback for Roche's exposure of their corruption. The women then formed an organization to oust the officials in the upcoming local election.[100] In an even more dramatic move, the county sheriff, Daniel A. Sullivan, a progressive opponent of Blakely and Arnold, offered Roche a deputy sheriff's position to continue her law enforcement work.[101] Roche accepted and turned up the heat.[102] "Women must fight the business interests in this campaign," she proclaimed at a women's club meeting the day after her discharge. As she saw it, saloons were businesses that, without regulation, exploited vulnerable consumers: "Night after night I have seen young boys . . . in the wine rooms, lying around, dead drunk on the tables, on the floor." But when she complained to the proprietors, she said, they informed her that they had "special permission from the board" to sell liquor as they wished. Her rousing conclusion: "We must have law enforcement and we women are going to win out if we demand it."[103] A few days later, a mass meeting was called for the "honest citizens of Denver" to hear Josephine Roche's story. Organizers warned, "The beast is not dead. Its claw was seen last week as it reached out of the mayor's office and struck down Josephine Roche." They demanded Roche's reinstatement.[104] Her case remained on the front pages of Denver's newspapers for weeks.[105]

Beyond the court of public opinion, Roche took her case to the Civil Service Commission and finally to district court. Because her police position was covered by civil service rules, she believed she was entitled to a hearing before she could be discharged. The Civil Service Commission agreed and on May 8 ordered the Fire and Police Board to reinstate her. The latter refused to act, and the mayor claimed that she was not covered by the civil service rules because she was "living in New York at the time of her appointment" and so was a nonresident of the city and should not have been appointed at all.[106] Rumors around city hall suggested just how determined the administration was to keep Roche out of city government. If she should win a court order for reinstatement, the plan was to charge her with incompetence.[107] If that didn't work, the administration had affidavits accusing her of what she called "the grossest immorality!" She assumed these came from "the pimps and rooming house keepers" whose businesses suffered from her campaigns.[108] Amid continuing upheaval, Roche took her case to a court of law. With Edward Costigan as her attorney, she filed a high-profile proceeding in district court against all remaining members of the Fire and Police Board.[109]

Before the case was resolved, Denver held its election for members of the new city commission. Sheriff Sullivan marked the event with a gesture that publicly supported Roche and commission government as well as female public authority more generally. The sheriff appointed fourteen women as deputies to join Roche in keeping order at the polls. "It was the first time in the history of Denver," announced the local newspapers, "that women deputies were appointed to uphold the law during an election."[110] For a moment, Roche succeeded in making law enforcement feminine, and women the heirs of Wyatt Earp.

But Election Day was no women's club meeting. Roche patrolled the city alongside the sheriff that day. "I went with him from one end of town to the other," she reported, "from morning until midnight." Because the police hated Sheriff Daniel Sullivan for his support of Roche and the reformers, many expected trouble between him and the cops. In fact, the sheriff carried a gun only as defense against the city's police force, not against its private criminals. "The expectations of a row were almost realized in two or three precincts," Roche later told friends in New York. At one polling place, a "policeman attempted to move him [Sullivan] out, . . . and before the Sheriff had sent him skulking across the street, the situation was tense. The policeman's hand went to his gun, so did Danny's." She mused, "It's a curious feeling to stand by a man about to be shot at and about to shoot." Mercifully, the two thought better of their impulses and left their guns holstered, but the near-shoot-out suggested just how much was perceived to be at stake in the election.[111]

To Roche's deep dismay, progressives decisively lost. Consistently construing her anti-vice campaign as an element in curbing corporate power, she lamented, "the old gang—the big corporations, the liquor interests and the 'big business' interests generally, have got back their old time grip." What she called the "crowning disgrace" was "the election of a man as Safety Commissioner who for years was one of the Republican machine's tools for all sorts of corrupt practices. . . . He is today part owner and proprietor of one of our worst places—a café with rooms upstairs for the purpose of private drinking and prostitution."[112] Moreover, voters poured taxpayer money into a private corporation to build a tunnel into Denver as well as giving "three miles of our streets" to the Burlington Railroad Company, "a corporation which," in Roche's estimation, "for years robbed and pillaged the city."[113] All in all, it was a dismal showing for the reformers, which Roche explained as the result of fears of losing tourists and conventions if Denver really did shut down its vice district.[114]

Since the new commission government replaced the Fire and Safety Board with a single elected commissioner of safety, Roche's lawsuit against the city now named that new official, Alexander Nisbet, as defendant in place of the board. Bent but hardly broken by the election, Roche made Nisbet a special target of her nocturnal investigations. She wrote cheerily to a friend in late May, "I'm off for a raid of some cafes. . . . Wish you were here. I'm after the new Safety Commissioner's place. Hope to get him indicted just as he goes into office!"[115] Only days before the swearing in, Roche filed three separate charges against Nisbet.[116]

These charges did not prevent the new government from forming on June 1 or Roche's case against the city from proceeding. Within the month, the district court ordered that Roche be reinstated as inspector of amusements.[117] Nisbet publicly claimed to welcome Roche back to the force, but for weeks made and broke appointments with her. When a grand jury failed to indict Nisbet on the evidence that Roche presented, she took her case to the district attorney, who also refused to indict him.[118] Roche was furious. She insisted that the evidence against Nisbet's wine room was as strong as the evidence that had "resulted in the indictment of more than a dozen café and cabaret proprietors, and the conviction and fine of one of them in the West Side Criminal Court."[119]

During the uncertain and frustrating weeks of summer, Roche felt terribly at loose ends. While many people thought she should take a job outside Denver, she could not bear to leave the city. But she could not stay without a real job. "The essential economic independence simply can't be sacrificed," she explained, "I would absolutely disintegrate if I abandoned that." She could not bear a "life of committee meetings—woman's club days, etc., etc."[120] By her mid-20s, Roche's identity was firmly rooted in public work and economic independence.

Those commitments did not preclude marriage to the right partner, however, and Roche had a chance to consider an offer of matrimony during her discombobulated summer in 1913. In July, her friend from Greenwich House, Read Lewis, having just finished law school in New York, headed west to take in some new sights before settling into full-time work. The two had written letters every week or so since Roche left New York, and they were quite close, so close indeed, that Read Lewis apparently intended to ask Roche to marry him. Very shortly before Lewis was to arrive in Denver, Roche received a remarkable letter from an old friend of Lewis's and his family. May Estelle Cook apologized to Roche for her "unwarranted impertinence" in writing, but she was just horrified when, before setting out for Denver, Read had informed her that "he was going to ask you to marry him although he wasn't the least bit in love with you, especially as he took it for granted that you were very much in love with him." Cook believed it her duty to inform Roche that

Lewis was heading west "with the matrimonial bee in his bonnet" and to share her opinion that Roche was too good for him. Roche immediately reassured Cook that her work meant everything to her and that she "could meet him on his own ground," presumably meaning that she was no more in love with Lewis than he with her.[121]

Earlier in 1913, confessions of marital unhappiness by a mutual friend occasioned a discussion of marriage between Roche and Lewis. They had agreed that marriage required, as Roche put it, "not only absolute, complete frankness, but an independence so great, and so surely established, and an understanding so perfect" that slights by one would not hurt the other.[122] Perhaps Lewis thought the two friends had developed such an understanding.

When Lewis arrived in Colorado, he seems to have had a good visit with Roche and her family, and she introduced him to her beloved western landscapes (figure 5). The two were compatible in many ways, and it may well be that she seriously entertained his proposal, not because she was in love with him but because they had achieved brutal frankness in their relationship and were independent, yet shared many fundamental values. Each remained committed to the Code they had outlined on the banks of the Hudson River in 1911. Letters exchanged between the two after Lewis's visit suggest that he held out hope of her saying yes even after he had left. In a cryptic paragraph, Roche wrote to him in August, "There is no if, as I thought you realized." She continued, "If, on my side, I've not made it clear yet please consider I've done so now by whatever means are most final." She later concluded, "I really think I feel more cordial . . . toward you than this letter sounds. Only you mustn't misunderstand, if you do, any longer."[123] However little she wished to marry Read Lewis, Roche remained committed to their friendship, which survived for sixty more years.[124]

Just about the time Lewis was heading out of Denver in late July, the new Denver government landed its final blow against Roche. She had been expecting Nisbet to fire her again or perhaps to change her duties dramatically, but a city attorney revealed to Roche that the safety commissioner had something more expansive in mind. He intended either to repeal or defang the public amusements ordinance and to abolish the woman's position as inspector of public amusements. Roche described herself as "sick over it." After much deliberation, she "felt that the only thing for me to do was to get out [of office]—for I knew of course that if I were out of the way they wouldn't bother with [repealing] it."[125] The decision to resign drained her. Although Roche was glad at last to have the ordeal behind her, she confessed shortly afterward, "I feel a hundred years old today and my bones feel as if they'd been broken."[126] Then, she sank lower. "You can't imagine—no one can who has never experienced failure or even defeat—what it is to have that feeling of hopelessness press down heavier upon you . . . to realize you've not even made people understand what you <u>wanted</u> to do, let alone not having been able to do it."[127]

She took refuge in her beloved mountains. As she reported to Read Lewis, "I came away alone—the best, the only thing for me. I won't attempt to describe just all it means to be absolutely alone—to have nobody near that you have to speak to, and nothing you have to do."[128] Although Roche would be forever in the public fray, to maintain her equilibrium, she had to balance frenzied society with time alone. Solitude refueled her, and solitude in the Rockies was as good as it got. During her two weeks away in August 1913, she stayed mostly at an inn on Long's Peak and spent long hours hiking. For three days of her solitary sojourn, she took her horse and pack into what she called the "wildest of the wilds." The mountain scenes enraptured her. She described her first few days as "exquisitely beautiful. . . . The atmosphere has been marvelously clear so that any climb has meant a view unequalled in loveliness—save by the next one." Nighttime expeditions thrilled her most: "The nights with the moon now in its full beauty make sleep intolerable. I've sat till the small hours by a frosty mountain streamlet, and on the edge of a magnificent pine forest on Twin Sisters' Mountain, scarcely able to move, or breathe lest the magic vision vanish. Long's with its surrounding peaks, its snow patches, and dark pine stretches, the marvelous valley below, with its timber, streams and meadows simply transport you into another world when seen by moonlight."[129]

After two weeks in the Rockies, the world-weary activist began to feel whole again, and she had come to believe that the previous year's trials and defeats had matured her. "I'm getting restless to be in things again," she wrote a friend, "I hope I'll show better wisdom in my rows this year—to say the least."[130] Reformers like Edward Costigan served as models of the resilience and persistence she determined to develop. "When I think of how Mike [nickname for Costigan] has gone through this sort of thing practically every day for twelve years and continues to be 'always there' with the same courage, why I realize I've not even begun to be tested."[131] By the time she returned to Denver, she pronounced the previous year "the most wonderful and interesting year of my life." In looking back, she actually sounded nostalgic: "I don't suppose there ever will be another year that will mean so much to me and teach me so much as this one has."[132]

The period between the elections of 1912 and fall of 1913 had been extraordinarily rich for Josephine Roche. Thanks to opportunities opened by her mentors in the West, Roche emerged as a fearless public leader.

That she felt temporarily defeated in many of her hopes for women, law, and justice did not diminish the fact of her leadership or the value of all she had learned both about exercising power and about having power trained against her. In her fight against Denver's business-controlled political establishment, she had demonstrated the kind of guts for which she would become well-known, and she had seen up close how the interconnections between business and government sometimes worked to exploit workers and consumers. She would continue to mull over all she had learned as she regrouped in fall 1913.

CHAPTER 4

SEEKING FUNDAMENTALS:
THE COLORADO COAL STRIKE, 1913–1914

When Roche returned to Denver after her restorative break in the Rockies, she faced hard decisions about what to pursue next. Her goal was to figure out what work was most "fundamental" to achieving social justice. "Sometimes I'm absolutely sure that our 'problems' are purely educational," she wrote Read Lewis. "Then I switch back to my feeling that the greatest service to be rendered is in public affairs."[1] Which was the more effective entry point for changing a society and, with that, the life chances of most Americans? Was it educating the next generation into new perspectives so that they would change the system when they took charge of it or establishing a new set of values within the system through electoral politics or government service? Roche wanted to hit injustice where it would hurt most, but she was not yet sure where the tender spot lay.

As she began probing for that spot in fall 1913, coal miners in Colorado provided guidance. They opened what turned out to be the country's "deadliest labor war," a conflict that eventually confirmed what Roche's experience as Inspector of Amusements had begun to reveal: progressive public policies could not, by themselves, achieve justice.[2] However important they were, progressive policies often went unenforced. Some additional element was required to make good on them, and the strike told Roche that the element was an aroused and organized citizenry, especially in the form of independent labor unions. By 1914, Roche had layered onto her social science progressivism the commitments of a labor progressive, who believed the self-organization of workers as crucial to achieving social justice as progressive public policies.

Roche's search for a new role in the fight for social justice took her in many different directions during fall 1913. One possibility was to organize a social ethics course for seventh- and eighth-grade boys and girls in which she could give students a bit of sex education, instruction in citizenship, and knowledge of "the modern position of woman."[3] She began raising funds for the venture, brought a mothers' organization on board, and enlisted the Denver public schools.[4] At the same time, loose ends from her police job demanded attention. More than two dozen of her cases came to trial that autumn, and she testified in most of them.[5] The prosecutor rarely took the cases seriously, and her opponents' first line of defense was to attack Roche's respectability by insisting that she had herself been swilling alcohol at the establishments she now wished to prosecute.[6] But in the end, twenty-two defendants pleaded guilty, so she came away with what she thought "a lot of convictions," totally worth the nine pounds she lost during two grueling weeks of testimony.[7]

In the midst of those two weeks, an unexpected opportunity came knocking. Frances Kellor, a reformer from New York City, recruited Roche to head Colorado's Progressive Service, a unique agency created by Progressive Party leaders in the aftermath of the 1912 elections.[8] Proposed by Kellor herself, the national Progressive Service was an educational wing of the Progressive Party. Its job was to disseminate information about the party, compile reading lists on issues that appeared on the platform, and even develop correspondence courses on them. The service also collected model laws on those issues and through state chapters drafted and introduced legislation "affecting the interests of working people, women and children."[9] The new unit of the party was separate from the explicitly "political" division, which devoted itself to getting candidates elected to office. Kellor led the educational body.[10]

When approached to carry on this work in Colorado, Roche agonized over whether it "was fundamental enough, with future enough to cast myself into it." She wondered if her social ethics course might not be more valuable in the long run, and she even toyed with the possibility of returning to the police force. Ultimately though, she concluded "that the educational work of the Progressive Service is the most, or one of the most vital things of the day. To go all over the state talking about facts— industrial, social, about conditions and a way of dealing with them, certainly appeals to me."[11] When she nevertheless expressed some remaining ambivalence, Read Lewis bucked her up: "At present there seem to be millions of jobs that have got to be done. Does it make so much difference where one does his patch of weaving on the social fabric?"[12]

Roche finally agreed to take charge of the Progressive Service in Colorado, and in her early organizing, acted as the boundary crosser that her birth on the 98th parallel had predicted. Despite women's long enfranchisement in Colorado, women in the political parties usually organized only other women, while men organized men, and they usually pursued their shared goals in gender-segregated groups. Roche upended that tradition, sometimes organizing men-only groups and doing her best to pull women and men into gender-integrated groups. In her first weeks of traveling, she organized a gender-integrated progressive club in Longmont, Colorado and repeated the success in Sterling.[13] In Colorado Springs, she organized among what she called "a most interesting little group of women here—feminists—of the foremost rank" and a "group of men corresponding to them in political work [who] are anything but feminists!" Predictably, "the job of making the two ends pull in some semblance of harmony" was strenuous.[14] Adept at reaching out to both sides, however, Roche succeeded—after seventy-eight individual home visits![15] Harnessing people to the same cart despite perceived differences thrilled her. "I have really been able to put my heart into it," she enthused of her Progressive Party work, "in a way I'd begun to despair of being able to do again."[16]

The conditions of Roche's travels were sometimes difficult, especially as the winter of 1913–1914 was, according to one historian, "one of the worst winters in living memory."[17] The hotels were cold and cramped; the dining tables not always clean.[18] When she arrived in Sterling, for instance, she stayed in what she called a "dingy little country hotel" in the midst of a "record-breaking blizzard." She had no bathtub or hot water and nearly froze each night of the several she was stranded in town.[19] Later on, she sometimes spent the night on trains and faced other kinds of miserable weather. During an organizing tour on the western slope of the Rockies, Roche arrived in the town of Rifle on a cold, blustery, and wet Saturday morning, having had no sleep at all. Despite the weather, she and her coorganizer, Roy McClintock, "got a soap box and had a street meeting for two hours." To their amazement, "a crowd of two hundred or more . . . stayed in spite of the steadily increasing storm and cold." She characteristically reported, "It was great!"[20]

It was great in part because Roche was fascinated by the small towns and agricultural districts where she had spent so little of her adult life. Her attitude toward those she met often combined condescension and respect. It is hard to imagine, for instance, a more acid contempt than Roche expressed for some of those she tried to organize: "The Lord pity me if there's anything much harder to do than rousing these well-to-do, smug ladies of the prosperous small towns!" she wrote back east. "Their vision ends with the hideous crayons of 'father' and 'mother' on their walls—and the fat, stupid baby wallowing on the hideous, flowered green carpet—But they're happy!"[21] At the same time, she confessed that, even where she found little progressivism, "something in the face of these slow . . . people as I watch them in meetings, or in little groups discussing, gives me the feeling, the conviction even, that in their solid, deliberate way they're working out in their minds and in actions, the most fundamental and lasting sort of a political democracy."[22]

For all the class arrogance and coercive potential within progressivism, this local organizing for discussion of public policy issues gave substance to progressives' claims of commitment to democracy. In fact, undergirding their support for direct democratic measures like the referendum, initiative, and recall was real confidence in an engaged and informed electorate. They had reason to believe in that deliberative electorate because they were active in organizing it. Colorado's party leader, Edward Costigan, laid out the process for a newcomer. Describing the Progressive Party as a "new movement for human rights," Costigan explained that it was "continuing its work between campaigns instead of merely showing activity at election time." This work occurred in local clubs, where members identified issues of greatest concern to them. He gave examples: "In farming communities these clubs discuss the farmer's problems and try to agree on farmers' needs." In urban areas, clubs considered issues related to public utilities and transportation. They also discussed "the needs of the workingmen and consumers to the end that the best wages and the lowest prices may be brought about." All issues "are being fully argued out." After several months of such deliberations, the state party intended to hold a large convention where "representatives of all these clubs will present their different views, to be acted on by and for the Progressive Party as a whole." In fact, "what is agreed on will really furnish the platform of the Progressive Party in the campaign of 1914; and during the coming fall and winter the principles for which the Progressive Party stands will be fully discussed all over Colorado."[23] Organizing the local discussion groups where this grassroots democratic process began was Roche's job, and she gave it her all.[24]

While doing so, Roche grappled with a new aspect of the question of fundamentals. This aspect was raised by some progressives' emerging interest in psychology and their suggestion that individual psychology and especially sexual relations lay at the root of all social problems. Roche was anguished by the turn. In January 1914, she lamented that two of her favorite novelists—Englishmen H. G. Wells and John Galsworthy—were shifting their focus from unjust social conditions to individual sexual relations. After reading Galsworthy's 1913 novel *Dark Flower*, she wondered whether he had "come to the belief, or feeling that after all [sex] is the vital, gripping thing in human life, and that social justice, political and industrial freedom are just as far off as ever until we first get into the open, and on a different basis, this struggling, upheaving, torturing thing that has wrecked or made perfect beauty of—depending on the point of view—human lives since time began? Is that the attitude he has come to—and Wells, too, in his very different way?"[25]

She just couldn't stand it. She resented seeing these two writers turn away from social analysis "to this . . . history simply of two human beings in their relation to each other." She admitted that in "biography all society is arraigned." But still, she continued to believe that the "fight for emancipation in sex matters can be carried to a successful end only when the economic and educational victory has been won. . . . I feel, more and more that the 'sex problem' . . . is largely the result of the social and economic injustices and limitations which do not allow from childhood the slightest individual expansion or expression." In the end, she wound up where she would stay for life: "I still feel the social and economic fight is the fight, and I cannot but feel an intense regret over the desertion of Galsworthy and Wells of this field of attention."[26]

Roche might not have been certain whether education, politics, or government service was the most fundamental entry point for creating a more equitable society, but she was certain that social and economic relations were more fundamental than sexual or psychological relations. Although she surely felt romantic and sexual attractions and she would marry briefly in the early 1920s, she was not much interested in stories or, perhaps, even the experience, of "two human beings in their relation to each other." She longed to be part of what she saw as the larger and more important struggle to correct the "economic injustices and limitations" that thwarted the fullest development of individual human beings. To Roche's mind, social and economic conditions were a tenderer spot in the anatomy of injustice than sexual relations or individual psychologies.

Roche's impatience with Galsworthy and Wells made perfect sense given the context in which she read their latest works. The fall of 1913 saw the opening of a miners' strike in Colorado's coalfields that was building toward what one historian would later call "the most ferocious conflict in the history of American labor and industry."[27] Although miners all over the state joined the strike, its heart pumped in Colorado's southeastern quadrant, where the largest coal company in the state, the Colorado Fuel and Iron Company (CFI), centered its holdings. New York's Rockefeller family held 40 percent of the stock in CFI, which, like all of the state's coal-mining firms, was supposed to be regulated by progressive mining laws that limited the work day to eight hours, protected miners' right to organize, outlawed payment in scrip, and mandated the election by miners of a check weighman at each mine. (A check weighman supervised the weighing of coal, which was crucial to miners because they were paid by the ton of coal mined each day.) But, especially in the southern counties of Huerfano and Las Animas, these laws were not enforced.[28] Worse still, CFI and other coal companies so completely controlled the election of sheriffs, judges, and other local officials that miners were fully at the mercy of their employers. Mine guards hired by the company were routinely deputized by the local sheriff so that the company's authority became government authority exercised at gunpoint.[29] In most southern mining camps, the company owned workers' houses, the local store, and the school. Coal companies in those closed camps controlled even the reading material that entered the communities.[30] Coal miners in southern Colorado, in other words, did not exercise even the most basic rights of democratic citizenship.

In 1913, the United Mine Workers of America (UMW), the largest labor union in the United States, opened a campaign to organize the miners in Colorado's southern coalfields.[31] In response, the state's three biggest companies, CFI, Victor-American, and the Rocky Mountain Fuel Company (RMF), Roche's father's firm, employed private detectives to patrol the streets of their coal towns with orders to keep union organizers out—by force of arms, if necessary.[32] Nevertheless, John Lawson, the UMW's local organizer, invited the coal operators to negotiate a labor contract. The miners' demands included union recognition, a wage increase, enforcement of the state's labor and mining laws, and miners' freedom to choose where to trade, live, and get medical care. The coal operators declined Lawson's invitation, and in September 1913, the union called a strike.[33]

Hoping for a large walkout, union leaders rented land near some of the mines and put up tents for miners and their families because, where the companies owned workers' housing, strikers would have to vacate their homes.[34] As the day of the strike neared, miners and their families began packing up by the thousands and trudging toward the tent villages set up at Ludlow, Forbes, and other towns in the state's southern coal-mining districts (figure 6). In the northern coalfields, miners more often owned their homes or rented from local landlords and so did not have to relocate, as they, too, brought their tools out of the mines in hopes of improving the conditions of their work. By September 23, between 70 percent and 95 percent of Colorado's coal miners were on strike. Thousands left the state for work elsewhere, while over 20,000 striking miners and their family members remained in Colorado.[35]

Roche immediately sided with the miners. "We're in the throes of a bitter strike here in the coal districts," she reported to friends in the East. "Practically all the mines are closed—tho the operators are trying to make it appear that fully half are running." Her father was one of those operators. "I don't dare talk about it with father for fear I'll say something to him I'll regret, but at times I feel the most unspeakable scorn and contempt for myself for staying quietly here [in Denver] when the most vital struggle of the day is fought so near at hand."[36]

Roche's judgment that the coal strike was the most vital struggle of the day, occurring as it did simultaneously with the prosecution of her vice cases, her attempt to create a sex education course, and her allies' ongoing struggle against Denver's political machine suggests that even before her fullest involvement with the strikers, she believed the workers' battle for their own empowerment the most significant manifestation of progressive reform. It was not that Roche saw the other campaigns as inconsistent with the workers' struggle—she always construed them as political and economic initiatives aimed at reducing corporate power—but that the workers' own fight seemed to her the supreme expression of the progressive impulse. She would later say of the strike, "Someway the thing has gripped me so that nothing else seems to compare with it as a vital, crying problem of human suffering."[37] Roche was in the process of deciding that the most fundamental entry point for attacking inequality was the point of production.

Early on, violence broke out. Initially, it was restricted to isolated skirmishes, but both sides armed themselves heavily, and more protracted gun battles erupted in October.[38] Colorado's Governor Elias Ammons, elected in 1912 with strong support from organized labor, reluctantly sent in the National Guard on October 28. He ordered the guardsmen only to protect property and any strikers who wished to return to the mines and explicitly forbade state troops to shield strikebreakers brought in from elsewhere. This way, the miners had a chance of gaining leverage with the companies by starving the state of coal and the companies of profits just as winter—the coal industry's big season—was coming on.[39]

At this moment in the strike, the Progressive Party of Colorado, for which Roche now worked, tried to organize a public debate between representatives of the miners and mine owners. But the owners, according to Roche, "refused point blank to attend, to speak or allow anyone to represent their side." The reason they gave was that the strike was "none of the public's business." Coal magnates in Colorado continued to see their property rights as so complete that they had no obligation to explain their position in a strike that clearly threatened public well-being as a Rocky Mountain winter approached. Roche was incensed: "Oh, I don't see how the miners have exercised one tenth the restraint they have, when they've been up against men with a point of view . . . like that!"[40] She and other progressives believed that the public had a compelling interest in any business that produced commodities crucial to the maintenance of life. Coal for home heating was one of those commodities. For Roche, property rights ended where human rights began, and she equated human rights with meeting the essential needs of workers and consumers.[41]

In the end, Colorado's Progressive Party sponsored a public presentation by a representative of the miners and Edward Costigan, who "defined the attitude of the Progressive Party toward Labor in general and this particular struggle" as well.[42] He also laid out a Progressive Party proposal to meet the immediate situation: the governor should supply current consumer demand for coal by mining the fuel on state property while calling a special session of the state legislature to pass a compulsory arbitration act. Should arbitration between the miners and operators fail, then the governor should take over and run all the state's coal mines until arbitration produced a settlement.[43] In Roche's view, Costigan's speech "championing the cause of union labor" met the highest standards of social science progressivism. It succeeded in "piling up facts so conclusively and treating the whole in such a scientific and historical way that no room for doubt was left in anyone's mind."[44]

On the last point, Roche was quite wrong. At least one mind was not swayed by Costigan's masterful oration, and it was the mind that mattered most. In late November, Governor Ammons capitulated entirely to the coal operators: he granted the National Guard permission to protect strikebreakers, who then flooded into the coalfields from out of state.[45] With this move, the governor destroyed the foundation of the strikers' power. If the companies could produce coal (and profits) without them, they lost their only bargaining chip. Making the miners' situation ever more hopeless, state troops developed such an intimate relationship with the coal companies that the state and the corporations became indistinguishable. Troops stayed in company-owned housing and received supplies from the companies. As men from other parts of the state mustered out of the National Guard units, mine guards and other employees of the companies mustered in. Eventually, the companies paid the troops' wages.[46] National Guardsmen appeared for all the world to be in the direct employ of the mine operators. From the strikers' point of view, their state government, in the institution of its National Guard, had abandoned any pretense of neutrality and taken the side of the coal companies against them.[47] Indeed, Colorado's state government had disappeared into the management of CFI, Victor-American, and the Rocky Mountain Fuel Company.

Roche's progressive community was aghast. In her words, "Governor Ammons has proved himself the most spineless of individuals."[48] Costigan, Lindsey, Creel (who returned to Colorado to cover the strike), and Roche, as well as their friend and now U.S. Congressman, Edward Keating, agreed that the conditions under which miners labored in the southern coalfields were "feudal" and that the strike was the fault of the operators who consistently prevented state laws from being enforced and kept the miners in virtual captivity, violating the most basic human rights.[49] Keating had won his congressional seat in 1912 on the promise of bringing "constitutional government to the counties of Las Animas and Huerfano."[50] When the strike broke out, he agitated for a congressional investigation of the coal conflict in Colorado, and in January 1914, he finally won.[51] Congressmen descended on Denver in February and held hearings there as well as in the southern counties. Costigan served as special counsel to the UMW during the hearings and cowrote a sixty-page brief for the striking miners.[52]

In Roche's organizing work for the Progressive Party, the strike became the most electrifying issue. Roche and McClintock discovered during stints in the southern counties of Pueblo and Fremont that although Costigan's advocacy for the strikers attracted new interest in the party from a wide range of workers, it caused consternation among many small business owners and professionals, who had provided the backbone of the party since 1912. In some cases, when Roche described conditions in the southern coalfields, places where workers did not enjoy the basic rights of free speech and assembly, she believed she won most listeners to the party's position that both operators and miners should exercise the same rights and claim the same protections from the state. But in other places, she and McClintock agreed, their explanations fell on deaf ears.[53] As early as February, McClintock averred that the strike had begun to sort out "sentimental Progressives" from "true believers in the cause of those who toil."[54] Faced with a real-life dispute between labor and capital, some members of the Progressive Party were not sure they supported the pro-labor planks of the party's platform. For others, the strike ignited or strengthened their commitment to the self-organization of workers.

At one point, having been on the road for four weeks straight, "living out of a suit case and having all sorts of adventures," Roche observed: "My trip has very largely resolved itself into a campaign on the industrial situation and our program in regard to it." It was a topic she felt "intensely upon." In Fremont County, she visited several large mining camps and interviewed both sides in the conflict. "I had a very intense hour with the commanding major, two captains and a lieutenant there," she reported. "Went thru the camps and had long talks with the strikers and attended a meeting at which they discussed the shooting up by the camp the night before by some drunken guards."[55] Her reconnaissance strengthened her commitment to the strikers' cause. By spring, McClintock was proposing she be slated for secretary of state on the Progressive Party ticket not only because she was now very well known among progressives all over Colorado but especially because she would "certainly have a labor commissioner who would enforce the law if she were in command."[56] Roche was not ready to run for office, but McClintock correctly assessed her commitment to workers' rights and foreshadowed her future on the campaign trail.

Not long after Roche's visit to the mine camps in Fremont County, new events blasted the party wide open. After the Congressional Committee investigating the strike completed its work in March and revealed what the investigators themselves considered shocking conditions in the coalfields, the militia unleashed increasing force against the strikers. Roche reported on March 12, "a brutal attack on the tent colony at Forbes . . . in revenge for some of the strikers testifying [before the congressional delegation]. The tents were entirely demolished. Children and women turned out homeless and feeling is at white heat." She predicted that "the bitterest part of the struggle" was yet to come.[57]

On April 20, 1914, Roche's prediction was fulfilled. A pitched battle broke out between a small contingent of state troops and a large body of strikers living in the tent colony at Ludlow. Once gunshots were exchanged, armed miners moved away from the tents in an effort to draw the militia away from their homes. The tactic failed. Some miners and many family members were still in their tents when gunfire became general. Mothers and children ran for cover in every place they could—some hid in a pump house; dozens jumped down a well; others crowded into makeshift cellars dug into the ground below their tent floors.[58] In the evening, one of the tents caught fire. No one is sure how, but numerous eyewitnesses—including guardsmen themselves—attested to the subsequent spread of the fire by deliberate action of the guardsmen.[59] As a result, eleven children and two women suffocated in an underground dugout. Meanwhile, the head of the strikers' group at Ludlow, Louis Tikas, was shot in the back. In all, eighteen miners or their family members died that day, along with one guardsman.[60] The events of April 20 came to be called the Ludlow Massacre (figure 7).[61]

Ludlow opened an entirely new phase in the strike and in the larger public's view of the conflict. John Lawson announced that miners must do everything they could to protect themselves now. "A striking miner's tent is his home," he was reported to have said, "as sacred to him as the mansions of the mine owner."[62] Ludlow convinced Lawson that the state was so completely in league with the companies that only armed struggle against the combined force could win the miners justice. Lawson's grim assessment opened a week and a half of virtual civil war in the southern coalfields. Striking miners swarmed several coal camps, burning tipples and dynamiting mines. They killed mine guards and terrorized operators. More men on both sides died, the bulk of them aligned with the coal operators.[63]

Roche and many other Coloradans believed that only federal troops could end the conflagration, and on April 28, President Woodrow Wilson obliged them. The troops began arriving two days later and disarmed both sides, bringing the bloodshed to an end by mid-May.[64] "Words cannot give a picture of the horrors, the brutalities, the sordidness, and the white heat of passion which have been and still are beating upon our exhausted emotions," Roche wrote after the troops arrived. "The coming of the Federal troops gave us our first respite from the hideous strain. But of course it's meant nothing in the way of solution—simply a cessation for the time they're here of the slaughter of men, women, and children."[65] Despite even Wilson's urging, operators never agreed to meet with union representatives, and the miners finally voted to end the strike in woeful defeat on December 7, 1914.[66] For all practical purposes, the UMW disappeared from the Colorado coalfields for more than a decade.

Many of Colorado's progressives were horrified by the deaths at Ludlow and the strike's revelation of injustice that coal miners daily endured. Lindsey was sure the strike meant that "Government ownership has simply got to come."[67] Moved in part by the strike, Dr. Caroline Spencer of Colorado Springs pledged her support of the Progressive Party "to the last ditch," and some Coloradans who identified themselves as "old Populists" heartily approved of Costigan's position on the conflict.[68] One physician, who had tended to oppose the strike in the beginning, visited the southern counties in late spring and, after interviewing ranchmen, storekeepers, and professionals identified with neither side in the strike, concluded, "the conditions in the southern Coal Districts are those of the feudalism of the middle ages rather than conditions that should prevail in an enlightened civilization." His interviews revealed that the "gunmen and thugs" who eventually wore National Guard uniforms "not only searched the homes of the strikers at their sweet will but also the homes of ranchers and other noncombatants. Anyone even suspected of sympathizing with the strikers were [sic] subjected to continual insult." He left the coalfields convinced that "The Battle of Ludlow was deliberately provoked" by the head of the guardsmen.[69]

An even larger group, however, was appalled by what they saw as the miners' subsequent disregard for lawful authority. The latter progressives were not concerned that the National Guard was by April largely constituted of mine guards and other men fully paid by the coal companies.[70] This group did not accept the argument of Roche and Costigan that no genuinely public or neutral authority intervened between the company and the miners, that the National Guard represented the mine owners pure and simple. Many Progressive Party members instead saw the miners as insurrectionists against the state of Colorado and feared what they construed as anarchy among the strikers. These Progressives began in June to suggest fusion with the state's Republican Party, which stood for law and order against the miners' violence.[71]

Roche's branch of Colorado's Progressive Party stood unequivocally with the strikers. When called on to proclaim the party's commitment to law and order, Costigan responded, "I want a brand of law and order that will apply impartially to both lawless elements in the strike matter." The reason for miners' lawlessness in 1914, he insisted, was that "For 25 years private business influences some of which are now parties to the existing industrial war . . . have dictated the appointment or election of our public officials, have written our laws, and have defied our laws when law did not suit their purposes." He reminded his listeners that, as a result, there had been as much bloodshed in the mines during peacetime as there was now in the mining districts because irresponsible mine owners routinely sacrificed miners' safety to profit.[72] In recognition of these conditions, he demanded law, order, and justice. He maintained that the strike situation forced all members of the Progressive Party to see what the national platform really meant when it supported organized labor and put human rights before property rights. If this reckoning forced realignments, so be it.[73]

As the campaign season heated up in unison with summer temperatures, Roche continued to organize throughout the state, now making the argument for law, order, and justice.[74] By mid-June, she was working less for the Progressive Service than for the campaigning unit of the party.[75] The party was pretty well broke by then, which meant Roche often worked without pay, a situation that thrust her into debt for the first time in her life. She admitted that her financial situation scared her, but she believed the workers' cause worth absolutely everything she had, a stance presaging her future with coal miners in Colorado.[76]

During her summer organizing, Roche discovered that Costigan was right about the strike forcing political realignments. As Pueblo County Progressives assembled in July, for instance, some of their leaders objected to any campaign slogan that included "Justice." They opposed the word because it seemed "an open bid to the strikers and against the corporations and they were opposed to anything but Law and Order by the constituted authorities." Moreover, some argued that since the Democratic Party had the labor vote sewn up, it made no political sense to appeal so directly to the miners.[77] Others who had voted a straight Progressive Party ticket in 1912 charged that the miners were in "armed Rebellion against the lawful authority of the State of Colorado" and that if Costigan, who openly supported the miners, were to be the party's gubernatorial candidate again, they would have to defect.[78] One newspaper editorial put it bluntly: "Those who do not stand for law and order stand for anarchy."[79] The Costigan/Roche camp, however, insisted that "Law and Order without Justice could be no permanent Law and Order."[80] As one activist said, "The cry of Law and Order" from the Republican Party just meant a "return under this cloak to their own peculiar brand of lawlessness and disorder. . . . It is just as lawless and disorderly to deport a striker or blacklist a union man without due process of law as it is for strikers to beat up a mine guard."[81]

Costigan won the Progressive Party's nomination for governor in 1914, committing the state party to the self-organization of labor and industrial justice. In the fall campaign, Roche coordinated the preparation and distribution of campaign literature and organized in the precincts.[82] Theodore Roosevelt publicly backed Costigan and the state party's position on the strike.[83] Still, the organization lost many people who had been leaders in the 1912 election, and although the party picked up many strike leaders, it did not win the mass of workers in the state, who had a traditional alternative in allegedly pro-labor candidates from the Democratic Party. Moreover, the southern strike districts were in summer 1914 gerrymandered in such a way that every precinct was bounded by fences surrounding the coal camps, which were patrolled by armed guards on Election Day.[84] The result was a statewide rout not only for Progressive Party candidates but also for progressive ballot measures like jury reform and adult probation.[85]

Colorado's Progressive Party had indeed been realigned. By identifying itself unabashedly with organized labor, it had shed those whose commitment to other aspects of the national platform helped them overlook the party's earlier support for unionization, and it gained new adherents among workers. For those, like Roche and Costigan, who led the party, industrial justice had become the overriding political conviction. They emerged from the ordeal of 1913–1914 as labor progressives, a particular group within the progressive movement who would by the end of the 1910s elevate the self-organization of labor to a place of prominence in their commitments equal to governmental regulation of corporations and state-sponsored social welfare measures. Their political coalition included a swath of working-class voters, which would continue to grow over the next decades.[86]

In years to come, Roche would claim that the coal strike was crucial to her political formation.[87] In fact, "to right the wrong of Ludlow" became one of her life-goals.[88] That the coalfield conflict generated in Roche a staunch commitment to organized labor when labor upheavals in New York did not is a testament to the power of interpretive communities. Roche's interpretive community in New York had responded to strikes and workplace accidents by advocating new laws rather than workers' organization.[89] In Colorado, by contrast, just laws for miners were already in place by 1913. Colorado's coalfields made clear that good laws alone did not ensure justice. Empowerment of the constituencies affected by unjust conditions was another critical element. Consequently, Roche's interpretive community in Colorado, dominated by men like Edward Costigan and Benjamin Lindsey, rallied to the self-organization of workers, which became a crucial component in Roche's understanding of how to diminish inequalities of wealth and power.

Labor progressivism was not peculiar to Colorado. Demonstrating the fact was a document produced by the U.S. Commission on Industrial Relations in 1915. Legislated in William Howard Taft's administration and formed during Woodrow Wilson's, the commission was charged to investigate labor conflicts that rocked the United States between 1910 and 1915. Colorado's coalfield conflagration was one of the hottest of those conflicts. Appointed to head the commission was George Creel's fellow Missouri progressive, Frank Walsh, and the majority report of the group echoed the convictions of Roche and her western progressive colleagues.[90]

Roche pored over the commission's report, and her emphatic underlinings and dog-eared pages reveal how passionately she supported its conclusions. It confirmed that inequality was the prime concern of labor progressives just as it was among social science progressives. In her copy of the report, Roche underscored with multiple red lines all evidence for the vast inequalities of wealth in the United States. She also dog-eared those pages.[91] She underlined the claim that one of the major causes of industrial unrest was the "unjust distribution of wealth and income."[92] She marked passages that concluded that workers had not received "a fair share of the enormous increase in wealth . . . which has taken place in this country as a result largely of their labors."[93] She marked sections that demonstrated that one-third to one-half of industrial workers lived in poverty; that fathers could not support their families alone; that high infant mortality was an especial problem among impoverished workers.[94] She underscored the recommendation of an inheritance tax to prevent the accumulation of wealth.[95]

Equally significant were sections on the right of workers to organize on their own behalf. Roche underlined numerous times in red the claim that another reason for labor unrest was the "denial of the right and opportunity to form effective organizations."[96] Every sentence of the report that insisted on labor's right to organize received the emphasis of Roche's colored pencils.[97] In blue, she emphasized the section on the specific wrongdoings of the Colorado Fuel and Iron Company and the recommendation that the Bill of Rights be strengthened so as to guarantee workers' civil liberties.[98] In years to come, Roche echoed the analysis of industrial democracy that the commission put forward. In the daily life of each worker, it insisted, an employer had even more influence than the state, and so if democracy were to have real meaning in the life of workers, the country must extend "the principles of democracy to industry."[99] Company unions and profit-sharing plans could not, according to the commission's report and Roche's insistent markings, substitute for the organization of workers by workers themselves.[100] "My ambition is to live to see all the workers of America organized in unions," Roche would declare decades later.[101] And, she was not alone.

The period from August 1913 through 1914 proved a pivotal period for Josephine Roche. She bounced back from a significant public defeat and reentered the political fray with all imaginable passion. She had not resolved every question about what arena was most fundamental to creating a more democratic and egalitarian society, but she *had* determined that, to her way of thinking, social and economic relations were more fundamental than individual psychologies or sexual relations and that the most powerful point in the production of inequality was the point of economic production. Relations between workers and employers were fundamental to the other structures of society. During these months, Roche had dug deep into electoral politics, honed her skill as a political organizer, and developed a desire to "right the wrong of Ludlow," though how she might concretely do that was as yet unclear. By the end of her western stint, Roche was as fully a labor progressive as a social science progressive, supporting with equal fervor the independent organization of workers and progressive public policies meant to trim the power of corporations in relation to workers and consumers. This combination of commitments Roche would carry through the 1920s, into the New Deal Era, and beyond.

CHAPTER 5

"PART OF IT ALL ONE MUST BECOME": PROGRESSIVE IN WARTIME, 1915–1918

Roche was so exhausted after the 1914 elections that she finally accepted Read Lewis's invitation to take a short break in the East. Little did she know that her brief vacation would whisk her into the maelstrom of global war. World War I had broken out during the campaign season, but Roche paid it little heed until her trip east early in 1915. In the face of wartime exigencies thereafter, Roche and her reforming communities agonized about the role they should play. Because they came to many different conclusions, historians have disagreed on the war's meaning for the reform movement, and the bottom line is that the war was neither the end nor the acme of progressive reform.[1] It was rather an intensification of the conflict between progressivism and conservatism, as the war simultaneously expanded resources for both opposition to and promotion of efforts to diminish inequalities. The outcome of that conflict was not determined during the war but afterward. Roche's experience provides a more intimate view, however, of the conflict that the war also ignited *within* progressivism. It forced progressives to prioritize their commitments, and by doing so, revealed in Roche's case important truths about her character. Roche's decisions showed that when forced to choose between remaining true to her full range of convictions and being effective on behalf of a few, she would choose effectiveness.

Incongruously, the conflagration that engulfed Europe in the last months of 1914 offered Roche an exciting opportunity for international social service. While she was in New York visiting friends, she was invited to participate in Herbert Hoover's Commission for Relief in Belgium, a humanitarian intervention of U.S. progressives in the European conflict. When Germany made its lightning march across Belgium in August 1914,

Hoover—engineer, businessman, and future U.S. president—was in London. As the Germans settled in to their occupation of Belgium, prompting Great Britain to blockade the country, reports of hunger among the Belgians began to circulate within the world community. In response, Hoover organized an enormous and improbable voluntary operation that purchased food from around the world and delivered it to Belgium and other occupied areas.[2] The cost of the endeavor was staggering, and Roche hired on to help Hoover raise funds to meet that cost.[3] Her original assignment was to go to Belgium to gather firsthand accounts of the situation there, which she could then use in fund-raising appeals back in the United States.[4]

Roche's telegram informing her parents of her plan elicited the only extant communications from her parents. That Roche saved only these missives suggests they represented her parents as she most wished to remember them, and understandably so: both her mother and father responded warmly to their daughter's first opportunity for European travel. Communicating his considerable spunk as well as deep affection for his only child, John Roche sent multiple telegrams. One of them exclaimed that he and her mother were "knocked off our feet" by her wire telling them of the chance to go to Belgium "and while we were counting on seeing our dear girl latter part of the week yet we are more than happy and glad that you have the golden opportunity to go abroad in the capacity you have been given," which he described as "going into the heart of this foreign war as a representative of a great national commission." Even as he nearly burst with pride, John Roche's parental concern also found voice: "but my dear child do be careful. This war is the world's greatest and brutal tragedy. You are now to be thrown into its very center." He signed off, "Worlds of love and kisses from us both Papa."[5]

Roche's mother wrote separately and in more cross-cutting tones. On the one hand, she was delighted for her daughter. "Very Precious Child," her long telegram opened, "Oh it is a wonderful chance for growth and development darling and we are so happy and proud of you." On the other hand, Ella Roche expressed ambivalence, if not outright hostility, toward Josephine's earlier political work. "I have always wanted you to speak—lecture," she effused, "and now you will have a full subject to talk upon." Ella Roche apparently did not consider the topics of her daughter's earlier speeches—women's suffrage, prostitution, economic justice, and political corruption—"full subjects." Perhaps Roche's mother, even more than her father, disapproved of her political activism.

Except for that one sour note, Ella Roche's telegram sang maternal care. Unable to resist motherly advice, Ella Roche instructed her daughter: "I hope you will continue to think of your carriage erect—chin in— head up." No doubt imagining Josephine rolling her eyes at the parental admonition, she hastened to say, "I know you will lovingly forgive your mother for all this—knowing it comes from a mother's devoted heart." She also said that she was awfully glad that "Jo" had her blue coat and wished she would buy some tights to keep her legs warm on the ship. "Oh I hope every good thing for my darling," she said in closing, "Good bye dearest girl."[6]

Wrapped in her parents' love and possibly her blue coat, Josephine Roche put to sea. Her ocean voyage spoke to both her adventurous spirit and her ambition to participate fully in the most significant events of the day, to be "in the thick of it."[7] Once Roche had reached London, however, Hoover decided she should not proceed to Belgium. He had secured assurances for her safe passage into the occupied territory but feared he would not be able to bring her out again for two or three months. Instead of pressing on, then, she scoured eyewitness reports on conditions in the occupied areas and visited Belgian refugee camps in England. With information from these sources, she returned directly to the United States.[8]

Roche's stateside work for the commission was much like her work for the Progressive Party. It created new grassroots organizations and allowed her the freedom of constant travel. Her first assignment took her to Vermont for a frantic ten-day organizing stint during which she sometimes gave three lectures a day, visited multiple towns, and set up permanent local committees to raise money for sending food to Belgium.[9] Once Vermont was organized, she went to Albany, where she helped to set up an office and mapped out a campaign for raising funds in New York State. Plan completed, she was off, traveling to about half the counties of the state, "delivering lectures, making addresses, organizing new local committees."[10] According to her bosses, "her work is most efficient and productive of splendid results."[11] But by mid-May 1915, the New York organization had completed its fund-raising projects, and money for administration was running out, so the commission cut Roche's position.[12] Within a few months, the group asked her to resume the work, but by that point, she was otherwise engaged.[13]

The suddenness of Roche's detachment from the commission left her a bit disoriented. "I still have a very bewildered feeling, a sense of unreality," she reported three months after the commission let her go, "for I cannot learn to adjust myself quickly to the reversal of my plans."[14] Nevertheless, she found plenty to do. She spent part of summer 1915 in New York, helping with the women's suffrage campaign.[15] She then returned to Denver, where Edward Costigan was still working on labor cases connected with the big coal strike, and she got to know John Lawson, leader of the strike, as he worked with Costigan on defending himself and other miners accused of murder.[16] In late summer, Judge Lindsey hired her as the chief probation officer for girls in his juvenile court.[17] Roche's job was to investigate any court case involving a girl. Many of them were rape cases, which prompted her to observe, "I have much still to learn about the depths to which human nature can sink."[18]

Local elections in 1916 further depressed Roche, and their outcome helps to explain why she would soon be ready to leave Denver more permanently. In the spring, Robert W. Speer, a former mayor of Denver, ally of utility and coal companies, and arch-nemesis of the city's progressive reformers, proposed an amendment to the city charter that would abolish the commission form of government—for which Roche had fought so hard in 1913—and establish an even more powerful mayoral government than had existed before.[19] The proposed amendment named Robert Speer as the next mayor should the amendment pass. Roche was apoplectic: "It seems incredible that anything so dreadful could happen—and yet."[20] She was right to worry: in May 1916, the amendment passed and established Speer as the most powerful mayor in the United States.[21] Roche plunged into "deep despondency." She explained, "So many weary, almost desperate years of fighting spent by so many splendid men and women, only to find ourselves in the situation today brings upon us." Bitterness surfaced: "Clearly the people want a czar, as well as a form of government that robs them of every vestige of democracy, so I can't see what there is for us but to hope they'll choke on it, and someday know better."[22] The political realignments of 1914 had transformed Denver from a sea of progressive possibility to a slough of progressive despond.

National elections seemed more hopeful. Roche loved everything about a presidential race: the spectacle, the spirit of competition, and the suspense as well as the chance to fight for high ideals. In 1916, Democrats renominated their incumbent president, Woodrow Wilson, who had not yet impressed Roche but who had so far kept the United States out of the European war and was leaning toward greater support of organized labor and women's suffrage as the campaign season opened. Theodore Roosevelt was expected to carry the Progressive Party banner again, but there was also talk of his return to the Republican fold as he gave increasing priority to military preparedness and a more aggressive U.S. foreign policy. As early as January 1916, Roche's excitement over the upcoming election began to grow. "I must confess to a thrill of admiration for T. R.," she wrote a friend, "Not that I agree with him at all on the universal military service, or Mexico, or lots of things, but oh I do love the way he hits out—and has been hitting long before his blows brought him any sympathy or praise. What a spectacle the campaign will be if . . . he and Woodrow are the contestants!" She savored the prospect of that particular matchup even though, "I should very probably not want to vote for either."[23]

Indeed, Roche was seriously considering a vote for the Socialist Party candidate in 1916, evidence of the easy alliances that progressives continued to forge with those farther left.[24] The Socialist Party's opposition to both U.S. involvement in World War I and all imperialistic elements of U.S. foreign policy appealed to Roche, as did its call for immediate passage of the women's suffrage amendment to the U.S. Constitution and the abolition of child labor; support for the initiative, referendum, and recall at the federal level; and the collective ownership of large industrial enterprises on which life and liberty depended.[25]

Still, since Colorado's Progressive Party promised to run good candidates for state offices, Roche remained active in the party early in 1916. At what Roche called a "right exciting and enthusiastic" state convention in May, she and Mabel Costigan were selected as delegates to the national convention in Chicago, and Roche was excited to go once more to "see the fireworks" in the Windy City.[26] Two conventions could not have been more different than the Progressive Party conventions of 1912 and 1916. The jubilation of 1912 crashed in despair four years later. Like other stalwarts, Roche attended the convention full of enthusiasm for the progressive platform and the party's potential for continuing outreach on behalf of its principles. She was then among those aghast when Roosevelt announced at the convention that he could not accept the party's nomination for president and instead threw his support to the Republican candidate, Charles Evans Hughes.[27] By that point, Roosevelt's top priority was preparedness for war, and Hughes stood firmly in favor. As if hawkishness were not bad enough in Roche's anti-war eyes, the Republican Hughes also opposed the recently passed Adamson Act, which granted the eight-hour day to interstate railroad workers.[28] Roche fumed that Roosevelt's endorsement of Hughes "was the act of an arch traitor."[29]

Immediately following Roosevelt's betrayal, Roche was not sure whether to go with Wilson or the Socialist candidate, but finally, with only a couple of weeks before the election, she came out for Wilson. Wilson's support for a federal law reducing child labor and the Adamson Act in addition to his keeping the United States out of the European war eased her conscience, but mostly she feared that a vote for anyone but Wilson gave a greater chance of victory to Hughes, a prospect she could not abide. By supporting the incumbent president, Roche disappointed some of her feminist friends. Her allies in the National Woman's Party urged her to work against Wilson because he would not advocate a federal amendment enfranchising women, but Roche argued that she could not make a decision based on only one issue—much as she desired a federal suffrage amendment. "I feel conclusively," she explained, "that I cannot repudiate all else that I commend because I condemn this suffrage record." She feared that "by voting against Wilson," she would help put in power "a party standing for the most reactionary elements in our civilization." In the end, she could not "subordinate all other matters of vital national and state concern to a particular method of obtaining suffrage."[30] Roche would never be a single-issue activist.

Election Day and its immediate aftermath, initially excruciating for Roche, eventually produced a narrow victory for Wilson, which Roche interpreted as a triumph of the West against the East. She reported to a friend traveling outside the United States: "The close contest in California, Minnesota, and New Hampshire kept us on pins and needles for days." Early on, "it looked like Hughes [for] sure, and then the western vote began to roll in. At least 90% of the Progressive vote went for Wilson in the middle and western country and now that California and New Hampshire are conceded to him, he is elected." She concluded with amazement: "It seems most remarkable that Wilson could win with N.Y., Mass., N.J., Indiana, Penn., Illinois, and all the other eastern states against him. We are too delighted for words out here."[31] Roche's political mentor, Ed Costigan, also observed a stark contrast between East and West in the 1916 election: "While the East has been thinking in terms of European War, the Progressives of the West have considered domestic peace and justice of greater immediate importance, and have voted accordingly."[32] Still working on cases produced by the armed conflict between labor and capital in 1914, Costigan, Roche, and their western colleagues sensed an urgent need to reform domestic social and economic relations that overrode every other concern.

Despite Wilson's campaigning on a peace platform in 1916, he took the United States into World War I shortly after his second inauguration. Prompted especially by German threats to American shipping, Wilson asked Congress for a declaration of war in April 1917, and Congress complied.[33] After the declaration, most progressives made some kind of uneasy peace with U.S. intervention in the war. They took refuge in Wilson's claims that U.S. participation aimed to end war itself through defeat of tyrannous government and the institution of international cooperation.[34] For most progressives, though, the war stood as a sobering reminder of how far the world had yet to go before achieving just human relations.

Even the official declaration of war did not move Roche to support U.S. involvement, which she feared would distract the country from its more important task of creating a democratic and egalitarian America, but she took some comfort from Wilson's increasing inclusion of her Denver crowd in his administration. She trusted her friends to do right even in an administration that might do some things wrong. Just before his war speech, Wilson appointed Costigan to the Federal Tariff Commission, and shortly afterward, he appointed George Creel to head the Committee on Public Information (CPI), which was "to have," in Roche's words, "complete charge of [government] publicity and information during the war." She was delighted that "our Denver men who fought so long and hard against such odds, and whom Denver steadily refused to recognize, are at last coming into their own."[35] Creel soon hired Harvey O'Higgins to assist him in his publicity campaigns, very nearly reconstituting the Denver gang in DC.[36] The hiring of her progressive network by the Wilson administration turned Roche's sights once again toward the East and the promise for progressive reform held out by the national government at a time when prospects for progressive change in Denver looked bleak.

With Speer in control of the local government, many progressive projects, including the juvenile court, were under attack. "Never were we so discouraged and the outlook so hopeless," Roche confided in spring 1917. "It is heartbreaking to see the most splendid work of seventeen years gradually eaten into by legislative and judicial attacks and undermined by hostile city and state departments."[37] The war increased her demoralization: "the war situation and all its attendant horrors is closing down more wretchedly each day, and what there is to look forward to I can't imagine."[38]

Although she admitted that in the West the war continued to seem somewhat abstract, Roche's horror of it intensified with every evidence of its increasing grip on the lives of her neighbors and especially the boys she knew through her work at the juvenile court. In September 1917, she watched as "Our first draft of boys left for training camp . . . and still I think we don't quite realize, out here, that we are at war, even yet." To her eastern friends, she remarked, "There is a sharp difference, I understand, between the East and West so far as the atmosphere of war time goes."[39] Indeed, Roche's description of preparations for war in the West reveals the sense of numbness that so many westerners felt in response to U.S. intervention in what seemed to them an exceedingly distant conflict.

Very soon though, Roche sampled the eastern experience of war. Late in 1917, the National Consumers' League invited her to study women's wages in Baltimore, Maryland. She accepted the offer. With the Costigans, George Creel, Harvey and Anna O'Higgins in Washington, DC, and Lindsey lecturing for the Red Cross in the East, she felt she was battling alone in the hopeless miasma of Denver. As she put it, "I'm sure I oughtn't to struggle on here where the few chances we had for interesting and original work are closing."[40] Just before Christmas, she boarded a train with Mabel Costigan, who had been in Denver for a visit, and headed back east. Even before she reached the East Coast, Roche felt the war more viscerally than before. When her train stopped in Chicago, she met a friend, Newton Jenkins, "in his uniform." She insisted, "It was my first acute realization of the war—so far it has been like a hideous but distant dream. But each minute here it is becoming more close and immediate." In fact, by the time she disembarked in New York, she felt "as tho I had entered upon a totally different planet from the one our western state is on—the difference in atmosphere is so great."[41]

Gradually, the atmosphere of the East worked a transformation on Roche, and her description of that transformation speaks volumes about the painful dilemmas of many a progressive in wartime. The conversion occurred during the first months of 1918. In January and February, Roche conducted research in Baltimore on weekdays and then spent weekends in Washington with her Denver friends. As she observed countless people bound up in the war effort, she was haunted by what she called "the eternal, ever deepening wonder, how can one be of most and finest service now," a question that she said was "never absent from one's mind." At that point, when the United States had been fully in the war for nearly a year, Roche admitted, "I haven't found my answer yet."[42] But the pressures were intense. By March, as she was finishing up her work for the Consumers' League, she described the effect of her "months in the East and particularly the time in W. [Washington]." They made her "feel as though some perfectly tremendous and personal, tho' invisible, presence were with me all the time, something holding utterly in itself the destinies of the future, and of which one must become a part if one cares at all about the future denouement."[43]

Even then, she resisted this powerful sense that she must, to be useful at all, throw herself into the war effort. There "seems something awful in abandoning oneself to that great thing; one cries out that there surely must be a way of carrying out the old ideals and realizing old visions without doing so." Miserably, no, she concluded: "to such protests there comes no answer from the presence about one, just the dreadful silence like someone listening, and which finally convinces as no answer could, that part of it all one must become, and suffer, and blunder, and go against one's highest dreams with it, or else be set apart utterly from the working out of human fate."[44]

There was the dilemma fully articulated. Should she set herself outside the stream of history as a pitiful little protest against its inexorable direction and by so doing render herself utterly irrelevant, or should she join the detestable flow in hopes of redirecting it just a little toward some small good that might otherwise go undone? The options were not good. As Roche saw it, and as so many others clearly did, she faced the decision whether to remain true to all of her values and thus doom herself to ineffectiveness or turn her back on some of her values in an effort to remain effective on behalf of others.[45] Given Roche's drive for engagement, once she saw the situation this way, she had to join the war effort.

Roche's reversal on the war could hardly have been starker. The same woman who late in 1917 mourned the abominable destructiveness of the conflict declared in summer 1918 that the war had catapulted the United States "much nearer the hoped for ideal democracy." A few months later, she gushed, "I can only realize that it is much the greatest time in history and be thankful that I'm living now—and the world has Wilson."[46]

This dramatic transformation occurred because once Roche felt the magnetic pull of history so powerfully that she wanted to stop resisting the war, the spring and summer of 1918 provided plausible grounds for doing so. By that time, some wartime initiatives seemed to be opposing inequalities of class and gender. In spring 1918, Wilson gave a boost to collective bargaining when he formed the National War Labor Board to mediate disputes between workers and employers and appointed labor progressive Frank Walsh to head it. The board was, according to one historian, "the most left-leaning government agency that Washington had ever seen," and the leading labor federation in the United States grew by a million members partly as a result of protections offered by the wartime government.[47] Indeed, workers emboldened by the country's critical need for labor, the government's apparent support for their right to organize, and their sense that employers were not fairly sharing war-created wealth initiated an extraordinary number of strikes during the war years, making it look as though the war might help to set relations between labor and capital on a more equitable basis.[48] Similarly, when the women's suffrage amendment reached the U.S. Senate in 1918, Wilson made what Roche characterized as "a powerful appeal" on its behalf, and the wartime economy's need for labor opened all kinds of new employment opportunities to American women, a fact recognized and supported by the Women in Industry Service, a federal agency established in 1918 to promote the welfare of women workers.[49] Perhaps the war would not destroy all things progressive as Roche had feared but might instead advance them.

Even so, Roche's decision to join Creel's CPI was a stunning choice for a former anti-war progressive. Keenly aware of widespread opposition to U.S. involvement in the war and envisioning the need for a citizenry fully devoted to the cause, Wilson had, almost as soon as he won the war declaration from Congress, created the CPI to publicize U.S. war aims both at home and abroad. He had then recruited George Creel to direct it. Both Wilson and Creel hoped that the CPI could forge a unified public in support of the war and, more grandiose (and sinister), create a single nation from a loosely connected, polyglot population. Once Creel had signed on to Wilson's war, he behaved exactly according to type: he could not understand how anyone of intelligence and moral standing could oppose U.S. intervention. He was determined to shape public opinion in such a way that all Americans shared a common commitment to making the world safe for democracy and would offer any sacrifice in service to that transcendent mission.[50]

Early on, Creel sought creative and fairly unobjectionable ways to get information about the war and the U.S. government to the American public. He published piles of pamphlets, produced movies and posters, and organized volunteer speakers (called Four-Minute Men) in virtually every American community to represent the administration's view of the war and the nation's needs in wartime. He also published the *Official Bulletin*, a daily report on the proceedings of government agencies in an effort to keep citizens informed of their government's operations.[51]

By early 1918, however, Creel was not providing straightforward information but had turned the CPI into what historian David Kennedy called "a crude propaganda mill."[52] His publications, posters, and movies increasingly vilified the Germans, peddled atrocity stories, and fomented suspicion of any American who questioned U.S. participation in the war. Although Creel lambasted vigilantes who punished pacifists or other dissidents, his own publicity machine played a prominent role in whipping up animus toward anyone who questioned the administration's wartime policies.[53] Materials published by the CPI even asked readers to report anti-war "whispers" to the Department of Justice.[54] Such suggestions posed profound dangers to political dissidents and discontented workers. Anyone who openly objected to U.S. participation in the war risked indictment for sedition or treason under the Espionage and Sedition Acts, passed in June 1917 and May 1918, and some of the administration's critics wound up in prison. In fact, the Department of Justice and the War Department helped to repress even labor activism, as they often equated resistance to employers with resistance to the war effort. Nowhere was that repression more pronounced than in Roche's beloved West.[55]

Roche never alluded to these aspects of wartime policy but seems to have concluded that the good she might do from within the Wilson administration outweighed the danger of associating herself with its repressions. Having decided she could not bear to stand on the sidelines of history, Roche accepted yet another opportunity opened to her by her Denver gang. This one was Creel's request that she form a new division within the CPI specifically to drum up support for the war among the 14.5 million Americans born abroad.[56] She started the work in May 1918 and named her new unit the Division of Work with the Foreign Born. By moving to Washington, DC, Roche completed the reconstitution of her western progressive community there. When Ben Lindsey wrote to any single member of the group in 1918 and 1919, he sent news to all the others and referred to them as the "round table" or "the gang."[57]

While getting immigrant communities on board Wilson's war train was the explicit goal of Roche's division, both she and Creel saw its work as a larger opportunity for integrating immigrants more fully in American life. Indeed, she did not construe her work for the CPI as being so much about the war—though she enthusiastically supported it in her outreach to foreign-language groups—as an effort "to try and work out better cooperation and understanding between them [foreign-language groups] and the English-speaking groups."[58] She furthermore insisted that the fuller participation of immigrants in American life required first overcoming "years of neglect and even injustice" toward immigrants by native-born Americans.[59] No doubt calling to mind the condition of miners in Colorado's coalfields just a few years before as well as the conditions in which her immigrant neighbors had lived in New York, Roche insisted, "The numerous un-American conditions and injustices to which so many immigrants have fallen victims must be wiped out."[60] To convince immigrants of the sincerity of American commitment to democracy and liberty and thus its stated war aims, native-born Americans must, according to Roche, rectify injustice and engage in a "mutual process of education" with the foreign-born.[61] It was especially this "mutual process of education" that the Division of Work with the Foreign Born meant to facilitate.

Roche's management of the division reflected her continuing commitment to democracy. Right off the bat, she decided to organize separate units devoted to communication with each of several language groups. She wanted a native speaker to head each unit. To identify a pool of candidates for those positions, she approached publishers of foreign-language newspapers and leaders of immigrant organizations across the country and asked them to recommend people from their language groups "to act as managers of the Foreign Language Bureaus of the division."[62] She meant this selection process to be so "thoroughly democratic" that her Division at the CPI might actually *represent* foreign-language groups to the federal government as well as communicate the federal government's concerns to those groups.[63] She claimed indeed that the "Managers of each language bureau were chosen by the foreign-language groups themselves—from their newspapers and organizations."[64] In this, Roche exaggerated the homogeneity of each language community as well as the democracy in her process of selecting managers, but her desire to create a site for genuine exchange between the federal government and the country's immigrant communities was sincere.

That exchange included only immigrant communities from Europe. In her first months, Roche hired directors from fourteen language groups and was working to hire more. The language groups were German, Italian, Swedish, Norwegian, Finnish, Ukrainian, Russian, Lithuanian, Hungarian, Yugoslavian, Czech, Polish, Danish, and Dutch.[65] Mexican and Asian immigrant communities received no attention in 1918. The reason was not that Roche failed to see these groups as potentially integral members of the American national community but that government officials did not perceive either Spanish-speaking communities or Asian-language speakers as likely to resist U.S. participation in the war. After the war, when Roche took her division out of the federal government and was no longer ruled by wartime imperatives, she worked to expand her agency to include non-European immigrant communities.[66]

While her division remained part of the Wilson administration, its work with the original European-descended groups aimed to establish multiple vectors of communication. She envisioned her agency as a mechanism through which the federal government communicated to immigrant communities and immigrant communities spoke to native-born Americans, including those in the national government. To facilitate the first goal, the directors were to circulate as widely as possible materials prepared by various government agencies, and these items reached 800 foreign-language newspapers a day by the war's end. The government materials predictably included news of the war and explanations of Wilson's commitment to a postwar world that supported the self-determination of European peoples and an international body devoted to peaceful settlement of international disputes. But releases went well beyond war news. Many articles provided information that immigrants in particular might need about naturalization and taxes. Still others contained information on such topics as health care, child rearing, and vocational training.[67] The division produced longer pamphlets on those same topics and hired immigrant speakers to act as the equivalent of Four-Minute Men in foreign-language neighborhoods.[68] In these ways, Roche opened a channel between the federal government and immigrant communities.

But she intended communication within that channel to flow both ways. To ensure that immigrant communities were empowered to speak through her agency, Roche asked the managers of each foreign-language bureau to gather a constant stream of information about their ethnic communities, which the division then disseminated through the English-language press. This aspect of the division's mission was made the more urgent by vicious attacks on some immigrant groups by vigilantes who suspected them of favoring Germany and its allies in the war. Roche saw as one of her tasks the defense of immigrants as loyal Americans.[69]

Some historians have argued that progressives' commitment to democracy diminished during World War I as many reformers devoted themselves to recruiting citizens to the national administration's policies rather than creating ways for the mass of citizens to make their interests known to policymakers.[70] This is a significant insight. In some cases, the direction of influence did seem to shift during the war. But Roche's wartime work, with its insistence on two-way communication between government and citizens, undermines blanket conclusions.

Within her division, too, Roche tried to embody her commitment to democratic equality between native- and foreign-born Americans. Before organizing her work, she interviewed people who had worked with immigrants at the Young Women's Christian Association (YWCA), Young Men's Christian Association (YMCA), and the Council of National Defense, among others, and discovered their belief that "all sorts of dreadful things" would happen if "we made our people [foreign-born writers and managers] really executives in their own line, giving them real responsibility." And in her interviews with foreign-language activists, she discovered "that all the experiences of foreign born workers with agencies for whom and with whom they've worked have been such as to make them feel very definitely their subordination and secondary place. Always," she explained to a friend, "they have been translators and interpreters . . . given no power of discretion, no latitude as to the exercise of their own judgment." She wanted her organization "to be the exception" to that rule, and it apparently was. The foreign-language managers were called in to discuss all the agency's big decisions during the years of Roche's leadership, and they were deeply disgruntled when later on new leadership pulled back from her democratic approach.[71] Moreover, Roche and her staff established such good relations with the editors of many foreign-language newspapers that when the armistice was signed in November 1918, the editors asked that the work of the division be continued, and Wilson's government kept it going until May 1919, when the last remnants of the CPI were finally dismantled.[72] To a remarkable extent, Roche created within Wilson's wartime government an agency genuinely devoted to democracy and cultural diversity.

Roche vividly articulated her goal as "the release of the neglected potentialities of our millions of new Americans into a fuller participation in our country's life."[73] She saw immigrants as a source of enrichment and renewal for the United States. For her, Americanization meant "the creation of a mutual sympathy and understanding which will eventually weld into one the many units composing our national destiny."[74] Her version of the melting pot envisioned the "active participation in a common purpose and life by the native born and foreign born together," not the disappearance of immigrant values or practices into an already existing and dominant American culture.[75] She thought it outrageous that patriotic fanatics urged suppression of the foreign-language press during the war and eradication of German from school curricula. For her, immi-

grants' own languages and institutions were not a threat to their participation in American life but precisely the instruments through which immigrants might participate, and she believed that immigrant cultures,
given full scope, would change America for the better.[76]

Roche believed that her work within Wilson's wartime government
could facilitate this change and that it would be a part of a larger global
rebirth. By mid-1918, she was willing to hope that the war was truly, to
use her words, a "movement for human liberty and the rights of nations
to govern themselves" as the president insisted it was. Grander yet, she
allowed herself to believe that the cause currently being fought on "the
battlefields of Europe" was for the "world commonwealth," and the
"principles of that democratic world-state."[77] She had warmed to the
idea of an international entity that might govern global relations in an
equitable way that guaranteed world peace. She seems to have accepted
the claims of the CPI that America's cause in the war was really the cause
of all peoples: a world in which self-governing nations cooperated to end
war forever.[78]

Having taken this leap of faith, Roche was, like other progressives,
deeply disappointed in the war's conclusion. By the time Wilson left for
Paris to negotiate a peace treaty in fall 1918, even Creel was somewhat
disillusioned with him. The administration's suppression of dissent of-
fended him as it did many others, and the subsequent failure of the peace
to usher in an era of international cooperation made U.S. participation
seem very nearly fraudulent.[79] In violation of Wilson's hopes for a peace
without victory, Germany and Austria were excluded from the peace
talks. The Allies, blaming Germany for the war, demanded reparations.
The peace conference refused seriously to entertain demands for independence by European colonies as Wilson's commitment to the self-
determination of peoples led some to hope it would.[80] Roche declared
early in 1919, "Everyone, of course, is feeling a rather dreadful reaction
and depression from the war and much that is taking place now. There
never was a time when faith and vision were so needed, and so hard to
have."[81] The U.S. Senate even refused to commit the United States to Wilson's League of Nations—an anemic version of the world-state that
Roche had rapturously envisioned. To make matters worse, many of the
initiatives tending toward more equitable labor relations were dismantled immediately following the war. As a result, organized labor declined
dramatically after 1919 and struggled miserably for the next decade.

The war years caused upheaval for Josephine Roche, sparking a series of
frenzied relocations between 1915 and 1918. Despite her initially fierce
opposition to U.S. involvement in the conflict, World War I opened remarkable opportunities for her, including her first foreign travel and her

first job in the federal government. Throughout, Roche's Denver crowd remained crucial to her prospects, as Lindsey saved her from unemployment in 1915 and Creel once again hired her for a job in which she pushed beyond the usual expectations of women. At the CPI, Roche directed an agency of men, an extraordinary position for a woman of her generation and a powerful confirmation that no restriction on women's possibilities was firm.

Roche's experience also illuminated the continuing vitality of progressivism through the war years. Her work at the CPI, an agency often associated with wartime repression, furthered the cause of democracy and cultural diversity, as she created a forum in which immigrant groups represented themselves to the federal government and a larger American public even as her agency tried to recruit immigrants to U.S. war aims. But more conservative forces were also given greater power by the U.S mobilization for war. These were forces that opposed organized labor, immigrants, and free speech. They were forces that supported corporate power over all other interests. In the postwar world, progressives would continue to contend with these forces, but on very different terms from before and during the war.

PART II

FIRST TEMPORARY REVERSAL OF PROGRESSIVE REFORM: ROCHE'S NEW DEPARTURES, 1919–1932

The decade following World War I represented the first temporary reversal within the Age of Reform. At the level of national politics and government, progressives lost power, as the new energy and status accorded anti-egalitarian forces during the war did not weaken, but the new assets invested in corporate regulation and the organization of labor were for the most part retracted. Progressive stalwarts like Josephine Roche nevertheless forged ahead with efforts to diminish inequalities of wealth and power at the state and local levels as well as in the private sector. Although embattled on many fronts after the war, reformers strengthened their links to organized labor and immigrant communities and initiated new institutional and policy departures that would serve as models under the New Deal. Indeed, by the end of the decade, Roche stood at the head of an experiment in labor-capital relations that became a beacon brilliantly connecting the Progressive Era and the New Deal.

CHAPTER 6

WORK AND LOVE IN A PROGRESSIVE EBB TIDE, 1919–1927

For several years after the war, Roche remained an itinerant reformer. In part, she moved around a lot because she had not yet situated herself at what she considered a fundamental site for rectifying inequalities; she was as a result never quite satisfied with where she was. In addition, during the decade after the war, unlike any other time in her life, Roche's days were significantly shaped by the family claim. In this decade, personal relationships forced some of Roche's frenzied mobility.

Roche's first postwar move was from Washington, DC to New York, and the circumstances of that relocation encapsulated both the embattlement and persistence of progressive reform. During the last months of 1918, Roche transferred most of the Division of Work with the Foreign Born to New York because so many foreign-language newspapers were published there and many immigrant associations were headquartered there. To facilitate more democratic relationships, she wanted her organization to be in the closest possible proximity to the communities it aimed to serve.[1] When the federal government withdrew support from Roche's agency in 1919, that withdrawal signaled the weakening of progressivism at the level of national politics, but it did not mean the end of Roche's work. Instead of folding up her tent, Roche transformed her former government agency into a voluntary organization called the Foreign Language Information Service (FLIS).[2] She did so especially because of the furious anti-immigrant forces unleashed in the United States as the war wound down. These forces were whipped up in part by Russia's Bolshevik Revolution in 1917, which lent credibility to arguments that any political dissent might ultimately threaten private property and other American institutions. Since many Americans associated political radicalism with foreign birth, immigrants in the United States suffered increased discrimination and violence in the aftermath of the Bolshevik victory. That situation convinced Roche and her staff that the work of "interpreting America to the alien and the alien to America" was as important after the war as it had been during the global conflict.[3]

Roche's FLIS embodied the thickening of connections between progressives and immigrant communities. To sustain her new venture, she sought funding from foundations and philanthropists as well as bankers and financiers.[4] She rejected the suggestion of charging foreign-language newspapers for her services because billing the papers would undermine the egalitarianism of her programs. She insisted that the communities most in need of the FLIS were precisely those who would not be able to pay.[5] She was determined not to serve only the elite among immigrant communities but to extend her reach as far as possible. That egalitarianism cost her enormous anxiety and put the whole enterprise constantly at risk. When government support ended in 1919, the organization lurched from one short-term grant to another until the Red Cross integrated the FLIS into its Department of Civilian Relief early in 1920.[6] At that point, Roche's friends sighed with relief that she had "saved her Americanization Bureau" and hoped "to see more of her."[7]

Roche intended the FLIS to continue, in part, as a conduit between immigrant communities and the U.S. government. To that end, the managers routinely translated press releases from federal agencies and sent them to 850 newspapers and 67,000 foreign language organizations and their branches. Those releases emanated from no fewer than 58 government agencies that sent daily notices to the FLIS for translation and dissemination. Regular contributors included the Children's Bureau, the Department of Labor, the Bureau of Internal Revenue, the Public Health Service, the Bureau of Immigration, and the Department of Agriculture.[8] In addition, thousands of immigrants every month sent queries to the FLIS, and, over and above sending individual replies, the organization published pamphlets to answer some of the most frequently asked questions. They ranged from "Venereal Diseases and How to Prevent Them" through "How to Become a Citizen" to "How Americans Won Their Liberty."[9]

The FLIS also remained a channel for communication from immigrant communities to a larger American public. To implement this aspect of her mission, Roche created an American Press Section that sent information on the foreign-born to the English-language press. Most of these press releases were translations of editorials first published in foreign-language newspapers. They served as direct messages from immigrant communities to English-only Americans. In addition, every month, the American Press Section produced two or three major articles on immigrant communities that were published in such venues as the *New York Times*, *New Republic*, *Christian Science Monitor*, and *Collier's*. Their goal was to ease fears of foreign-language groups and oppose anti-immigrant policies and violence. On top of its journalistic work, the FLIS undertook case work for immigrants anxious for help with income taxes, health care, passports, education, and naturalization. In early 1920, the organization was responding to about 1,000 such pleas every month.[10] In addition, the FLIS offered legal aid.[11] In a single month during 1920, for instance, Roche was trying to arrange pro bono representation for 109 individual legal cases.[12] Her staff of 65 was stretched to its limit.[13]

By March 1921, Roche was pleading with the Red Cross for increased funding. She needed more staff to respond to the deluge of requests for information and advice, and she wanted to add several new languages to the FLIS repertoire, especially Greek, Spanish, Arabic, Chinese, and Japanese.[14] Roche was also emphatic that her managers should be meeting in person with representatives of their language groups all over the country. Democracy required it. She insisted, "if the Bureau's work is to continue to be based on the fundamental needs of, and in sympathetic cooperation with the foreign born," the staff had to get out into communities. "A long absence by Managers from the field," she argued, "inevitably undermines the Bureau's work."[15] Roche wanted her agency to be an integral part of immigrant communities, not to become a separate bureaucratic entity claiming to speak on behalf of those whose real and changing concerns it could not possibly know. In defense of her request for more money, Roche pointed out that the FLIS had drawn over 600,000 foreign-born members to the Red Cross in just over a year.[16] Clearly, some immigrant communities believed they were benefiting from Roche's efforts, and she was reaching enormous numbers of people.

Roche would not abide any diminution of her efforts. In spring 1921, the Red Cross, facing financial pressures of its own, recommended that the FLIS downsize to twenty staff members, cut the American Press Section, and end its casework with individual immigrants.[17] Roche and her staff found these reductions unacceptable. Eliminating the American Press Section and casework would shut off much of the communication from immigrants to English-only Americans, reducing the FLIS to a one-way telegraph from the government to immigrant groups. Rather than accept what she considered an anti-democratic curtailment of her work, Roche took the risk of unhitching her organization from the Red Cross. After a mad scramble, she won funding from various foundations, including the Commonwealth Fund and the Laura Spelman Rockefeller Memorial Fund. Every grant was for only a fixed period.[18] Still, for Roche, keeping the fullest possible program in operation was worth continual anxiety about funding.

Beyond sustaining the FLIS's established work, Roche envisioned her organization as a sort of Progressive Service for immigrants. She hoped to foster alliances among immigrant communities that would empower them politically. To this end, Roche proposed a committee with at least half its members foreign-born Americans, who would work toward developing government activities "in the interest of the immigrant."[19] The group would identify common interests, devise public policies, and lobby for passage and implementation of those programs. The proposal demonstrated Roche's dual commitment to progressive legislation and a citizenry organized to promote its own interests. Given the shoestring budgets on which the FLIS dangled over the years, Roche's vision was never fully realized, but it reflected the persistence of progressive ideals after World War I.

Roche's vision was shared by her devoted staff, and by none more passionately than Edward Hale Bierstadt, who, for a brief time, won Roche's love. It is easy to see why Roche fell in love with Bierstadt. Born in New York City in 1891, Bierstadt was witty and well-read, a progressive, playwright, and drama critic.[20] During the war, he heroically enlisted in the American Expeditionary Force and served on the staff of hospitals in both England and France.[21] On his return to New York, Bierstadt defended free speech and radicalism against repression by both government agencies and self-styled patriotic groups.[22] Roche hired him in September 1919 as an associate director at the FLIS in charge of the American Press Section, from which position he wrote fervent defenses of immigrants and castigations of their detractors.[23]

On July 2, 1920, Bierstadt married his boss, Josephine Roche.[24] Given that Roche had probably not met Bierstadt long before she hired him in fall 1919, theirs was a whirlwind romance. They married less than a year after they met and in a service so sudden that Ben Lindsey did not find out about it until the Costigans wired him the morning of the ceremony.[25] There is no sign that her parents attended the nuptials or that the couple took any time away from work to celebrate. In fact, the marriage looks like a wildly impetuous move by two besotted lovers. In a note to Read Lewis a few days after the event, Roche reported that she and Edward returned home "after hunting a minister madly all over Westchester County."[26] The wedding was apparently not long in the planning stages.

Like many other members of the second generation of college-educated women, Roche expected to combine her public career with marriage, and her belief in the possibility of doing so was fueled by her political community. Feminist men like George Creel, Ben Lindsey, and Ed Costigan accepted and even expected that their wives would continue public work after their weddings. Lindsey's wife, Henrietta, to whom he was married in 1913, worked with him at the juvenile court. Mabel and Ed Costigan were a political team. Creel's wife remained on the stage and made more money than he did; the two agreed early in their marriage to split their expenses fifty-fifty.[27] Roche had also closely observed the egalitarian marriage of Mary and Vladimir Simkhovitch at Greenwich House. She had every reason to believe that she also could continue her public mission while married.

Roche and Bierstadt certainly were political and intellectual soul mates. His defense of free speech, resting as it did on his belief that moral codes and laws change "with the flux and flow of time as change all other things" set him squarely among historical relativists like Roche and her beloved teacher and now friend, James Harvey Robinson.[28] And as fiercely as Bierstadt championed free speech, he even more vehemently supported immigrants. In the context of anti-immigrant and anti-radical violence following the war, Bierstadt wrote, "My country, right or wrong . . . is the creed of fools and weaklings: fools because they cannot see the truth, and weaklings because they dare not face it."[29] He condemned the idea of the melting pot because too many Americans imagined it to mean that only "elements they consider alien to themselves" should dissolve away.[30] He went on to explain, "If there is no reciprocity in Americanization, there is only harm. . . . Americanization must mean the blending of all nationalities on American soil, including our own; it must not mean simply the engulfing of all other nationalities in ours. That is egomania."[31]

Roche and Bierstadt fiercely opposed the conviction, growing among Americans, that immigrants threatened their cherished institutions.[32] So widely had that notion spread by 1921 that Congress set quotas on immigration from each European country.[33] In 1924, anti-immigration advocates won an even more stringent quota law that very nearly cut off immigration from areas outside Northern and Western Europe.[34] Immigration restriction was a conspicuous victory of the conservative forces given increasing power after World War I. Roche's and Bierstadt's shared opposition to it, and the broader fit between their progressive ideals seemed to make them ideal partners.

To friends who routinely urged Roche to take a break now and then, the marriage must have seemed a blessing. In the year following their vows, Roche and Bierstadt spent several weekends lollygagging in the country and a full month in Colorado with Roche's parents.[35] The couple also socialized regularly when in New York. They were in frequent contact with the family of James Harvey Robinson, whose latest project, the New School for Social Research, Roche heartily endorsed. They also palled around with a range of progressive writers and activists.[36] Roche had long been a friend of left-leaning Sonya Levien, avid suffragist and editor at *Metropolitan* magazine, who became a screenwriter in the 1920s and went on to pen scripts for such big hits as *Quo Vadis* and *Okla-*

homa.[37] Other writers in Roche's crowd included the legendary play-wright Eugene O'Neill and Sidney Howard. Howard interested Roche because of an exposé he wrote on employers who spied on their workers to prevent unionization.[38] She hired him at the FLIS.[39] In the course of their early acquaintance, Howard wrote his first play, and over the Thanksgiving holiday in 1920 he regaled Roche and Bierstadt with anec-dotes from his first professional encounter with the theater. "As it was his first venture in dramatics and his first experience with folks theatrical," Roche wrote after an evening at Howard's apartment, "his adventures have been highly entertaining."[40] Howard would, only five years later, win the Pulitzer Prize for Drama, and in 1931, his first of two Academy Awards for screenwriting. The second, awarded posthumously, was for *Gone with the Wind*.[41]

Despite their interesting friends, however, Roche soon believed she had made a mistake in marrying.[42] In 1922, she filed for and was granted a divorce, and Bierstadt left the FLIS.[43] Because divorce records in New York are sealed for one hundred years and Roche left no private record of her marriage or divorce, we cannot know why the marriage failed. In earlier discussions with Read Lewis, Roche had insisted that she couldn't "see how any person can have a feeling of obligation, of duty . . . without its ultimately meaning the death of any affection, love, or even comrade-ship between them."[44] Perhaps the sense of duty in her marriage destroyed her love. Certainly, Roche's previous life and the life she led afterward suggested that domesticity was not among her interests and that she pre-ferred to devote every waking hour to her public work. Perhaps only after they married did she and Bierstadt realize their hopes for domestic life were incompatible.

Whatever pushed them apart, Roche retained no record at all of her two-year experiment with matrimony, and she does not seem to have been tempted to marry ever again. Her commitment to progressive re-form was all-consuming and would continue to be so for another fifty-plus years. Had Roche remained in this particular marriage—as rooted as Bierstadt was in New York—her subsequent contributions to American life would have been quite different from what they turned out to be, al-most certainly narrower in scope and less transgressive of gender norms. The decision to divorce and remain unmarried freed Roche to take up whatever work she believed most likely to create a more just world, and she made full use of that freedom.

As her marriage to Bierstadt unraveled, Roche worked frantically to set the FLIS firmly enough on its financial feet that she could pass it on to some other leader. Her funders urged her to remain at the helm through the fall 1922, which she dutifully did.[45] But early that year, she recruited an old friend to join her as assistant director with the clear intention of grooming him to run the organization when she left.[46] That acquaintance was none other than Read Lewis, who, since graduating from law school and asking Roche to marry him, had developed his cross-cultural chops as an assistant to the U.S. Ambassador to Russia. In late fall 1922, Roche turned the FLIS over to Lewis, for whom the organization became a life's work.[47]

By that time, Roche had proven herself a capable manager of men and yet dramatically softened her public self-presentation. In 1922, Roche projected a much more conventionally feminine persona than she had during her term as a police officer. In photographs published during the 1920s, Roche sometimes wore necklaces, brooches, or earrings, favored collars with small bows or a slight ruffle, and wore no hat, exposing the thick wavy hair that she swept away from her face and pinned at the back of her head (figure 8). She no longer wore tailored suits but dresses and blouses that in no way hinted at masculine imitation. She had lost considerable weight as well, making her square jaw more pronounced than it had been earlier, when her face was nearly as round as her rimless spectacles. She favored this more conventional feminine image for the remainder of her career.[48] Perhaps she thought she might encounter less resistance to her authority in unconventional arenas if she did not reject more superficial markers of femininity.

Her more conventional appearance may have made Roche more comfortable as well in the new job she landed in Washington, DC. Apparently eager to get out of Bierstadt's town, Roche returned to the national capital late in 1922, this time as head of the Editorial Division of the U.S. Children's Bureau. The move established Roche within an important network of women reformers. Created by Congress in 1912, the Children's Bureau represented one of the signal achievements of women progressives. The small agency, nestled in the Department of Labor, was proposed as a clearinghouse for information about and model policies promoting child welfare. At the head of the campaign to create the bureau were such leading progressive lights as Jane Addams, Lillian Wald, and Florence Kelley—women who pioneered the social settlement movement in the United States and rose to national prominence as progressive activists. Having created the Children's Bureau, they succeeded in getting a woman appointed its first chief. Julia Lathrop then built the Children's Bureau into a female-dominated federal unit that, through alliances with women's voluntary organizations, developed child welfare policies often adopted by the states as well as the federal government.[49]

Until her service at the Children's Bureau, Roche had operated at the margins of its woman-centered reform network. Her work on delinquent girls was part of the network's project; her research for the National Consumers' League put her in touch with its leaders. But even while pursuing those assignments, Roche was more intimately involved with her progressive community in Colorado, which was led by men. Because of that positioning, Roche was used to gender-integrated initiatives that looked to electoral politics and labor organization as primary vehicles for social change. The women in the Children's Bureau were used to policy initiatives spearheaded by women in gender-segregated organizations. Indeed, women in the Children's Bureau established their authority in public life by creating new areas of policy and professional expertise where women could thrive without competing against men. As a younger woman closely mentored by men, Roche expected to vie with men for jobs and leadership. That Roche could become an integral member of the female-dominated Children's Bureau network without losing her place in the male-led Denver gang was another testament to her gift for straddling boundaries.

Although Julia Lathrop and Roche hit it off, Lathrop's successor at the bureau proved an even more important friend.[50] Grace Abbott, who took over the bureau in 1921, shared many life experiences with Roche. Both were from Nebraska, where Abbott's older sister attended Brownell Hall, Roche's high school alma mater. Like Roche, Abbott earned a master's degree in political science (hers from the University of Chicago) and lived in a social settlement for a time. Abbott eventually led an organization, the Immigrants' Protective League, dedicated to smoothing immigrants' transition to American life. Once they met at the Children's Bureau in the early 1920s, the two women became fast friends, and the relationship anchored Roche securely in the national women's reform community in which Abbott was a major player.[51] So enduring and profound was their friendship that when Abbott died in 1939, Roche delivered a eulogy at her memorial.[52]

Roche's leadership at the FLIS prepared her well to head the Editorial Division of the Children's Bureau. In that position, she edited reports from all of the bureau's divisions, prepared a weekly news summary from the agency, wrote news releases based on the bureau's research, and produced a weekly radio talk on child welfare.[53] Most important to Roche was her role in agitating for the Child Labor Amendment. Women reformers had long been involved in efforts to end child labor, seeing it as perhaps the worst example of corporate exploitation of working-class families.[54] After two federal anti–child labor laws were declared unconstitutional, children's advocates shifted into a new gear, resolving to amend the constitution so that Congress could regulate what they considered an abhorrent labor practice.[55] Roche arrived at the bureau in the midst of its campaign for the constitutional amendment. Straight away, she joined Abbott as a member of the Permanent Conference on the Abolition of Child Labor, a group chaired by Samuel Gompers, president of the American Federation of Labor (AFL).[56] Roche took charge of publishing leaflets supporting the amendment.[57] When Congress passed it in 1924 and sent it to the states for ratification, Roche's division closely followed editorial opinion in the states, hoping to intervene at crucial points on the measure's behalf.[58] Although prospects for ratification looked good while Roche remained with the Children's Bureau, the opposition ultimately defeated it in most states. By the early 1930s, only nine states had ratified, and the amendment would never become part of the U.S. Constitution.

Before that defeat was clear, the declining health of Roche's father forced her to leave the Children' Bureau. Although brief, her stint at the female-centered federal agency was significant. It positioned Roche at yet another political and cultural intersection. Just as she internalized perspectives of both the East and the West, social science progressivism and labor progressivism, so did she now stand in the overlap between reforming networks dominated by women and by men. This location would prove a crucial component of her efficacy as a leader in Franklin Roosevelt's New Deal government.

Her father's health had begun to deteriorate early in Roche's tenure at the Children's Bureau, and by early 1925, Roche felt she must return to Denver to help care for him.[59] At that point, her father was still making his daily trek to the offices of Rocky Mountain Fuel (RMF), where he was now president. She attended him in the evenings. By summer 1926, he was in constant pain but still managing to work every day. At night, though, according to Roche, he had "to sit up much of the time and get relief only through hot cloths which I put on. . . . The doctors seem powerless to help, or even relieve him much. How little medicine can do at times, and how little we really know about human ills!"[60] At the same time, Roche's mother was failing. Through 1926, Ella Roche was ambulatory and enjoyed riding around in a car, so Roche hired a chauffeur to drive her around most of each day. But eventually, her mother needed nursing care as well, and Roche had two increasingly dependent parents to care for. Because her father did not want her mother to know how bad his situation was, Josephine tried to put a good face on his condition, and Ella Roche was so little in touch with daily life that she apparently did not know the difference.

Finally, in September 1926, John Roche collapsed. From then on, he stayed at home, could not take food for several weeks, and eventually could not make himself understood because his tongue and throat had "hardened." At that point, Roche hired two nurses so that her father had round-the-clock care.[61] Until December, he could express his needs by writing, but at that point, he became too weak even to write. Roche was anguished. "It is only a question of time now, and after these months of suffering and wretchedness for father and with the doctors all saying positively he has nothing else to look forward to, I can only hope it may not be prolonged for worse ordeals for him."[62]

Even though she never had children or a dependent partner, Roche learned between 1925 and 1927 what it was to feel the conflict between work and family responsibility. When she returned to her parents' home, she also returned to the juvenile court, where Ben Lindsey was fighting for his political life and that of the juvenile court itself. Roche took charge of not only work with girls but also much of the court's administration. Given the needs of her parents, she confided in December 1926, "I have had great difficulty in coming to any decision as to whether I am justified in trying to go on with my work at all and even the little I am in the office seems wrong sometimes, but I have also the problem of keeping mother from knowing about the seriousness of the situation—a not impossible task because she is so far from herself . . . and my being at the office every day, for a time at least, helps in the plan. And it certainly helps me, for I am forced to think of other people's troubles for a bit."[63]

Whatever good it did Roche to escape to the court each day, she had returned to the agency only because she was drawn back to Denver for her parents' sake, and she rejoined the progressive outpost in Denver's government as it was about to be destroyed. In the mid-1920s, the Ku Klux Klan won control of many offices in Colorado on the promise of restoring law and order to a state the Klansmen claimed was awash in crime. Lindsey's court, accused by the Klan of interfering in the patriarchal prerogatives of men in their families and coddling juvenile offenders, was a target. In 1924, Lindsey won reelection to his judgeship by only a handful of votes, and the Klan introduced a bill to move the state's juvenile courts into the criminal court system. That transfer would destroy the juvenile justice program that Lindsey had labored for over twenty years to build. Lindsey initially held his own, as the Klan fell from grace in 1925. But the new victors were not progressives; they were conservatives overwhelmingly associated with the largest corporate interests of the state and devoted to fiscal restraint and small government. Lindsey was nearly as repugnant to them as to the Klan. Between 1925 and 1927, the Klan and their more mainstream conservative successors contested Lindsey's close election to the court and condemned him for being soft on crime as well as for his increasingly vocal support for birth control and easier divorce for couples without children.[64]

The strain of caring for her parents and working at the court produced a nearly desperate need in Roche for a place of refuge. In the fall of 1926, she rented a small apartment not far from her parents' home, of which she said, "I hope to go into solitary confinement and read and rest a few hours a week." She admitted, "It seems mad to take it when I can't live there and can only hide out for a brief time on Sundays and evenings, but I've felt an increasing need of a place all my own if only for half an hour's retreat."[65]

Her refuge would prove all the more important to Roche as she faced profound losses in 1927. The first was the death of her father on January 13, 1927. John J. Roche died without a will, and Colorado law dictated that in such cases a man's wife and children should inherit his estate equally. Ella Roche was by the time of her husband's death so ill that Josephine had hired a full-time nurse to care for her.[66] While grieving her father's death and working under enormous pressure at the juvenile court, Josephine Roche took on the role of administrator of her father's estate.[67]

An itinerant reformer for nearly twenty years, Roche had traveled light in her adulthood, but suddenly, at forty, she found herself possessed of various kinds of property. Her father's estate included small landholdings in Arapahoe County, Colorado; Neligh, Nebraska; and Chiapas, Mexico, as well as stocks and bonds. Roche had so little interest in the land that she let it go for taxes.[68] But she was intrigued by the almost 20,000 shares of stock in the Rocky Mountain Fuel Company and a smattering of shares in other companies that ranged from the Michigan Land Company to RCA.[69] In these assets, Roche's limber mind eventually saw the possibility of reshaping labor-capital relations in the coalfields of Colorado, and as a result, she took a mighty interest in them. But that interest did not manifest itself until several months after her father's death. In the meantime, she had her mother to care for and a rapidly deteriorating situation to handle at the court.

In fact, as her mother's condition worsened in spring 1927, Lindsey was in his final months at the juvenile court. The state's Supreme Court ruled that the judge's 1924 election was invalid, and, until a new election could be held, a successor was to be appointed by local officials. Lindsey fought the decision, but by June 1927, had exhausted all legal options.[70] Roche reported that the situation at the court was "a fearful strain," and she suffered the appalling experience of having her case files "rifled . . . and all my confidential correspondence stolen" by the court's opponents.[71]

Her mother's death and Lindsey's final ouster were almost simultaneous. Her mother died on June 28, 1927, and was buried two days later. On the day of the funeral, the final proceedings against Lindsey concluded, and Roche felt she must go straight from the cemetery to the court to stand by Lindsey and his wife as they retrieved the judge's personal belongings under the watchful eye of the county sheriff. Roche described the day as "very dreadful."[72] Prolonging the tension, Roche and other staffers at the court had decided to resign en masse as of July 1, the day after her mother's funeral, in protest against the treatment of Lindsey and the directions that the court was being forced to take—toward criminal court procedures with punishment rather than child guidance as their goal. The week following the resignation was, she reported, "a nightmare" because "I was responsible for all court moneys, records, etc., and after resigning had instantly to see to the final audit of books, turning over of bank balances, records, etc." To make matters worse, "the County Commissioners had ordered the sheriff's office to watch us and my every move was under the scrutiny of a deputy sheriff."[73] Roche herself had once worn the badge of the office that now supervised her dismantling of Denver's juvenile court, a vivid illustration of the shift in progressive fortunes since Roche's tenure in law enforcement.

After discharging her courthouse duties, Roche was exhausted. She took a few days in mid-July to rest up with the Costigans on the shores of Palmer Lake, "trying," she said, "to get my jangled nerves quieted before taking on the many things of a more personal nature awaiting me."[74] She hoped soon to sort through "all the family things" so that she could close down her parents' apartment by August 1. She expected to keep her own small refuge for a while longer as she decided what to do next. To Read Lewis, she confessed, "I do want to try and get in better shape mentally and physically before I take on a new job. So I plan to be without one for 2 or 3 months."[75]

Still, only about a week after she had finally left the court and before she had moved everything from her parents' home, she wrote, "It is the most amazing feeling to be without <u>anything</u>—no work, no personal ties or responsibilities, after two such intense years of never being free from both for an instant." Remarkably, jangled as her nerves remained, she did not like her liberty: "And when I think of how I used to think utter freedom would be the height of human bliss and contrast my present feelings with it, I realize how completely our attitudes shift and change."[76] Even though she claimed the need to collect herself before taking on a new job, she was already restless.

This restlessness would help create a unique departure for Roche, one that finally situated her directly within the relationship between labor and capital. After spending the years between 1915 and 1927 flitting from one job to another, never satisfied that what she was doing was the most important thing she might be doing, she was, as she rested at Palmer Lake, on the verge of work she considered truly fundamental in its power to reduce inequality. Her new endeavor would represent her biggest break from reigning gender conventions and make it clear that progressivism had not died even though conservatism had gained the upper hand in many forums during the 1920s. Indeed, even as conservatives in Denver celebrated their long-sought victory over Judge Lindsey and his juvenile court, Roche was imagining a new site from which to strike at them. The ensuing history would demonstrate that the drama of Roche's first forty years was perfect preparation for the greater theatrics and achievements of her mid-life and old age.

MIGRATING TO A "TOTALLY NEW PLANET": ROCHE TAKES OVER ROCKY MOUNTAIN FUEL, 1927–1928

O rphaned and unemployed in 1927, Josephine Roche contemplated her future. Her father's lawyers advised her to sell her stock in the Rocky Mountain Fuel Company (RMF) and live off the proceeds. She could then follow the conventions of Denver's elite and devote herself to afternoon bridge or fulfill her sense of social responsibility by funding progressive causes. Neither option appealed. In fact, in this midlife moment of decision, Roche defied every sort of convention. In the windfall of her inheritance, the grieving reformer saw a slender chance to right the wrong of Ludlow. And she took it. In a blazing exhibition of nerve, she amassed enough shares to become the majority stockholder of her father's coal company, kicked out the sitting management, and transformed the mining operation into a progressive enterprise that welcomed organized labor back to the coalfields of Colorado. Although the destruction of the juvenile court in Denver was a striking illustration of conservatism's power in the late 1920s, Roche's response to her inheritance was equally powerful evidence of progressivism's persistence. Roche's experiment in progressive industrialism, moreover, exemplified a process ongoing among progressives more generally during the first temporary reversal in the Age of Reform. With national politics resistant to their initiatives, progressives tried out ideas for diminishing inequality in other venues.

Once Roche was free of her duties at the juvenile court, she became more and more engrossed in the workings of RMF. During the final months of her father's illness, she had worked every evening with what she called his "confidential secretary" to keep the company running.[1] Her involvement increased as she became executor of her father's estate. At some point in that process, she explored his office and discovered that RMF had engaged in all the anti-union practices that she had come to abhor during the coal strike in 1913–1914. As one analyst later put it, "She found in the company's offices the paraphernalia of war," especially "the records of expenditures for [anti-union] detectives and [armed] mine guards."[2] Indeed, the company had long been spying on its workers to keep them from organizing.[3] To make matters worse, some of the most notorious anti-labor participants in the 1913–1914 strike had since been hired by RMF and remained in its employ.[4] They included Walter Belk, who in 1913 worked as a hired gun for the coal operators, and Judge Jesse Northcutt, who not only delivered rulings favoring coal operators but also funded the transportation of gunfighters who bolstered anti-union forces.[5] Men whom Roche considered villainous were on the payroll of a company in which she had become the largest stockholder.

By September 1927, Roche saw her shares in the coal company as a grand opportunity "to do something" she felt might "be a little worth while in the strictly economic and merciless field of business."[6] Until then, she later reminisced, "It had never occurred to me that I might be put in a position demanding that I act from within industry, instead of protesting from without."[7] Once she found herself with this possibility, however, she realized that she had what she called "a complete laboratory to thresh out all the theories I had evolved in my research work."[8] She then determined to use her windfall to "take over the management [of RMF] . . . and pave the way to operating under a union contract."[9] By inviting the United Mine Workers of America (UMW) back to the coalfields of Colorado and running a coal company in the interests of workers as well as consumers and investors, she felt she had a chance to rectify the injustices that produced the Ludlow Massacre. In that hope, she declined her lawyers' advice to sell her shares in the company: "And miss my chance to help all those miners' families? Definitely, no."[10]

When Roche first took this chance, RMF was quite extensive. Some of its mines were in southern Colorado, where the 1913 conflict had first exploded. There, RMF mined heavy bituminous coal as a neighbor to Colorado Fuel and Iron (CFI), the largest coal producer in the state. The company also owned mines in the mountainous western part of the state. But the bulk of RMF's production centered in the northern coalfields of Colorado, straddling Boulder and Weld counties. On that flat land sweeping up to the Rocky Mountains, the company mined sub-bituminous coal (usually called lignite), which was especially good for household use because it produced less smoke than bituminous coal.[11] Roche focused her attention on those northern fields, where production moved the company from the third- to the second-largest coal producer in Colorado early in her tenure.[12]

Once Roche decided to venture into the world of industrial production, her fondest wish was immediately to overhaul RMF's relation to workers by instituting collective bargaining. To her great frustration, however, she could not move as comprehensively as she desired. Although she was RMF's largest stockholder, she did not yet control a majority of the company's stock, and other members of the board of directors opposed collective bargaining. Indeed, the directors shared the opinions of most coal operators in Colorado, who reviled organized labor, refused to negotiate with any but individual workers, and believed that the solution to strikes was the imprisonment of union organizers. They believed that property rights were simple and absolute: as property owners, they had the right to dictate working conditions, and workers had no independent rights in the operation.[13] Given this attitude, RMF's board elected as president in place of Roche's father the second largest stockholder, an infamously anti-labor real estate baron, Horace W. Bennett.[14] For the moment, Roche had to settle for changes in company policy that fell short of her progressive vision.

Those changes were not insignificant. Roche's holdings granted her the power to appoint a new general manager and vice president. For both roles, she selected Merle D. Vincent, a prominent Denver lawyer who had held firm as an ally of Roche and Edward Costigan during the Progressive Party's realignment in 1914.[15] Vincent was a staunch labor progressive willing to help Roche transform RMF into a proving ground for egalitarian ideals. While arguing with the RMF board over the miners' right to unionize, Roche worked with Vincent to install pro-labor personnel wherever in the company they could, and they started by firing both Northcutt and Belk.[16]

Even as Roche made these down-payments on a new labor policy at RMF, discontent rivaling that of 1913 was roiling Colorado's coalfields. The conditions producing that dissatisfaction violated every tenet of labor progressivism—not to mention American commitments to civil liberty and democracy—and were as evident at RMF as at other coal operations in the state. Workers were paid in scrip instead of cash; many lived in company housing and were required to shop in company stores; they had suffered multiple wage cuts since 1925; they exercised no power over their working conditions. In fact, miners lacked even the freedom to protest when the company paid them for less coal than they mined or delivered unusable coal dust to their company homes for winter heating.[17] The UMW remained ineffectual. Responding to these conditions, the Industrial Workers of the World (IWW) initiated an organizing campaign in 1927, and in October called the miners out in the name of higher wages, shorter hours, mine safety, and union recognition. Some observers estimated that half of Colorado's coal miners participated, and the most enthusiastic were in the northern fields where Roche's holdings were centered.[18] Workers eventually shuttered all of RMF's mines except the Columbine, located in Weld County directly east of Boulder.

The strike put Roche in a difficult spot. She was on record supporting the miners' right to organize and agreed with strikers that conditions in the coalfields were deplorable. She was outraged by other operators' arguments that jail time for strikers would "cure strikes."[19] Moreover, as violence began to erupt, Roche insisted that "the operators and their sympathizers were the first to start violence and trouble."[20] At the same time, Roche did not yet have the power to run RMF as she wished, and she would not have closed a deal with the IWW even if she had. Committed to satisfying all parties with a material interest in coal, Roche wanted to negotiate a contract with miners that not only improved their working and living conditions but also stabilized production so that consumers could count on coal during the winter months and investors could bank on dividends. She was out to demonstrate that private enterprise *could* meet obligations to all those with a legitimate interest in it: workers, consumers, and investors. Doing so required stable production, and stabilizing production required a no-strike pledge from workers for the duration of any contract.[21] The IWW did not negotiate contracts. Believing in the solidarity of workers across regions and occupations, the IWW could not agree to restrain workers from striking, especially in the event of a strike by other workers in their own industry.[22] The IWW did not share Roche's hope that investors, consumers, and workers might be served with equal justice by private enterprise. Capitalism was, in the view of the IWW, an inevitably unjust system. The goal of the IWW's activism was eventually to bring capitalism down.[23] Although Roche and the IWW remained in communication throughout the 1927 strike, the two could not ultimately come to terms.

Roche did her best nonetheless to walk a progressive line between the IWW and the anti-labor coal operators. Through Vincent, she pleaded with Governor William "Billy" Adams not to activate the National Guard against strikers, and she wrested from RMF's board a daily wage increase for the company's miners.[24] She won this agreement by insisting a higher wage would get the company's mines up and running and in this way best the competition. In Roche's words, "it was a good business proposition."[25] She promised no interference with the IWW's pickets at RMF mines so long as miners already on the payroll were allowed to work if they wished to. The IWW agreed to that stipulation, and many strikers from the northern fields began to rally each morning at the company's Columbine Mine.[26] RMF did not import workers from outside the usual workforce and refrained from amassing a body of armed guards at its mines as other operators did.[27] In fact, Roche ordered that "the gates [of the mines] were to be left open and that there was to be no shooting, even though the mines were destroyed."[28] Above all, she was desperate to avoid a repetition of Ludlow.

While Roche and IWW leaders warily accommodated each other, participants elsewhere were not so cautious. On November 4, Colorado's governor, a conservative Democrat who promised a square deal to workers but behaved nonetheless as a protector of coal operators, appointed an ex-military officer, Louis N. Scherf, to command a new state police force to patrol the minefields. On Sunday, November 20, a segment of the new force approached the Columbine Mine. Upon hearing about this ominous development, Roche rushed to Governor Adams, asking that the police be ordered away from RMF's mines. The governor acquiesced.[29] But his instruction reached Scherf too late. On Monday morning, November 21, the usual demonstrators arrived at the Columbine Mine and, when confronted by Scherf's group, refused to disperse. Fighting broke out, and six miners were killed, with many others injured.[30] An anguished Roche telegrammed friends in Washington to report that the worst "has happened . . . strikers killed several seriously wounded this morning . . . can't yet believe it."[31]

Roche's response to the disaster at the Columbine Mine revealed much about her character. Given that she failed to prevent the very anti-labor violence she most dreaded and that she was an only child still grieving the loss of her parents—her mother had died only five months before the Columbine disaster and her father less than a year before—Roche might have sailed toward safe harbor at this point. She might have sold her shares in RMF, moved back to New York, and resumed the directorship of the Foreign Language Information Service.[32] Instead, she chose to stick it out at RMF. "If I had failed," she later explained, "the whole idea of better working conditions in the mines would have been discredited."[33] In November 1927, the odds of failure were extremely high. Roche was willing nevertheless to risk her fortune, her reputation, and her future ease on a slim chance to promote greater justice in the coalfields of Colorado. In a year of devastating personal loss, she took the biggest risk of her life. By staying the course at RMF, she demonstrated not only the "guts" she would in future demand of those around her but also her inclination to take personal comfort from public struggle. This was recognizably the same woman who had decided that even an egalitarian marriage might siphon too much energy from the reforming work she found more fulfilling than domesticity. Josephine Roche satisfied virtually every personal need in public action.

Indeed, the violence at Columbine pushed Roche fully into the public spotlight. While most coal operators blamed the IWW for the shootings, Roche countered that the fundamental cause of the violence was the inhumane condition of work and life in the Colorado coalfields.[34] To the press immediately after the incident, Roche defended the miners: "I do not believe the pickets were armed Monday or had deliberate intention of injuring anyone."[35] There would have been no violence, she argued, if Scherf had not incited it.[36]

After the shootings, the strike moved rapidly toward conclusion. Governor Adams sent the National Guard to the northern fields. The IWW cancelled most picketing.[37] Colorado's Industrial Commission began hearings in December and in its final report delivered a scathing indictment of the coal operators for comprehensive violations of state laws governing the coal industry and insupportable conditions in the mining camps. The report pointed to the lack of unionization as a primary culprit in causing the strike and urged "restitution of collective bargaining through non-company unions."[38] The strike officially ended in February 1928. The IWW claimed victory because of the solidarity demonstrated by miners and the wage increases won at virtually every mine.[39] Roche argued that solidarity and wage increases were not enough: unless other conditions that caused periodic upheavals in the coalfields were ameliorated, violence would inevitably reerupt.[40]

Determined to reform those conditions, Roche redoubled her efforts to gain control of RMF. In early 1928, she devised a strategy that demonstrated her increasing understanding of the company and her willingness to play hardball in pursuit of social justice. Instead of trying to persuade the current board of directors to accept collective bargaining, she reached out to shareholders beyond the board, asking for their proxies in electing a new set of directors. She shrewdly approached investors outside of Colorado in hopes they were less inflamed by recent labor conflicts in the state. By March, she held enough proxies to appoint any board she chose, and she immediately assembled a pro-labor board.[41] At the meeting where Roche announced her triumph, the original board exploded in a "stormy scene." But the anti-union directors were powerless; Roche had the votes to do as she pleased.[42] Adding sheen to her victory, Horace Bennett was so disgusted that he allowed Roche to buy his shares in the company. That purchase made Roche the majority stockholder at RMF.[43] She gleefully announced: "I now have control."[44]

As thrilled as she was, Roche confessed that the unfamiliarity of her experience at RMF caused her to "wonder if I am myself, so completely has this new task and life taken me from nearly all my former experience and daily habits."[45] In fact, she confided to Read Lewis, "it seems as though I have migrated to a totally new planet and left behind every familiar experience."[46]

Despite operating light years from her comfort zone, Roche had no trouble hiring a progressive managerial team once she had full control of the company. She initially promoted Vincent to the offices of president and general manager, appointed herself vice president, and hired Edward Costigan as general counsel.[47] In a move meant to rectify a specific injustice committed in the strike of 1913–1914, Roche engaged John Lawson as another vice president. Lawson had been one of the leading organizers of the coal strike in 1913–1914, and he had suffered profoundly for it, saved from life in prison only by the legal efforts of Edward Costigan.[48] Fay Springer served as secretary and treasurer of the company. Springer had been with RMF since the 1910s and worked her way up to secretary and assistant treasurer under Roche's father. She then gave her all to the new direction of the company when Josephine Roche took over. She was rewarded not only with promotion to secretary/treasurer but also with a seat on the board of directors.[49] Indeed, Roche, Lawson, Vincent, and Springer constituted the majority of the new board of directors.[50] Over the years, these players occasionally traded offices—Roche would become president of the company in 1930 with Vincent as vice president— but until 1933, this same team ran the operation.[51]

Shortly after her coup, Roche invited the full managerial staff to lunch at her home in Denver. Guests included executives from headquarters as well as the local superintendents of each mine. She announced to them that "40 years of industrial warfare were over," because she was inviting the miners to organize and enter into a collective bargaining agreement with management at RMF.[52] "If we can just put it over . . . it will mean putting over for the first time in mining history a policy of recognition of human rights, and showing it can succeed."[53] Roche instructed her team that RMF would blacklist no one active in the recent strike and that she intended to develop "a scientific production and marketing program for the first time in this insane situation."[54]

Roche enjoyed the power she wielded at RMF both because it gave her resources to try to improve the lives of coal miners and because it so dramatically violated reigning gender norms. Although 25 percent of adult women were in the labor force in 1930, about half of those workers were in domestic service or clerical work. According to the U.S. census, women constituted only 3.3 percent of all managers in manufacturing and mechanical industries, and the overwhelming majority of those were supervisors on the shop floor rather than higher-ups. Of women employed in trade, only 0.3 percent were proprietors or managers. Most of those were owners of small businesses devoted to such things as dressmaking or millinery.[55] At the same time, the coal industry was nearly all male. It employed some women as clerks in offices, but coal camps offered few opportunities for employment for women, and the president of the UMW was so committed to domesticity for women that he refused to allow the wives of miners to form an auxiliary to support the union![56] Roche was the only female coal operator in the United States during the late 1920s and early 1930s.[57]

When Roche became an industrialist, however, her innovation did not prove an opening wedge for other women aspiring to industrial or business leadership. That was in part because, although her seizure of the helm at RMF received lots of positive press, she was usually represented as a social worker or an idealist who took over a business rather than as a businesswoman.[58] One writer referred to her as an industrial "Joan of Arc."[59] Roche contributed to this way of understanding her work by arguing that profits were not her ultimate concern; humanizing industrial relations was. Roche's goal indeed was to change the meaning of running a business just as in 1913 she had hoped to infuse new meaning into law enforcement. She wanted ownership of a business to carry with it a commitment to meeting the needs of workers and consumers as well as investors. She wanted to imbue private property with public responsibility. In this way, her self-representations as well as those of the press deemphasized the gender breakthrough of her role as chief executive officer of a major industrial enterprise and probably discouraged the public from thinking of her as a real industrialist at all. This obscuring of gender innovation produced a conservative undertow that diminished the power of Roche's example to move other women into executive positions.

Moreover, Roche's leadership at RMF was construed more as a victory for organized labor than women's advancement. As soon as she took over the company, the progressive and labor press praised her experiment and did so all the more vociferously because it occurred in the context of a dramatically declining labor movement nationwide. Even employers who offered high wages and additional benefits usually opposed labor unions, so Roche's pro-labor management was a rarity. In response, the *Nation* made Roche a trustee of the publication.[60] The *New Republic* featured her work at RMF as soon as she undertook it, and the *Survey* proved a longtime friend.[61] Edward Keating, Roche's old progressive ally from Colorado, edited the newspaper *Labor* and routinely held up her experiment as a model of progressive labor relations. The *Colorado Labor Advocate*, published by the State Federation of Labor, adored her and the experiment at RMF.[62] Even the *Progressive Labor World* became a fan.[63] The *New York Times* took an immediate interest in her work at RMF, and always featured it under the by-line of a labor reporter and not in the women's pages.[64]

Those reporters began their coverage in late spring 1928 when Roche was in a position genuinely to transform labor relations at RMF. In May, she announced that "whenever the miners are organized in a union affiliated with the American Federation of Labor, the Rocky Mountain Fuel Company is ready to recognize and contract with their organization."[65]

Roche's choice to negotiate a labor contract only with an affiliate of the American Federation of Labor reduced the miners' options to the UMW, and it located her at the center of a spectrum of thought regarding labor relations in the late 1920s.[66] Rabidly anti-labor coal operators and the IWW occupied the opposing ends of the spectrum. Between those poles were several shades of opinion that claimed the mantle of "industrial democracy," a concept that achieved wide currency during and after World War I, even though advocates disagreed vehemently about what exactly "industrial democracy" meant.

Roche's largest competitor in Colorado's coalfields, John D. Rockefeller Jr., offered one definition. Although he shared his fellow coal operators' belief that capital ultimately exercised full authority over the workplace, he caused a commotion in the late 1910s when, in the interest of diminishing hostility between managers and miners at CFI and salvaging his reputation as a humanitarian after the battle at Ludlow, he developed an Industrial Representation Plan for his coal company.[67] Rockefeller's system allowed elected representatives of his employees to meet with managers to discuss common concerns and submit grievances.[68] Rockefeller's was one of many employee representation schemes to emerge between World War I and the Great Depression. They were part of a wave of experiments in welfare capitalism that often improved workers' living standards while conceding them virtually no new power.[69]

Despite the apparent goodwill of such plans, many progressives and workers remained skeptical.[70] Employee representation plans denied workers any independent base of power, cut off workers in one firm from those in another, and, because employee representatives only *advised* managers, conceded no real power to workers or the public. Without connection to workers outside their own firms, employees had no resources to support them in case of a strike, and without the strike, they had no genuine leverage in negotiations. In the actual distribution of power, employee representation plans recognized no other interests than those of owners. The most noticeable achievement of such plans was to stave off independent labor organization.[71]

Roche rejected employee representation plans. In April 1928, the *Survey* made the mistake of suggesting that her intentions for RMF paralleled those of Rockefeller's plan. Roche shot back, "Nothing could be further from our announced plan and intention than to put into operation the Rockefeller or any Company union plan." She continued, "Our original statement of policy, all our succeeding statements, and every practical step we have taken, are based on our recognition of labor's right to organize independently in an organization of its own choice and to deal collectively and on equal terms with capital."[72] She argued that a company union was no union at all precisely because workers had interests that differed from those of owners and "independent rights in the determination of working and living conditions."[73] Workers must organize themselves so that they were free to identify their own interests and formulate collective decisions that their elected representatives would then take to negotiations with managers.

With the IWW disqualified, however, Roche was left with the UMW as the only possible bargaining agent for the miners at RMF. It was, to say the least, an uninspiring group. Although the UMW had come out of World War I as the largest labor union in the United States, claiming several hundred thousand members and a commitment to nationalizing the coal industry as well as forming a labor party, by 1928 the union had dwindled to about 80,000 members.[74] Its treasury was correspondingly small, and precious resources were spent on big salaries for union officials like the autocratic president, John L. Lewis. During the 1920s, Lewis took over the union's newspaper, abolished elections for union officers in many districts so that he could appoint officers loyal to himself, and assumed control of the union's treasury.[75] In the mid-1920s, with new competition from oil and gas driving down coal consumption and small nonunion mines successfully competing for the remaining customers, Lewis began accepting wage cuts.[76] Edward Costigan warned Roche that the UMW suffered from a "lack of industrial statesmanship and constructive thinking in the group headed by John L. Lewis."[77]

Colorado's UMW bore out the charge. O. F. Nigro was president of the union's District 15, which encompassed Colorado and New Mexico, and he showed more interest in preserving his cushy position in John L. Lewis's hierarchy than in organizing workers. Indeed, since Ludlow the union failed to initiate any effective organizing drives in the state. Nigro continually discouraged activism among miners, insisting that the small number of UMW members made conflicts with employers impractical. His laziness ensured things would stay that way. During the 1927 strike, Nigro urged John L. Lewis not to support the miners' walkout, which he predicted would soon fall apart.[78] Nigro's opposition to the strike alienated not only the IWW but also the state's more moderate State Federation of Labor, which urged his support. Nigro absolutely refused, preposterously accusing the IWW of being a puppet in CFI's campaign to destroy the UMW![79]

Roche hoped things might change. She wanted to negotiate with the UMW in part because it was at least ostensibly affiliated with the American Federation of Labor (AFL), and she believed that RMF needed the support of a broad labor movement in order to survive. The teamsters who hauled coal from RMF mines were affiliated with the AFL, and the Denver Trades and Labor Assembly as well as the State Federation of Labor were connected with the national federation as well. Roche wanted her enterprise to plug into this preexisting community of unions. In fact, in spring 1928, she and Vincent began meeting with AFL-affiliated unions in Denver to explain their intentions for RMF and their hopes for wide labor support of RMF's experiment.[80]

Roche sought multiple kinds of aid from her labor allies. Most immediately, she imagined the unions as leaders in a movement to promote sales of her union-mined coal. With the local business community aghast at her outreach to organized labor, she knew RMF would face intense opposition, maybe even boycotts of its coal and refusal of credit from local banks.[81] Consequently, before RMF had negotiated its first union contract, Roche won tentative support for her company from the Denver Trades and Labor Assembly, which conditioned its final approval on the company's connection with the AFL.[82] The very night that Roche publicly announced her intention to negotiate a contract with "an affiliate of the American Federation of Labor," she and Vincent invited local representatives of organized labor to a dinner in Denver, where an organizer from the UMW confirmed the progress he was making in organizing RMF's miners. That meeting opened a campaign among workers in Colorado to buy coal exclusively from RMF. One attendee wrote to his local of the Brotherhood of Locomotive Firemen and Enginemen, "the least our membership could do would be to patronize the Rocky Mountain Fuel Company, to the exclusion of all others, and prevail on our friends, and those we do business with, to do likewise."[83] Very shortly, organized labor in Colorado created a Central Coal Committee to "mobilize the purchasing power of the organized workers in support of union firms."[84] The committee's major purpose was marketing RMF's coal.[85]

Setting aside her qualms about the UMW, then, Roche spent the summer of 1928 negotiating with Percy Tetlow, an aide to John L. Lewis in the UMW's central office, and the distasteful Nigro.[86] Those discussions culminated on August 16, 1928, when Roche and the UMW signed what one commentator called an "Industrial Magna Carta."[87] It was a historic union contract in that it gave organized labor a foothold in the coalfields of Colorado after more than a decade of exclusion and proclaimed a new relationship between labor and capital. Opening with a "Declaration of Principles," the contract declared its first purpose was "to promote and establish industrial justice." Such justice was to rest on "collective bargaining between mine workers and operators through free and independent organization." Stabilizing the coal industry in order both to preserve jobs and to assure consumers a dependable supply of fuel was another goal, this one to be achieved through "cooperative endeavor and the aid of science" as well as through rendering strikes unnecessary by "the investigation and correction of their underlying causes." The contract explicitly acknowledged a "public interest" in the coal industry and pledged to protect that interest by defending "our joint undertaking against every conspiracy or vicious practice which seeks to destroy it."[88]

Some provisions of the contract simply committed RMF to the requirements of existing state law. It specified the eight-hour day and the right of miners to elect a check-weighman.[89] The election of a check-weighman was crucial to the workers paid on a tonnage basis. To realize the full profit from their labor, tonnage miners depended on receiving credit for all the coal they mined, and one of their perennial grievances was that the person who weighed their coal at day's end under-reported their production. Even though Colorado law required that miners be allowed to elect a check-weighman, nonunion miners were usually left at the mercy of company weighmen.[90] Not so at Roche's RMF.

The contract also contained provisions not touched by law. It raised the basic daily wage to $7.00, which was the highest miners' wage anywhere in the country except Montana.[91] It also specified a grievance procedure.[92] The contract responded to some issues with age-old roots in the mining industry. One such issue had to do with laying tracks for mine cars. At the bottom of each mine shaft, tunnels sometimes several miles long led to the various rooms where miners dug coal. Coal cars traveling on what looked like train tracks hauled the coal from the rooms to the mine shaft, where it was then pulled to the surface in a sort of elevator car. In nonunion mines, miners were generally not paid for all the hours spent laying track. This unpaid labor was a persistent grievance. In the RMF contract, the company took responsibility for laying the track that carried coal cars to each mining room, and miners themselves were to lay the track only in their own rooms. Another issue was water at the mine face. Miners often lost wages because their work rooms were wet or even flooded.[93] The RMF contract specified that the company had to pay for labor that kept the mines dry. Cave-ins posed yet another threat to miners' earnings. In nonunion mines, miners often worked without pay for a full day or more as they cleaned up a collapsed area of a mine.[94] The RMF contract ruled that miners would be paid for coal they lost to any collapse. Finally, wherever a majority of the miners wanted a bathhouse, the company would build one; miners agreed to help pay for the washrooms at a rate not to exceed $1.00 per month per man.[95]

Some provisions of the contract openly upheld the power of ownership, but even these provisions did not concede unrestricted freedom to management. "The right to hire and discharge, the management of the mines and the direction of the working forces are vested exclusively in the Company, and the U.M.W. of A. shall not abridge this right," opened one section of the contract. But that right was immediately qualified: "If any employee shall be discharged or suspended by the Company and it is claimed an injustice has been done," the issue was to be investigated and pursued through the usual grievance procedure.[96] Similarly, the company reserved the right to lower wages but only under specified conditions: if 51 percent of the coal mined in Boulder and Weld counties (not including that mined by RMF) were produced by miners making less than $6.77 a day, then RMF could lower wages so long as it always paid at least 23 cents more per day than the average basic daily wage of those other producers.[97]

Finally, the contract contained a unique provision that was never fully realized but reflected Roche's earlier experience with the Children's Bureau and foreshadowed her work in the Roosevelt administration and the UMW thereafter. This provision contemplated a Department of Medicine, Health, and Sanitation for RMF miners and their families. The department was to be run by a licensed physician who would hire as many nurses and doctors as necessary not only "to render the best and most skilled medical and surgical service possible to employees and their families" but, further, to provide prenatal and obstetrical care to the "wives of the employees" as well as to establish a program of preventive health care by improving sanitation in the camps and "making available, through consultation and visitation of doctors and nurses, information on general health matters and specialized service and information on matters affecting children's health and development."[98] This Department of Medicine was to be run jointly by miners and owners. To sustain it, the miners were to be charged $1.00 per month for unmarried men and $1.50 per month for married men and their families, which was already the fee charged to miners for their (much hated) company doctors. Any cost of the department that exceeded these fees was to be "paid by the Company."[99]

The commission governing the Department of Medicine embodied Roche's belief in the equal contributions of labor and capital to the industrial enterprise as well as the value of face-to-face relationships between the two interests. She deplored absentee owners of industry (like John D. Rockefeller Jr.). Roche insisted that industrial democracy could prevail only if workers and owners regularly met together to discuss their perspectives and came to know the conditions of each others' daily lives. The process of negotiating the union contract was one kind of such meeting, but Roche did not believe a series of meetings every two years was nearly enough. Echoing Roche, Vincent argued indeed that "day-to-day contact with miners" was a necessary "guide" to labor policy at RMF.[100] Roche often sat among the men at union meetings so as to know what was happening on the ground in the mines, and she invited miners to visit her whenever they wished at the offices in Denver.[101] Confirming that both she and the miners took this outreach seriously, one miner who had worked at the Columbine Mine between 1929 and 1931 wrote to her in 1935: "I've saw you at Local several times and also in the office at Denver."[102] Similarly, when a reporter visited Roche in her office in 1934, she found the company president in conference with three miners who had come to suggest that she open a new room in their mine. "They may be right," Roche admitted to the surprised visitor, "I'm going to talk it over with the chief engineer."[103] Another investigator noted early in Roche's tenure as president of the company that "All of the men know her. . . . Around the camps they speak of her as 'Josephine,' but in this there is no suggestion of familiarity—rather of affectionate regard."[104]

Roche believed in the value of talk. Even before she took over the company, she explained the corroding effect of unexpressed grievance. "Rather than incur the possible displeasure of the foreman or superintendent, the man [a miner] will nurse his grievances in silence. This is bad for the man and bad for the company he works for. Such a man never will give his best efforts. . . . It would pay the employers to have some ways and means, satisfactory to the men, of investigating the complaints of individuals or groups, adjusting them if they are reasonable, or if arbitrary, giving the miners convincing reasons why they are so."[105] To increase the likelihood that miners would feel free to express their opinions, Roche and Vincent assured foremen that their reputations with the higher management would not be hurt by complaints from miners. "When a man or group of men are willing, frankly, to complain or kick, and talk about a grievance," they insisted, "the problem is half-settled. . . . When, however, for any reason, there is a reluctance to make a complaint or discuss a condition, the problem is much more difficult, and will remain difficult until it is faced, discussed and settled."[106]

Accordingly, Roche opened an experimental channel for exchange between workers and managers called the Joint Advisory Board. This committee seems to have been suggested by officers at RMF and taken up by union representatives in 1931. Its purpose was to provide a forum where "practical coal miners" could learn the details of running the company and officers of the company could become more familiar with the details of life underground. Those involved in the early discussions emphasized "the necessity of the men and the company being in close personal touch for the common good."[107]

The group of managers and workers who outlined the Advisory Board's form and function imagined it as a democratic space that might integrate workers more directly into decisions reserved to management by the union contract. Each mine elected two members-at-large and then one member for each fifty workers. An equal number of representatives from the managerial team were appointed. Ten miners and ten managers constituted a quorum, and the group was chaired by a miner. The board met monthly and was intended to make recommendations on every point of managing the mines, including employment, production, marketing, and finance.[108] Union leaders believed this committee, where "freedom of thought and action" were "assured . . . by both the United Mine Workers of America and the Coal Company" might create a genuinely democratic citizenry in industry.[109]

The board was in full operation for only a couple of years because union leaders came to believe its work was more appropriately conducted by the union itself, but the board's brief history demonstrated both that miners came to believe they were free to speak their minds to management—realizing a wholly new relationship between workers and employers on Colorado's coalfields—and at the same time that managers in the end held the high cards on any issue outside the union contract.

One of the most controversial issues taken up by the board was job rotation. Even before the advisory group was created, workers at RMF had suggested that instead of laying men off every spring and summer when demand for coal decreased, the company should allow miners to share whatever work the company had. Managers agreed to try it.[110] The experiment unfolded in the context of deepening economic depression, and workers generally preferred it to layoffs. Despite rising production costs and an increasing number of accidents, job sharing remained in effect in 1930 and 1931. In spring 1932, however, managers—not including Roche, who was traveling—returned to seasonal layoffs without consulting the miners. Managers claimed that job sharing proved too expensive and dangerous at a point when the company was operating close to the edge of bankruptcy because of the ongoing economic downturn.[111]

Workers at RMF were, predictably, upset about the unilateral decision, and the Joint Advisory Board took it up. Miners argued that the problems of increasing accidents and costs could be worked out through better planning. They offered concrete solutions to the problems and urged managers to rehire the men who had been laid off. Miners' forthrightness suggested they genuinely believed in their right to speak their mind to management.[112] Vincent, however, confirmed the remaining *inequality* of power between workers and managers by refusing to rehire anyone immediately.[113] The limits of democracy in the company were exposed.

But the struggle was not over, and it was Vincent who lost his job in the end. Roche was so unhappy with his handling of this issue (and others) that she asked for his resignation.[114] By January 1933, she was herself both president and general manager of RMF. She reinstituted job rotation in the spring of 1933 and explicitly disavowed the unilateral decision to end the practice the year before. By that time, the Joint Advisory Board had been dissolved at the request of the union, but not before its operation threw back the curtain to reveal the very real inequality between workers and owners at RMF. Experience with the Advisory Board also revealed, however, that Roche herself was dead-set on implementing workers' preferences for the management of the company.[115]

Miners at RMF believed that Roche's progressive labor policy constituted a genuine improvement over previous labor relations in Colorado's coalfields. RMF not only paid the highest daily wages of any mining concern in Colorado even through the worst years of the Great Depression but also increased the real annual earnings of its miners between 1928 and 1931.[116] Workers at RMF enjoyed greater stability of employment from the late 1920s through the early 1930s than even in better economic times.[117] By 1931, every coal camp had a bathhouse.[118] Other conditions of labor were dramatically improved. Before Roche took over the company, miners walked from the bottom of the mine shaft to and from their work rooms every day. These hikes could be several miles. The men carried their picks, shovels, blasting powder, and lunch pails the entire distance and arrived at the face already worn out. They were not compensated for this travel time. After the UMW signed the contract with Roche, the company delivered the miners' tools to their workplaces, and the miners rode from the shaft to and from the coal face in small cars called "mantrips."[119] They were now paid for dead work (which included laying track, building supports for underground ceilings, draining wet work areas), and miners were not required to live in company housing or to trade at the company store. They were paid in cash not scrip.[120] Roche had also returned control of the local schools to their counties.[121] One miner who had worked at RMF since 1923 claimed that, because of the freedoms now exercised by workers at RMF and the power they wielded through their union, a miner at RMF "feels like an American citizen, the equal of any man in the world. Working conditions are improved out of all semblance to the old conditions."[122]

In the first years after her parents died, Josephine Roche made the most dramatic moves of her life. She defied every expectation of women by taking over a coal company, where she established a labor policy aimed to realize her social science and labor progressivism. That policy recognized the independent rights of labor in industrial enterprises and tried to hold those rights in balance with what Roche perceived as the equal rights of investors and consumers. Roche's recognition of labor and consumer rights was, however, anathema to her competitors in the coalfields of Colorado. As the U.S. and world economy contracted after 1929, those competitors mounted a vicious campaign to drive her out of business. Her achievement of a union contract in 1928 was a signal victory, but it was only the beginning of her exploration of the totally new planet that was industrial production in the coalfields of Colorado.

CHAPTER 8

"PROPHET OF A NEW AND WISER SOCIAL ORDER," 1929–1932

A s Josephine Roche and the miners at Rocky Mountain Fuel (RMF) implemented their "industrial Magna Carta," they faced two major threats. One was the Great Depression. The other was the determination of Roche's competitors to drive her out of business because of her labor policy. When Roche took over RMF, the United States and most of the industrialized world were on the brink of the most profound economic downturn of the twentieth century. That global economic contraction made Roche's competitors the more eager to force her out of the coalfields and made it harder for her to maintain high labor standards. Remarkably, she held on, heralded by progressives as a "prophet of a new and wiser social order."[1] In the process, she established her place within an emerging political elite that would soon dominate national politics and government. Indeed, Roche's work at RMF was one of many threads tying the Progressive Era to the New Deal.

Like all business owners, Roche needed credit. In her case, that need became increasingly urgent in 1929 because RMF was deeply in debt to bondholders, who expected interest payments every April 1 and October 1; much of the company's mining equipment needed replacement; and, early in the year, Merle Vincent discovered that the company owed back taxes for 1917 through 1924. Beyond these obligations, Roche wanted to create the medical department contemplated in her union contract as well as to mechanize the mines more fully.[2] To complicate matters, Roche was personally in debt. In order to buy out Horace Bennett, she had sold all her marketable securities and taken out a loan, which was due, regrettably, April 1, 1929.[3]

Finding money to meet these needs was a monumental challenge. RMF had long been a bad credit risk. In the 1920s, coal was what some called a "sick industry," meaning it produced more coal than consumers needed. Cut-throat competition, low prices, and instability were the result. At the time of John J. Roche's death, the industry had been so volatile that he could borrow for the company only on his personal responsibility. Once his daughter took over, only one bank offered her credit even on those terms, and, soon after she signed the union contract, the president of that lone supportive institution died. At that point, no bank in Colorado would extend credit to her.[4] Edward Costigan discovered early in 1929 that a local association of businesses explicitly conspired to cut off credit and customers from RMF because of Roche's encouragement to unionization.[5] As April 1 drew nearer, Roche realized she would not be able to repay her personal loan and that the bank planned to use the occasion to force her company into receivership.[6] That would spell the end of her experiment in progressive industrial relations.

To protect that experiment, Roche whipped up a fund-raising tour that illuminated and helped to create connections among progressives who otherwise operated at independent scattered sites in the 1920s. Because Colorado's elite refused her credit, Roche focused her fund-raising efforts on her second home, New York, where she spent three frenetic months, publicizing her labor policy at RMF and begging for money to support it. As a result, RMF became a joint enterprise of eastern and western progressives, men and women, labor organizations and middle-class reformers.

One of her first contacts demonstrated the connections between organized labor and middle-class reformers, which had been solidifying since the 1910s. Sidney Hillman, president of the Amalgamated Clothing Workers of America (ACW), led a union committed to the sort of industrial democracy Roche was trying to create at RMF, a regime in which organized labor worked with employers to stabilize production and thus ensure a reliable supply of goods to consumers as well as higher living standards and more power to workers.[7] When Roche approached Hillman in January 1929, she explained, "Your work has furnished so much help to us in what we have been doing and planning [at RMF] that I should consider it a great privilege if I might have a little time with you."[8] Her meeting with Hillman opened a long-lasting relationship between the two, one strand of which ran through the Amalgamated Bank of New York.[9] Run by the ACW and committed to serving the labor movement, the Amalgamated Bank suited Roche so well that she opened an account there through which she received and repaid the monies raised during her eastern trip.[10]

Roche then appealed to every labor leader and progressive she could locate. The International Brotherhood of Electrical Workers supported her work and got her in to see the officers of the AFL.[11] She scored a contribution from Herbert H. Lehman, then lieutenant governor of New York under the new governor, Franklin D. Roosevelt.[12] Oswald Garrison Villard, editor of the *Nation*, extended her a loan big enough to repay her personal debt.[13] For longer-term needs, he sent her to the Garland Fund.[14] Norman Thomas, who was just becoming the perennial presidential candidate of the Socialist Party, assured Roche, "You're doing a grand job!"[15] Paul Kellogg, editor of the *Survey*, and Supreme Court Justice Louis Brandeis introduced her to multiple financiers.[16] Paul Warburg, architect of the Federal Reserve System, contributed to the cause.[17]

The women's progressive network and professors from Columbia came through like gangbusters. Lillian Wald invited potential donors to dine with Roche at her Henry Street Settlement.[18] Progressive social worker Pauline Goldmark and future New Deal congresswoman Caroline O'Day extended aid.[19] Mary Dreier of the New York Women's Trade Union League wrote a check.[20] The National Board of the Young Women's Christian Association received Roche warmly.[21] Arthur Suffern of the Federal Council of the Churches of Christ in America sent her to a faculty member at Columbia for both money and further contacts.[22] While in the northerly precincts of Manhattan, Roche visited her former professor, James Harvey Robinson, who contributed, as did Henry Seager.[23]

The fund-raising tour demonstrated that Roche's hope for more egalitarian labor-capital relations represented a widely shared progressive vision, and it integrated Roche into a circle of progressives who would achieve power in the New Deal. Most obviously, the trip edged her close to the future president, Franklin Roosevelt, as she won the admiration of his lieutenant governor. But labor leaders like Hillman and progressive lawyers like Brandeis were also part of what historian Steve Fraser has identified as the "new political elite" that would shape the New Deal.[24] By publicizing Roche's western experiment in industrial relations, the trip also garnered attention from the left wing of the Taylor Society, which operated as a sort of think tank for those interested in stabilizing mass-production industries through collective bargaining and industry-wide economic planning.[25] Roche was soon a member and developed a critical friendship with comember Mary van Kleeck.[26]

When she returned to Denver in late spring 1929, Roche brought much-needed capital for RMF. As it turned out, though, that cash would only briefly tide the company over. Natural gas from a recently laid pipeline soon began to lure Colorado customers away from coal, and in October, the stock market crash sent demand spiraling even more sharply downward.[27] And then there were Roche's competitors, who were determined to drive her out of business by lowering their prices on coal below the cost of production. The price war had begun in 1928, but Roche expected it to abate in 1929. Competition from gas and the stock market crash discouraged abatement.[28]

In late 1929, despite the U.S. economy's slipping into what would be the longest economic depression in its history, prospects for RMF were far from hopeless. Miners across Colorado's northern coalfields were demanding wages equal to those at RMF, and Roche believed that equal wages would put RMF in a very competitive position. Moreover, even despite the general downturn in coal sales, RMF actually increased production in 1929. That increase moved Roche's company from the third largest producer of coal in Colorado to number two. Her increased sales resulted from the campaign led by the region's unions: union members and their supporters in Colorado were turning to Roche's coal for home heating. By early 1930, Roche had also begun negotiating profitable contracts with industrial customers.[29] All in all, Roche had reason to hope that the deficit registered in 1929 was an anomaly and that she would be able to pull RMF into the black in 1930.[30] Few dreamed that the economic downturn would deepen and then endure for a decade.

Even greater cause for hope was the formation of the Northern Colorado Coal Producers' Association. Roche understood full well that one company acting alone could not stabilize the hypercompetitive and declining coal industry. So long as individual firms competed against each other for anything other than a rapidly expanding market, pressures to lower prices would result in declining wages and worsening work conditions. Only when some mechanism set a floor under wages, limited hours, and prohibited selling below cost would consumers be assured a reliable supply of goods and workers a decent standard of living. In this conclusion, Roche joined many labor leaders and progressives who had by the 1920s come to believe industrial justice required industry-wide economic planning.[31]

Sold on this scenario, Roche was committed to organizing the coal industry in whatever small steps she could and so was thrilled in January 1930, when operators in Colorado's northern coalfields formed an association aimed to stabilize their industry.[32] Most importantly, members of the Northern Coal Producers' Association devised a code of trade practices to govern their conduct.[33] Foreshadowing similar agreements negotiated by hundreds of industries under the New Deal, this code forbade practices that signatories identified as unfair. The major problem was pricing. On that issue, the northern coal operators agreed that all prices should yield cost plus—that is, they would not sell any coal below the cost of production. Signatories also agreed to publish their prices so that customers could shop for the best price, and they agreed not to offer secret rebates, discounts, or other terms of sale that lowered prices to select customers.[34]

The coal producers' code revealed the character of the coal industry. While the violent and exploitive tenor of labor relations in the coal industry had long been clear to any observer, the code illuminated the dark side of relations among owners themselves and even their deceptive and discriminatory relations with customers. Prohibitions in the code suggested that coal operators routinely spied not only on workers but also on each other. Lying about competitors and cutting secret deals with customers were standard operating procedures. Roche was increasingly immersed in and trying to transform a viciously cut-throat and deceitful business culture. Establishing transparency and cooperation here seemed an eminently worthwhile but highly improbable proposition.[35]

And so it proved. Over the course of 1930 and 1931, as the coal industry began to feel the full effects of the Great Depression, most operators broke ranks. They failed even to sell their coal at cost plus.[36] What's more, no coal operator in the northern fields undertook collective bargaining with miners. As her own sales declined, Roche continued paying higher wages and guaranteeing better working conditions than her competitors, and these were expensive commitments.[37]

UMW officials were no help. When Roche signed the original union contract, she had expected the UMW to use RMF as a base from which to organize miners throughout the northern coalfield, and by doing so raise her competitors' production costs to equal her own.[38] But no organizing campaign materialized. O. F. Nigro and John L. Lewis resisted every suggestion that they mount an organizing drive in Colorado. When miners fairly begged him for organizers, Nigro treated the requests as an affront. He complained to Lewis, "For the last several months I have been importuned almost to the point of distraction, by a number of members and some local unions of this district, to appoint two or three organizers and start an organization campaign."[39] He repeatedly "tried to dissuade some of these local unions from" approaching the international board for aid in organizing miners.[40]

The refusal of Nigro and Lewis to organize miners in Colorado pushed Roche into alliance with their opponents inside the union and in the larger labor movement. Roche worked hand in glove with UMW locals and Colorado's State Federation of Labor, bypassing Nigro altogether whenever she could.[41] She also hired miners from Illinois, who openly opposed Lewis's leadership.[42] In public addresses, she celebrated the leadership of the State Federation of Labor and Sidney Hillman's ACW with nary a word of praise for the UMW. Nigro bitterly resented these occasions and reported them to Lewis as "the usual plethora of propaganda" from RMF.[43]

Intensifying the strain between UMW officials and more progressive elements, Roche's beloved friend and mentor, Edward Costigan, returned to the political campaign trail in 1930. To Roche's delight, his venture confirmed the renewed electoral appeal of progressive reform. Costigan sought a seat in the U.S. Senate because of the rapid spread of economic misery following the stock market crash in 1929. Predictably, he put forward a full progressive platform, featuring programs long advocated by reformers across the country and prefiguring policies of the New Deal. It included an "elastic program of federal building and works, increased or diminished, as need arises, to parallel in some measure our unemployment demands." It advocated old age and unemployment insurance, opposed child labor, and demanded improved federal employment agencies. It promised "legislation recognizing the rights and dignity of labor."[44] The State Federation of Labor was so wildly in Costigan's corner that Nigro felt forced to back him in public. Privately, however, the UMW leader hoped Costigan would lose. He referred to Costigan and Roche as "political racketeers," who, by joining the Progressive Party in 1912, "doublecrossed their own party for personal gain, on some fancied grievance based on moral issues."[45] The majority of Colorado's voters disagreed. Costigan's campaign, which Roche called "a whale of a fight," won him a seat in the U.S. Senate.[46]

While making that fight for Costigan, Roche also negotiated a new contract with the miners at RMF. She spent two weeks of July in all-day conferences with representatives of the miners. Although she must have had anxieties about the process because of the shrinking economy and her lack of faith in UMW officials, her dominant mood was elation. The negotiations constituted for her "a most interesting two weeks" that spared company business any "dull moments."[47] The new contract generally maintained commitments made in 1928. Basic daily wages remained the same despite the deterioration of coal markets, and the company recommitted itself to creating the Department of Medicine, a project delayed by lack of funds.[48]

Fulfilling the commitments of the 1930 contract, however, proved impossible. Any hope for stabilizing wages and prices through the Northern Coal Producers' Association had evaporated so utterly by spring of 1931 that RMF officially withdrew from the group.[49] Adding more difficulty, companies in Colorado's southern coalfields, led by CFI, abruptly cut wages and slashed prices, directly threatening Roche's sales. Moreover, the method by which southern companies cut wages underscored the exploitiveness of relations prevailing between workers and owners in the coal industry and the dilemmas those conditions posed for anyone trying to change them.

The method for accomplishing the wage cut was intended to outwit a state law requiring employers to give the State Industrial Commission thirty days' notice of any decrease in wages. Notice allowed the commission to determine the legitimacy of a proposed cut. Although the commission had no power to enforce its determination, its proponents hoped publicity alone might restrain employers from implementing wage cuts rejected by the independent body. Instead of following those steps in 1931, the southern coal companies closed their mines and laid off their workers. Managers then circulated petitions among the now-unemployed miners, asking their companies to resume operation at a lower wage than the one paid before the layoffs. The companies argued that these petitions constituted an agreement negotiated between workers and management, which allowed the mines to reopen with lower wages and without any notice to the State Industrial Commission.[50]

Even the lethargic UMW was moved to action by this ploy. Nigro joined Roche and the State Federation of Labor in protesting the wage cuts. They argued that the petitions did not constitute a legitimate agreement between workers and managers because they were so obviously coerced.[51] Testimony before the State Industrial Commission confirmed coercion. One miner reported that he had approached signers of the petitions "under cover of darkness," and that they were "all scared to death."[52] Company managers took the petitions to married men who were in debt to the company stores and so could not leave to look for work elsewhere. These men readily signed, according to one foreman, "because they did not want to starve to death."[53] Roche and the state's labor leaders argued that these practices constituted coercion.[54] The State Industrial Commission heard testimony from May through July, and in August and September, denounced the wage cuts and urged collective bargaining.[55] But, the commission found no "direct proof" that the petitions were coerced, and the wage cuts stood.[56]

While arguing before the Industrial Commission, Roche intensified the conflict between her and the southern operators by taking it national and making it personal. On August 1, she fired off a public telegram to New Yorker John D. Rockefeller Jr., majority stockholder of CFI. In Roche's mind, Rockefeller embodied much that was wrong with the current organization of industry: he was the quintessential absentee owner, willfully ignorant of the lives of the workers who produced his wealth; he lived in luxury without earning a penny of the millions that fell to him. Roche's passionate (and imperious) telegram implored Rockefeller to stop the "anti-social methods" being used by his company to cut the wages of miners. Referring darkly to the "loss of life and property in 1914," she urged her foe to change the course of his company in order to "prevent a recurrence of the human and economic waste which will result from the action taken by your company in cutting miners' wages 20 percent."[57] Rockefeller ignored Roche's entreaty. The national press, however, reported Roche's plea and represented Rockefeller as oblivious to the desperation of his workers. The *New York Times* reported that in response, Rockefeller "had no comment" and was "spending the Summer at his estate in Seal Harbor, Me."[58] What a contrast to Roche, who was in her Denver office or out at the mines every day, frantically trying to stave off disaster for her company and the cause of progressive industrialism. Roche was the anti-Rockefeller, and she gained celebrity status in part because of the contrast.

The issue of price and wage cuts remained red-hot through 1931 and into 1932. Even as the State Industrial Commission was hearing testimony on wage cuts in the southern coalfields, operators in the northern fields also reduced wages.[59] In July 1931, when Roche discovered that other northern operators had been secretly discounting their products all winter, she lowered her own prices to match. In response, her competitors lowered prices further. Out-and-out price war was on. Roche was forced to lower her own prices to remain competitive.[60]

The miners at RMF could hardly ignore the conflict. At a union meeting on August 4, leaders reported that owners of the nonunion mines had created a "slush fund" of $100,000, which "is now being used to lower the price of coal," and, once they had "put the Rocky out of business," will "reduce our wages to possibly three dollars per day." Those present declared, "The fight is on, freedom or serfdom." They vowed to redouble their efforts to sell union coal, to organize "our fellow workmen in the other mines," and "make it known to the entire country, we stand ready to save ourselves and the company at all costs, even if we have to dig coal for nothing."[61]

As RMF's well-informed miners looked toward autumn, they worried right along with Roche about making the October 1 payment of bond interest. If the company failed to pay, bankruptcy loomed, threatening unionized mining in Colorado. In response, some workers at RMF circulated their own petitions, offering to loan RMF half their wages for three months in order to make the interest payment on the bonds and thereby "defend our union contract and wage scale against the conspiracy and systematic attempt of non-union operators to reduce wages and reduce coal miners to a condition of economic slavery."[62] Their petitions argued that the wage cuts RMF's competitors were trying to put over in non-union mines were a calamity to coal miners. "We therefore give notice," one petition read, "to all non-union operators that we and the Rocky Mountain Fuel Company will mine and put coal in every market at prices which will meet any and every price made by non-union operators who are viciously taking advantage of widespread unemployment and hunger to crush out the right of workers to fair wages and decent American living standards, until this conspiracy is broken."[63] Not all miners at RMF signed the petitions, but enough signed to make the interest payment on

October 1. When the company offered to repay the loan of wages with interest, the workers refused the interest and did not set a repayment date.[64] For the moment, RMF's miners had dramatically saved the company.

Roche's competitors, naturally, roared their disapproval. They argued that Roche was doing the same thing she had opposed their doing: she lowered wages without thirty days' notice and evaded the legal requirement of notice by coercing workers to sign a petition that made it seem they voluntarily accepted the cut.[65] Evidence suggests that Roche did originally propose the loan of wages, though company supervisors did not circulate petitions. UMW district president Nigro wrote to John L. Lewis in August 1931: "For some weeks agents and some officers of the Rocky Mountain Fuel Company have put out feelers to find if our men were willing to waive two or three paydays, beginning with the payday due on 29th of August, and this money due to them would be paid back later."[66] On August 18, Nigro reported an urgent phone call from Roche, "requesting an immediate conference." At the meeting, "she began to hint about the question of waiving on the part of our men of two or three paydays." Nigro reported that "she was ill at ease and seemed that she could find no words to speak plainly on the subject." Nigro enjoyed her discomfiture but eventually assured Roche that, though he would not press the miners to waive their pay, he would not stand in the way if miners voluntarily offered their wages.[67]

Despite surely knowing that Roche initially suggested the loan of wages, the State Federation of Labor supported it, and had nothing but praise for RMF throughout the ordeal.[68] Even Nigro admitted that the company was in terrible financial shape and probably could not survive without the loan (or temporary wage cut, depending on your point of view).[69] When Roche's competitors tried to find disgruntled miners to testify against RMF during summer 1931, they came up empty-handed.[70] Similarly, when social science investigator Mary van Kleeck interviewed miners about the issue some years later, she could find no evidence of intimidation at the time that miners signed the petitions. In fact, some miners did not sign and were paid their full wages. Moreover, the company did pay back the wages, and the loan did not affect the basic wage scale.[71] Claims that the workers "voluntarily" made the loan were not entirely misleading.

Nevertheless, many miners surely felt compelled to sign the petitions that effectively cut their wages for three months. In August 1931, Roche was out in the coalfields day after day speaking with miners about the wage and price situation and, in her words, "not getting home until long after midnight."[72] As she had promised, she opened the company's books to workers to demonstrate that her anxieties about impending disaster were well-founded.[73] Her continuous, direct contact with workers meant that miners knew all about the company's situation and surely had the effect of pressuring workers to sign on to any scheme that might save their jobs. Intensifying that pressure, the State Federation of Labor and Colorado's Central Coal Committee—all institutions of labor itself—were clearly on Roche's side, and the UMW offered no objections. Resistance took extra courage when the workers' own organizations urged them to give up a portion of their wages to keep the company—and thus the cause of organized labor—alive. The line between compulsion and freedom was hardly clear in a situation of such economic desperation.

By the time of the miners' loan, it was clear, however, that the contraction of markets for coal was part of a much more general economic downturn that had no end in sight. While unemployment had been creeping up in many cities and the coal industry before the stock market crash in 1929, unemployment thereafter threatened workers in virtually all sectors of the U.S. economy. Whereas in 1929, only 3 percent of the national labor force had been officially unemployed, that percentage more than doubled during 1930, and it nearly doubled again in 1931. A conservative estimate was that in 1931, nearly 16 percent of the labor force was out of work, and over the next two years that figure reached a devastating 25 percent.[74] Bank failures, too, told the tale of an economy spiraling into desperation. In 1929 alone, 659 banks failed; in 1930, another 1,352 closed their doors; in 1931, yet another 1,456 banks failed. In the years between 1930 and 1933, Americans lost over $2.5 billion to bank failure, and the money supply shrank, according to some estimates, by a full third.[75] The result was a wave of price cutting, wage cuts, and layoffs that sent millions of Americans into bread lines and worse.

Despite the vagaries of her situation in 1931, Roche's public assessment was that her company was one of several in the United States that was proving the viability of a new economic system "based on recognition of human rights." Anxious to generate support for progressive industrialism even in the midst of economic contraction, she gave speeches, wrote articles, and delivered radio addresses denouncing wage cuts. She argued that the devastation of the depression had emerged because of dramatic inequalities of wealth that increasingly confined economic resources to a few and left the majority of Americans to struggle against want. Just as she had dog-eared pages of the *Report of the U.S. Commission on Industrial Relations* in 1915 that cited great inequalities of wealth in the United States, Roche in 1931 constantly emphasized the "injustice and short-sightedness" of the "increasing concentration of wealth and large incomes in the hands of a few." Her evidence of growing inequality was that in the late 1920s, only 13 percent of the U.S. population owned 90 percent of the wealth; that in many years when workers incomes declined, dividends on common stock increased; and that during the 1920s, when real wages did increase, dividends on industrial stock increased phenomenally more. Inequality of wealth, she insisted, doomed the United States to its current misery because a few wealthy families did not constitute a mass market. Only by spreading purchasing power across a broad population could a mass-production economy survive. "Prosperity comes," she explained in one radio address, "when goods are sold; goods are sold when people have money to buy, and the people who chiefly make the markets are the wage earners, the farmers, the small-salaried men and women who constitute over 80% of our public." Mass production required mass purchasing power. By redistributing wealth more equitably across the population, she insisted, the depression might be eased and future disasters averted. She concluded that there was no such thing as overproduction. "Under consumption is our modern tragedy."[76]

In this analysis of the Great Depression, Roche set herself squarely in the progressive community that had supported RMF during her eastern fund-raising trip in 1929. That group, becoming increasingly cohesive in the face of the depression, generally insisted that a high-wage, low-price economy was not only possible but absolutely necessary to sustaining the mass production that new technologies and corporate organization made possible. The more equitable distribution of wealth—or purchasing power, as they generally called it—was a crucial component of maintaining the new mass production economy that had fully congealed in the United States by the 1920s.[77]

Even as Roche held out RMF as evidence for the profitability of industrial relations that recognized "human rights," her company was teetering on the brink of failure. She owed her own workers thousands of dollars in loaned wages; she owed friends and investors tens of thousands of dollars; and she could not shake any credit out of the financial establishment in Denver. Determined nonetheless to keep her experiment in progressive industrialism alive, she stepped onto the slippery slope of secret deals. Late in 1931, she negotiated a secret loan from the highest echelon of the UMW, probably to pay back the wages loaned by the workers to RMF. The details of that negotiation are undocumented. Roche may have approached the detested John L. Lewis, or perhaps he approached her. The international headquarters of the UMW had good reason for wanting Roche's workers repaid: union mines in Wyoming feared for their own viability if Roche underpriced them. To keep those mines in the union camp, the UMW needed to stabilize Roche's situation.[78]

What is clear is that the emergency loan made to Roche by the UMW in 1931 was only the first of many such advances over the course of the Great Depression. She received at least two loans in 1932 and another two in 1933. Unlike the loans received by RMF through Roche's public fund-raising, those from the UMW carried no interest, and the early loans were not secured with any collateral.[79] Over the years, John L. Lewis would secretly contribute hundreds of thousands of dollars to Roche's company from the union's coffers, and the practice set a precedent for similar loans to other union-friendly companies.[80] The loans to RMF were not illegal, but they did fly in the face of Roche's commitment to sharing company information with miners and including them in decisions. The loans betrayed her commitment to transparency and democratic decision making. According to Roche's own standards, the coal miners whose union dues were keeping her company afloat ought to have been apprised of this use of their hard-earned wages and allowed to debate it. In accepting Lewis's loans without consulting the rank-and-file workers who made them possible, Roche acquiesced in the culture of deception endemic to the coal industry. While striving to create a new culture of transparency and cooperation, she practiced subterfuge and autocracy. When she believed she had to compromise democratic openness on this one transaction to keep other aspects of her progressive experiment afloat, she chose the compromise.

Even with secret loans, however, RMF could not indefinitely avoid wage cuts. In spring 1932, Roche's competitors in the northern coalfields openly reduced their basic daily wage from $6.72 to $5.00 despite opposition from the State Industrial Commission. At that point, she and Nigro petitioned the commission for approval of wage cuts at RMF. As required in the union contract, Roche kept her employees' wages at least 23 cents above those paid by other northern operators, but this move was a major blow to her desire to keep wages high both for the miners and for the larger economy that depended, in her view, on the widest possible distribution of purchasing power.[81] In the summer of 1932, she and the miners were back at the bargaining table, negotiating their third contract, and the end result finally capitulated to the Great Depression. The basic daily wage was set at $5.25.[82]

Despite that disappointment, RMF received consistently positive publicity not only among progressives but also in the mainstream national press. The experiment seemed to demonstrate that capitalism could be just. Private enterprises, organized to ensure human rights first, might ultimately satisfy the claims of all who had legitimate interests in them: workers, consumers, and investors. Because of that hopeful message, by 1932 Roche had emerged as a progressive celebrity. Her biography appeared in the *Woman's Journal*, and *Independent Woman* touted the wonders she achieved as head of a major industrial concern.[83] When she denounced wage cuts as a response to the depression in 1931, her arguments were repeated in newspapers across the country.[84] In spring 1932, she was invited to speak before the United Press in Los Angeles, and her call for a wider distribution of purchasing power appeared in the *New York Sun*, *Chicago Illustrated Times*, and *Boston Globe* as well as smaller-town newspapers between the coasts.[85]

This publicity produced myriad invitations to speak. Roche was asked to describe her industrial experiment at labor gatherings and on local radio programs.[86] The Philadelphia Labor College asked her to speak at a Conference on New Relations between Labor and Capital.[87] The Episcopal Church invited her to speak on labor relations in 1931.[88] That fall, she was, as she herself reported, "speaking every day and often twice a day at every and all kinds of meetings."[89] She became a popular speaker at women's clubs.[90] In spring 1932, the Catholic Church in Los Angeles invited her as a delegate to a convention to consider solutions to the "world's economic ills."[91] Senator Edward Costigan was so impressed by her work at RMF that he lauded her on the floor of the Senate as "a prophet of a new and wiser social order," before entering into the record a verbatim transcript of one of her radio addresses.[92] She became so renowned that in 1932, Smith College awarded her first of several honorary degrees, and at least one editorialist suggested she deserved a Nobel Prize.[93]

Just a few months after Roche accepted her honorary degree from Smith, American voters elected a new president. The Republican incumbent, Herbert Hoover—former humanitarian and World War I boss of Josephine Roche—had presided over a failing economy without taking steps bold enough to communicate concern for the nation's massive suffering much less to diminish it. Given the perception of Hoover as an uncaring and ineffectual leader, virtually any Democrat had a good shot at the country's highest office by 1932. The particular Democrat to step into that fortunate spot was Franklin D. Roosevelt, governor of New York. Although Roosevelt's gubernatorial record generated enthusiasm among progressives, his plans for a presidential administration were murky.[94]

Roosevelt's opacity during the campaign worried Roche. She worked on his campaign with many misgivings. "I'm helping a little," she explained to Read Lewis, "an occasional talk at small meetings, but have a very small amount of time—and between us—not an awful lot of enthusiasm for our national or state candidates." She did believe that electing Roosevelt was the "best chance and practically our only hope for some gains these coming four years." If only Roosevelt would accept the "counsels of the ablest and most progressive, like Costigan," she thought, then the Democrats had "an amazing chance" to improve things, but if he failed to do that, "it's just going to be the ghastliest travesty ever." She agreed with Lewis that the socialist Norman Thomas "made a gorgeous campaign and his program and platform were most satisfying," but a vote for him seemed impractical.[95] Thus did Roche explain her participation in Roosevelt's campaign, which the National Democratic Committee praised nonetheless as "a superb piece of work."[96] Whether negligible or superb, her work paid off. Roosevelt won by a landslide in Colorado as well as the rest of the country, opening up possibilities for moving progressive values from the coalfields of Colorado into national policy.

In the years between her father's death and the election of Roosevelt, Josephine Roche created a remarkable experiment in progressive industrial relations at the Rocky Mountain Fuel Company. It was remarkable for its recognition of workers' right to organize in the context of Colorado's violently anti-labor industrial and political culture. It was remarkable for its attempts to involve workers in managerial decisions, and it was remarkable for its genuine improvement of workers' material lives even in the midst of a devastating economic depression. It was also remarkable because it was instituted by a woman.

For all its uniqueness, however, Roche's experiment in industrial relations represented a set of values widely shared by a national progressive community. The receptiveness of eastern progressives to her appeals for financial support, her popularity with even the mainstream press by 1932, and her growing renown among leaders of organized labor and progressives from Los Angeles to Philadelphia demonstrated that her vision of private enterprise satisfying the demands of three major interests—workers, consumers, and investors—resonated with a broad progressive public. Progressivism was very much alive in the early days of the Great Depression, and Roche's enterprise was one of the concrete links between the progressivism of the 1910s and that of the 1930s.

1   Josephine Roche at six weeks with her nurse, 1887. Courtesy Harmon Lewis.

2 Josephine Roche around the time of her graduation from Brownell Hall, 1904–1905. Courtesy Harmon Lewis.

3 Roche's cherished deputy sheriff badges, 1913. Josephine Roche Collection, box 10, folder 3, Archives, University of Colorado at Boulder Libraries.

4   Roche as Denver's first policewoman, 1912.
The Denver Public Library, Western History Collection, WH 2129.

5   Roche with her parents, Ella Aspinwall Roche and John J. Roche, in the
Rocky Mountains, ca. 1913. The Denver Public Library, Western History Collection,
Biography Folder.

6   Families living in the Ludlow tent colony before the Ludlow Massacre, ca. 1913.
The Denver Public Library, Western History Collection, X-60458.

7 Ludlow tent colony after the conflagration, April 1914. The Denver Public Library, Western History Collection, Ed Doyle Collection, X-60483.

8 Roche as head of the Foreign Language Information Service, early 1920s. Edward P. Costigan Papers, box 54, folder 9, Archives, University of Colorado at Boulder Libraries.

9 Roche as a gubernatorial candidate in Colorado, summer 1934.
The Denver Public Library, Western History Collection, WH2129.

10   Roche with Secretary of the Treasury Henry Morgenthau on the day she was sworn
      in as assistant secretary of the treasury, December 1934. Library of Congress,
      Prints and Photographs Division, photograph by Harris and Ewing, reproduction
      number LC-DIG-hec-37931.

11   Roche with Mabel and Edward Costigan (both seated to the left of Roche), her politi-
      cal mentors and second parents, 1936. Library of Congress, Prints and Photographs
      Division, photograph by Harris and Ewing, reproduction number
      LC-DIG-hec-39900.

12 Roche as director and trustee of the United Mine Workers Welfare and Retirement Fund, Washington, DC, 1955. Photograph by Chase Photography, Bethesda, Maryland. Courtesy the George Meany Memorial Archives, Silver Spring, Maryland.

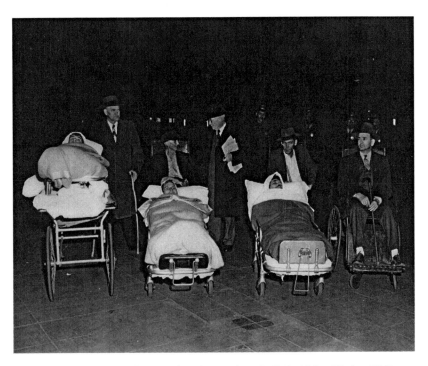

13 Disabled miners, beneficiaries of Roche's work at the United Mine Workers Welfare and Retirement Fund, arrive in Washington, DC, for physical rehabilitation at area hospitals, 1949. Photograph by Harris and Ewing. Courtesy Robert Kaplan Papers, Manuscripts and Archives, Yale University Library.

14 Roche with her longtime ally, labor titan John L. Lewis, in the early 1940s.
Courtesy History Colorado, scan #10029087.

15 Two miners in a waiting room of the Miners' Memorial Hospital at Beckley, West Virginia, 1959. Photograph copyright Fred J. Maroon. Courtesy Robert Kaplan Papers, Manuscripts and Archives, Yale University Library.

16 Mothers and babies at a health clinic established by the United Mine Workers Welfare and Retirement Fund in Beckley, West Virginia, 1959. Photograph copyright Fred J. Maroon. Courtesy Robert Kaplan Papers, Manuscripts and Archives, Yale University Library.

17 Roche with her godson, William E. Owens, on his graduation from high school in 1958. Also pictured are Owens's father, Ted, and Roche's longtime assistant, Mildred Lea. Courtesy William E. Owens.

18 Roche at a West Virginia press conference in 1972, campaigning for Arnold Miller and other candidates nominated by Miners for Democracy to run the United Mine Workers of America. Photograph copyright Earl Dotter.

PART III

SECOND BURST OF PROGRESSIVE REFORM: HEIGHT OF ROCHE'S RENOWN, 1933–1948

The vision of a new and wiser social order that inspired Josephine Roche also drove much of the social and economic program enacted by Franklin Roosevelt's administrations and those of his successor, Harry S. Truman. To respond to the calamitous and, by the time of his inauguration, apparently chronic, contraction of the U.S. economy, Roosevelt pulled together progressives who had spent the 1920s adapting to the economic and political changes reshaping American life since World War I. Although some of these reformers had joined forces before, the Roosevelt administration wove progressives into the most cohesive and effective community they would ever constitute. Women and men, easterners and westerners, social scientists and workers, native-born and immigrant Americans coalesced in this progressive community. Together, they produced the New Deal, organized U.S. participation in World War II, and emerged from the war hopeful of dramatically diminishing inequality through an expansive welfare state and national labor movement. The long New Deal Era that stretched from 1933 to 1948 represented the second and hottest flaring up of progressivism within the twentieth century's Age of Reform.[1] As one flame in the New Deal's progressive fire, Roche rose to the pinnacle of her renown and power.

CHAPTER 9

WORKING WITH THE NEW DEAL
FROM COLORADO, 1933–1934

Josephine Roche's experience at Rocky Mountain Fuel (RMF) primed her for the New Deal. As Franklin Roosevelt's administration began to grapple in 1933 with the devastation caused by the Great Depression, Roche was asked to serve in several capacities. Early on, the most important was in the National Recovery Administration (NRA), an attempt to stabilize the U.S. economy through industry-wide economic planning. Shortly after that, Roche broke through yet another gender barrier by running for governor of Colorado. She took this bold step because the sitting state executive refused to cooperate with the relief programs of the New Deal, and Roche wanted Colorado effectively linked with the national government. She did not succeed, but her gubernatorial bid was nevertheless significant. It demonstrated both the centralizing force that Washington exerted through the New Deal and some of the bases for resistance. It also drew a direct line between progressivism in the early twentieth century and progressivism in the New Deal, highlighting a range of tactics for diminishing inequality that New Dealers brought straight from the Progressive Era into the 1930s.

When Franklin Roosevelt was inaugurated in March 1933, the United States was at the end of the worst winter of the Great Depression. Unemployment reached its official peak with at least 25 percent of the workforce unemployed; less conservative estimates went as high as 33 percent. Unemployment had expanded beyond the "sick" industries of coal and textiles, beyond mass production in autos and electrical appliances, beyond the drought-devastated farms of the Great Plains. By 1933, even the most diversified local economies felt the full force of economic contraction. Among workers still employed, as many as half were working only part time, and hourly wages were decreasing. Local charities could not come close to meeting the need for relief, and local governments were decimated by impossibly low tax returns. In the winter of 1932–1933, the city of Chicago could not pay its teachers. With over 5,000 bank failures between 1930 and 1932, the governors of thirty-four states closed their remaining banks in 1933. Especially ominous, on the morning that Franklin Roosevelt was inaugurated, the governors of New York and Illinois, the centers of the country's financial system, closed their banks. The financial system of the United States had collapsed.[1]

In the first hundred days of his administration, the new president responded to the economic disaster with a torrent of legislation aimed to shore up the financial system and increase the purchasing power of a broad swath of wage-earning Americans. In his first days as president, Roosevelt declared a bank "holiday" and provided federal money to private banks to stave off more failures. To prevent another stock market crash, he initiated regulation of the securities industry, and to assuage the fears of banking customers, he offered legislation that insured depositors' savings. To increase purchasing power and ease the despair gripping so many unemployed Americans, the administration created a massive program of emergency relief run by the efficient social worker from New York, Harry Hopkins. Hopkins's Federal Emergency Relief Administration (FERA) poured money into the states for, among other things, straightforward cash assistance to those in need. The administration also organized the Civilian Conservation Corps, a cadre of young unemployed men who pursued a range of conservation projects in America's public parks and forests as well as on the nation's farms. Another jobs program was embedded in the National Industrial Recovery Act (NIRA), which created the Public Works Administration (PWA).[2]

Roche's experience at RMF made her an obvious choice to participate in these early New Deal programs. She was initially appointed to two advisory boards. One was the State Advisory Board of the PWA in Colorado, appointment to which emphasized Roche's feminist pioneering: she was the only woman out of 145 advisers appointed to PWA boards. She was also named to the national advisory committee for the U.S. Employment Service, created in 1933 to fund state employment offices that would match unemployed workers to jobs in the private sector.[3]

Most importantly, Roche was among the industrialists who negotiated a production code for the coal industry under the auspices of the NIRA. Congress hoped that the NIRA would stabilize wages and prices by ending the cutthroat competition in industries like coal that drove wages and prices inexorably downward in the face of shrinking markets. In imperfect form, the NIRA embodied commitments to both protective labor policies and the self-organization of labor that Roche and so many other progressives had promoted since the 1910s. The act authorized each industry to produce a code of fair competition that had to set minimum wages and maximum hours within the industry and recognize labor's right to organize and bargain collectively. The NIRA protected producers from anti-trust suits and authorized the president to issue a code if any industry failed to do so. The codes were to end on June 16, 1935.[4] To implement these provisions of the NIRA, the president created the National Recovery Administration (NRA) with General Hugh Johnson at its head, and eventually over 500 industries wrote codes.[5]

The process of code making that emerged during the summer of 1933 embodied Roche's progressive belief that workers and consumers had a legitimate interest in the operation of private enterprises. Although employers from larger enterprises usually produced the first draft of a code for their industry, competing groups sometimes produced alternatives, and the process required public hearings at which employers, workers, and members of the public testified. Draft codes next went before industrial, labor, and consumer advisory boards for comment. Ultimately, the president had to sign off. Enterprises that abided by the codes were supposed to display the symbol of the NRA—a blue eagle in an orange frame—in their establishments so that consumers could reward their cooperative spirit.[6]

Roche was the nation's only female coal mine operator and a natural leader in the work of code making. She had rehearsed the part when helping to produce the code of fair trade practices with northern coal operators in Colorado. Indeed, she had so long advocated the kind of industrial organization contemplated by the NIRA that she was often heralded by the press as having been a new dealer before the New Deal.[7] Fittingly then, Roche was among a group of coal industry representatives invited to Washington to discuss whether the coal industry would support the NIRA even before the legislation passed. On June 5, the group pledged support.[8] All coal operators were then invited to a conference in Chicago to discuss a draft code on June 16, 1933, the very day the NIRA became law.[9]

Over the course of the summer, coal operators produced multiple, competing codes. The distinguishing characteristic of the Chicago draft was its capitulation to the competitive regionalism of the coal industry: it allowed each coal-producing area to set its own wage and hours standards.[10] Roche was among coal operators who countered with a demand for uniform wages and hours across the industry. Roche and her allies employed union miners and were worried that regional variations in wages would allow nonunion operators to underprice them. In July,

Roche's group convened a conference in Washington that included the president of the United Mine Workers of America (UMW), John L. Lewis.[11]

The NIRA had begun to work a remarkable transformation on John L. Lewis. For evidence, one had to look no further than his sudden change of lieutenants in Colorado, where Lewis finally replaced the ineffectual O. F. Nigro with an energetic Frank Hefferly. Lewis explained to Nigro that the NIRA required a major organizing drive in Colorado and, generously attributing Nigro's ineffectuality to ill health, that the UMW must appoint someone healthy enough to spearhead the drive.[12]

As Hefferly's appointment hinted, the New Deal was converting John L. Lewis to a labor leader with whom Josephine Roche could forge a powerful political partnership. Building that partnership began with drafting the proposal for a uniform national coal code in July 1933. Even this draft was not all Roche hoped for, but her influence was everywhere in evidence. Like her union contract at RMF, it opened with a statement of the industry's duty to serve all interests invested in coal: workers, consumers, and shareholders. Positing that a single, national minimum wage would generate greater purchasing power than variable wages would, signatories set a national minimum wage of $5.00 per day.[13] They stipulated an eight-hour day and forty-hour week, despite John L. Lewis's argument for a six-hour day and Roche's support for that limitation. The proposal also required some of the work conditions already embedded in Roche's contract with the UMW: it allowed miners to choose their own check-weighmen and forbade employers to require that miners live in company housing or shop at company stores.[14] At the close of the conference and in recognition of her leadership, Roche was among the group of six operators selected to sign the draft code and present it to President Roosevelt.[15]

The code-setting process revealed sharp conflicts among coal operators. Many insisted that the NRA could not force them to bargain collectively with their workers; others, that the code should not set wages; many, that operators must be allowed to retain their company unions.[16] Some scoffed at any maximum hours standard.[17] Even Roche's nearest competitors in Colorado sent their own proposal to the NRA, which prompted her to fire off a protest announcing that she, who produced 30 percent of the coal produced in the lignite fields of Colorado, did not subscribe to the proposal submitted by the Northern Colorado Coal Producers' Association. She petitioned the NRA not to approve any agreement for northern Colorado until she had been allowed to testify to the success of higher wages than the northern operators proposed.[18]

By the time of Roche's protest, the NIRA was already making a huge difference in the organization of the coal industry—and others as well.

Responding to the provision that protected workers' right to organize, coal miners sprang into action all over the country, organizing themselves into locals of the UMW and surprising union officials with their eagerness for membership. Between June and August, more than 300,000 miners signed membership cards, and they pressed hard for local contracts and a national coal code.[19] Their demands in negotiations with employers and the NRA confirmed that the issues addressed by Roche's union contract were the ones that mattered most to them.[20] Miners' activism was pushing the coal industry as a whole toward the progressive industrialism achieved with Roche at RMF.

Roche's most dramatic opportunity to plead the case for her vision of progressive industrialism came during public hearings on the coal code held in Washington's sweltering Commerce Building during August 1933.[21] On the fourth day of testimony, Roche ascended the platform, reportedly "a modish figure" in a gray dress, gray shoes, and a gray straw hat, and "electrified the conference with an impressive appeal for adoption of a national code recognizing the mutual interests of management, miners and consumers."[22] Speaking without a prepared manuscript, Roche vehemently defended a uniform national code and the necessity of protecting workers' right to bargain collectively. The problems of the coal industry were not local or regional, she argued, but nationally "interrelated and interdependent." As a result, only national planning could manage the industry effectively. She quoted at one point the preamble of her now-famous contract with the UMW and insisted that her experience in the coal industry demonstrated that high wages could be maintained even as prices declined.[23]

Roche's testimony did not, of course, produce harmony among coal operators. By September 12, it was not clear they would agree to any code, even if wage differentials were allowed for different parts of the country.[24] The operators' intransigence ignited anger among miners. In mid-September, 30,000 restive miners took a "holiday" from mines in Pennsylvania, where labor conflict had erupted throughout the summer.[25] The UMW, which was not in fact controlling the strikers, threatened to broaden the action if operators did not sign on to the national code. The workers' threat to close down the coal industry moved Roosevelt to acknowledge his power to impose a code if coal operators failed to produce their own. Under duress, most operators signed on September 16.[26]

For all its imperfections, the coal code was a huge victory for miners. It did for the mass of coal miners what Roche's contract with the UMW had done for those at RMF. It increased wages for most and assured the eight-hour day. It guaranteed miners the right to choose their checkweighmen, set up a grievance procedure, and prohibited child labor, payment in scrip, and the requirement that miners live in company housing and shop in company stores.[27] The latter were issues on which Roche had been closely questioned at the August hearings. She had assured NRA administrators that her company survived quite well when it released its workers from the requirement of company housing, operated its stores on a cash basis, and left the miners free to shop where they would.[28]

Although Roche signed the coal code, she immediately filed a complaint because it permitted wages to vary across the country. To get the code passed, the NRA agreed to divide the country into five major coal districts, each district then splitting into subdistricts for the purposes of setting wages. RMF was in District V, which encompassed most of the West. That major district was then subdivided into seven smaller areas. Roche's area was Subdistrict L, which included only northern Colorado. Wages in her small district were set at $5.00 per day, and she wanted an immediate revision because her most recent union contract committed her to $5.25. If her closest competitors paid only $5.00 a day, she was clearly disadvantaged.[29] Far worse, though, coal operators in southern Colorado won a minimum wage of $4.44 a day, and these operators were openly competing against Roche for business in Denver.[30] The southern operators contended that super-cheap coal from Oklahoma, Arkansas, Missouri, and even western Kentucky was making its way into their markets, and as wages in those areas were set between $3.75 and $4.00 a day, they could not endure a wage hike.[31] All of this confirmed Roche's argument that the problems of the coal industry were national. Conditions in one area affected the others. Allowing wages to vary from area to area set up a situation in which competition could continue to exert downward pressure on wages.

Fortunately for Roche and coal miners, the code's protection of collective bargaining compensated to some degree for variable minimum wages. Once the coal code was promulgated, UMW organizers in Colorado went to work on Roche's northern competitors and brought them at last into collective bargaining agreements that stipulated wages equal to those paid by RMF. As Frank Hefferly, new president of the UMW in Colorado, put it, "the operators in the northern Colorado Producers' Association . . . finally agreed with us to negotiate a scale comparable with the Rocky Mountain Fuel contract on the basis of $5.25."[32] Hefferly then shifted his attentions to the southern Colorado coalfields, which had by April 1934 signed contracts with the UMW that raised wages to $5.10 per day.[33]

Early in 1934, Roche was fairly optimistic about the code. She explained, "the fact that the same wage scale is now in effect because of the union contract made possible at last by the Code has helped greatly in preventing the ruthless price cuts our competitors have been so prone to indulge in." She admitted, however, that administration of the code remained inadequate, and she was serving on the Code Authority for the Northern Field in Colorado to try to put the full intent of the code into practice.[34]

As new industries were devising codes and existing codes were being improved, though, individual enterprises in many industries were ignoring them. Even in coal, where many operators lobbied to extend the NIRA beyond the two years Congress had originally given it, others hated the law and simply refused to comply.[35] One irate operator fulminated that a proposed amendment to the coal code "combines the law of the jungle with the worst features of a military despotism and so far as the Alabama field is concerned the amendments are and will continue to be null and void."[36] Some version of that sentiment was fairly common among employers in many industries. Moreover, workers and consumers were disappointed that businesses often raised prices to compensate for increased wages with the net result of little increase in purchasing power and, thus, little economic recovery.[37] The ultimate effect of the NRA remained uncertain in 1934.

In the early months of that year, while Roche continued to wrangle for higher wages in coal, she was also keeping an eye on her home state's relationship with other New Deal programs. She did not like what she saw. Despite having a Democrat in the governor's chair, Colorado was slow to work with the Roosevelt administration in setting up programs of economic relief. In fact, Colorado's legislature failed to raise the matching funds required for the state to receive monies from FERA. After pouring federal funds into the state for several months without receiving the requisite matches, Harry Hopkins threatened to cut off further monies. Colorado's Governor Edwin Johnson was livid. He saw Hopkins's administration of FERA as high-handed interference in the state's sovereignty and Hopkins's insistence on hiring professional social workers to run FERA programs as an affront to Johnson's freedom to dispense patronage. Only in January 1934, when the state's unemployed threatened violence, did the legislature finally identify sources of matching funds for the FERA programs. Federal money started flowing into the state's treasury once again, but Governor Johnson remained hostile to Washington's dictates.[38]

During the standoff between Hopkins and Johnson, some observers wondered whether Colorado needed a new governor and proposed that Josephine Roche might be just the person for the job.[39] By spring 1934, newspapers speculated freely about the possibility of a gubernatorial run for the coal magnate, and one source insisted that her "friends" in Washington were keen that she run.[40] Presumably, those friends included the Costigans, Edward Keating, and Oscar Chapman, the latter a Colorado progressive who had been appointed assistant secretary of the interior in

1933. When Roche was in Washington to testify at coal hearings in April, she surely discussed the possibility with her Colorado gang.[41] By May, Oswald Garrison Villard was lobbying to announce her candidacy in the *Nation*, and Roche herself was finally convinced.[42] During a visit to Washington that month, she telegrammed the chair of Colorado's Democratic State Central Committee, proclaiming that she would like to announce her candidacy for governor of Colorado (figure 9).[43] The next day, May 24, the *Rocky Mountain News* carried the story, and in a portentous line concluded: "Party leaders in Colorado are surprised."[44]

Roche's new political ambition set her sprinting toward another gender hurdle. By 1934, only two women had actually served as governors of U.S. states, and both achieved their positions by association with a husband. In 1925, Nellie Tayloe Ross took the governor's chair in Wyoming following a special election required by her governor-husband's death, and Miriam "Ma" Ferguson served as governor of Texas in place of her impeached husband. Not until 1974 would any U.S. state elect a woman governor in her own right.[45] Roche was yet again reimagining women's possibilities, and the courage it took to break this ground was recognized by women all over the country. One wrote to admire Roche "for your nerve," and another exclaimed, "you are a brave woman to try it!"[46]

One of the reasons that Roche seemed to have a shot at the governorship was her perfection of what we might call New Deal womanhood. That version of femininity combined enough stylishness to demonstrate an appreciation of male/female difference—as in Roche's reportedly "modish" outfits—with an explicit rejection of female dependency. When Roche, attired in her snappy gray ensemble, had testified at the coal code hearings in August, an NRA official asked an aide to "pull out a chair for Miss Roche." She responded, "I am perfectly willing to take Mr. Richberg's questions standing."[47] The audience applauded. Trendy feminine dress combined with a refusal of chivalry seemed to be an appealing version of womanhood among New Dealers. A reporter captured that gender balance when he claimed that Roche's "mental processes, her self-sufficiency and her dynamic energy are essentially masculine and have made her blood brother to other captains of industry, yet she is completely feminine in manner and appearance."[48]

Even with that kind of approval, however, the gubernatorial race posed a formidable challenge. Back in Colorado after her announcement, Roche opened a blazing campaign. In June, she received her first significant endorsement: The State Federation of Labor backed her despite its generally good relations with Governor Johnson, who was a certain contender for a second term.[49] The *Rocky Mountain News* followed suit shortly thereafter, editorializing, "The Rocky Mountain News sincerely believes that Josephine Roche will be the greatest governor Colorado ever had."[50] Progressives all over the state were delighted by her announcement, and many women metaphorically hurled their hats into the air. "More power to you!" exclaimed a representative female fan.[51] The *Nation*, of course, endorsed her early on, and progressive women across the country contributed to her campaign.[52] Grace Abbott, about to retire from the Children's Bureau, promised to get to Colorado as soon as she could and was a great presence on the campaign trail.[53] Because of Roche's staunch support for organized labor and federal labor standards, national labor organizations lined up behind her. John L. Lewis had pledged his support while she was still in Washington, and William Green, president of the American Federation of Labor, endorsed her as well.[54]

Roche's first official challenge was getting on the Democratic primary ballot. To do so, Roche needed to win 10 percent of the delegates at the state's Democratic Party Assembly, scheduled to meet on July 30. Her likely challengers were Edwin Johnson, the incumbent governor, and William "Billy" Adams, who had been governor for three terms before Johnson. Both men were deeply ensconced in the Democratic Party's regular organization in Colorado. Both were well versed in the patronage politics that Roche frankly opposed. They were both fiscal conservatives, shaken by the massive spending that Roosevelt's Washington encouraged, and neither welcomed federal interference in business or what they saw as the state's prerogatives.[55]

Roche's campaign countered the localism and conservatism of these Democratic men with an enthusiastic dedication to New Deal progressivism. Her slogan, "Roosevelt, Roche, and Recovery," proclaimed that one of her major commitments was full cooperation with the New Deal government. Unlike her Democratic opponents, Roche welcomed federal programs aimed at relieving unemployment and promoting economic recovery. In fact, she insisted in her campaign appearances that the first duty of government was "human welfare" and that the goals of "economic democracy and social justice" required "a new union of effort by state and Federal governments."[56] Just as she had argued that the problems of the coal industry were national and thus required a national solution, so she asserted in her gubernatorial race, "We realize today no individual, no community, no state is self-sufficient and able independently to develop and to achieve the necessary and desired things of life. . . . As a great national unit we must work together."[57]

In these convictions, Roche's campaign recalled the nationalism of Theodore Roosevelt's Progressive Party and, in other ways, too, drew a straight line between progressivism early in the century and that coming to the fore in the New Deal. To identify the aim of her nationalist vision, she often used the phrase, "the conservation of human resources," quoting directly from the Progressive Party's 1912 platform.[58] Her policy proposals, too, borrowed from the earlier endeavor. At the top of her agenda was a progressive state income tax. Following the populists, the Progressive Party had supported a federal income tax, which became a reality during Woodrow Wilson's administration. Since its establishment, however, the federal tax had been levied on so few people that it played little ongoing part in national politics. As the NRA foundered, some progressives identified a widely levied income tax capable of funding aid to lower-income earners as a better way to maximize purchasing power. In 1934 and 1935, New Dealers followed through with new tax laws. Together with modifications of the tax code enacted during World War II, these moves helped to create greater economic equality by mid-century than ever before in U.S. history.[59]

Committed to that same end, Roche took up the cause of a graduated income tax at the state level. Colorado's state government did not yet have the power to levy an income tax and so depended solely on property taxes, which fell inordinately on farmers and small businessmen. Roche was eager to ease this tax burden and rest state government instead on revenues from those most able to pay. To justify the switch from property to income taxes, she contended that a "broadening of the base of income distribution and wealth ownership is fundamental" to our goal of "security for all men, women and children."[60]

Other issues also demonstrated continuities between Roche's campaign in 1934 and the Progressive Party's national and state campaigns in 1912. She promised to support a system of old-age pensions, unemployment insurance, and more fully funded public health initiatives. She pushed to strengthen and expand the civil service system and to solidify the state's ability to ensure safe working conditions in coal mines. More broadly, she aimed to reignite progress against "child labor, sweat shop slavery, pitiful wages, needlessly long working hours, yellow dog contracts, and other evil industrial conditions," progress that she believed had been stymied by the conservative policies of the 1920s. She pounded every podium with the point that to improve the standard of living for the mass of Americans and to achieve anything approximating social justice required an activist government both at the national and at the state level.[61]

Roche combined in her political vision a familiar progressive emphasis on both enhancing democracy and relying on science. In the first radio address of her campaign, she committed herself to the "life-saving fundamental principles of democratic self-government." Drawing on the populist emphases of progressivism in the West and prefiguring the rhetoric of Franklin Roosevelt's 1936 presidential campaign, she denounced the wealthy, castigated Wall Street, and demanded that ordinary Americans "take back into our own keeping the America that our fathers created and is ours, to put a stop to the encroachments on the Constitution and the flouting of the Declaration of Independence by those who talk glibly about American traditions, while in every act violating true Americanism in behalf of the privileged few."[62] At the same time, she advocated responsible management of state spending, insisting on a "scientifically worked out plan for elimination of administrative waste." She pledged herself repeatedly to "scientific values" and "to a willingness to apply in the field of economic and social science the knowledge and intelligence which have in the field of natural science liberated and so vastly aided mankind."[63]

Most important, Roche hammered home her belief that the current economic emergency was not a fluke that required only temporary measures to get Americans back to the *status quo ante*. She fervently maintained that the Great Depression was instead the result of the very structure of America's political economy in the 1920s. To get the country out of the current disaster and prevent another one demanded in her words "reconstruction" not simply "recovery." She dismissed the "amazing prosperity" of the 1920s as "mythical and nonexistent save for the privileged few." Sometimes she called it the "deceptive prosperity" of the 1920s. Over and over again, she chanted the statistics that showed rising dividends for the elite while many workers' standards of living declined. The United States could not return to the policies of the 1920s because they could not sustain a mass-production economy that required mass purchasing power to survive. Americans needed instead policies that assured "prosperity for all."[64] The Great Depression was, in the telling of Josephine Roche and progressives like her, the most powerful possible argument for promoting economic equality.

Roche's platform appealed to many Coloradans, and their support was enough to win her more than the 10 percent of delegates she needed when Colorado's Democratic Party met in late July. At that convention, hundreds of delegates chose the candidates to appear on the party's primary ballot in September. Three survived the vote: Edwin Johnson, Billy Adams, and Josephine Roche.[65] That combination of contenders set off the hottest political race in the state in 1934 and one of the hottest state races ever in Colorado history. One local newspaper referred to it as a "40-day war raging for state Democrats."[66]

From early August until the September 11 primary, Roche campaigned zealously. Driving her old Buick—described by one friend as "nothing so much as a worn-out, spavined Dobbin"—Roche bounced along the state's bumpy roads, introducing herself where she was not yet known and reconnecting with those she knew from previous campaigns. Sometimes, she had her office assistant, Mildred Lea, at her side; sometimes, she drove alone. In a few short weeks, she visited nearly all of the sixty-three counties of the state, logging more than 8,000 miles over the Rocky Mountains and across the state's eastern plains.[67]

In her speedy tour of the state, Roche spoke to a broad spectrum of groups. She kept her relations with organized labor solid, and the State Federation of Labor opened offices for her in all of its strongholds.[68] She spoke to associations of Italians, Jews, Scandinavians, and Poles; she sought out young people and college grads.[69] She reached out to Spanish-speaking voters. In Otero County, one of the Spanish-speaking priests "sent out the word to his people to vote for" Roche.[70] The founder of the Spanish-American Citizens Association of Denver campaigned for her among Spanish speakers all over the state.[71] She spoke repeatedly to African American groups, who were concentrated in Denver and offered their support not only because of Roche's own commitment to equality of opportunity but because her ally, Senator Edward Costigan, cosponsored an anti-lynching bill in the U.S. Congress. At one event, 2,000 people turned out to hear Roche and Costigan in East Denver's African American neighborhood.[72] As one supporter put it, the New Deal was of "great import to all citizens of the state and of particular importance to the negro group." Because of Roche's work for relief and the "man down under," this black activist committed to her election.[73] In keeping with national trends, black Americans in Colorado were moving into the Democratic Party, and Roche began seriously to consider the special burdens of racial difference.

Roche spoke in a range of venues to groups of all sizes. She took tea with Catholic women at Denver's Brown Palace Hotel. She spoke at dance halls and churches. She mounted platforms in vacant lots and attended barbeque picnics. She met potential supporters at high schools, stores, and grain elevators.[74] She spoke to "a packed audience in the Pueblo City Auditorium."[75] At the county fairgrounds in Loveland, she proclaimed to 1,200 people, "From this day on, we members of a great democracy are going to demand from politics the philosophy that human rights are the first charge of government."[76] She drew such a large crowd at Walsenburg that nearly 1,000 people reportedly followed her to a church auditorium "when they discovered that the court house wouldn't hold them."[77]

The race was tight. Support for Roche was exceptionally strong in Denver, and she had solid backing in Boulder, Colorado Springs, and Pueblo—all cities on the eastern edge of the Rockies—as well as in Crested Butte and Grand Junction, towns out in rugged mining areas on the western slope of the mountains. Those receiving and administering federal relief were united behind her.[78] In August, her star was definitely rising. Local polling suggested that Roche could win the primary so long as both Adams and Johnson stayed in the contest but that she would face trouble in a head-to-head battle with only one of them.[79] Indeed, the old guard of the state's Democratic Party so feared losing the race that U.S. Senator Alva Adams intervened to strengthen the chances of a victory for his more conservative forces. Early in August, Senator Adams convinced his relative, Billy Adams, to withdraw from the gubernatorial race and throw his support behind the incumbent, Edwin Johnson. Alva Adams feared that if the Roche/Costigan forces won the governorship, giving progressives' control of patronage in the state government, they would dominate the state party indefinitely.[80]

Even with more conservative Democrats united against her by mid-August, Roche looked strong. Observers both inside the state and outside insisted that the race was too close to call, and Edwin Johnson campaigned like his life depended on it. He allegedly offered bribes to potential voters in the coal camps and called on Spanish-speaking Americans, for whom he generally showed only contempt, to repay him with their votes for stopping the execution of a Mexican boy accused of murder.[81] Wielding the power of incumbency, Johnson shifted state highway funds to areas where he was uncertain of support and falsely accused Roche of threatening to cut off beneficiaries of federal relief if they refused to vote for her.[82]

Simultaneously, the right-wing *Denver Post* opened a scurrilous campaign that both red-baited Roche and associated her with sexual impropriety. In a particularly striking example, the *Post* headlined a front-page article with inch-high red letters that screamed, "SO THE PEOPLE MAY KNOW," which set up the contest between Johnson and Roche this way: "Shall Democrats keep control of the Democratic Party or shall they surrender their party to the Reds?"[83] The article went on, "A vote for Miss Roche, Denver divorcee and ex-policewoman, is a vote to turn the Democratic Party over to the Reds."[84] In that line, the *Post* not only accused Roche of communism but also condemned her for failing to uphold its notion of proper womanhood. Divorce and service on the police force were construed as stains on Roche's character.[85]

In other stories, too, the *Post* brought up Roche's divorce, and sometimes it associated her with sexual lasciviousness. "Tax Orgy Threatens Small Home Owner" was one memorable headline to a story in which the *Post* warned, "Her nomination would launch the wildest orgy of profligate public spending Colorado has ever seen." The article continued, "The Communist element sees in Miss Roche's candidacy an opportunity to get control of the state government and use that control to take away from everybody who has property and give that money and property to those who have been too lazy or too improvident to lay up anything for themselves."[86] That Roche's platform aimed to ease the tax burden on small property owners and that she was herself a corporate property owner was of no interest to the *Post*, which wished to smear Roche by any means available.

Only a few days before the September 11 primary, Roche answered the *Post* directly. In a radio address delivered over the Denver airwaves, she said, "Every fight for human beings waged in the past has met with the same animosity and unscrupulous attacks as this fight is encountering— the same slanderous personal whisperings and other falsehoods; the same ignorant, vicious propaganda . . . the same groundless, wholly manufac- tured, purely pretended fears of radicalism." She answered those charges and then "having brushed off some of the inconsequential dust of the campaign," she sighed, "let us turn to the only things citizens are truly interested in—our issues. Here," she continued with gleeful sarcasm, "I am indeed fortunate, because I seem to have an uncontested field."[87]

On the day of the primary, voters surged to the polls, pushing the turn- out to record numbers.[88] Over 135,000 voters marked ballots in the Democratic gubernatorial primary on September 11, and by September 13 the election was still too close to call. Johnson was leading, but several counties had not yet reported, and Roche refused to concede until all votes were counted. At that point, she had won Denver by a landslide despite the *Post*'s smear campaign. She was also winning in Mesa County, way out west, where organized labor enthusiastically supported her, and in Boulder, where she had mines and the support of progressives at the state university. Gunnison, also a mining county in the west, was being disputed, but she would eventually pull that one out, too. She ran so close to Johnson in El Paso County, home of Colorado Springs, that one paper called that county for her early on. She was neck-and-neck with Johnson in Pueblo, too. In fact, according to one source, Roche won 11,000 more votes than the previous highest vote winner in any Democratic guberna- torial primary. But still, she lost the primary to Edwin Johnson by 12,000 votes.[89]

Roche's defeat had many causes. Certainly, sexism played a part. Some voters, even though they agreed with Roche's views, could not bring themselves to vote for a woman. Right after Roche's announcement, one supporter in Denver warned, "There are still a few who feel that the Gov- ernor of Colorado should wear trousers."[90] Another reported, "I have already spoke about her [Roche] to six of my friends, who are enthusias- tic about her candidacy, except one, who is a woman, and she objected on account of Miss Roche's sex."[91] Years after the election, one of her sup- porters told Roche of an experience he had had on the campaign trail for her in 1934. As he was giving a speech in Durango, he recalled, "I noticed an old man with a long beard out in the front of the not too large audi- ence. He kept nodding his head in agreement, and I thought there I made at least one vote, but after the speaking was over, he came up to me and said, 'that was a mighty fine speech, but young feller, we don't want a woman governor, do we now?' "[92] On the basis of just such evidence, one reporter concluded, "it is also true that Miss Roche is a woman and for that reason many are planning to vote against her, despite the fact that they subscribe to her principles."[93]

Probably even more important than gender to Roche's loss were issues related to political organization, patronage, and competition between local and national elites. As incumbent governor, Johnson enjoyed the benefit of patronage that he had been bestowing on Coloradans for two years. Many owed him political fealty, and many of Roche's supporters reminded her repeatedly how important patronage was to the way Coloradans voted.[94] Before the Democratic Assembly, one woman instructed Roche that all of the delegates from her county were "bandwagonists, in other words they want to jump the safe way, the way that will give them jobs, appointments." She regretted, "Even those who believe in you will not risk their political future."[95]

In addition to having patronage on his side, Johnson's longer immersion in the state's party apparatus and support from the very well-established Adams family meant that his political organization was far better developed. Roche had effective support in Denver, Boulder, Colorado Springs, and Pueblo. But her organization in other places was spotty—reportedly not as good as Costigan's had been in 1930.[96] Organized labor could not make up for Johnson's organizational advantage both because many of Colorado's counties were strictly agricultural and because Johnson enjoyed some support from workers, having been their candidate in 1932. Indeed, some members of the State Federation of Labor thought the organization should endorse both Johnson and Roche.[97]

Perhaps most important, however, Roche was very closely associated with a national political elite centered in Washington rather than the local Democratic Party. She was, after all, the New Deal candidate. Johnson, unknown at the national level and exclusively focused on Colorado, painted Roche as an outsider not genuinely interested in the state. She had announced her candidacy from Washington rather than Denver. She had not observed political courtesy by informing U.S. Senator Alva Adams that she intended to run.[98] She had not been an integral participant in the local Democratic Party. Instead, she consulted with New Deal administrator Harry Hopkins on issues related to relief and child labor in Colorado, and figures from outside, like Grace Abbott, invaded the state on her behalf.[99] Local party stalwarts, then, were disinclined to support her. The anger of patronage seekers who had resented Roche's appointments to the Denver police force in 1912 and juvenile court in 1915 came back to haunt her as Johnson echoed their accusations that Roche was an interloper unfairly favored with unearned rewards. Although she had campaigned for many individual Democrats—Woodrow Wilson in 1916 and Edward Costigan in 1930 as well as Franklin Roosevelt in 1932— these were flashes in the political pan rather than the consistent participation on the ground as a committeewoman or party loyalist that was so important to electoral success in local or statewide office. "What did Josephine Roche ever do for the Democratic Party?" was on the lips of many opponents.[100] Roche was a national progressive, not a Colorado Democrat, and that lack of local party identity hurt her in the gubernatorial campaign. Her experience in the primary race demonstrated indeed that the nationalizing process of the New Deal was contentious, uneven, and ultimately incomplete.

Roche's supporters offered every sort of comfort after her defeat. One lawyer thanked her: "You raised the banner of progressivism and all we did was to follow." He went on, "The splendid way you conducted your campaign made thousands of friends for you and for your progressive cause."[101] Another politico of long experience wrote, "I count it a pleasure and honor to have served in your cause. I recall what Bryan said after he was unjustly defeated in 1896, 'It is better to have run and lost than never to run at all.' "[102] The Young Men's Democratic Club of El Paso looked to her for further leadership: We "shall await your call that we may carry on."[103]

Confirming her status as a national progressive rather than a local Democrat, however, Roche also received thanks and condolences from Washington. Paul Shriver, another Coloradan serving in Roosevelt's State Department, penned a note to say, "Although the progressive movement appears to have had a temporary set-back in Colorado, your truly splendid fight has gone far toward impressing upon our citizens the real necessities of the hour and you have placed all of us under obligations to you for what you have done."[104] He later said that her campaign had "better prepared" the Roosevelt camp "for the campaign of 1936" and asked her to make "any suggestions you may care to make directed toward that end."[105]

Shriver's invitation made clear that Roche's gubernatorial effort solidified her place in the national political elite now dominating the New Deal government. Although she would remain connected to Colorado for twenty years more, her stronger associations were in the East. Roche's early moves after the primary blared this message. She did not stay in Colorado to campaign for Edwin Johnson against his Republican opponent but by October was speaking outside the state on behalf of the Women's Division of the Democratic National Committee. She also attended conferences in Washington and worked in New York for two progressive candidates who had contributed to RMF in 1929. Herbert Lehman was running for governor of the Empire State, and Caroline O'Day for U.S. representative. In November, both won their races, and Roche was overjoyed.[106]

To make such frequent trips between Denver and the East Coast, Roche joined an airborne elite in the early 1930s. Commercial flight remained in its infancy during the Great Depression, but Denver had a small municipal airport, and the adventurous Roche started making good use of it as soon as the New Deal was under way.[107] Indeed, although she could not have known it, during the summer of 1933 she had begun a decade and a half of regular air-commuting between Denver and Washington. To save time, she often flew at night and was mesmerized by the stars she could see through the portholes as she drifted off to sleep.[108]

Roche needed access to air travel ever more urgently in fall 1934, as the Roosevelt administration constantly invited her to Washington. While the New Deal government had initially drawn on Roche's business experience, late in 1934 the administration turned to her for a different project: the development of a permanent national program of social welfare. New Dealers were already doing welfare work, of course, through their jobs programs and FERA, but these were construed as temporary responses to an emergency situation. Progressives in the administration wanted more. By the 1930s, many who had advocated state-level programs of health insurance and old-age pensions in the 1910s much preferred national programs because they promised greater stability, pooled resources from a broader base, and created equality across states lines. These activists succeeded in putting unemployment and old-age insurance on the national Democratic platform in 1932. When Roosevelt asked Roche's friend and colleague from their Columbia days, Frances Perkins, to serve as his secretary of labor, she accepted on the condition that he genuinely meant to press toward those goals.[109] Some of Roosevelt's other supporters also hoped for a program of health insurance and permanent, elastic public works programs that would grow or shrink as economic cycles demanded.[110] With the massive suffering caused by the depression eroding opposition to interventionist government, progressives saw their main chance to realize a full-blown system of national social insurance and public assistance.

While Roche was running for governor of Colorado, Roosevelt began to follow through on that possibility. He organized a committee within his cabinet, the Committee on Economic Security (CES), to craft a plan that would prevent the vagaries of life—unemployment, old age, and illness—from sinking individuals and families into destitution. Perkins chaired the group, and as it went to work, she also formed an advisory council to provide ideas from outside the administration and to generate public buy-in for whatever program ultimately emerged. Perkins tapped Roche for a spot in the advisory group just about a week before the 1934 general elections. The first meeting of the council convened in Washington on November 15.[111]

Even before Roche made it to Washington for that meeting, however, the wheels were set in motion for her deeper involvement in the economic security program. The administration approached her about appointment as assistant secretary of the treasury, from which position she would oversee the Public Health Service (PHS) and the welfare of the Treasury's 56,000 employees.[112] The PHS had long been in the Treasury because of its origin in an eighteenth-century system of marine hospitals paid for by a tax collected by the Treasury.[113] By the 1930s, the nation's chief medical officer was the surgeon general, and the Treasury official who oversaw the PHS a fiscal expert simply keeping track of the PHS budget.[114] By putting Roche in charge of the PHS, Roosevelt was in essence creating a new position. One observer labeled it "Minister of Health," an office entrusted to a nonmedical person with broad expertise in social and economic welfare. Such a person might direct the PHS as an integral component of a comprehensive social welfare program, which is precisely what Roche would do.[115]

That possibility was not immediately apparent, however, and Roche did not accept right away. She took the opportunity of her trip to Washington in mid-November to gather information and discuss the offer with friends. In addition to meeting with Secretary of the Treasury Henry Morgenthau, she conferred with the Costigans and Keatings. She dined at the White House.[116] Satisfied by those discussions, Roche said yes, and, on November 15, the Roosevelt administration announced her appointment as assistant secretary of the treasury. The press described her as "breathless with excitement" at her elevation to the "Little Cabinet," a nickname for the assistant secretaries of the federal government's executive departments.[117]

As soon as she could, Roche rushed back to Denver to put things in order at RMF. She and the board of directors elected a long-standing employee, J. Paul Peabody, to the company presidency.[118] She then packed a few necessities, enjoyed the acclaim of 600 friends at a celebratory dinner, and returned to Washington to open an entirely new chapter in her life.[119]

During the early years of the New Deal, Roche performed as a citizen-adviser to the Roosevelt administration. She brought to that work the progressive commitment to diminishing inequality that had long driven her activism. In fact, framing the Great Depression as an inevitable consequence of growing economic inequalities, Roche and other progressives regained a sort of political traction at the national level that they had lost during the 1920s. They used that traction to implement a set of policies not only to arrest further economic decline in the 1930s but also to reduce class inequalities in the future. When Colorado refused Roche's gubernatorial leadership in 1934, Roosevelt scooped her up for service to her progressive ideals as a full-fledged member of the New Deal administration.

CHAPTER 10

AT THE CENTER OF POWER: ROCHE IN THE NEW DEAL GOVERNMENT, 1934–1939

S erving as assistant secretary of the treasury in the New Deal government carried Josephine Roche to the height of her renown and power. Between 1934 and 1938, her central responsibility was health policy, but the full range of her involvement in the New Deal went well beyond that core focus.[1] She also shaped one of the most significant pieces of federal legislation in the twentieth century, the Social Security Act, and oversaw the implementation of such New Deal programs as the National Youth Administration (NYA), all the while pushing for more effective regulation of industry and the unionization of American workers. As she dashed from one New Deal initiative to another, Roche was celebrated as an icon of female achievement, who represented the new level of power achieved by women in politics and government during the 1930s.

During Roche's stint as a Washington insider, the scope of the progressive project expanded. Class inequality remained the primary concern, but Roche never lost sight of gender inequities, as her constant attention to women's organizations attested, and like many of her closest allies, she began to struggle consistently with racial inequality. The inadequacy of Roche's efforts in that regard illuminated the difficulty that many progressives faced in effectively fighting a fuller range of inequalities. Indeed, progressives' policies sometimes created new sources of racial and gender inequality. But the greater traction that racial justice gained on the progressive agenda in the 1930s was permanent.

As Roche flew back to Washington after her farewell dinner in Denver, she had time to imagine how she would give substance to her new position at the Treasury. It was hers to define, and the context was promising. Although her own electoral bid had failed, Democratic congressional victories in 1934 improved the chances for national progressive policies. The enthusiastic response to her appointment also boded well. Some observers rejoiced because they believed her appointment indicated the president was tilting his administration more emphatically toward the progressive wing of the Democratic Party.[2] Organized labor, of course, divined in it a good omen, and all read it as a victory for women.[3] "Congratulations!" one celebrant exclaimed, "Thank heaven my dreams for women are coming true."[4] A Vassar graduate working in the Treasury reported that she was "thrilled" that Roche was coming to her department: "All of us here in the Treasury anticipate with delight and joy your coming to this fascinating old building and its people and problems."[5]

The delight and joy intensified when Roche took the oath of office on December 7, 1934 (figure 10).[6] At the ceremony, she was surrounded by old friends and new colleagues as well as "a battery of reporters and newsreel photographers." Wearing a familiar black dress belted at the waist and featuring a wide white strip of cloth across the bodice, she took the occasion to condemn the Republican administrations of the 1920s and express confidence in the country's future. When she returned to her office, she found it overflowing with celebratory flowers, which she immediately shared with the clerical staff, keeping a few chrysanthemums and roses for herself.[7] Only days later, the Colorado State Society honored Roche with a reception at Washington's elegant Willard Hotel, and the Newspaper Women's Club soon sponsored a tea for her.[8] It was a glorious welcome to the nation's capital.

All the festivities recognized that Roche came to Washington as the second-highest-ranking woman in the New Deal government. Secretary of Labor Frances Perkins, the first woman ever to hold a position in the cabinet, was the only woman who outranked her. But Roche and Perkins were hardly alone. The New Deal government boasted an unusually large number of female executives because President Roosevelt established a better record than any of his predecessors at elevating women to high office. He appointed 23 women, including Roche, to Senate-confirmed posts, and by 1938 nearly 200 women held executive positions in the administration.[9] Keen on advancing the sorority, Roche assembled an exclusively female staff at the Treasury. She hired Vassar grad Mary Switzer as her executive assistant and also relied on personal assistant Mildred Lea and secretary Josephine Coe.[10]

New Deal enhancements of women's power represented a mix of gender innovation and convention, and that mix helps to explain how women's prospects for public authority could both improve dramatically in the 1930s and remain inferior to men's. In most cases, women moved into high-level federal positions because the New Deal vastly expanded the federal bureaucracy in policy areas already associated with female professional authority, especially social welfare, which increased the power and opportunities of women without disturbing the existing gender division of labor.[11] Someone like Josephine Brown, for instance, a rural county welfare director before the New Deal, found herself in the upper echelons of federal power during the 1930s—first, in the Federal Emergency Relief Administration (FERA) and, later, the Works Progress Administration (WPA)—because the New Deal created unprecedented federal programs that depended on social work expertise.[12] Likewise, the New Deal recognized consumers as a discrete economic interest when women were widely assumed to be the nation's primary consumers. Consequently, as New Deal initiatives asked that consumers be represented on advisory boards and committees, they advanced women to higher-level federal positions, again, without establishing women's authority in any new field of expertise. Women's economic opportunities and governmental power genuinely increased in the 1930s but mostly in circumscribed fields. Josephine Roche's appointment made a more striking break from gender conventions than some female appointments, as it located her within Henry Morgenthau's economic policymaking circle and charged her with supervising the militarily organized and ferociously male and scientific Public Health Service (PHS). But even in Roche's case, gender innovation mixed with convention, as her new position was often associated with social welfare as well as fiscal and science policy. The most common pattern of change for women in the New Deal government was new growth on old wood.

Similarly, New Deal Washington promoted rituals in its social arena that undercut the authority of high-ranking women. Take tea, for example. Roche routinely attended formal teas sponsored by individual officials or agencies in Roosevelt's administration. At these lavish functions, only women poured tea, and in most cases, the women who served were the wives of male government officials. But it was not unusual for Roche or Perkins to take a shift behind the tea table as well.[13] That men never poured tea and that women, regardless of their position in the official hierarchy of the New Deal government, poured tea together, meant that the ritual of a Washington tea did not recognize distinctions among women but only a distinction between women and men. It drew a rigid gender boundary that associated women with domesticity and service to men and, by doing so, subordinated women to men. Over the course of her term in Washington, Roche often poured tea as one of the only women who herself held a high-ranking position, and she was often serving men who were her equals in government. In these settings, Roche, Perkins, and other female officials were equated with wives of men with similar rank rather than with their male peers. However impressive the official titles of women in the federal hierarchy of the 1930s, their power and accomplishment were undermined in the closely related realm of Washington society.

Undaunted by these ambiguities, Roche worked with verve in her groundbreaking position at the Treasury. She captained her female team in the agency's grand Greek Revival building, where her large office suite commanded a view of the White House lawn. Roche chain-smoked cigarettes as she worked in those stately surroundings, periodically burning holes in official documents as hot ashes dropped onto their pages.[14] Adding a grace note to her noxious habit, she sometimes inhaled through the Alaskan cigarette holder given her by Secretary of the Interior Harold Ickes only a few months into her government service.[15] A confirmed workaholic, Roche smoked many of her cigarettes after eating lunch at her desk. She took no interest in distractions like vacations or even an occasional weekend of leisure during her New Deal years. As one newspaper explained, "Her work has always been her life."[16] Even though Roche attended two or three major social events each month, by Washington standards, she was nearly a recluse. Local society pages described her as "one of many brilliant people in Government who either because they aren't eager to play the social game, or haven't the leisure, take little part in the whirl here."[17]

In keeping with her focus on work, Roche wasted no time commuting. She rented a two-room apartment just a few blocks from her office and walked to and from work each day. The small apartment featured open fireplaces framed by built-in bookcases, a kitchenette, and a bath.[18] It was cozy and convenient for one; not a place for entertaining crowds—though Roche did bring from Denver a set of silverware for six and a silver tray for visitors' cards.[19] She occasionally hosted a friend or two for dinner, but Roche's home in Washington was primarily a place for solitude.

She needed the break after long, frenetic days crammed with obligation. Her mornings usually included a conference with Morgenthau and his other assistant secretaries, where she debated economic policy; each evening concluded with a memo to Morgenthau, summarizing her day's work. These digests recorded such constant appointments that the two doors between Roche's office and its outer chamber functioned as a revolving door. While Roche showed a visitor out through one door, her office assistant brought the next one in through the other.[20] Prominent among her visitors were labor leaders and members of Congress as Roche was a conduit between the administration and what she called the "Progressive group" in Congress as well as organized labor.[21]

The first legislative project to absorb Roche as assistant secretary of the treasury was the economic security program. Once she joined Roosevelt's administration, she had to resign from the Advisory Council to the Committee on Economic Security (CES), but Morgenthau announced that Roche would represent the Treasury on the cabinet committee it-self.[22] That committee, chaired by Frances Perkins, also included Harry Hopkins, Secretary of Agriculture Henry Wallace, and Attorney General Homer Cummings. Edwin Witte, an expert on unemployment compensa-tion, served as executive director of the committee, and Arthur Altmeyer, a social scientist from Wisconsin and assistant secretary of labor, chaired the technical board. The latter was responsible for actually drafting a bill.[23] As soon as Morgenthau dubbed Roche his representative on the cabinet committee, the CES elected her to the bill-drafting technical com-mittee, and she was assigned to both its executive committee and the subcommittee on unemployment compensation.[24] The president expected draft legislation from the group before the end of December 1934, which meant late nights of study for Roche, who attended meetings of the CES even before she was officially sworn in as assistant secretary.[25]

Roche's deepest involvement was with unemployment compensation, and here she represented the left edge of progressivism within the CES. She favored a fully national program that excluded as few workers as possible. She shared the preference with Henry Wallace and the majority of the Technical Subcommittee on Unemployment Compensation.[26] Only a uniform federal program guaranteed that all workers would receive the same benefits, that workers would not be disadvantaged by changing jobs or moving from one state to another, and that they would receive the highest possible and most reliable benefits. Because all employers across the country would be pooling their money in such a program, the fund would not be threatened by downturns in particular industries or re-gions. Roche did not want workers taxed to fund the system so that it might have at least a slight redistributive effect. At one point, Roche and her allies won the day, and the CES geared up to recommend a national system. Howls of protest from some states, many employers, and legal experts skeptical of the constitutionality of a national program sent the CES back to the drawing board.[27]

Indeed, the particulars of the bill proved so contentious as the CES faced its December deadline that a determined Frances Perkins finally scheduled an evening meeting of the committee at her home on December 21, 1934. Once members arrived, Perkins took the phones off the hook and announced that nobody would leave until the shape of the economic security program was settled. The legendary caucus lasted until 2 am, by which time Roche's smoking habit must have shrouded every head in a thick haze.[28]

At the interminable meeting, Roche was outvoted on the general struc-ture of unemployment compensation. With a conservative judiciary threatening to kill much of the New Deal program, the issue of constitu-tionality induced caution. Instead of a single national program, the CES recommended a state-federal system under which states were allowed to develop their own plans of unemployment compensation, even schemes that permitted individual plants or industries to opt out of the public unemployment fund and create their own. As an advocate of organized labor, Roche was adamant that workers who moved from a plant with its own fund to one in the public system should continue to be covered as though they had not changed jobs. Otherwise, Roche claimed, the legislation "would greatly advantage employers financially sound and powerful and would tend to prevent free organization of workers."[29] She won the point that even small businesses—those with four or more workers—should participate. And the CES agreed that employees should not be taxed for the unemployment program; employers alone should fund it.

Negotiations among committee members actually did continue beyond the December 21 marathon, and Roche was totally engaged in that process. After reading her many comments on one draft of the unemployment and old-age pension provisions of the proposed bill, Witte responded that if the committee accepted all of her proposals, "we will not get the support of any employer other than yourself."[30] Still, Roche kept up the pressure for as generous, comprehensive, and redistributive a Social Security program as she could get.

The president sent the CES's economic security bill to Congress in January 1935. It included the unemployment compensation measure that Roche helped to shape and a federal program of old-age pensions as well as substantial increases in funding for the PHS and new monies for maternal and infant health programs for poor women and children. It proposed means-tested public assistance programs for indigent elderly Americans and poor children of single parents. It did not mention health insurance or a permanent program of public works. Before Roche joined the CES, Roosevelt had decided that the latter programs were so controversial they might torpedo the entire effort and so must be excised from the omnibus bill. The CES continued to work on those issues nonetheless, expecting to address them in separate legislation after the first bill passed.[31]

Even though the economic security bill seemed paltry by Roche's standards, it was to become one of the most significant pieces of federal legislation in the twentieth century. Deeply rooted in progressive ideals that had produced state-level experiments in social insurance and public assistance since the Progressive Era, when it passed in August 1935, the Social Security Act established the federal government's new and permanent responsibility for the economic security of American citizens. Roche then assisted Arthur Altmeyer in organizing the Social Security Board and expanding the program's reach.[32] By the end of the century, the measure would affect the lives of virtually all Americans and significantly reduce poverty among the elderly and temporarily unemployed. Roche was by any measure thoroughly "in the thick of it" as she had always wished to be.[33]

During negotiations over the economic security bill, conflict with her boss at the Treasury emerged as a persistent irritant for Roche, and that conflict illustrated some of the divisions within the New Deal administration. Henry Morgenthau first tangled with Roche over who should pay for unemployment compensation. Morgenthau believed that both employees and employers should pay into that insurance fund, shrinking its redistributive effect. To Roche's relief, Morgenthau agreed not to press his preference, but he fought harder on funding old-age pensions. The issue there was whether to make the old-age pension system entirely self-sustaining through earmarked taxes or to expect general revenues eventually to subsidize the program. Roche and other members of the CES agreed that an indefinitely self-financed system would require immediate taxation too great for Congress to accept and, moreover, they desired the redistributive effect of using general revenues. After the issue was settled within the committee, Morgenthau raised a ruckus with Perkins, who finessed the language of the bill enough to satisfy him. Roche remained his representative on the committee, but this rift foreshadowed others.[34]

Morgenthau succeeded in defeating the CES on one deeply cherished point. When the House Ways and Means Committee was deliberating on the provision for old-age pensions, Morgenthau testified against covering agricultural workers and domestic servants. Assuring pensions to these employees was especially important to the CES because they were among the neediest workers and included disproportionate numbers of African American, Asian American, Mexican American, and female workers. Morgenthau, however, insisted that the Treasury would never be able to collect payroll taxes from such far-flung workers and employers. In this, the Treasury secretary played into the hands of southern congressmen who preferred to exclude black workers in any case. Morgenthau's betrayal of the CES rankled long after the incident and confirmed Roche's sense that her values clashed with those of the secretary she allegedly served.[35] It also meant that the old-age pension program as passed by Congress benefited white male workers in ways it did not benefit women workers or African Americans, Asian Americans, or Mexican Americans. It institutionalized racial and gender inequality in a new forum.[36]

Racial justice nevertheless emerged during the New Deal as an increasingly urgent concern among a broader range of progressives than before, including Josephine Roche. In fact, Roche's response to racial injustice in the 1930s embodied white progressives' raised consciousness of racial inequality as well as their general failure to envision or implement effective anti-racist policies. This combination was captured in an appearance that Roche made at the annual convention of the National Association for the Advancement of Colored People (NAACP) in 1935. Her position as the principal speaker in a Sunday session of the convention recognized Roche's commitment to racial justice. Her speech reiterated her support for an anti-lynching bill recently debated on Capitol Hill, referring to it as "that particular measure which we who meet here today hold so vital and important to our progress and our realization of a juster social order." She furthermore conceptualized the pursuit of African American advancement as one dimension of the larger cause of "social and economic justice" and as integral to the movement for "human rights" and "human cooperation."[37]

At the same time, Roche demonstrated that her vision of a just social order had not fully absorbed racial justice. As an example of the "broader" cause of social and economic justice, she pointed to the Social Security bill then pending before Congress.[38] While she herself had advocated versions of the bill that would have offered genuine benefit to the majority of African American workers, she knew well that Congress had amended the bill to exclude from its insurance programs the occupations that employed the majority of black workers. As it stood in summer 1935, the bill promised its most reliable and highly regarded benefits—unemployment compensation and old-age pensions—to a minority of black Americans and thereby institutionalized racial inequality in a new and far-reaching federal program. That Roche could put forward this particular bill as an example of the broader progressive goal of social justice without any mention of its capitulation to white supremacy suggested that she had not yet fully integrated race with class in her conception of social justice.

Roche's response to racial discrimination within the federal civil service evinced a similar shortfall. On the one hand, she was determined to end discriminatory hiring practices that restricted most African American civil servants to janitorial positions, but on the other, she was willing to accept racially segregated offices to achieve that end. While at the Treasury, Roche was especially eager to meet African American demands for clerical positions. In her attempts to hire more black clerks, however, Roche came up against the expectation, apparently widespread within the federal bureaucracy, that black employees should work in the same room as white employees only if the white workers explicitly agreed to it. In 1937, Roche reported to Morgenthau that one black woman had been successfully placed as secretary to a Treasury official who "expressed himself as willing to have her work in the room with him." Dissatisfied with that single, hard-won victory, she floated the possibility of creating an all-black section within the Bureau of Internal Revenue. She argued that "Although . . . I am not in favor personally of extending segregation," it would be better to establish a segregated section "where colored Civil Service employees might have a chance to work for the Federal Government" than not to hire black people in higher positions at all. Trying to negotiate openings for one person at a time seemed to "deprive the colored group of an economic chance as well as a social chance."[39] Like some other white progressives in the New Deal government, most notably Secretary of the Interior Harold Ickes, Harry Hopkins, and later, Henry Wallace, Roche genuinely wished to promote racial justice, but she failed to imagine the full-scale assault on segregation and discriminatory hiring that racial justice would require.[40]

Symbolic gestures came easier. Roche was one of the many New Dealers who supported black opera star Marian Anderson when the Daughters of the American Revolution infamously denied her a performance space in their grand hall in downtown Washington.[41] The concert was relocated to the Lincoln Memorial, where Roche sat with other dignitaries on the sponsor's platform as Anderson regaled a racially integrated crowd on Easter Sunday in 1939.[42] The concert identified some members of the Roosevelt administration with the cause of racial justice and participated in a nascent process of making racial segregation unacceptable among members of a national political elite, but that process had only just begun in the late 1930s.

Roche's growing awareness of racial injustice, however clouded, allied her with the more progressive edge of the New Deal, and so did her involvement with the National Youth Administration (NYA). In 1935, Harry Hopkins, now running the Works Progress Administration (WPA), an innovative federal jobs program, developed a special project for young people. He wanted Roche to chair the executive committee of the new unit, and she was delighted by the prospect. Morgenthau, however, resisted. The Treasury secretary wanted Roche to run instead a new agency to regulate alcohol.[43] When Roche announced her preference for youth over alcohol, a vexed Morgenthau phoned the president with Roche in his office and insisted that she not be snatched away from the alcohol agency to serve the "youth movement." The president responded that he specifically wanted Roche for the NYA and thought she could manage both![44]

Morgenthau behaved horribly. Following his unsatisfactory conference with the president, he all but commanded Roche to hire an administrative assistant of his choice to help with the NYA. When she refused, Morgenthau warned that he could "not have an Assistant Secretary of the Treasury that is a failure and if the Youth Movement is not run properly" he would "hold her personally responsible."[45] Morgenthau's petulant condescension did not help his cause with Roche: when the Federal Alcohol Administration moved into the Treasury, she took it on only until a permanent supervisor could be recruited.[46] She remained chair of the NYA's executive committee for years.

The appeal of the NYA was clear. It connected Roche with more progressive New Dealers than those at the Treasury—people like Hopkins and Aubrey Williams, the NYA's executive director—and reconnected her to the young people who had been her concern in the juvenile justice movement. The goal of the NYA was to prevent young Americans from slipping into despair and losing faith in American institutions because of the Great Depression. The program supported part-time work for high school, college, and graduate students who would otherwise have to quit school for lack of money. It also funded job training for out-of-school youth aged sixteen to twenty-five.[47] Roche's executive committee began meeting in July 1935 to iron out details like the monthly stipend for each kind of student, eligibility requirements, and procedures for establishing eligibility. In keeping with her dedication to democracy, Roche insisted that young people themselves establish a major presence on her advisory board, and the NYA became one of the New Deal's most successful programs at serving racial minorities in proportion to their numbers in the general population. It also set precedents for future federal aid to American youth.[48]

Roche's experience at the NYA demonstrated further the easy alliances that progressives continued to forge with those farther left. Lee Pressman, general counsel for the WPA, was a member of the Communist Party when he served briefly on the NYA's executive committee. He impressed Roche so profoundly that she introduced him to her by-then great friend, John L. Lewis, and Lewis eventually hired Pressman as counsel to the Committee for Industrial Organization, an emerging militant wing of the labor movement. Roche and Pressman remained close allies for many years.[49] Although Roche may have known nothing about Pressman's Communist Party membership, her association with him was emblematic of progressives' openness to the left in the New Deal Era. Those alliances were facilitated by the Communist International's Popular Front policy in the years between 1935 and 1939, when party members were encouraged to link arms with anyone who opposed fascism.[50] But they were also a result of the longer-term inclination of progressives to ignore ideological distinctions in favor of pragmatic policymaking coalitions.

Despite her expanding New Deal portfolio, Roche managed to be of continuing use to the labor movement. An early opportunity resulted from termination of the National Recovery Administration (NRA), which in May 1935 the Supreme Court declared unconstitutional. The high court objected that the NRA both regulated intrastate commerce, a power the Constitution did not grant to Congress, and delegated too much discretion to the executive branch in developing industrial codes.[51] Although

Roche was dissatisfied with the NRA's coal code, she was very disappointed to see the experiment in economic planning end prematurely, especially as her data revealed a decline in wages, an increase in unemployment and work hours, and a widespread resort to child labor after the NRA's demise.[52]

Roche and other progressives moved swiftly to create programs that would preserve as much as possible the goals of the NRA. One of those goals was to sustain economic planning in basic industry. Roche, naturally, focused on coal and helped to craft the Bituminous Coal Conservation Act (BCCA), which was enacted almost immediately.[53] When the BCCA was challenged in court, Roche testified in its defense. From the witness box in November 1935, Roche countered the claim that Congress had, by creating a commission to set wages in the coal industry, once again dabbled in intrastate commerce. She argued that the relation between employer and worker—even in an enterprise located in only one state—was not an exclusively local relation, as the plaintiffs maintained, because wages in one locale inevitably affected those in other locales without respect for state borders. All commerce in coal was at some level interstate commerce.[54] The Court was not convinced, but since the majority opinion condemned only the BCCA's labor provisions, Roche, John L. Lewis, and other New Dealers drafted an alternative law that regulated only prices.[55] By the time the Bituminous Coal Act of 1937 found its way to the Supreme Court, a key conservative had retired and Roosevelt had chastened the body by threatening to increase the number of justices. This time around, the court upheld the law, and the National Bituminous Coal Commission became an agency within the Department of the Interior.[56] Roche labored continuously to make the new legislation effective, and economic planning on a much reduced scale remained part of the New Deal.[57]

Another measure replacing the defunct NRA had been on the drafting table even before the NRA ended. The National Labor Relations Act, sponsored by New York Senator Robert F. Wagner and often called the Wagner Act, aimed more adequately to safeguard workers' right to organize than the NRA had done. Roche was an outspoken advocate of the bill, and it passed in July 1935, setting up the National Labor Relations Board to supervise union elections and investigate unfair labor practices.[58]

To Roche's delight, the New Deal's support for unionization ignited labor organizing to such a degree that the number of unionized workers tripled in the 1930s and would continue to increase until one-third of the nonagricultural workforce was organized in the 1950s.[59] Making good on federal support was the development of a new and aggressive wing of the labor movement, led by the transformed John L. Lewis. "I dream of a mass labor movement," Lewis declared in 1936, "which will establish collective bargainers on a basis of equality with corporation managers. We need a labor movement that will embrace the teeming millions."[60] To organize those millions, Lewis and a few allies organized the Committee for Industrial Organization (CIO) within the larger American Federation of Labor (AFL) and pushed for organizing workers by industry rather than by craft. Ideally, industrial unions pulled all workers within any industry—male and female; black and white; unskilled, semi-skilled, and super-skilled—into massive unions that then had the power to shut down the industry in defense of their interests. The UMW, an older example of industrial organizing, had by 1935 become the largest and wealthiest union in the AFL, which empowered Lewis to lead the new initiative.[61]

Roche wholeheartedly backed the CIO. Given her hope to see every American worker organized in an independent union, the CIO's commitment to organizing the "teeming millions" was precisely Roche's vision for the future.[62] She carefully followed the group's organizing drives and helped to form the CIO's political branch, Labor's Non-Partisan League.[63] To a labor progressive like Roche, industrial unions promised to make American democracy real by granting all workers citizenship rights in their workplaces and by drawing workers into active participation in American politics.[64] Because national "policies and legislation reach today into every home," Roche insisted, Americans "with more vigor and alertness than ever before . . . must function as citizens in public affairs." Indeed ignorance and indifference among the citizenry could not be tolerated "in a progressive democracy."[65] She credited the labor movement with enrolling the mass of Americans as active members in the body politic where their engagement was essential for the achievement of economic and social justice. Roche's staunch advocacy of a powerful national government in no way eroded her support for energetic grassroots activism. Indeed, she believed an aroused citizenry, fully participating in public life, was the only hope for continuing strides toward equality. The CIO promised precisely the robust democratic participation that Roche and all labor progressives thought essential to a free and just society.[66]

In recognition of her support for industrial organizing, when the CIO broke away from the AFL in 1938 and created the independent Congress of Industrial Organizations (also the CIO), Roche was invited to speak at the founding convention. She was introduced as "the greatest woman of our time."[67] Lauding the delegates' intention to reduce "economic and social inequalities," Roche attributed to their convention "a significance as vital and far-reaching as was that of the first great constitutional convention which gave us the basis for our political democracy, for today," she continued, "you write the constitution of industrial democracy."[68]

Roche later said of the founding convention: "I do not think anything I have been privileged to have anything to do with has ever seemed so vital to me."[69] The claim rang true, as the founding of the CIO promised to fulfill hopes that had crystallized for Roche on the coalfields of Colorado in 1913–1914.

In the same year as the CIO's declaration of independence, Congress completed its replacement of the NRA by passing the Fair Labor Standards Act (FLSA). The FLSA abolished child labor in most industries and set a minimum wage and maximum hours in a significant swath of occupations.[70] Because Congress excluded from the FLSA workers in the service sector, retail, and agriculture, women and racial minorities were once again less likely to benefit than white men. This outcome belied progressives' original intent, but reformers like Roche contented themselves with having established the right of the federal government to intervene directly in the wage relation, and they assumed the restricted reach of the legislation could be expanded.[71] Together with the Wagner Act and regulatory legislation like the BCA, the FLSA took steps toward reinstituting many of the NRA's key components and sustained progressives' hopes that public policy was a viable tool for reducing inequality.

Roche's enthusiasm for the New Deal's economic security program and her connections to the labor movement as well as women's organizations made her an enormous asset in Roosevelt's reelection campaign in 1936, which she referred to as "the grand and glorious campaign."[72] In June, she touted the Social Security Act at a women's luncheon at the Democratic National Convention, conferred with party operatives about a public health plank in the Democratic platform, and discussed ways to shape the campaign for women voters.[73] She went on to make radio addresses and speeches on behalf of the president and the New Deal throughout the fall. She carried special authority with women's groups and labor associations, both of whom saw her as one of their own and were inclined as a result to credit her arguments.[74] One of Roche's auditors in the fall campaign captured the sentiment of many when she thanked Democratic headquarters for sending "such an excellent speaker and such a splendid person as Miss Roche. She was magnificent."[75]

In this particular presidential contest, Roosevelt's rhetoric took the same populist tone that Roche had struck in her 1934 gubernatorial bid. The Wagner Act, progressive taxation, and regulatory legislation had alienated many business interests from the New Deal by 1936, and Roosevelt consequently condemned those interests as greedy "economic royalists" who wished to stall progress against economic insecurity. He mobilized against the business elite a coalescing electoral base among farmers, progressives, African Americans, and urban workers, the latter often first- or second-generation immigrants.

Roche had no difficulty articulating the president's message. Explicitly identifying herself as a progressive, Roche chastised the Republicans as "the same masters that ruled in the privilege-dominated decade of 1920–30" and lauded Roosevelt's leadership, under which "human rights have broken through the grip of privilege."[76] As she had in her own drive for office, she campaigned now on the New Deal's "principle that human welfare, human conservation, is definitely a charge of government." Gains in employment, production, sales, and stock market values bore out her claim that all Americans benefited from New Deal policies. Roosevelt's administration was, she proclaimed, "a people's government," and those who opposed his reelection were "royalists, both political and economic." She denounced selfish businessmen for approving government debt in times of war but opposing it for "human conservation." "Apparently a deficit written in the red blood of millions of human lives is preferable to them," she vividly surmised, "to a red ink one written on paper."[77] In response to those who accused the New Deal's devotion to security of "undermining liberty," Roche responded that there could be no liberty where workers' wages would not support them, where a single illness wiped out a lifetime's savings, and where millions suffered soul-crushing deprivations. "Security," Roche insisted, in what might have been the New Deal's motto, was the "basis of liberty."[78]

Roche's campaign appearances for the president represented only a sliver of her public-speaking docket in the late 1930s. Even outside the campaign, she was ever in the limelight and indeed, in the mid- to late-1930s achieved her greatest renown. The press sought her out for interviews, covered her many speeches, and publicized her social life (figure 11). Reporters were taken with her "electric personality," and described her as "a volatile sort of person, high strung, and given to rapid gestures." She was, according to all, "charming" and radiant with an intensity "which makes itself felt as you approach her—like the electric impulses given off by a powerful battery."[79] She cut a dashing figure as she rushed around the capital city in her fashionable hats and flowy dresses. She was wildly popular. Radio stations in the mid-1930s broadcast dramatic reenactments of episodes from her life, and schools in Colorado displayed her photo next to those of President Roosevelt and famed aviator Charles Lindbergh.[80] In March 1935, the founder of the League for a Woman President named Roche as one of two women especially qualified to hold the nation's highest office. That same year an opinion poll named Roche "the most prominent woman business executive in the country."[81] First Lady Eleanor Roosevelt identified Roche as one of the women who "inspired" her, and, later that spring, Roche received the National Achievement Award from an honor society called Chi Omega. The annual award was given to a woman who contributed to the "culture of the world."[82] A year later, *American Women: The Official Who's Who among the Women of the Nation* named Roche one of America's ten most outstanding women.[83]

Roche was so highly regarded that she clocked several speaking engagements a month throughout her tenure at the Treasury. Sometimes, she spoke to all-female groups like the Women's International League for Peace and Freedom or the National Council of Catholic Women.[84] When, in March 1935, she spoke before a regional meeting of the Women's Division of the National Democratic Party, one analyst touted Roche's evening speech as "the high spot" of the meeting, and the indomitable politico Molly Dewson exclaimed, "You certainly were superb at Detroit; you just broke loose!"[85] Other times, she addressed mixed crowds like the National Democratic Club, where in April 1935 she was the only woman to speak before 2,000 people gathered for the organization's annual Jefferson Dinner. She spoke on the Chautauqua circuit along with Amelia Earhart and Upton Sinclair, before social scientists, and with Jewish charities.[86] By 1937, the New York State chair of the League of Women Voters, who had heard many speakers in her day, reported, "Of many women to whom I have listened, I believe that Frances Perkins, Josephine Roche and Dorothy Thompson are about at the top of the list."[87]

Roche's experience in the New Deal government highlighted its kinship to early twentieth-century progressivism. Although it represented a watershed in U.S. history in that it vastly expanded the role of the federal government in social and economic life, the New Deal's ideas, goals, and even many of its specific programs had long been on the progressive agenda. This same combination of continuity and innovation marked Roche's work in the field of health policy, where she would make another of her most significant marks and demonstrate her genius for administration.

CHAPTER 11

GENERATING A NATIONAL DEBATE ABOUT FEDERAL HEALTH POLICY, 1935–1939

Despite her many other roles, Josephine Roche's primary obligation in the New Deal government was oversight of health policy. She fulfilled that obligation in two ways. Within the Treasury Department, she took charge of the Public Health Service (PHS) at a moment of explosive growth, championing a vastly expanded mandate for the agency and building a more effective public health infrastructure in the states. Outside the Treasury, she spearheaded a campaign to elevate health care to the status of a "basic American right."[1] In the course of that campaign, Roche patched together a national health plan, which she used to generate a nationwide conversation about the role of the federal government in health care. Indeed, while other contributors were crucial to devising the health plan, Roche was the policymaker who took the issue of federal intervention in health care to the American public. She was responsible for generating an ongoing public conversation about governmental responsibility for America's health, a discussion that continued into the twenty-first century.

In her health work, Roche demonstrated her considerable administrative gifts and made good on her unique position as a trusted member of multiple reform networks. Indeed, many of the health programs of the New Deal could not have been implemented without the special combination of qualities and connections that Roche brought to the job.

Roche's leadership in the field of health policy emerged from her work with the Committee on Economic Security (CES) and her responsibility for the PHS. Title VIII of the Social Security Act appropriated 10 million new dollars for the PHS, effectively tripling the federal health budget.[2] As supervisor of the PHS and a coauthor of the social security bill, Roche became a significant spokesperson for that eye-popping increase. Two million of the new dollars were earmarked for beefing up staff and research at the PHS itself. The other eight million dollars were for states that needed help building local public health infrastructures.

Like other provisions of the bill, Title VIII perpetuated public policy goals originated in the Progressive Era. The first permanent, full-time county health agency was established in 1911 as part of the progressive impetus to involve local governments in the protection of health. By 1935, several hundred county health departments had been created, but the vast majority of counties had no effective health agency. About 2,000 of these underserved counties were in rural areas so poor they could not fund preventive measures against diseases like malaria, typhoid fever, pellagra, and tuberculosis—much less take on industrial hygiene, prenatal care, or cancer studies.[3]

As soon as the Social Security Act passed, Roche set up an administrative apparatus that allowed her to start disbursing the PHS's new money. The act gave her wide discretion in choosing which local initiatives to fund. Reflecting Roche's commitment to workers, a quarter of the states used some of their initial windfall for projects protecting workers from occupational injuries and illnesses and for research on hazards endemic to the industries in their regions. Roche was also eager to use some of her new funds to improve working conditions affecting the health of migratory workers and to experiment with new ways of ensuring health care in rural areas.[4] In some states, she funded laboratories for testing local water supplies and in others public vaccination programs to fight smallpox, typhoid, diphtheria, and rabies. Training programs for public health nurses and the creation of local health clinics were priorities in states with some public health work already in place.[5]

As she was allocating Social Security funds to the states, Roche was also expanding the mission of the PHS. She took a very broad view of the agency's charge. In 1936, she shaped and promoted legislation to enlarge the PHS's role in eradicating stream pollution, and she oversaw plans to build a new research facility for the National Institute of Health (NIH) in Bethesda, Maryland.[6] She organized the PHS's responses to both flood and drought emergencies in 1936 and 1937, arranging for delivery of vaccines to stricken areas, fresh water to desperate communities, and researchers to test for toxins in water, soil, and air.[7] She obtained money for cancer research at NIH, and advocated special projects for treatment of venereal diseases as well as cancer. She hired a new surgeon general in 1936 and persistently sought monies from other agencies for particular health initiatives in the states. She joined discussions of and provided resources for creation of health care co-ops among impoverished farmers in the Dakotas.[8]

Indeed, Roche was a point person for a movement to stretch the very meaning of public health not only to include measures to prevent disease but also to provide medical treatment. Even as a member of the CES, she supported expanding the purview of public health to include the actual provision of health care.[9] As she became more expert on health issues, she found that the kinds of preventive health measures to which public health officials had devoted themselves for decades—developing vaccines and instituting quarantines, draining swamps, and purifying water—had succeeded in reducing communicable diseases to such an extent that chronic illnesses like cancer and heart disease now killed more people than communicable diseases did, a stunning shift in human history. The biggest threats to public health now required treatment of individual patients. In light of the "unequal distribution of medical services," this new situation demanded in Roche's view that public health practitioners move into medical care itself, especially care of those who could not otherwise afford treatment.[10]

To many sectors of the medical profession, Roche's position was a declaration of war. The leadership of the American Medical Association (AMA) saw it as a threat to private doctors' incomes and autonomy, and they fought every perceived incursion into the treatment of disease with a ferocity that few elected officials had the courage to meet. Roche, however, was happy to strap on her armor. She did so as commander of a small but energetic fighting corps, the Interdepartmental Committee to Coordinate Health and Welfare Activities (Coordinating Committee).[11] Once the Social Security Act passed, Frances Perkins persuaded Roosevelt to create the Coordinating Committee to bring order to the proliferating health and welfare programs scattered throughout the New Deal government, and she recommended Roche to chair it.[12] Perkins knew Roche was an able administrator uniquely positioned to negotiate peace among competing agencies.

The Coordinating Committee was also, in the vaguest possible language, asked to follow through on proposals for health care that had been dropped from the original economic security bill.[13] Perkins and the president knew Roche was perfect for that duty not only because of her work with the PHS but also because she had consulted with the CES's technical committee on medical care after the economic security bill was finished and been the most vociferous advocate of amending the bill to include a cash benefit for those unemployed due to disability. She had approached President Roosevelt directly about that matter despite Perkins's objections, and so her passion on the subject of health care was well-known.[14]

Members of Roche's Coordinating Committee represented federal agencies involved in health or welfare programs. They included assistant secretaries of agriculture, interior, and labor.[15] Roche's good friend from Colorado, Oscar Chapman, represented the Department of the Interior, and Arthur Altmeyer initially spoke for Labor. Altmeyer was soon appointed director of the new Social Security Board, however, and Roche retained him as the board's spokesperson. She also added Aubrey Williams to represent the Works Progress Administration (WPA).[16]

Coordinating existing health and welfare programs took top priority. To begin, Roche had her staff simply identify government programs dealing with health and welfare. The results were daunting. In the area of maternal and child hygiene alone, her staff found programs in six different permanent agencies of the federal government. In the area of food and nutrition, they identified fifteen agencies with relevant programs, and the pattern held in other areas of welfare policy as well.[17] In each policy area, Roche named subcommittees to study the programs in their field and then recommend ways to eliminate duplication and fill gaps in service.

In short order, Roche began to develop working agreements among the various agencies.[18] The easiest seem to have involved the PHS and the Department of Agriculture.[19] The most contentious were those between the PHS and the Department of Labor. In areas like industrial hygiene and maternal and infant health, the PHS and Department of Labor had contended for authority since the early 1920s. The two fought for leadership on the same issues, and they had genuinely different priorities. As far as the Department of Labor was concerned, the health and safety of workers was not simply a matter of identifying workplace toxins but also of empowering workers against exploitive employers. State health departments had proven notoriously uninterested in industrial hygiene and were often antagonistic toward organized labor.[20] Moreover, policymakers in the Children's Bureau, also an agency in the Department of Labor, believed that maternal and child health was not just a matter of medical care as doctors in the PHS assumed but of health education and more equitable income distribution.[21]

So intense was the rivalry between the Children's Bureau and the PHS that Roche's appointment to oversee the PHS sparked ecstatic celebration at her former federal agency. "We in the Children's Bureau are almost bursting with pride and joy in your appointment. Nothing could be grander!" exclaimed the bureau's Katharine Lenroot on hearing of Roche's appointment to oversee the health service.[22] Rumors immediately circulated (even in the *Washington Post*) that Surgeon General Hugh Cumming, who had bitterly fought the Children's Bureau for years, would be shown the door as soon as Roche took over the PHS.[23] Sophonisba Breckinridge, a social scientist long active in the bureau's battle against the health service, wrote: "When I first heard the news [of your appointment], having a very mean streak in my heart, I did wish that I might have been present when Surgeon General Cumming was informed of the appointment, but I really have no malice, even toward the Surgeon General. I am only so grateful that there is in the government so ingenious, as well as public spirited, an official as the one who worked out this plan."[24] A former bureau physician, Anna Rude, wrote to Roche: "My feministic reminiscences of 1919–1923 make me smile at the irony of fate which puts you in charge of the USPH Service!"[25]

One of the signal achievements of Roche's life was overcoming these conflicts. Her success in this regard flowed at least in part from her habit of boundary crossing. Roche had never belonged exclusively to one reform community but had participated in both male and female reform networks, in both social science progressivism and labor progressivism, in both western and eastern progressive communities. Roche's immersion in multiple reform communities made her a perfect bridge between the women in the Children's Bureau and the men in public health.Indeed, intent on sowing cooperation where competition threatened common projects, Roche actually made a friend of Surgeon General Hugh Cumming. By the time Cumming left office in early 1936, he signed a photo for her, "with admiration, esteem, and real affection."[26] When Roche resigned from the Treasury in 1937, Cumming telegrammed from Paris: "Resignation distressing. Thanks for many courtesies."[27] That Roche was able simultaneously to establish a warm relationship with Cumming and retain the trust of women in the Children's Bureau attests to her gifts as an administrator and to the breadth of her progressive vision.

Moreover, her broad experience and varied connections allowed Roche to stay focused on the big picture of social justice and to help train her colleagues' eyes on that same sweeping canvas. In a meeting with representatives of the Department of Labor and the PHS in spring 1936, for instance, Roche opened with a passionate reminder of why those present were doing the work they did: "We are all after the same objective," she insisted, "to make our present technical information useful in protecting human lives." She urged both sides "to look at the situation from the angle of service to humanity rather than from the technical angles." She worried that "Lives are being sacrificed every day and hour because technical knowledge is not being used to serve people in the way that it should." It was her goal to develop a mechanism for putting expert knowledge in direct service of humanity.[28]

This she did. The agreements that Roche was able to negotiate in areas like industrial hygiene, public health nursing, and child hygiene resulted in such smooth relations among formerly contentious agencies that all involved were amazed. Roche reported to Morgenthau in spring 1936 that relationships between the Children's Bureau and the PHS were "so friendly and cooperative these days that it is fairly simple to get problems adjusted."[29] Perkins confirmed that relations between the PHS and the Division of Labor Standards "in protection of workers from health hazards in industry" were now "most friendly and the joint approach to problems is rendering a much greater service to the States than would otherwise be possible."[30] Workers in the field agreed. One state health official wrote to Roche early on: "It seems to be the consensus of opinion [among state health officers] that the happy relations and good cooperation now so in evidence between the Public Health Service and the Children's Bureau is largely due to your skilled management."[31] A public health nurse just back from professional meetings in fall 1936 reported, "I can't resist telling you my impression of the tremendous progress which has been made by the Public Health Service and the Children's Bureau in carrying out the health work of the Social Security Program." She had been very concerned about whether the two agencies could work together in the states, but she glowed: "It is a pleasure to report that . . . there is every indication of good understanding of the work of the two federal agencies and a happy relationship between the staffs of the Children's Bureau and Public Health Service. I am sure much of this is due to the work of the Interdepartmental Committee under your leadership."[32]

Once Roche had achieved this nearly miraculous integration of existing health and welfare programs, she turned the Coordinating Committee's attention to the more controversial issue of federal provision of medical care. The CES's technical committee on medical care had prepared the ground on the issue and in spring 1935 laid out a series of recommendations. They included two kinds of aid to bolster health security: replacement of wages lost due to illness and a program to provide actual health care.[33] Members of the CES referred to the two strands as "disability insurance" and "health insurance."[34] Having discovered that many areas of the country had no adequate medical facilities, the CES also expressed hope that, especially in rural areas, any national health plan would include federal monies for building community hospitals, clinics, and diagnostic facilities as well.[35]

Given that health insurance was in the 1930s largely untested even in the private sector, policymakers felt greater trepidation about it than about old-age insurance or unemployment compensation. Illness seemed so unpredictable that it was hard to imagine insuring against it. In response, Isidore Falk, a Ph.D. in public health who conducted much of the research for the CES technical committee on medical care, proposed to Roche in May 1935 that a health survey be designed simply to determine the incidence of illness in the country.[36] Before doing so, Roche conducted a smaller pilot project with a slightly different emphasis. With her own PHS funds and support from the private Milbank Memorial Fund, she commissioned studies of illness strictly among the unemployed. The results, released in September 1935, revealed that the rate of illness among "families hit hardest by the depression" was 56 percent higher than among "their more fortunate neighbors." Roche concluded that poverty and illness were integrally related and that the administration must act fast to "conserve one of our most valued national resources—the health and vitality of our people."[37]

To make the strongest possible case for a comprehensive federal health program, Roche built on her initial study by organizing the National Health Inventory, to that point the largest survey ever of the nation's health. The effort put social science progressivism to work on a massive scale. Drawing over $3 million from the WPA, Roche hired 5,000 people as canvassers. These interviewers went door to door in eighty-six communities and ultimately interviewed 865,000 families with nearly three million members. The Census Bureau helped Roche determine which communities were representative of national trends, and, at each home, interviewers asked a multitude of questions: was anyone in the household currently sick; had anyone had been sick in the last twelve months; had work time been lost to illness; and did anyone suffer a chronic condition. She studied the availability of medical facilities in various parts of the country and tried to determine how many Americans were blind or deaf, how many had asthma, arthritis, or rheumatism.[38] To increase cooperation with the health inventory, Roche hit the airwaves and print media, explaining the purpose of her canvass and urging potential interviewees to welcome her scouts.[39] As the field work wound down in summer 1936, about a thousand workers in Detroit—most of them women—began hand-tabulating results.[40]

In the midst of her historic survey, Roche faced her most serious conflict at the Treasury. Early in 1936, Henry Morgenthau began urging President Roosevelt to decrease federal spending on jobs programs. Roche argued herself blue in the face against the proposition. In meetings at the Treasury, Roche insisted that work relief programs should not be cut but increased because of the "desperate need for work of hundreds of thousands who are not on relief, but on the margin."[41] Morgenthau, convinced the private sector could pick up the slack, would have none of it and convinced the president to cut spending in fiscal 1937.[42]

The health survey was affected almost immediately. In view of impending cuts in WPA funding, early in 1937 Harry Hopkins issued pink slips to seventy of the women tabulating results from Roche's survey. His staff had determined that these particular workers should be eligible for benefits from Social Security's Aid to Dependent Children program and so should not go hungry if laid off. The women, however, saw this move as a demotion from self-supporting worker to recipient of charity. They resisted. Remarkably, they won the support of their sister workers and led a strike to protest their layoffs. Roche took up their cause, conducting negotiations by phone through a weekend in March. At the end of it, Hopkins rescinded the pink slips, and the women returned to work.[43] It was a glorious victory for these particular women, but it did not presage a future of job security for those in publicly funded jobs or even those working on the health survey. By summer 1937, the devastating effects of the budget cuts were fully in evidence. Roche reported to Morgenthau that, when she finally had to start laying off people from the health survey, two people committed suicide. At that point, she warned him that with the WPA forced to cut so many jobs, "it's hard on people" and she thought he ought to know "there could be publicity."[44]

The results of government cutbacks extended well beyond Roche's health survey. By fall 1937, they produced what came to be called the Roosevelt Recession, which threw four million workers out of their jobs—a dramatic increase in unemployment after steady declines in joblessness during the president's first term. Slashing federal spending also decreased industrial production by 40 percent, sent the stock market tumbling, and depressed corporate profits. The progress of organized labor was temporarily halted by the resurgence of unemployment, and Roosevelt's relationship with the CIO was strained.[45]

Given her exasperation with Morgenthau and disappointment that Roosevelt would heed his advice, Roche may not have been entirely disappointed when, in fall 1937, Rocky Mountain Fuel (RMF) unexpectedly demanded her attention. J. Paul Peabody, the man serving as president of her coal company, suddenly died, and Roche decided she must return to Denver to run the company.[46] President Roosevelt and Morgenthau urged her to make her separation from the Treasury only temporary, and they kept her job open, hoping she would return.[47] But Roche had had enough of Morgenthau, and would never return to the Treasury.

When news got out that Roche was leaving the Treasury, sorrowful letters flooded her office. Official regrets came from the likes of Harold Ickes, Frances Perkins, and Mary McLeod Bethune, the latter writing: "It just grieves me to know that you are [going] away."[48] Eleanor Roosevelt hoped that Roche would return soon, "for the country certainly needs you."[49] Private citizens registered their dismay.[50] The public health community expressed anxiety. When Michael Davis, chair of the Committee on Research in Medical Economics, heard of her resignation, he wrote: "Your leaving Washington at this time represents a public loss which hits hard the people who are interested in public health and medical services in this country. Your leadership in shaping policies, your support of officials who could not otherwise resist pressures, your skill in developing cooperation where formerly isolationism and antagonism existed, have brought the most important advances in the public health and medical programs of the federal government that this generation has known."[51]

Women in the Treasury were disconsolate. "I can't believe the three grand years of work together by the Treasury columns are really over," lamented her assistant, Mary Switzer. "Three golden years—for me—To have . . . the immeasurable opportunity of being touched by your mind— guided by your true and undeviating standards is to have an immortal influence that will never leave me."[52] Another woman in the Treasury drew a weeping stick figure on a farewell note to Roche and labeled the figure "Washington."[53]

On leaving the Treasury, Roche did not relinquish the chair of the Coordinating Committee or her work with the National Youth Administration. The health survey had given her precisely the evidence she needed to make the case for a comprehensive national health program, and she wanted to push that project into its next phase. During the summer of 1937, Roche had consulted with various administration officials about the possible shape of such a plan and a strategy for winning legislation to put it into operation. She believed that buy-in from the Social Security Board, the PHS, and the Children's Bureau was the crucial first step to creating a successful health program.[54] Consequently, she lodged responsibility for drafting legislation in the medical care subcommittee of her Coordinating Committee. All interested bureaus were represented there, with the Children's Bureau representative in the chair. In September 1937, just after tendering her letter of resignation from the Treasury, Roche called a meeting of the subcommittee to bring its members into a conversation about the role that the federal government should play in sustaining Americans' health. At its close, Roche charged the subcommittee to "formulate plans for a national medical care program."[55]

In the discussions that followed, Roche pushed the subcommittee for a "comprehensive program." That goal required overcoming the group's initial caution. Some members argued that the first step should be a plan that would reach only those already enrolled in government relief programs. The conservative approach made sense for several reasons. First, the federal government had a bit of experience with such a plan, as the Federal Emergency Relief Administration had provided health care to some of its beneficiaries in 1933 and 1934. Second, doctors might object less if the plan helped only those who could not afford health care otherwise.[56] Caution was also warranted by the fact that health insurance was so new-fangled that no one was clear exactly how or whether it would work. And finally, many state health officers explicitly opposed "a program of general medical care administered by themselves."[57] They could not fathom adding yet another major responsibility to their teetering stacks of obligation. Despite the objections, Roche argued that any national health program must provide at least for all those she called "medically indigent," a category that included not just those already on some sort of government relief but also Americans who were able to provide their own housing, food, and clothing but could not afford health care, especially in the event of a long illness or major surgery.[58] Her health survey suggested that the lowest percentage of Americans to be reached by such a plan would be about one-third of the population.[59] Some commentators thought Roche's minimum hardly "comprehensive," but among federal policymakers, it was an ambitious goal.

Once she had the subcommittee working toward a plan, Roche reached out to the American public. Even as she packed up her office to leave the Treasury, she bombarded mass audiences with the results of her health survey. In speeches delivered all over the country and articles for the mass media, she reiterated her findings: "The greatest single cause of death in the United States is poverty." Medical science had made breakthroughs that allowed it to prevent previously unavoidable diseases and to cure previously incurable illnesses. But these "medical miracles" were not available to many Americans because they simply could not afford them. Moreover, the poorer people were, the more they needed medical services. Roche's data showed that poorer Americans were sick more often and longer than Americans with higher incomes and that they were the least likely to have access to medical care. Indeed, the poorer you were, the more likely you were to die of diseases that wealthier people routinely weathered.[60] Illness was one of the most common causes of economic insecurity just as poverty was a common precondition for illness.[61]

In December 1937, Roche's medical subcommittee finalized its plan. The group announced that the goal of their proposal was to make "equal opportunity for health a basic American right."[62] Least controversial, the plan recommended disability insurance to replace wages during temporary illness or permanent disability, federal money for building and maintaining community hospitals, and expansion of PHS and maternity and infancy programs already in the Social Security Act. Riskier, it proposed federal grants-in-aid to the states to provide programs of medical care either through insurance schemes, public medical services, or some combination of the two. The proposal permitted tremendous variation among the states, something Roche generally rejected in federal social programs but was willing to accept in this area of so little experience. She imagined that after accumulating some know-how through experimentation in the states, policymakers would learn how best to proceed, and more prescriptive policy might follow. To that end, the plan suggested continuing consideration of a more general health care program for the full citizenry, which might include compulsory health insurance and/or a program of public health services funded by general revenues.[63]

Despite its modesty, Roche knew the plan would generate widespread controversy. She could count on opposition from the politically powerful AMA, and she was sure fiscal conservatives and even moderates would blanch at the price tag, which she estimated would grow to $850 million per year (spread among federal, state, and local governments). Given that the PHS's entire annual budget was between $15 and $20 million at the time, this new set of expenditures seemed astronomical.[64]

Roche had a plan for building support. Once she had the committee's report in hand, she took it to the president and asked if the Coordinating Committee could introduce its proposal through a national health conference. Her idea was to bring together representatives of various interests—agriculture, labor, business, civic associations, medicine, social welfare—to discuss each aspect of the proposal. In advance of the conference, only invited participants would see the specific recommendations. The general public would be learning just Roche's data on the *need* for federal aid for health care. Roche wanted to save full disclosure of the plan—and especially its cost—for the time of the conference itself—that is, only after she had fully established the need for federal intervention. Roosevelt agreed to the convention.[65]

With a health plan completed, the president on board, and the way forward mapped out, Roche asked to be released from chairing the Coordinating Committee. By early 1938, RMF was in enough financial turmoil to require her full attention, and her additional responsibilities in Washington stretched her too thin. Roosevelt, however, refused her resignation. He may have wanted to keep Roche connected to the administration because of her alliance with the CIO, which, especially because of the recession caused by his reduction of spending in 1937, was wary of him. Losing Roche would corrode one of his links to a vital segment of the labor movement.[66] Or maybe the president honestly wanted to keep alive the possibility of enacting a major health plan. Roche was certainly the best bet to lead that initiative. Whatever his motive, the president kept Roche in the New Deal government for another year. She reluctantly agreed to remain at the helm of the Coordinating Committee through the National Health Conference.[67]

Despite her ambivalence, Roche organized the conference with energy, perspicacity, and a commitment to democratic policymaking. Indeed, she took the issue of federal aid to health care through the process envisioned by the Progressive Service in 1913 and 1914: an issue of common concern had been identified and a policy proposed. Now, the broadest possible public would be brought into the discussion to accept, reject, replace, or modify the recommendations. The conference would help citizens sift through the problems involved and possibilities for resolution by bringing together specially interested parties—providers and consumers of health care—to share their views and debate them in full public view. Roche kept the conference small enough, she hoped, for a free and wide-ranging exchange of ideas, anticipating that the delegates would identify common ground and show her committee where the sticking points were. From this process might emerge a refined plan with enough support among the public and special interests to survive the legislative obstacle course that lay ahead.[68]

In choosing delegates for the conference, Roche operated on the assumption that airing the full range of opinion was best for the cause. She recruited representatives of various economic, professional, and regional interests and those with genuinely varied views on health care and government activism. Representatives of the AMA appeared, as did those from organized labor. The Chamber of Commerce and AT&T sent delegates, as did medical reformers. Women's groups like the League of Women Voters, the Women's Trade Union League, and the National Council of Jewish Women were represented, as was the National Association for the Advancement of Colored People (NAACP) and the national association of black doctors. Surgeons attended, and government bureaucrats came. Radio executives and the American Legion sent delegates. Representatives of farmers, the public health profession, and medical schools participated.[69]

On a hot and humid July 18, 1938, Roche called to order 176 official delegates at Washington's mercifully air-conditioned Mayflower Hotel.[70] She acknowledged the difficulties in achieving health security for all Americans, but proclaimed, "we may take courage from the advances on other front lines of attack on our economic and social inequalities." The New Deal had established "the principle that certain insecurities which individuals alone are powerless to withstand must be met through public action" and provided a hopeful basis on which to proceed.[71] She outlined the intense experience ahead. All conferees attended every session over a three-day period. The first day was devoted primarily to demonstrating the deficiencies in the existing system of health care. The second day focused on the proposals of the Coordinating Committee.[72] Each session addressed one or two recommendations, usually explained by a member of the Coordinating Committee, and then several respondents provided formal commentary before the floor was thrown open to discussion. As evidence for the genuinely democratic structure of the conference, Roche invited Dr. Olin West, secretary of the AMA and a ferocious opponent of the health plan, to return to the podium at the close of the second day to give his appraisal of the day's discussion. West had spoken with passion the first day of the conference, and Roche knew he would oppose the recommendations put forward the second day, but she gave West the fullest possible opportunity to articulate his objections.[73]

In general, conferees did not dispute the evidence for deficiencies in the nation's health care. Serious conflicts emerged over the proper response to those deficiencies. The leadership of the AMA fundamentally opposed any kind of health insurance or centralized authority over medicine, warning that any insurance system or federal authority would eventually threaten the personal relationship between doctor and patient—not to mention the incomes of physicians. Used to working as individual practitioners with individual patients, these doctors resisted any scheme that would embed them in a bureaucracy or even in group practices with other doctors. Preserving doctors' autonomy and incomes was the first priority of the leadership of the AMA. Hospital administrators—themselves often doctors—objected to any plan that would produce competition with their institutions. For them, the proposed aid to communities for building hospitals sent up red flags.[74]

Representatives of medical consumers offered dramatic evidence of need for federal aid, sometimes reviled the doctors, and other times offered comprehensive alternatives to the Coordinating Committee's plan. Florence Greenberg, activist in Chicago's Steel Workers Organizing Committee, gave perhaps the most riveting testimony. "I speak as the representative of the organized wives of workers," she began. "My people are asking that our government take health from the list of luxuries to be bought only by money and add it to the list of 'inalienable rights' of every citizen." Greenberg then narrated real-life stories of working-class illness. They included, "The Mexican family, whose little girl got double pneumonia twice, and finally died of an abscessed lung after 3 years of suffering." The girl had left a hospital "because the relief authorities would not pay for her care any more." In response to such horrors, Greenberg brought with her a 12-point health program that included improved housing, compulsory health insurance, and the "concentration of medical care in people's health centers."[75] Her proposals far exceeded the vision of Roche's Coordinating Committee.

Indeed, representatives of labor generally pushed for a more liberal program. Lee Pressman, by this time general counsel for the CIO, objected to reliance on state governments to organize health care, insisting that only a fully federal system of health insurance supported by progressive taxation would provide health care to all on an equal basis.[76] Even William Green, president of the AFL, advocated a compulsory plan of government-administered health insurance for all families earning between $1,000 and $5,000 a year, which he suggested could be organized through the workmen's compensation programs already active in the states.[77]

When Roche closed the conference on July 20, she was upbeat. She concluded that no one disputed the need for expanding access to health care. Furthermore, no one seemed to object to increased expenditures for public health and maternal and infant health measures, building hospitals in areas that were demonstrably underserved, or funding medical care for those who were simply too poor to buy health care at all. Little criticism splattered the proposal to replace wages lost due to disability. Differences flared mainly over whether and how government should be involved in providing health care for families who might be able to pay for routine health care but would be bankrupted by a long-term illness or major surgery. And, even there, she insisted, the objections to government involvement seemed to stem from fears of interference in the doctor-patient relationship, anxiety about maintaining the quality of care, and eagerness to allow for local and regional differences, all of which the proposals of the Coordinating Committee addressed. By placing responsibility for actual care in state governments, local and regional differences would be accommodated, and none of the proposals directly intervened in the relationship between doctors and patients.[78] Roche invited delegates to continued conversation as her committee stitched together its final proposals for Congress.

The immediate response of delegates to the conference was overwhelmingly favorable. Older progressive and founding mother of industrial medicine Alice Hamilton enthused: "It was really, all in all, the very best meeting of its kind that I have ever attended and I was not the only one to feel this way. You did not over-load your program, you left ample time for discussion from the floor."[79] Mary Dublin, a younger progressive representing the National Consumers' League, concurred, "The reports were unique for clarity and forceful presentation of undeniable need. The meetings moved with magnificent dispatch and provided for truly democratic representation of opinion."[80] Dr. Frederic Besley from the American College of Surgeons thanked Roche for inviting him to the conference. "The arrangement of the program and the excellent manner in which you gave every faction an opportunity for an expression of opinion was unusually excellent," he observed before going on to express his "firm conviction that the rank and file of the medical profession will cooperate wholeheartedly in any such program as you are proposing, which will make for better care of the patient whose health welfare is paramount and transcends every other consideration."[81] Dr. John Peters, a New Haven doctor rebellious against the AMA leadership, lauded the conference as "the most impressive and inspiring meeting I have ever attended. . . . I feel that this is a magnificent attempt to analyze the situation of medical care and to synthesize a solution on the basis of fact."[82] Robert Neff, administrator of the University Hospitals at the State University of Iowa, claimed, "It was an epoch making event and I believe the most significant affair which has ever taken place in the field of public health and medical care."[83] Industrialist Charles Taussig agreed that Roche had done "a swell job" of organizing the conference.[84] Even Emma Puschner, representing the American Legion, agreed that the conference allowed "freedom of expression from all points of view."[85]

The general public was genuinely engaged in the debate. During the conference, one delegate from a middle-class women's organization described public interest as "at white heat."[86] Polls bore her out. They showed that the majority of U.S. voters approved higher taxes to provide health care to those who could not provide it for themselves.[87] Press coverage was widespread, and, after the conference, Roche was swamped with requests to speak all over the country—from Baton Rouge to Iowa City; from Buffalo to Nashville; from Beckley, West Virginia, to Seattle.[88] When the Coordinating Committee published a summary of the health conference, it was overwhelmed by orders for the publication.[89] And the National Health Conference unquestionably sparked local and union organizing on health care issues all over the country.[90] Roche had generated a vital public conversation about governmental responsibility for America's health.

After several months of follow-up, which included meetings with nineteen groups wishing for further input, Roche's Coordinating Committee sent its recommendations to the president.[91] They advocated a phased-in program. As Roche explained, the proposal recommended a ten-year implementation schedule during which "we shall learn by doing."[92] The proposals also left lots of leeway for those drafting the final legislation. The first recommendation was for expansion of the public health services and maternal and child health programs supported in the Social Security Act. The second was for building hospitals in areas demonstrably underserved. The next recommendation was for grants-in-aid to the states to provide medical services to whomever they chose and by whatever method they chose, but with the clearly expressed hope that aid would extend not only to the indigent but also to "moderate income groups." The final recommendation was for insurance to cover a portion of wages lost during temporary or permanent disability. In her memo to the president requesting his support, Roche suggested that the program would cost the federal government $65 million the first year and at its peak might cost the federal government about $450 million per year, figures that flipped the wigs of most commentators.[93]

The president assured Roche that he would submit the report to Congress. How hard he would press for action, however, was not clear. The health plan, which seemed to progressives a logical extension of the New Deal's commitment to diminishing inequality, came under consideration at an unpropitious moment. Not only had the 1938 elections returned a more conservative legislature to Capitol Hill but also the president was increasingly focused on the possibility of war in both Asia and Europe. He did not intend to spend precious political capital or economic resources on expanding the New Deal when he believed that all resources might soon be required to defend U.S. interests against Germany's encroachments in the Atlantic or Japan's in the Pacific. He did send Roche's recommendations to Congress in January 1939 with a firm statement as to the importance of the issues involved, but rumors whispered that the president wanted Congress "to handle the bill entirely." He would go along if Congress took the lead, but he did not intend to expend his own resources on the legislation.[94]

Roche became bracingly aware of the president's detachment when she attempted to meet with him as her committee's recommendations reached his desk. She made a trip to Washington in December 1938 specifically to talk with him and then described the experience as "one long postponement of my appointment with the President." During her wait, she suffered "increasing apprehension that he wasn't going to do anything about our national health program. I discovered," she explained vaguely, "all sorts of forces had been at work (that's what happens when you aren't on the spot all the time)—so I had to do some quick planning and acting, which means in Washington all sorts of unpleasant things."[95]

Especially given the president's reserve, Roche was deeply grateful when Senator Robert Wagner took an interest in the health plan.[96] In February 1939, Wagner submitted legislation that embodied many of the committee's proposals but significantly watered them down.[97] Roche publicly expressed no disappointment. Any move forward might at least establish the principle of federal responsibility for health care and, in doing so, open the way to fuller intervention in the future. Indeed, even as Wagner drew up his bill, Roche was consulting with Secretary of the Interior Harold Ickes about the possibility of using monies from his Public Works Administration to build some of the hospitals contemplated in her report.[98] She was willing to tap every resource that might fund even a piece of the plan. On May 4, 1939, she testified on behalf of Wagner's legislation in the Senate, refraining from complaint about the bill's failure to embody the full recommendations—modest as she believed them to be—of her committee.[99]

On that same day, Roche finally succeeded in resigning from the Coordinating Committee. Rocky Mountain Fuel's truly desperate situation motivated her, but so did hopes for a more effective platform from which to pursue not only her health plan but also other expansions of the New Deal program.[100] Roche could not know at the time of this resignation that it portended a much bumpier relationship with the Roosevelt administration than she had previously enjoyed.

CHAPTER 12

UNMOORED DURING WARTIME, 1939–1945

J osephine Roche's new difficulties with Franklin D. Roosevelt were created by World War II. As during World War I, U.S. involvement in this new global conflict funneled fresh resources to both progressives and their opponents, leaving the outcome of their competition to the postwar period. Roche's experience provided glimpses of both the war's progressive and conservative tendencies as well as the dilemmas generated within progressive souls. Difficulties at Rocky Mountain Fuel (RMF), however, gave World War II an even more discouraging cast for Roche than World War I had. Indeed, miseries fueled by her coal company eroded Roche's connection to the Democratic Party and weakened her confidence in government as an ally in the cause of diminishing inequality. These losses set Roche slightly out of sync with the larger progressive movement and left her by war's end institutionally unmoored.

The institutional breaks began after a significant personal loss. In January 1939, Senator Edward Costigan died. Costigan had been Roche's political touchstone and personal friend, a mentor who encouraged her every wild progressive experiment, whether it was running a coal company or mounting a gubernatorial campaign. All through the 1930s, she credited Costigan with "much of the inspiration" for her mission in life.[1] To be at his bedside when he died, she raced back to Denver from a trip to the East Coast and arrived just in time. "It seems cruelly ironical that after three years of always being near, I should on this last trip have reached home only fifteen minutes before the end," she wrote to Read Lewis. "But I am thankful for those minutes and for the years of unbelievably rare and wonderful friendship and inspiration . . . they are the realities which will always burn."[2]

Mabel Costigan, ten years Roche's senior and a constant presence since Roche's college days, remained Roche's best friend, and after Edward Costigan's death, she and Roche created a quasi-family that included Roche's personal assistant Mildred Lea and Beatrice Owens, the nurse who cared for Senator Costigan in his final years. Bea's husband, Ted, and eventually the Owens's children were members of the fictive kin group as well.[3] In fact, Roche was godmother to Bea's son, William. Whenever Roche was in the Mile-High City during the early 1940s, she visited the child she called "my boy," dined with him and his parents, and developed a lifelong attachment to them. Although Roche always lived alone, she did not want for intimate attachments.[4]

As was her pattern, however, Roche did not seek solace so much in personal relationships as she did in work. "It has probably been fortunate," she observed only days after Costigan's death, "that I have been exceptionally overwhelmed with company matters which have left me little time to think or feel.... Work having dominated me so long, continues to bring an automatic response from me under even these circumstances."[5]

Matters at RMF were indeed overwhelming. When Roche resumed control late in 1937, the company was in bad shape. Because of the depressed economy and competition from oil and gas, production at RMF fell by nearly half between the late 1920s and late 1930s.[6] Moreover, taxes increased, and RMF's mines needed substantial improvements.[7] Finding money for new equipment was especially challenging. Although RMF usually made an operating profit in the 1930s, it consistently required loans to pay interest on the bonds issued before Roche took the wheel. As in 1931, she sometimes obtained those loans secretly from the United Mine Workers of America (UMW), the later loans secured with company stock. When equipment failures shut down one of the company's most productive mines in 1938 and coal markets declined precipitously, Roche faced bankruptcy if she could not find additional loans or renegotiate the terms of her debt to bondholders.[8]

She tried both. To purchase urgently needed equipment, Roche acquired a loan from the Reconstruction Finance Corporation (RFC), a federal agency created to loan money to otherwise stable businesses unable to obtain credit because of the economic downturn.[9] She then moved to restructure her debt. In February 1939, she asked her creditors to accept a lower interest rate and later maturity date on her bonds. The majority accepted immediately.[10] In addition, Roche took steps to mechanize more fully.[11] Since John L. Lewis agreed that only mechanization would assure the long-term profitability of a firm in which his union now held a significant interest, he proposed to loan Roche $100,000 if she hired Coal Mine Management (CMM) to oversee the mechanization process and initiate a major sales campaign. Roche gratefully consented, and CMM signed on to run RMF for five years. The company soon paid off the RFC loan.[12]

Roche was relieved to relinquish the daily operation of RMF, especially as she had reason to hope for a new job in Washington. In spring 1939, national newspapers were touting her as the most likely candidate to head the new Federal Security Agency (FSA), recently created to unite the federal government's health and welfare activities in one unit.[13] The FSA was part of a larger federal reorganization intended to streamline the new version of government born from the New Deal. It gave permanent administrative homes to the many independent units created in the 1930s and shifted some divisions from existing departments into more appropriate agencies. Into the new FSA moved New Deal creations like the Social Security Board, National Youth Administration (NYA), and Civilian Conservation Corps. From older departments came the Public Health Service (PHS), Office of Education, and U.S. Employment Service.[14]

Roche was the most qualified candidate to lead the FSA. She had with great results already overseen the PHS and the NYA, helped to create the Social Security Board, and worked closely with Arthur Altmeyer to get the board up and running. She served on the advisory board for the U.S. Employment Service. She had proven her administrative acumen, was loyal to the New Deal, and had strong supporters, most especially the unions affiliated with the Congress of Industrial Organizations (CIO).[15] The *Washington Post* was so convinced of her eventual appointment that it actually announced on June 14: "Josephine Roche Reported Offered Welfare Post."[16]

FDR stunned even his closest associates when instead of appointing Roche he named machine politician, Paul McNutt, to the position. McNutt had no experience in Washington and had been a corrupt, authoritarian, and anti-labor governor of Indiana.[17] When word got out that the president was considering the McNutt appointment, Frances Perkins and Attorney General Frank Murphy begged him not to follow through.[18] Henry Morgenthau later said that neither he nor Harry Hopkins could understand McNutt's appointment, and Washington insider Lowell Mellett reported, "I haven't heard of anybody that does understand it."[19]

Many factors prevented Roche's appointment to the FSA, but two major reasons stood out.[20] First, as the president explained to Secretary of the Interior Harold Ickes, Roche was "too close to John L. Lewis" for her to head the FSA.[21] The open split between the CIO and the American Federation of Labor (AFL) in 1938 forced the president to walk a tightrope between the rival factions in the labor movement. Roche's close association with the CIO made her appointment dicey in that regard. Even more important though, the president wanted at the FSA someone who would accept no increases in social spending while the military budget grew. With Adolf Hitler occupying Czechoslovakia and threatening Poland and with Japan an ongoing anxiety, the president's priorities had by summer 1939 shifted from social welfare to war planning. The fascist threat, to Roosevelt's mind, demanded substantial increases in U.S. military might with a concomitant lull in expanding domestic programs.[22] He confided to his closest associates, "I am sick and tired of having a lot of long-haired people around here who want a billion dollars for schools, a billion dollars for Public Health." He needed an administrator at FSA who would, he said, "tell Aubrey Williams [at the NYA] that just because a boy wants to go to college is no reason he should finance it."[23] At the moment of this declaration, Roche remained chair of the NYA's executive committee and would not have put the brakes on Aubrey Williams. She was, moreover, the very person asking for millions of new dollars for public health. She would have fought tooth and nail for more resources to battle inequality, and she would have opposed military spending. Not so McNutt. Since serving in World War I, McNutt had been a member— even National Commander—of the American Legion, which testified annually on behalf of increasing the military budget.[24] FDR could rest assured that his new lieutenant at FSA would not badger him for resources to diminish inequality at home when he wanted the money to fight enemies abroad.

McNutt's appointment was announced on July 11, 1939, and although Roche kept her own counsel about the decision, other progressives were not so restrained. Their interpretation of McNutt's appointment expressed their sense of dimming prospects for the progressive project more generally. Harold Ickes reported that progressives were trying "to put a good face on the matter, but I can't take it this way myself."[25] Attorney General Frank Murphy agreed that "the liberal cause had fallen on difficult, if not evil, days."[26]

They were not alone. Roche struggled against the same sense of despair in the National Consumers' League (NCL), an organization central to the struggle for economic justice since its founding in 1899. By the 1930s, the NCL had a long history of lobbying for minimum wage and maximum hours laws, factory safety measures, and other progressive policies. The NCL was extremely interested in Roche's health plan and in 1938 elected her its first woman president. She accepted the position enthusiastically, hoping to work with the NCL to establish "for all our people the social and industrial democracy on which our general welfare and progress depend."[27]

Especially after the McNutt appointment, Roche made the NCL a priority, hoping it might provide a base from which to protect the New Deal and press for its expansion. She led the group first in opposing attempts by a new and more conservative Congress to weaken the Wagner and the Fair Labor Standards acts. The assaults were so powerful that the NCL's young general secretary, Mary Dublin, mourned in August 1939, "Things these days are too disheartening to talk about. I spent last week in Washington fighting against the destruction of the Wages and Hours Law and am leaving in a few hours to make one last and, I know, futile attempt."[28] Despite her own disappointments, Roche successfully bucked up her younger protégé and their organization. In the fall, Dublin reported that Roche had been, "a tremendous source of inspiration and encouragement" and that she had fueled a "much more cooperative" spirit on the NCL board, where she "built the fires again" from embers that had nearly gone cold.[29] What's more, the Fair Labor Standards Act and Wagner Act were for the moment successfully defended.[30]

One of the reasons that Dublin and Roche hit it off so famously was that Dublin rallied to the cause of Roche's health plan.[31] Roche had no doubt hoped to lead the charge for health care legislation from the director's office at the FSA, but when that fell through, she searched for an alternative headquarters. In summer 1939, she, Dublin, and a small group of allies agreed that the NCL was a logical coordinator for their campaign to build interest in the health program and press for passage.[32] In September, Roche volunteered to chair the effort if the NCL would host it. Roche and Dublin assured the NCL board that they could raise money for the campaign independent of the league's budget.[33]

The board's response was another of 1939's disappointments. Although members supported the health plan, the NCL was on the ropes financially and desperate to protect and, if possible, strengthen the minimum wage and maximum hours law as well as the Wagner Act.[34] Feeling those prized measures still under siege, the board feared taking on additional projects and asked Roche to wait on the health bill.[35] Roche more graciously accepted the postponement than Dublin, who, in the weeks following, drummed up support for the health plan in meetings with state chapters and used that support to keep the issue alive at the organization's next annual convention.[36]

At the convention, Roche demonstrated the persisting breadth of her progressive vision and her continuing commitment to diminishing inequalities of both wealth and power. In her presidential address, she envisioned the health bill as one small part of a grander program of progressive social reconstruction for which the New Deal had only laid a foundation. Although she judged New Deal legislation "sound and progressive," it was just the meagerest beginning of realizing democracy in the daily life of American citizens. To progress toward that goal, Roche urged passage of Senator Wagner's health bill and the extension of Social

Security's benefits to all excluded groups. She then zeroed in on protecting industrial democracy. For Roche, nourishing the independent organization of workers remained on par with progressive public policy in achieving social justice. One reason, she explained, was that industrial democracy undergirded economic stability by more evenly distributing wealth: "In economic terms it means collective bargaining, fair industrial relationships, the broadening of purchasing power on which the nation's prosperity depends." A lesser understood but equally important aspect of industrial democracy was its necessity to political democracy. Restating the tenets of labor progressivism, she declared, "Only as men and women of labor acquire a secure status as citizens of industry can they meet effectively their responsibilities and exercise their rights as citizens of a self-governing political democracy."

Even more than the crying need for health care, Roche was alarmed by escalating attacks on industrial democracy. A committee of the U.S. Senate, operating since 1936, had uncovered evidence of employers' massive and often violent repression of workers' speech, assembly, and organization, and Roche deplored this "denial of civil liberties." These practices, she claimed, "strike at and destroy the most valuable asset of our body politic—a free thinking, independent electorate." Only as industrial democracy triumphed, she argued, would "all the resources of our citizenship" be "released and made available for wise and courageous use in the solution of the economic and social problems which still confront us."[37] An expanding economic democracy depended, to Roche's mind, on a vital political democracy. Inequalities of wealth and power were interlaced and required a broad range of remedies. Roche's long-standing progressive agenda was fully intact.

Although Roche was frustrated by the modesty of New Deal accomplishments, she remained firmly attached to the New Deal government. In fact, by December 1939, she was chair of a resurrected Interdepartmental Committee to Coordinate Health and Welfare Activities (Coordinating Committee).[38] On the face of it, the president's decision to reactivate the Coordinating Committee made no sense at all. The FSA should have made the committee redundant. However, after war broke out in Europe in September 1939, FDR's desire for an unprecedented third presidential term strengthened. Paul McNutt also had aspirations to the White House, and FDR did not want McNutt to win any backers through leadership on health care.[39] Moreover, FDR hoped for support from the CIO and the West, two constituencies potentially alienated when he passed over Roche to head the FSA.[40] To compensate, the shrewd politician revived the Coordinating Committee, appointed Roche to chair it, and promised support for a small portion of Roche's health plan—federal aid to community hospitals.

Roche had bigger dreams for the Coordinating Committee. FDR offered her its chair only two weeks after the NCL board declined to sponsor a movement for her health plan.[41] Chairing the Coordinating Committee gave her a platform from which to press for the entire plan as women's groups, including the League of Women Shoppers, and organized labor assured her they awaited her leadership.[42] By mid-December, she was conferring with committee members and devising a bill for community hospitals.[43] She also began coordinating the health and welfare activities still scattered beyond the FSA and initiated a plan for aid to migrant labor.[44]

Reactivating the Coordinating Committee while also managing RMF proved quite a juggling act. During 1940, Roche's commuting life became so extreme that she was in the air nearly as much as on the ground. When in the capital, she lived at the Carlton Hotel, a 1920s establishment only two blocks north of the White House, kept appointments in the hotel lobby, and used "a capacious handbag for her office."[45] Regardless of age or stature, Roche traveled light, her home, the progressive cause itself. She remained a peripatetic reformer.

Crises at RMF diluted Roche's effectiveness in Washington. In 1940, the company needed additional funds to pay off loans and taxes as well as to continue the modernization project that CMM had begun. To those ends, Roche applied in February for a second loan from the RFC.[46] Despite FDR's request for "sympathetic consideration" of her application, however, the RFC found the company on such shaky ground that it rejected her appeal.[47] Roche desperately hoped to avoid bankruptcy and strategized ways to convince the RFC to reconsider her application. Before the issue could be resolved, though, some of Roche's attention turned to the upcoming presidential election, and eventually, the loan and election became dramatically entwined.

Roche's frustrations with FDR did nothing to diminish her standing as a leading light within the Democratic Party. As such, she participated fully in the activities of Democratic women when they geared up for another presidential election. In late 1939, she spoke before large Democratic gatherings in the West, and in May 1940 joined other Democratic women for a three-day institute in Washington.[48] Hailed at the latter gathering as one of the "Democratic party celebrities," Roche argued that what women wanted most on the Democratic platform was a commitment to peace and an end to unemployment.[49] She also urged expansion of Social Security to currently excluded groups, passage of the health plan, and protections of civil liberties.[50]

Party leaders hoped for Roche's full attention during the presidential campaign. Given other demands, Roche initially planned to keep her participation in June's Democratic Convention to a minimum. She agreed to speak before an assembly of Democratic women and to have her address broadcast on the radio, but she did not intend to participate beyond that.[51] In the end, though, she felt that too many important issues were at stake to stint on the convention. Indeed, at the last minute Roche was roped into chairing an all-day meeting of the Women's Advisory Platform Committee, where prominent Democratic women produced more than a dozen planks advocating everything from federal aid to education and abolition of the poll tax to Roche's health plan and a national conference on unemployment.[52]

They also drafted an alternative plank to the Equal Rights Amendment (ERA). Since its introduction in 1923, the proposed constitutional amendment, which required that women and men be treated equally by the law, had been a thorn in the side of activists who supported protective labor legislation for women workers. Like most in her progressive cohort, Roche believed that the ERA would abolish these gender-specific laws and so could not support it. Some Democratic women, however, advocated the amendment, and their voices grew louder once the Fair Labor Standards Act passed in 1938. With a federal minimum wage and maximum hours law for both women and men—a gender-neutral law that the ERA did not threaten—they could not see why the ERA should pose a problem. But it did: many state laws continued to mandate better working conditions for women than federal law required. Women workers as well as progressives like Roche were loath to risk those laws by sponsoring the ERA.[53] The alternative developed by Roche's platform committee expressed unwavering commitment to women's right to paid labor and also recognized women's peculiar liabilities in the labor market. It committed the Democratic Party to strenuous "efforts to achieve equality of opportunity for women and men without impairing the social legislation which promotes true equality by safeguarding the health, safety, and economic welfare of women workers."[54] Roche still believed that women sometimes needed special treatment in order to achieve equality.

Although it is unclear what Roche thought about FDR's nomination for a third term as president, she certainly remained committed to the New Deal and the Democratic Party platform in the summer of 1940. The party's platform included all of the women's recommendations except federal aid for education and opposition to the poll tax.[55] Roche's article on the national health plan was used with her blessing as a "handbook" for the election, and she spoke throughout the election season to "non-partisan groups" on issues like labor standards, the New Deal youth program, and industrial democracy.[56]

But Roche was disappointed enough in FDR himself and simultaneously so frantic about her company's survival that she undertook an act of political ruthlessness that illuminated not only her own comfort with political deal making but also the deep involvement of a larger women's political network in political wheeling and dealing. Roche's threat was this: she would not campaign on behalf of the president unless she received the loan requested for RMF from the RFC. She issued her ultimatum early in September, when the women's Democratic Party network already had an inkling that things were not as they should be for Josephine Roche. Eleanor Roosevelt's intimate friend, newspaper reporter Lorena Hickok, confided that Roche "seems awfully worried and depressed about something, and I think it's business."[57] It was. Although most of RMF's bondholders had accepted Roche's adjustment of their terms, a handful threatened to sue the company to get their original interest rate and maturity date.[58] Roche's only hope for avoiding bankruptcy was a substantial loan from the RFC, and she held her campaigning energies hostage to that hope. If FDR did not pry a loan loose from the RFC, he would receive no support from Roche on the campaign trail.

By mid-September, the Women's Division of the National Democratic Committee was nearly begging Roche to campaign on behalf of the president. Dorothy McAllister, head of the Women's Division, was eager for Roche to appear at a number of stage events as well as on the radio. When McAllister tried to schedule Roche for the appearances, she cagily responded that although she had already arranged to speak to several groups in the Midwest, she would "be able only to talk issues."[59] She would not be able to promote FDR himself. She did not spell out for McAllister the *quid pro quo* that would free her tongue, but a few days later explained her situation to Molly Dewson, former head of the Women's Division.[60] Dewson telephoned the president to ask for his help in securing a loan for Roche from the RFC. He agreed to try.[61]

Dewson also revealed Roche's situation to McAllister, who then contacted Eleanor Roosevelt. McAllister explained, "Whether Miss Roche can make several important speeches in this campaign depends on what action can be taken to meet her difficulty." McAllister acknowledged that Dewson had already gone to the president, but she wanted all the help she could get in launching Roche into the campaign: "We are eager to have Miss Roche on the National Forum of the Mutual Broadcasting Company . . . and wish to schedule her for speeches in Illinois, Indiana, and Ohio. I would greatly appreciate it if you would speak to the President to find out how soon Miss Roche will know about whether something can be done."[62]

As McAllister penned those words, several anti–New Deal newspapers exposed what they construed as scandalous dealings between Roche and John L. Lewis. Roche was trying to get a federal loan, they maintained, in order to pay back hundreds of thousands of dollars secretly lent to her company by the UMW. Reporters suggested that Lewis was promising to endorse the president for the moment only because he wanted the money the president could ostensibly free up for Roche.[63] These reports may well have been correct. RMF owed the UMW over $300,000—very near the amount Roche had requested from the RFC specifically to pay back loans—and Lewis, who had hoped the Democratic Party would nominate an isolationist candidate for the presidency, was mum about the fall election. Lewis himself definitely approached the president to ask for help in getting Roche the RFC loan.[64]

These public revelations of influence peddling and backroom deals in no way deterred Roche or her female allies from continuing their attempts to win federal money for RMF. Women earlier in the twentieth century had often argued for their participation in electoral politics by promising to clean them up, but their New Deal heirs suggested a different trajectory. Democratic women in the 1930s were embedded deeply enough in the institutions of American politics not to bat an eye over Roche's secret deals with Lewis or to apologize for pulling every string they could to release public money for her private enterprise. Federal dollars in return for political endorsement? No problem. These women played hardball. On October 5, Eleanor Roosevelt invited Roche to dinner at the White House and reported that the president had spoken to the chair of the RFC on her behalf. On October 9, Roche met at the White House with the president and Sam Husbands, a member of the RFC board.[65]

The uncertainty was excruciating. On October 11, Roche reported to McAllister that the White House meeting was "more than generous," but since the "situation remains unchanged as yet," she could not commit to work for the Women's Division.[66] At that point, McAllister nearly gave up on Roche and, according to Lorena Hickok, felt "very gloomy."[67] Nevertheless, McAllister reached out to Roche on October 18 to see if she would participate in an upcoming broadcast discussion between Democratic and Republican women.[68] Only the night before, John L. Lewis had met with the president in the wake of press reports that Lewis was leaning toward Roosevelt's Republican opponent in the presidential election. That night, October 17, the political break between the two men was definite.[69] The next day, the president reported to Lewis that Husbands would recommend to the RFC board a loan of $175,000 for Roche. "I have spent many hours in trying to get this matter straightened out for my friend Miss Roche," the president pointed out to Lewis, "but I am very glad to have done so if it works out so that she can keep on going."[70]

Husbands's recommendation was utterly inadequate, but Roche refused to believe it was a final offer. She replied to McAllister on October

21, "Have had your wire before me ever since it arrived hoping so to answer yes. Instead of matter being concluded as I had every reason to expect new investigator sent out Friday. Is still here. Endless negotiations and nothing settled. Therefore don't see how I can be counted on. Sorry beyond words."[71]

The drama reached its climax. On October 23, at a meeting of the RFC, the board officially approved a loan for RMF. It was less than half of what Roche requested, and the terms were impossible.[72] Roche received a phone call laying out the decision on October 24.[73] The next day, John L. Lewis announced his support for the Republican presidential candidate, Wendell Wilkie. Lewis also promised that if Roosevelt won the election, he would take it as a vote of no confidence in his CIO leadership and resign from the organization's presidency.[74] The election was less than two weeks away.

Shortly after Roche received the devastating news about the loan, McAllister reached her by phone. An exasperated Roche explained it was "time for a little reciprocity"; that she was "fed up"; that she wanted $450,000 for machinery and would be able to repay this loan just as she had the first one. But the RFC had offered "terms they knew she could not meet." She would have to "spend every minute left in October financing her business," and so could not possibly help with the campaign. McAllister concluded that Roche was "trying to whisper she is not behind FDR."[75]

McAllister's conclusion was not universally accepted. Roche remained chair of both the executive committee of the NYA and the Coordinating Committee and was thus still part of FDR's administration. Although Roche wired Lewis "congratulating him on a courageous speech" endorsing Wilkie, she reported to members of the Consumers' League that her telegram did not "necessarily mean [her own] support of Mr. Wilkie." She did not publicly endorse any presidential candidate in 1940, but in a speech for the Consumers' League just days before the election indicated "support and admiration for the [current] administration." She told a friend privately that "if Mr. Wilkie goes in, I won't be in Washington at all, and if the President wins, I won't be there as much as in the past."[76] The friend interpreted her remarks to mean that "she is for the President but cannot openly oppose Lewis."[77]

The bulk of evidence suggests that Roche voted for Roosevelt even though she was disappointed in him. Wilkie was a Republican businessman, and Roche had no love for that species. The Democratic platform included planks that she herself had written; she remained officially attached to Roosevelt's administration; and even after the election she occasionally dined at the White House.[78] Moreover, during the campaign Roche repeatedly expressed her hope to Dorothy McAllister that she would eventually be able to accept invitations to speak on Roosevelt's behalf, suggesting that, had the loan come through, she would have spoken out for Roosevelt. It was public campaigning Roche withheld, not her vote.

Still, the Democratic Party ceased to be a vehicle for Roche's reform activities after 1940. Only six years later, she would make the extraordinary claim, "I never was in politics. There were certain principles some of us thought were worth fighting for and we used the political mechanism to do it." But she was "completely out" of politics now.[79] This statement, from a woman who in 1914 had referred to politics as a "fine, just thing," was a stunning indicator of just how disaffected from politics Roche had become.[80] The mounting disappointments of 1939–1940—ranging from FDR's refusal to give effective support to her health plan through appointment of McNutt to head the FSA to reductions in social spending—sobered Roche as to the possibilities of using the "political mechanism" for progressive ends. But she had remained firmly attached to the Democratic Party through each of those disappointments until the president failed to stabilize her coal company. That politics could not ease RMF's difficulties seems to have been the deciding factor in Roche's estrangement from the electoral field. She would eventually leave the Democratic Party and register as an independent, holding fast to the privilege of voting but never again publicly entering the electoral fray.[81]

If Roche renounced party politics, however, she had no intention of leaving public life. Only two days after the election, she attended a meeting of the NCL board in New York; two weeks later, she made speeches in California; and in December, she was back on the East Coast, praising the New Deal and urging its extension.[82] That same month, Mary Dublin, perhaps sensing Roche's need for some cheering up, urged her not to give up leadership on the health bill: "You are everything that's good, courageous, and wise," the younger woman assured her mentor. "More people than you will ever know share my sense of gratitude in knowing you and through you getting a new concept of what a person can be. . . . You're the one person everyone . . . looks to, to carry the health fight particularly."[83]

Indeed, throughout 1941, with increasing unofficial U.S. interventions in the European war and pressures for the same in Asia, Roche remained active on the lecture circuit. Managed by the W. Colston Leigh speakers' bureau, Roche crisscrossed the country pleading with groups as diverse as the National Lawyers Guild and the Inland Empire Education Association not to let the war distract them from the urgent need for justice at home. She urged her listeners to hold the U.S. government accountable to its own professed values. According to wartime rhetoric, government officials proclaimed their interventions in the war to be yet another venture mounted on behalf of democracy and freedom. But in Roche's view, the United States had so far failed to complete the democratic project within its own borders. As she often put it, "Our task is not only to defend democracy but to achieve it for all."[84] She insisted that Americans could not claim to have achieved democracy at home until every man, woman, and child enjoyed full Social Security, a goal far from fulfillment.[85] Moreover, she warned, "the democracy we love can be destroyed even more readily . . . by . . . economic and social injustice within our nation than by any force from without."[86] She cited massive data demonstrating economic inequalities in the United States—less than 3 percent of American families "dominate American economic life"—which, to her mind, revealed "our uncompleted task of achieving democracy."[87]

When the Japanese attacked Pearl Harbor and Germany openly declared war against the United States in December 1941, Roche must have had a sense of déjà vu. Just as she and many other peace-promoting progressives had opposed U.S. military involvement in World War I but had then come to support the war effort, so did she and most other progressive opponents of U.S. participation in World War II accept the necessity of armed conflict late in 1941.[88] Her acquiescence in taking up arms, however, did not assuage her fears, increased by her experience in World War I, that organized labor might be crushed, social programs gutted, or civil liberties abandoned as a result of this latest global conflagration. These anxieties prevented Roche from developing the kind of enthusiasm for World War II that she had eventually expressed in World War I.

Roche's participation in the war effort was also limited by trouble at RMF, the early years of World War II representing the lowest point of her life. Only a few months after the bombing of Pearl Harbor, she was forced back into active leadership of the company because the manager from CMM not only failed to increase sales but even started missing board meetings and omitting to open his mail.[89] Consequently, RMF could not pay for new equipment, and manufacturers threatened to repossess it. In summer 1942, Roche had to terminate the contract with CMM, which trapped her in Denver, lashed to a tumultuous and deteriorating business.[90] Just weeks after returning to the company, she confessed, "The day to day struggle, in today's industrial situation, to maintain the things I've so long fought for there, has been taking every bit of my days and nights. . . . I feel terribly isolated and most of the time worse than futile."[91] It was no wonder. Roche's company was in desperate condition, and the very governmental regulation she had championed seemed to threaten the survival of her company as well as the interests of workers.

The threats came, ironically, from federal policies that managed wartime production and seemed to represent the victory of progressive ideals. World War II vastly expanded economic planning and pushed millions of new members into unions. The War Production Board, Office of Price Administration, and War Labor Board were crucial agencies in the planning effort, and having won representation within those agencies, labor leaders promised no strikes during the war. That bargain inadvertently helped to produce an economy in which war contracts sent corporate profits through the roof while workers' wages stagnated. Roche saw the imbalance as a betrayal of progressivism despite the unprecedented level of economic planning and the millions of new workers flocking into unions.[92]

Coal miners shared Roche's perception. In 1943, 400,000 miners defied the no-strike pledge. Their initiative was no mystery: not only were coal miners' wages held steady while profits increased but miners also faced hellacious levels of death and injury. In 1942–1943, nearly 3,000 miners were killed on the job, and 34,000 were injured.[93] In response to the miners' rebellion, FDR ordered Secretary of the Interior Harold Ickes to take over the mines. In the midst of that upheaval, Roche reported that she was "necessarily living on a day to day basis" and "keeping very close to the mine situation." Indeed, she was traveling nearly every day from her Denver office to the two mines she still had running in Boulder and Weld counties.[94]

Despite the peculiar fragility of her own company, Roche opposed all restrictions on organized labor. Echoing her explanation of strikes in 1914 and 1927, she insisted that the miners' strike in 1943 resulted from unjust conditions in their industry and that the solution was not to punish the miners but to correct the conditions. "What is increasingly and desperately needed today is economic statesmanship which will act courageously and constructively to eliminate our mounting economic inequalities," she insisted. "To attempt merely to penalize the inevitable consequences of these inequities would surely prove an unsound and shortsighted policy not aiding the very objective for which it was mistakenly adopted, namely the furtherance of the war effort." She unequivocally opposed "any legislation to prohibit strikes or to penalize labor leaders or unions that call strikes in the war industries."[95] Ultimately, coal miners benefited from their walkout—Ickes negotiated an industry-wide union contract—and other workers soon followed suit in defiance of both the Roosevelt administration and their own union leadership.[96] In Roche's view, the lesson here was that workers kept progressivism alive; government agencies took steps to diminish inequality only because of workers' independent collective action.

As Roche urged pro-labor policies on Roosevelt's wartime administration, she struggled with the administration's management of coal production. That the administration was managing production at all held out hope for the benefits that Roche had advocated in her work for the National Recovery Administration and subsequent regulation of the coal industry. From her perspective in the 1940s, however, the government was not equitably distributing its orders for coal, and the formula for setting coal prices omitted crucial expenses.[97] In December 1943, the Office of Price Administration finally heeded her pleas to include those costs.[98] But RMF still suffered from the squeeze between what Roche called the "manpower shortage" and the "ever-mounting volume of work imposed on the Company by innumerable Government agencies, demanding reports," and "constantly changing rules and regulations."[99] With an office staff reduced 50 percent by the war, she dreaded the daily mail because it so often brought additional government requests for information. Many of the reports were "obligatory." Others, she admitted, were optional.[100] But Roche complied with every request because she believed in the higher purposes served by data gathering. She did not, however, have the staff to fulfill those purposes without enormous hardship. Her situation at RMF during the war unsettled Roche's confidence in public policy as an instrument for diminishing inequality. She still saw government as a necessary ally in pursuing social justice, but she was newly cautious about its reliability and efficacy.[101]

The moment finally came when RMF could no longer avoid bankruptcy. A tiny fraction of bondholders continued to refuse the new terms Roche had set in 1939, and so far as these creditors were concerned, their bonds matured in 1943. Roche could not pay, and her creditors sued. After staving off bankruptcy through the country's worst ever economic disaster, Roche finally succumbed in 1944, when the coal industry was booming because of wartime needs. She filed on February 12, 1944, and, as painful as it was to admit (temporary) defeat, she probably heaved a sigh of relief to turn the company over to someone else. This time, trustee Wilbur Newton took the reins and spent more than a year evaluating Roche's leadership and the financial prospects of her beloved but increasingly precarious experiment in labor progressivism.[102]

While RMF went through reorganization, Roche gratefully fled Denver. It was like coming up for air after being, in her words, "literally buried" in the coal mines.[103] Revealingly, she escaped not to Washington but to New York, where, after a brief stay at the Cosmopolitan Club, she took a small apartment on East Fifty-third Street.[104] The city offered the balm of old friends, especially Read Lewis and Mary van Kleeck, the latter especially dear since publishing a study of Roche's work at RMF in the early 1930s.[105] But the move away from both Denver and Washington signified something deeper than a longing for old friends.

The move to New York announced Roche's new unease with government, politics, and RMF as bases from which to pursue progressive reform. New York offered civil society alternatives. Although Roche stepped down from the presidency of the NCL in mid-1944, she remained on its board of directors and chaired a committee on full employment.[106] She did that work not from the NCL office, however, but from a desk at the Common Council for American Unity (CCAU), the new name for her World War I creation, the Foreign Language Information Service (FLIS).[107] Read Lewis remained executive director of the organization, and Roche served on its governing board as she had since the 1920s.

The FLIS had changed its name in 1939 to signal an expanded purview. In keeping with the deepening interest of progressives in issues of racial justice, the CCAU opposed "group discrimination" of any kind rather than focusing exclusively on incorporating foreign-language groups into the political life of the United States.[108] In its official mission statement, the CCAU dedicated itself to "overcome intolerance and discrimination because of foreign birth or descent, race or nationality" and "to encourage the growth of an American culture which will be truly representative of all the elements that make up the American people."[109] The CCAU was marrying the Progressive Era interest in integrating European immigrants into American life to an increasingly vivid interest in justice for African Americans and Asian Americans.

World War II infused the struggle for racial justice with new power. As Roche put it, "The war has sharply focused" Americans on "our long-standing discrimination and intolerance because of race or national origin."[110] The hypocrisy of fighting racism in Germany with a racially segregated American military could hardly be obscured, and African Americans insisted that if they were to defend America's ostensible democracy against racist fascism, then the United States must eradicate racism from its own institutions. Bearing out the progressive potential of the war effort, black activists' threat of a march on Washington in 1941 moved FDR to prohibit government contractors from discriminating on the basis of race when hiring. He also created the Fair Employment Practices Committee (FEPC) to enforce the prohibition during the war. The establishment of a permanent FEPC then became a cause célèbre among those concerned with racial freedom, and Roche advocated the measure both through the CCAU and within the NCL, which went on record advocating a permanent FEPC in fall 1944.[111]

Even earlier in the war, Roche engaged the issue of racial justice. As an adviser to the federal Office of Civilian Defense, she raised what she called "the great problem of minority groups in the defense effort." While creation of the FEPC was a start, Roche believed the country needed to go further. She advocated a National Advisory Council comprising representatives of minority groups, which would plan a program for eliminating racial discrimination throughout the nation. Federal aid should then fund whatever program the council devised. Most important from

Roche's perspective was that members of minority groups themselves should lead the campaign against racial discrimination. Racial paternalism would not do; only genuine democracy would.[112]

From her position in the CCAU, Roche attended to other issues of racial justice as well. The organization opposed discrimination against Asians in U.S. immigration and naturalization law; argued for "fair play" for Japanese Americans forcibly removed from their homes on the West Coast; opposed racial segregation by law or practice; and denounced anti-Semitism.[113] Roche and the CCAU also supported decolonization efforts across the globe.[114]

As World War II came to its dramatic conclusion in summer 1945, Roche was thinking as much about coal as about race relations, however. Wilbur Newton released his meticulous research on RMF, which found no mismanagement of the company and concluded that it had survived as long as it had by the "sheer will" of Josephine Roche.[115] The company often produced an operating profit, as Roche continually claimed, but the indebtedness contracted long before her tenure sentenced the company to failure in the context of shrinking markets. One commentator concluded, "Miss Roche has given 18 years of her life and virtually all of her personal fortune to keep afloat an enterprise that was doomed before she took it over." Roche's experiment was, according to this assessment, "magnificent, but it was not business."[116]

To interpret Roche's experiment as "not business" was a way of dismissing economic justice from the responsibility of business. To the contrary, Roche's experiment at RMF *was* business. Roche's progressive industrialism was not foreordained to collapse because of its commitment to economic justice but because of declining markets in coal and a mountain of debt created by her (anti-labor) predecessors. Her company went into bankruptcy for reasons that no individual owner could possibly have prevented regardless of her labor policy. In fact, operators who had the most oppressive imaginable labor policies went into bankruptcy long before Roche did. Her biggest and richest competitor in Colorado, Rockefeller's Colorado Fuel and Iron Company, found it difficult to meet expenses early in the 1930s and nipped immediately into bankruptcy court to dodge its debts. Countless others followed suit. Roche was among the last of her coal mining cohort to accept the healing shelter of Chapter 10.[117]

Roche's accomplishment at RMF was to use her position as an industrialist for progressive ends despite the decline in the coal industry. By borrowing on her own credit and finally integrating the UMW into the ownership of the company, she made a stand for the self-organization of workers, for a model of industrial management that recognized a public interest in private enterprise, and for stability over competition. She used

the platform built for her by RMF to promote planning in basic industries and cooperation among labor, industry, and government. Her efforts
had long-term ramifications even if these did not include saving her particular coal company from bankruptcy. And, in fact, after the company
came out of court in 1946, it diversified and survived for the remainder
of the twentieth century, with the UMW initially its most powerful
stockholder.[118]

When RMF emerged from bankruptcy, Roche returned as president for
several years, but she found little to interest her in the work because she
was shutting down the mines and had no relationship with workers. The
company would never again provide a base for her activism. Indeed, as
World War II ended in the late summer of 1945, Roche was very much at
sea. Unlike others in her progressive community, many of whom were
buoyed by the war's support for economic planning, union membership,
and racial justice, she was disappointed in electoral politics as a method
for diminishing inequalities of wealth and power and had largely left
government service. She still believed that government must play a role in
creating a more equitable world, but she was more cautious than before
about government interventions. Even a sympathetic administration was
not entirely reliable in times of crisis, and she saw that progressive social
legislation, once achieved, was never secure. Sometimes, rather than expanding social welfare measures, progressives expended every bit of their
energies simply trying to prevent the retraction of measures already won.
These sobering insights set Roche searching for new methods of diminishing inequalities in American life.

CHAPTER 13

BECOMING A COLD WAR LIBERAL, 1945–1948

etween 1945 and 1948, Josephine Roche continued to reassess methods for diminishing inequality. Disaffected from politics, more wary of government, and no longer a progressive captain of industry, she sought new paths toward social justice. After 1945, her search proceeded in tandem with the emergence of the Cold War, which powerfully shaped her options. By the end of 1948 in fact, Cold War imperatives had moved Roche to disavow her former alliances with the Left, constricted her reform agenda, and lowered her expectations for social change. In these ways, Roche was very much back in sync with her cohort of New Deal progressives. Her journey in the late 1940s vividly illustrated the processes by which many New Dealers became Cold War liberals, a set of conversions that presaged the second temporary reversal in the Age of Reform.

Roche's postwar search for new ways of diminishing inequality began in Europe, where in fall 1945 she attended a meeting of the International Labor Organization (ILO), an association formed in 1919 to promote workplace justice as a foundation for world peace, and then opened an investigation of the French and British coal industries. Suffering terrible fuel shortages by war's end, both France and Britain had nationalized their coal industries, and Roche was interested in how nationalization was affecting workers and whether the mines in each country would be able to retool fast enough to provide fuel for winter heating and industrial production. To satisfy her curiosity, she proposed to tour French and British coalfields after her ILO meetings in Paris. Other progressives were eager for her findings: New York's *Herald Tribune* contracted for her observations; Mary van Kleeck commissioned a report for the Russell

Sage Foundation; and Paul Kellogg asked her to write articles for the *Survey Graphic*.[1]

In September 1945, Roche set off on her adventure. It began with a few days of preliminary research in London. Given all Britain had endured during the war, simply locating life's necessities proved a challenge.[2] Roche required help from the American Embassy just to find a bed in a Women's Army Corps barracks, where she slept, in her words, "after a fashion" for ten days. She had no bureau, no chair, no place even to prop up the bag where her clothes remained throughout her stay. While pursuing her research, she was served by her habit of homelessness: "I made notes standing in corridors and on street corners." She admitted, "As my days were packed with conferences this was a bit strenuous and messy."[3]

She soon left for France and the ILO's gathering at the Sorbonne. This was Roche's first visit to France, and she was deeply moved by the Sorbonne's "centuries-old buildings with their breath-taking beauty." Indeed, the "paneled lecture rooms where France's greatest men of science, letters and the arts have taught and lectured through the decades" elicited an echo of James Harvey Robinson's belief that higher learning was liberatory: the Sorbonne's scholars had been, in Roche words, "pioneers in freeing the minds and spirits of mankind."[4] In her postwar context, she took hope from both that history and the ILO conference, where representatives of government, labor, and business agreed no other task was so urgent as "restoring to activity the paralyzed industrial and economic functions of Europe."[5] The ILO organized committees to study basic industries in each country and make recommendations for increasing production as soon as possible. Roche's investigations in coal served that effort.[6]

She headed first to the mines of the Nord and Pas-de-Calais, where two-thirds of French coal was mined. There Roche demonstrated both physical courage and insatiable curiosity when she went underground herself—reportedly the first woman ever to descend into a French coal mine—to observe the hand mining on which France now depended for heat and industrial renewal. At one point, she was 1,500 feet below ground, crawling on her hands and knees to reach a coal face. The tunnels were so small that she could not sit up, and the miners had to "coil themselves up" to pick away at the coal, which they then set on a conveyor belt that took each precious chunk to the mine shaft. She observed the process while lying flat on her stomach and trying to scoop up any piece of coal that fell off the belt. She concluded from such experiences that the French were miraculously increasing production as a result of effective industrial planning, which included incentives to workers for efficient labor. Ultimately, mechanization would be necessary to increase

BECOMING A COLD WAR LIBERAL   213

production adequately, but she had faith the French were on track to do that.[7]

Her confidence in the British future was not so firm. Once back in Britain, she began a whirlwind tour of coal country arranged by the Ministry of Fuel and Power. Her itinerary was so packed that Roche claimed it "would have knocked out a husky male of twenty five." As a petite woman of fifty-nine, she was proud to keep up. The tour opened in Wales. With Cardiff as her home base, she spent ten days in the rocky Welsh hills, setting off at 7:00 each morning to visit mines. She went down into at least one mine a day and walked the mile or more to each mine face, "usually bent double" because of the low ceilings. At each mine, she talked with coal officials and miners, union representatives, and staff at the local rehabilitation centers and canteens.

From Wales, she sped to the coalfields of northern England. She kept the same pace there for eight days before exhaustion left her vulnerable to accident. At a mine near Nottingham, she fell and broke her wrist. The mishap forced her to stay in a small Nottingham hospital for six days and bypass mines in Newcastle and Durham, but she "felt right proud" when, on the seventh day, she got up and caught the train to Edinburgh. For over twelve hours, she rode the train without food, water, or heat. Carrying her bags with her good arm, she detrained in Edinburgh and then managed the same sort of schedule in the Scottish mines that she had kept in Wales. When finally she returned to London, she was delighted to find a flat where she got enough heat to raise the indoor temperature to 55 degrees. She had lost 26 pounds since leaving the United States and, by then, her good arm complained about doing the work of two. She endured two weeks of such nerve pain that she could "barely manage to dress." Still, she located a typewriter and pecked out several articles for her impatient editors at the *Herald Tribune*.[8]

The articles for the New York newspaper, subsequent essays for *Survey Graphic*, and confidential report to the Russell Sage Foundation evinced Roche's recalibration of the place of politics, government, and the self-organization of workers in the campaign to diminish inequality. She found in Britain that coal production was declining disastrously and continued to do so even after the Labour Party nationalized the industry, which had for a decade been the major goal of the British miners' federation. To Roche's mind, the steady decline in production was no mystery because the nationalization bill drafted by the Labour government said not a word about the welfare of miners. All particulars in regard to wages, hours, and other conditions of labor were left to negotiations between the coal miners' union and a new National Coal Board. Overworked, undernourished, and demoralized miners who had barely made it through the war and now were desperate for improvement in their material lives were, Roche thought, understandably disappointed that they received no statutory protections from the nationalization scheme while owners of coal mines received guarantees of compensation for their property.[9]

This situation confirmed Roche's disillusionment with politics. What she saw as the Labour Party's betrayal of the miners moved her toward John L. Lewis's position that the labor movement must remain independent of political parties. British miners would have been better off, in her view, if their national union had bargained with employers on an industry-wide basis for higher wages, safer mines, shorter hours, and better health care rather than pressing for nationalization. Putting all their eggs in the electoral basket, they had simply exchanged one set of employers for another. They had won themselves a single governmental employer with whom they would have to continue bargaining to achieve any improvement in their daily lives. "The chief need in the English coal mines, where production remains a million tons a week below pre-war levels, appears to be a strong national union headed by a leader who can get results," Roche concluded.[10]

Moreover, the Labour government faced a situation that, according to Roche, could be improved only through economic reconstruction that could have been effected without nationalization. Small, high-cost mines had to be shut down, other small operations consolidated, and the industry substantially mechanized in order to approach the output necessary to heat British homes and run British industry, not to mention raise wages and benefits for miners. She also argued that production would have to be planned on a regional basis. She was, in the end, recommending a sort of National Recovery Administration for the British coal industry and outlining a vision for coal that she and John L. Lewis would pursue in the United States during decades to come.[11]

While Roche's articles on British coal made nationalization look like a bad bargain for workers, she did not condemn all governmental economic intervention or even every nationalization scheme. Her recommendation for regional planning within the British coal industry suggested a significant role for government, and she lauded the French nationalization effort because it increased production through regional planning and incentives to workers. Moreover, Roche praised and participated in the tripartite commissions of labor, government, and business set up by the ILO.

What had crystallized for Roche was a belief that, in the achievement of economic justice, the crucial thing was not whether government or private interests operated an industry; the crucial issue was whether workers maintained independent power. Roche had long championed an independent labor movement, of course, and her belief in its necessity had only increased over the decades. But in the 1940s, "independence" explicitly acquired a new dimension for her. Roche was now convinced that workers must remain as independent of political parties and government agencies as of employers. Independence did not suggest severing all ties; achieving greater equality required workers to recruit politicians and government agencies—and even employers—to their cause whenever they could. But the British case confirmed, to her mind, what her own wartime experience had begun to suggest, which was that even governments allegedly sympathetic to workers could as easily oppress as liberate them. A movement of worker-citizens ever free to scrutinize and resist government action and political deals as well as company policies was the *sine qua non* for diminishing inequality. She now saw the self-organization of workers as the foundation from which all other elements in the edifice of social justice must be built. Other elements were also necessary, but they were dust in the wind without this foundation.

When Roche flew back to the United States in March 1946, she was only months away from connecting in a whole new way with the movement of worker-citizens in the United States. In the meantime, she returned stateside not only as a reporter on the European coal situation but also as the reelected president of Rocky Mountain Fuel (RMF). The company had just emerged from reorganization, and her plan was to liquidate its holdings and move on. Given that she did not plan to put her mines back into operation, the work at RMF was not nearly as interesting to her as it had once been. She explained, "Getting a new corporation set up . . . with no redeeming human factors in the way of mine operations . . . has been an experience I've found extremely wearing—not 'my beat.' "[12]

Roche would not walk someone else's beat for long. Even as she completed her articles for the *Survey Graphic* and issued new stock from RMF, she was drawn back to the nation's capital, this time not to serve in government but to advise John L. Lewis, who needed her help because he was entering territory unknown to him and well known to Roche. It was the field of social welfare. At the behest of coal miners themselves, a workforce unusually at risk for injury and illness, Lewis was trying to establish a miners' welfare program funded by coal operators and run by the union. Had Roche's 1939 health plan become law, miners might not have needed to haggle with their employers for health care and disability insurance; had the New Deal's social insurance and public assistance programs been more generous, miners might not have worried about finding supplemental aid for their widows and orphans or for themselves in old age. But, with the failure of a national health plan and little progress on improving existing New Deal programs, miners pushed their union leaders to consider such benefits an object of collective bargaining. Lewis made his first effective move in this direction during contract negotiations in 1946. When he demanded that coal companies fund a welfare program for miners, the operators balked, and Lewis called the miners out. With much of the country dependent on coal for both home heating and industrial production and the government's wartime economic powers still in place, President Harry Truman, who had moved into the White House on Franklin Roosevelt's death in 1945, ordered his secretary of the interior to seize the mines. Secretary Julius Krug and Lewis then negotiated a contract for the coal industry that included a health and retirement plan for miners.[13]

Because of continued disputes between the union and the operators as well as dramatically unsettled labor law, the Krug-Lewis Agreement was never enforced in its original form, but that government-negotiated contract laid the groundwork for mine operators to accept greater responsibility for their employees' health and old age. To help him build on that underpinning, Lewis began informally consulting with Roche in fall 1946. Lewis soon afterward convinced coal operators to establish a private welfare and retirement program funded by a royalty on each ton of coal mined and run by three trustees, one each representing the operators, the union, and the public.[14] Roche was, of course, the ideal adviser on such a project because of her work on the Social Security Act and national health plan, and Lewis officially hired her as a part-time consultant in 1947.[15] "There could be no greater privilege or honor," she wrote to Lewis, "than to work in this capacity in helping to develop the Welfare and Retirement program which offers such infinite possibilities for progress, both human and industrial. Thank you."[16]

Advising Lewis on development of the welfare fund set Roche firmly back on her beat at a critical historical moment. It was crucial in part because coal miners were not alone in trying to convince employers to fund the kinds of social welfare programs the New Deal had so far failed to provide. Other unions were also attempting to wrest supplemental retirement pensions and health care from employers. In the absence of an expanding New Deal, unions were pressing for a newly robust private sector in social welfare, and Roche's relationship with the UMW allowed her to pioneer—yet again—in this new realm of American life.

The late 1940s represented a decisive juncture in another way, too: progressives and conservatives were battling for domination of American politics. While progressives came out of World War II hoping for massive expansions of the welfare state, continuation of at least some aspects of wartime economic planning, a permanent Fair Employment Practices Commission, and, in some quarters, even gender equity in the workplace, conservatives had equally high hopes for reestablishing the primacy of private capital, rolling back the new powers of the central government, and maintaining existing social hierarchies at home, at work, and in politics.[17]

International affairs boosted the conservative cause. In the first several years following World War II, a global rivalry between the capitalist United States and the communist Soviet Union was solidifying into Cold War, a process that handed conservatives a devastating weapon against campaigns for more egalitarian public policies. The new geopolitical competition encouraged conservatives to associate any allusion to class division, social responsibility for individual welfare, or explicit governmental intervention in private economic enterprises with communism, which, given the Soviet Union's emergence as a global power opposing U.S. interests, carried much greater weight than when the *Denver Post* smeared Roche as a Red in 1934. Such accusations now carried a suspicion of disloyalty to the United States. Aided by this new advantage, corporate America succeeded in winning legislation that severely restricted the power of labor unions (the Taft-Hartley Act of 1947); white supremacists dug in their heels against a permanent Fair Employment Practices Commission; and employers pushed most women workers out of the high-paying jobs they had won during the war.

Progressives did not roll over and play dead in the face of these losses. Into 1948 at least, they continued to push back against conservatives' onslaught. The battle over health care offered a prime example. President Truman reopened that front in 1946 by signing the Hill-Burton Act. Hill-Burton provided federal funds for building community hospitals in underserved areas, one of the recommendations in Roche's original health plan. Pushing further, Truman's administration organized a national health conference in 1948 that was direct heir to Roche's 1938 conference and signaled Truman's intention to press for compulsory national health insurance, a significant advance over Roche's original health plan, which seemed feasible because of a more progressive Supreme Court. Roche and Isidore Falk, who was still working on health care at the Social Security Administration, helped to choose participants for the conference, and Roche was delighted that "some of the best qualified representatives of professional and lay groups" agreed to attend.[18] She was one of them, of course, and attended as the representative of the UMW.[19]

Conservatives and progressives put forward proposals. One of Roche's anxieties was that conferees might support a health plan offered by Senator Robert Taft, an arch-enemy of the New Deal and the labor movement. Coauthor of anti-union legislation in 1947, Taft had proposed a health care bill that, according to Roche, threatened " 'second class citizenship' in the matter of medical care" by providing publicly funded medical care on the basis of the "strictest means test" and nearly turning administration of the program over to the American Medical Association (AMA).[20] She wanted a comprehensive plan run in the public interest rather than a plan exclusively for the poor run in the doctors' interest. However slim the chance of success, progressives like Roche continued in early 1948 to push for their broadest hopes.

During the health conference, a variety of reformers made their case for those hopes. Roche joined with representatives of fourteen other organizations, including the American Federation of Labor (AFL), individual unions from the Congress of Industrial Organizations(CIO), the National Consumers' League (NCL), and the National Association for the Advancement of Colored People (NAACP), to propose a compulsory national health insurance program that incorporated existing voluntary health plans—like health cooperatives and union health care programs—so long as they met federal standards. National health insurance for those outside these voluntary plans might be financed, they suggested, by earmarked contributions from those able to pay and general revenues for those unable to do so.[21] Unions thus expressed their hope to protect any welfare benefits they might wrench from employers through collective bargaining, but they imagined those programs as components of a more comprehensive national system of health insurance to which they also remained firmly committed.[22]

As it turned out, the health conference did not generate as much support for compulsory health insurance as the Truman administration had hoped it might; the Republican Congress blocked health care legislation in any event; and the AMA mounted a campaign identifying Truman's plan with communism.[23] Conservatives decisively won this round in their fight against progressives, a denouement that would have seemed unbearably grim to Roche had she not found her new path toward diminishing inequality.

Only days before the health conference opened, John L. Lewis hired her as the full-time director of the United Mine Workers of America Welfare and Retirement Fund.[24] As such, Roche was charged with building from the ground up a set of welfare programs in aid of coal miners across the country, which she would then run on a daily basis. She considered the appointment a supreme privilege and argued that the Welfare Fund embodied progressive principles enunciated in the Progressive Party campaign of 1912.[25] In many ways, Roche's work at the fund would indeed promote the mission to which she had committed herself in the 1910s. She would improve the living standards of hundreds of thousands of coal miners and support the labor movement in the bargain.

But some aspects of Roche's political thinking were changing by 1948, and those changes illustrated the immediate postwar outcome of the battle between conservatives and progressives. Along with her new anxieties about the reliability of politics and government as allies in the fight to diminish inequality, Roche's nonchalant collaborations with the Left came to an end. In this, she was part of a broad trend. Beginning in the late 1940s, alliances between progressives and the Left, which had given the period between 1890 and 1948 a special political fertility, were shredded by the anti-communist crusade unleashed by the emerging Cold War.[26]

Indeed, by the late 1940s, the anti-communist crusade had gained so much power in American politics that many progressives felt they had to vilify the Left if they were to remain effective in public life at all. Some of the first evidence of that trend came in the form of President Truman's own loyalty program, which in 1947 began investigating the political affiliations and ideals of federal employees. A whiff of association with the Left could for several years thereafter doom a career in policymaking.[27] And that move emanated from within a Democratic administration full of progressives. Better known were the proceedings spearheaded by conservatives in the House Un-American Activities Committee (HUAC) and slightly later interrogations by the senatorial committees of Joseph McCarthy and Pat McCarran, all of which treated virtually any critique of American institutions or support for cooperation with the Soviet Union as a threat to the survival of the United States. In the overheated political atmosphere of the late 1940s and early 1950s, even having associated with people who expressed admiration for the Soviet Union before World War II raised suspicions of disloyalty. To put it lightly, U.S. political culture lost its range; political speech was severely constrained.[28]

Josephine Roche had precisely the kind of past that might in this new context have brought her under suspicion. She had been an open and enthusiastic supporter of the early CIO, which had rather famously hired Communist Party members as organizers; she had in the 1930s sponsored the League of Women Shoppers, a pro-labor organization accused of communist affiliation by HUAC as early as 1939.[29] Along with Mary Dublin, Roche had called for the dismantling of that first HUAC in the late 1930s and urged the NCL to denounce it in the strongest possible terms.[30] At that same time, Roche had been consulting regularly with Lee Pressman, a member of the Communist Party. Roche was a good friend of Mary van Kleeck, who endured FBI surveillance for decades because of her alleged Soviet sympathies.[31] Roche had acted in political theater staged by the Workers Alliance in 1940 and spoken before the National Lawyers Guild in 1941, both organizations with Communist Party connections. During the late 1930s, she, like other progressives in the Roosevelt administration, attended social functions at the Soviet Embassy, and in early 1937 she accepted a linen tablecloth from the Soviet ambassador, which she promised to use when he and his wife came to dine with her "most informally."[32] After the war, she briefly belonged to socialist Norman Thomas's Post War World Council, which advocated general disarmament, and she declined a position on the board only because she feared other obligations would prevent her from attending meetings.[33] She worked closely with Isidore Falk on Truman's National Health Assembly when Falk was accused of trying to foist "socialized medicine" on the United States at the behest of the ILO, another suspect organization with which Roche had deep and recent connections.[34]

By summer 1948, the dangers associated with Roche's résumé were frighteningly clear. She was well aware of Truman's loyalty program because she had close friends in the administration. No one remotely keeping up with current events could be ignorant of the indictment of American Communist Party leaders on charges of conspiring to overthrow the U.S. government in summer 1948.[35] Roche could not have been unaware either of the sensational drama unfolding in HUAC, where in early August, Whittiker Chambers testified that Alger Hiss had been a communist while working in the federal government during the 1930s, hardly a crime but in the context of the anti-communist frenzy a situation that sparked suspicions of espionage and treason. Roche's former friend Lee Pressman was subpoenaed less than a month later, also accused of being a communist while working in the New Deal government during precisely the period when Roche befriended him and introduced him to John L. Lewis.[36]

The presidential campaign of 1948 gave special vehemence to these proceedings and helped (temporarily) to drive progressivism from American politics. In that turbulent political year, multiple parties vied for the presidency. The Republicans offered a pro-business Thomas Dewey, and the Democrats, the pro-labor incumbent Harry Truman. A new Progressive Party, advocating cooperation with the Soviet regime, sharing of atomic technology, and disarmament, nominated former New Dealer Henry Wallace for the top spot, while southern white Democrats, rejecting their party's support for racial justice, formed the States' Rights Democratic Party, also known as the Dixiecrats. Conservatives used HUAC proceedings to paint the Truman administration, heir to the New Deal government, as riddled with communist spies. Truman and the Dixiecrats burnished their own anti-communist *bona fides* by rabidly denouncing third-party candidate Henry Wallace.

In this context, having just taken the reins of the UMW's Welfare and Retirement Fund, Roche was asked to testify at a loyalty hearing on behalf of her dear protégé, Mary Dublin—now Mary Dublin Keyserling. By 1948, Dublin Keyserling headed a unit in the Department of Commerce that studied the effects of international trade on the U.S. economy. She faced a loyalty hearing because unidentified accusers alleged, among other things, that she had belonged to several communist-affiliated organizations in the late 1930s and had associated with communists or Communist Party sympathizers. One specific allegation was that she was seen having tea with Mary van Kleeck in the 1930s. This sort of past was enough to tar her with suspicion of disloyalty to her country and, short of that, threatened her employment in the federal government. On August 24, 1948, Roche testified before the Loyalty Board of the Department of Commerce that Mary Dublin Keyserling was loyal to the United States, having never so much as hinted approval of the Soviet Union since their association began in 1938. In the end, the Loyalty Board would accept that judgment.[37]

But Roche went well beyond defending Dublin Keyserling. She took the opportunity of this hearing to distance herself from communism and the Soviet Union in the crudest possible ways. She referred to members of the Communist Party as "Commies" and explained that "particularly during '40 and '41 I was very, very sensitive to what I felt was the great danger of some of our liberal people being too sympathetic toward the Russian group." In condemning the "muddy-minded liberalism that was floating around" in the early 1940s, Roche referred to liberals sympathetic to the Soviet regime as "screwballs" and even denounced her old ally, Henry Wallace, for his current use of the name "progressive," which she considered "an outrage, a name taken in vain." She emphatically disassociated herself from the newest Progressive Party.[38]

Except for supporting cooperation with the Soviet Union, the Progressive Party platform of 1948 actually exemplified Roche's commitments. It promoted price controls on necessities of life just as did a consumers' group that Roche helped to form in New York City in 1947.[39] It advocated the civil rights of all minority groups, just as did the Common Council for American Unity (CCAU). It argued for the extension of Social Security to all groups and universal health security, goals that Roche adamantly supported. It opposed the restrictions on labor organizations set by the Taft-Hartley Act in 1947, legislation anathema to Roche and all supporters of organized labor. It proposed to advance the cause of peace through disarmament and full U.S. participation in the United Nations, hopes of the Post War World Council to which she belonged as recently as 1946. The only explanation for Roche's disgust with the Progressive Party of 1948 was its endorsement of cooperation with the Soviet Union.

It seems possible that Roche had by 1948 become virulently anticommunist. Her testimony before Dublin Keyserling's Loyalty Board would certainly suggest so.[40] But, it also seems possible that Roche exaggerated her anti-communism at the loyalty hearing. If she were to do Dublin Keyserling any good in that context, Roche had to establish her own unassailable commitment to the American institutions and values that Dublin Keyserling was suspected of rejecting. Moreover, Roche must have worried that she herself, having many of the same associations as Dublin Keyserling, might come under suspicion by anti-communist crusaders and thereby threaten the fragile experiment in social welfare that she was just undertaking at the United Mine Workers of America Welfare and Retirement Fund. Roche believed with all her heart that, if given a chance to create a full welfare program, the fund might improve the lives of individual miners and, with that, boost the labor movement at a moment when it was severely embattled. Only weeks before her testimony for Dublin Keyserling, she called her directorship of the fund "the most significant opportunity" of her life. "There are many battlefields," she had said, "but never so great a one as this."[41] Given that the fund was under attack by coal operators and that conservatives in Congress were restricting union authority in every way they could, Roche had to have felt her own past affiliations with the Left might well put the fund at risk. One business publication had warned upon Roche's taking charge at the fund that "every move she makes is going to get careful scrutiny from the Coal industry" because the enterprise was so "controversial" and the operators remained largely opposed to it.[42] With so much at stake, Roche had every reason to amplify her anti-communism in 1948.

Whatever her motive, Roche's testimony before the Loyalty Board represented a significant historical shift. Long in easy association with the Left, Roche disavowed not only communists themselves but also those willing to ally with communists on particular issues. Because Henry Wallace accepted the endorsement of the Communist Party and promoted cooperation with the Soviet Union in world affairs, Roche not only denounced him and his third-party effort but also renounced her own identity as a "progressive." Just as she said in Dublin Keyserling's loyalty hearing that Wallace's party took the name "progressive" in vain, so she castigated the party a year later, when she declared that she had been a progressive "when the word 'progressive' had not been desecrated by the people who are using it today."[43] Since one of the identifying characteristics of progressives had long been their alliances with those farther left and Roche no longer approved such alliances—either out of a sincere change of heart or from more pragmatic motives—it made sense for her to stop identifying as a progressive in 1948. The postwar anti-communist crusade thus transformed many a former progressive into a Cold War liberal.[44]

But there was more to Roche's transformation from progressive to liberal than her new unwillingness to ally with the Left. In the next decade, she narrowed her reforming focus to one group of workers rather than remaining explicitly focused on the broad program of social and economic reconstruction that she and other progressives had long pursued and that Roche had been adamant to keep ever before her. As an example of the broader trend, a comprehensive national health plan was off the table for twenty years after Truman's initiative in the late 1940s. Piecemeal reforms were the best that reformers hoped for.

Roche's telescoped focus pointed to one of the profound effects of anti-communism in the late 1940s and 1950s. By discouraging sweeping programs for social change, it pulled apart the various campaigns for social justice that had in the 1930s been coalescing and forced each to go it alone in the postwar world. In the 1930s and early 1940s, Roche herself had repeatedly insisted that each campaign, each piece of legislation, each organization or government agency must be seen as part of the larger program for human welfare. "Our various fields are but small lots, separated from each other only by imaginary lines," she had proclaimed in the 1930s, "in one great general field where we must do joint battle for our common cause—security for all human beings."[45] By the late 1940s, because of the Cold War and its empowerment of the anti-communist crusade at home, that larger project of social reconstruction was no longer within the bounds of acceptable political speech because it implied a broad critique of American institutions—including unrestrained capitalism, white supremacy, and patriarchy. As a result, labor unions especially committed to racial justice lost traction. Issues of class were muted in mainstream organizations dedicated to racial justice. And the interests of workers and consumers were construed as largely antithetical rather than joined in opposition to corporate interests.[46] Struggles for social justice continued through the 1950s, but they did so mostly as individual campaigns focused on one group or issue rather than as part of a sweeping program for diminishing inequality in American life.

This narrowing of focus represented a significant change from the progressivism of the 1930s and early 1940s and warranted a new name: Cold War liberalism rather than progressivism. It signaled the beginning of the second temporary reversal in the Age of Reform. And, unlike the first reversal, this one changed Josephine Roche herself, constricting the scope of both her agenda and her alliances. In Roche's case, the ground had been prepared for change during the war, when she began to cast a more wary eye on politics and government as allies in the cause of diminishing inequality. Other progressives took different paths, and the timing of their conversions varied. But by the early 1950s, Cold War liberalism had supplanted progressivism as the main alternative to conservatism in American politics.

PART IV

SECOND TEMPORARY REVERSAL OF PROGRESSIVE REFORM: ROCHE BUILDS A PRIVATE WELFARE SYSTEM IN THE COALFIELDS, 1948–1963

The second temporary reversal of progressive reform was under way by 1948, when Josephine Roche denounced "Commies," screwball liberals, and Henry Wallace's Progressive Party. During this second reversal, progressivism was not so much subordinated by conservatism in national political life as transformed into the less ambitious, critical, and visionary Cold War liberalism. As during the first temporary reversal, however, Roche continued to experiment with new ways of diminishing inequality. She did not explicitly connect her experiments with a broader movement for social reconstruction as she had before, and she would for a few years even lose her grip on the commitment to democratic decision making that had marked her institutional leadership in the decades previous. But even still, Roche's postwar experiment in building a private social welfare program for coal miners embodied ideals she had formed in the early years of the twentieth century. Progressivism thus lived on in bits and pieces within Cold War liberalism, and Roche's work at the United Mine Workers of America Welfare and Retirement Fund provided proof.

CHAPTER 14

CREATING "NEW VALUES, NEW REALITIES" IN THE COALFIELDS, 1948–1956

D espite the contraction of her reforming efforts in the late 1940s, Josephine Roche had high hopes for her new work at the United Mine Workers of America Welfare and Retirement Fund. She proclaimed in fact that her goal as director of the fund was to "build new values, new realities" in America's coalfields.[1] Remarkably, she did just that. Although initially under siege from many directions, Roche managed to build a private social welfare system that did for one group of workers what she had hoped the New Deal would do for all: guarantee world-class health care and a dignified retirement. This creative work in the private sector did not mean Roche had given up on public policy: she imagined her health program as a template for or component of a larger federal health care program that might develop somewhere down the road. But she also saw her work at the fund as a direct support to the labor movement, which she believed even more crucial now to the task of diminishing inequality. Roche therefore construed her postwar efforts in the private sector as a continuation of her early twentieth-century mission to right the wrong of Ludlow.

When Roche moved into the director's office of the Welfare Fund in April 1948, she reensconced herself in the nation's capital (figure 12). This time, her work occupied several stories of a modern office building overlooking leafy McPherson Square, only a few blocks from her old digs at the Treasury Building and within sight of the national headquarters of the United Mine Workers of America (UMW) union. She joyously reentered her New Deal community. Her good friend Arthur Altmeyer remained at the head of Social Security programs. She still had economist friends in the Department of Commerce. Edward Keating, whom Roche had known since the 1910s, resided in the capital city. Martha Eliot, with whom Roche had worked closely on the New Deal health plan, returned in 1951 to head the Children's Bureau, and Clara Beyer continued her work in the

Department of Labor until the late 1950s.[2] Most important, Coloradan Oscar Chapman held high positions at the Interior Department, including eventually that of secretary.[3] These New Dealers offered Roche not only friendship but also useful contacts, which she shamelessly exploited for information about and support of projects near and dear to the fund. Indeed, she shared with John L. Lewis a relish of political intrigue.[4]

Roche's intent as director of the Welfare Fund was to deliver state-of-the-art health care and income assistance to the hundreds of thousands of bituminous coal miners and their families who were concentrated in Appalachia and fanned out over twenty-six states stretching from Georgia to Alaska.[5] She hoped to supplement the inadequate retirement pensions coal miners received from Social Security, support miners' widows and orphans, and compensate for the failure of a national health program by replacing wages lost due to disability and providing health care at no cost to miners themselves. Instead of offering health or disability *insurance*, however, Roche set out to build a health care *service* that would feature everything from maternity care to cancer treatment, preventive medicine to advanced medical research.[6]

Realizing these hopes was an enormous challenge in part because coal miners were among the nation's most vulnerable workers. A conservative survey in the 1940s counted 1,120 job-related deaths annually among bituminous coal miners and over 50,000 injuries.[7] The injuries permanently disabled nearly 2,000 men each year, a number that did not include those sickened by inhalation of coal dust. Tuberculosis and pneumonia killed coal miners at a rate far exceeding that of the general population, and a more mysterious lung ailment sometimes called "miner's asthma" caused additional widespread disabilities and death.[8] Because coal mining communities so often lacked effective sanitation facilities, gastrointestinal maladies were rampant, and nervous disorders naturally plagued families whose breadwinner risked life and limb every single workday.[9]

Implementing Roche's vision was also a challenge because it faced many powerful opponents. In fact, it seemed possible that the work would not go forward at all. Although coal companies had been forwarding royalties to the miners' trust fund since 1946, the companies had blocked use of the monies by filing a series of lawsuits. No retirement pensions had been paid and no general medical program established when Roche became director. Only emergency aid to victims of mining accidents was dribbling out to beneficiaries.[10] As the lawsuits snaked through the court system, trustees of the fund wrangled over eligibility requirements and benefit levels. The Taft-Hartley Act (1947) required that any union-negotiated welfare fund be operated by a board of trustees that included representatives of workers, employers, and the public.

In extremely contentious discussions, the UMW fund's three-member board temporarily agreed on eligibility requirements for beneficiaries of death and disability payments as well as retirement benefits. If the fund were ever allowed to start paying out pensions, for example, a miner who had reached sixty-two years of age and mined for twenty years would receive $100 a month from the fund.

To Roche's great relief, shortly after she assumed leadership of the fund, the legal logjam broke. In June 1948, Judge T. Alan Goldsborough ruled against the coal operators in a case holding up the bulk of the fund's assets. In response, Roche moved like lightning to begin creating new realities in the coalfields.[11] By early September, the fund delivered its first pension check to a retired miner in Rock Springs, Wyoming, and two months later, Roche had paid over half a million dollars in current pensions and nearly four million in retroactive pension payments. She had also authorized grants to over 40,000 disabled miners, miners' widows, and orphans.[12] By that time, too, Roche had furnished the fund's offices, identified hundreds of coal companies delinquent on royalty payments, and replaced the man John L. Lewis had put in charge of medical services. Indeed, by September 1, 1948, Roche had installed her own choice, Dr. Warren F. Draper, to oversee the fund's medical work.[13] Draper was a former New Dealer who shared her progressive vision of health care.

Roche and Draper began their partnership by implementing a remarkable rehabilitation program for severely disabled miners. As soon as she took office, Roche began locating coal miners paralyzed by mine accidents and then transporting them to the finest rehabilitation facilities in the country. Between July and November 1948, she hospitalized 99 stricken miners, some of them bedridden for as long as twenty-eight years. She had also identified nearly 500 more men needing the same care. Roche's research revealed appalling examples of medical neglect: some of the men were so misshapen by their injuries and subsequent lack of medical attention that their twisted bodies would not fit on stretchers; they had to be carried out of mountain hollows on their own beds to reach ambulances or railcars that whisked them on to treatment centers (figure 13).[14] It took Roche's medical staff a year to arrange for treatment for what she called this "backlog of human misery." By then, Roche could report that hundreds of "these indescribably tragic cases have been hospitalized and almost half of these hopeless and neglected men are now out of bed and getting around again." Many were learning new vocations.[15] Roche's early work at the Welfare Fund demonstrated some of the most dramatic possibilities imaginable for "human conservation."

To generate new programs with dispatch, the wiry and intense Roche, still chain-smoking in her early sixties, worked constantly and expected nearly the same from her subordinates. She rarely took a day off, and in

1948 had everyone at the fund working five-and-a-half days a week. She gave her employees Thanksgiving Day off but not the following Friday. She closed the offices for Election Day and Armistice Day, but did not close until noon on Christmas Eve. On Good Friday, she allowed supervisors to let employees attend services between noon and 3:00 but required everyone back at their desks thereafter.[16] She could not understand how anyone could want a day off when coal miners were suffering.[17]

In keeping with her mission, Roche moved during her first few months at the fund to steel John L. Lewis's spine in a struggle to increase miners' benefits. Lewis represented the miners on the fund's board of trustees and, in early negotiations, had been outvoted on the age of eligibility for a retirement pension from the fund. Lewis's original hope had been for any miner with twenty years of work in the coalfields to retire at sixty, but the coal mine owners had temporarily defeated him by commissioning an actuarial report. Actuaries, whose job was to predict future costs of insurance schemes, generally argued that insurance plans should offer only benefits for which they could set aside enough money to guarantee the benefits through the lifetime of every beneficiary. This approach—sometimes called a "fully funded plan"—had set actuaries against the old-age pension plan in the Social Security Act because their standards would have meant prohibitive start-up costs. Instead, New Deal policymakers designed a pay-as-you-go program that served current beneficiaries from current receipts. Beneficiaries were protected by a reserve fund built up before any benefits were paid, but, in rejection of actuarial science, the reserve was not calculated to guarantee lifetime payments to each beneficiary. If costs sufficiently outran receipts at some point, taxes would have to be increased or benefits cut. That was the risk taken and one that progressives like Roche adamantly supported. True to form, the actuaries hired by the coal operators at the fund advised a much less generous pension than Lewis called for, and the issue remained contentious when Roche became director.[18] Once apprised of the situation, Roche generated reams of data and arguments to help Lewis win a retirement age of sixty for bituminous coal miners.[19]

Roche's case against the actuaries exposed her continuing commitment to many progressive ideals and spotlighted the postwar relocation of some New Deal battles to the private sector. For starters, Roche channeled progressive historian James Harvey Robinson when she explained that the actuaries' claim to extrapolate future costs of a pension program represented a "wholly unsubstantiated, theoretical position," which attempted "to contemplate the manifold uncertainties of the future," a patently impossible task.[20] She argued, moreover, that hard data—the touchstone of social science progressivism—had proven the futility of actuarial predictions: "<u>actual experience</u> demonstrates the absurdity and unreliability of . . . actuaries 'projections' and dire prophecies," she insisted.[21] "How wrong" the actuaries had been in the case of Social Security, for instance, "has been amply proven," she informed Lewis. "The ten-year experience of the S.S. Fund shows that a <u>not-fully funded</u> plan is practicable."[22] Social Security's pay-as-you-go pension program was indeed building assets even as it paid out benefits.[23]

In this campaign, Roche replayed arguments made on behalf of Social Security's pension plan in her New Deal days and sometimes even faced down the same individual opponents. One was the trustees' actuary, Russell Reagh, with whom Roche had tangled at the Treasury in the 1930s. According to Roche, Reagh had been "brought to the Treasury by . . . as reactionary an anti-labor bird as could be found," and he had consistently opposed Social Security. What was worse in her view, Reagh remained at the Treasury while "he works on the side for the Duponts . . . and has a very fancy country estate."[24] Feathering his own nest by working for the notoriously anti–New Deal and anti-union Duponts was an abomination in Roche's view; facing Reagh in her private-sector work confirmed her sense that she was fighting the same battle against inequality here that she had fought in the New Deal government.[25]

Roche's conflict with Reagh also illuminated both her relationship to John L. Lewis and her postwar personality. Most importantly, in this episode as in most others at the fund, Roche led Lewis. She was the partner who understood actuarial science and could identify the deceptive practices it used to thwart liberal advancement. But in addition, Roche communicated her understanding with a sometimes shocking dose of acid. After one particularly galling exchange with Reagh, Roche raged against his "utter lack of mental integrity," and after explaining to Lewis the misunderstanding that one of Reagh's forms would inevitably create, she concluded, "No more misleading or ill-founded table could be devised. . . . He could ask nothing better than for us to fall into his crude little trap and type in the figures for his tables, so that he could say the Fund's own experience—its own data—proves the impossible future cost of the pension program." Roche referred to this move as, "The 'last gasp' effort of Reagh to bulwark his fraudulent estimates."[26] Roche had always had a sharp tongue and at times shown contempt for her opponents, but, in her youth and midlife, those qualities had been balanced by self-deprecation and self-critique. Since that time, she had been immersed in the secretive and deceptive business culture of the coal industry and then in a political world of backroom deals and betrayals. Add to those experiences the general paranoia of the early Cold War, and it is easy to understand, perhaps, how a more cynical and guarded Roche emerged in the postwar period.

In fact, in the late 1940s, Roche described herself as "a suspicious person," and her behavior at the fund bore out the judgment.[27] After information about the fund was leaked to the press early in 1949, she established a complete lock on such news.[28] From that point on, Roche had to approve not only every press release and article written by staff members but also every professional presentation given by any member of her staff, including the doctors. As her bureaucracy grew to include medical directors in far-flung places like Denver and St. Louis, she required that every letter or pamphlet they sent to beneficiaries or health care providers be approved by her first.[29] She chose, moreover, not to serve on policy-making bodies in her first years at the fund because she did not want to share information that might in any way be used against her fledgling agency. She forbade other members of her staff to do so as well.[30]

The suspicious and irascible streak in Roche's personality—so much more evident in the late 1940s than before—was given fullest expression in her relationship with John L. Lewis. With him, she felt completely free, and she expected him not only to accept her vitriolic excesses but even to enjoy them. He did: Lewis considered Roche a paragon of virtue. Toward the end of the 1950s, in a note attached to an accolade Roche received from the American Labor Health Association, Lewis wrote: "A tribute, worthy of a goddess, coming from the hearts of men."[31] Given to biting insult himself, Lewis encouraged the same in Roche. Theirs was a liberating relationship, in which Roche felt no obligation to tamp down her fury or moderate her invective. She loved Lewis for giving her that freedom.

During the 1950s, the press sometimes intimated that this love had a romantic tinge. The petite, white-haired Roche and gigantic, bushy eyebrowed Lewis, both unmarried by that time, did see each other nearly every weekday through the decade (figure 14). They often met in the dining room at the Carlton Hotel, where they lunched separately and then Lewis approached Roche's table to conduct various kinds of business. This was a regular ritual and one interpreted by the press as courtship.[32] What reporters could not know was that Roche almost always had specific business to discuss with Lewis at those lunchtime encounters. When either Roche or Lewis missed the lunchtime rendezvous, they spoke on the phone, or Lewis lumbered over to the fund's stately offices late in the afternoon.[33] But there is no evidence of romance. They were a determined and effective team, perhaps enjoying the eros of shared mission in time of siege. But they were almost certainly not lovers.

Just as John L. Lewis required no restraint of Roche's meanest feelings, so he temporarily uncapped her dreams for the welfare of miners. As Roche reported to the press in spring 1949, she and Lewis agreed that "the degree of human need in the mine fields would be the measure of the [UMW's welfare] program's ultimate extent, and not the availability of funds."[34] After becoming so discouraged in the late New Deal years by the excruciating effort required to win and maintain nothing but "minimums" in social programs, what an exhilarating change for Roche to be told that she need not consider current revenues a limit on the benefits she could imagine for the miners. Rather, she was to determine the extent of need, and Lewis would find a way to get her the money. Lewis insisted that protecting the health of miners and their families, supporting those disabled by mine work, and providing a dignified retirement to those grown old underground should be considered a cost of doing business, and he intended to extract that cost from coal mine owners, whatever it took.

Given this freedom, by March 1949, Roche had taken significant strides toward fulfilling the mission she and Lewis shared. In addition to sending more and more disabled miners to rehabilitation centers, Roche was paying monthly stipends to disabled miners, including supplements for their spouses, children, and other dependents. She was paying retirement pensions of $100 over and above Social Security's monthly stipends. Miners' widows and orphans also received monthly income support from the fund in addition to one-time payments of $1,000 to the family of any miner who died. Roche had also begun to pay for medical care for "the cases of most shocking neglect."[35]

Just as Roche was then beginning to expand the medical program, Lewis entered a season of tumultuous contract negotiations. As the union and coal operators battled through the summer, some companies stopped sending royalties to the fund, while Roche continued to pay at least $2 million per week in benefits. By September, with no contract in the offing and fund resources dwindling, the trustees voted to stop paying benefits.[36] Two days later, nearly 400,000 miners went on strike, chanting, "No welfare, no work."[37] Emotions ran high both in the coalfields and the offices of the fund. The operators' trustee resigned.[38] When the new industry representative announced his commitment to actuarial science, Lewis refused to seat him, and Roche started searching for skeletons in his closet.[39] By December, Roche was laying off staff from the fund, and several coal companies took the union to court for failure to comply with the Taft-Hartley Act.[40]

As the coal cases made their way through the courts in early 1950, Roche worked closely with Oscar Chapman, now secretary of the interior, to convince President Truman to take over the mines. By doing so, Roche hoped to avert fines for contempt of court that seemed sure to be levied against the UMW when miners refused to return to work despite an injunction requiring them to do so. On February 20, Chapman privately approached Truman to try to stave off the Justice Department's plan to file contempt charges against the union. He asked the president to seize the mines. Truman was open to the suggestion, but indicated he would not take over the mines until all of Taft-Hartley's procedures had been followed. Truman wanted to demonstrate that the anti-labor law was a failure in that, even after its procedures had been followed to the letter, no coal would be mined.[41]

On March 2, 1950, Judge Richmond B. Keech surprised the president, Chapman, Roche, Lewis, and the coal operators by refusing to find Lewis or the union in contempt of court, and on March 3, the president sent a message to Congress, drafted by Oscar Chapman, asking for power to seize and operate the mines.[42] If the administration took over the mines, mine revenues would flow into the U.S. Treasury rather than into the accounts of mine owners, and the workers would have to return to work under provisions of the 1948 contract. Neither side wanted this outcome, but it was the operators' hopes that had been most clipped by the combination of Keech's decision and Truman's message to Congress. Only hours after Truman's request went to the Capitol, the majority of operators reached agreement with Lewis on principles for a new contract, and two days later they signed the National Bituminous Coal Wage Agreement of 1950.[43]

That agreement was momentous. The miners won an increase in wages and royalties for the fund, and Roche was named the fund's "neutral" trustee. All observers recognized that Roche was anything but neutral and that her appointment gave control of the fund to representatives of the miners.[44] Her appointment was an ingenious way of circumventing the Taft-Hartley Act's prohibition of union control of union-negotiated welfare funds. In return, mine owners won compliance with Taft-Hartley on eligibility for the fund's benefits: union membership did not confer eligibility; only employment in a company signatory to the union contract did.[45] And the miners gave up the right to strike during the two-year term of the contract.[46] Unbeknownst to anyone at the time, the 1950 agreement would remain the basis of labor relations in the coal industry for more than a decade. Wages would increase and the royalty to the fund would rise from 30 to 40 cents per ton of coal mined, but the basic parameters of agreement were now set for years to come.[47]

With Roche and Lewis occupying two of the three positions on the fund's board of trustees, they formed an indomitable team. The new industry representative was Charles Owen, and his first two years as a trustee were nothing but frustration. Roche routinely ignored his requests for information and sometimes refused to send him agendas in advance of meetings.[48] Before each meeting, Roche and Lewis decided which issues to raise as well as how they would vote, and then proceeded to outvote Owen on every one. Within a few months of gaining control, they gave Roche full power over money in the Trust Fund, agreed to keep the fund's money in the National Bank of Washington—a bank in which the UMW held a controlling interest—and nixed Owen's motion to turn over the fund's benefits to a commercial insurance company.[49]

For all the power that Roche now exercised at the fund, the eight agonizing months of suspended benefits in 1949–1950 had caused some soul searching. She saw more clearly the suffering that might result from overextending the fund's resources. As a result, she resumed benefits more slowly than she might otherwise have done, restoring one-time death benefits in May 1950 and retirement pensions in June. She was especially cautious as she contemplated the medical plan.[50] In fact, Roche conceded in spring 1950 that the fund could not afford to offer miners and their families complete medical and hospital care at no cost to miners themselves. With a 30-cent royalty established by the new contract, she accepted the necessity of tailoring benefits to revenues.

In keeping with her commitment to democratic decision making, Roche invited representatives of the miners to help make decisions about what medical benefits to fund and which beneficiaries to cover. To facilitate the discussion, she and Draper drafted a proposal and submitted it to the presidents of the union's regional districts. Roche saw these men as representatives of rank-and-file miners even though most were handselected by John L. Lewis, who had long ago ended most elected representation within the union hierarchy. Still, the presidents were in touch with their members and on the issue of health benefits had an inkling of members' preferences. Roche was not completely mistaken in identifying these presidents with the rank-and-file. But rank-and-filers were not united in their hopes for the fund, and the district presidents clearly favored the interests of one constituency over all others.

The proposal for health care that Roche and Draper sent to the district presidents bore the imprint of the New Deal. Closely tracking the reasoning of Roche's Coordinating Committee in the 1930s, she and Draper assumed that the best thing they could do was provide care for those least able to afford it. Since working miners had reliable income, they were presumed to be able to pay for most of their own health care. Consequently, Roche and Draper proposed a comprehensive plan of home, office, and hospital care for retired and permanently disabled miners and help for working miners only in cases of catastrophe, like long-term illness or hospitalization.

When the district presidents met with Roche and Draper, their priorities caught the New Dealers by surprise. Instead of supporting the plan to cover those most in need, the presidents, at first hesitantly and then with intensifying ardor, insisted that the working miner deserved priority. "We must take care of our working men," stated one president. "Working members and families should come first," agreed another. "The people in the mines should be given first consideration," echoed the president from District 5. It was after all the working miner who preserved the union, they argued, and who would be counted on to back the union during all contract negotiations. Working miners wanted their families, widows, and the "old-timers" taken care of, but they expected something for themselves as well. Roche and Draper were flabbergasted. At one point, Roche said, "I had thought that the pension, disability, death benefits, etc. were considered just as much a benefit to the young men as to the old men." One president irritably agreed, "Every working man is getting plenty from the protection of this Organization, for his widow, children and for hospital care when he needs it most."[51]

The majority of presidents, however, disagreed, and Roche listened intently. The logic of a union welfare plan, she learned, was different from a public plan. While in the 1930s, pollsters had found that the American public was willing to pay taxes to provide health care to those who could not provide it for themselves, Roche and Draper subsequently learned that workers expected a private plan to cover the worker first. The active worker was considered most entitled to benefits because his own sacrifice and labor had won the benefits in the first place. By the end of their conference, Roche and Draper had begun revising their proposal, and Roche insisted to the presidents, "We feel we must have closer contact with you personally, not only through correspondence. We hope to have frequent meetings like this to discuss plans and new steps, and I hope to visit the District offices personally."[52]

Roche's response to the district presidents demonstrated that in 1950 she remained committed to the kind of democratic decision making she had instituted at the Foreign Language Information Service (FLIS), Rocky Mountain Fuel (RMF), and the National Youth Administration (NYA): those affected by a decision ought to have a say in it. Indeed, so seriously did Roche take the testimony of the miners' representatives that, from this point on, she put working miners at the center of her concern. All other considerations had to be secondary because she believed that preserving the union was the fundamental requirement of her work. Only the union gave workers some voice in the wages they earned, the housing and medical care they received, the hours they worked, and the safety of conditions under which they worked. Without the union, workers were powerless. Moreover, absent the union, there was no fund. Even though the fund was a legal entity separate from the union, and she was required by law to act in the interest of the beneficiaries of the fund rather than in the interest of the union, Roche did not see the two organizations as practically independent. And so, when Roche became convinced by the district presidents that the union's preservation—which required rock-solid commitment from the men currently underground—required the fund to give priority to the working miner rather than to those unemployed, disabled, or elderly, she fastened her intentions firmly to serving that miner above all others.

Roche's revised medical plan reflected the priorities of the district presidents while still spreading benefits as broadly as possible. As it emerged piecemeal, the program paid for all costs of hospitalization for working miners, disabled miners, unemployed miners, and miners pensioned by the fund as well as miners' dependents, including wives, minor children, and the miner's and his wife's parents if the parents were living with the miner and financially dependent on him. It also covered outpatient care by specialists. For a while, widows and orphans continued to receive medical benefits indefinitely, though that benefit was soon restricted to one year following the miner's death. The fund also paid for some especially expensive drugs and, of course, rehabilitative services. What Roche and Draper had excised from their original health plan was home and office care. All routine medical care by general practitioners was to remain the responsibility of miners or the union local.[53]

Roche's decision to accept the district presidents' health care priorities also meant reducing income assistance programs to disabled miners, widows, and orphans. When she resumed those programs in 1950, she cut their maximum monthly benefit in half. More dramatically, when the cost of the medical program increased beyond expectations only four years later, she ended sustained income assistance to widows, orphans, and disabled miners altogether. When she terminated these income support programs in 1954, Roche claimed they had never been imagined as a permanent part of the fund's obligations. But in reality, the income replacement programs had taken priority over medical care to working miners in Roche's initial estimation. Only after absorbing the preferences of the district presidents did she shift the fund's priorities.[54]

In fall 1950, when the final shape of the health program was announced, Roche was so fully absorbed in her work for the fund that she finally withdrew entirely from management of RMF. She described her work at the fund as "engrossing and demanding beyond words" and was still spending virtually every day of the week in the office with no vacations at all. Her only absences from Washington in 1950 were for RMF board meetings, including a final confab in October, where she "performed the long overdue act of resigning, both as president and director." The UMW had a controlling interest in the company, and one of its own was selected as president. "It was a perfect time for me to resign," she sighed, "and the relief is enormous."[55]

Indeed, Roche's work at the fund absorbed her more fully than any other work she had ever done. When she resigned from RMF, she withdrew from most voluntary organizations as well, and, after a lifetime of itinerancy, only rarely left Washington. As she confided to an old friend later in the 1950s, she did not go regularly "even to New York."[56] In fact, during the next two decades, she rarely ventured out of the fund's immediate neighborhood, keeping her living quarters within walking distance of the office.[57] Consistent with earlier preferences, she lived in small apartments or at the Carlton Hotel, places that required minimal attention and provided the restorative privacy she required after action-packed days at the fund.[58]

In 1952, that action ceased to include friction with Charles Owen, the industry representative on the fund's board of trustees. Owen's decision to stop fighting with Roche and Lewis signaled larger shifts in the coal industry. By 1952, many of the big coal operators, especially in the North, sought cooperation with the UMW because of marked declines in the demand for coal—especially due to competition from oil and gas—and increasing competition from small, nonunion mine companies in the South—especially Kentucky and Tennessee. Those small operations could pay union wages and still underprice the big companies because they did not pay royalties to the fund, and they were often small enough even to avoid federal safety regulations. Their costs were thus lower than those of the big companies.[59] Roche and Lewis preferred the big companies because they seemed safer for miners, supported the fund, and were more likely to hire union workers. By 1952, Lewis and Roche accepted the sincerity of the big operators' wish to cooperate with them, and an eerie peace settled over meetings of the fund's trustees.[60]

This peace permitted Roche to expand the fund's services to such a degree that they were billed by the mid-1950s as the largest nongovernmental welfare program in the world.[61] In the early 1950s, the fund's old-age pensions were the most generous in basic industry; the fund rushed aid to miners' families in the event of disaster; disabled miners received medical treatment from the fund unequaled by any other private health plan; mortality rates declined measurably in the coalmining regions; and even its opponents conceded that the fund was noticeably improving health care within its precincts.[62] In fall 1951, the fund won the first of numerous awards for its medical program, this one from the U.S. President's Committee on Employment of the Physically Handicapped.[63]

The diminution of morbidity and mortality in the coalfields resulted from extraordinary departures in health care. Unlike most commercial health insurance companies, Roche's fund took responsibility for the quality of care received by beneficiaries. It began doing so by dividing the country's coal-mining districts into ten areas and assigning a medical director to each one. The directors, all medical doctors, were responsible for identifying physicians, hospitals, and clinics that provided acceptable care. Once approved, these doctors and facilities billed the fund directly for services rendered to eligible miners and their families. All the miners had to do was flash the provider with their fund-issued health cards.[64]

At first, the medical directors were liberal in their approval of doctors and facilities. With time, however, misgivings about many physicians and hospitals grew, and hopes for improved care from these providers diminished. In fact, the directors' investigations of hospitals and doctors confirmed miners' anecdotal reports that health care in coal-mining areas was often inadequate, sometimes incompetent, and at times, fraudulent. Of course, some doctors and hospitals were doing exemplary work under challenging circumstances. In many areas, however, no hospital served miners at all, and general practitioners performed surgeries and treated conditions they were in no way qualified to handle. Many areas relied on hospitals that did not meet requirements for accreditation. In one Kentucky hospital, investigators found "an accumulation of rubbish and filth in the hallways and rooms, unwashed windows dark with grime, and . . . even an accumulation of dust on a microscope." One patient reported going nineteen days without a change of bedclothes. In another hospital, fund investigators discovered an operating room cooled by a large electric fan situated just outside a doorway. "When the fan blows, it picks up dust and dirt from a manure pile located about twenty feet away. The air is blown across the floor of the operating room and should a patient be on the operating table, fatal contamination would be a natural consequence."[65] Local doctors, who owned many of the hospitals, made money from hospital charges as well as their own individual bills. They sometimes profited even from the hospital pharmacies. These incentives encouraged long hospital stays, lots of prescriptions, and unnecessary surgeries.[66] In some places, most extracted appendixes were perfectly healthy, and unnecessary tonsillectomies were so common that the fund stopped paying for them in 1952.[67]

The fund's initial responses to these problems indisputably improved health care. Under pressure from the fund, some hospitals began working toward accreditation, and some doctors helped to recruit specialists to their communities as well as to improve their own care. In Tennessee, the state medical society organized a special group devoted to improving health care in the state's mining districts, the results of which were inspirational.[68] Where no public health unit functioned, the fund lobbied states to take up the kinds of preventive health measures for tuberculosis, diphtheria, typhoid, and dysentery that Roche had extended to many areas through her work at the Public Health Service (PHS) in the 1930s.[69] Moreover, the fund sponsored research on a range of miners' lung diseases that were hard to diagnose, disregarded by the medical establishment, and unrecognized by workmen's compensation programs, and would eventually be called "black lung." The fund educated doctors on the existence and treatment of the devastating but controversial condition, and, of course, paid for treatment.[70]

Despite these improvements, the fund locked horns with many doctors and medical societies. By 1954, Roche determined that fund beneficiaries in some areas had hospital stays twice as long as patients paying their own bills and openly considered withdrawing fund approval from doctors whose record of unnecessary surgeries and excessive hospitalizations was demonstrable. Most local medical societies rallied to the defense of their members, setting up terrible conflicts with the fund, especially in eastern Kentucky and West Virginia.[71] The fighting was so intense that one national publication referred to it as part of "Labor's War with the Doctors."[72]

Clashes between the fund and local health care providers stood to reason because Roche and Draper were guided by a vision of health care first developed in the Progressive Era and completely at odds with the way medicine was generally practiced in the postwar United States.[73] This vision imagined doctors giving up individual, fee-for-service practices and associating in group practices at health centers where they could consult with each other about patients' care. Doctors would earn a salary or retainer for particular groups of patients and provide all necessary care without charging for individual visits or services. Roche had long been in conversation with reformers who believed this reorganization of medicine necessary before compulsory national health insurance could succeed. She took their arguments to heart and worked toward their vision in her work at the fund.[74]

This progressive legacy was highly controversial. The doctors ruling the American Medical Association (AMA) and most local medical societies remained adamantly opposed to progressive proposals, and they often denied the necessities of medical practice—hospital privileges and malpractice insurance—to doctors who cooperated with the fund's reorganizing initiatives.[75] They were also willing to spend enormous sums of money to fend off such threats to their lucrative independent practices. In 1949, the AMA had spent one and a half million dollars defeating President Truman's proposal for compulsory health insurance.[76] They also won legislation in some states that outlawed all direct-service health programs, which were health plans like the fund that provided service rather than indemnifying consumers for some portion of their medical bills.[77]

Although initially eager to avoid offending local doctors, Roche did experiment from the beginning with new systems of health care delivery where she could. She gave her medical directors freedom to create group medical practices in out-patient clinics wherever they could argue this was the only way to draw specialists to certain communities, and she encouraged paying retainers to doctors caring for particular groups of miners wherever directors could get away with it.[78] In 1951, she made a more grandiose move. She announced that the fund would build its own hospitals in areas of Appalachia underserved by medical professionals and so poor they could not attract federal monies for community hospitals.[79]

Roche's hospital plan fully realized in one area of Appalachia the progressive vision for health care.[80] It created an integrated system of ten health care centers, each a memorial to miners killed or disabled in the course of their work. Seven of the hospitals were located in eastern Kentucky; two in West Virginia; one in Virginia. The hospitals operated as one system with centralized administration for such things as billing and ordering. They shared dieticians and librarians. Three of the hospitals were large, multipurpose centers; the others, satellites to the larger facilities. Each of the larger hospitals offered between 100 and 200 beds; the smaller ones, 50 to 85. Each hospital featured an out-patient clinic, health education programs, well-baby clinics, and various forms of specialized care. Eventually, the hospitals sent mobile health units into even more rural areas, and all facilities were open to the larger community as well as beneficiaries of the fund.[81]

The hospital project proved to be an economic development program for parts of Appalachia, a sort of health care Tennessee Valley Authority (TVA), especially welcome because of the continuing downturn in the coal industry. The fund built its hospitals in some of the poorest counties in the country, and the projects included not only hospitals and clinics but sometimes housing for new doctors.[82] Roche required that union labor be employed to build the facilities, and, once built, the hospitals hired workers of every skill level, from groundskeepers and janitors to highly specialized doctors. In many areas, the hospitals offered such high-paying jobs that local employers complained about the competition for workers.[83]

Unlike some architects of private pension and health plans in the postwar period, Roche did not see her program as a way to stave off universal, tax-supported health care measures. In fact, she did not see any of the benefits offered by the fund as *competitive* with public programs. She saw her work in the private sector rather as a spur to public social welfare programs. Wherever she could, Roche used fund resources to pressure the states to expand their services, and she saw her programs as developing and modeling first-rate social welfare practices that other providers, including government, might someday emulate.[84] In the case of her health program, she also saw her work as providing an initial layer of change—the reorganization of medicine—that some reformers thought necessary before a compulsory national health program could be feasible. Roche thus saw her work in the private sector as a building block toward more universal Social Security.

Indeed, despite her reduced confidence in government as a partner in diminishing inequality, Roche remained deeply committed to the principles embedded in the Social Security Act and to their expansion. In this, she was of one mind with postwar liberals generally. In 1953, for instance, she quietly opposed moves by Dwight D. Eisenhower's presidential administration to prevent expansion of Social Security's old-age pensions.[85] Behind the scenes, she also pressed for the extension of the Social Security system to include disability insurance, which her own health plan had proposed in the 1930s and which finally came to fruition in 1956. She lobbied in addition for more sustained unemployment compensation, a federal agency to coordinate programs for the handicapped, and, when the time was right, another attempt to move the federal government into health care.[86]

Roche's role in these developments occurred behind the scenes in the early and mid-1950s not because she no longer cared about public Social Security programs but because Roche feared that public appearances by any representative of the fund risked further alienating the doctors with whom the fund was locked in conflict. For example, Roche allowed Warren Draper to participate in private sessions of a presidential commission on health care in 1952, but when the commission moved toward public hearings, Roche dropped an iron curtain between the fund and the more public forum, fearing that even a "chance remark" taken out of context might offend the doctors she was working so hard to recruit to the fund's vision of high-quality health care.[87] For that moment, public silence seemed the better part of valor.

Moreover, Roche no doubt feared drawing anti-communist crusaders' negative attention to her nascent medical program. Medical opponents of the fund routinely accused it of trying to "socialize medicine," a particularly fearsome accusation in the early Cold War context. Since representatives of the fund would inevitably oppose conservatives on Social Security issues, their participation in any public debate might give right-wingers motive to join the medical opposition to the fund's health program. In the early 1950s, when the anti-communist crusade was in full swing and Roche's medical program was in a delicate stage of development, she had reason to fear that the uncontrollable give and take in a public forum might jeopardize her health care experiment in the coalfields.

Roche did everything she could to ward off suspicions of the fund, and the hospital project helped. She associated her enterprise with fundamental American values by breaking ground for the first hospital on July 4, 1953. Before Thanksgiving, construction was under way on all ten centers, and only two years later, the hospitals began to open. Shortly thereafter, the chain of ten hospitals was dedicated in a widely publicized ceremony. On June 2, 1956, Roche and Lewis rode a festively decorated train into Beckley, West Virginia, location of the largest of the memorial hospitals. They delivered celebratory speeches before thousands of miners, union officials, and medical leaders. In her oration, Roche tied the hospitals to the longer history of progressive reform, referring to them as part of the fund's commitment to "human conservation," a phrase she still borrowed from the Progressive Party platform of 1912.[88]

Miners and their families treated the dedication ceremony as a major festival. According to reporters, they streamed out of mountain hollows and laid out picnic lunches to celebrate. They toured the sleek modern facility their labor had created. Even if journalists exaggerated when they described the miners as "awed" by and "wide-eyed" at the gleaming medical equipment and pristine bathrooms of the hospitals, those descriptions may not have been far off the mark. After all, some of those miners lived in unpainted two- or three-room cabins with no running water. The contrast between their homes and what one hospital architect called "the glassiest hospital in the world" could hardly have been starker. That the fund's state-of-the-art hospitals would become a source of pride for at least some miners was perfectly plausible.[89]

The glassy hospitals drew new people to Appalachia's rural communities and developed the brain power already there. Some of the finest physicians in the country relocated to Appalachia to be part of this innovation in health care. All the hospitals trained medical residents and interns from top-notch medical schools. Within two years of opening, some of the hospitals won research grants from the National Institutes of Health (NIH). One of the big, central hospitals trained registered nurses, and the other two offered programs for licensed practical nurses. The chain also trained medical technicians.[90] The goal of the fund was eventually to hire all of its nurses and technicians from the local population, an enormous boon to depressed communities.[91] Roche pointed out with delight the benefit to mountain women of the nearly 700 nursing and 245 nursing aides positions.[92] Another point of pride was that the hospitals hired dozens of disabled miners and their families, and all photographs of the facilities emphasized their racial integration (figures 15 and 16).[93]

By the time the hospitals were dedicated, the fund was routinely winning awards and public praise.[94] That year, the fund received the prestigious Albert Lasker Award from the American Public Health Association "for brilliant and dedicated scientific planning which has created a model program of health services for a million and a half workers and their families."[95] Congress found the fund, in contrast to many other union programs, to be "honestly and well administered; in fact, the medical program is outstanding," and the general program "of incalculable benefit to the beneficiaries."[96] In 1958, the Harvard School of Public Health used the fund as a "case study in our required Public Health Practice course."[97] In 1958, the American Labor Health Association paid tribute to Roche and her work at the fund.[98] Visitors from Europe and Latin America visited the fund to learn from its example, and, perhaps most astonishing, in 1959 the United States Information Agency (USIA) saw the fund as such a point of national pride that it extolled its programs in 200 local publications outside the United States.[99]

By the mid-1950s, it seemed that Roche's fund could do no wrong. It was acknowledged in labor circles as the standard setter for health plans.[100] Experts in rehabilitative medicine credited the fund with helping to establish Physical Medicine as a specialty, and those eager for the reorganization of health care appreciated the push toward group practice and salaried doctors. Even the more conservative *Reader's Digest* praised the fund for providing an example of "free enterprise social security."[101] Although Roche supported public health care and saw her work at the fund as building infrastructure that might one day make a national public health care system feasible, she happily associated her efforts exclusively with private initiatives if doing so was necessary to protect this first stage in the building process. In the Cold War context, when she had to fend off accusations that even her preference for group practice and salaried doctors promoted "socialized medicine," she welcomed commentators willing to see her innovations as consistent with American ideals.[102] By 1956, the fund was winning the point as *Reader's Digest* hailed its accomplishments as congruent with America's free-enterprise system. Indeed, the accolades from *Reader's Digest*, Congress, and USIA were evidence that Roche was helping to win the public relations battle over the reorganization of medicine. The victory extended only to group practices and some authority for third parties—like the administrators of health plans—in health care matters, but it was a remarkable feat, one that helped to change the shape of health care for virtually all Americans in the later twentieth century.[103]

That triumph was attributable in large part to Roche's administration of the fund and the iron grip she established on publicity about its programs. In comparison even to such well-run hospitalization plans as Blue Cross, Roche's administrative costs at the fund were mind-bogglingly low. She generally kept the administrative cost of the fund at 3 to 4 percent of expenditures.[104] Her closest competitors spent twice that percentage.[105] In forum after forum, investigators expressed astonished admiration for her efficiency, for the sleek integrity of an enterprise that put virtually all of its resources into direct services for beneficiaries.[106] On visiting the fund's offices, veteran administrator Arthur Altmeyer observed to Roche, "I must say that I have never had an opportunity to observe an organization which clicked with the efficiency and precision that yours does."[107]

Moreover, Roche was prescient in her view that she should control every word that left the fund's offices. She knew the fund was battling for hearts and minds. To give the fund the highest chance of winning that battle, Roche set up an office of public information to generate positive press about her operation, and she hired her old friend George Creel to run it. In 1951, she began producing a glossy, illustrated annual report that explained the operations of the fund in such gripping terms that some readers wrote to say they found it "deeply moving."[108] Recognizing the potential value of the annual report for generating public support, Roche from the first hired a professional writer to complete the final editing and write a press release to highlight the points that would be of greatest interest to the mass media.[109] Roche's annual reports presented not only all revenues and expenditures of the fund but also photos of miners receiving state-of-the-art health care at the Memorial Hospitals, children whose lives were saved by surgeries or medications provided by the fund, retirees glowing with happiness as they left the mines for the last time. Sidebars featured letters from miners, widows, and orphans grateful for the fund's life-sustaining aid. The annual report explained why health care costs were so high and why the fund might suggest group practices in some areas to guarantee higher quality care at costs the fund could afford.[110] Roche wrote multiple drafts of every report, hired the finest photographers to provide eye-catching photos, and circulated the masterpiece as broadly as she possibly could.[111] Partly as a result of Roche's public relations campaign, after 1956, she and Draper would no longer feel they had to refuse to speak in public forums about the fund's medical work.

By 1956 indeed, much of Roche's caution-inducing context had changed. The most virulent brand of anti-communism was discredited by Joseph McCarthy's overreach, and the threats posed by congressional anti-communists consequently diminished.[112] The Eisenhower administration had lost a bid to stymie expansion of the federal Social Security program, and the fund's hospital chain was completed. In fact, the fund had pretty well laid to rest the accusation that it was socializing medicine and had instead convinced most Americans that its program was a star in the cap of the all-American free-enterprise system. At that point, Roche no longer felt the need to operate so clandestinely as in the early 1950s. Battles between the fund and local doctors, though continuing, could be carried on in public without substantial threat to the fund.[113] Roche began to breathe a little easier.

With the dedication of the miners' memorial hospitals in 1956, Roche had brought the UMW's Welfare and Retirement Fund from nearly nothing to a premier private welfare program. In the ten years since its inception, it had spent almost one billion dollars on nearly a million beneficiaries.[114] Roche had defeated the actuaries and other conservative opponents who would have forced her to offer more limited benefits to fewer beneficiaries and made innovation in the medical field impossible. Without abandoning hope for expanded public Social Security programs, she laid building blocks for change that would eventually sweep the nation in medical care. It is no wonder that, for the first time in her life, Roche was utterly absorbed by one thing. She had remarkable power at the fund, and she exercised it to the fullest, carrying many of her Progressive Era commitments into the postwar period. Indeed, from the reorganization of health care to support for organized labor, Roche carried strands of early twentieth-century progressivism into Cold War liberalism.

CHAPTER 15

DEMOCRATIC DENIALS AND DISSENT AT THE MINERS' WELFARE FUND, 1957–1963

D uring the late 1950s, two trends marked Josephine Roche's work at the miners' Welfare Fund. First, she reemerged into public life, having gained confidence that her latest creation was no longer at risk from hostile coal operators, anti-communist crusaders, or recalcitrant doctors. Second, her commitment to democracy eroded. By 1960, Roche had built an effective bureaucracy committed to improving health care among miners and to preserving their union. But, unlike bureaucracies Roche had assembled before, this one became frozen in its priorities and deaf to the preferences of those it claimed to serve. This attenuation of democratic commitment was one of the principal reasons that, despite the survivals of progressivism in her work at the fund, Roche could no longer be considered a progressive. Ironically, however, the lack of democracy within the fund generated such anger in the coalfields that it helped to spark the final eruption of progressive reform in twentieth-century America during the 1960s.

In the late 1950s, the dissatisfactions of miners were mostly contained within the union and the fund. What the outside world saw was a vital experiment in social welfare, which included what one journalist called the "giant United Mine Workers' medical empire."[1] Indeed, Roche's health care domain extended from Appalachia to Alaska; she managed tens of millions of dollars a year; and she enjoyed the accolades even of former opponents.[2] As a result, Roche gained a new confidence that allowed her, among other things, to push harder and more publicly for the reorganization of medicine.[3] In 1957, she asked the fund's medical administrators to cut from their lists of approved physicians any doctor who, after years of work with the fund, refused to stop overhospitalizing, overoperating, or overcharging. Nearly a third of previously approved physicians were cut off.[4] She also began more openly favoring group practices over individual medical practitioners.[5] And, she experimented with what came to be known as "managed care." After a decade of small trials using primary care physicians to coordinate a patient's care, Roche allowed Warren Draper in 1962 to make managed care a goal for 50 percent of the fund's beneficiaries.[6] That process went so well that, by 1968, the fund publicly aimed to put all its beneficiaries under managed care, and 70 percent of its managing doctors were on retainers.[7]

In another sign that Roche was no longer running scared, she agreed to chair the National Conference on Labor Health Services in 1958. Sponsored by the American Labor Health Association, the conference convened in the same Mayflower Hotel where Roche had gaveled the first national health conference to order twenty years before. From the podium all these years later, Roche waxed eloquent about the gains made in preserving the nation's health since that first convention. But she also warned that much work was yet to be done, and because unions were among the few groups moving forward on this front, strong and inventive unions were the main hope for improving the medical care of most Americans. Conferees publicly heralded all the practices reviled by the American Medical Association (AMA)—group practices, salaried doctors, community health centers—as the way of the future and shared strategies for moving in those directions.[8]

Roche's greater confidence also moved her back into policymaking circles. In 1959, the federal Department of Health, Education, and Welfare asked Roche to serve on an advisory committee for a White House Conference on Aging, and she actually said yes.[9] More important, she agreed to serve on Arthur Altmeyer's Advisory Committee on Social Security, a group organized to make recommendations for the Democratic Party platform in 1960.[10] With unemployment chronic among coal miners and an ever-growing segment of America's blue-collar workers, Roche pushed for unemployment insurance to cover the full period of any workers' joblessness, and she pressed for public provision of health care.[11] The health care proposals before the advisory committee focused exclusively on the elderly, a constituency especially in need and politically appealing because commercial insurers had little interest in covering them.[12] None of the proposals satisfied Roche, whose positions on national health policy had changed since the 1930s. She was now adamant, for instance, that the states *not* be given jurisdiction over any portion of health care because she felt the states had failed miserably in the tasks assigned them by the New Deal and so would never be able to offer adequate health care.[13] She believed instead that any national health plan should be administered by the Social Security Administration as a fully federal program, and should pull all beneficiaries—well-off or poor—into the same program.

Furthermore, Roche believed that the federal plan should hew as closely as possible to her hopes for the fund's health program. It should pay for full medical care—hospitalization, doctors' bills, surgery, and even preventive and restorative medicine. Predictably, no bill before Altmeyer's advisory committee served as many people or offered coverage as comprehensive as Roche preferred, and the proposal in the Democratic Platform fell short of her vision.[14] What she had once called the "political mechanism" continued to frustrate Roche's highest hopes for diminishing inequality, but at least health care had reappeared on the nation's political agenda, and Roche was once again making a public case for grander policies.

Even as Roche was worrying about national inequalities in health care, however, she grew less concerned about inequalities of power within the Welfare Fund itself. In the late 1950s, her attention to democratic personal relations and decision making waned. It was not that Roche refused all contact with beneficiaries of the fund. Occasionally, she met in her office with delegations of miners who had a complaint, and she met with dissatisfied groups at biennial conventions of the UMW.[15] But she did not maintain regular meetings with the district presidents or routinely visit the districts as she anticipated in 1950, and no procedure was ever put in place for consulting with miners in advance of changes in policy at the fund. After 1950, Roche met with miners in ad hoc situations about decisions that she had already made.

Indicative of Roche's changing relationship with the miners was the tone of her correspondence. In the early 1950s, when Roche had received inquiries about the fund's rejection of applications for benefits, she had taken great pains to explain the rejections and to identify alternative sources of help. By the late 1950s, she was fending off supplicants rather than engaging them. Her letters simply repeated that the fund could not aid the applicants and discouraged further contact.[16] Roche was aware of the change. Addressing a convention of the UMW, she distinguished herself personally from herself as director of the fund and regretted the tone she felt she had to take in the latter role. "Some day, perhaps, when I am not Director of the United Mine Workers of America Fund I can write an answer to some of the letters that are written to me as I personally would like to write them, not as Director of the Fund. As Director of the Fund I write them exactly as they must be written. . . . The answers . . . have earned for me . . . the title of the "No" woman. I do not like to be a "No" woman . . . but whenever it is necessary to safeguard your Trust Fund . . . we just move in and function."[17]

Powerfully capturing the erosion of democracy in the fund was an exchange between Roche and a group of miners unhappy with the fund's mental health services. Psychiatric care was not routinely covered by the fund because state mental hospitals provided services. But miners often hated the public asylums, which were usually far from home and at times a perfect horror of debilitated patients. In response, the fund hired psychiatrists at the memorial hospitals and provided out-patient psychiatric care where it could. In fact, by the late 1950s, the fund was sending mental health professionals to rural communities in mobile health units. But these experiments did not reach everyone, and some groups of miners continued to protest against sending their mentally ill dependents to public institutions.[18]

Officers of one union local in West Virginia took up the issue in 1959. Their pleas for a hearing with the central office of the fund revealed both their sense of entitlement to a fair hearing and their resistance to the more general bureaucratization of the fund. In a letter to the trustees, the local officers explained their habit of meeting with their Area Medical Administrator whenever they were "dissatisfied with his handling" of "nervous disorders and border line mental cases." The last time they had asked for such an appointment, however, their administrator asked them instead to "write him concerning the case." A letter would have saved the miners a trip to the administrator's office in Morgantown, but they did not want to be spared the travel because they did not trust the written word. "We feel," they explained, "that writing cases to him would not bring any concrete results."[19] They knew that a letter was easier to ignore than a flesh-and-blood human being and that their more minimal educations disadvantaged them in a written exchange. They could be more effective if they were looking the administrator in the eye and making their case with their whole selves to his whole self. Face-to-face oral communication created greater equality between miners and administrators at the fund.

Even though the miners had apparently disapproved the dispositions of many earlier cases of mental illness, they had not gone over the administrator's head with their protests until he refused to see them in person. What drove them to seek redress higher up was the sense that they were being forced into a subordinate position from which they would not be able to make their case effectively. Thus, they appealed to the trustees. "We insist the International Trustees of the Welfare and Retirement Fund . . . make an investigation and send an investigator to our Local Union." When "the investigator arrives, we will present in detail our grievances.[20] By demanding that the trustees send someone to hear them out *in person*, the miners revealed their sense of entitlement to a voice in fund decisions and pointed to the only method of communication through which they believed they could achieve a fair hearing, which was the oral rather than written word.

Roche denied that hearing. She responded in off-putting legalese: "The official Trust Fund notice dated October 1, 1957 sent to all beneficiaries holding Fund-issued hospital forms, and to all Local Unions and Districts with covering letter, clearly states in paragraph #2 that Trust Fund payments are not authorized for any hospitalization or medical care of beneficiaries for whose illnesses or incapacities treatment and care are available to them, as to other citizens, by or in public supported agencies or institutions." She went on to say that the area administrator's decision in the current case "has been in conformity with these regulations." She concluded not only that the "decision in matters such as your letter presents is not subject to further discussion or review" but also that under "regulations of the Trustees, investigations such as you suggest are not authorized."[21] Roche's letter was a "Case Closed" stamp. In it, she made clear that area administrators had every right to reject oral communication and that miners had no say in the policies of what they believed to be *their* welfare fund. Her message was that the trustees made the rules; the area administrators implemented them; and the miners had no other choice than to accept them.

For Roche, bureaucracy and democracy had at last parted ways. From her early career through the New Deal, Roche had built bureaucracies that established two-way communication and depended on face-to-face relationships between managers and clients or employees. Like many other progressives, she had made bureaucracy and democracy compatible. At Rocky Mountain Fuel, Roche had gone so far as to fire her general manager because of his unilateral decision to lay off workers rather than continue the job sharing miners themselves preferred. She had started off on this same foot at the fund, when in 1950 she revamped her health care program in accordance with advice from the union's district presidents. But by the late 1950s, the fund was not democratic. Although John L. Lewis was ostensibly the mouthpiece of miners at the fund, he was no longer directly in touch with miners, and his lieutenants in the field were more likely to squash discontent with the fund or union than act as spokesmen for it. No other official conduit permitted miners to shape the fund's policies. There were only means for the fund to notify miners of decisions already made. Roche no longer sought to create the democratic personal relations or decision-making procedures that marked her earlier work. Her commitment to diminishing inequalities in health care, to improving the material lives of miners, had trumped her commitment to democratic decision making within her institution. This priority of efficiency over democracy was a hallmark of Cold War liberalism.

Although the anti-democratic bureaucratization of the fund was a betrayal of Roche's earlier progressivism, her need for efficient ways to manage an impossible workload was understandable. Her daily docket overflowed with obligation. She tracked revenues, projected expenses, invested monies, monitored delinquent royalty payments, and initiated lawsuits against delinquent operators. She generated forms and instruction manuals to keep up with changing eligibility requirements for benefits. She repaired buildings and replaced equipment when floods damaged the miners' hospitals.[22] She tried to figure out how to protect the fund's doctors from retaliation by local medical societies, supported research on what would come to be known as black lung, managed salaries and benefits for the fund's own employees, kept abreast of legislation affecting benefit programs, and testified before Congress on those issues. She met with government and foreign dignitaries interested in programs of the fund, vetted every speech and article that left the fund's offices, and spoke to UMW conventions.[23]

As if this were not enough for a woman who turned seventy in 1956 and soon required hearing aids in both ears, Roche did have a bit of a nonwork life.[24] She did all she could, for instance, to support her godson, Bill Owens (figure 17). By the late 1950s, "her boy" was applying to colleges, and Roche was greasing the wheels for him at several institutions. Bill's family had relocated to the Washington, DC, area, and she lunched with them fairly often and celebrated holidays with them routinely, usually hosting a dressy Christmas dinner at the Carlton Hotel. She never missed Bill's or his sister's birthday.[25] Fastidious about her appearance, Roche had her hair done every week and shopped at the upscale Garfinkel's Department Store.[26] She occasionally invited the Altmeyers, Read Lewis, or Mildred Lea to dinner at her apartment. She somehow remained in touch with the artistic community and hosted in one of her small apartments an exhibit of abstract paintings, poignantly confiding to her godson that she thought artists were the happiest people she knew.[27]

Especially demanding of Roche's remarkable stamina was the need to shore up the fund's bottom line. Late in the 1950s, many factors converged to thin the financial ice under the fund. First, the coal industry continued to decline. Competition from oil and gas decreased coal production from 688 million tons in 1947 to 392 million tons in 1954. Membership in the UMW correspondingly declined from 400,000 members in 1945 to around 200,000 in 1955. Sharpening that decline was an increasing market share among nonunion mines, which by the early 1960s accounted for 25 percent of U.S. coal production. Since the fund drew its revenues from royalties paid on each ton of coal mined by companies signatory to the UMW's wage agreements, the decrease in production diminished the fund's revenues, as did production by mines not signatory to the union contract.[28] Second, the fund was incurring enormous expenses from the health program. Inflation in the cost of health care resulted in part from measures pioneered by the fund but also from expensive technological and pharmaceutical advances in the treatment of disease. In addition, the miners' hospitals were, as it turned out, never full. The fund was thus spending a lot of money maintaining empty hospital beds.

Rising costs and decreasing revenues eventually required the unthinkable: major cutbacks in benefits. Roche began to worry about the possibility in 1958.[29] With the fund's income still falling early in 1959, she informed her staff that they must decide just how low their reserve funds could sink before they curtailed benefits and, in that event, who would take the hit. Having internalized the priorities of the union's district presidents in 1950, Roche argued that the working miner above all must be protected. The least "disastrous" place to cut would be hospital and medical care for retired miners.[30]

In the end, medical care for pensioners was not cut, but this first discussion of potential reductions was revelatory. It confirmed that Roche figured the good of the union into her decisions at the fund, even though, legally, the two institutions were separate, and why she did so. As things stood in 1959, cutting medical benefits from pensioned miners would have been one of the *most* disastrous benefits to cut, rather than the least, if the welfare of current beneficiaries were the only consideration. The reason was that in the late 1950s elderly Americans were the group least likely to qualify for private health insurance, and they were the population most in need of health care. They also generally had lower incomes than miners currently working. Consequently, cutting their medical benefits would have been far more damaging than cutting medical benefits to younger, working miners. But cutting the medical benefits of pensioned miners might well have been the "least disastrous" choice for the good of the miners' *union*. As Roche would subsequently note, coal companies were just beginning to hire hundreds of new miners each month as coal-fired electrical facilities were built and put into service. These new miners had yet to join the UMW.[31] Free, state-of-the-art medical care would be a potent incentive. A powerful reason, then, not to cut benefits for working miners was to motivate younger miners to join the union and thereby keep their companies signed on to the union's wage agreements. That way, their employers would pay royalties to the fund, and benefits could continue and even expand. In Roche's mind, the good of the fund and the union were often indistinguishable.

In summer 1959, no benefit reductions were made, but the fund's financial sky darkened. Later in the year, as expenditures exceeded receipts by more than $10 million, Roche and her staff worked feverishly to project income and expenses.[32] They toyed with various ways of cutting benefits to see what kinds of savings each reduction might produce.[33] Eventually, Roche warned John L. Lewis and the industry trustee, Henry Schmidt, about the probable need to reduce benefits and persuaded them to vote for specific reductions calibrated to particular benchmarks in the fund's reserves. Shortly thereafter, Lewis announced his resignation as president of the UMW and his intention to continue as the union's trustee at the fund.[34]

The year 1960 brought the first major reductions. In the spring, reserves dropped so low that Roche prepared to end medical benefits on July 1 for miners unemployed for more than a year or working in a managerial position. By her calculations, over 59,000 people would lose benefits, the bulk of them among "older groups." Underscoring Roche's lack of regard for democratic processes, she refused to notify beneficiaries of the reductions until July 1 to prevent a rush for medical services in anticipation of the cutback.[35] Her administrative doctors, informed of the reductions in April, were stunned and remonstrated that they should have been notified earlier so they could solicit state agencies or private philanthropies to help those cut off.[36] They dreaded the storm of protest that would blow through their offices, and Roche agreed they were heading into severe turbulence. She insisted, however, it could not be avoided if the fund were to remain solvent.[37]

The letter canceling benefits went out over Roche's signature.[38] Howls of protest went up, and she spent weeks responding.[39] As she did so, Roche knew well that this was only the beginning of a sustained state of siege: at the June meeting of the trustees, she had convinced Lewis and Schmidt that if the cash balance of the fund dropped below $70 million, they would have to cut benefits even further. When that happened, she intended to protect not only working miners but also her pioneering medical program: she proposed to cut the pensions of retired miners rather than their health benefits. In fall 1960, when it became clear that reserves would indeed dip below $70 million, Roche called Lewis to tell him that she planned to reduce retirement pensions from $100 a month to $75. To remove any more beneficiaries from the medical program, she argued, would nearly destroy it, and she could not let that happen.[40] At Roche's insistence, then, the trustees announced on December 30, 1960 that pensions would be cut by 25 percent beginning with checks sent on February 1, 1961.[41]

Needless to say, cutting miners' pensions was a shocking development. A decade before, Roche had helped to engineer for coal miners one of the most generous private pensions in all American industry. But, as other unions increased their pensions through the 1950s, the fund expanded its health program instead. By 1960, miners' pensions no longer led the pack, and the 1961 reductions dropped them even further behind. Retirees felt the reduction as an egregious betrayal of trust. They had earned their pensions fair and square and, with only thirty days' warning, they lost 25 percent of this monthly income. How could this be?[42]

Looking back from February 1961, it might have seemed that the actuaries had been right. The pay-as-you-go pension system was doomed to failure. But they were not right. By their calculations, the fund should have reached insolvency much earlier and without building its "medical empire." Actuaries in the 1940s predicted that the pension program would soon be insolvent even if only the early pension and disability program were continued. Had the fund stuck with only those programs, it could have paid benefits indefinitely.

As it was, however, even Roche's medical program would have to face more cuts before the worst was over. A national economic contraction that began in 1957 took its worst toll on the coal industry in late 1960 and early 1961. As a result, the fund's income fell to its lowest level since the early 1950s.[43] In addition, the fund faced potentially devastating legal challenges. As the coal industry stumbled through the 1950s, small mining operations went in and out of business, some of them run by miners themselves when they were laid off by larger companies. It was increasingly common for these small concerns to hire union members and sometimes pay a union wage but, in order to charge prices competitive with bigger companies, withhold royalties from the fund.[44] In many cases, Roche took such companies to court for violation of the Coal Wage Agreement. But in other instances, she let the delinquencies pile up while continuing to pay the miners' health bills.[45]

Roche's variable treatment of small companies resulted from a deceptive maneuver sometimes practiced by union representatives and mine operators. The procedure required a small operator to sign the Bituminous Coal Wage Agreement and then contract a secret oral agreement with the union representative that replaced the written contract. The new oral pact often forgave the royalty or the union wage rate but allowed miners to receive full benefits from the fund based on the (now fake) written contract. Forgiveness of the royalty or the union wage helped to keep many companies afloat and union members employed in a bad labor market.[46] Roche did not know about all of these secret oral agreements, but she did know about at least 700 of them. In these 700 cases, she continued to pay benefits to miners whose employers she knew were no longer legally signatories to the Coal Wage Agreement.[47]

Incidents in 1962 made her covert participation in these deals clear. At that time, the fund was following a routine procedure in taking several Tennessee companies to court for nonpayment of royalties. Before the cases were decided, the UMW urgently contacted Roche, pleading with her to withdraw the suits. As it turned out, the written union contracts on which her suit was based had been superseded by secret oral agreements between union representatives and employers. These oral agreements explicitly allowed the operators not to pay royalties to the fund or to pay only what they could. These operators were no longer, then, actually signatories to the Coal Wage Agreement. Given that her suits were based on what looked like valid written union contracts, Roche could have persisted with them, but such a course risked exposing the duplicity of the UMW. In the end, she spared the union that exposure—against her legal counsel—dismissing the cases and withdrawing health benefits from those employed by the apparently but not actually "delinquent" companies.[48]

In these instances, Roche had not known about the secret agreements. But the experience in Tennessee forced her to face the risks to the fund that her knowledge of many other such cases entailed. Just days after the imbroglio over the Tennessee lawsuits, Roche convened some of her staff and announced that the fund must stop benefits to several thousand additional miners because, as her notes put it, the "Fund definitely has information in files and field investigations to show written contracts throughout Districts 19 and 30, where no royalties have been paid the Fund, are as much 'sham' contracts as those on which litigation was based. Trust Fund has financial obligation to move in promptly to make sure no further dissipation of Fund monies."[49] Two days later, she brought Lewis into the loop and convinced him, too, that she simply had to withdraw benefits from the miners working for these allegedly delinquent companies because she was fully aware—and had been for years—that the companies no longer considered themselves signatories to the Coal Wage Agreement. Their secret arrangements with the union meant they were not genuinely delinquent and their employees were legally ineligible for benefits. Lewis reluctantly agreed to Roche's decision, and she prepared to cancel the health cards of nearly 4,000 workers in over 700 companies in Kentucky and Tennessee.[50]

The new cancellation notices went out in September 1962 and ignited fury in the coalfields. Thousands of miners converged in the parking lot of the memorial hospital at Hazard, Kentucky, pledging to strike their mines to force their employers to pay the royalties.[51] Miners were confused and outraged about suddenly losing benefits when their status had not otherwise discernibly changed: they remained dues-paying members of the UMW, and they believed their employers signatories to the Coal Wage Agreement.[52] To the miners and the outside world, it looked like the fund canceled benefits in these instances *instead of* taking the delinquent companies to court to get the royalties they owed.[53] Observers at the time assumed the move was ordered by Lewis to drive small operators out of business or to cut costs. But Roche was the one who ordered the cancellation because she knew the secret oral agreements meant there *were* no delinquent royalties in these cases. This knowledge she never revealed publicly.

This episode offers an opportunity to reflect on the damage done to our understanding of the past by sexist assumptions about who has been in charge of crucial decisions. The cancellation of benefits in 1962 has been misunderstood by reporters, lawyers, and even historians as a cost-cutting measure or an attempt to put small, nonunion mines out of business.[54] These misunderstandings have stood because of Roche's success in covering her knowledge of the secret agreements between hundreds of operators and union representatives. Roche was so successful in covering her knowledge in part because of the ubiquitous assumption that John L. Lewis made all the decisions at the fund and Roche was simply his rubberstamp. Few of those who have written about the union or the fund have entertained the possibility that Roche made the decisions and commanded Lewis's acquiescence and have not, as a result, mined the records of Roche's work independent of Lewis.[55] But Roche's dominance was the norm in fund operations, and only in her records do we learn what really happened in 1962: when Roche realized that her documentable knowledge of "sham" contracts put the fund in legal jeopardy, she ordered the cancellation of benefits for miners employed by offending mines. Lewis had to go along. The labor titan was not exaggerating when he once told the press that Roche made the decisions at the fund: "All the trustees do is hold the light."[56]

The 1962 cancellations generated ire and inquiries from miners, miners' lawyers, and even congressional representatives. Roche was especially shaken by the threat of a congressional investigation into the union's relations with the fund.[57] Consequently, she conducted a full and systematic audit of royalty payments and instituted a rigid policy for prosecuting delinquent companies.[58]

In the course of that clean-up, Roche and Lewis faced an especially dicey situation, one that, had it come to light at the time, would surely have sparked congressional investigations. The situation involved the West Kentucky Coal Company, an operation that as early as 1960 was significantly in arrears to the fund. By 1963, that debt remained, which was not unusual, except that the UMW owned 64 percent of the company's common stock! Had Roche gone after West Kentucky Coal to recover delinquent royalties, she would have been demanding payment from the union itself. Miners, Congressmen, and the general public would have blown sky high at the scandal of the union's failure to pay royalties into its own members' Welfare Fund. And, of course, Roche was on the wrong side of the law when she held back from taking the company to court to get those royalties: she was legally bound to run the fund in the interest of the fund's beneficiaries, not in the interest of the UMW. She and Lewis were as a result sweating bullets in 1963 as they desperately tried to identify a buyer for the union's shares in the company, which, finally, they did. The buyer paid the royalty debt—with a loan from the union—and Roche and Lewis were off the hook on that score.[59]

Josephine Roche was deeply implicated in the union's shady dealing. During the late 1950s and early 1960s, she knew full well that many coal companies to whose employees she was providing generous health benefits had colluded with the miners' union to avoid various obligations imposed by the Bituminous Coal Wage Agreement. She was thus in violation of the laws that governed the fund. She may also have conspired with Mildred Lea, her assistant of many years, to cover their knowledge of the sham contracts and other union misdeeds. In spiral notebooks where Lea kept track of Roche's daily appointments and where several entries in the late 1950s vaguely alluded to oral agreements between the union and some employers where the fund continued health benefits despite delinquent royalties, someone glued many of the notebooks' pages together. The glue is so firm that a reader cannot possibly see what is on the pages now stuck together. It may be that Mildred Lea spilled coffee on those pages or simply needed to correct some of the entries, but it may also be that these mysteriously glued pages—now lost to history and snoopy lawyers or congressmen—contained evidence of explicit decisions to continue paying benefits even where Roche knew employers did not consider themselves bound by the Coal Wage Agreement.[60]

Roche's motive for overextending benefits was perfectly laudable. She wanted to spread the benefits of the fund to as many coal miners as she could, and the law requiring her to act in the interest of beneficiaries and not in the interest of the union failed to recognize the very real relationship between the two. Indeed, the law most immediately governing the fund was the anti-labor Taft-Hartley Act, whose purpose was to curb the increasing power of the union movement after World War II. Nevertheless, Roche operated outside the law and eventually, under threat of having her illegal generosity discovered, had to withdraw benefits from miners who had every reason to believe they were entitled to them. Transparency at the fund and miners' own involvement in decisions about eligibility requirements and benefit levels would have prevented the profound sense of betrayal coal miners suffered in the early 1960s. The ramifications of that betrayal eventually reverberated well beyond coal country, but not before Roche threw one more match into the exceedingly dry tinder of the eastern Kentucky coalfields.

In October 1962, only weeks after canceling the health benefits of thousands employed by "delinquent" coal companies, Roche shocked miners further by announcing she would have to close four of the memorial hospitals in eastern Kentucky if she could not find a buyer for them. The problem was that miners often used nonfund hospitals closer to home, leaving memorial hospital beds empty. When a beneficiary went to a nonfund hospital, the fund paid twice, once for maintaining the empty bed at a memorial hospital and again for the bed at the non-fund facility. The situation was financially untenable.[61] Roche hoped that local communities might take over the hospitals, but they were too poor even to maintain the hospitals, much less to purchase them.[62] Eastern Kentucky was one of the poorest areas in the United States. Because of mechanization in the coal industry—a trend generally encouraged by the UMW—and the downturn in coal use, unemployment rates in Appalachia were twice the national average.[63] Around Hazard, Kentucky, where one of the threatened hospitals was located, between one-third and one-half of coal miners relied on government aid to get through the winter of 1962–1963, and in some counties of eastern Kentucky more than half the residents had relied on government food commodities since 1957.[64]

When Roche added to this misery the cancellation of health cards and a threat to close the hospitals, the coalfields of eastern Kentucky exploded. Miners organized pickets at nonunion and "delinquent" mines. Reenacting scenes from American coalfields earlier in the century, local law enforcement agencies allied with the mine operators. Violence was common. Dynamite destroyed coal trucks, mine tipples, and every kind of equipment. Picketers shut down a goodly portion of targeted mines by December 1962 and thought their union would support them, but the union disavowed responsibility for the protests and, of course, had to remain aloof from actions against employers with whom union representatives had cut secret deals. Baffled protesters bitterly denounced both the UMW and the fund for inexplicably deserting them.[65]

Although many of these same protesters had suffered horribly for many years, it was not until Roche canceled their health benefits and threatened to shutter their hospitals that their misery converted to what one observer called a "burning crisis." The miners' health benefits and the memorial hospitals had taken on not only material but also symbolic meaning. One analyst explained, "Some of those miners worship that hospital card more than anything else." Another claimed that the hospital card was "the most precious asset left" to many miners. Upon hearing that the hospitals might close, one miner warned, "If they do, the people around here would be destroyed. They're our only hope." Reporters drawn to the area by violence in the winter of 1962–1963 explained that miners "look on the hospitals as their personal property."[66] Bearing out that assessment, the leader of the pickets said of the miners: "We helped build those hospitals."[67]

Beyond the health care and jobs the hospitals offered, miners saw the hospitals as *theirs*. Their life-risking labor underground had built those hospitals, and they believed they had a *right* to them. That unelected officials at the fund could take them away was galling in the extreme.

Roche's announcement of the potential closing of the hospitals in Kentucky thus violated two cherished expectations of the miners: the expectation of first-rate health care and the expectation of a say in the decisions affecting the health care they now saw as their right. Roche had succeeded in creating "new values, new realities" in the coalfields. Miners, until recently offered paltry and even appalling medical care, had developed a sense of entitlement to the country's premier health care. When that right was threatened, they used every means at their disposal to reclaim it. They picketed mines and blew up property; they condemned their duplicitous and ineffective union as well as their heartless and undemocratic Welfare Fund. They began to see their cause as connected to others among those shut out of power in the United States: miners eventually reached out to young dissidents in an emerging student movement and activists in the increasingly powerful struggle for racial justice. One miner-protester said, "we are just going to have to get out on the streets like the colored people."[68]

Early in their protests, even as they challenged employers, their union, and the fund, miners also called on the federal government for aid. One demand was that the government ensure what miners saw as their right to effective unionism. "The Government's got to act to get the operators and the union together to make a contract," the leader of the pickets insisted. Recognizing his demand as a call for renewal of New Deal commitments, he declared further, "Roosevelt did it. Truman did it. Why can't Kennedy do it?"[69] Picketers were equally clear, however, that the bargaining of even a farsighted and creative union could not solve all the problems of eastern Kentucky, caused as they were by a sweeping, though as yet largely unrecognized, deindustrialization of the American economy. A much larger political and economic community would need to bring its resources to bear, which is why miners turned to the federal government for more than a goad to collective bargaining. In the immediate, they needed food, shelter, and clothing.[70] But mostly, they wanted jobs. They envisioned a full-scale public works program akin to that of the New Deal.[71] By spring 1963 indeed, coal miners paralleled the ever-strengthening civil rights struggle by threatening a "miners' march on Washington for jobs and unionism in Southeastern Kentucky."[72] One set of observers hailed the miners as the "first soldiers in the war on poverty."[73] Immiserated miners were rekindling progressive reform.

As picketers in Kentucky set their sights on federal aid, so did Josephine Roche. Her immediate attention focused like a laser: she wanted federal money to keep the miners' hospitals open. In December 1962, the United Presbyterian Church expressed interest in operating the hospitals but had no capital to purchase them, and Roche would not give them away for free. She hoped the presidential administration of John F. Kennedy might supply funds for purchase and began pulling strings to that end.[74]

The administration was eager to help. During his presidential campaign in 1960, Kennedy identified Appalachian poverty as a special interest, and the Area Redevelopment Administration (ARA) was created in 1961 in part to respond. By early 1963, however, little of concrete value to the area had materialized.[75] Only after violence erupted in eastern Kentucky did the administration finally direct a concerted effort toward the region. In the early months of 1963, emphasizing that "social unrest taking the form of violence to the hospitals is a real possibility," the administration flew into action, trying to find a way to keep the hospitals open.[76] Kennedy created a cabinet-level task force to figure out how the federal government might help save the miners' hospitals.[77]

As a result, by 1965, all ten miners' memorial hospitals had been preserved. Cooperation among several federal agencies, the state of Kentucky, and the Presbyterian Church, all negotiating with the hard-nosed Josephine Roche, made the save possible.[78] The ARA pulled together a grant for purchase of five hospitals, which it was able to offer the Presbyterians once they created a nonprofit corporation.[79] With incredible swiftness, the Presbyterians created Appalachian Regional Hospitals, Inc. (ARHI), which on October 1, 1963, took ownership of half of the miners' hospitals and was already in negotiations with Roche for the other half.[80] The subsequently formed federal Office of Economic Opportunity (OEO) and Appalachian Regional Commission (ARC) as well as the state of Kentucky provided further support, allowing ARHI to purchase the remaining hospitals and maintain their operation as a unit. Federal intervention thus preserved Roche's progressive vision of health care in Appalachia.

Roche had been right to think that her work in the private sector might stimulate rather than stifle expanded public responsibility for Social Security. Because of benefits from their *private* health plan, miners had come to expect high-quality and comprehensive health care. When their private plan then failed to provide it, they believed the *public* sector owed them a hand in maintaining it. In fact, Roche's and the miners' outreach to the federal government in 1962–1963 revealed an expectation that the public sector was ultimately responsible for miners' health and well-being. Even though the miners had developed their sense of entitlement to state-of-the-art health care through a private sector organization, when the private sector failed them, they saw their government as the guarantor of that right as well as jobs, unionization, and the necessities of life.

Sometimes, historians have claimed that workers in the postwar era came to see their employers rather than the larger national community as the ultimate source of economic security.[81] The miners' case suggests otherwise. It reveals that even those who won substantial benefits from the private sector nevertheless saw the public sector as the ultimate underwriter of their well-being. Indeed, miners' demands for health security, jobs, and effective collective bargaining became part of the pressure in the 1960s to expand federal Social Security programs and corporate regulation. Their protests helped to push the United States into its last progressive moment of the twentieth century. Some of Roche's fondest wishes would be fulfilled in that moment even as she was herself under severe attack by a new generation of progressives.

PART V

THIRD BURST OF PROGRESSIVE REFORM: ROCHE RECLAIMS THE FULL PROGRESSIVE AGENDA, 1960–1976

Josephine Roche's involvement in discussions of the Democratic Party platform in 1960, the coal miners' uprising in 1962, and the subsequent flow of federal resources to Appalachia were all part of the twentieth century's third burst of progressive reform. The progressivism of the 1960s and early 1970s was like earlier iterations in featuring broad social movements dedicated to diminishing inequalities of wealth and power and in the vigorous expansion of public policies intended to regulate industry and distribute the benefits of the country's productive capacity to a wider range of citizens. But in other ways, this final chapter in the Age of Reform contained new priorities and conceptions that justify the name New Progressivism. Racial justice topped progressive concerns in this era; the labor movement was tainted by apparent accommodations to corporate interests; and bureaucracy was considered anathema rather than a weapon against injustice. Because of these differences, older activists like Roche were sometimes viewed by younger progressives as part of the problem instead of the solution to social and economic inequality. Pushed by new progressives, however, Roche eventually denounced the anti-democratic processes she had accepted in the 1950s and returned to the fuller progressive agenda of her earlier career. Her reconversion embodied a trend common to many postwar liberals, who once again made common cause with those farther left to produce this final surge of progressive reform in the twentieth century.

CHAPTER 16

CHALLENGED AND REDEEMED BY THE NEW PROGRESSIVISM, 1960–1972

O nce the miners' hospitals were safely preserved, Josephine Roche had reason to think the future looked bright. Coal production was picking up. The U.S. presidency was occupied by New Dealer Lyndon B. Johnson. The struggle for racial justice was winning landmark legislation that promised to end many forms of racial discrimination, and young people were taking to the streets, mouthing some of the same values that Roche's generation had extolled: equality, democracy, curbs on corporate power. A new mass movement on behalf of women's advancement was in the offing as well, making the 1960s all the more like the moment of Roche's introduction to progressive reform. Pushed by these social movements and the president, Congress was in the midst of a major expansion of federal responsibility for social and economic welfare that in some particulars built directly on the New Deal. Progressivism was again in full swing. Before the third explosion of progressive reform had burned out, however, Roche experienced political whiplash: she was in very short order lauded, vilified, and finally redeemed by the new progressive movement.

In the 1960s, the decade of her late seventies and early eighties, Roche carried on much as she had a decade earlier. She walked everywhere at a clip many younger colleagues could not match, stood ramrod straight, and gave off the kind of energy that commanded attention the minute she breached a threshold. Age did not diminish her charisma.[1] Her work habits and friendships remained much the same as well. She worked relentlessly, punching in at the office even the day after Thanksgiving and during the week between Christmas and New Year's.[2] She stayed in touch with her Progressive Era buddy, Read Lewis, who still lived in New York, and the many friends who dated from her New Deal days: the Altmeyers and Keyserlings, Clara Beyer, John L. Lewis, and Mildred Lea. She continued to preside over holidays with the Owens family.[3]

Some of Roche's daily rhythms did change in the 1960s. She spent lots of time with doctors, especially to have her hearing aids adjusted and eyes checked. Her vision deteriorated enough that she had to replace her signature pince-nez with thick eyeglasses, and age shrank her so much that her heavy glasses sometimes overwhelmed her tiny face. She usually went out to lunch with Mildred Lea, the length of her lunch breaks halved since Lewis retired from the UMW in 1960.[4] She went home every day by 4:30 and, in an acknowledgement that she could not live forever, made a will in 1965, leaving whatever she might own at the time of her death to the Owens family. In a demonstration of iron determination, when the surgeon general's warning in 1964 convinced her that cigarette smoking really was hazardous to health, she gave up smoking cold turkey.[5]

Remarkably, nicotine withdrawal did not dull Roche's ability to parry ominous moves by Congress and coal operators that same year. Since 1961, when Roche abruptly reduced miners' pensions, Congress had been anxious about the apparent instability of private pension plans and considered a range of measures that might shore them up.[6] Roche kept her finger on the pulse of those discussions and, by December 1964, was so convinced that Congress would mandate vesting for all pension plans that she broke down and hired an actuary.[7] In that same month, representatives of a new generation of coal operators threatened the fund by offering their own health insurance packages and pensions independent of the union contract. These operators hoped to win workers' loyalty to themselves and, ultimately, break the union, sparing themselves the royalty to the fund and depriving workers of workplace power.[8]

Fortunately for Roche, coal production increased just in time for her to check the operators' advance. In 1963, the electrical industry turned decidedly to coal for meeting skyrocketing demand for electricity, and by late 1964, the resulting surge in coal production fully registered in the revenues of the fund. Consequently, when several operators first offered their own independent pension plan in December 1964, Roche was able to counter with warp speed. She decided to raise the fund's monthly pensions from $75 to $85 and lower the retirement age from sixty to fifty-five. Expanding eligibility rather than more significantly raising the monthly pension was meant to ease the lives of middle-aged miners, who continued to suffer from extraordinarily high unemployment. In the bargain, Roche hoped to keep a larger pool of unemployed miners from turning to work in nonunion mines. Early retirement on a low income was more appealing to many than a higher income working for a union-buster. Once Roche had sold her staff on this course, she brought John L. Lewis into the loop, and on January 4, 1965, the board of trustees voted the changes. Only thirteen days passed between the moment Roche received word of the operators' rival pension plan and revisions to the fund's own pension package.[9]

When income from royalties continued to increase through the mid-1960s, Roche edged pensions higher and improved other benefits as well. In fall 1965, she restored pensions to $100 per month and two years later increased them to $115.[10] By that time, she had also extended health coverage to miners' dependent children between ages eighteen and twenty-two, and she would soon increase the one-time death benefit sent to widows and other miners' survivors.[11] As the fortunes of the fund improved, Roche tried to spread the new wealth as broadly as possible across coal mining's various constituencies, with the working miner always uppermost among her priorities.

In the mid-1960s, Roche saw promise not only in the revival of the coal industry but also in the legislative whirlwind generated by President Johnson. As she surveyed the federal policy-scape from her perch overlooking McPherson Square, she detected the same kind of progressive energy as in the New Deal Era, a situation gratifying both because Roche was recognized as a progenitor of this progressive renewal and because she welcomed the possibility of diminishing inequalities of wealth and power on a broader scale than the immediate postwar period had allowed. Although the political winds had originally shifted with the election of John F. Kennedy in 1960, they reached gale strength after Kennedy's assassination in November 1963. The new president, Lyndon Johnson, explicitly dedicated his administration to racial and economic justice. In his first State of the Union address in January 1964, Johnson promised "a progressive administration" and famously declared "all-out war on human poverty and unemployment." Well aware of miners' plight in eastern Kentucky, he pledged "a special effort in the chronically distressed areas of Appalachia," and simultaneously urged the current Congress to build a reputation for doing "more for civil rights than the last hundred sessions combined."[12] However skeptical of politicians, Roche had to admit this one was intriguing.

True to his word, only two months after his State of the Union speech, the new president started rolling out anti-poverty legislation. Although many dimensions of the War on Poverty seemed startlingly new, the president's legislative program drew heavily on progressive precedents.[13] Johnson's opening shot was the multifaceted Economic Opportunity Act (EOA), which contemplated, among other things, job training initiatives that mimicked the New Deal's Civilian Conservation Corps and a version of the college work-study programs that Roche's National Youth Administration had pioneered.[14] It created Volunteers in Service to America (VISTA), a sort of domestic Peace Corps reminiscent of Progressive Era social settlements.[15] Only a few weeks later, in a move prompted in no small part by the ongoing activism of unemployed coal miners, the president proposed a massive redevelopment project for Appalachia modeled on the New Deal's Tennessee Valley Authority (TVA).[16] The EOA was signed into law in the summer 1964 just after that year's landmark Civil Rights Act, and the Appalachian Recovery Act was signed into law in March 1965.[17]

President Johnson's War on Poverty was one part of an even grander vision, which he called the "Great Society." Eager to complete and outdo the New Deal, the president eventually extended federal funding to primary and secondary education and the arts, reopened immigration, and involved the federal government in reviving American cities and cleaning up the environment.[18] The scope and humanity of Johnson's vision recalled, and in its effective commitment to racial justice surpassed, the largest ambitions of earlier progressives. As Johnson described his ideal, the Great Society "demands an end to poverty and racial injustice. . . . But that is just the beginning. The Great Society is a place where every child can find knowledge to enrich his mind and to enlarge his talents. . . . It is a place where the city of man serves not only the needs of the body and the demands of commerce but the desire for beauty and the hunger for community."[19]

Roche saw much of the Great Society as a revival of hopes that had been dashed in the 1940s. With her vivid red pencil, she underlined that very sentiment in a tribute to her friend and long-time colleague Arthur Altmeyer. "Almost two decades before the War on Poverty," the admirer reported, "Altmeyer was issuing documented evidence of America's need for what he called a 'war on poverty,' " but at that time few were willing to follow him into battle.[20] In a separate speech, Altmeyer himself explicitly identified Roche as a forerunner of Johnson's poverty warriors: "The tragedy is that the first war on poverty that I think FDR had in mind—Harry Hopkins had in mind—Josephine Roche had in mind . . . died at birth largely because of the oncoming war. . . . It was not until 1960 that we really picked up where we left off 25 years ago."[21] Lyndon Johnson was not alone in seeing the Great Society as a legacy of the New Deal.

No single element of the new president's program was more significant to Roche than his commitment to health care. In his first State of the Union address, Johnson pledged to meet the "health needs of all our older citizens," and in 1965, he signed a set of amendments to the Social Security Act that made substantial progress toward that goal, expanding once more the New Deal program that Roche had helped to craft.[22] Medicare and Medicaid, the two lead amendments, went a long way toward realizing Roche's earlier hopes for health security. For Americans who reached age sixty-five with significant employment history, Medicare provided hospital insurance and, for a small premium, supplemental insurance for doctors' care, home health services, and other out-patient services. In addition, Medicaid provided new funding to the states to support health care for the medically indigent of any age.[23]

With the passage of Medicare and Medicaid, most of Roche's 1938 national health plan was finally enacted—in spirit if not detail. The Hill-Burton Act of 1946 committed federal monies to building community hospitals; disability had been insured in 1956; and now the aged and a significant portion of the medically indigent were provided considerable health care. Wilbur Cohen, soon to be secretary of health, education, and welfare, confirmed her legacy when, after recalling her leadership of the 1938 National Health Conference, he concluded, "many of the proposals emanating from that Conference have since been enacted into law."[24]

If Roche felt a sense of victory, however, she did not express it. By this time, she had developed much higher expectations for health care than she dared in the 1930s, and she now believed that the federal government should take full responsibility for public social welfare programs, leaving nothing to the states because of the inadequacies of most state-run welfare programs and the inequalities created between states by decentralized programming. Old friends like Ben Cherrington perhaps captured Roche's own assessment when he gave her "credit for the shift in public attitude towards programs of this type including the President's program, weak as it is in comparison with the need."[25]

More laudatory in identifying Medicare as a culmination of Roche's work was Senator Wayne Morse, Oregonian Democrat, who delivered a paean to Roche on the floor of the U.S. Senate a few months before the new health legislation took effect. Morse's tribute recognized Roche's earlier work in government as well as her more recent work in the private sector as contributions to this new progressive moment in U.S. history. "In just a matter of months now," he began, "medical care for the aged will no longer be the dream that it was almost a half-century ago. Instead it will be a reality—a reality made possible in no small part by the historic struggle of one of this country's most illustrious citizens, Josephine Roche." Morse waxed eloquent about Roche's long crusade, citing her chairmanship of the Coordinating Committee, design of the country's first health inventory, and organization of the first national health conference as foundations for Medicare. He went on to say that her work at the Welfare Fund demonstrated "in a practical way what was only theory in 1938." Quoting an award Roche received in the 1950s, Morse soared: "The medical care program of the United Mine Workers of America Welfare and Retirement Fund created and operated by you and your colleagues exemplifies the best in medicine, in social accomplishment and social consciousness."[26]

The last time Roche had inspired a speech on the floor of the U.S. Senate was 1932, when Edward Costigan heralded her as "a prophet of a
new and wiser social order" because of her work at Rocky Mountain
Fuel (RMF). In 1965, when she was again saluted in that forum, she appeared as one whose prophetic leadership had been fulfilled. That Roche
would draw this sort of public attention in the 1930s and the 1960s indicated the intimate relationship between the two eras. That the first of the
speeches pictured her in the vanguard of big changes and the latter at the
conclusion of them was also significant.

Roche was acclaimed as an antecedent of the new progressives but not
as one of their current leaders. The Johnson administration called Roche's
fight for a national health plan in the 1930s "monumental" and her subsequent work in health care "a great humanitarian service outstanding
for its vision and achievement."[27] The University of Colorado at Boulder
awarded Roche an honorary degree.[28] The Social Security Administration
hounded Roche for an interview about her role in crafting the Social Security Act and chairing the Coordinating Committee. When one intrepid
interviewer finally wrangled an appointment, however, he reported afterward that Roche was not interested in being interviewed. She was sure
that other people could tell the story of the 1930s better than she, and,
more to the point, if she were to give accurate information on events so
long ago, she would have to dig through old documents to confirm her
memory and "she cannot afford to" expend that time "as long as she is
busy with her job as Director of the United Mine Workers Welfare and
Retirement Fund."[29]

Roche's impatience with the backward glance was in some ways admirable. She was unwilling to reminisce casually lest she misremember
something, and she seemed to believe her current work for miners more
important than how—or whether—she was remembered to history.
When old progressives urged a memoir on her, Roche always responded
that she just could not take the time because "So much remains to be
done and there are so many new problems and challenges for which solutions seem almost impossible."[30]

At the same time, Roche's stubborn refusal of an interview had a self-
protective quality, for she actually did care how she was remembered to
history. She had since 1956 been weeding her papers and making untold
"trips to the incinerator" with the rejects in that process.[31] She periodically sent Read Lewis documents she thought he might value, but she
destroyed virtually all other evidence of her interior life or intimate relationships.[32] She had promised her papers to the University of Colorado,
though other institutions asked for them, and, through the process of
selecting which documents to save and which to discard, she presented
herself to the future as a strictly public person, who battled continually

for social justice and was often a female first—policewoman in Denver, president of a coal company, gubernatorial candidate, member of the president's "Little Cabinet," and director of the mine workers' Welfare Fund.[33] Roche was thus privately shaping a triumphalist version of herself as a scrappy fighter in the avant-garde of social change.

However engaged she was in the present, Roche was not averse to looking back so long as she controlled the focus of the gaze. She confided in 1968, "I do like to think back to 40 years ago on occasion." She was glad to run her mind over, for instance, "the constructive results that, to some extent did come from our [RMF's] successful contract . . . with the United Mine Workers of America."[34] She was not ready, however, to submit herself to questions that might produce a more complex narrative of her past. Why face questions about her shady dealings with the UMW in the 1930s, for example, or her conflict with Roosevelt in 1940, or the bankruptcy of her company during World War II? Her accomplishments were extraordinary, but Roche knew her feet were made of clay, and she had no interest in exposing them to an interviewer. Perhaps she understood, too, that the younger generation of progressives was looking not only for their political origins but also for the flaws in their predecessors that would explain the continuing need for reform.

Admittedly, Roche's work at the fund in the mid-1960s remained supremely absorbing. Once the Social Security amendments passed, she had to figure out how the fund would mesh its work with Medicare.[35] The health benefits provided by the fund were more comprehensive than those offered by the new program, and Roche ultimately arranged for the fund to pick up any medical costs that Medicare left uncovered.[36] The federal plan also generated new hopes among miners, some of whom assumed the medical costs of the fund would decrease precipitously as Medicare went into effect. Imagining those savings added to the increasing revenues produced by coal's revival, they hoped for improved benefits from their welfare plan.[37] Some beneficiaries wanted the new money spent on preventing the fluctuation of benefits that so disrupted lives in the early 1960s. They pressed for a fully funded pension system in place of the more unpredictable pay-as-you-go plan.[38] Others asked that new resources be paid out in immediate benefits. Some demanded that pensions increase to $150 or even $200 per month; others wanted income support or additional health care for widows and disabled miners. Few seemed satisfied with the status quo.[39]

Roche heard the escalating demands for change. "We [at the fund] know perfectly well how much you want more benefits for more people," she said at one convention of the UMW. "We know there are still many human needs throughout the mining industry, just as there are throughout this whole great country of ours . . . which seem to be appalling and particularly challenging." She assured her audience, "We care, with all our hearts." But the fund operated under many constraints. "While we want to do more about benefits, you must keep in mind that there is no greater disservice, no greater evil that could befall you and your members and all the beneficiaries of the Trust Fund than for us to lack the courage to constantly go on assuring the preservation of your trust. We will not let it become insolvent."[40]

One reason that Roche hesitated to increase benefits was that Medicare failed to produce a windfall for the fund. Roche had been skeptical from the beginning.[41] She was sure that medical costs would rise as a result of the new program, and, given that she would continue to pay for any pensioners' health care uncovered by the federal program, she did not bank on substantial savings. Her wariness was prescient. In the first year of Medicare, daily hospital charges paid by the fund increased 16 percent instead of the average 6 percent, and doctors fees went up 8 percent instead of their usual 3 percent. Very shortly, the fund's expenditures for medical care exceeded those before Medicare.[42] Another reason for Roche's reluctance to move too quickly was her experience of economic recession just a few years before. She knew how rapidly the economy could shrink, how volatile the coal industry was, and how painful it was to cut benefits once they were established. As she would put it later, "We had a bitter lesson in knowing how unwise it was to attempt to do too much without knowing our sources of income."[43] Her goal was to build up a substantial reserve so that she would have on hand enough resources to pay a full year's obligations at any point. The experience of twenty years at the fund had made her extremely cautious about new spending.

Roche's caution set her on a collision course with increasingly discontented miners. Every retrenchment of benefits, going back to 1954, when Roche had ceased monthly stipends for disabled miners and widows, had created pools of material want and resentment in mining communities across the country. Retractions of health benefits from unemployed miners in 1960 and the subsequent withdrawal of health cards from thousands in 1962 sharpened the bitterness against the fund. Moreover, miners disabled on the job could retain their health benefits from the fund for only four years unless they reached retirement age or returned to work in the mines. To disabled workers, that revocation of health care, however reasonable by industry standards, seemed cruel and arbitrary as they watched the bank accounts of the fund grow. By 1968, some groups of miners had begun to form organizations independent of the union to protest what seemed like arbitrary eligibility requirements and insufficient benefits from their increasingly wealthy fund.[44]

The miners' militancy both contributed to and was explained by a national eruption of protest in the late 1960s. The general upheaval was caused by persisting racial and economic injustice in the context of dramatically rising expectations as well as by President Johnson's foreign policy. All the while the president had been unfurling his Great Society programs, he had also been expanding U.S. involvement in a civil war in Southeast Asia. As the president committed increasing numbers of U.S. troops to the Vietnam War and the possibility of achieving an acceptable peace dimmed, opposition to the war increased, more and more often taking the shape of mass demonstrations, resistance to military service, and sometimes violence. Early in 1968, President Johnson was so besieged that he decided not to run for reelection. Within a week of Johnson's surprising announcement, civil rights leader Martin Luther King Jr. was assassinated. In response, more than 100 towns and cities exploded with the frustration of African Americans for whom the promises of the Great Society had not yet materialized.[45] In June, Democratic presidential contender, Robert F. Kennedy, was assassinated, and when the Democratic National Convention opened in Chicago later that summer, the city's police met thousands of anti-war protesters with tear gas and batons. Race riots flared through the summer.[46]

The tumult of 1968 resulted in the presidential election of Republican candidate, Richard M. Nixon, a red-baiter loathed by Josephine Roche.[47] Candidate Nixon promised to bring American troops home from Vietnam victorious and to end the violence in American streets. By offering himself as the law and order candidate, Nixon unwittingly echoed Coloradans who in 1914 had opposed Roche's Progressive Party platform after the Ludlow Massacre. In 1968, Roche may well have been thinking once again, "Law and Order without Justice could be no permanent Law and Order."[48] Nixon's own disregard for the law would ultimately force him out of office, of course, but not before coal miners—among other activists—forced him to advance the cause of social justice and keep alive the new Progressive Era.

The precipitating event in the coal miners' drama occurred in Farmington, West Virginia. At 5:40 am on November 20, 1968, with ninety-nine men working Mine 9 of the Consolidated Coal Company, a powerful explosion collapsed portions of the mine and ignited a fire that set off additional explosions. Twenty-one men escaped. Seventy-eight did not. The fire, fed by coal dust and methane gas, burned out of control for days, sending thick columns of smoke 500 feet in the air. After nine days, unable to extinguish the fire any other way, the company plugged up the mine. The seventy-eight miners were entombed in their workplace. Capturing the front pages of the country's newspapers and television's nightly news, the disaster grieved the country.[49]

The Farmington disaster set in motion a chain of events that transformed the UMW, its Welfare Fund, federal social policy, and the life of

Josephine Roche. By riveting national attention to the preventable dangers of coal mining at a time when Americans were increasingly dependent on coal to feed their appetite for electricity and doing so in the context of renewed progressive reform, the Farmington explosions provided an opening for more effective regulation of the coal industry.[50] While hope remained that the seventy-eight trapped miners might be rescued, the outgoing Johnson administration scheduled an emergency conference on mine safety.[51] The conferees, meeting on December 12, 1968, sought to pressure the incoming Nixon administration to support more stringent safety regulations, including more consistent mine inspections, fines for violating safety regulations, and even a limit on coal dust in mines.[52]

It worked. In 1969, with Roche and the fund in support, Congress passed the Coal Mine Health and Safety Act, which not only ramped up federal oversight of coal mine safety but also included a federal program of workmen's compensation for those disabled by coal miners' pneumoconiosis, commonly called black lung.[53] Because x-rays often detected no lung damage in cases of black lung, many states still refused to recognize it in their workmen's compensation programs.[54] The Coal Act was landmark legislation: it involved the federal government in workmen's compensation for the first time, these programs having been strictly state programs since their origins in the Progressive Era, and it laid the foundation for further federal oversight of occupational health and safety issues, resulting ultimately in the Occupational Safety and Health Act (OSHA) of 1970.[55] Farmington and the miners' subsequent threat of massive strikes helped to extend the Great Society into the Nixon years.

Farmington also crystallized miners' dissatisfaction with their union and the fund. As for the union, in 1968, its president was William A. "Tony" Boyle. After John L. Lewis's retirement from the union's presidency in 1960, his old lieutenant, Thomas Kennedy, had taken the reins but then died in 1963. Boyle, who had been an assistant to Lewis for over a decade, moved into the presidency. Since then, Boyle had misstepped repeatedly with much of the rank and file. Unlike Lewis, who was charismatic, towering, and eloquent, Boyle was self-important, insecure, and petulant.[56] More important, he had been slow to negotiate a new contract once the coal industry turned around, and when he finally did, he failed to win provisions the miners wanted most, which were hedges against unemployment and improved safety measures. Indeed, unable to get Boyle to take them seriously any other way, some miners finally took the union to court in December 1964 to try to force compliance with a 1959 federal law that protected miners' right to elect their district officers.[57]

Boyle's response to the disaster at Farmington was, for many miners, final confirmation of his indifference to their well-being. In the face of that firestorm, John L. Lewis would have thundered against the greed of coal operators whose unforgiveable contempt for the welfare of their workers had blown up Mine 9 and murdered the seventy-eight fine men whose widows and orphans were now grieving and destitute. Tony Boyle excused the company. "As long as we mine coal," he yawned, "there is always this inherent danger of explosion." With astounding insensitivity to the stricken wives, parents, children, and siblings of trapped miners, Boyle praised Consolidated Coal: "This happens to be one of the better companies, as far as cooperation with our union and safety is concerned."[58] Boyle could hardly have done anything more alienating to rank-and-file miners. He seemed nothing but an errand boy for Consolidated Coal.

As for the fund, Farmington inspired organization among disabled miners and widows long dissatisfied with Roche's policies and drew powerful allies to their cause. West Virginia miners suffering from black lung, for instance, organized the Black Lung Association in January 1969 as attention to Farmington gave them hope of forcing West Virginia to make coal miners' pneumoconiosis compensable under the state's workmen's compensation program. They scored a nearly incredible victory within weeks and were poised for broader battle.[59] Although Roche had since the 1950s promoted the study and treatment of black lung, her withdrawal of monthly cash stipends from disabled miners and widows in 1954 and her inability (or refusal, in the eyes of beneficiaries) to offer health care indefinitely to both groups finally came to roost. Disabled miners and widows wanted all the benefits the fund had offered in the early 1950s and since revoked.[60]

Disaffected miners were aided by a new generation of progressive activists and Great Society programs. Anti-corporate consumer firebrand Ralph Nader took the part of the dissidents, researching the policies of the Welfare Fund and the union and exposing their questionable relationship. Nader and other progressives saw the union and the fund as corrupt bureaucracies just like corporations, who exploited rather than protected their members.[61] Moreover, many VISTA volunteers living in mining communities as part of the president's anti-poverty program came to share the perspectives of the people they served. VISTA volunteers provided significant resources to protesting coal miners, and Office of Economic Opportunity (OEO) monies were used to train unemployed miners as community organizers.[62]

Congressional progressives allied with protesting miners, too. Early in April 1969, a Democratic representative from West Virginia, Ken Hechler, called on his colleagues to investigate the fund.[63] Hechler was moved by the miners' building rage over the fluctuation of benefits. Why was it that disabled miners and widows, once supported by the fund, no longer were? Why had pensioners suddenly suffered a 25 percent reduction in 1961? Why had thousands had their health care revoked in the early 1960s? Resentments over these denials led to further accusations against the fund that included failing to report fully on its operations, stockpiling unnecessary reserves, failing to invest the fund's reserves wisely, and neglecting aged and disabled miners.[64]

Roche was genuinely worried about a congressional investigation.[65] In mid-April, she issued a point-by-point rebuttal of Hechler's charges. She answered some of his accusations honestly and directly, and, though sincere people might disagree, Roche's position on these points was justifiable. In response to the charge that her reserves were too great, she insisted that her reserves were not nearly so large as that of many other pension funds with fewer obligations or as large as would be required by legislation pending in Congress at that very moment. Her reserves would cover just over a year's worth of benefits; they would not come close to guaranteeing benefits for the fund's current beneficiaries into the foreseeable future. Although Roche did not mention this, even some miners complained that these reserves were not large enough to guarantee their retirement security.[66] On the issue of reserves, she was on very solid ground.

In other instances, however, Roche ignored the spirit of the indictment altogether. In response to the charge that the fund "fails to make full report on its operations," Roche rehearsed the list of annual reports that she submitted to various governmental agencies, union members, and the press, which itemized the revenues, expenditures, investments, and procedures of the fund. She was not wrong to insist that nearly everything reformers were now complaining about had been public knowledge for years, and that the fund could not legitimately be found guilty of hiding that information. But the point at issue was not really the raw numbers in the assets and liabilities columns. What really needed explaining was the basis on which decisions were made about which benefits to cut or expand, whose lives to improve or ruin, and which companies to call on the carpet for delinquent royalties and which ones to forgive. When miners complained about lack of transparency, they were concerned about their own lack of involvement in the decision-making process, not a lack of information about decisions already made. That is why some local unions had insisted for years that "members should have a vote on who runs and takes care of the fund," and delegates from one union local had in 1964 suggested that two "rank and file men" should serve on the "Welfare Board and have them reelected every four years."[67] Roche ignored the central issue in the complaint about transparency, which was undemocratic decision making at the fund.

Roche also evaded the central issue in the charge that the fund had neglected old and disabled miners. When the accusation was phrased in this way, Roche had ample evidence to dispute it. She had honestly spent over a billion dollars on old-age pensions since taking over the fund, aided tens of thousands of disabled miners in one way or another, and in fact broken entirely new ground in the field of disability treatment.[68] She could with pride point to a shelf-full of awards for her leadership on disability issues that made this accusation, at one level, preposterous. At another, however, it was absolutely true. Beginning in 1950, Roche had absorbed the priorities of the union hierarchy: to aid the working miner above all. The result had been constantly fluctuating benefits for the disabled, retired, and widowed. Legally, she, leading the board of trustees, had had every right to cancel monthly stipends to the widowed and disabled in 1954, to change eligibility requirements for health care in 1960, and to reduce monthly pensions for retirees in 1961. Given limited resources, the fund simply could not meet the material needs of all coal miners in the United States. But with every reduction, Roche had alienated another constituency and made the fund seem indifferent to the needs of those it was created to serve.

What the miners' misery ultimately demonstrated was that no private welfare plan could amass the resources necessary to provide economic security to all workers in an industry. This was a job for the larger political community: the failures of the fund were an argument for universal federal programs of Social Security. Although some miners and a broad coalition of progressives would make that case stringently in the early 1970s, most miners focused on reforming institutions closer to home.

In 1969, the combination of genuine deprivation among so many miners on the one hand and heightened expectations fueled by Roche's programs and the Great Society on the other produced an irrepressible wave of protest among coal miners. Inspired by this rank-and-file activism and his own deep dissatisfaction with Tony Boyle's administration of the UMW, Joseph "Jock" Yablonski, a long-standing stalwart of the UMW's leadership, took the astonishing step on May 29, 1969, of announcing he would challenge Tony Boyle in the upcoming election for the union presidency. Yablonski's move opened the first genuinely competitive election for the union leadership since the 1920s. Yablonski took up the rank-and-file call for greater democracy within the union, increased benefits from the Welfare Fund, and more attention to miners' health and safety.[69]

Even though many of Yablonski's supporters were attacking the fund as well as the union, Roche supported his bid for the presidency. She and John L. Lewis were disgusted with Boyle's thuggish and self-serving leadership, his insensitivity to miners' suffering, and his failures at the negotiating table. Although in many of his faults Boyle followed directly in Lewis's footsteps—especially his refusal of democracy within the union—Roche saw the two leaders as utterly different. For all his vanity and hunger for power, Lewis, in Roche's view, genuinely cared about the welfare of coal miners and other working-class Americans. Lewis had seen his job as directing to miners through increased wages and benefits a greater share of the wealth their labor created. He had a vision of the coal industry that Roche largely shared, which was a stable and efficient industry, made so by mechanization and the industry-wide planning that consolidation could achieve. Because of machine-driven high productivity, Lewis's and Roche's ideal coal industry could pay top wages and support miners and their families in sickness and old age. Lewis was autocratic, and he failed to grasp that the mechanization he promoted also created new forms of danger to miners—increased coal dust, for instance, that caused debilitating lung disease—and that deindustrialization and automation elsewhere in the economy meant miners unemployed by mechanization would have nowhere else to go. But, at least in Roche's mind, Lewis sincerely meant to do right by as many coal miners as he could. Boyle, on the other hand, cared only for himself and his cronies, lacked vision, and saw the union as a vehicle, not for improving working-class living standards and thereby achieving a modicum of social justice, but for his own aggrandizement.[70]

Roche could not openly take sides in union politics because of the fund's legal independence from the union. She nevertheless hoped Yablonski would defeat Boyle, and Yablonski hoped she would intervene with Lewis on his behalf. She did.[71] But the legendary labor leader made no immediate public statement for either candidate, and only two weeks after Yablonski's announcement—on June 11, 1969—John L. Lewis died.[72] Since before his death Lewis had not renounced Boyle, his own appointee to the union hierarchy, Boyle claimed that he remained Lewis's choice for union leadership.

When the eighty-nine-year-old Lewis died, Roche lost a beloved friend and partner in what they both saw as their crusade for social justice. In Lewis's memory, Roche collected files full of newspaper articles recounting his career and analyzing his leadership.[73] Poignantly, she pored over those articles and reminisced about her long association with Lewis while herself propped up in a hospital bed. About a week and a half before Lewis died, Roche had hastily arranged a trustees meeting at his home so that they could certify a new industry trustee. In that haste, as Roche later put it, "I fell down and, ridiculously, demobilized myself."[74] Hospitalization for a broken hip meant that she received the news of Lewis's death while herself out of commission.

Another octogenarian might have, under these circumstances, considered retirement. The fund was under fire from discontented rank-and-file miners, younger progressives, and congressional committees. Roche was eighty-two and at least temporarily bedridden. Her cherished collaborator at the fund had died, and Warren Draper, another steadfast colleague, was retiring. Was it time to hand the baton to a new team? Roche thought not. She intended to soldier on at the fund with or without her original squad.

Roche probably had an inkling that Lewis's death would introduce yet another source of conflict into her life. In fact, it was hard to imagine any other trustee with whom she might work so amicably as Lewis, and sure enough, she soon found herself brawling with the union's new trustee at the fund. On June 23, 1969, UMW officials named their president, Tony Boyle, to replace Lewis as the union's representative on the fund's board of trustees.[75] At that point, Roche remained confined to a hospital bed, though, predictably, she was in regular telephone contact with her office and held staff meetings in her hospital room.[76] Furious about Jock Yablonski's challenge to his presidency, Boyle resolved to use his position as trustee of the fund to help him retain leadership of the union. The day after he was named trustee, he called a meeting of the board. With Roche indisposed, Boyle met with the coal operators' trustee, George Judy, while officers of the fund observed in Roche's stead. At what he had billed as a "pro forma" meeting, Boyle proposed raising the monthly pensions of miners from $115 to $150 effective August 1.[77] Judy went along. Since two votes constituted a majority of the board, the motion passed. The fund's astonished observers informed Boyle and Judy that Roche could be reached by telephone or personal visit, and they provided data demonstrating the threat that such an increase in pensions would pose to the solvency of the fund. Boyle ignored them and asked that notice of the pension increase go out under his name with July's pension checks. It did, and Boyle instantly became a hero to many pensioners and near-pensioners, garnering him votes in the upcoming presidential election.[78]

To justify his support for Boyle's proposal, Judy later told colleagues that Boyle had said he held Roche's proxy in his pocket. Judy claimed that he assumed the pension increase would, as a result, go through no matter what he did, and so he made the decision unanimous. But of course, Boyle had not held Roche's proxy, and Judy soon resigned from the board of trustees.[79]

Roche did not publicly denounce Boyle in 1969; she fought him in private. At the next meeting of the trustees, she announced that she would never have voted for the pension increase and warned that Boyle's self-promoting step threatened the solvency of their entire enterprise.[80] In a complete reversal of Lewis's extreme deference to Roche, Boyle tried to bully her into submission as he did everyone who opposed him. He called meetings without consulting her and issued peremptory memos declaring decisions he and the new industry representative, C. W. Davis, had made. Roche did not give an inch. She let Boyle know in no uncertain terms that he and Davis could not take decisions without appropriately scheduled board meetings and so his alleged "decisions" were bogus. The power struggle between the two was intense, with Boyle determined to use the fund to empower him in the union and Roche equally determined to prevent him from destroying everything she had built since 1948.[81]

The struggle between Roche and Boyle was not nearly so intense, however, as that between Boyle and Yablonski. When Boyle won the union presidency on December 9, 1969, his victory precipitated chaos in the coalfields. Arguing that Boyle triumphed through manipulation of the fund, fraud, and brute intimidation, the Yablonski camp filed court cases as well as complaints with the Department of Labor. They called for a new election.[82] Chaos then turned to horror: on December 31, 1969, Jock Yablonski, his wife, and his twenty-five-year-old daughter were murdered in their beds. Although no evidence immediately tied Boyle to the crime, Yablonski's supporters were convinced the murders were associated with the election, and no one who knew Boyle could think him incapable of ordering the murders.[83] Roche had to know she was going head to head with a brutal and potentially murderous opponent.

Even before the slayings, Roche considered herself embattled.[84] Boyle was doing everything he could to undercut her at the fund. Mayhem ruled the union. Congress was still considering an investigation of the fund, and in August 1969, a new lawsuit had been filed against Roche, Boyle, the union, and the fund. It was brought by the Association of Disabled Miners and Widows, a group of about 4,000 who believed they ought to be eligible for benefits the fund denied them. The group alleged, among other things, that the eligibility requirements for pensions and health benefits were "arbitrary and capricious," that trustees had looted the fund for personal gain, and that the trustees had mismanaged the resources of the fund. The shortened name of the case was *Blankenship v. Boyle*.[85]

Discovery of the Yablonskis' bodies intensified scrutiny of the union and the fund. The FBI opened an investigation of the murders; the Department of Labor examined Boyle's election; and the Senate Subcommittee on Labor scheduled hearings on the election as well. Management of the fund was of interest to the Senate because Boyle was suspected of manipulating the fund to bolster his chances of election.[86] The Senate hearings began early in February, but Roche did not testify until March, by which time five people had been indicted in the conspiracy to murder

Jock Yablonski, and the FBI had become convinced the planning included many more conspirators, possibly including Boyle himself. The Department of Labor had also made progress, turning up so much evidence of fraud in the December election that it asked the Justice Department to file suit to set aside the election results.[87]

This was the context in which Roche made her last appearance before a congressional committee. She was by this time extremely thin, bony even, and heavily spectacled.[88] She walked with a knobbed cane.[89] Before she spoke, an observer might have thought her frail. Once she spoke, "frail" would have been the last word that came to mind. When Roche appeared before the Senate's subcommittee in a session broadcast on national television, senators were already convinced that Boyle had misused the fund to bolster his chances of retaining the union presidency, a clear violation of his position as trustee. They were especially curious, then, about the pension increase that Boyle had engineered in June. From Roche, they wanted to know whether Boyle actually had her proxy when the pension increase was passed and whether the fund was in a financial position to grant the increase. "Mr. Boyle did not have any proxy," she stated bluntly. "He did not have any statement in memorandum form or in verbal form whatsoever to give him any authority to speak for me. . . . I certainly could not have done otherwise than oppose [the pension increase] if I had been present at the meeting." Roche went on to say that such a dramatic increase in pensions required careful study of the fund's future revenues and obligations to determine whether the increase was sustainable. And even if the fund could have increased its obligations at that time, many other needs were crying to be met. The trustees would have needed to weigh those—especially the needs of the working miner— against the needs of pensioners.[90] When asked whether she believed Boyle had acted so impetuously in order to influence the union's presidential election, Roche confessed that she felt "very strongly" on the question but had no firm proof of Boyle's motive. When pressed, she admitted believing that his action at the fund "had a part to play in the election."[91]

Enraged by Roche's testimony, Boyle and his supporters ginned up a letter-writing campaign demanding her resignation from the fund. They denounced her as a betrayer of the union and coal miners everywhere. Some accused her of lying. Dozens of union locals called for her resignation.[92] She refused. "Think how bored I'd be without a fight," she'd said in the 1930s.[93] She was not about to descend into boredom at this late date. Believing, however, that her position at the fund barred her from public involvement in union politics, Roche could battle Boyle only surreptitiously, a task made more complicated by the fact that, on issues related to the fund, many miners construed Roche and Boyle as equally culpable. They were both trustees of the fund that many accused of arbitrarily denying them benefits.

As Roche watched for her opportunity to strike at Boyle, his opposition in the union organized. At a memorial for Jock Yablonski in April, anti-Boyle activists formed Miners for Democracy (MFD), an organization devoted to carrying on Yablonski's reform campaign.[94] MFD kept up the pressure to have the 1969 election overturned, and while that issue remained in the courts, they ran candidates for district offices in the few union districts where elections still took place.[95] Those tumultuous campaigns were paralleled by wildcat strikes through the summer of 1970, many of the strikes spearheaded by disabled miners, aided by VISTA volunteers, dissatisfied with the fund's eligibility requirements for health care benefits.[96] Indeed, it seemed that new organizations of insurgents were forming in every hollow of coal-mining country. Their complaints fell into two broad categories: lack of democracy in the union and insufficient benefits from the fund.[97]

These upheavals—edged as they were with violence and scandal—threw the UMW and the fund constantly into the headlines, which gave Roche her secret shot at Boyle. In June 1970, an investigative reporter from *Reader's Digest*, Trevor Armbrister, approached Roche for an interview. Instead of assuming her usual sphinx-like silence, she granted the interview on condition that Armbrister not name her as his source. After the interview, Armbrister professed his admiration to Roche for holding the fort against Boyle at the fund and called her "courageous."[98] His story on corruption in the UMW came out in October 1970 and reported that, before he died, John L. Lewis had confided to "intimates" that his appointment of Boyle as a vice president of the union was "the worst mistake I ever made." In that quotation, Lewis's intimate, Josephine Roche, contributed her lance to the campaign against Boyle. Through her, Lewis spoke from the grave.[99]

In 1970, Roche was in a bizarre position. In trying to undermine Boyle, she made common cause with many of the very people who were challenging her policies at the fund. Some of the disabled miners, widows, black lung activists, and pro-democracy advocates who coalesced in opposition to Boyle were also activists who sued Roche and the fund for capricious eligibility requirements, mismanagement, and collusion with the union. Indeed, her opposition to Boyle tacitly allied Roche with forces that would eventually eject her from the fund.

Before the courts ruled on the 1969 election or tried those suspected of murdering the Yablonskis, Roche and Boyle faced federal district judge Gerhard Gesell as codefendants in *Blankenship v. Boyle*. The case came to trial in 1971 and represented another alliance between miners and a new generation of progressive activists. The group that initially brought the suit, the Washington Research Project, had been founded in 1969 by civil rights leader Marian Wright Edelman especially to monitor federal anti-poverty programs.[100] *Blankenship v. Boyle* was divided into two segments. Charges that the fund's eligibility requirements were arbitrary and capricious were tried later. In 1971, the charges at issue focused on mismanagement. In general, they accused Roche and Boyle of colluding to use assets of the fund to benefit the union at the expense of the fund's beneficiaries. It was a breach of trust and conspiracy case. As to specifics, the suit charged that the fund hoarded excessive cash reserves and left unconscionable amounts of cash in a non-interest-bearing checking account at the Washington National Bank, a bank in which majority ownership belonged to the union. By doing so, the suit charged, the fund strengthened the union and deprived fund beneficiaries of income from interest-earning investments. When the fund did invest, according to plaintiffs, it favored electrical companies in order to influence the companies to buy union-dug coal. This investment policy allegedly robbed beneficiaries of dividends that might have made more liberal benefits possible.[101]

When Roche entered the witness box, she defended some of her policies and regretted others. She agreed that she had left too much cash in the non-interest-bearing checking account at the Washington National Bank in the years between 1965 and 1968. "The fiscal requirements certainly didn't justify what we had on deposit. I know that perfectly well," she admitted.[102] But she explained that she "favored maintaining an amount equal to several months' expenditures in cash" because that was the only way she could be sure she would have enough money on hand in case of a crisis.[103] Roche and Lewis had been "scarred" by the Depression, she explained, as well as their experiences at the fund, and were consequently wary of tying up too much of their principal in investments that could crash or make the funds inaccessible in the case of an emergency, including a strike or recession.[104] The judge found this position ridiculous, but it was probably sincere. At the moment the lawsuit was filed, the fund had about $28 million in checking accounts, the equivalent of two to three months' worth of benefits, which were hovering between $10 and $14 million per month.[105] Given RMF's bankruptcy in the 1940s, the inability of the fund to pay benefits for several agonizing months during a strike in 1949–1950, and the necessity of selling assets at a steep loss in the late 1950s when recession forced the fund to dip into its reserves to pay benefits, Roche's experience actually did warn against tying up resources in obligations she could not sell off on short notice without loss.[106] A temporarily flush coal industry could make hard-earned wisdom look foolish—even corrupt. But Roche was right to assume that economic good times were transitory.

Once the coal industry picked up in the mid-1960s and Roche became convinced that she had enough cash on hand to cover emergencies and that she could count on steady revenues, she testified, she started arguing with Lewis that they should invest more of their cash. She succeeded in 1968 and began investing more of the fund's assets.[107] She also argued that they should invest in instruments other than electrical companies. Although tens of millions of the fund's dollars were invested in electrical utilities, by 1969 more of the fund's assets were invested in state and municipal bonds than in utilities and more in Certificates of Deposit (CDs) invested through the Bank of Washington than in electrical utilities. Roche's CDs were earning a respectable 5 1/2 percent and 6 1/4 percent.[108] Her investment strategy was actually not so lopsided as her opposition suggested.

Judge Gesell was especially interested in determining whether the trustees might have used the fund to benefit the union rather than the beneficiaries of the fund. Here was tricky ground because some of the distinctions that the law, the plaintiffs, and the judge wanted to draw between what was good for beneficiaries of the fund and what was good for the union were simply not as clear as they wished them to be. For instance, although there was certainly potential for abuse in depositing the fund's resources in a bank directed largely by the union, given that the union made the fund possible and only because of union contracts was the fund kept in existence, it was in the interest of the fund's beneficiaries that the union remain strong. If interest and fees at two banks were roughly equal, it would surely be better for the fund's beneficiaries to put their assets in the institution that kept the union viable than to put them in an institution with no relation to their interests or values.

Drawing a clear distinction between the interests of the union and the fund was in reality not always possible, and Roche justified most of what she was accused of in the breach of trust case by making precisely that point. She saw the fund as ultimately dependent on a strong union. Benefiting the union where she could seemed to her a legitimate strategy for protecting her beneficiaries' long-term interests. Some of the defendants in *Blankenship* even argued that the law allowed the fund to give "collateral advantages" to the union's interests, and Judge Gesell admitted the difficulty of distinguishing between the good of the union and the fund's beneficiaries to some extent in his final decision.[109]

Still, the laws governing the fund did not concede gray areas. Indeed, the law most immediately governing the fund was the anti-union Taft-Hartley Act of 1947, which aimed specifically to prevent unions from using employer-funded welfare plans as "war chests" for the unions themselves.[110] Since the law required that Roche make decisions at the fund without reference to the good of the union, she was culpable on several counts—more than the plaintiffs, their lawyers, or the judge ever discovered—and Judge Gesell found her to be so. He concluded that her deposits in the National Bank of Washington created a conflict of interest between the fund and the union, that the amounts she kept in non-interest-bearing accounts robbed beneficiaries of income they might otherwise have enjoyed, and that the investment in utility stocks constituted a breach of trust because those investments were aimed at getting the utilities to buy union coal. He also found her revocation of benefits from employees of delinquent employers to be an unnecessary punishment of beneficiaries for their employers' behavior. Gesell did not, of course, discover the secret agreements that actually motivated the revocation. Boyle alone he found responsible for the illegitimate increase of pensions in 1969.[111]

Gesell's remedies included Roche's ouster from the fund. He commanded Roche and Boyle to step down from their trusteeships of the fund by June 30, 1971, and required the new trustees to decide whether Roche should continue as the fund's director. She was eighty-four years old and had run the fund for more than two decades. This was a shocking way for an illustrious career to end. Roche publicly expressed no self-pity, resentment, or remorse, however. She worked her heart out until her last day on the job, generating and distributing monthly reports on investments, acting on questions of eligibility for benefits, and tracking expenditures.[112] She must have understood that her eviction from the fund resulted from her remarkable success in building new values and new realities in the coalfields of the United States. It was because she had created a sense of entitlement to first-rate health care and income support among coal miners and their families—but was unable fully to provide them—that she was forced out of the fund. Perhaps that realization prevented Roche from wallowing in self-pity or self-reproach. In any case, she clocked out of the fund for the last time on July 15, 1971, when the new trustees named the fund's comptroller, Tom Ryan, as acting director.[113]

Roche did not yet leave the public scene, however. In fact, she was to make a final public overture that brought her back to the full progressive creed of her youth and demonstrated that far from harboring any ill will toward those who had ejected her from the fund, she identified with them.

Roche's redemption occurred in the midst of continuing tempests within the UMW. In early 1972, the conspirators in the Yablonski murders began going to court, and one after another was found guilty. During those trials, Boyle was convicted in separate proceedings of embezzlement from the union and illegally contributing to political candidates. He was sentenced to a federal penitentiary. Only weeks after this conviction, Boyle's 1969 election was overturned in district court on the grounds of "massive vote fraud and financial manipulation." A new election was scheduled for December 1972. Nearly a year after the election, Boyle was indicted on conspiracy charges in the murder of the Yablonskis, and he was found guilty in spring 1974.[114]

Roche voraciously read newspaper coverage of these events. She organized files on every suspect in the Yablonski murders, underlining with her red and blue pencils the names of each, the union districts they were from, and whether they had ever held a position in the union. She seemed to be piecing together her own theory of the case.[115] Roche also followed the rulings on the 1969 union election. Once the courts ordered a new election in 1972, MFD selected its candidates, their presidential hopeful, a West Virginian named Arnold Miller, who suffered from black lung and had supported Jock Yablonski in 1969. Boyle ran for reelection even though he had been convicted of crimes against the union itself.[116]

As the date of the new election approached, Roche made a dramatic move. On November 9, 1972, she publicly denounced Tony Boyle, endorsed MFD, and contributed $1,000 to Miller's campaign (figure 18). Roche opened her formal statement, "I have devoted my entire life to improving the working and living conditions of active and retired coal miners and their families throughout the United States." She went on to identify her "closest working associate and one of my dearest friends" as John L. Lewis. "Just before his death," she announced, "Mr. Lewis confided to me that his deepest concern was that W. A. 'Tony' Boyle would destroy the Welfare Fund just as he was destroying the Union." Confirming her decades-old belief that the fund depended on a strong union, Roche went on, "With others, I share the deep conviction that the Welfare and Retirement Fund can only be saved by revitalizing the top leadership of the Union." And then she proclaimed: "Today I am announcing my full and complete support for the UMWA Miners for Democracy." Just to make sure that no one continued to believe that Boyle might have been Lewis's choice of heir to the UMW presidency, she clarified, "Mr. Lewis was ill in 1969 and died shortly after Joseph Yablonski announced his candidacy for the UMWA Presidency. Had Mr. Lewis lived he would not have been neutral. He would have supported Jock Yablonski with all his vigor."[117] With this announcement, Roche turned her back on the autocratic governance of the UMW, resuming her earlier commitment to democratic decision making.

Roche was not satisfied with issuing a single statement; she actively campaigned on Miller's behalf. Her statement in support of MFD was printed in newspapers all over coal country. She was interviewed by journalists in Washington.[118] On the day that balloting began, Roche appeared on national TV in a segment on *CBS Morning News*.[119] In the meantime, accompanied by counsel to MFD and steadying herself with her trusty cane, she flew to Charleston, West Virginia, to take her message personally to the coalfields.[120] The trip created an iconic moment. Not only was Roche campaigning against a candidate widely suspected of murdering the last man to run against him, but, remarkably, sitting with her at the press conference in Charleston were several of the plaintiffs in the *Blankenship* case, the dissidents whose complaints had ended her tenure at the fund. The disabled miners, too, backed Arnold Miller.[121]

Roche's appearance with the victors in the *Blankenship* case demonstrated that she did not take their challenge to her administration of the fund personally. When she had insisted over the years that she understood that mining communities had deep and legitimate needs she simply did not have the resources to meet, she meant it. She did not blame disabled or unemployed miners, widows, or pensioners for protesting her policies; she recognized their needs as real and profound. She also felt kinship with the young legal team that had helped miners oust her from the fund.[122] Roche's openness to these young progressives, even when they had attacked her policies and the institution to which she had devoted herself for more than two decades, symbolized the historical connections between the Progressive Era and the Great Society, between Roche's generation of progressive activists and the generation of the 1960s.

In fact, during her campaign for Arnold Miller, Roche routinely tied 1972 to 1914. When rehearsing her own biography for reporters, she invariably began with the Ludlow Massacre, and in one interview, she explicitly likened Jock Yablonski to Louis Tikas, one of those shot down by National Guardsmen at Ludlow in 1914. "From Louis Tikas to Joseph Yablonski, seven decades of murder," she mourned in one interview. In Roche's view, Jock Yablonski was yet another in a never-ending series of martyrs to the cause of labor rights in the coalfields. For her, MFD carried on the struggle of miners at Ludlow, and, by promoting their cause, she continued the work she had begun as a young woman in the West.

What Roche did not openly admit was that labor relations had changed so substantially since Ludlow that though workers continued to be exploited by their employers, they were also sometimes exploited by their own institutions. Tony Boyle and some of the other conspirators eventually convicted in Jock Yablonski's murder were not state militiamen in the pay of mine operators but union men themselves, and Roche had been intimately allied with the autocratic union that produced those murderers.[123] Perhaps her staunch support for the autocracy of John L. Lewis is what Roche referred to when she told one national TV interviewer during Arnold Miller's campaign, "I've made lots of mistakes."[124]

Whether or not Roche ever admitted to herself that she had given support to the very anti-democratic practices she now disparaged is unclear. But she did explicitly support the new democratic practices that MFD promised within the union and that the courts finally enforced in the 1970s. She told an interviewer that she was thrilled that the "miners from the mine pits" finally had the "opportunity to elect . . . their own representatives and know that the things that are nearest to them in the way of safety and progress in the mines . . . have a chance now that they haven't had before, because it was just word from the top and that was it."[125] No longer supporting "just word from the top," Roche had resumed her commitment to democracy.

CHAPTER 17

ONLY TEN MINUTES LEFT?
EPILOGUE AND ASSESSMENT

While Josephine Roche was campaigning for Arnold Miller in November 1972, a reporter asked whether she would at last consider writing her memoirs. As usual, she refused. "I only have 10 minutes left," she retorted, "and I'm afraid I didn't fight hard enough."[1] By one way of accounting, the relentless reformer had three and a half years left; by another, she lives on still.

Until her death on July 29, 1976, Roche stayed in touch with developments in the institutions that meant most to her. She was pleased with the directions taken at the United Mine Workers of America. Miller won his election in 1972 and moved quickly to reform the union. His administration held elections for district offices, built up the union's safety division, and opened the pages of the union's newspaper to the rank-and-file. Miller stopped charging union dues to pensioners and abolished locals that enrolled no active miners. In 1974, he negotiated a new contract that raised wages and benefits.[2]

The fund also underwent profound changes, the outcome of which was not yet clear by the time Roche died. Believing the coal industry was on an upswing and that a higher royalty on increasing production would provide enough revenue to meet new obligations, reformers followed through on their promise to increase the level of benefits as well as the number of beneficiaries of the fund. For precisely the reasons that Roche had been so cautious—the general unpredictability of the economy, the peculiar instability of the coal industry, and astronomical increases in medical costs—the reformers quickly reached a point where they could not meet these obligations.[3] As a result, only six years after Roche's retirement and a year after her death, the reformers began sloughing off the unique features of her health program. They returned to fee-for-service payments to doctors and required miners to pay deductibles and copayments for services that had previously been free. The changes destroyed some of the medical clinics serving miners in Appalachia and decreased health care usage because miners could not always afford the new out-of-pocket expenses. In addition, the 1978 union contract handed the health care of working miners to employers, who insured them through commercial insurance plans. Under the new health plans, less care was covered; miners paid more than when Roche was in charge; and no one oversaw the quality of care. The fund became strictly a welfare agency serving the retired and disabled rather than an active player in recalibrating the relationship between labor and capital or in reshaping American health care. Indeed, in the shift of responsibility for the medical care of working miners, workers lost a significant measure of their independence from employers, and the union some of its appeal.[4]

The failure of the union to maintain control of working miners' health care was yet another blow to an already weakening labor movement. Because of automation, its own corruption, globalization, and the determination of anti-union interests, the labor movement declined dramatically after 1970. While a third of the nonagricultural labor force was unionized in the early 1950s, that percentage fell to 24.1 percent in 1979 and 13.9 percent in 1998. By 2012, only 11 percent of the total U.S. workforce was unionized, including just 6.6 percent of workers in the private sector. The deterioration of the union movement in the late twentieth century was part of the reason that economic inequality, significantly diminished by progressive achievements in the mid-twentieth century, began to increase again in the 1970s.[5]

Roche's system at the fund, dedicated to remaking American medicine and sustaining a strong union in addition to improving the living standards of coal miners, had preserved a broader social justice agenda for the fund than that of the reformers who took her down. Despite Roche's narrowed political vision in the 1940s, she was able to see how her activity in a circumscribed field might reverberate well beyond it. When she became convinced that her fund could not provide for every need of the country's coal miners, Roche chose to provide benefits for the groups that she could while also achieving two broader goals, bolstering the labor movement and transforming American medicine. In the end, the law did not allow her to continue pursuing those broader goals through the fund.

For historians, those goals were significant in part because of their continuity with earlier periods of progressive reform. Roche carried her commitment to diminishing inequality from the earliest twentieth century through the New Deal and into the post–World War II world. Her work at the miners' Welfare Fund demonstrated that ideals and even concrete plans for reform generated in the Progressive Era and sustained

during the New Deal survived within Cold War liberalism, creating institutions and expectations that helped to ignite the final burst of progressive reform in the 1960s. Roche's long life, which began as industrialization transformed American institutions in the late nineteenth century and
ended as deindustrialization was doing the same in the 1970s, helps us
see that near-century as an Age of Progressive Reform with temporary
reversals in the 1920s and 1950s.

Roche did not live to see the new, deindustrialized age in American
history. Before her death, she moved to the Fernwood Nursing Home in
Bethesda, Maryland, just outside of Washington, DC. Visited regularly by
Mildred Lea and the Owens family, Roche spent her last months on the
sidelines. Early in 1976, she was diagnosed with breast cancer. It had
metastasized, and she died in July at age 89.[6]

Even though obituaries of Josephine Roche in 1976 rehearsed many
of the highlights of her amazing career, she had by then faded from
Americans' collective memory.[7] She had lived so long that few remembered the headlines trumpeting her breakthroughs as a policewoman in
the 1910s, as a progressive industrialist in the 1920s, or as assistant secretary of the treasury in the 1930s. Her obscurity resulted in part from
Roche's own desire to hide from public view during the anti-communist
frenzy of the late 1940s and early 1950s.[8] Her low profile during those
years probably helped the miners' Welfare Fund survive, but it also
moved Roche off the front pages of American life. When she reemerged,
she was an old woman eventually represented in print as little more than
a rubberstamp to John L. Lewis.

That representation is worth investigating because it helps us understand further how such an important and previously well-known woman
could disappear from American history. The rubberstamp representation
began with the 1971 judicial opinion of Judge Gerhard Gesell in *Blankenship v. Boyle*. In that opinion, Gesell, who would officiate later in trials connected to Watergate and other federal scandals, went beyond finding Roche guilty of breach of trust.[9] He belittled her intelligence,
questioned her independence, and disparaged her business experience.
He attributed her investment decisions, if not to corruption, then to "na-
ivete" and claimed that she "idolized John L. Lewis and felt entirely con-
fident to follow his leadership in financial matters, apparently without
independent inquiry." At another moment, he wrote, "The Fund's affairs
were dominated by Lewis until his death in 1969. Roche never once disagreed with him."[10] Even though Gesell did not have the evidence that
would later vindicate Roche's fiscal caution, he did have evidence against
this portrait of her as slavishly subservient to John L. Lewis. That Gesell
would nevertheless paint Roche as naïve, dependent, and mindlessly devoted to a powerful man attests more to widespread assumptions about

women's fundamental nature than to a careful evaluation of the evidentiary record. The assumption of women's subordination to men seems to have fixed Gesell's attention on the parts of the record that confirmed Roche's subservience to Lewis and deflected his focus from evidence to the contrary.

It is easy to see how Gesell came to his assessment. For starters, he did not have full evidence of Roche's relationship with John L. Lewis. Roche and Lewis hashed out most of their decisions off the official record, and Gesell was not looking into the lion's share of decisions made at the fund, most of which Roche clearly controlled. In addition, Roche spoke in extravagant praise of John L. Lewis every chance she got, including at the trial. Gesell had no way of knowing that Roche spoke in extravagant praise of everyone she admired, not just John L. Lewis, and so he read more into her effusiveness than he should have. Most important, Roche explicitly testified at trial that she on occasion deferred to Lewis's judgment on financial matters, contrasting her "personal experience against his wisdom."[11]

But the record contained evidence against Gesell's characterization of Roche as well. Roche testified to her ultimately successful arguments with Lewis both to invest their cash and to diversify their investments, demonstrating that she exercised independence from and disagreed with Lewis on issues before the court. Gesell also ignored Roche's many years as president and general manager of Colorado's second-largest coal company when he claimed that Roche had substantial experience in welfare matters but "her business experience was more limited."[12] And, of course, union executives and industry trustees at the fund deferred to Lewis to a greater degree than Roche ever did, and Gesell did not represent these men as naïve dependents of John L. Lewis. Expectations of women's subservience to men and their affinity for welfare but not business were assuredly at work in Gesell's representations of Roche.

Popular writers followed suit. In the 1970s, several journalists narrated the dramatic implosion of the UMW, and they echoed Gesell's representations of Roche. In mass-marketed books that would later be cited in important works by historians, Roche was treated as an inconsequential yes-woman to John L. Lewis. One reported that Lewis dominated the fund and "Josephine Roche was there with him, holding the crucial vote in her hands, to do the will of Lewis." Roche's judgment was, he wrote, for "John L. Lewis to form as he wished." Another popular writer claimed, "Roche was completely in accord with his [Lewis's] wishes, whatever they were." In each of these works, Roche was put forward as anything but the irascible, no-nonsense powerhouse she was, hired by Lewis to direct the fund because he needed her expertise, and on whose judgment, advice, and creativity he and the fund utterly relied. She was just, according to them, "a little gray lady who administered the Fund."[13]

The point is not to blame earlier representers of Josephine Roche. The point is rather to see in these inaccurate pictures of Roche the toll that sexism has taken on our understanding of the American past. Although many factors played into Roche's historical obscurity, one of the most significant was the assumption of female subservience that so dampened the imaginations of even smart and curious observers that they could not see a woman as head of a vast, innovative, and powerful institution like the United Mine Workers of America Welfare and Retirement Fund—and especially not an old, gray-haired woman with a cane, thick glasses, and hearing aids. One reason to tell Roche's story is make sure that we can, from now on, detect power in old women.

Another reason is that Roche's legacy to American life is so vast. She had a hand in crafting policies and erecting institutions that affected virtually every American during the second half of the twentieth century. She presided over the immense expansion and modernization of the U.S. Public Health Service in the 1930s and participated in drafting the founding legislation of the American welfare state, the Social Security Act of 1935. Social Security's disability insurance as well as Medicare and Medicaid bear the mark of her leadership in devising and promoting the first national health plan in American history. Indeed, Josephine Roche generated the national conversation Americans are still having about the relationship between health care and U.S. citizenship. Additionally, an organizational heir to her Foreign Language Information Service, the Immigration and Refugee Services of America, persisted in serving immigrants in the twenty-first century, and Roche's Appalachian hospitals continue even today to operate as a pathbreaking medical unit, fulfilling the vision for health care that progressives developed early in the twentieth century.[14] In 2010, under the name of Appalachian Regional Healthcare and somewhat reorganized, Roche's chain of hospitals was designated the Outstanding Rural Health Organization in the nation by the National Rural Health Association. In 2013, it remained the largest employer in southeastern Kentucky.[15]

Although the UMW's health service did not survive the 1970s, the legacy of Roche's years at the helm of the Welfare Fund lives on. She and her staff participated in pioneering managed care, one of the permanent directions of health care for the rest of the century, and she, along with others in the labor movement, pointed the way toward solving some of the country's current health care predicaments. Prepayment plans that replace fee-for-service health care and group practices collaborating in community clinics go a long way toward controlling the cost and quality of health care and in the process expand accessibility. They remain crucial elements in the health care mix of the twenty-first century.[16]

Roche's years at the fund offer important lessons, too. They highlight not only the inevitable inadequacy of private social welfare schemes but also the need for democracy in our health care system. Although coal miners in general were receiving a quality of health care in the 1960s unimaginable a decade earlier, many were profoundly dissatisfied. Why? To receive care, miners had to tangle themselves in a bureaucracy that treated them as dependents rather than decision-makers and then changed the rules of the game without consulting them. Miners were not citizens in their health care system; they were at the mercy of decisions made by others. Ultimately, they revolted against their exclusion from decisions that so directly shaped their lives—and deaths. Roche's experience at the fund suggests that if we are to create a health care system with which Americans are truly satisfied, we must not only increase access to care, lower costs, and maintain high quality but also address issues of governance. Coal miners in the 1960s demanded a health care system in which patient-citizens shared power in deciding how to distribute health care resources. They never got it, but their history suggests that only such a system is consistent with democratic ideals and social peace.

Rocky Mountain Fuel stood as another of Roche's legacies. She lived to see the company roar back to life in the early 1970s when oil and gas reserves were drilled on the company's land; new water rights were discovered; and farmers flocked to its fertile fields. Some of the company's real estate was developed for recreational and residential use. In this new incarnation, Roche's enterprise funneled valuable income to America's coal miners, as their union still owned about a third of the company's stock. Roche was delighted when Gerald R. Armstrong, a corporate reformer, expressed interest in running the company in 1972–1973. She encouraged him to gather as many proxies as he could and made calls on his behalf. He was elected president of RMF in April 1973 and ran the thriving company until 2006.[17] Recently, some of RMF's land in Lafayette, Colorado, was set aside as a wild area and named the Josephine Roche Open Space; on another plot in 2012, the Boulder County Housing Authority opened seventy units of affordable housing for seniors in a development named the Josephine Commons.[18]

These memorials would have pleased Josephine Roche. They embody the kind of tribute she called for on the death of her friend, Grace Abbott, in 1939. The only memorial worthy of Abbott, Roche insisted, was "to hold ourselves relentlessly" to the task of correcting the "inequalities, widespread denials and fears, threateningly in violation of democracy's commitments." To give Abbott the "honor which is her due" meant continuing to battle "the destructive force of economic and social injustice reaching into every phase of human life."[19] Ongoing efforts to diminish inequalities of wealth and power would, in other words, be the memorial most cherished by Josephine Roche. Her life illuminates a powerful political heritage for any who wish to build that memorial.

ABBREVIATIONS

ARA	Area Redevelopment Administration
BLP	Benjamin Barr Lindsey Papers, Library of Congress, Washington, DC
CCHWA	Records of the Interdepartmental Committee to Coordinate Health and Welfare Activities, FDRL
CRB	Commission for Relief in Belgium (1914–1930) Collection, Hoover Institution, Stanford University, Stanford, California
CSFLP	Colorado State Federation of Labor Papers, Archives, Norlin Library, University of Colorado, Boulder
ECP	Edward P. Costigan Papers, Archives, Norlin Library, University of Colorado, Boulder
ER	Eleanor Roosevelt
FA	United Mine Workers of America Health and Retirement Fund Archives, West Virginia Collection, University Libraries, University of West Virginia, Morgantown
FDRL	Franklin D. Roosevelt Presidential Library, Hyde Park, New York

IRSA   Immigration and Refugee Services of America Records, Immigration History Research Center, University of Minnesota, Minneapolis

MKP   Mary van Kleeck Papers, Sophia Smith Collection, Smith College, Northampton, Massachusetts

NARA   National Archives and Records Administration, College Park, Maryland

NCLR   Records of the National Consumers' League, Library of Congress, Washington, DC

RC   Josephine Roche Collection, Archives, Norlin Library, University of Colorado, Boulder

RLP   Read Lewis Papers, in private hands, copies in author's possession

RMF   Rocky Mountain Fuel Company

SSA   Social Security Administration Archives, RG 47, National Archives and Records Administration, Baltimore, Maryland

UMW   United Mine Workers of America

UMW Archives   United Mine Workers of America Archives, Historical Collections and Labor Archives, Pennsylvania State University Libraries, State College, Pennsylvania

VAO   Roche File, Vassar Alumnae Office, Vassar College, Poughkeepsie, New York

Citations of newspaper articles, when not from a manuscript collection, are from Proquest: Historical Newspapers.

NOTES

INTRODUCTION

1 "11 Women Hailed by Mrs. Roosevelt," *New York Times*, Mar. 9, 1935, 17.

2 Mary Margaret McBride, "Woman President Boom Is Gaining," *Kentucky New Era*, Feb. 28, 1935, 3; "Women Leaders Open Drive for Presidency of the U.S.," *Christian Science Monitor*, Feb. 12, 1935, 1.

3 "Bamberger Poll Honors Mining Woman," *Star Eagle*, Mar. 11, 1935, folder 7, box 35, RC.

4 "Mrs. Simpson Is Left Out of List of Famous Women," *Washington Daily News*, Jan. 1937, folder 2, box 36, RC. Durward Howes, ed., *American Women: The Official Who's Who among the Women of the Nation*, vol. II (Los Angeles, 1937), xxvi, 583.

5 Mrs. Olive Douglas Bostick to Roche, Nov. 30, 1934, folder 2, box 30; Angelina Martorano to Roche, Oct. 15, 1935, folder 1, box 33, RC.

6 "Miss Roche to Get Medal," *New York Herald Tribune*, Apr. 2, 1935, 2. *The Eleusis of Chi Omega*, Sept. 1935 and Chi Omega Award, folder 7, box 8, RC. *Proceedings of the Founding Convention of the CIO*, Pittsburgh, PA, Nov. 1938, 197.

7 James R. Mock and Cedric Larson, *Words That Won the War: The Story of the Committee on Public Information* (Princeton, NJ, 1939), 220.

8 Senator Morse, "Tribute to Josephine Roche," *Congressional Record*—Senate—Oct. 13, 1965, 25884–25885, in Josephine Roche File, Revolving File, SSA.

9 Quoted in "Denver's Dynamic Josephine Roche Takes Treasury Post," *Washington Post*, Dec. 1934, folder 6, box 35, RC.

10 Roche was among a generation of left-feminists who very nearly disappeared from public life. Landon R.Y. Storrs, *The Second Red Scare and the Unmaking of the New Deal Left* (Princeton, NJ, 2013); Daniel Horowitz, *Betty Friedan and the Making of The Feminine Mystique: The American Left, the Cold War, and Modern Feminism* (Amherst, MA, 1998).

11 Roche's memory will be taken up in chapter 17. As for her treatment by historians, the only full-length biography is Elinor McGinn, *A Wide-Awake Woman: Josephine Roche in the Era of Reform* (Denver, 2002). Roche is included in Susan Ware, *Beyond Suffrage: Women and the New Deal* (Cambridge, MA, 1981); alluded to in Melvyn Dubofsky and Warren Van Tine, *John L. Lewis: A Biography* (New York, 1977); and fully integrated into Richard P. Mulcahy, *A Social Contract for the Coal Fields: The Rise and Fall of the United Mine Workers of America Welfare and Retirement Fund* (Knoxville, TN, 2000). Brief biographical sketches exist, and she makes cameo appearances elsewhere, but she remains mostly unknown even among historians of twentieth-century America.

12 I use "Great Society" to refer not only to the domestic programs established by Lyndon B. Johnson's administration but also to their elaboration in the 1970s. For a similar understanding, see Sidney Milkis and Jerome M. Mileur, "Preface," in *The Great Society and the High Tide of Liberalism* (Amherst, MA, 2005), xvii, as well as Hugh Heclo, "Sixties Civics," and R. Shep Melnick, "From Tax and Spend to Sue and Mandate: Liberalism after the Great Society," in the same volume at 58 and 387–405.

13 Richard Hofstadter, *The Age of Reform from Bryan to F.D.R.* (New York, 1955). Hofstadter distinguished between populism, progressivism, and the New Deal in ways I do not, but he saw them all as connected in opposition to conservatism.

14 This is a direction at least vaguely suggested by several historians of policy and social movements in the last few years. See, for instance, Ira Katznelson, "Another History," *Dissent* 59 (Spring 2012): 72–73; Nelson Lichtenstein, "Introduction," *American Capitalism: Social Thought and Political Economy in the Twentieth Century*, ed. Nelson Lichtenstein (Philadelphia, 2006), 4–5; Alan Brinkley, "Liberalism and Belief," *Liberalism for a New Century*, ed. Neil Jumonville and Kevin Mattson (Berkeley, 2007), 75–89; Otis Graham Jr., "Liberalism after the Sixties: A Reconnaissance," in *The Achievement of American Liberalism: The New Deal and Its Legacies*, ed. William Chafe (New York, 2003), 293–295, 299.

More common has been the claim that progressivism ended earlier. Some, like Robert Wiebe and Michael McGerr, see the end of the Progressive Era either during or immediately following World War I. Robert H. Wiebe, *The Search for Order, 1877–1920* (New York, 1967); Michael McGerr, *A Fierce Discontent: The Rise and Fall of the Progressive Movement in America, 1870–1920* (New York, 2003). Some, like Gary Gerstle, see the 1920s as a period of dramatic transition from progressivism to liberalism. Gary Gerstle, "Protean Character of American Liberalism," *American Historical Review*, 99 (Oct. 1994): 1043–1073. Many, including most women's historians, have seen the New Deal as the culmination of progressive reform. Robyn Muncy, *Creating a Female Dominion in American Reform, 1890–1935* (New York, 1991); Theda Skocpol, *Protecting Soldiers and Mothers: The Political Origins of Social Policy in the United States* (Cambridge, MA, 1992); Linda Gordon, *Pitied but Not Entitled: Single Mothers and the History of Welfare* (New York, 1994); Landon R.Y. Storrs, *Civilizing Capitalism: The National Consumers' League, Women's Activism, and Labor Standards in the New Deal Era* (Chapel Hill, NC, 2000); Daniel T. Rodgers, *Atlantic Crossings: Social Politics in a Progressive Age* (Cambridge, MA, 1998); Kevin Mattson, *When America Was Great: The Fighting Faith of Postwar Liberalism* (New York, 2004), 95–113. James Henretta and Alan Brinkley have detected a major shift in the progressive tradition beginning in the late 1930s. James A. Henretta, "Charles Evans Hughes and the Strange Death of Liberal America," *Law and History Review* 24 (Spring 2006): 115–171; Alan Brinkley, *The End of Reform: New Deal Liberalism in Recession and War* (New York, 1995). As for female reformers in particular, Estelle Freedman suggested continuities into the 1940s. See her *Maternal Justice: Miriam Van Waters and the Female Reform Tradition* (Chicago, 1996). See also the many possibilities for periodization suggested by Elisabeth Israels Perry, "Men Are from the Gilded Age, Women Are from the Progressive Era," *Journal of the Gilded Age and Progressive Era* 1 (Jan. 2002): 25–48.

15 I use the term "social science progressivism" here rather than "social justice progressivism" because I want to differentiate the group that emphasized public policy as the method of reform from the group that emphasized labor organizing. Both social science and labor progressives advocated social justice.

The notion of social science progressivism has long been implicit in the historical literature. See, for instance, Nancy Cohen, *The Reconstruction of American Liberalism, 1865–1914* (Chapel Hill, NC, 2002); Wiebe, *The Search for Order*; Rodgers, *Atlantic Crossings*, 76–111; Mary O. Furner, *Advocacy and Objectivity: A Crisis in Professionalization of American Social Science, 1865–1905* (Lexington, KY, 1975); Thomas L. Haskell, *The Emergence of Professional Social Science: The American Social Science Association and the Nineteenth-Century Crisis of Authority* (Urbana, IL, 1977); Ellen Fitzpatrick, *Endless Crusade: Women Social Scientists and Progressive Reform* (New York, 1990); Dorothy Ross, *The Origins of American Social Science* (Cambridge, UK,1991).

For labor progressivism, see Joseph A. McCartin, *Labor's Great War: The Struggle for Industrial Democracy and the Origins of Modern American Labor Relations, 1912–21* (Chapel Hill, NC, 1997).

16 Roche, "Women in Industry," Fresno, CA, Nov. 25, 1940, folder 4, box 8, RC.

17 Gerry Dick, typescript interview with Roche, Oct. 9, 1937, folder 2, box 36, RC.

18 Most obviously, the drive to reduce inequalities lay at the center of social justice progressivism, a category encompassing those intent on raising the living standards of working-class families through public welfare and social insurance programs, protective labor legislation, and/or the organization of labor unions. The same drive motivated the West's populist progressives, who supported progressive income taxes, the direct election of senators, and several methods of direct democracy, including the referendum, initiative, and recall of elected officials. Reducing inequalities of power moved those good government reformers who wanted to disseminate power beyond a small cadre of political bosses or corporate interests. Women's suffragists hoped to eliminate political inequality between women and men. Progressives who pressed for government regulation of industry often did so to bolster the power of workers or consumers in relation to corporations. Anti-vice reformers often saw commercialized vice as exploitation of consumers (in the case of alcohol) or workers (in the case of prostitution). Those opposed to racial discrimination were pressing for greater equality. Maureen A. Flanagan captured the multitude of progressivisms in *America Reformed: Progressives and Progressivisms, 1890s–1920s* (New York, 2007). In addition to the historians cited elsewhere in this introduction, my thinking about progressive reform in the early twentieth century has been informed by Allen F. Davis, *Spearheads for Reform: The Social Settlements and the Progressive Movement, 1890–1914* (New York, 1967). Peter G. Filene, "An Obituary for the Progressive Movement," *American Quarterly* 22 (Spring 1970): 20–34. Richard L. McCormick, "The Discovery That Business Corrupts Politics: A Reappraisal of the Origins of Progressivism," *American Historical Review* 86 (April 1981): 247–274; James T. Kloppenberg, *Uncertain Victory: Social Democracy and Progressivism in European and American Thought, 1870–1920* (New York, 1986); Nell Irvin Painter, *Standing at Armageddon: The United States, 1877–1919* (New York, 1987); Seth Koven and Sonya Michel, " 'Womanly Duties': Maternalist Politics and the Origins of Welfare States in France, Germany, Great Britain, and the United States, 1880–1920," *American Historical Review* 94 (October 1990): 1067–1108; Alan Dawley, *Struggles for Justice: Social Responsibility and the Liberal State* (Cambridge, MA, 1991); Evelyn Brooks Higginbotham, *Righteous Discontent: The Women's Movement in the Black Baptist Church, 1880–1920* (Cambridge, MA, 1993); Glenda Elizabeth Gilmore, *Gender and Jim Crow: Women and the*

Politics of White Supremacy in North Carolina, 1896–1920 (Chapel Hill, NC, 1996); Leon Fink, *Progressive Intellectuals and the Dilemmas of Democratic Commitment* (Cambridge, MA, 1997); Michael Denning, *The Cultural Front: The Laboring of American Culture in the Twentieth Century* (New York, 1997); Sidney M. Milkis and Jerome M. Mileur, eds., *Progressivism and the New Democracy* (Amherst, MA, 1999); Elizabeth Sanders, *Roots of Reform: Farmers, Workers, and the American State, 1877–1917* (Chicago, 1999); Deborah Gray White, *Too Heavy a Load: Black Women in Defense of Themselves, 1894–1994* (New York, 1999); Maureen A. Flanagan, *Seeing with Their Hearts: Chicago Women and the Vision of the Good City, 1871–1933* (Princeton, NJ, 2002); Robert D. Johnston, *The Radical Middle Class: Populist Democracy and the Question of Capitalism in Progressive Era Portland, Oregon* (Princeton, NJ, 2003); Shelton Stromquist, *Re-inventing "The People": The Progressive Movement, the Class Problem, and the Origins of Modern Liberalism* (Urbana, IL, 2006); Doug Rossinow, *Visions of Progress: The Left-Liberal Tradition in America* (Philadelphia, 2008); and Sidney M. Milkis, *Theodore Roosevelt, the Progressive Party, and the Transformation of American Democracy* (Lawrence, KS, 2009).

19 W. Colston Leigh, brochure, "Josephine Roche," 1944–1946, folder 2, box 8, RC.

20 I am thus in agreement with the many scholars who have argued for the late 1940s as a major turning point in what I would call the progressive tradition. See, for instance, Robert Korstad and Nelson Lichtenstein, "Opportunities Found and Lost: Labor, Radicals, and the Early Civil Rights Movement," *Journal of American History* 75 (Dec. 1988): 786–811, and Lichtenstein, "From Corporatism to Collective Bargaining: Organized Labor and the Eclipse of Social Democracy in the Postwar Era," in *The Rise and Fall of the New Deal Order, 1930–1980*, ed. Steve Fraser and Gary Gerstle (Princeton, NJ, 1989), 122–152; Ellen Schrecker, *Many Are the Crimes: McCarthyism in America* (Princeton, NJ, 1998), esp. 368–373. In addition, see Patricia Sullivan, *Days of Hope: Race and Democracy in the New Deal Era* (Chapel Hill, NC, 1996); Horowitz, *Betty Friedan and the Making of* The Feminine Mystique; Storrs, *Second Red Scare*; Carol Anderson, *Eyes off the Prize: The United Nations and the African American Struggle for Human Rights, 1944–1955* (Cambridge, UK, 2003); Meg Jacobs, *Pocketbook Politics: Economic Citizenship in Twentieth-Century America* (Princeton, NJ, 2005), esp. 221–261; Gary Gerstle, "The Crucial Decade: The 1940s and Beyond," *Journal of American History* 92 (Mar. 2006): 1292–1299; Michael Kazin, "The Fall and Rise of the U.S. Populist Left," *Dissent* 59 (Spring 2012): 67–70; Ira Katznelson, *Fear Itself: The New Deal and the Origins of Our Time* (New York, 2013).

21 In calling the Great Society an episode of progressive reform, I am revising not only the nomenclature of most participants in the social movements and policymaking circles of the 1960s but also historiographical conventions. Historians generally refer to the Great Society as an expression of liberalism (not progressivism), and they most often identify the origins of that liberalism in the New Deal (not the Progressive Era). One writer, for instance, has claimed that "liberalism" was "literally born in the early New Deal." (Ronald Rotunda, quoted in Jerome M. Mileur, "The Great Society and the Demise of New Deal Liberalism," in *The Great Society and the High Tide of Liberalism*, 418.) See also William Chafe, introduction, in *The Achievement of American Liberalism: The New Deal and Its Legacies*, ed. William Chafe (New York, 2003), xii, where he claims that the New Deal "constitutes the beginning point for any discussion of liberalism."

But I think it makes sense to use the "progressive" label for liberal social movements and policymakers in the 1960s because that identification makes clear their connections to earlier episodes of reform and highlights their renewed openness to alliances with more radical social movements, a characteristic that distinguished their outlook from the liberalism of the late 1940s and 1950s.

In the 1960s and early 1970s, many politicos who had narrowed their vision of social justice in the immediate postwar period reexpanded it and were willing once again to make common cause with those farther left. These new progressives, for the most part, continued to call themselves liberals, and historian Doug Rossinow has recently argued that liberals and leftists remained mutually antagonistic rather than cooperative through the 1960s (*Visions of Progress*, esp. 196–202, 233–260). My own vision is quite different. As I see it, the Left and postwar liberals, despite genuine and often violent hostility between them, shared commitments to reducing inequalities of wealth and power and, as a result, after the rupture of the 1940s reunited on general directions for public policy in the 1960s.

In developing the anti-poverty programs of the Great Society, for instance, the liberal Sargent Shriver consulted with Michael Harrington, the nation's foremost socialist. Anti-poverty legislation contained explicitly liberal emphases like job training as well as the New Left's insistence on the "maximum feasible participation" of poor people themselves in devising programs aimed to alleviate poverty. Within a few years, liberals in Americans for Democratic Action joined leftists in Students for a Democratic Society in opposing the Vietnam War, and a similarly broad group supported a guaranteed annual income, national health insurance, the right of farm workers to unionize, and women's reproductive freedom. Between 1968 and 1972, the Democratic Party moved leftward, and liberals in that party and outside it openly associated with mass movements for equality in which leftists actively participated. Perhaps one of the most vivid illustrations of liberals' renewed openness to the Left was a contribution in 1971 by the liberal United Presbyterian Church to the defense fund of communist Angela Davis as she faced trial for kidnapping, murder, and criminal conspiracy. The religious body feared that an avowed communist might have trouble winning a fair trial and so offered aid.

On the coalition supporting guaranteed annual income, see Marisa Chappell, *The War on Welfare: Gender, Family, and the Politics of AFDC in Modern America* (Philadelphia, 2009). On the alliances of leftists and liberals in the women's movement of the 1960s and 1970s, see Sara M. Evans, "Comment: Liberalism and the Left," *Radical History Review* 71 (Spring 1998): 41–45. For leftists and liberals united in opposition to the Vietnam War, see Rossinow, *Visions of Progress*, 249; Maurice Isserman and Michael Kazin, *America Divided: The Civil War of the 1960s* (New York, 2000), 278; Allen J. Matusow, *The Unraveling of America: A History of Liberalism in the 1960s* (New York, 1984), esp. 376–394; Maurice Isserman, *The Other American: The Life of Michael Harrington* (New York, 2000), e-book location 4376. On left and liberal support for national health insurance in the early 1970s, see, for instance, Jack Newfield, "A Populist Manifesto: The Making of a New Majority," *New York Magazine*, July 19, 1971, 39–46; Paul Starr, *The Social Transformation of American Medicine* (New York, 1982), 392–405; Maurice Isserman, *The Other American*, Kindle edition, location 4864. On the United Farm Workers, see, for instance, Julie Leininger Pycior, *LBJ and Mexican Americans: The Paradox of Power* (Austin, TX, 1997); Margaret Rose, "'Woman Power Will Stop Those Grapes': Chicana Organizers and Middle-Class Female Supporters in the Farm Workers' Grape Boycott in Philadelphia, 1969–1970," *Journal of Women's History* 7 (Winter 1995): 6–36; Randy Shaw, *Beyond the Fields: Cesar Chavez, the UFW, and the Struggle for Justice in the 21st Century* (Berkeley, 2008); José-Antonio Orosco, *Cesar Chavez and the Common Sense of Nonviolence* (Albuquerque, NM, 2008). For other evidence of the convergence of the New Left with 1960s and 1970s liberals, see Michael Kazin, *American Dreamers: How the*

Left Changed a Nation (New York, 2011), Kindle edition, locations 4585, 4608, 4875–4876; Jefferson Cowie, *Stayin' Alive: The 1970s and the Last Days of the Working Class* (New York, 2010). On the Presbyterians and Angela Davis, see George Dugan, "United Presbyterians End Assembly on 10th Day," *New York Times*, May 27, 1971, 35.

To my way of thinking, then, the Great Society constituted a final burst of progressive reform in which the heirs of New Deal progressivism reopened exchanges and alliances with the Left to produce dramatic departures in corporate regulation (as evidenced in, for instance, creation of the Environmental Protection Agency in 1970 and the Occupational Health and Safety Administration in 1971), challenges to inequality (as demonstrated by passage of the Civil Rights Act and Economic Opportunity Act in 1964), and renewed commitment to democratic participation (as promoted by the constitutional amendment abolishing poll taxes in 1964, the Voting Rights Act of 1965, and the requirement of maximum feasible participation in the Economic Opportunity Act of 1964).

22 In the early 1990s, historians began to understand early twentieth-century progressivism as organized in part by gender, with women and men reformers often operating in gender-exclusive organizations and forming gendered political networks that pursued overlapping but gendered agendas. While this literature illuminated aspects of progressivism that we had not seen before and enriched women's and gender history, Roche's story helps us move beyond his-and-her versions of progressive reform.

Paula Baker, "The Domestication of Politics: Women and American Political Society, 1780–1920," *American Historical Review* 89 (June 1984): 620–647, and *Moral Frameworks of Public Life: Gender Politics and the State in Rural New York, 1870–1930* (New York, 1991). Koven and Michel, "Womanly Duties"; Kathryn Kish Sklar, "Historical Foundations of Women's Power in the Creation of the American Welfare State, 1830–1930," *Mothers of a New World: Maternalist Politics and the Origins of Welfare States*, ed. Seth Koven and Sonya Michel (New York, 1993), 43–93; and Sklar, *Florence Kelley and the Nation's Work: The Rise of Women's Political Culture, 1830–1900* (New Haven, CT 1995). Skocpol, *Protecting Soldiers and Mothers*; Gordon, *Pitied but Not Entitled*; William H. Chafe, "Women's History and Political History: Some Thoughts on Progressivism and the New Deal," *Visible Women: New Essays on American Activism*, ed. Nancy A. Hewitt and Suzanne Lebsock (Urbana, IL, 1993), 101–118; Muncy, *Creating a Female Dominion in American Reform*; Maureen A. Flanagan, "Gender and Urban Political Reform: The City Club and the Woman's City Club of Chicago in the Progressive Era," *American Historical Review* 95 (Oct. 1990): 1032–1050; and Flanagan, *Seeing with Their Hearts*.

23 Roche's life also forces us to reckon with a broader vision of women's political and professional networks than appears in the current historical literature. Robyn Muncy, "Women, Gender, and Politics in the New Deal Government," *Journal of Women's History* 21 (Fall 2009): 60–83.

24 For instance, Phelps Adams, "Practical Theorist Wins Office," *New York Sun*, Nov. 1934, folder 6, box 35, RC.

25 Emmanuel Saez, "Striking It Richer: The Evolution of Top Incomes in the United States," Sept. 3, 2013, elsa.berkeley.edu/~saez/saez-UStopincomes-2012.pdf, accessed Feb. 1, 2014. Anthony B. Atkinson, Thomas Piketty, and Emmanuel Saez, "Top Incomes in the Long Run of History," *Journal of Economic Literature* 49 (Mar. 2011): 3–71. See also Wojciech Kopczuk, Emmanuel Saez, and Jae Song, "Earnings Inequality and Mobility in the United States: Evidence from Social Security Data since 1937," *Quarterly Journal of Economics* 125 (2010): 91–128. Economic Policy Institute, "Inequality," from *The State of Working America*, 12th ed., 2012, http://stateofwork

ingamerica.org/chart/swa-wealth-figure-6b-share-total-household, accessed Feb. 14, 2014.

26 Economic Policy Institute, "Inequality," from *The State of Working America*, 12th ed., 2012, http://stateofworkingamerica.org/chart/swa-wealth-figure-6b-share-total-house hold, accessed Feb. 14, 2014.

27 Michael Norton and Dan Ariely, "Building a Better America—One Wealth Quintile at a Time," *Perspectives on Psychological Science* 6 (Jan. 2011): 9–12.

28 William Owens, interview with author, Ellicott City, MD, May 26, 2005. "Pointed Advice," *The Pittsburgh Press*, Feb. 10, 1935, 3.

29 "Battler for Miners," *Business Week*, Apr. 8, 1967, VAO.

30 For instance, Nicholas von Hoffman, "One More Battle," *Washington Post*, Nov. 24, 1972, B1.

31 Roche to Read Lewis, Aug. 13, 1911, RLP.

32 Quotation in Roche to Read Lewis, Aug. 13, 1911, RLP.

33 Nicholas von Hoffman, "One More Battle," *Washington Post*, Nov. 24, 1972, B1.

CHAPTER 1   CHILDHOOD IN THE WEST, EDUCATION IN THE EAST, 1886–1908

1 Birth announcements for Josephine Roche appeared in *Neligh Leader*, Friday, Dec. 3, 1886, 3, and *Neligh Republican*, Wednesday, Dec. 8, 1886, 4. Thanks to the Nebraska Historical Society for these citations.

2 Walter Prescott Webb, *The Great Plains* (New York, 1931). For pointing out Neligh's telling location, thanks to James C. Olson and Ronald C. Naugle, *History of Nebraska*, 3rd ed. (Lincoln, NE, 1997), 2–4.

3 Ella Aspinwall taught at Platteville Normal School: Marian Watkins to Josephine Roche, 1935, folder 4, box 30, RC. Her attendance at the school in 1869–1873 is in school catalogues for those years. E-mail message, Angie Reinecke, Archives Assistant, University of Wisconsin, Platteville, to Angela Cavallucci, Oct. 9, 2007, in author's possession. Her teaching at the school is confirmed in school catalogues. E-mail message, Angie Reinecke, Archives Assistant, University of Wisconsin, Platteville, to Angela Cavalucci, Oct. 17, 2007, in author's possession.

4 D. J. Gardner to Josephine Roche, Aug. 28, 1934, folder 5, box 22; Mrs. Dorrit Roecker to Josephine Roche, June 11, 1934, folder 5, box 22; G. M. Morrissey to Josephine Roche, July 1, 1935, folder 1, box 33; RC. Consul Willshire Butterfield, *History of Lafayette County, Wisconsin* (Chicago, 1931), 493, 535. N.A., *History of LaFayette County, Wisconsin* (Chicago, 1881), 727.

5 Dr. George Strassler combed through Deed Books in the Antelope County Clerk's Office in Neligh, Nebraska, and found that in October 1880, a parcel of land was sold to the firm of Roche, Ray, and Hall for $300. A year later, the men sold part of that piece; in 1882, after Roche had married Ella Aspinwall, they sold another part of that land to the cashier of the First National Bank. E-mail message, Dr. George Strassler to Robyn Muncy, Jan. 2, 2008, in author's possession.

6 A. J. Leach, *A History of Antelope County* (Chicago, 1909), 155, 159. I surmise that he was the founder from information in *Nebraska State Gazetteer, Business Directory and Farmers List, 1890–91*, Antelope County, 305.

7 Leach, *History of Antelope County*, 152, 156–57. *Compendium of History Reminiscence and Biography of Nebraska* (Chicago, 1912), 74, 65, https://archive.org/details/compendiumofhist00inalde, accessed Feb. 14, 2014.

8 *Nebraska State Gazetteer, Business Directory and Farmers List for 1890–91,* Antelope County, 305.

9 "Early Burials in Laurel Hill Cemetery," *Nebraska Ancestree,* vol. III, no. 3 (Winter 1984–1985).

10 *Neligh Leader,* Friday, Dec. 3, 1886, 3.

11 Euphan Macrae to Josephine Roche, Nov. 16, 1934, folder 8, box 32; Ella Roche to Josephine Roche, Feb. 10, 1915, folder 11, box 10, RC.

12 Mabel Cory Costigan, "A Woman's Way with Coal Mines," *Woman's Journal,* Mar. 1929, VAO.

13 Leach, *History of Antelope County,* 24–26.

14 Ibid., 58–59, 127.

15 Ibid., 85–89.

16 "U.S. Debt to Lewis," *Rocky Mountain News,* Apr. 12, 1950, folder 4, box 53, RC.

17 Leach, *History of Antelope County,* 150, 161, 164–166. Nancy Cohen, *The Reconstruction of American Liberalism, 1865–1914* (Chapel Hill, NC, 2002), 27.

18 Leach, *History of Antelope County,* 165–166.

19 Michael Kazin, *A Godly Hero: The Life of William Jennings Bryan* (New York, 2006), 23, 27.

20 Ibid., 27.

21 On this point, I am in agreement with Charles Postel, *The Populist Vision* (New York, 2007). See also Elizabeth Sanders, *Roots of Reform: Farmers, Workers, and the American State, 1877–1917* (Chicago, 1999).

22 Olson and Naugle, *History of Nebraska,* 264–265. Lawrence Goodwyn judged the Nebraska Populists to be a "shadow movement" that lacked the substance given the movement elsewhere by participation in the cooperative movement. Goodwyn, *The Populist Moment: A Short History of the Agrarian Revolt in America* (New York, 1978), 139–144, 216–222. My own judgment is much more in line with Kazin, *Godly Hero,* 41, 45–46.

23 Dr. George Strassler searched advertisements for the First National Bank of Neligh in the local newspapers, especially the *Neligh Leader.* Roche was president of the bank in 1893 and gone by 1895. E-mail message, Dr. George Strassler to Robyn Muncy, June 20, 2007, in author's possession.

24 Roche's bank merged with another four years after he left, and the new institution was soon accused of malfeasance. The merger is documented in local papers researched by Dr. George Strassler at the Antelope County Historical Society in Neligh, and the accusation against the bank was recorded in J. Sterling Morton and Albert Watkins, *History of Nebraska* (Lincoln, NE, 1905–1913), 675.

25 Josephine Roche testimony, Transcript of Proceedings in John L. Lewis and Josephine Roche and Henry G. Schmidt v. James M. Pennington et al., Civil Action 3431, U.S. District Court for the Eastern District of Tennessee, May 5, 1961, folder 19, box 2, Robert Kaplan Papers, Manuscripts and Archives, Sterling Memorial Library, Yale University, New Haven, CT.

26 John Roche was a manager in the Stockyards Exchange Building in 1898 and by 1899 secretary-treasurer of the Omaha Cattle Loan Company, according to *McAvoy's City Directory and Business Directory,* Omaha, 1897–1907. Researched at the Douglas County Historical Society in Omaha by Dr. George Strassler. E-mail message, Dr. George Strassler to Robyn Muncy, Jan. 27, 2008, in author's possession. Olson and Naugle, *History of Nebraska,* 250–251.

27 Mrs. H. Ward Gordon to Josephine Roche, Nov. 16, 1934, folder 7, box 31, RC.

28 Mrs. H. Ward Gordon to Josephine Roche, Nov. 16, 1934, folder 7, box 31; Phelps Adams, "Practical Theorist Wins Office," *New York Sun,* clipping, Nov. 1934, folder 6, box 35; Josephine Roche to Dr. and Mrs. Thomas Parran, July 30, 1937, folder 6, box 33; Mrs. Daniel Daughhetee to Josephine Roche, May 1937, folder 5, box 30, RC.

29 Euphan W. Macrae to Josephine Roche, Nov. 16, 1934, folder 8, box 32, RC. Academic Record of Josephine Aspinwall Roche, Registrar's Office, Vassar College, Poughkeepsie, NY. Fanny Clarke Potter, *Historical Sketch of Brownell Hall, 1863–1914* (Omaha, NE, 1914).

30 Helen Lefkowitz Horowitz, *Alma Mater: Design and Experience in the Women's Colleges from Their Nineteenth-Century Beginnings to the 1930s* (Boston, 1984), 3–6, 30.

31 Nancy Woloch, *Women and the American Experience*, 3rd ed. (Boston, 1999), 607. Lynn D. Gordon, *Gender and Higher Education in the Progressive Era* (New Haven, CT, 1990), 2.

32 Josephine's appearance is clear in photos like *Vassarion*, 1908, 58, Special Collections, Thompson Library, Vassar College, Poughkeepsie, NY.

33 *Vassarion*, 1905, 21–28, 44–45. Gordon, *Gender and Higher Education in the Progressive Era*, 140, 143.

34 *Vassarion*, 1908, 58.

35 "Democracy," *Vassar Miscellany*, May 1907, 438–440, Special Collections, Thompson Library, Vassar College, Poughkeepsie, NY. Horowitz, *Alma Mater*, 152.

36 See, for instance, Editorial, "Intelligent Culture," *Vassar Miscellany*, Mar. 1908, 334; "Table Talk," ibid., Feb. 1907, 286–288; "Democracy," ibid., May 1907, 438–440.

37 Academic Record of Josephine Aspinwall Roche.

38 Leach Biographical File, Special Collections, Thompson Library, Vassar College.

39 Speech to Association of Collegiate Alumnae, published Feb. 1908, clippings, Leach Biographical File.

40 *Vassarion*, 1908, 232; ibid., 1907, 169; ibid., 1906, n.p. For the routines of the Hellenic Society, see for instance, *Vassar Miscellany*, Nov. 1907, 114; ibid., Apr. 1907, 355; ibid., Feb. 1905, 243.

41 "The Eternal(?) Feminine," *Vassar Miscellany*, May 1908, 436–437.

42 Editorial, ibid., Oct. 1904, 28–29.

43 Editorial, ibid., Jan. 1905, 196.

44 For such a description of Roche, see Phelps Adams, "Practical Theorist Wins Office," *New York Sun*, Nov. 1934, folder 6, box 35, RC. For Roche's own opinion, see "Miss Roche Wins Woman's Prize as Promoter of Industrial Peace," *Christian Science Monitor*, Apr. 9, 1935, 6.

45 Horowitz, *Alma Mater*, 193–194, 222. "A Field for Cooperation," *Vassar Miscellany*, Nov. 1907, 104.

46 Ellen Carol DuBois, *Harriet Stanton Blatch and the Winning of Woman Suffrage* (New Haven, CT, 1997), 104–105. Gordon, *Gender and Higher Education*, 134.

47 *Vassarion*, 1907 and 1908, n.p.

48 Ibid., 1908, 94, 165.

49 Editorial, *Vassar Miscellany*, Nov. 1904, 89–90.

50 *Vassarion*, 1908, 165.

51 Membership in the society was competitive: *Vassar Miscellany*, Nov. 1904, 83. Roche's membership: *Vassarion*, 1905, 108; ibid., 1906, 33; ibid., 1907, 113; ibid., 1908, 219.

52 Horowitz, *Alma Mater*, 162–163.

53 Debate reserved to men: Gordon, *Gender in Higher Education*, 145.

54 *Vassarion*, 1908, 100–102.

55 Ibid., 1908, 100–102.

56 *Vassar Miscellany*, Dec. 1904, 129.

57 Ibid., Apr. 1905, 360.

58 *Vassarion*, 1905, 181; ibid., 1906, 77; ibid., 1907, 173; ibid., 1908, 223.

59 Robert A. Woods and Albert J. Kennedy, eds., *Handbook of Settlements* (New York, 1911). The best history of the social settlements is Allen F. Davis, *Spearheads for Reform: The Social Settlements and the Progressive Movement, 1890–1914* (New York, 1967).

60 Mary Kingsbury Simkhovitch, *Neighborhood: My Story of Greenwich House* (New York, 1938).

61 For general information on this transitional period, see, for instance, Steven J. Diner, *A Very Different Age: Americans of the Progressive Era* (New York, 1998).

62 *Vassar Miscellany,* Apr. 1908, 393, 395–396.

63 Woods and Kennedy, eds., *Handbook of Settlements*; Davis, *Spearheads for Reform*; Mina Carson, *Settlement Folk: Social Thought and the American Settlement Movement, 1885–1930* (Chicago, 1990); and Robyn Muncy, *Creating a Female Dominion in American Reform, 1890–1935* (New York, 1991), 3–37.

64 *Vassar Miscellany,* Nov. 1904, 84. The first installment on workers' budgets had been published by Louise Bolard More as *Wage Earners' Budgets: A Study of Standards and Cost of Living in New York City* (New York, 1907). Simkhovitch, *Neighborhood: My Story of Greenwich House*, 151.

65 *Vassar Miscellany,* Feb. 1907, 242. On the history of social science progressivism, see Kathryn Kish Sklar, Kevin Bales, and Martin Bulmer, eds., *The Social Survey Movement in Historical Perspective* (Cambridge, UK, 1992); Mary O. Furner, *Advocacy and Objectivity: A Crisis in Professionalization of American Social Science, 1865–1905* (Lexington, KY, 1975); Thomas L. Haskell, *The Emergence of Professional Social Science: The American Social Science Association and the Nineteenth-Century Crisis of Authority* (Urbana, IL, 1977); Ellen Fitzpatrick, *Endless Crusade: Women Social Scientists and Progressive Reform* (New York, 1990); Dorothy Ross, *The Origins of American Social Science* (Cambridge, UK, 1991). Daniel T. Rodgers, *Atlantic Crossings: Social Politics in a Progressive Age* (Cambridge, MA, 1998), 76–111.

66 Academic Record of Josephine Aspinwall Roche. Gordon, *Gender in Higher Education*, 133–134.

67 Herbert Mills Biographical File, Special Collections, Thompson Library, Vassar College; Gordon, *Gender and Higher Education*, 133–134, 148; and *The Eleusis of Chi Omega*, Sept. 1935, folder 7, box 8, RC.

68 Interview of Roche by Gerry Dick, Oct. 9, 1937, folder 2, box 36; "Denver's Dynamic Josephine Roche Takes Treasury Post," *Washington Post*, Dec. 1934, folder 6, box 35, RC.

69 Charles Larsen, *The Good Fight: The Life and Times of Ben B. Lindsey* (Chicago, 1972), 3–54.

70 Larsen, *The Good Fight*; Elizabeth J. Clapp, *Mothers of All Children: Women Reformers and the Rise of Juvenile Courts in Progressive Era America* (University Park, PA, 1998), 63.

71 Costigan, "A Woman's Way with Coal Mines," *Woman's Journal*, Mar. 1929, 20–21, 37; Academic Record of Josephine Aspinwall Roche; *Vassar College Catalog, 1907–1908.*

72 *Vassar Miscellany,* Feb. 1906, 274.

73 Kathleen Dalton, *Theodore Roosevelt: A Strenuous Life* (New York, 2002), 233–235, 291–299. Muncy, *Creating a Female Dominion*, 39–43.

74 Josephine Roche, "Reclaiming the Western Lands," *Vassar Miscellany*, Jan. 1908, 202–206.

75 "A Vassar Girl Policeman," *Poughkeepsie News-Press*, July 9, 1913, VAO.

76 Costigan, "A Woman's Way with Coal Mines," *Woman's Journal*, Mar. 1929, 21.

CHAPTER 2   ASPIRING FEMINIST AND SOCIAL SCIENCE PROGRESSIVE, 1908–1912

1   Roche's address: *Vassarion*, 1908, 58, Special Collections, Thompson Library, Vassar College, Poughkeepsie, New York.

2   Benjamin Lindsey and Harvey O'Higgins, *The Beast* (New York, 1910), 196. Keating: R. Todd Laugen, *The Gospel of Progressivism: Moral Reform and Labor War in Colorado, 1900–1930* (Boulder, CO, 2010), 15–31.

3   Charles Larsen, introduction, *The Beast* (1910; Seattle, 1970), xix.

4   George Creel, *Rebel at Large: Recollections of Fifty Crowded Years* (New York, 1947), 85–97.

5   Benjamin Lindsey to Harvey O'Higgins, Apr. 10, 1911, box 31; Benjamin Lindsey to Roche, Apr. 5, 1911, box 31; Benjamin Lindsey to Roche, Aug. 14, 1913, box 42, BLP. Harvey O'Higgins to Sojo, Jan. 15, 1910; Feb. 20, 1910; June 4, 1912; May 7, 1912; Jan. 9, 1917, folder 12, box 5, RC.

6   Richard McCormick, "The Discovery That Business Corrupts Politics: A Reappraisal of the Origins of Progressivism," *American Historical Review* 86 (Apr. 1981): 247–274.

7   Eleanor Flexnor, *Century of Struggle: The Woman's Rights Movement in the United States* (1959; New York, 1970), 62–112, 142–178, 216–239, 248–261.

8   Lindsey and O'Higgins, *The Beast*, 301–321.

9   *Thirteenth Census of the United States: 1910*, vol. 4, *Population* (Washington, DC, 1912), 231, 253.

10   Roche to Benjamin Lindsey, Sept. 1909, box 23, BLP.

11   James Harvey Robinson, *The New History: Essays Illustrating the Modern Historical Outlook* (1912; New York, 1965), 131.

12   Student Record of Josephine Aspinwall Roche, Political Science, Columbia University Archives, New York City. Grace Robinson to Roche, Jan. 2, 1926; ibid., Dec. 1926, RLP.

13   Quotation: Rosalind Rosenberg, *Changing the Subject: How the Women of Columbia Shaped the Way We Think about Sex and Politics* (New York, 2004), 110–111.

14   Course Description, History 252, *Columbia University Bulletin of Information, Courses Offered by the Faculty of Political Science*, 1910–1911, 19.

15   Robinson, *The New History*, 247, 252–255, 263–266. Harvey Wish, introduction to Robinson, *The New History*, xviii.

16   Robinson, *The New History*, 128–130, 135. Vladimir G. Simkhovitch, *Marxism vs. Socialism* (New York, 1913), 33.

17   Simkhovitch, *Marxism vs. Socialism*, 33. Brilliant analysis of American pragmatism: James T. Kloppenberg, *Uncertain Victory: Social Democracy and Progressivism in European and American Social Thought* (New York, 1986). Recent treatment of pragmatism: William J. Novak, "The Myth of the 'Weak' American State," *American Historical Review* 113 (June 2008): 752–772, esp. 764–765.

18   Rosenberg, *Changing the Subject*, 110. Quotation: Robinson, *The New History*, 14.

19   Robinson, *The New History*, 61–62.

20   Course descriptions, *Columbia University Bulletin of Information Courses Offered by the Faculty of Political Science*, 1909–1910, 33, 36. Simkhovitch, *Marxism vs. Socialism*, 30–31.

21   Simkhovitch, *Marxism vs. Socialism*, viii.

22   Ibid., xi, 289–293.

23   Ibid., 187–216; vii–viii.

24   Doug Rossinow, *Visions of Progress: The Left-Liberal Tradition in America* (Philadelphia, 2008).

25   Annelise Orleck, *Common Sense and a Little Fire: Women and Working-Class Politics in the United States, 1900–1965* (Chapel Hill, NC, 1995), 53–63; Nan Enstad, *Ladies of Labor, Girls of Adventure: Working Women, Popular Culture, and Labor Politics at the Turn of the Twentieth Century* (New York, 1999), 84–160.

26   Probation Commission: Mary E. Odem, *Delinquent Daughters: Protecting and Policing Adolescent Female Sexuality in the United States, 1885–1920* (Chapel Hill, NC, 1995), 113–115. Night court: Barbara Meil Hobson, *Uneasy Virtue: The Politics of Prostitution and the American Reform Tradition* (1987; Chicago, 1990), 160.

27   Strikers' views: Orleck, *Common Sense and a Little Fire*, 59–62. Roche interviewing them: Josephine Aspinwall Roche, "Economic Conditions in Relation to the Delinquency of Girls," M.A. Thesis, 45–46, folder 4, box 10, RC.

28   Harvey O'Higgins to Sojo, Jan. 15, 1910, folder 12, box 5, RC.

29   Orleck, *Common Sense and a Little Fire*, 63; Jo Ann E. Argersinger, *The Triangle Fire: A Brief History with Documents* (Boston, 2009); and Richard A. Greenwald, *The Triangle Fire, the Protocols of Peace, and Industrial Democracy in Progressive Era New York* (Philadelphia, 2005). Roche's witnessing the fire: "Denver's Dynamic Josephine Roche Takes Treasury Post," *Washington Post*, Dec. 1934, folder 6, box 35, RC.

30   The notion of an "interpretive community" began in Stanley Fish's work, *Is There a Text in This Class? The Authority of Interpretive Communities* (Cambridge, MA, 1980). See also Anne Ruggles Gere, *Intimate Practices: Literacy and Cultural Work in U.S. Women's Clubs, 1880–1920* (Urbana, IL, 1997). I repurpose the phrase here to refer to a political community.

31   Course descriptions, *Columbia University Bulletin of Information Courses Offered by the Faculty of Political Science*, 1909–1910, 40–41. Course descriptions, ibid., 1910–1911, 42–43.

32   Course descriptions, *Columbia University Bulletin of Information Courses Offered by the Faculty of Political Science*, 1909–1910, 40. Josephine Aspinwall Roche, Student Record, Columbia University. Course descriptions, *Columbia University Bulletin of Information Courses Offered by the Faculty of Political Science*, 1910–1911, 43.

33   Course descriptions, *Columbia University Bulletin of Information Courses Offered by the Faculty of Political Science*, 1910–1911, 46. See also Henry Rogers Seager, *Social Insurance: A Program of Social Reform* (New York, 1910).

34   Simkhovitch, *Marxism vs. Socialism*, 221–223. On the distance imposed between activism and the professoriate, see Mary O. Furner, *Advocacy and Objectivity: A Crisis in Professionalization of American Social Science, 1865–1905* (Lexington, KY, 1975).

35   Roche participated in producing one of the classics of the literature, Ruth True, *The Neglected Girl* (New York, 1914). Her M.A. thesis predated two of the other classics, Robert A. Woods and Albert J. Kennedy, eds., *Young Working Girls: A Summary of Evidence from Two Thousand Social Workers* (Boston, 1913), and Sophonisba P. Breckinridge and Edith Abbott, *The Delinquent Child and the Home: A Study of the Delinquent Wards of the Juvenile Court of Chicago* (1912; New York, 1916).

36   Slippery slope: Ruth Alexander, *The "Girl Problem": Female Sexual Delinquents in New York, 1900–1930* (Ithaca, NY, 1995), 33–34, 42; Elizabeth Lunbeck, *The Psychiatric Persuasion: Knowledge, Gender, and Power in Modern America* (Princeton, NJ, 1994), 187–190, 199–207. Offenses of girls brought before the juvenile courts: Odem, *Delinquent Daughters*, 135–136. A large and rich literature addresses these issues, including Joanne J. Meyerowitz, *Women Adrift: Independent Wage Earners in Chicago, 1880–1930* (Chicago, 1988), and Kathy Peiss, *Cheap Amusements: Working Women* *and Leisure in Turn-of-the-Century New York* (Philadelphia, 1986). Hobson, *Uneasy Virtue*; Ruth Rosen, *The Lost Sisterhood: Prostitution in America, 1900–1918* (Baltimore, 1983); Estelle B. Freedman, *Their Sisters' Keepers: Women's Prison Reform in America, 1830–1930* (Ann Arbor, MI, 1981), and *Maternal Justice: Miriam Van Waters and the Female Reform Tradition* (Chicago, 1996); Regina G. Kunzel, *Fallen Women, Problem Girls: Unmarried Mothers and the Professionalization of Social Work, 1890–1945* (New Haven, CT, 1993); and Elizabeth Alice Clement, *Love for Sale: Courting, Treating, and Prostitution in New York City, 1900–1945* (Chapel Hill, NC, 2006).

37 Hobson, *Uneasy Virtue*, 150–152. Range of motives: Mara L. Keire, *For Business and Pleasure: Red-Light Districts and the Regulation of Vice in the United States, 1890–1933* (Baltimore, MD, 2010); Jennifer Fronc's review of Keire's book in *American Historical Review* 116 (Feb. 2011): 184–185.

38 Roche, "Economic Conditions in Relation to the Delinquency of Girls," 4–9, and introductory material, appendix A.

39 Ibid., 39–43.

40 Ibid., 11–14.

41 Cf. Edith Abbott, *Women in Industry: A Study in American Economic History* (New York, 1910), 308–309, 313–316; Louise Bosworth, *The Living Wage of Women Workers* (New York, 1911); and Elizabeth Beardsley Butler, *Women and the Trades: Pittsburgh, 1907–08* (Philadelphia, 1909). See also Alice Kessler-Harris, *A Woman's Wage: Historical Meanings and Social Consequences* (Lexington, KY, 1990), 6–18.

42 Roche, "Economic Conditions in Relation to the Delinquency of Girls," 15.

43 Ibid., 15.

44 Simkhovitch, *Marxism vs. Socialism*, 33.

45 Roche, "Economic Conditions in Relation to the Delinquency of Girls," 15.

46 Ibid., 16.

47 Ibid., 17. Larger picture: Kessler-Harris, *A Woman's Wage*, 10–11.

48 Rebecca J. Mead, " 'Let the Women Get Their Wages As Men Do': Trade Union Women and the Legislated Minimum Wage in California," *Pacific Historical Review* 67 (Aug. 1998): 317–347, esp. 326–327.

49 Roche, "Economic Conditions in Relation to the Delinquency of Girls," 20, 23. In using the phrase "sex commodity," she was especially drawing on feminist Charlotte Perkins Gilman's analysis as evidenced in Roche's thesis, bibliography, n.p. See also Judith A. Allen, *The Feminism of Charlotte Perkins Gilman: Sexualities, Histories, Progressivism* (Chicago, 2009).

50 Roche, "Economic Conditions in Relation to the Delinquency of Girls," 21. Roche's phraseology here is very close to Simkhovitch, *Marxism vs. Socialism*, 18.

51 Roche, "Economic Conditions in Relation to the Delinquency of Girls," 43.

52 Ibid., 42.

53 Ibid., 43.

54 Greenwich Village: Christine Stansell, *American Moderns: Bohemian New York and the Creation of a New Century* (New York, 2000). Shift in middle-class sexual standards in the 1920s: Clement, *Love for Sale.*

55 Odem, *Delinquent Daughters*; Alexander, *The "Girl Problem."*

56 Josephine A. Roche, *Wage Earning Women and Girls in Baltimore: A Study of the Cost of Living in 1918* (New York: National Consumers' League, 1918), folder 12, box 10, RC.

57 Roche, "Economic Conditions in Relation to the Delinquency of Girls," 43–49.

58 Nancy Woloch, *Muller v. Oregon: A Brief History with Documents* (Boston, 1996). Reformers preferred protective laws for men and women: Landon R. Y. Storrs, *Civiliz-*

ing Capitalism: The National Consumers' League, Women's Activism, and Labor Standards in the New Deal Era (Chapel Hill, NC, 2000).

59 Roche, "Economic Conditions in Relation to the Delinquency of Girls." Roche, *Wage Earning Women and Girls in Baltimore.*

60 See, for instance, Nancy F. Cott, *The Grounding of Modern Feminism* (New Haven, CT, 1987), 117–142. The debate over protective labor legislation divided women reformers through the 1960s. See, for instance, Dorothy Sue Cobble, *The Other Women's Movement: Workplace Justice and Social Rights in Modern America* (Princeton, NJ, 2004). A debate has continued over the decades about how to refer to reformers who wanted to open new opportunities for women but also advocated protective labor legislation. Nancy F. Cott, "What's in a Name? The Limits of 'Social Feminism'; or, Expanding the Vocabulary of Women's History," *Journal of American History* 76 (Dec. 1989): 809–829. Jacquelyn Dowd Hall, "Women Writers, the 'Southern Front,' and the Dialectial Imagination," *Journal of Southern History* 69 (Feb. 2003): 3–38. I am going with "progressive feminist" because it sets these activists who wanted to expand women's lives directly into the larger progressive movement of which they were most assuredly a part.

61 Roche, "Economic Conditions in Relation to the Delinquency of Girls," 32.

62 Roche to Read Lewis, Dec. 2, 1912, RLP.

63 Nan Enstad, *Ladies of Labor*, 91. Jennifer Guglielmo, *Living the Revolution: Italian Women's Resistance and Radicalism in New York City, 1880–1945* (Chapel Hill, NC, 2010), 189.

64 To the extent that northern progressives supported racial segregation, the same dynamic applied: rather than restrain perpetrators of racial violence, segregation restricted African Americans' freedom.

65 Josephine Roche, Curriculum Vitae, 1921, folder 15, box 4, IRSA.

66 For the study of Italian wage-earning girls, she visited eighty-six families. Josephine Roche, "The Italian Girl," in *The Neglected Girl*, 109.

67 Roche, "Economic Conditions in Relation to the Delinquency of Girls," 8.

68 Social surveys: Martin Bulmer, Kevin Bales, and Kathryn Kish Sklar, eds., *The Social Survey in Historical Perspective* (Cambridge, UK, 1992), especially Kathryn Kish Sklar, "Hull House Maps and Papers: Social Science as Women's Work in the 1890s," 111–147; Stephen P. Turner, "The World of the Academic Quantifiers: The Columbia University Family and Its Connections," 269–290.

69 Harvey O'Higgins, "Lucia Ancilotti," *Collier's*, Dec. 28, 1912, 13–14. O'Higgins, "The Paladino Family," *Collier's*, Feb. 17, 1912, 11–12, 33ff. Harvey O'Higgins, "The Gianellis," *Collier's*, Apr. 6, 1912, 42. See also Roche, "The Italian Girl."

70 Roche, "Economic Conditions in Relation to the Delinquency of Girls," 10.

71 Ibid., 9.

72 O'Higgins, "The Gianellis," 42.

73 Ibid.

74 Ibid.

75 Roche, "The Italian Girl."

76 O'Higgins, "Lucia Ancilotti," 13–14. O'Higgins, "The Paladino Family," *Collier's*, Feb. 17, 1912, 11–12, 33ff. O'Higgins, "The Gianellis," 42. See also Roche, "The Italian Girl."

77 Mary Kingsbury Simkhovitch, *Neighborhood: My Story of Greenwich House* (New York, 1938), 90.

78 Ibid., 90.

79 Ibid., 98, 93.

80 Roche to Dr. Simkhovitch, Nov. 1951, folder 7, box 2, Mary Simkhovitch Papers, Arthur and Elizabeth Schlesinger Library on the History of Women, Radcliffe Institute for Advanced Study, Harvard University, Cambridge, MA.

81 Roche to Read Lewis, July 1911, RLP.

82 "Credo 1911," enclosure Roche to Read Lewis, May 13, 1962, RLP.

83 Roche to Read Lewis, Aug. 13, 1911, RLP.

84 Roche to Ben Lindsey [prior to Feb. 13, 1912], box 36; Roche to Lindsey, spring 1912, box 37, BLP.

85 Roche to Lindsey, spring 1912, box 37, BLP.

86 Anna O'Higgins to Ben Lindsey, June 2, 1912, box 37, BLP.

87 "Routed Suffragists Win," *New York Times*, July 6, 1912, 3.

CHAPTER 3   EMERGENCE AS A PUBLIC LEADER, 1912–1913

1 Roche to Read Lewis, Jan. 2, 1914, RLP.

2 Lindsey to Dear Sir, July 20, 1912, box 38, BLP. See also R. Todd Laugen, *The Gospel of Progressivism: Moral Reform and Labor War in Colorado, 1900–1930* (Boulder, CO, 2010), 36–39.

3 Laugen, *Gospel of Progressivism*, 37–38.

4 George Creel, *Rebel at Large: Recollections of Fifty Crowded Years* (New York, 1947), 100–101.

5 Creel was an exception. Creel, *Rebel at Large*, 101–102.

6 Certificate filed with the Secretary of State, Colorado, June 29, 1912, box 38; "State Progressives Start Party Tonight," *Denver News*, June 29, 1912, box 331; C. E. Fisher to Lindsey, July 20, 1912, box 39; Lindsey to Costigan, July 18, 1912, box 39, BLP. "Progressives Unite on Plans for Their Party in Colorado," *Denver News*, June 26, 1912; "New Political Party Is Organized in Colorado," *Greeley Tribune*, July 1, 1912; "Progressives Meet August 1 in Denver to Nominate," *Denver News*, July 11, 1912; "Costigan Moose Candidate for Governor," *Denver Republican*, Aug. 2, 1912, box 331, BLP.

7 Roche to Read Lewis, Aug. 1912, RLP.

8 Ibid., Apr. 16, 1914, RLP.

9 See, for instance, Frances A. Kellor, "A New Spirit in Party Organization," *New American Review* (1914): 879–892; Theodore Roosevelt, "The Progressive Party," *Century Magazine*, Oct. 1913, 826–836; Jane Addams, "My Experiences as a Progressive Delegate," *McClure's Magazine*, Nov. 1912, 13.

10 Melanie Gustafson, "Partisan Women in the Progressive Era," *Journal of Women's History* 9 (Summer 1997): 7–30, esp. 26–27, note 37. John Allen Gable, *The Bull Moose Years: Theodore Roosevelt and the Progressive Party* (Port Washington, NY, 1978), 267, note 76. See also "Suffragists O.K. New Party," *Chicago Daily Tribune*, Aug. 9, 1912, 4, box 331, BLP.

11 Roche to Read Lewis, Aug. 1912, RLP.

12 Ibid., Aug. 1912, RLP.

13 Gustafson, "Partisan Women in the Progressive Era." See also Melanie Gustafson, Kristie Miller, and Elisabeth Israels Perry, eds., *We Have Come to Stay: American Women and Political Parties, 1880–1960* (Albuquerque, NM, 1999).

14 Roche to Read Lewis, Aug. 1912, RLP.

15 "Progressive Party Platform," http://teachingamericanhistory.org/library/index.asp ?document=607, accessed June 23, 2011. Progressive Party's commitment to direct democracy: Sidney M. Milkis, *Theodore Roosevelt, the Progressive Party, and the Transformation of American Democracy* (Lawrence, KS, 2009).

16   Allen Davis, "The Social Workers and the Progressive Party, 1912–1916," *American Historical Review* 69 (Apr. 1964): 671–688.

17   Pamphlet, "To the Women Voters," 1912, folder 2, box 13, Theodore Roosevelt Collection-Progressive Party Papers, Houghton Library, Harvard University, Cambridge, MA.

18   Gable, *Bull Moose Years*, 60–74. "Republican Party Platform of 1908," http://www.presidency.ucsb.edu/ws/index.php?pid=29632#axzz1Q8N0LMTW, accessed June 23, 2011.

19   Sidney Milkis and Daniel Tichenor, "Direct Democracy and Social Justice: The Progressive Party Campaign of 1912," *Studies in American Political Development* 8 (Fall 1994): 316–317, 320. Gable, *Bull Moose Years*, 64–66.

20   Gable, *Bull Moose Years*, 63.

21   Milkis and Tichenor, "Direct Democracy and Social Justice," 320 and n. 135. Evelyn Brooks Higginbotham, *Righteous Discontent: The Women's Movement in the Black Baptist Church, 1880–1920* (Cambridge, MA, 1993), 226.

22   "TR Wins, Predicts Lindsey at Big Bull Moose Luncheon," *Denver Republican*, Aug. 31, 1912; "200 Bull Moosies Hear Third Party Orators," *Denver News*, Aug. 31, 1912, box 331, BLP. Robyn Muncy, "'Women Demand Recognition': Women Candidates in Colorado's Election of 1912," in *We Have Come to Stay*, 45–54.

23   "Twelve Amendments Carry," *Denver News*, Nov. 10, 1912, box 332, BLP. See also Minutes of a Meeting RE Administration of the Mothers' Compensation Law, Nov. 14, 1912; Ida L. Gregory to Mayor and Board of Supervisors, Nov. 18, 1912, box 134, BLP.

24   Student Record of Josephine Aspinwall Roche, Political Science, Columbia University Archives, New York. *Columbia University Bulletin of Information: History, Economics and Public Law,* 1912–1913, 30–31.

25   George Creel to Roche, Oct. 13, 1912, folder 6, box 10, RC.

26   On the national movement toward such measures: Joanne Meyerowitz, *Women Adrift: Independent Wage-Earners in Chicago, 1880–1930* (Chicago, 1988), 64–65. Estelle B. Freedman, *Their Sisters' Keepers: Women's Prison Reform in America, 1830–1930* (Ann Arbor, MI, 1981), 127.

27   Alice Rohe, "Denver's Petticoated Copper," *Sunday News*, Dec. 1, 1912, folder 5, box 10, RC.

28   Creel, *Rebel at Large*, 105.

29   Roche to Read Lewis, Sept. 8, 1913, RLP.

30   Ibid., Nov. 1912, RLP.

31   Alice Rohe, "Denver's Petticoated Copper."

32   Lindsey to William Allen White, Nov. 22, 1912, box 40; "Twelve Amendments Carry: Women's and Miners' Bills Obtain Greatest Majorities," *Denver News*, Nov. 10, 1912, box 332, BLP.

33   Rohe, "Denver's Petticoated Copper."

34   Ibid.

35   Roche to Read Lewis, Nov. 1912, RLP.

36   "Appeal from Order of Discharge of the Fire and Police Board," 1913, folder 6, box 10, RC. Parents' opposition: "Denver's Dynamic Josephine Roche Takes Treasury Post," *Washington Post*, folder 6, box 35, RC. Her feelings: Roche to Read Lewis, Nov. 1912, RLP.

37   Night sticks: Creel, *Rebel at Large*, 102–103. That Roche wore her badge: Creel, *Rebel* *at Large,* 106; Rohe, "Denver's Petticoated Copper"; photo of Roche in "Women Deputies Patrol Polls," *Denver Express,* May 20, 1913, folder 5, box 10, RC.

38 Deputy sheriff badges, City of Denver, folder 3, box 10, RC.

39 Raine: see Creel, *Rebel at Large,* 97; Raine to Lindsey, Sept. 10, 1912, box 39, BLP. Raine and Roche remained friends until his death: see correspondence in folder 2, box 6, RC. William MacLeod Raine, *Famous Sheriffs and Western Outlaws* (Garden City, NY, 1929), contains stories he published in mass media between 1903 and 1927; *Brand Blotters* (New York, 1909); *Wyoming: A Story of the Outdoor West* (New York, 1908). In another of Raine's novels, the plot in many ways foreshadows Roche's work at Rocky Mountain Fuel: William MacLeod Raine, *Ridgway of Montana: A Story of Today, in Which the Hero Is Also the Villain* (New York, 1909).

40 Roche herself juxtaposed her college sports to her new job as policewoman in the interview with a Denver journalist. Rohe, "Denver's Petticoated Copper."

41 Photographs are in, for instance, " 'Miss Officer' Josephine Roche," *Washington Post,* Dec. 3, 1912, 3. "Maternal" is in Anna O'Higgins to Ben Lindsey, Oct. 26, 1913, box 136, BLP.

42 Roche to Read Lewis, Dec. 30, 1912, RLP.

43 "A Vassar Girl Policeman," *Poughkeepsie News-Press,* July 9, 1913, VAO. Creel, *Rebel at Large,* 105–106. Lindsey to Mrs. Warren Hayden, Dec. 12, 1912, box 41, BLP.

44 Roche to Read Lewis, Dec. 30, 1912, RLP.

45 Ibid., Dec. 2, 1912, RLP.

46 Ibid., Dec. 2, 1912, RLP.

47 Ibid., Dec. 2, 1912, RLP.

48 Ibid., Dec. 30, 1912, RLP.

49 Thomas J. Noel, *The City and the Saloon: Denver, 1858–1916* (1982; Niwot, CO, 1996), 35, 88, 98, 108. See also "The Youthful Delinquent: A New Way to Deal with Him," *New York Times,* Feb. 25, 1906. Cronin v. Adams, 192 U.S. 108 (1904), http://caselaw.lp.findlaw.com/cgi-bin/getcase.pl?linkurl=%3C%linkurl3E&friend=%3C%20riend%%3E&court=us&vol=192&invol=108, accessed Feb. 14, 2014. Lincoln Steffens, "Ben B. Lindsey: The Just Judge," *McClure's Magazine* 28 (1907), 162–176.

50 Noel, *City and the Saloon,* 37.

51 Ibid., 37–40.

52 Ibid., 99–103, 107. On the mayor, see also Laugen, *The Gospel of Progressivism,* 12–13, 17–19, 24–30, 35–39.

53 Noel, *City and the Saloon,* 86. See also Mary Murphy, "Bootlegging Mothers and Drinking Daughters: Gender and Prohibition in Butte, Montana," *American Quarterly* 46 (June 1994): 174–194, esp. 178–181; Mara L. Keire, *For Business and Pleasure: Red-Light Districts and the Regulation of Vice in the United States, 1890–1933* (Baltimore, MD, 2010), 31.

54 Noel, *City and the Saloon,* 87.

55 Creel, *Rebel at Large,* 104. Other such districts in the West: Mark Wild, "Red Light Kaleidoscope: Prostitution and Ethnoracial Relations in Los Angeles, 1880–1940," *Journal of Urban History* 28 (Sept. 2002): 720–742. Crib districts elsewhere: Keire, *For Business and Pleasure,* 33.

56 Wide spectrum of anti-prostitution reformers: Barbara Meil Hobson, *Uneasy Virtue: The Politics of Prostitution and the American Reform Tradition* (1987; Chicago, 1990), 150–152.

57 Creel, *Rebel at Large,* 105.

58 Ibid., 106.

59 Ibid., 105.

60   Ibid., 105–106.

61   Ibid., 109–110.

62   Ibid., 106.

63   Ibid., 108.

64   On this issue, I agree with Robert D. Johnston, *The Radical Middle Class: Populist Democracy and the Question of Capitalism in Progressive Era Portland, Oregon* (Princeton, NJ, 2003), 96–98.

65   Lindsey to Miss Morgan, Feb. 21, 1913, box 41, BLP.

66   Creel, *Rebel at Large*, 109–110.

67   Ibid., 109–110.

68   David J. Pivar, *Purity and Hygiene: Women, Prostitution and the "American Plan," 1900–1930* (Westport, CT, 2002). Kristin Luker, "Sex, Social Hygiene, and the State: The Double-Edged Sword of Social Reform," *Theory and Society* 27 (1998): 601–634, esp. 610.

69   Thomas C. Mackey, *Pursuing Johns: Criminal Law Reform, Defending Character, and New York City's Committee of Fourteen, 1920–1930* (Columbus, OH, 2005), 6.

70   Mary E. Odem, *Delinquent Daughters: Protecting and Policing Adolescent Female Sexuality in the United States, 1885–1920* (Chapel Hill, NC, 1995), 113–114.

71   Creel, *Rebel at Large*, 109–110.

72   Ibid., 109–111. "George Creel Tells of Work to Wipe Out Vice in Denver and Warns of Red Light Menace," *News*, Feb. 5, 1913, folder 5, box 10, RC.

73   Creel, *Rebel at Large*, 110, 112. Roche, "Girls Lost Low Wage Fight," clipping, 1912; Roche, "Girls Driven to Wrong in Denver by Ignorance, Low Pay, and Fatigue," *Denver Express*, Mar. 15, 1913, folder 5, box 10, RC.

74   Creel, *Rebel at Large*, 110. "A Vassar Girl Policeman," *Poughkeepsie News-Press*, July 9, 1913, VAO.

75   Luker, "Sex, Social Hygiene, and the State," 611.

76   "Twenty-two Women of Redlight District Sent to Jail," *Rocky Mountain News*, Jan. 23, 1913, folder 5, box 10, RC.

77   *Thirteenth Census of the United States: 1910*, vol. 4, *Population* (Washington, DC, 1912).

78   "A Vassar Girl Policeman," *Poughkeepsie News-Press*, July 9, 1913, VAO. Roche, "Girls Lost Low Wage Fight," clipping, 1912; Roche, "Girls Driven to Wrong in Denver by Ignorance, Low Pay, and Fatigue," *Denver Express*, Mar. 15, 1913; and other newspaper articles in folder 5, box 10, RC.

79   Just for example, see Paul S. Boyer, *Urban Masses and Moral Order in America, 1820–1920* (Cambridge, MA, 1978).

80   For additional evidence on the point, see Laugen, *The Gospel of Progressivism*, 56–60.

81   Roche to Read Lewis, May 24, 1913, RLP.

82   "George Creel Tells of Work to Wipe Out Vice in Denver and Warns of Redlight Menace," *News*, Feb. 5, 1913, folder 5, box 10, RC. Creel, *Rebel at Large*, 114–115.

83   Roche to Read Lewis, Feb. 9, 1913, RLP.

84   Ibid.

85   Creel, *Rebel at Large*, 116–117.

86   Roche to Sonya Levien, Aug. 30, 1913, Roche file, Sonya Levien Papers, Huntington Library, San Marino, CA.

87   Roche to Read Lewis, Mar. 23, 1913, RLP.

88   Lindsey to Miss Morgan, Feb. 21, 1913, box 41; Lindsey's Secretary to Theodore Roosevelt, Mar. 8, 1913, box 41; Lindsey to William Hard, Mar. 26, 1913, box 41; Lindsey to Madeleine Doty, Mar. 29, 1913, box 41; Lindsey's Secretary to Christopher

Ruess, Apr. 17, 1913, box 42; Lindsey to Richmond Pearson Hobson, May 15, 1913, box 42; Lindsey to Harry H. Tammen, May 15, 1913, box 42; Lindsey to Hon. George Kindel, June 17, 1913, box 42; Lindsey to Mr. and Mrs. J. P. Wright, June 29, 1913; box 42; Dr. Martin to Lindsey, Sept. 12, 1913, box 43, BLP.

89 Roche to Read Lewis, Apr. 7, 1913, RLP.

90 Roche to Sonya Levien, Aug. 30, 1913, Roche file, Levien Papers.

91 Roche to Read Lewis, [1913], RLP.

92 "Violate Liquor Law on Blakeley's Say So, Miss Roche Says," *Rocky Mountain News*, Mar. 13, 1913, folder 15, box 10, RC.

93 "Mayor's Critic Out of Office," *Rocky Mountain News*, Apr. 25, 1913, folder 5, box 10, RC.

94 Roche to Read Lewis, Mar. 23, 1913, RLP.

95 Hobson, *Uneasy Virtue*, 155–157. Freedman, *Their Sisters' Keepers*, 127. Odem, *Delinquent Daughters*, 96–98, 111. Mara Keire confirms that progressives elsewhere also saw their anti-vice campaigns as directed mainly at corporate power. See Keire, *For Business and Pleasure*, 69–90.

96 "Report of the Morals Commission of the City and County of Denver Concerning Licensed Cafes and Restaurants," 1913, 11, folder 5, box 10, RC.

97 Roche to Read Lewis, May 7, 1913, RLP.

98 "Mayor's Critic Out of Office," *Rocky Mountain News*, Apr. 25, 1913; "Discharge Was Spite, Not Economy, Assert Miss Roche's Friends," *Denver Republican*, Apr. 25, 1913, folder 5, box 10, RC.

99 "Hear Josephine Roche's Story at Central Presbyterian Church Tuesday Night," *Denver Express*, Apr. 28, 1913, folder 5, box 10, RC.

100 "Women Brand Ousting of Josephine Roche as Infamous Outrage," *Denver Express*, Apr. 26, 1913, folder 5, box 10, RC.

101 "Hear Josephine Roche's Story at Central Presbyterian Church Tuesday Night," *Denver Express*, Apr. 28, 1913, folder 5, box 10, RC. On Sullivan, see Roche to Read Lewis, May 24, 1913, RLP.

102 "Miss Roche Takes Oath as Deputy," *Denver Express*, May 1913, folder 5, box 10, RC.

103 "Grand Jurors Will Ask Woman to Prove Charges of Graft," *Denver Post*, Apr. 26, 1913, folder 5, box 10, RC.

104 "Hear Josephine Roche's Story at Central Presbyterian Church Tuesday Night," *Denver Express*, Apr. 28, 1913, folder 5, box 10, RC.

105 File full of newspaper reports, folder 5, box 10, RC.

106 "Arnold Won't Observe Order," *Rocky Mountain News*, May 8, 1913, folder 5, box 10, RC.

107 Ibid.

108 Roche to Read Lewis, May 7, 1913, RLP.

109 "Miss Roche Again on Force Court Orders Reinstatement," *Denver News*, July 9, 1913, folder 5, box 10, RC.

110 "Women Deputies Patrol Polls; Absence of Trouble Features," *Denver Express*, May 20, 1913, folder 5, box 10, RC.

111 Roche to Read Lewis, May 24, 1913, RLP.

112 Ibid.

113 Ibid.

114 Ibid.

115 Ibid.

116 Ibid., May 30, 1913, RLP.

117   Roche to Sonya Levien, Aug. 30, 1913, Roche file, Levien Papers. "Miss Roche Again on the Force," July 9, 1913, folder 5, box 20, RC.
118   Roche to Sonya Levien, Aug. 30, 1913, Roche file, Levien Papers.
119   Quote is from Roche's letter of resignation, Aug. 4, 1913, Roche file, Levien Papers. "Miss Roche Out, Attacks Rush," *Denver News*, Aug. 5, 1913, folder 5, box 10, RC.
120   Roche to Read Lewis, May 30, 1913, RLP.
121   May Estelle Cook to Roche, July 4, 1913; May Estelle Cook to Roche, July 12, 1913; May Estelle Cook to Roche, July 27, 1913, RLP.
122   Roche to Read Lewis, Apr. 7, 1913, RLP.
123   Ibid., Aug. 30, 1913, RLP.
124   Ibid.
125   Roche to Levien, Aug. 30, 1913, Roche file, Levien Papers.
126   Roche to Read Lewis, Aug. 1913, RLP.
127   Ibid., Sept. 8, 1913, RLP.
128   Ibid., Aug. 15, 1913, RLP.
129   Ibid.
130   Ibid., Aug. 30, 1913, RLP.
131   Ibid., Sept. 8, 1913, RLP.
132   Roche to Levien, Aug. 30, 1913, Roche file, Levien Papers.

CHAPTER 4   SEEKING FUNDAMENTALS: THE COLORADO COAL STRIKE, 1913–1914

1   Roche to Read Lewis, Sept. 28, 1913, RLP.
2   Quotation is Thomas G. Andrews's from *Killing for Coal: America's Deadliest Labor War* (Cambridge, MA, 2008).
3   Roche to Sonya Levien, Aug. 30, 1913, Roche file, Sonya Levien Papers, Huntington Library, San Marino, CA.
4   Roche to Read Lewis, Sept. 8, 1913, RLP.
5   Roche to Sonya Levien, [Nov.] 1913, Roche file, Levien Papers.
6   Roche to Read Lewis, [Nov. 1913], RLP.
7   Roche to Sonya Levien, [Nov.] 1913, Roche file, Levien Papers.
8   E.L.M. Tate to E. P. Costigan, Oct. 17, 1913, folder 22, box 6, ECP.
9   Frances Kellor to Lindsey, Nov. 7, 1912, box 40, BLP.
10   Pamphlet by Frances Kellor, "The Progressive Service," Jan. 25, 1913, box 41, BLP. John Allen Gable, *The Bull Moose Years: Theodore Roosevelt and the Progressive Party* (Port Washington, NY, 1978), 154.
11   Roche to Read Lewis, Nov. 1913, RLP.
12   Read Lewis to Roche, Nov. 12, 1913, RLP.
13   "Longmont Moosers Begin Work for 1914 Campaign, *Rocky Mountain News*, Nov. 22, 1913; "Miss Roche Urges Women to Support Progressives," *Rocky Mountain News*, Nov. 29, 1913; "Progressive Club Chooses Officers," *Sterling Advocate*, Dec. 5, 1913, folder 8, box 10, RC.
14   Roche to Read Lewis, Dec. 18, 1913, RLP.
15   Ibid., Dec. 22, 1913, RLP.
16   Roche to Sonya Levien, [Nov.] 1913, Roche file, Levien Papers.
17   Andrews, *Killing for Coal*, 251.
18   Roche to Read Lewis, Nov. 27, 1913, RLP.
19   Ibid., Dec. 5, 1913, RLP.
20   Ibid., Feb. 23, 1914, RLP.

21 Roche to Read Lewis, Nov. 30, 1913, RLP.
22 Ibid., Dec. 5, 1913, RLP.
23 Costigan to J. C. Scott, Aug. 28, 1913, folder 19, box 6, ECP.
24 Roche to Sonya Levien, [Nov.] 1913, Roche file, Levien Papers. Lindsey to Kellor, Feb. 21, 1914, box 41; Lindsey to Anna and Harvey O'Higgins, Mar. 5, 1914, box 137, BLP.
25 Roche to Read Lewis, Jan. 1, 1914, RLP.
26 Ibid.
27 George S. McGovern and Leonard F. Guttridge, *The Great Coalfield War* (Boston, 1972), vii.
28 Ibid., 20–21, 23.
29 Ibid., 23, 28–36.
30 Ibid., 24, 27–29. Andrews, *Killing for Coal*, 197–229.
31 Andrews, *Killing for Coal*, 247.
32 McGovern and Guttridge, *Great Coalfield War*, 86–88.
33 Ibid., 102.
34 Ibid., 102–103.
35 Ibid., 103–105, 107. Andrews, *Killing for Coal*, 246–250.
36 Roche to Read Lewis, Sept. 28, 1913, RLP.
37 Ibid., Feb. 23, 1914, RLP.
38 McGovern and Guttridge, *Great Coalfield War*, 114–119, 122–127.
39 Ibid., 134; Andrews, *Killing for Coal*, 254–256.
40 Roche to Read Lewis, Nov. 1913, RLP.
41 Roosevelt had emphasized human over property rights in his presidential campaign of 1912. Sidney M. Milkis, *Theodore Roosevelt, the Progressive Party, and the Transformation of American Democracy* (Lawrence, KS, 2009), 55.
42 Roche to Read Lewis, Nov. 1913, RLP.
43 Ibid., Nov. 27, 1913, RLP.
44 Ibid., Nov. 1913, RLP.
45 McGovern and Guttridge, *Great Coalfield War*, 156–158.
46 Andrews, *Killing for Coal*, 257.
47 McGovern and Guttridge, *Great Coalfield War*, 156–161, 205–206.
48 Roche to Read Lewis, Nov. 27, 1913, RLP.
49 Creel, *Rebel at Large: Recollections of Fifty Crowded Years* (New York, 1947), 126–132. Dr. L. P. Barbour to S. A. Coston, June 15, 1914, folder 2, box 7, ECP. Roche to Read Lewis, Mar. 8, 1914, RLP.
50 McGovern and Guttridge, *Great Coalfield War*, 155.
51 Ibid., 176.
52 Edward P. Costigan and James Brewster, "Conditions in the Coal Mines of Colorado," Brief for the Striking Miners, presented to Hearing before a Subcommittee of the Committee on Mines and Mining, House of Representatives, 63 Congress, Washington, DC, 1914, folder 1, box 12, RC.
53 R. M. McClintock to Costigan, Feb. 13, 1914, folder 2, box 7, ECP.
54 Ibid.
55 Roche to Read Lewis, Feb. 23, 1914, RLP.
56 McClintock to Costigan, Mar. 11, 1914, folder 2, box 7, ECP.
57 Roche to Read Lewis, Mar. 12, 1914, RLP.
58 McGovern and Guttridge, *Great Coalfield War*, 211–223.
59 Ibid., 223–225, 234.
60 Andrews, *Killing for Coal*, 273.
61 McGovern and Guttridge, *Great Coalfield War*, 228–230, 237–239.

62 Quoted in ibid., 188.

63 Ibid., 239–268. Graham Adams, *Age of Industrial Violence, 1910–1915* (New York, 1966), 160. Andrews, *Killing for Coal*, 273–284.

64 McGovern and Guttridge, *Great Coalfield War*, 267–268.

65 Roche to Read Lewis, May 5, 1914, RLP.

66 McGovern and Guttridge, *Great Coalfield War*, 301, 310.

67 Lindsey to William Allen White, June 15, 1914, box 138, BLP.

68 Roy McClintock to Costigan, June 22, 1914, folder 4; Otto Thurm to Costigan, June 9, 1914, folder 5, box 7, ECP.

69 Dr. L. P. Barbour to S. A. Coston, June 15, 1914, folder 2, box 7, ECP.

70 Payment scheme: McGovern and Guttridge, *Great Coalfield War*, 204–206; Andrews, *Killing for Coal*, 257.

71 Costigan to Clarence Dodge, May 16, 1914, folder 2; Ira DeLong to Edwin Miller, June 15, 1914, folder 2; John Crone to Costigan, June 29, 1914, folder 2; J. Homer Dickson to Costigan, June 29, 1914, folder 10; Costigan to Edwin Miller, June 13, 1914, folder 4, box 7, ECP. Lindsey to William Allen White, June 15, 1914, box 138; George Eisler to Lindsey, June 27, 1914, box 47; E. E. McLaughlin to Lindsey, June 18, 1914, box 47, BLP.

72 Costigan to Clarence Dodge, May 16, 1914, folder 2, box 7, ECP.

73 Costigan to Edwin Miller, June 13, 1914, folder 4, box 7, ECP.

74 See, for instance, John Crone to Costigan, June 29, 1914, folder 2, box 7, ECP; George Eisler to Lindsey, July 27, 1914, box 47, BLP. Roche to Costigan, folder 17, box 7, ECP.

75 Letterhead of the party: James Causey to Lindsey, June 16, 1914, box 138, BLP.

76 Roche to Read Lewis, Mar. 9, 1914, and June 16, 1914, RLP.

77 L. F. Cornwell to Costigan, July 8, 1914, folder 2, box 7, ECP.

78 Fred Robinson to Costigan, July 26, 1914, folder 5, box 7, ECP.

79 "Colorado's Comeback," *Pueblo Chieftain*, Aug. 12, 1914, box 334, BLP.

80 L. F. Cornwell to Costigan, July 8, 1914, folder 2, box 7, ECP.

81 O.K.D. to Costigan, n.d., folder 2, box 7, ECP.

82 Roche to Costigan, folder 17; Marie Dieker to Costigan, 1914, folder 10, box 7, ECP. Campaign materials in folder 6, box 7, ECP.

83 Theodore Roosevelt to Progressives of Colorado, Oct. 11, 1914, folder 5, box 7, ECP.

84 J. S. Temple to Costigan, Oct. 27, 1914, folder 5, box 7, ECP. Lindsey to William Chenery, Nov. 5, 1914, box 48, BLP; Fisher to Costigan, Nov. 6, 1914, folder 11, box 7, ECP. Costigan to Hiram Johnson, Dec. 28, 1914, folder 12, box 7, ECP. McGovern and Guttridge, *Great Coalfield War*, 307, 340.

85 Lindsey to William Chenery, Nov. 5, 1914, box 48, BLP.

86 See Joseph A. McCartin, *Labor's Great War: The Struggle for Industrial Democracy and the Origins of Modern American Labor Relations, 1912–1921* (Chapel Hill, NC, 1997). In 1914, Prohibition became in Colorado an anti-worker movement rather than an anti-corporate movement. What had been considered moral reform at this point in Colorado's history split off from pro-labor reform. R. Todd Laugen, *The Gospel of Progressivism: Moral Reform and Labor War in Colorado, 1900–1930* (Boulder, CO, 2010), 56–60.

87 See, for instance, Roche to Edward Keating, Nov. 3, 1928, folder 5, box 4; Gerry Dick, typescript interview with Roche, Oct. 9, 1937, folder 2, box 36, RC. See also documents on Roche's gubernatorial campaign in 1934; her speeches through the 1930s and early 1940s, all in Roche Collection, for evidence of continuity of thought with this moment.

88 Roche quoted in "Denver's Dynamic Josephine Roche Takes Treasury Post," *Washington Post*, Dec. 1934, folder 6, box 35, RC.

89 For instance, George Martin, *Madam Secretary: Frances Perkins* (Boston, 1976), 76–90, 170–172. Elisabeth Israels Perry, *Belle Moskowitz: Feminine Politics and the Exercise of Power in the Age of Alfred E. Smith* (New York, 1987), 83.

90 McCartin, *Labor's Great War*, 18–24.

91 Roche's copy of Basil Manly, *Final Report of the U.S. Commission on Industrial Relations* (Washington, DC, 1915), 26–27, folder 3, box 12, RC.

92 Ibid., 22, 32.

93 Ibid., 8–9.

94 Ibid., 10–12, 14–15.

95 Ibid., 22, 32.

96 Ibid., 22.

97 Ibid., 82–86, 90–91.

98 Ibid., 43–44, 50, 56–57, 68, 150–151, 74–75, 78–79.

99 "Manly Report Urges Decent Militia; Hits at Oppression," clipping, folder 5, box 12, RC.

100 Roche's copy of Manly, *Final Report*, 85–91.

101 Gerry Dick, typescript interview with Roche, Oct. 9, 1937, folder 2, box 36, RC.

CHAPTER 5   "PART OF IT ALL ONE MUST BECOME": PROGRESSIVE IN WARTIME, 1915–1918

1 Jonathan M. Hansen refers to the "collapse of American progressivism in the face of World War I" in *The Lost Promise of Patriotism: Debating American Identity, 1890–1920* (Chicago, 2003), 158. Michael McGerr sees the war as both the "climax of progressivism" and "its death knell" in *A Fierce Discontent: The Rise and Fall of the Progressive Movement in America, 1870–1920* (New York, 2003), xvi. For apogee, see Joseph A. McCartin, *Labor's Great War: The Struggle for Industrial Democracy and the Origins of Modern American Labor Relations, 1912–1921* (Chapel Hill, NC, 1997), 3, and Robyn Muncy, *Creating a Female Dominion in American Reform, 1890–1935* (New York, 1991), 95–101.

2 Herbert Hoover, *The Memoirs of Herbert Hoover: Years of Adventure, 1874–1920* (New York, 1951), 150–181.

3 Ibid., 160, 170.

4 Memorandum of agreement between Miss Josephine Roche and the Commission for Relief in Belgium, Feb. 13, 1915, Roche file, folder 6, box 262, CRB.

5 John J. Roche to Josephine Roche, [1915], folder 11, box 10, RC.

6 Ella Roche to Josephine Roche, Feb. 10, 1915, folder 11, box 10, RC.

7 Roche to Read Lewis, Aug. 13, 1911, RLP.

8 Commission for Relief in Belgium, [May 1915], letter of recommendation describing Roche's work for the commission, folder 6, box 262, CRB.

9 "Miss Roche Tells of Work of Feeding the Belgians," *Rutland Herald*, Mar. 27, 1915; Roche to G. W. Giddings, Mar. 25, 1915, folder 6, box 262, CRB.

10 Commission for Relief in Belgium, [May 1915], letter of recommendation describing Roche's work for the Commission, folder 6, box 262, CRB. Methods of organizing: voluminous correspondence between Roche and G. W. Giddings or the commission's Organization Department, April–May 1915, folder 6, box 262, CRB.

11 Untitled and unsigned document, May 18, 1915; G. W. Giddings to Miss Josephine Roche, May 15, 1915, folder 6, box 262, CRB.

12 Untitled and unsigned document, May 18, 1915; G. W. Giddings to Miss Josephine Roche, May 15, 1915, folder 6, box 262, CRB.

13 Roche to Read Lewis, Nov. 21, 1915, RLP.

14 Ibid., Aug. 9, 1915, RLP.

15 See Lindsey to Roche, June 7, 1915, box 50, BLP. "Suffragists Start an Essay Contest," *New York Times*, July 4, 1915, S4.

16 Roche to Read Lewis, July 16, 1915; Aug. 23, 1915; Sept. 15, 1915; Nov. 7, 1915; and Dec. 1915, RLP.

17 Josephine Roche, "Wage-Earning Women and Girls in Baltimore," 1918, folder 12, box 10, RC.

18 Roche to Read Lewis, Sept. 1915, RLP.

19 Robert Speer's political machine: Charles Larsen, *The Good Fight: The Life and Times of Ben B. Lindsey* (Chicago, 1972), 60–64; J. Paul Mitchell, "Boss Speer and the City Functional," *Pacific Northwest Quarterly* 63 (Oct. 1972): 155–164; R. Todd Laugen, *The Gospel of Progressivism: Moral Reform and Labor War in Colorado, 1900–1930* (Boulder, CO, 2010), 24–26.

20 Roche to Read Lewis, Mar. 1916, RLP.

21 Edgar MacMechen, ed., *Robert Speer, A City Builder* (Denver, n.d.), 56–57.

22 Roche to Read Lewis, May 1916; Apr. 22, 1916, RLP.

23 Ibid., Jan. 21, 1916, RLP.

24 Ibid., June 1916, RLP.

25 Socialist Party Platform, 1916, http://www.presidency.ucsb.edu/ws/index.php?pid =29634#axzz1RvIFokVZ, accessed July 12, 2011.

26 Roche to Read Lewis, May 1916, RLP.

27 Mabel Cory Costigan, "A Woman's Way with Coal Mines," *Woman's Journal*, Mar. 1929, VAO. "Astounded": Edward Costigan to Edwin Miller, June 14, 1916, folder 10, box 8, ECP.

28 Maureen A. Flanagan, *America Reformed: Progressives and Progressivisms, 1890s–1920s* (New York, 2007), 224.

29 Roche to Read Lewis, June 16, 1916, RLP.

30 Roche to Dr. Caroline Spencer, Oct. 23, 1916, folder 7, box 6, RC.

31 Roche to Read Lewis, Nov. 12, 1916, RLP.

32 See, for instance, Statement of Edward Costigan on the National Election of 1916, Oct. 1, 1916; Memorandum of Statement Given to New York Times, Nov. 10, 1916, folder 13, box 8, ECP.

33 Woodrow Wilson, *War Messages*, 65th Congress, 1st Session Senate Document No. 5, Serial No. 7264, Washington, DC, 1917, 3–8.

34 Flanagan, *America Reformed*, 215–217.

35 Roche to Read Lewis, Apr. 22, 1917, RLP.

36 Lindsey to Harvey O'Higgins, Sept. 25, 1918; O'Higgins to Lindsey, Nov. 12, 1918; O'Higgins to Lindsey, Nov. 22, 1918, box 59, BLP.

37 Roche to Read Lewis, Apr. 22, 1917, RLP.

38 Ibid., July 1, 1917, RLP.

39 Ibid., Sept. 9, 1917, RLP.

40 Ibid., Dec. 16, 1917, RLP.

41 Ibid., Dec. 23, 1917, RLP.

42 Ibid., Jan. 29, 1918, RLP.

43 Ibid., Mar. 17, 1918, RLP.

44 Ibid.

45 Roche's dilemma was widely shared among progressives. David M. Kennedy, *Over Here: The First World War and American Society* (New York, 1980), 35.

46 First quote: Roche to Read Lewis, July 22, 1918; second from Roche to Read Lewis, Nov. 3, 1918, RLP.

47 McCartin, *Labor's Great War*, 91.

48 Alan Dawley, *Struggles for Justice: Social Responsibility and the Liberal State* (Cambridge, MA, 1991), 198–200.

49 Roche to Read Lewis, July 22, 1918, RLP.

50 George Creel, *Rebel at Large: Recollections of Fifty Crowded Years* (New York, 1947), 158–163.

51 Creel, *Rebel at Large*, 158–176. Kennedy, *Over Here*, 41, 55–61.

52 Kennedy, *Over Here*, 61.

53 Ibid., 61–63, 74.

54 Stephen Vaughn, *Holding Fast the Inner Lines: Democracy, Nationalism, and the Committee on Public Information* (Chapel Hill, NC, 1980), 78.

55 Dawley, *Struggles for Justice*, 188–189, 200–203.

56 Vaughn, *Holding Fast the Inner Lines*, 3.

57 See, for instance, Lindsey to Harvey O'Higgins, Nov. 9, 1918, box 59; Lindsey to Harvey O'Higgins, Feb. 5, 1919, box 60, BLP.

58 Roche to Read Lewis, May 6, 1918, RLP.

59 Roche in George Creel, *Complete Report of the Chairman of the Committee on Public Information 1917; 1918; 1919* (Washington, DC, 1920), 81.

60 Ibid., 102.

61 Ibid., 102.

62 Ibid., 81.

63 Ibid., 80.

64 Roche, "Report of the Division of Work with the Foreign Born of the Committee of Public Information from May 1918–May 1919," folder 2, box 11, RC.

65 Roche in *Complete Report of the Chairman of the Committee on Public Information*, 81.

66 Statement of Expenditures of the Foreign Language Information Service, Feb. 1st–Sept. 30, 1920, page 11, folder 15, box 4, IRSA.

67 Documents in Records of the Committee on Public Information, Division of Work with the Foreign Born, RG 63, NARA.

68 Kennedy, *Over Here*, 353.

69 Roche in *Complete Report of the Chairman of the Committee on Public Information*, 83. Her stand-alone report is in folder 2, box 11, RC.

70 Alan Dawley, *Changing the World: American Progressives in War and Revolution* (Princeton, NJ, 2005), 123. See also Kevin Mattson, *Creating a Democratic Public: The Struggle for Urban Participatory Democracy during the Progressive Era* (University Park, PA, 1998), 111–115.

71 Roche to Read Lewis, Apr. 23, 1923, RLP.

72 Roche in *Complete Report of the Chairman of the Committee on Public Information*, 80. L. E. Stein to Mr. Munroe, Nov. 9, 1920, folder 14, box 4, IRSA.

73 Roche in *Complete Report of the Chairman of the Committee on Public Information*, 102. Roche's language here came close to that of the cultural gifts movement that would emerge in the 1920s. Diana Selig, *Americans All: The Cultural Gifts Movement* (Cambridge, MA, 2008).

74 Edward Hale Bierstadt, *Aspects of Americanization* (Cincinnati, 1922), 24.

75 Her emphasis. Roche, "The Place of the Foreign Language Press in an Educational Program," paper presented to the National Conference of Social Work, June 22–29, 1921, folder 3, box 11, RC.

76   See Harvey O'Higgins, "The Gianellis," *Collier's*, Apr. 6, 1912, 12. Bierstadt, *Aspects of Americanization*, 121.

77   Roche in *Complete Report of the Chairman of the Committee on Public Information*, 81–82.

78   Vaughn, *Holding Fast the Inner Lines*, 70.

79   Kennedy, *Over Here*, 89–90.

80   Dawley, *Changing the World*, 238–255.

81   Roche to Read Lewis, Mar. 15, 1919, RLP.

CHAPTER 6   WORK AND LOVE IN A PROGRESSIVE EBB TIDE, 1919–1927

1   Roche to Read Lewis, Nov. 3, 1918, RLP.

2   Lindsey to Roche, Feb. 15, 1919, box 60, BLP.

3   "The Work of the FLIS," n.d., folder 14, box 4, IRSA.

4   Roche to Read Lewis, n.d., folder 6, box 9, IRSA.

5   Will Irwin, "FLIS," *Collier's*, Feb. 14, 1925, VAO.

6   Memo from L. E. Stein to Mr. Munroe, Nov. 9, 1920, folder 14, box 4, IRSA.

7   Harvey O'Higgins to John J. Roche, Feb. 17, 1920, folder 12, box 5, RC.

8   L. E. Stein to Mr. Munroe, Nov. 9, 1920, folder 14, box 4, IRSA.

9   "Summary of the Work of the Foreign Language Information Service Bureau," 1920, folder 15, box 4, IRSA.

10   L. E. Stein to Mr. Munroe, Nov. 9, 1920, folder 14, box 4, IRSA. Number of cases: "The Work of the FLIS," n.d., folder 14, box 4, IRSA.

11   Roche to Frank Persons, Mar. 17, 1921; Expenditures of the Bureau of FLIS, Feb. 1–Sept. 30, 1920, folder 15, box 4, IRSA.

12   Roche to L. E. Stein, Aug. 1920, folder 15, box 4, IRSA.

13   Staff size: Mr. Joy to Mr. Persons, Apr. 19, 1921, folder 15, box 4, IRSA.

14   Expenditures of the Bureau of FLIS, Feb. 1–Sept. 30, 1920, folder 15, box 4, IRSA.

15   Roche to Frank Persons, Mar. 17, 1921; Expenditures of the Bureau of FLIS, Feb. 1–Sept. 30, 1920, folder 15, box 4, IRSA.

16   Roche to Frank Persons, Mar. 17, 1921, folder 15, box 4, IRSA.

17   Mr. Joy to Mr. Persons, Apr. 19, 1921, folder 15, box 4, IRSA.

18   Roche, Memos to File, Mar. 10, 1922; Mar. 20, 1922; Mar. 22, 1922; Apr. 6, 1922; n.d.; Sept. 12, 1922, folder 1, box 1, IRSA.

19   Roche, "A Study of the Needs and Problems of the Foreign Born and of What Is Being Done to Meet Them," for Commonwealth Fund, folder 1, box 11, RC.

20   Edward Hale Bierstadt, ed., *Portmanteau Plays by Stuart Walker*, 4th ed. (Cincinnati, 1921), xvi–xvii. Louise Burleigh and Edward Hale Bierstadt, *Punishment: A Play in Four Acts* (New York, 1916).

21   Edward Hale Bierstadt, *More Portmanteau Plays by Stuart Walker* (Cincinnati, 1919), v.

22   Edward Hale Bierstadt, Barrett H. Clark, and Sidney Howard, *Jurgen and the Censor: Report of the Emergency Committee Organized to Protest against the Suppression of James Branch Cabell's Jurgen* (New York, 1920).

23   See, for instance, Edward Hale Bierstadt, *Aspects of Americanization* (Cincinnati, 1922).

24   "E. H. Bierstadt Marries," *New York Times*, July 3, 1920, 15. Lindsey to Mr. and Mrs. Edward Costigan, July 2, 1920; Henrietta Lindsey to Mrs. E. H. Bierstadt, July 16, 1920; Lindsey to Harvey O'Higgins, July 12, 1920, box 63, BLP.

25 Lindsey to Mr. and Mrs. Edward Costigan, July 2, 1920; Henrietta Lindsey to Mrs. E. H. Bierstadt, July 16, 1920; Lindsey to Harvey O'Higgins, July 12, 1920, box 63, BLP.

26 Roche to Read Lewis, July 6, 1920, RLP.

27 George Creel, *Rebel at Large: Recollections of Fifty Crowded Years* (New York, 1947), 141–144.

28 Bierstadt, Clark, and Howard, *Jurgen and the Censor*, 32.

29 Bierstadt, *Aspects of Americanization*, 16.

30 Ibid.

31 Ibid., 24.

32 Ibid., 124–136.

33 Alan Dawley, *Changing the World: American Progressives in War and Revolution* (Princeton, NJ, 2005), 291.

34 Ibid., 292.

35 Roche to Read Lewis, July 17, 1920; Oct. 4, 1920; Dec. 6, 1920; Sept. 25, 1921, RLP.

36 Ibid., Feb. 9, 1919, RLP.

37 Sonya Levien to Jo, Mar. 10, 1914, folder 6, box 4, RC. Levien Obituary, *Washington Post*, Mar. 21, 1960, folder 14, box 5, RC. See also Roche to Levien, Aug. 30, 1913, and other letters in Roche file, Sonya Levien Papers, Huntington Library, San Marino, CA.

38 On O'Neill, see William E. Owens, interview with author, Ellicott City, Maryland, May 26, 2005. Roche to Sidney Howard, July 25, 1932; June 9, 1934; July 18, [1929], box 7, Sidney Coe Howard Papers, Special Collections, Bancroft Library, University of California, Berkeley, CA. And Roche to Mrs. Sidney Howard, Dec. 20, 1941, folder 13, box 3, RC.

39 FLIS, Personnel List, Feb. 28, 1921, folder 14, box 4, IRSA.

40 Roche to Read Lewis, Dec. 6, 1920, RLP.

41 Guide to Papers of Sidney Coe Howard, Special Collections, Bancroft Library, University of California, Berkeley, CA, http://cdn.calisphere.org/data/13030/3q/tf2f59n63q /files/tf2f59n63q.pdf, accessed July 18, 2011.

42 Roche, Memo to File, Apr. 18, 1922, folder 1, box 1, IRSA.

43 Divorce Record Index #21922–1922, Division of Old Records, County Clerk's Office, Manhattan, New York. *Bulletin* 1, no. 4 (June 1922), a publication of the FLIS, shows that Bierstadt was no longer on staff by summer 1922. Records of the American Council for Nationalities Service 1921–1971, microfilm edition, University Publications of America, reel 24, Library of Congress, Washington, DC.

44 Roche to Read Lewis, Apr. 7, 1913, RLP.

45 Roche, Memos to File, Apr. 6, 1922; Apr. 18, 1922; n.d. [Spring 1922]; Sept. 12, 1922; "What the January and February Curtailments Have Meant," Mar. 10, 1922; Minutes Advisory Committee, Mar. 10, 1922, folder 1, box 1, IRSA.

46 *Bulletin*, 1, no. 1–2 (Jan.–Feb. 1922); 1, no. 3 (Mar. 1922); 1, no. 4 (June 1922); 1, no. 7 (Oct. 1922); 1, no. 8 (Nov. 1922); 1, no. 9 (Dec. 1922). Will Irwin, "FLIS," *Collier's*, Feb. 14, 1925, folder 1, box 11, RC.

47 Daniel Erwin Weinberg, "The Foreign Language Information Service and the Foreign Born, 1918–1939: A Case Study of Cultural Assimilation Viewed as a Problem in Social Technology," Ph.D. diss., University of Minnesota, 1973 (Ann Arbor, MI, 1974), 42–43. Read Lewis's adventures in Russia during the Revolution are documented in the RLP.

48 For her look in the early 1910s, see photos in "T. R. Wins, Predicts Lindsey at Big Bull Moose Luncheon," *Denver Republican*, Aug. 31, 1912, clipping, folder 5, box 5; "Women Deputies Patrol Polls; Absence of Trouble Features," *Denver Express*, May 20, 1913, folder 5, box 10; "Miss Roche Again on Force," *Denver News*, July 9, 1913, folder 5, box 10; RC and "'Miss Officer': Josephine Roche," *Washington Post*, Dec. 3, 1912, 3. For the 1920s, see photos of Roche in folder 9, box 54, ECP. The latter photos appeared in such publications as "Woman Heads Foreign Information Service," clipping, South Bend, Indiana, May 7, 1922; *Collier's*, Feb., 14, 1925, 21; "Woman Social Worker Inherits Vast Holdings in Strike-Bound Mine," Camden, New Jersey, *Courier*, Jan. 18, 1928, VAO.

49 Robyn Muncy, *Creating a Female Dominion in American Reform, 1890–1935* (New York, 1991), chapter 2.

50 Roche to Read Lewis, n.d., folder 6, box 9, IRSA.

51 Muncy, *Creating a Female Dominion*, 89–90. Lela B. Costin, *Two Sisters for Social Justice: A Biography of Grace and Edith Abbott* (Urbana, IL, 1983), 163, 165, 180.

52 "Grace Abbott," Roche's remarks reprinted from *Welfare Bulletin*, Feb. 1940, folder 2, box 1, RC.

53 Katharine Lenroot, General Memorandum on Editorial Division, Nov. 14, 1922, file 1-3-7, box 164, Central File, 1921–1925, Children's Bureau Records, RG 102, NARA (hereafter CBR).

54 Kathryn Kish Sklar, *Florence Kelley and the Nation's Work: The Rise of Women's Political Culture, 1830–1900* (New Haven, CT, 1995), 151–152, 159–161, 234–240.

55 Muncy, *Creating a Female Dominion*, 80. Costin, *Two Sisters for Social Justice*, 103. Molly Ladd-Taylor, *Mother-Work: Women, Child Welfare and the State, 1890–1930* (Urbana, IL, 1994), 91–97.

56 Meeting of the Permanent Conference for the Abolition of Child Labor, Nov. 20, 1923, frames 184–188, reel 123, Samuel Gompers Letterbooks, microfilm edition, Library of Congress, Washington, DC. Thanks to Peter Albert and Amy Rutenberg for these documents.

57 Correspondence between Roche and the AFL, Apr. 24, 1923–July 25, 1923, file 6-1-0-1, box 185, Central File 1921–25, CBR.

58 Roche, Annual Report of the Editorial Division, year ending June 30, 1924, file 1-4-1-13, box 164, Central File 1921–25, CBR.

59 Roche to Grace Abbott, Oct. 18, 1923, file 1-3-7, box 164, Central File, 1921–25, CBR.

60 Roche to Read Lewis, Labor Day, [1926?], RLP.

61 Ibid., Oct. 30, 1926; Dec. 12, 1926, RLP.

62 Ibid., Dec. 12, 1926, RLP.

63 Ibid.

64 R. Todd Laugen, *The Gospel of Progressivism: Moral Reform and Labor War in Colorado, 1900–1930* (Boulder, CO, 2010), 153–186.

65 Roche to Read Lewis, Labor Day, [1926?], RLP.

66 Ibid., Jan. 1, 1927, RLP.

67 John J. Roche Probate File, County Court, City and County of Denver, Colorado, opened Jan. 31, 1927, and closed Feb. 24, 1931.

68 Dr. George Strassler to Robyn Muncy, e-mail message reporting information from the Antelope County Clerk's Office on Roche's holdings at Neligh, Nebraska, Feb. 26, 2008, in author's possession.

69 John J. Roche, Probate File.

70 Charles Larsen, *The Good Fight: The Life and Times of Ben B. Lindsey* (Chicago, 1972), 193–199.

71 Roche to Read Lewis, June 22, 1927, RLP.

72 Ibid., July 13, 1927, RLP.

73 Ibid.

74 Ibid.

75   Ibid.
76   Ibid.

CHAPTER 7   MIGRATING TO A "TOTALLY NEW PLANET": ROCHE TAKES OVER ROCKY MOUNTAIN FUEL, 1927–1928

1   Roche to Read Lewis, Dec. 12, 1926, RLP.
2   Mary van Kleeck, *Miners and Management: A Study of the Collective Agreement between the United Mine Workers of America and the Rocky Mountain Fuel Company and an Analysis of the Problem of Coal in the United States* (New York, 1934), 37.
3   Reports from anti-labor spies, folder 8, box 11, RC.
4   Typescript page, no title, folder 3, box 15, RC.
5   George S. McGovern and Leonard F. Guttridge, *The Great Coalfield War* (Boston, 1972), 90, 120. See also typescript page, no title, folder 3, box 15, RC.
6   Roche to Read Lewis, Sept. 2, 1927, RLP.
7   Roche to Edward Keating, Nov. 3, 1928, folder 5, box 4, RC.
8   Roche quoted in "Cutting Wages Retards Recovery Says Colorado Woman Mine Owner," *New York Sun*, Apr. 6, 1932, VAO.
9   Quotation is from Merle Vincent statement, quoted in Donald McClurg, "The Colorado Coal Strike of 1927," *Labor History* 4 (Winter 1963): 68–92, esp. 83.
10   Sigrid Arne, "She Runs Mines: Josephine Roche," *St. Paul Pioneer Press*, May 25, 1934, folder 4, box 17, RC.
11   Van Kleeck, *Miners and Management*, 48. "The Coal the Public Wants," flyer, folder 5, box 17; "A Short Story of Coal and Colorado's Coalfields," pamphlet by RMF, folder 5, box 19; "Leaving Bad Impressions," an advertisement for Rocky Mountain Fuel's "lignite" coal, *Rocky Mountain News*, Mar. 19, 1928, folder 4, box 17, RC.
12   Third largest: "State Coal Industry Headed toward Another Strike," *Rocky Mountain News*, Mar. 19, 1928, 8, folder 4, box 17, RC.
13   Roche, handwritten notes on testimony before the Industrial Commission on Nov. 28, 1927, folder 1, box 15, RC.
14   "Commission Refuses to Permit Wage Cuts by Petition Method," *Colorado Labor Advocate*, Sept. 24, 1931, 1, Archives, Norlin Library, University of Colorado, Boulder.
15   Attachment, Roche to Wilbur Newton, Feb. 29, 1944, folder 16, box 20, RC.
16   Typescript page, no title, folder 3, box 15, RC.
17   "Miss Roche Cites Own Guffey Law," *New York Times*, Nov. 13, 1935, 4. "Statement of Miners to Industrial Commission of Colorado," 1927, folder 1, box 15; A. K. Payne to George Peart, Sept. 16, 1927, folder 6, box 15; memo on conversation with Mrs. Petroff, May 3, 1928, folder 4, box 15, RC.
18   McClurg, "The Colorado Coal Strike of 1927," 68–77.
19   Handwritten memo by either Roche or Vincent, last week of Oct. 1927, folder 4, box 15, RC.
20   Roche to Read Lewis, Nov. 2, 1927, RLP.
21   Statement by officials of Rocky Mountain Fuel, Mar. 18, 1928, appendix II in van Kleeck, *Miners and Management*, 243–245, and the first contract that Roche would sign in Aug. 1928.
22   Melvyn Dubofsky, *We Shall Be All: A History of the Industrial Workers of the World*, 2nd ed. (1969; Urbana, IL, 1988), 73, 155, 165.
23   "Coal Miner of the West!" Industrial Workers of the World mailing [1927]; "Miners of Colorado: Build a New Strong Fighting Union on a National Basis," Industrial

Workers of the World flyer; "Coal Men of Colorado," Industrial Workers of the World flyer, folder 2, box 15, RC. For the last claim, see van Kleeck, *Miners and Management*, 54; Dubofsky, *We Shall Be All*, 78–79, 126, 139, 152, 155–167.

24   McClurg, "The Colorado Coal Strike of 1927," 83–84. Wage increase: Vincent to Ben Cherington, Nov. 2, 1927, folder 4, box 15, RC.

25   Roche to Read Lewis, Nov. 2, 1927, RLP.

26   McClurg, "The Colorado Coal Strike of 1927," 84.

27   Ibid., 83–84.

28   Typed sheet, n.d., probably corrective to an article in *Nation*, Dec. 7, 1927, folder 3, box 15, RC.

29   Roche, Statement to the *Rocky Mountain News*, Nov. 25, 1927, folder 4, box 15, RC. In re William Adams, R. Todd Laugen, *The Gospel of Progressivism: Moral Reform and Labor War in Colorado, 1900–1930* (Boulder, CO, 2010), 181–186.

30   Strike notes, handwritten by Roche or Vincent; Roche to Costigan, Nov. 21, 1927; Roche, Statement to *Rocky Mountain News*, Nov. 25, 1927, folder 4, box 15, RC. McClurg, "The Colorado Coal Strike of 1927," 84–85.

31   Roche to Edward Costigan, Nov. 21, 1927, folder 4, box 15, RC.

32   William E. Owens, interview with author, May 26, 2005, Ellicott City, MD; Elinor McGinn, *A Wide Awake Woman: Josephine Roche in the Era of Reform* (Denver, 2002), 70.

33   Arne, "She Runs Mines."

34   Roche's Handwritten Notes on Hearings before the Industrial Commission, Nov. 28, 1927, folder 1, box 15, RC.

35   Roche to Edward Keating, Nov. 26, 1927, folder 5, box 4, RC.

36   Strike notes, handwritten either by Vincent or Roche, folder 4, box 15; Roche to Edward Keating, Feb. 1, 1928, folder 5, box 4, RC.

37   McClurg, "The Colorado Coal Strike of 1927," 84–86.

38   Charles J. Bayard, "Colorado Coal Strike," *Pacific Historical Review* 32 (August 1963): 250.

39   McClurg, "The Colorado Coal Strike of 1927," 88–90.

40   "Woman Social Worker Inherits Vast Holdings in Strike-Bound Mine," *Camden Courier*, Jan. 18, 1928; Middletown *Herald Times*, Feb. 11, 1928, VAO.

41   Roche, Memorandum to Wilbur Newton, Feb. 29, 1944, folder 16, box 20; "Denver's Dynamic Josephine Roche Takes Treasury Post," *Washington Post*, Dec. 1934, folder 6, box 35, RC.

42   W. C. Murphy Jr., "The Woman Who Has Challenged the Rockefeller Billions," *St. Louis Post-Dispatch*, Sept. 20, 1931, 4, Roche File, box 83, Honorary Degrees, Smith College Archives, Smith College, Northampton, MA.

43   Josephine Roche, Statement, July 20, 1928, folder 4, box 13; "Denver's Dynamic Josephine Roche Takes Treasury Post," *Washington Post*, Dec. 1934, folder 6, box 35; Roche, Memorandum to the Trustee, Wilbur Newton, Feb. 29, 1944, folder 16, box 20, RC.

44   Roche to Read Lewis, Apr. 2, 1928, RLP.

45   Ibid.

46   Ibid., Sept. 2, 1927, RLP.

47   "State Coal Industry Headed toward Another Strike," *Rocky Mountain News*, Mar. 19, 1928, 8.

48   McGovern and Guttridge, *Great Coalfield War*, 315, 326, 337, 339–340. Documents in folder 4, box 73, addendum to RC.

49   Roche, Memorandum to Wilbur Newton, Feb. 29, 1944, folder 16, box 20, RC.

50   RMF, *Annual Report for 1928*, folder 2, box 13, RC.

51   RMF, annual reports, folders 2 and 4, box 13, RC.

52   "Denver's Dynamic Josephine Roche Takes Treasury Post," *Washington Post*, Dec. 1934, folder 6, box 35, RC.

53   Roche to Read Lewis, Apr. 2, 1927, RLP.

54   Statement by Officials of Rocky Mountain Fuel, Mar.18, 1928, appendix II in van Kleeck, *Miners and Management*, 243–245. "State Coal Industry Headed toward Another Strike," *Rocky Mountain News*, Mar. 19, 1928, 8. Roche to Read Lewis, Apr. 2, 1927, RLP.

55   Sophonisba P. Breckinridge, *Women in the Twentieth Century: A Study of Their Political, Social, and Economic Activities* (New York, 1933), 108, 126, 140, 173. Angel Kwolek-Folland, *Incorporating Women: A History of Women and Business in the United States* (New York, 2002), 9.

56   Warren Van Tine and Melvyn Dubofsky, *John L. Lewis: A Biography* (New York, 1977), 201.

57   Marian J. Castle, "Josephine Roche, Coal Operator," *Forum and Century*, 92 (Aug. 1934), 103–105. In a recent encyclopedia of women in business, coal is not even indexed. Carol H. Krismann, *Encyclopedia of American Women in Business*, 2 vols. (Westport, CT, 2005), 95–96, 112–113, 379–380, 469–470, 554.

58   By the mid-1930s, Roche appeared in the press more consistently as a businesswoman or industrialist without any qualifying descriptor, but by then she was also a federal administrator, a laborite, and much else. For early representations, see "Woman Social Worker Inherits Vast Holdings in Strike-Bound Mine," *Camden Courier*, Jan. 18, 1928, VAO; Mabel Costigan, "A Woman's Way with Coal Mines," *Woman's Journal*, Mar. 1929, VAO. Sigrid Arne, "She Runs Mines: Josephine Roche," *St. Paul Pioneer Press*, May 25, 1934, folder 4, box 17, RC. Louis Stark, "A Woman Unravels an Industrial Knot," *New York Times Magazine*, Feb. 7, 1932, 6ff.

59   "Joan of Arc of the Coalfields": Arne, "She Runs Mines."

60   McGinn, *A Wide-Awake Woman*, 68, citing letters in the RC.

61   See, for instance, *New Republic*, Sept. 19, 1928, and *Survey*, Dec. 15, 1928, referenced in Mary Anderson to Staff of the Women's Bureau, May 19, 1929, frame 359, reel 1, Mary Anderson Papers, Papers of the Women's Trade Union League and Its Principal Leaders, microfilm edition (Woodbridge, CT, 1985).

62   Roche to Edward Keating, 1931; July 22, 1931, folder 5, box 4, RC. See also "Miss Roche Risks Personal Fortune to Protect Miners," June 9, 1931, *Labor*; "Josephine Roche Is Honored as Rival Cuts Wages of Miners," July 5, 1932, folder 7, box 17, RC. "Entire New Staff of Officers Elected by UMWA Local," *Colorado Labor Advocate*, June 25, 1931, 5; "A Mass Meeting of Miners Emphasizes Need of Organization," *Colorado Labor Advocate*, Aug. 20, 1931, 1.

63   "Josephine Roche Is Honored as Rival Cuts Wages of Miners," *Progressive Labor World*, July 7, 1932, VAO.

64   Louis Stark, "A Colorado Mine War Peace Pact," *New York Times*, Sept. 23, 1928, XX3. Stark, "A Woman Unravels an Industrial Knot," 6.

65   Statement of the Rocky Mountain Fuel Company, issued May 29, 1928, reprinted in van Kleeck, *Miners and Management*, 245–247.

66   The communist option was not represented in the Colorado coalfields yet. The National Miners' Union formed in 1928 and operated in Ohio, Pennsylvania, West Virginia, and Kentucky. Robert H. Zeiger, *John L. Lewis: Labor Leader* (Boston, 1988), 50.

67   Ben Lindsey to Harvey O'Higgins, Feb. 24, 1919; Lindsey to O'Higgins, Feb. 28, 1919; O'Higgins to Lindsey, Mar. 2, 1919, box 60, BLP.

68   Ben Selekman and Mary van Kleeck, *Employes' [sic] Representation in Coal Mines: A Study of the Industrial Representation Plan of the Colorado Fuel and Iron Company* (New York, 1924), 61–96.

69   Selekman and van Kleeck, *Employes' Representation in Coal*, 396. Howell John Harris, "Industrial Democracy and Liberal Capitalism," in *Industrial Democracy in America: The Ambiguous Promise*, ed. Nelson Lichtenstein and Howell John Harris (Cambridge, UK, 1993), 60–65. Van Kleeck, *Miners and Management*, 15, 18, 36. Sanford M. Jacoby, *Modern Manors: Welfare Capitalism since the New Deal* (Princeton, NJ, 1997), 21–23.

70   Harvey O'Higgins to Ben Lindsey, Feb. 28, 1919, box 60, BLP. Selekman and van Kleeck, *Employes' Representation in Coal*, conclusion.

71   Selekman and van Kleeck, *Employes' Representation in Coal*, 384–389.

72   Roche to Editor of the *Survey*, Apr. 11, 1928, folder 12, box 6, RC. See also, "Rocky Mountain Fuel Announces Liberal Policy," *Rocky Mountain News*, Mar. 19, 1928, folder 4, box 17, RC.

73   "State Coal Industry Headed toward Another Strike thus Price Cutting, Vincent Avers," *Rocky Mountain News*, Mar. 19, 1928, 8. See also Statement by Officials of Rocky Mountain Fuel, Mar. 18, 1928, appendix II in van Kleeck, *Miners and Management*, 243–245.

74   Dubofsky and Van Tine, *John L. Lewis*, 133, 147. Zeiger, *John L. Lewis*, 18.

75   Dubofsky and Van Tine, *John L. Lewis*, 81–83, 99–101. Zeiger, *John L. Lewis*, 38–40.

76   Dubofsky and Van Tine, *John L. Lewis*, 135. Zeiger, *John L. Lewis*, 32–35. "Miners of Colorado: Build a New Strong Fighting Union on a National Basis," Industrial Workers of the World flyer, folder 2, box 15, RC. Van Kleeck, *Miners and Management*, 71.

77   Costigan to Roche, Apr. 1927 or 1928, folder 1, box 73, RC.

78   O. F. Nigro to John L. Lewis, Mar. 24, 1927, folder 24, box 71, UMW Archives.

79   Nigro to Percy Tetlow, Mar. 31, 1928, and Percy Tetlow to John L. Lewis, Feb. 24, 1928, folder 25, box 71, UMW Archives.

80   A. J. Chipman to Officers and Members of Denver Lodge 273, June 9, 1928, folder 5, box 17, RC.

81   Roche to Read Lewis, Apr. 2, 1927, RLP.

82   Roche to Editor of the *Survey*, Apr. 11, 1928, folder 12, box 6, RC.

83   A. J. Chipman to the Officers and Members of Denver Lodge 273, June 9, 1928, folder 5, box 17, RC.

84   Vern Hill and J. O. Stevic to Merle Vincent, Apr. 21, 1930, folder 5, box 17, RC.

85   Ibid.

86   Louis Stark, "A Colorado Mine War Peace Pact, *New York Times*, Sept. 23, 1928, XX3. Percy Tetlow to Merle Vincent, July 3, 1928; John L. Lewis to Merle Vincent, Aug. 22, 1928, folder 1, box 16, RC. See also Maier B. Fox, *United We Stand: The United Mine Workers of America, 1890–1990* (Washington, DC, 1990), 309.

87   "Industrial Magna Carta" is Louis Stark's phrase in "A Woman Unravels an Industrial Knot," 6, 17.

88   Agreement by and between the Rocky Mountain Fuel Company and the United Mine Workers of America, Dist. No. 15, 1928–1930 (hereafter 1928 contract), folder 12, box 15, RC.

89   *The Compiled Laws of Colorado, 1921* (Denver, 1922), 1071, sec. 113; 1179, sec. 24. Stipulated in the 1928 contract at pp. 4 and 8, folder 12, box 15, RC.

90   Van Kleeck, *Miners and Management*, 75–76. Selekman and van Kleeck, *Employes' Representation in Coal*, 218.

91   Van Kleeck, *Miners and Management*, 71.

92   Selekman and van Kleeck, *Employes' Representation in Coal*, 274–275.

93   1928 contract, 12–13, folder 12, box 15, RC. Routine grievances: Carter Goodrich, *The Miner's Freedom* (1925; New York, 1977), 31–39.

94   1928 contract, 12, folder 12, box 15, RC. Selekman and van Kleeck, *Employe's Representation in Coal*, 219–222.

95   1928 contract, 14–15, folder 12, box 15, RC.

96   Ibid., 8, folder 12, box 15, RC.

97   Ibid., 17–18, folder 12, box 15, RC.

98   Ibid., 15–16, folder 12, box 15, RC. Children's Bureau programs: Robyn Muncy, *Creating a Female Dominion in American Reform, 1890–1935* (New York, 1991), 93–123.

99   1928 contract, 15–16, folder 12, box 15, RC.

100 Van Kleeck, *Miners and Management*, 38.

101 Stark, "Woman Unravels an Industrial Knot," 17. The men may well have considered this attendance a sort of spying, but I can find no evidence of that sentiment, and she did not attend all the meetings.

102 Walter Thomas to Roche, Mar. 18, 1935, folder 7, box 34, RC.

103 Arne, "She Runs Mines."

104 Stark, "Woman Unravels an Industrial Knot," 17.

105 "Woman Social Worker Inherits Vast Holdings in Strike-Bound Mine," *Camden Courier*, Jan. 18, 1928, VAO.

106 Written statement of the management of Rocky Mountain Fuel, quoted in van Kleeck, *Miners and Management*, 141.

107 "Duties of Advisory Board and Its Possible Functions," late 1931, folder 1, box 18, RC.

108 "Joint Advisory Board," folder 1, box 18, RC.

109 "Duties of Advisory Board and Its Possible Functions," late 1931, folder 1, box 18, RC.

110 Roche to Oswald Garrison Villard, May 12, 1931, folder 3, box 5, RC.

111 Van Kleeck, *Miners and Management*, 144–148. RMF, annual reports, 1930, 1931, 1932, folder 4, box 13, RC.

112 See, for instance, Minutes by Miner Jack Green, "At the Vulcan to Improve Output through Cooperation," Jan. 19, 1932, folder 20, box 105, MKP.

113 Minutes by Miner Jack Green, "At the Vulcan to Improve Output through Cooperation," Jan. 19, 1932; Confidential Report on Grant Case, Spring 1932 and attachments, folder 20, box 105, MKP.

114 Roche to Read Lewis, Sunday [1933], RLP.

115 Van Kleeck, *Miners and Management*, 151, 155–160.

116 Ibid., 167.

117 Ibid., 173.

118 HMJ to Merle Vincent, Feb. 12, 1931, folder Insurance Data #1, box 27, Rocky Mountain Fuel Collection, Denver Public Library.

119 Van Kleeck, *Miners and Management*, 143.

120 Ibid., 144, 142. Agreements, 1928, 1930, 1932, folder 12, box 15, RC.

121 Gerald Armstrong, telephone interview with author, Sept. 29, 2008.

122 Statement by Miner Jack Green, Lafayette, Colorado, "Union-Management Cooperation in the Rocky Mountain Fuel Company," Mar. 26, 1932, folder 20, box 105, MKP.

CHAPTER 8   "PROPHET OF A NEW AND WISER SOCIAL ORDER," 1929–1932

1   "Miss Josephine Roche, New Type of Industrial Leader," Remarks of Senator Edward Costigan, in the Senate of the United States, June 15, 1932, 72nd Congress, First Session, *Congressional Record*, folder 3, box 18, RC.

2   Roche, Memorandum to the Trustee, Feb. 29, 1944, folder 16, box 20, RC. Merle Vincent to Roche, Mar. 13, 1929; Roche, "Note on Financing," folder 2, box 16, RC.

3   Roche to Oswald Garrison Villard, Feb. 15, 1930, folder 3, box 5, RC.

4   Arthur Suffern to Marion Hedges, Mar. 12, 1929, folder 7, box 3; Paul Kellogg to Henry Bruere, Mar. 12, 1929, folder 12, box 6, RC.

5   Edward Costigan to Roche, Spring 1929, folder 1, box 73, RC.

6   Arthur Suffern to Marion Hedges, Mar. 12, 1929, folder 7, box 3, RC.

7   Sidney Hillman in his Report of the General Executive Board of the ACWA, "Documentary History of the Amalgamated Clothing Workers of America, 1924–26," containing the Report of the General Executive Board and Proceedings of the Seventh Biennial Convention of the Amalgamated Clothing Workers of America, May 10–15, 1926, Montreal, Canada, 10–14.

8   Roche to Sidney Hillman, Jan. 23, 1929, folder 5, box 1, RC.

9   Ibid., Feb. 20, 1929, folder 5, box 1, RC.

10   Amalgamated Bank of New York Statement, folder 2, box 17, RC. Roche to Jacob Potofsky, July 25, 1929; Roche to Jacob Potofsky, Aug. 9, 1929; Jacob Potofsky to Roche, Mar. 1931, folder 5, box 1, RC.

11   Marion Hedges to Roche, Mar. 19, 1929, folder 15, box 3, RC.

12   Raymond Ingersoll to Roche, Apr. 12, 1929; Ingersoll to Roche, May 28, 1929, folder 2, box 4, RC. Amalgamated Bank of New York Statement, folder 1, box 17; Roche, Memorandum to the Trustee, Feb. 29, 1944, folder 16, box 20, RC.

13   Roche to Oswald Garrison Villard, Oct. 23, 1929; Roche to Villard, Feb. 15, 1930; folder 3, box 5, RC. Amalgamated Bank of New York, Statement, folder 2, box 16, RC.

14   Oswald Garrison Villard to Roche, Mar. 14, 1929, folder 3, box 5, RC.

15   Norman Thomas to Roche, May 29, 1929; Roche to Thomas, July 31, 1929; Thomas to Roche, Aug. 3, 1929, folder 15, box 6, RC.

16   Paul Kellogg to Henry Bruere, Mar. 12, 1929; Kellogg to Everett Macy, Mar. 12, 1929; Kellogg to Sam Lewisohn, Mar. 12, 1929, folder 12, box 6, RC. Louis Brandeis to Roche, May 27, 1929, and other letters from Brandeis in folder 3, box 2, RC.

17   Roche, Memorandum to the Trustee, Feb. 29, 1944, folder 16, box 20, RC.

18   Lillian Wald to Roche, Apr. 17, 1929, folder 7, box 7, RC.

19   Pauline Goldmark to Roche, May 22, 1929, folder 12, box 32, RC. Amalgamated Bank of New York Statement, folder 2, box 16, RC.

20   Amalgamated Bank of New York Statement, folder 2, box 17, RC.

21   Frances Rice Behringer to Roche, Apr. 18, 1929; Lucy Carner to Roche, Apr. 4, 1929, folder 9, box 7, RC.

22   Arthur Suffern to Roche, Mar. 11, 1929; Suffern to Marion Hedges, Mar. 12, 1929, folder 7, box 3, RC.

23   Amalgamated Bank of New York Statement, folder 2, box 17; Harry Seager to Roche, Feb. 21, 1930; Seager to Roche, May 18, 1930; Roche to Seager, Mar. 3, 1930, folder 7, box 6, RC.

24   Steve Fraser, "The 'Labor Question,'" in *The Rise and Fall of the New Deal Order, 1930–1980*, ed. Steve Fraser and Gary Gerstle (Princeton, NJ, 1989), 62.

25   Fraser, "The 'Labor Question,'" 62.

26 Roche to Mr. and Mrs. Morris L. Cooke, Mar. 6, 1930, folder 12, box 2, RC.

27 *Time*, July 10, 1939, folder 4, box 17, RC.

28 Roche to Oswald Garrison Villard, Feb. 15, 1930, folder 3, box 5; RMF, annual report, 1929, folder 4, box 13, RC.

29 Roche to Oswald Garrison Villard, Feb. 15, 1930, folder 3, box 5; RMF, annual report, 1929, folder 4, box 13, RC. Mary Anderson to Staff, May 19, 1929, frame 359, reel 1, Mary Anderson Papers, Papers of the Women's Trade Union League, Arthur and Elizabeth Schlesinger Library on the History of Women, Radcliffe Institute for Advanced Study, Harvard University, Cambridge, MA.

30 Roche to Oswald Garrison Villard, Feb. 15, 1930, folder 3, box 5; RMF, annual report, 1929, folder 4, box 13, RC.

31 Fraser, "The 'Labor Question.'" Melvin Dubofsky and Warren Van Tine, *John L. Lewis: A Biography* (New York, 1977), 148.

32 RMF, annual report, 1929, folder 4, box 13, RC.

33 "The Northern Coal Producers' Association," pamphlet, folder 8, box 17, RC.

34 "Code of Trade Practices of the Northern Colorado Coal Producers' Association," folder 8, box 17, RC.

35 O. F. Nigro to John L. Lewis, Feb. 6, 1930, folder 30, box 71, UMW Archives. Morris Llewellyn Cooke to Roche, Feb. 11, 1930, folder 12, box 2, RC.

36 RMF, annual report, 1930, folder 4, box 13, RC.

37 Vern Hill and J. O. Stevic to Merle Vincent, Apr. 21, 1930, folder 5, box 17, RC.

38 O. F. Nigro to John L. Lewis, Apr. 3, 1929, folder 27, box 71, UMW Archives.

39 Ibid., Feb. 7, 1931, folder 34, box 71, UMW Archives.

40 Ibid., Feb. 7, 1931, folder 34, box 71, UMW Archives.

41 See, for instance, ibid., Oct. 4, 1929, folder 29, box 71, UMW Archives.

42 Ibid., Oct. 22, 1929; Nov. 22, 1929, folder 29, box 71, UMW Archives.

43 Ibid., June 8, 1930, folder 32, box 71, UMW Archives.

44 Primary Announcement on the U.S. Senatorship, folder 6, box 73, RC.

45 O. F. Nigro to John L. Lewis, July 30, 1930, folder 31, box 71, UMW Archives.

46 Roche to Read Lewis, July 22, 1930, folder 11, box 3, RC.

47 Ibid.

48 Mary van Kleeck, *Miners and Management: A Study of the Collective Agreement between the United Mine Workers of America and the Rocky Mountain Fuel Company and an Analysis of the Problem of Coal in the United States* (New York, 1934), appendix III, 248–277.

49 RMF to Northern Coal Producers' Association, Mar. 24, 1931, folder 8, box 17, RC.

50 See documents in folder 8, box 1, CSFLP. "Intimidation Used to Inforce Pay Cut Hearing Reveals," *Colorado Labor Advocate*, July 9, 1931, 1.

51 Statement of Merle D. Vincent for the Colorado Industrial Commission, May 18,1931, folder 5, box 18, RC. On research by and conclusions of State Federation of Labor, see documents in folder 8, box 1, CSFLP.

52 Charlie Hutton to Jim, Spring 1931, folder 8 1/2, box 1, CSFLP.

53 "Miss Roche Risks Personal Fortune to Protect Miners," *Labor*, June 9, 1931, folder 7, box 17, RC.

54 See State Federation of Labor's Argument before the Commission, Roche's letter attached, folder 8 1/2, box 1, CSFLP.

55 Transcripts of hearings, May, June, and July 1931; Decision rendered in re Bluff Spring Leasing Company; Report on the Hearings at Walsenburg and Trinidad, Sept. 1931, folder 5, box 18, RC.

56 Thomas Annear, *Investigation of the Coal Industry in Colorado Report on the Hearings at Walsenburg and Trinidad*, Sept. 3, 1931, folder 11, box 1, CSFLP.

57 Telegram, Roche to John D. Rockefeller Jr., Aug. 1, 1931, folder 7, box 17, RC.

58 Quotation is from "Rockefeller Is Silent," *New York Times*, Aug. 4, 1931, VAO. See also, "Asks Rockefeller to Halt Wage Cut," *New York Times*, Aug. 3, 1931, VAO; W. C. Murphy, "The Woman Who Has Challenged the Rockefeller Billions," Sunday Magazine, *St. Louis Post-Dispatch*, Sept. 20, 1931, box 83, Honorary Degrees, Archives, Smith College, Northampton, MA.

59 Roche to Edward Keating, night letter, [1931], folder 5, box 4, RC.

60 Roche, interview with press, forwarded to Edward Keating, July 22, 1931, folder 5, box 4, RC.

61 "Coal Committee Report of Meeting Held in Lafayette," Aug. 4, 1931, folder 20, box 105, MKP.

62 Petition at Industrial Mine, [1931], folder 10, box 17, RC.

63 Ibid. See also Roche to Oswald Garrison Villard, Aug. 29, 1931, folder 3, box 5, RC.

64 Van Kleeck, *Miners and Management*, 114–115.

65 N. C. Brooks to Merle D. Vincent, Sept. 19, 1931, folder 8, box 17, RC. "Miners' Loan to Rocky Mt. Fuel Firm Hit," *Rocky Mountain News*, Nov. 1931, folder 7, box 17, RC.

66 O. F. Nigro to John L. Lewis, Aug. 17, 1931, folder 38, box 71, UMW Archives.

67 Ibid., Aug. 18, 1931, folder 38, box 71, UMW Archives.

68 Loan of wages: "Union Miners to Loan Rocky Mountain Fuel Co Half Their Wages during Price Cut War," *Colorado Labor Advocate*, Aug. 27, 1931, 1.

69 O. F. Nigro to Lewis, Aug. 17, 1931, and Aug. 18, 1931, folder 38, box 71, UMW Archives.

70 Roche to Keating, night letter, [1931], folder 5, box 4, RC. "Intimidation Used to Inforce Pay Cut Hearing Reveals," *Colorado Labor Advocate*, July 9, 1931, 1. See also O. F. Nigro to John L. Lewis, July 8, 1931, with attachments, folder 36, box 71, UMW Archives.

71 Van Kleeck, *Miners and Management*, 114–116.

72 Roche to Oswald Garrison Villard, Aug. 29, 1931, folder 3, box 5, RC.

73 Louis Stark, "A Woman Unravels an Industrial Knot," *New York Times Magazine*, Feb. 7, 1932, 6.

74 U.S. Bureau of the Census, *Historical Statistics of the United States, Colonial Times to 1957* (Washington, DC, 1957), 70.

75 Alan Brinkley, *American History: A Survey*, 11th ed. (Boston, 2003), 679.

76 Roche, "When Prosperity Comes," radio address over KOA, Oct. 7, 1931, folder 11, box 17, RC.

77 Meg Jacobs, *Pocketbook Politics: Economic Citizenship in Twentieth-Century America* (Princeton, NJ, 2005), 2–7.

78 Thanks to Peter Albert for this citation. Maier B. Fox, *United We Stand: The United Mine Workers of America, 1890–1990* (Washington, DC, 1990), 309–310.

79 Records of Amalgamated Bank of New York show loans from the United Labor Bank and Trust in Feb. and July 1932 and two more such loans in 1933, folder 1, box 17, RC.

80 Report of the Trustee, Wilbur Newton, July 1944, folder 5, box 21, RC. Fox, *United We Stand*, 310–315.

81 Roche and O. F. Nigro to Industrial Commission of the State of Colorado, May 18, 1932; Merle Vincent to Industrial Commission, May 24, 1932, folder 5, box 18, RC.

82 Memorandum of Changes in Agreement for Period Beginning Sept. 1, 1932, and ending Aug. 31, 1934, reprinted in van Kleeck, *Miners and Management*, 277–289.

83 Mabel Cory Costigan, "A Woman's Way with Coal Mines," *Woman's Journal*, Mar. 1929, 20–21, 37. Nancy Cattell Hartford, "Josephine Roche—Industrialist," *Independent Woman*, Nov. 1932, 393, 420.

84 "Asks Rockefeller to Halt Wage Cut," *New York Times*, Aug. 3, 1931; "Rockefeller Is Silent," *New York Times*, Aug. 4, 1931, VAO. Stark, "A Woman Unravels an Industrial Knot," 6ff.

85 "Cutting Wages Retards Recovery, Says Colorado Woman Mine Owner," *New York Sun*, Apr. 6, 1932; "Mine Owner Attacks Cuts," *Des Moines Tribune*, Apr. 5, 1932; "Vassar Graduate Operator of Successful Coal Mine," *Passaic Herald-News*, Apr. 5, 1932; "Vassar Graduate in Business," *Boston Globe*, June 21, 1932; "Vassar Grad, Mine Co. Head Calls Wage-Cutting Unsound," *Chicago Illustrated Times*, Apr. 6, 1932, VAO.

86 Roche, "When Prosperity Comes," radio address over KOA, Oct. 7, 1931, folder 11; "Organized Labor the Hope of the Nation," *Railway Clerk*, 1931, folder 7, box 17, RC.

87 "Proceedings of Conference on New Relations Between Labor and Capital," Feb. 2–3, 1929, folder 4, box 11, RC.

88 "Old Marriage Ideal Urged upon Church," *New York Times*, Sept. 24, 1931, 32.

89 Roche to Read Lewis, Nov. 28, 1931, RLP.

90 "Miss Roche to Address Club Women Thursday," *Fort Collins Express-Courier*, Feb. 2, 1932, folder 5, box 11, RC. "Between You and Me," *Independent Woman*, clipping, mid-1930s, 361, Gerrittson Collection: Women's History Online, 1543–1945. Eudora Ramsay Richardson, "Social Security—Theme of Institute Meetings," *Independent Woman*, May 1935, 150.

91 "Catholic Meet Seeks Cure of Economic Ills," *L.A. Examiner*, Apr. 5, 1932, folder 7, box 17, RC.

92 "Miss Josephine Roche, New Type of Industrial Leader," Remarks of Senator Edward Costigan, in the Senate of the United States, June 15, 1932, 72nd Congress, First Session, *Congressional Record*, folder 3, box 18, RC.

93 Honorary degree, folder 6, box 8, RC. "Josephine Roche Is Honored as Rival Cuts Wages of Miners," *Progressive Labor World*, July 9, 1932; "Smith Class Urged to Resist 'Ballyhoo,'" *New York Times*, June 21, 1932; *Smith Alumnae Quarterly*, Aug. 1932, 445–447, VAO. Nobel Prize: editorial, 1932, unknown paper, VAO.

94 William E. Leuchtenburg, *Franklin D. Roosevelt and the New Deal, 1932–1940* (New York, 1963), chapter 1.

95 Roche to Read Lewis, Oct. 6, 1932, RLP.

96 Nellie Tayloe Ross to Roche, Dec. 15, 1932, folder 1, box 6, RC.

PART III   SECOND BURST OF PROGRESSIVE REFORM: HEIGHT OF ROCHE'S RENOWN, 1933–1948

1 I am not alone in linking the 1930s and 1940s in this way. See, for instance, Nelson Lichtenstein, *State of the Union: A Century of American Labor* (Princeton, NJ, 2002), and Ira Katznelson, *Fear Itself: The New Deal and the Origins of Our Time* (New York, 2013).

CHAPTER 9   WORKING WITH THE NEW DEAL FROM COLORADO, 1933–1934

1 Anthony Badger, *The New Deal: The Depression Years, 1933–1940* (Chicago, 1989), 11, 18–22, 24, 31, 35, 67. James S. Olson, *Saving Capitalism: The Reconstruction Finance Corporation and the New Deal, 1933–1940* (Princeton, NJ, 1988), 29.

2   Badger, *The New Deal*, 66–73, 97, 190–196.

3   Franklin Roosevelt to Roche, July 26, 1933, folder 5, box 6, RC. "Public Works Boards for 48 States Named," *Washington Post*, July 27, 1933, 2. "U.S. Drafts 50 to Help Solve Job Problem," *Washington Post*, Aug. 13, 1933, 14. See also Biographical Notes, folder 634, box 61, Mary Elizabeth Switzer Papers, Arthur and Elizabeth Schlesinger Library on the History of Women, Radcliffe Institute for Advanced Study, Harvard University, Cambridge, MA.

4   National Industrial Recovery Act, Public-No. 67–73rd Congress, H.R. 5755, June 16, 1933.

5   National Recovery Administration, *Codes of Fair Competition*, vols. 1–23 (Washington, DC, 1933–1935).

6   Badger, *The New Deal*, 84–86. Process of code-making: Landon R. Y. Storrs, *Civilizing Capitalism: The National Consumers' League, Women's Activism, and Labor Standards in the New Deal Era* (Chapel Hill, NC, 2000), 96.

7   See, for instance, Phelps Adams, "Practical Theorist Wins Office," *New York Sun*, Nov. 1934, folder 6, box 35, RC.

8   D. W. Buchanan to Roche, May 29, 1933; Roche to D. W. Buchanan, May 31, 1933; Charles O'Neill to All Bituminous Coal Producers, June 7, 1933, and enclosure, folder 9, box 18, RC.

9   Charles O'Neill to All Bituminous Coal Producers, June 7, 1933, and enclosure, folder 9, box 18, RC.

10   Report of the Code Committee, June 19, 1933, folder 9, box 18, RC.

11   James P. Johnson, "Drafting the NRA Code of Fair Competition for the Bituminous Coal Industry," *Journal of American History* 53 (December 1966): 521–541. "List of Coal Operators Participating in National Bituminous Coal Code Conference," Washington, DC, July 7–13, 1933, folder 9, box 18, RC.

12   John L. Lewis to O. F. Nigro, May 27, 1933, folder 44, box 71, UMW Archives.

13   Draft Coal Code, July 13, 1933, vol. no. A—part III, box 14, Records Maintained by the Code Record Unit, 1933–1935, Records of the National Recovery Administration, RG 9, NARA (hereafter NRA Records).

14   Ibid. John L. Lewis's request for the 6-hour day is in J. G. Puterbaugh to Hugh Johnson, July 12, 1933, vol. no. A—part I, box 13, Records Maintained by the Code Record Unit, NRA Records.

15   Senator Essington et al. to the President, July 13, 1933, folder 9, box 18, RC. To the President of the United States, July 13, 1933, vol. B, box 15, Records Maintained by the Code Record Unit, NRA Records.

16   Melvyn Dubofsky and Warren Van Tine, *John L. Lewis: A Biography* (New York, 1977), 188.

17   Transcripts of Hearings on the Coal Code, Aug. 1933, box 114, Records Maintained by the Library Unit, NRA Records.

18   Roche to NRA, July 28, 1933, two separate letters, vol. B, box 15, Records Maintained by the Code Record Unit, NRA Records.

19   Dubofsky and Van Tine, *John L. Lewis*, 184–187. Maier B. Fox, *United We Stand: The United Mine Workers of America, 1890–1990* (Washington, DC, 1990), 312.

20   See, for instance, Proposed Code Submitted by Miners of Carbon County, Utah, Summer 1933, signed by hundreds of miners, vol. A–part V, box 12, Records Maintained by the Code Record Unit, NRA Records.

21   Transcripts of Hearings, Aug. 1933, box 114, Records Maintained by the Library Unit, NRA Records.

22   George Sanford Holmes, "Denver Woman Electrifies Hearing on Industrial Code," *Rocky Mountain News*, Aug. 13, 1933, folder 6, box 18, RC.

23 Transcript of Proceedings, Coal Code Hearing, Aug. 12, 1933, National Recovery Administration, folder 9, box 18, RC.

24 Transcript from Sept. 12, 1933, box 115, Transcripts of Hearings, Records Maintained by the Library Unit, NRA Records.

25 F. Etaplin to Hugh Johnson, Sept. 13, 1933, vol. B, box 15, Records Maintained by the Code Record Unit, NRA Records.

26 "Coal Code Signed in Bitter Battle," *Washington Post*, Sept. 17, 1933, 1.

27 Labor provisions of the Coal Code are in Dubofsky and Van Tine, *John L. Lewis*, 190–191, and Fox, *United We Stand*, 314.

28 Transcript of Proceedings, Coal Code Hearing, Aug. 12, 1933, National Recovery Administration, folder 9, box 18, RC.

29 Roche to Kenneth Simpson, Deputy Administrator, National Recovery Administration, Sept. 7 and 12, 1933, folder 9, box 18, RC.

30 See, for example, Roche to Mr. Wayne Ellis, Mar. 24, 1934, vol. A–part II, box 13, Records Maintained by the Code Record Unit, NRA Records.

31 Memorandum of Conference on New Mexico and Northern and Southern Colorado Coal Rates, Sept. 13, 1933, vol. A–part V, box 12, Records Maintained by the Code Record Unit, NRA Records.

32 Frank Hefferly testimony, Hearings on Amendment 1 of the Bituminous Coal Code, Apr. 1934, vol. III-D, box 116, Transcripts of Hearings, Records Maintained by the Library Unit, NRA Records.

33 Ibid.

34 Roche to Read Lewis, Jan. 7, 1934, RLP.

35 Eagerness to continue the National Industrial Recovery Act: Transcript of Meeting of Bituminous Coal Industrial Board, Jan. 4, 1935, box 118, Transcripts of Hearings, Records Maintained by the Library Unit, NRA Records.

36 Alabama operator to Hugh Johnson, Mar. 31, 1934, box 12, Records Maintained by the Code Record Unit, NRA Records.

37 Badger, *The New Deal*, 88–91.

38 James Wickens, "Depression and New Deal in Colorado," in *The New Deal: The States and Local Level*, vol. 2, ed. John Braeman et al. (Columbus, OH, 1975), 269–310.

39 One of the earliest speculations: *Morgan County Herald*, clipping, Nov. 23, 1933, folder 2, box 29, RC.

40 Drew Pearson and Robert S. Allen, "The Daily Washington Merry Go Round," *St. Louis Post-Dispatch*, Mar. 27, 1934; "Woman May Enter Race for Governorship of Colorado," *Pueblo Star Journal*, Mar. 27, 1934, folder 2, box 29, RC.

41 "Woman May Enter Race for Governorship of Colorado," *Pueblo Star Journal*, Mar. 27, 1934, folder 2, box 29, RC.

42 Edward and Mabel Costigan to Roche, May 11, 1934, folder 1, box 73, RC.

43 Roche to Honorable James A. Marsh, Chair, Democratic State Central Committee, May 23, 1934, folder 8, box 22, RC.

44 "Josephine Roche Runs for Governor," *Rocky Mountain News*, May 24, 1934, folder 3, box 28, RC.

45 Zoe Oxley and Richard Fox, "Women in Executive Office: Variation across American States," *Political Research Quarterly* 57 (Mar. 2004): 113–120, esp. 113.

46 Brave woman: Margaret Henderson to Roche, Sept. 9, 1934, folder 5, box 22, RC. Nerve: Mrs. Bertie Hagan to Roche, June 18, 1934, folder 5, box 22, RC.

47 Transcript of Proceedings, Coal Code Hearing, Aug. 12, 1933, National Recovery Administration, folder 9, box 18, RC.

48 Phelps Adams, "Practical Theorist Wins Office," *New York Sun*, Nov. 1934, folder 6, box 35, RC. Journalists routinely praised the femininity of Roche's clothing. Ray Tucker, "Chairwoman for Youth," *New York Times*, July 14, 1935, folder 7, box 35; "Now Who Will Take Court Place of Van Devanter," newspaper clipping, n.d., no paper identified, folder 3, box 33, RC.

49 The endorsement came on June 7, 1934.

50 "A New Deal and a Square Deal," *Rocky Mountain News*, n.d., clipping, folder 1, box 28, RC.

51 Marguerite Higgins to Roche, June 18, 1934, folder 5, box 22, RC.

52 Oswald Garrison Villard, "Issues and Men: Josephine Roche for Governor of Colorado," *Nation*, June 13, 1934, 665. Edith Abbott to Roche, 1934; Sophonisba Breckinridge to Roche, Aug. 1934, folder 5, box 22, RC.

53 Roche to Lillian Wald, June 9, 1934, folder 5, box 22; "Election of Miss Roche Urged by Grace Abbott," clipping, n.d., folder 1, box 28, RC.

54 "AFL Indorses Josephine Roche," *Labor*, Sept. 4, 1934, 1. On Lewis: "Colorado Woman in Governor Race," *New York Times*, May 27, 1923, 20.

55 Robert G. Athearn, *The Coloradans* (Albuquerque, NM, 1976), 277.

56 Radio address, Aug. 8, 1934, folder 10, box 24, RC.

57 Press release, July 5, 1934, folder 10, box 24, RC.

58 Speech to Business and Professional Women's Clubs, July 17, 1934, folder 10, box 24, RC.

59 Badger, *The New Deal*, 88, 102–105.

60 Press release, July 5, 1934, folder 10, box 24, RC.

61 Sweat shop quotation: Press release, July 19, 1934, folder 10, box 24, RC.

62 Radio address, Aug. 8, 1934, folder 10, box 24, RC.

63 Roche, "Economic Values and Human Needs," Aug. 10, 1934, folder 10, box 24, RC.

64 For example, Roche, "Rebuilding America for Present and Future Citizens," Aug. 23, 1934; Press release, July 19, 1934, folder 10, box 24, RC.

65 "Declaration of Acceptance of Designation by Assembly," July 30, 1934, folder 2, box 25, RC.

66 "40-Day War Raging for State Democrats," *Rocky Mountain News*, Aug. 1, 1934, folder 1, box 28, RC.

67 "[S]pavined Dobbin": Oswald Garrison Villard, "Issues and Men: Josephine Roche for Governor of Colorado," *Nation*, June 13, 1934, 665. Roche, radio address, Denver, Sept. 5, 1934, folder 10, box 24, RC. Mildred Lea: William E. Owens, interview with author, May 26, 2005, Ellicott City, MD.

68 *Colorado Labor Advocate*, Aug. 2, 1934, folder 3, box 26, RC.

69 "Elect Roche Governor," *Jewish News*, Aug. 31, 1934; "Enthusiastic Groups Rally to Miss Roche," *Rocky Mountain News*, Sept. 4, 1934, folder 1, box 28, RC.

70 A. E. Harris to Roche, July 21, 1934, folder 1, box 23, RC.

71 E. M. Quintana to Roche, n.d., folder 3, box 23, RC.

72 "Miss Roche Thrills East Denver Audience Thursday Night," n.d., folder 4, box 28, RC.

73 Maude Abner to Roche, June 11, 1934, folder 2, box 23, RC.

74 Roche schedules, folder 4, box 24, RC.

75 " 'Vital Issues Predominate This Fall,' Says Roche," *Rocky Mountain News*, n.d., folder 1, box 28, RC.

76 "Crowds Hail Miss Roche in 'Sugar Bowl,' " [Sept. 2, 1934], folder 1, box 28, RC.

77 "Constructive Campaign Urged by Josephine Roche in Speech," *Walsenburg Independent*, Aug. 31, 1934, folder 5, box 28, RC.

78 See, for example, C. T. Hoffnagle to Roche, Sept. 6, 1934, folder 2, box 23, RC.

79 A. E. Harris to Roche, July 21, 1934; Mrs. Margaret Garner to Roche, Aug. 4, 1934, folder 1, box 23, RC.

80 Neil West Kimball, Capitol Comment, *La Jara Gazette*, Nov. 15, 1934, folder 12, box 4, MSS-011, John A. Carroll Papers, Auraria Library, Archives and Special Collections, University of Colorado, Denver.

81 Bribes in coal camps: Florence Coates to Roche, n.d.; Mike Rinn to John Carroll, Sept. 8, 1934, folder 1, box 23, RC. Johnson's appeal to "Mexicans": Lito Gallegoes to Miss Roche, Aug. 4, 1934, folder 2, box 23, RC.

82 "Just among Ourselves," *Salida Mail*, Sept. 14, 1934, folder 5, box 27, RC.

83 "So the People May Know," *Denver Post*, Sept. 9, 1934, folder 1, box 28, RC.

84 Ibid.

85 Other rumors: J. C. McCaffrey to John Gross, Aug. 4, 1934, folder 15, box 4, CSFLP.

86 "Tax Orgy Threatens Small Home Owner," *Denver Post*, Sept. 4, 1934, folder 1, box 28, RC.

87 Josephine Roche, radio address, Denver, Sept. 5, 1934, folder 10, box 24, RC.

88 *Rocky Mountain News*, clipping, folder 1, box 29, RC.

89 N.t., *Colorado*, Sept. 21, 1934, folder 2, box 26, RC.

90 Dexter Brown to Roche, n.d., folder 2, box 23, RC.

91 Unknown to Hon. Alva B. Adams, June 2, 1934, folder 2, box 23, RC.

92 Willard Fraser to Roche, June 7, 1965, folder 4, box 9, RC.

93 John Farnham, "Sex May Defeat Woman Candidate," *New York Times*, Sept. 9, 1934, E7.

94 See, for instance, Pat Keating to Roche, June 22, 1934, folder 4, box 23, RC.

95 Helen Noland of Durango to Roche, July 2, 1934, folder 1, box 23, RC.

96 See correspondence in, for instance, folder 1, box 23, RC.

97 Correspondence in folder 15, box 4, CSFLP. Eighth Biennial State Labor Political Convention, June 7, 1934, folder 6, box 24, RC.

98 This point was made by Neil West Kimball, "Capitol Comment," *La Jara Gazette*, Nov. 15, 1934, folder 12, box 4, Carroll Papers.

99 Harry Hopkins to Roche, June 29, 1934, folder 18, box 3, RC.

100 "A Battle for Miss Roche," *Julesburg Grit-Advocate*, Aug. 23, 1934, folder 2, box 27, RC.

101 Foster Cline to Roche, Sept. 19, 1934, folder 6, box 22, RC.

102 Albert Craig to Roche, Sept. 13, 1934, folder 6, box 22, RC.

103 Ralph Harris to Roche, Sept. 12, 1934, folder 5, box 22, RC.

104 Paul Shriver to Roche, Sept. 12, 1934, folder 6, box 22, RC.

105 Ibid., Sept. 24, 1934, folder 6, box 22, RC.

106 Herbert Lehman to Roche, Nov. 19, 1934; Roche to Caroline O'Day, Nov. 10, 1934; Caroline Wolfe to Roche, Oct. 8, 1934; Roche to Caroline Wolfe, Oct. 17, 1934; Ritchie, secretary to Miss Roche, to Mrs. Caspar Whiney, Nov. 27, 1934, folder 7, box 25, RC. Herbert Lehman to Roche, Nov. 24, 1934, folder 8, box 32, RC.

107 "Miss Josephine Roche Flies to Capital for Coal Parley," *Rocky Mountain News*, Sept. 14, 1933, folder 6, box 18, RC.

108 Clarice Feldman to Robyn Muncy, e-mail message, Feb. 28, 2011, in author's possession.

109 Kirstin Downey, *The Woman behind the New Deal: The Life of Frances Perkins, FDR's Secretary of Labor and His Moral Conscience* (New York, 2009), 121–125.

110 A program of flexible public works coordinated to business cycles was proposed as early as 1921: Report of Committee on Public Works—Long-Range Planning of Public Works, Adopted Oct.10, 1921 in Herbert Hoover, *Report of the President's Conference on Unemployment* (Washington, DC, 1921). Employment stabilization through public works had long been an interest of Senator Robert Wagner. "The Wagner Proposals to Prevent Unemployment," *Congressional Digest* 10, no. 1 (Jan. 1931): 9; Roger Biles, "Robert F. Wagner, Franklin D. Roosevelt, and Social Welfare Legislation in the New Deal," *Presidential Studies Quarterly* 28 (Winter 1998): 139–152, esp. 142; Paul Starr, *The Social Transformation of American Medicine* (New York, 1982), 265–270.

111   Frances Perkins to Roche, Oct. 29, 1934, folder 4, box 41, RC.

112   Roche to Henry Morgenthau, Nov. 11, 1934, Roche file, box 240, Henry Morgenthau Papers, FDRL. The 50,000 employees: "Josephine Roche Sworn as Public Health Head," *New York Herald Tribune*, Dec. 8, 1934, VAO.

113   Josephine Roche, "Guarding the Nation's Health," *Labor Information Bulletin*, n.d., folder 7, box 35, RC.

114   Interview with Mary Switzer by Mr. Shafel of the United Press, Oct. 28, 1937, folder 8, box 31, RC.

115   Michael Davis to Roche, Oct. 16, 1935, Roche file, box 71, Michael Davis Papers, New York Academy of Medicine Library, New York City.

116   Roche to Henry Morgenthau, Nov. 11, 1934, Roche file, box 240, Morgenthau Papers. Jean Eliot, "Miss Roche Brings Charm and Ability to Treasury Post," *Washington Herald*, Nov. 1934, folder 6, box 35, RC.

117   "[B]reathless": "Josephine Roche Appointed Assistant to Morgenthau," *Philadelphia Record*, Nov. 1934, folder 6, box 35, RC. Joining the "little cabinet": photo caption, *New York American*, Nov. 17, 1934; "Miss Roche Gets Treasury Post as Health Head," *New York Herald Tribune*, Nov. 16, 1934; VAO.

118   "Miss Roche Quits Job as Head of Fuel Firm," *New York Herald Tribune*, Dec. 5, 1934, VAO.

119   "Over 600 Attend Dinner in Honor of Josephine Roche," *Colorado Labor Advocate*, Nov. 1934, folder 6, box 35, RC.

CHAPTER 10   AT THE CENTER OF POWER: ROCHE IN THE NEW DEAL GOVERNMENT, 1934–1939

1   All of Roche's work in the field of health will be analyzed in the next chapter.

2   See correspondence in boxes 30 and 31, RC.

3   UMW Local Union # 2483 to Roche, Nov. 17, 1934, folder 2, box 30, RC. Phelps Adams, "Practical Theorist Wins Office," *New York Sun*, Nov. 1934, folder 6, box 35, RC.

4   Mrs. Lamar Rutherford Lipscomb to Roche, Nov. 16, 1934, folder 8, box 32, RC.

5   Gabrielle Forbush to Roche, Nov. 16, 1934, folder 2, box 30, RC.

6   Osgood Nichols, "Denver's Dynamic Josephine Roche Takes Treasury Post," *Washington Post*, Dec. 1934, folder 6, box 35, RC.

7   Nichols, "Denver's Dynamic Josephine Roche Takes Treasury Post." "Woman Mine Owner Finds Flowers Too Much," *Pittsburgh Post Gazette*, Dec. 19, 1934, folder 6, box 35, RC. Photos in "First Day on the Job," *New York American*, Nov. 17, 1934, and "Josephine Roche Sworn in as Public Health Head," *New York Herald Tribune*, Dec. 8, 1934, VAO.

8   "Society Is Host to Miss Roche," *Washington Post*, Dec. 17, 1934, 10. "Women's Group Plans Two Parties," *Washington Post*, Dec. 16, 1934, 82.

9   Susan Ware, *After Suffrage: Women in the New Deal* (Cambridge, MA, 1981), 1, 142–157; Cynthia Harrison, *On Account of Sex: The Politics of Women's Issues, 1945–1968* (Berkeley, CA, 1988), 53, 255. Karen Keesling and Suzanne Cavanagh, *Women*

Presidential Appointees Requiring Senate Confirmation, 1912–1977, microfilm edition (Washington, DC, 1978). Women in executive positions: Lucille Foster McMillin, *Women in the Federal Service* (Washington, DC, 1938), 6, 39. Mary Elizabeth Pidgeon, *Women in Federal Service, 1923–1947*, U.S. Women's Bureau Bulletin #230 (Washington, DC, 1949), 16, 22, 27, 28. Thanks to Kristen Kelley for this research in federal positions.

10 *Official Register of the United States* (Washington, DC, 1937).

11 Ibid. See also Ware, *After Suffrage*, 87–115, 143. Landon R. Y. Storrs, *Civilizing Capitalism: The National Consumers' League, Women's Activism, and Labor Standards in the New Deal Era* (Chapel Hill, NC, 2000), 96–99.

12 Beverly Stadum, "The Marriage of Professional Social Work and Public Relief," *The Professionalization of Poverty: Social Work and the Poor in the Twentieth Century*, ed. Gary R. Lowe and P. Nelson Reid (New York, 1999), 43.

13 See for instance, "Morgenthau Tea Is Given for Officials," *Washington Post*, Dec. 12, 1934, 13. "Mrs. Hull Holds At-Home Today at the Carlton," *Washington Post*, Feb. 6, 1935, 11. "Mrs. Morgenthau, Mrs. Cummings, and Mrs. Farley Entertain at Season's Final Cabinet at-Homes," *Washington Post*, Apr. 15, 1937, 18.

14 Burn in Unknown to Roche, Dec. 30, 1936, folder 7, box 32, RC. Chain-smoker: Jane Eads, "Washington Daybook," Sept. 1, 1948, VAO.

15 Harold Ickes to Roche, Mar. 14, 1935; Roche to Ickes, Mar. 15, 1935, folder 2, box 32, RC. That she often used a cigarette holder, see "The Fascinating Ladies," *Washington DC Times-Herald*, Feb. 17, 1940, Roche file, VAO.

16 "Denver's Dynamic Josephine Roche Takes Treasury Post," *Washington Post*, Dec. 1934, folder 6, box 35, RC.

17 Quote about Roche: "About the Town," *Washington Post*, Oct. 29, 1937, folder 1, box 44, RC. Defining the social whirl: "Suzanne Wilson Takes Up Art," *Washington Post*, Jan. 12, 1937, 13. Mary Switzer confirmed that Roche knew "about everyone who should be known" in DC but that "she isn't terribly social." Mr. Shafel of the United Press, typescript interview with Mary Switzer, Oct. 28, 1937, folder 2, box 36, RC. Roche described herself as having "little time to go about socially" in an interview with Gerry Dick, typescript, Oct. 9, 1937, folder 2, box 36, RC. Nevertheless, she appeared to go out constantly: "Mrs. Ickes' Luncheon Honors First Lady," *Washington Post*, Feb. 1, 1935, 13; "Mrs. Hull Holds At-Home Today at the Carlton," *Washington Post*, Feb. 6, 1935, 11; "White House Dinner Fetes Supreme Court Justices," *Washington Post*, Feb. 3, 1935, 15; Evelyn Peyton Gordon, "Capital Society Entertained at Supper Party by Assistant Treasury Chief," *Washington Post*, Feb. 10, 1935, S1; "Soviet Embassy Dines Officials; Counselor's Guest List Includes Miss Roche and the Packers," *Washington Post*, Apr. 18, 1935, 12. Roche's own entertaining: Newspaper clipping, May 18, 1937, folder 3, box 33, RC; "Notes of Society," *Washington Post*, Feb. 22, 1936, X14; "Notes of Society," *Washington Post*, July 24, 1937, 8; "Notes on Society," *Washington Post*, Feb. 11, 1938, 18; newspaper clipping, May 1935, folder 10, box 34, RC.

18 Address: Harriet Holther to Roche, Jan. 10, 1935, and Roche to Horace H. Westcott and Co., Jan. 20, 1936, folder 3, box 35, RC. Apartment: Gerry Dick, interview with Roche, typescript, Oct. 9, 1937, folder 2, box 36, RC.

19 Roche to Mrs. Gaines, Feb. 1, 1935, folder 8, box 31, RC.

20 Roche's office: Lorania King Francis, "Mass of Impressive Duties Fails to Lessen Personal Charm of Miss Josephine Roche," *Providence Evening Bulletin*, Nov. 22, 1935, VAO.

21 Roche to Henry Morgenthau, May 20, 1935, Roche file, box 240, Morgenthau Papers, FDRL.

22 Henry Morgenthau to Frances Perkins, Nov. 28, 1934, Roche file, box 171, RG 56, entry 193, Department of the Treasury Records, Central Files of the Office of the Secretary, 1917–1956, NARA. Minutes of the CES, Nov. 27, 1934, http://www.ssa.gov /history/reports/ces/ces8minutes.html, accessed Aug. 10, 2011.

23 Executive Order and "Committee Members," Members file, box 1, SSA. Linda Gordon, *Pitied but Not Entitled: Single Mothers and the History of Welfare* (Cambridge, MA, 1994), 206. Edwin Witte, "Possible General Approaches to the Problem of Economic Security," CES General File, box 1, SSA.

24 Minutes of the CES, Nov. 27, 1934, http://www.ssa.gov/history/reports/ces/ces8minutes .html, accessed Aug. 10, 2011.

25 Minutes of CES, Dec. 4, 1934, www.ssa.gov/history/reports/ces/ces8minutes.html, accessed Aug. 10, 2011.

26 "Report of Committee on Unemployment Insurance," Sept. 26, 1934, Reports and Minutes of Committee on Unemployment Insurance File, box 1, CES, SSA. Roche and Wallace's agreement, see Frances Perkins, *The Roosevelt I Knew* (New York, 1947), 90–91.

27 Perkins, *The Roosevelt I Knew*, 90–91.

28 Ibid., 292.

29 Roche to Witte, Dec. 26, 1934, Roche file, General Correspondence, box 59, CES, SSA.

30 Witte to Roche, Dec. 27, 1934, Roche file, General Correspondence, box 59, CES, SSA.

31 H.R. 4120, A Bill to alleviate the hazards of old age, unemployment, illness and dependency; to establish a Social Insurance Board in the Department of Labor, to raise revenue, and for other purposes, 74th Congress, 1st Session, Jan. 17, 1935.

32 Roche to Morgenthau, Feb. 20, 1936; Apr. 20, 1936; Apr. 21, 1936, all in Roche file, box 240, Morgenthau Papers.

33 For instance, Jennifer Klein, *For All These Rights: Business, Labor, and the Shaping of America's Public-Private Welfare State* (Princeton, NJ, 2003), 78–115, 259–275; National Partnership for Women and Families, "Social Security, Poverty, and Old Age," http://www.nationalpartnership.org/site/DocServer/SocialSecurityPovertyOldAge .pdf?docID=1089, accessed Aug. 11, 2011. Roche's quotation: Roche to Read Lewis, Aug. 13, 1911, RLP.

34 Perkins, *The Roosevelt I Knew*, 293–96.

35 Ibid., 297–298.

36 On the ways that the New Deal more generally institutionalized gender and racial inequality, see Alice Kessler-Harris, *In Pursuit of Equity: Women, Men, and the Quest for Economic Citizenship* (New York, 2001); David R. Roediger, *Working toward Whiteness: How America's Immigrants Became White* (New York, 2005), 199–244; David M. P. Freund, *Colored Property: State Policy and White Racial Politics in Suburban America* (Chicago, 2007); Ira Katznelson, *Fear Itself: The New Deal and the Origins of Our Time* (New York, 2013).

37 Roche's daily reports to Morgenthau tracked the progress of the anti-lynching bill. See, for instance, Roche to Morgenthau, Apr. 30, 1935, Roche file, box 240, Morgenthau Papers. Roche, address before the National Association for the Advancement of Colored People, St. Louis, Missouri, June 30, 1935, folder 3, box 36, RC.

38 Roche, address before the National Association for the Advancement of Colored People.

39 Roche to Morgenthau, Mar. 1, 1937, Roche file, box 241, Morgenthau Papers.

40 Harvard Sitkoff, *A New Deal for Blacks: The Emergence of Civil Rights as a National Issue: The Depression Decade*, 30th anniv. ed. (1978; New York, 2008), 33–36, 50–61; Patricia Sullivan, *Days of Hope: Race and Democracy in the New Deal Era* (Chapel Hill, NC, 1996), 43–55, 178–180; Laurence J. W. Hayes, "The Negro Federal Government Worker: A Study of His Classification Status in the District of Columbia, 1883–1938," *Howard University Studies in the Social Sciences* 3, no. 1 (1941): 14,73, 77–78, 80–90; Desmond King, *Separate and Unequal: African Americans and the US Federal Government*, rev. ed. (New York, 2007), 3–15, 23, 31–32, 67, 80. [Unknown] to Mr. President, May 20, 1935, and Thompson to McReynolds, Feb. 7, 1934, Personnel-Segregation of Employees in Treasury, 1933–1935 folder, box 101, Central Files, 1933–1956, Department of the Treasury Records, NARA. Leslie S. Perry to Morgenthau, Jan. 12, 1937, and Leslie S. Perry to Morgenthau, July 16, 1937, folder 12, box 273; Andrews, "Report on Segregation in Government Departments," Aug. 10–17, 1928, folder 10, box 403; Letters between Andrew Mellon and James Weldon Johnson, Apr. and May 1928, folder 10, box 403, part I, series C, National Association for the Advancement of Colored People Papers, Library of Congress, Washington, DC. Thanks to Mary-Elizabeth Murphy for citations from the NAACP Papers.

41   Sitkoff, *A New Deal for Blacks*, 245.
42   "Throng Honors Marian Anderson in Concert at Lincoln Memorial," *New York Times*, Apr. 10, 1939, 15; Ernest K. Lindley, "Voice from the Temple," *Washington Post*, Apr. 12, 1939, 9.
43   Memo, Meeting with Roche, June 25, 1935, 150, book 7, Morgenthau Diaries, FDRL.
44   Memo, Meeting with Roche, June 25, 1935, 150; Meeting with Roche, June 27, 1935, 179, book 7, Morgenthau Diaries.
45   Memo, Meeting with Roche, July 16, 1935, 85, book 8, Morgenthau Diaries.
46   "Josephine Roche New Head of FAA," Jan. 11, 1936, folder 1, box 36, RC.
47   Felix Bruner, "$50,000,000 Sets Up a Unit to Aid Youth," *Washington Post*, June 27, 1935, 1.
48   Commitment to youth on the board: Roche to Morgenthau, June 28, 1935, and Morgenthau's handwritten response, Roche file, box 240, Morgenthau Papers. Ironing out details: many minutes, National Youth Administration file, box 13, Aubrey Williams Papers, FDRL. On her pride in serving black youth and the failure to achieve equality for them, see Roche, "The National Youth Administration," address for the Conference of Democratic State Committee of New York, June 8, 1937, folder 3, box 36, RC; Roche to Morgenthau, June 3 and June 4, 1936, Roche file, box 240, Morgenthau Papers; Mary McLeod Bethune to Roche, Nov. 3, 1937, folder 2, box 37, RC. Sitkoff, *New Deal for Blacks*, 55.
49   Federal Security Agency, *United States National Youth Administration, Final Report Fiscal Years 1936–1943* (Washington, DC, 1944), 30. Gilbert J. Gall, *Pursuing Justice: Lee Pressman, the New Deal, and the CIO* (Albany, 1999), 31, 47–53.
50   Communist Party membership: Gall, *Pursuing Justice*, 34.
51   G. Edward White, *The Constitution and the New Deal* (Cambridge, MA, 2000), 110–111. Richard A. Maidment, *The Judicial Response to the New Deal: The US Supreme Court and Economic Regulation, 1934–1936* (New York, 1991), 83–95.
52   Roche to Morgenthau, June 6, 1935, Roche file, box 240, Henry Morgenthau Papers.
53   "Coal Code Upheld," *New York Times*, Nov. 17, 1935, folder 4, box 19, RC.
54   "Guffey Coal Act Backed in Court by Miss Roche," Nov. 1935, [*Herald Tribune?*], VAO.
55   Justice Sutherland's decision, folder 1, box 20, RC. Thomas H. Coode and John F. Bauman, *People, Poverty, and Politics: Pennsylvanians during the Great Depression* (Lewisburg, PA, 1981), 148–151. Roche's involvement in second bill: Memo, Roche to Morgenthau, May 20, 1936, and Memo, Roche to Morgenthau, June 1, 1936, Roche file, box 240, Morgenthau Papers.
56   "Bituminous Coal Act of 1937," and majority opinion are in folder 3, box 20, RC.

57   "Statement of Josephine Roche before Representatives of the U.S. Bituminous Coal Commission," Jan. 15, 1938, folder 3, box 20, RC. Other successes of economic planning: Anthony Badger, *The New Deal: The Depression Years, 1933–1940* (Chicago, 1989), 147.

58   "Josephine Roche Is Ardent Backer of Disputes Bill," *Labor*, May 21, 1935, folder 7, box 35, RC.

59   Roger H. Zieger, *American Workers, American Unions, 1920–1985* (Baltimore, MD, 1986), 26.

60   "Mine Workers Defy A.F. of L.," *Washington Post*, Jan. 31, 1936, 1.

61   Zeiger, *American Workers, American Unions*, 41–46.

62   See documents in folder 11, box 65, RC.

63   James O'Connor to Roche, Oct. 13, 1936; Roche to O'Connor, Oct. 14, 1936, folder 5, box 33, RC. In spring 1936, she began working with John L. Lewis to organize a group of labor unions devoted to Roosevelt's reelection. Roche to Morgenthau, Apr. 23, 1936, Roche file, box 240, Morgenthau Papers.

64   Lewis, radio address, Mar. 15, 1938, multiple copies in Roche's possession, folder 11, box 65, RC.

65   Roche, "The New Citizenship," address at Mount Holyoke College Founder's Day Exercises, Nov. 8, 1935, folder 3, box 36, RC.

66   In the vast literature on civil society, some argue that labor unions are not a part of civil society, but I am not alone in construing them this way. See, for example, Jeffrey C. Isaac, "The Poverty of Progressivism and the Tragedy of Civil Society," *Varieties of Progressivism in America*, ed. Peter Berkowitz (Stanford, CA, 2004), 145–188, esp. 152–154; Peter Levine, "The Legitimacy of Labor Unions," *Hofstra Labor and Employment Law Journal* (Spring 2001): 529–573. On the debate itself, see, for instance, Robert D. Putnam, *Bowling Alone: The Collapse and Revival of American Community* (New York, 2000); Michael W. Foley and Bob Edwards, "The Paradox of Civil Society," *Journal of Democracy* 7 (1996): 38–52; Don E. Eberly, "The Meaning, Origins, and Application of Civil Society," *The Essential Civil Society Reader: Classic Essays in the American Civil Society Debate*, ed. Don E. Eberly (New York, 2000), 3–29; Theda Skocpol and Morris Fiorina, eds., *Civic Engagement in American Democracy* (Washington, DC, 1999).

67   Delegate Thomas Kennedy, Nov. 17, 1938, *Proceedings of the First Constitutional Convention of the Congress of Industrial Organizations*, Pittsburgh, PA, Nov. 14–18, 1938, 197.

68   Roche, *Proceedings of the First Constitutional Convention of the Congress of Industrial Organizations*, 198.

69   Roche to Ralph Hetzel, Dec. 6, 1938, folder 13, box 3, RC.

70   Storrs, *Civilizing Capitalism*, 177–205.

71   Ibid., 196–205.

72   Roche to Mrs. Charles Tillett, Nov. 23, 1936, folder 1, box 31, RC.

73   "Pageantry and Sport Fill Convention Week," *Christian Science Monitor*, June 22, 1936, 3. Roche to Morgenthau, June 8, 1936, and June 15, 1936, Roche file, box 240, Morgenthau Papers.

74   Fall campaign: Roche folder, box 18, Papers of the Women's Division of the Democratic National Committee, FDRL. Speeches to labor: Roche to Morgenthau, Aug. 18, 1936, Roche file, box 240, Morgenthau Papers.

75   Mrs. Kenneth Gould to Betty Lindley, Oct. 28, 1936, folder 3, box 35, RC. See also documents in folder 2, box 33, RC.

76   Roche, "Radio Broadcast under the Auspices of Labor's Non-Partisan League, the National Progressive League, and the Good Neighbor League," Washington, DC, Oct. 1,

1936, folder 3, box 36, RC. "Warns against Privilege," *New York Times*, Oct. 12, 1936, 21. Press release, "Roche at American Labor Party Forum," Brooklyn Academy of Music, Oct. 11, 1936, folder 3, box 36, RC.

77   Roche, address before the Federation of Democratic Women's Clubs of Ohio, Sept. 26, 1936, folder 3, box 36, RC.

78   Roche, address before the United Mine Workers Convention, Jan. 30, 1936, folder 3, box 36, RC.

79   "Mass of Impressive Duties Fails to Lessen Personal Charm of Miss Josephine Roche," *Evening Bulletin*, Nov. 22, 1935, VAO.

80   Olive Douglas Bostick to Roche, Nov. 30, 1934, folder 2, box 30; Angelina Martorano to Roche, Oct. 15, 1935, folder 1, box 33, RC.

81   "Finds Women of Presidential Stamp Plentiful," *New York Herald Tribune*, Oct. 2, 1935, VAO. "Bamberger Poll Honors Mining Woman," *Star Eagle*, Mar. 11, 1935, folder 7, box 35, RC.

82   "Mrs. Roosevelt Lists 11 Women as 'Inspiration,'" *Washington Post*, Mar. 9, 1935, folder 7, box 35, RC. The Chi Omega award is in folder 7, box 8, RC. "[C]ulture of the world": "Miss Roche to Get Medal," *New York Herald Tribune*, Apr. 2, 1935, VAO. Full ceremony: *The Eleusis of Chi Omega*, Sept. 1935, folder 7, box 8, RC.

83   "Mrs. Simpson Is Left Out of List of Famous Women," *Washington Daily News*, Jan. 1937, folder 2, box 36, RC. Durward Howes, ed., *American Women: The Official Who's Who among the Women of the Nation*, vol. II (Los Angeles, 1937), xxvi, 583.

84   Roche "The Government and Social Justice," National Council of Catholic Women, Annual Convention, Nov. 19, 1935, folder 2, box 36, RC.

85   "Women Democrats to Meet in Detroit," *Washington Post*, Mar. 16, 1935, 12. Molly Dewson to Angel Josephine, Mar. 28, 1935, folder 9, box 30, RC.

86   "To Speak at Jefferson Dinner," *New York Times*, Apr. 20, 1935, 15. "Chautauqua Opens Today," *New York Times*, July 7, 1935, N4. "Milbank Conference to Open Here Today," *New York Times*, Mar. 27, 1935, 3. "Jewish Women Plan Annual Luncheon," *Washington Post*, Nov. 3, 1935, F7.

87   "Women Defended on Public Speaking," *New York Times*, Nov. 30, 1937, 25.

CHAPTER 11   GENERATING A NATIONAL DEBATE ABOUT FEDERAL HEALTH POLICY, 1935–1939

1   *The Nation's Health*, Discussion at the National Health Conference, July 18–20, 1938 (Washington, DC, 1939), 16.

2   Roche, address before Women's National Democratic Club, Jan. 11, 1935, folder 3, box 36, RC. PHS's appropriation in fiscal 1935 was just under $5 million if one excluded over $4 million appropriated for the Immigration Service. 73rd Congress, Session II, Mar. 15, 1934, *United States Statutes at Large*, vol. 48, pt. 1, chapter 70, HeinOnLine, http://www.heinonline.org.proxy-um.researchport.umd.edu/HOL/Page ?handle=hein.statute/sal048&id=1&size=2&collection=statute&index=statdocs#1, 48 Stat. 1928–1934, 434–436, accessed Feb. 15, 2014.

3   "Statement of Miss Josephine Roche," before the Finance Committee of the U.S. Senate, in *Economic Security Act: Hearings before the Committee on Finance, Seventy-Fourth Congress First Session, on S. 1130 A Bill to Alleviate the Hazards of Old Age, Unemployment, Illness, and Dependency, to Establish a Social Insurance Board in the Department of Labor, to Raise Revenue, and for Other Purposes* (Washington, DC, 1935), 374–407.

4　Roche to Morgenthau, June 19, 1936, Roche file, box 240, Henry Morgenthau Papers, FDRL.

5　Developing infrastructure: Roche, "Education for Living," address before General Federation of Women's Clubs, Washington, DC, May 15, 1936; Roche, "Remarks to the Third National Conference of State Labor Commissioners," Nov. 10, 1936, folder 3, box 36, RC. See also Roche, Report on Social Security and Public Health, [1936], folder 6, box 33, RC; Roche to Morgenthau, Dec. 7, 1936, Roche file, box 240, Morgenthau Papers. For Progressive Era precedents: Christopher C. Sellers, *Hazards of the Job: From Industrial Disease to Environmental Health Science* (Chapel Hill, NC, 1997); Barbara Sicherman, *Alice Hamilton: A Life in Letters* (Cambridge, MA, 1984).

6　Stream pollution: Roche to Morgenthau, May 21, 1936, and June 9, 1936, Roche file, box 240, Morgenthau Papers. For various bills, see Herman G. Baity, "Aspects of Governmental Policy on Stream Pollution Abatement," *American Journal of Public Health* 29 (Dec. 1939): 1297–1307. New research facility: Roche to Morgenthau, June 24, 1936; Nov. 16, 1936; Dec. 15, 1936; Apr. 1, 1937, Roche file, box 240, Morgenthau Papers.

7　Floods: Roche to Morgenthau, Mar. 19, 1936; Mar. 23, 1936; Feb. 12, 1937; Apr. 2, 1937; Apr. 9, 1937, Roche file, box 240, Morgenthau Papers. Drought: Roche to Morgenthau, Dec. 10, 1936, and Dec. 23, 1936, Roche file, box 240, Morgenthau Papers.

8　Roche to Morgenthau, Sept. 11, 1936, folder 2, box 33, RC. Hiring: Roche to Morgenthau, Jan. 23, 1936; Feb. 12, 1936; Mar. 24, 1936, Roche file, box 240, Morgenthau Papers. She obtained monies from PWA, for instance, to extend emergency health services in several states. See Roche to Morgenthau, Jan. 22, 1936, Roche file, box 240, Morgenthau Papers. VD and cancer: Roche to Morgenthau, Dec. 21, 1936; Dec. 30, 1936; Mar. 31, 1937, Roche file, box 240, Morgenthau Papers. "Resettlement Administration," n.d.; "Resettlement Administration," Dec. 11, 1935, conference notes, Interdepartmental Committee to Coordinate Health and Welfare Activities, Miss Roche's Office; minutes of the conference of Technical Committee on Medical Care, Aug. 11, 1937, no folders, box 43, CCHWA, FDRL. Roche to Morgenthau, Apr. 5, 1937, Roche file, box 240, Morgenthau Papers. Analysis of some of the medical care experiments funded by PHS and other New Deal sources: Jennifer Klein, *For All These Rights: Business, Labor and the Shaping of America's Public-Private Welfare State* (Princeton, NJ, 2003), 131–150.

9　Technical Board on Economic Security, Minutes, Mar. 4 and 5, 1935, Minutes of Executive Committee file, box 1, Committee on Economic Security, SSA.

10　Roche, "Medical Care as a Public Health Function," address before the American Public Health Association, Oct. 5, 1937, folder 3, box 36, RC. See also, Roche, "Medical Care as a Public Health Function," *American Journal of Public Health* (Dec. 1937), folder 3, box 38, RC.

11　See, for instance, Roche to Morgenthau, Jan. 2, 1935, Roche file, box 240, Morgenthau Papers. Edwin Witte to Roche, Jan. 10, 1935, General Correspondence file, box 59, CES, SSA. Documents in Interdepartmental Committee folder, box 1, Official File 1731, Franklin Delano Roosevelt Papers, FDRL (hereafter FDR Papers).

12　Perkins to Roosevelt, Aug. 2, 1935; Perkins to Early, Aug. 14, 1935; Early to Roosevelt, Aug. 15, 1935, Interdepartmental Committee folder, box 1, Official File 1731, FDR Papers. Roosevelt to Roche, Aug. 19, 1935; Roche to Roosevelt, Aug. 21, 1935, Roche Correspondence folder, box 5, CCHWA.

13　Roosevelt, "Statement of the President," Aug. 15, 1935, folder 4, box 37, RC.

14　Isidore Falk to Roche, Feb. 1935, folder 216, box 42, Isidore S. Falk Papers, Manuscripts and Archives, Sterling Memorial Library, Yale University, New Haven, CT. Vociferous support: Edwin E. Witte, *The Development of the Social Security Act* (Madison, WI, 1963), 187–188. Roche to Morgenthau, Mar. 15, 1935, Roche file, box 240, Morgenthau Papers.

15 Roosevelt, "Statement of the President," Aug. 15, 1935, folder 4, box 37, RC.

16 Roosevelt, Executive Order 7481, Oct. 27, 1936, folder 5, box 6, RC; "The Interdepartmental Committee on Health and Welfare Activities," Apr. 14, 1939; "The Interdepartmental Committee to Coordinate Health and Welfare Activities" [1936], Interdepartmental Committee folder, box 32, CCHWA.

17 "Purposes of the Program of Research for the Interdepartmental Committee," Miscellaneous folder, box 32, CCHWA.

18 "The Interdepartmental Committee on Health and Welfare Activities," Apr. 14, 1939, Interdepartmental Committee folder, box 32, CCHWA.

19 Minutes of Conference of Technical Committee on Medical Care, May 5, 1937, no folder, box 43; "Progress Report," Sept. 1937, no folder, box 45; Resettlement Administration folder, box 7, CCHWA.

20 Roche to Lee Pressman, Mar. 20, 1939, folder 13, box 5, RC.

21 Robyn Muncy, *Creating a Female Dominion in American Reform, 1890–1935* (New York, 1991), 142–150.

22 Editorial Division of the Children's Bureau to Roche, Nov. 1934, folder 2, box 30; Katharine Lenroot to Roche, Nov. 1934, folder 8, box 32; Anna Rude to Roche, Nov. 27, 1934, folder 2, box 34, RC.

23 "Miss Roche's Rule May Mean Ouster of Dr. Cumming," *Washington Post*, Nov. 19, 1934, 3. "Exit of Cumming Seen in Prospect," *Washington Star*, Dec. 1934, folder 6, box 35, RC.

24 Breckinridge to Roche, Nov. 19, 1934, folder 3, box 30, RC.

25 Rude to Roche, Nov. 27, 1934, folder 2, box 34, RC.

26 Photograph of Cumming, Feb. 12, 1936, folder 3, box 71, RC.

27 Warren Draper to Roche, Dec. 24, 1963, folder 2, box 3; Cumming to Roche, Oct. 28, 1937, folder 2, box 37, RC.

28 Roche, "Remarks to Representatives of Labor and PHS," Apr. 10, 1936, folder 3, box 36, RC.

29 Roche to Morgenthau, May 8, 1936; Nov. 20, 1936, Roche file, box 240, Morgenthau Papers.

30 Perkins to Roche, Apr. 23, 1936, folder 6, box 33, RC.

31 A.J.U. Chesley to Roche, Feb. 28, 1936, folder 5, box 30, RC.

32 Alma C. Haupt to Roche, Nov. 9, 1936, no folder, box 43, CCHWA.

33 Health insurance section, "Message of the President Recommending Legislation on Economic Security," Jan. 17, 1935, folder 4, box 41, RC.

34 Roche, address to the Milbank Memorial Fund Dinner, Mar. 28, 1935, folder 3, box 35, RC.

35 Ibid.

36 Falk to Roche, "Preliminary Memo Concerning Health, Sickness, and Disability Survey," May 21, 1935, folder 216, box 42, Falk Papers.

37 Roche, "Cost of Depression in Health Revealed," *New York Times*, Sept. 1935, folder 7, box 35, RC.

38 "Bell-Ringers for Health," *Literary Digest*, Oct. 5, 1935, folder 7, box 35; Roche, "A National Health Survey," *Science Newsletter*, Feb. 1, 1936, folder 4, box 36; Roche, address to the Public Health Association, Oct. 7, 1935, folder 3, box 36; Roche, "The National Health Inventory," radio address, NBC, Oct. 14, 1935, folder 3, box 36; "Points to Remember," Aug. 28, 1936, folder 5, box 33, RC. Number of communities: "Statement of Josephine Roche at Hearings before Subcommittee of Senate Committee on Education and Labor," May 4, 1939, folder 1, box 8, RC. Some sources say eighty-

three communities: Roche's testimony before the Senate Committee on Education and Labor, *Hearings before a Subcommittee of the Senate Committee on Education and Labor* (Washington, DC, 1939), 118.

39 "Bell-Ringers for Health," *Literary Digest*, Oct. 5, 1935, folder 7, box 35; Roche, "A National Health Survey," *Science Newsletter*, Feb. 1, 1936, folder 4, box 36; Roche, address to the Public Health Association, Oct. 7, 1935, folder 3, box 36; Roche, "The National Health Inventory," radio address, NBC, Oct. 14, 1935, folder 3, box 36, RC.

40 Roche, "Points to Remember," Aug. 28, 1936, folder 5, box 33, RC.

41 Roche to Morgenthau, Mar. 3, 1936, Roche file, box 240, Morgenthau Papers.

42 Meeting notes, Aug. 24, 1936, and Aug. 26, 1936, 168–172, 316–318, book 30, Morgenthau Diaries, FDRL.

43 Roche to Morgenthau, Mar. 3, 1937; Mar. 9, 1937, Roche file, box 241, Morgenthau Papers.

44 Meeting Notes, June 28, 1937, 86–100, book 74, Morgenthau Diaries.

45 Alan Brinkley, *The End of Reform: New Deal Liberalism in Recession and War* (New York, 1995), 28–29.

46 Roche to Roosevelt, Sept. 14, 1937, folder 5, box 6, RC.

47 "Miss Roche Leaves But 'May Be Back,'" *New York Times*, Oct. 31, 1937, folder 1, box 37, RC.

48 Mary McLeod Bethune to Roche, Nov. 3, 1937, folder 2, box 37, RC.

49 Eleanor Roosevelt to Roche, Nov. 4, 1937, Resignation folder, box 32, CCHWA.

50 See folder 2, box 37, RC.

51 Michael Davis to Roche, Oct. 28, 1937, folder 2, box 37, RC.

52 Mary Switzer to Roche, handwritten note, n.d., folder 2, box 37, RC.

53 Josephine Coe to Roche, n.d., folder 2, box 37, RC.

54 For Roche's strategy, see Roche to Morgenthau, Oct. 22, 1937, folder 2, box 33, RC.

55 Minutes of conference re Medical Care, Sept. 28, 1937, no folder, box 43, CCHWA. The story of developing a national health plan has been told elsewhere, with different emphases: Paul Starr, *The Social Transformation of American Medicine* (New York, 1982), 266–279; Klein, *For All These Rights*, 131–149.

56 FERA: "Revision of Memorandum Concerning Emergency Medical and Health Needs," to Roche, Jan. 12, 1935, folder 216, box 42, Falk Papers.

57 "Tentative Draft," meeting of Committee on Medical Care, Nov. 20, 1937, folder 208, box 14, Martha May Eliot Papers, Arthur and Elizabeth Schlesinger Library on the History of Women, Radcliffe Institute for Advanced Study, Harvard University, Cambridge, MA.

58 Minutes of Committee on Medical Care, Nov. 20, 1937; Minutes of Conference on Medical Care, Nov. 29, 1937, no folders, box 43, CCHWA.

59 "Summary Progress Report of the Technical Committee on Medical Care to the Chair of the Interdepartmental Committee to Coordinate Health and Welfare Activities on Federal Participation in a National Health Program," Dec. 15, 1937, box 9, CCHWA.

60 See, for instance, "Abundant Life," Oct. 15, 1937, and "Poverty the Most Deadly," Oct. 15, 1937, folder 2, box 36, RC.

61 *The Nation's Health*, 11–12. Interdepartmental Committee to Coordinate Health and Welfare Activities, *The Need for a National Health Program* (Washington, DC, 1938), 1–3, 21–25.

62 *The Nation's Health*, 16.

63 Minutes of meeting of Technical Committee on Medical Care, Feb. 10, 1938, no folder, box 43, CCHWA. Starr, *The Social Transformation of American Medicine*, 276.

64 Clippings, folder 1, box 38, RC.

65 Minutes of meeting of Technical Committee on Medical Care, Feb. 10, 1938, no folder, box 43, CCHWA. See, for example, press releases in Mar.–June 1938, no folder, box 26, CCHWA.

66 "Roosevelt Adds 2 Left-Wingers to Guest List for Cruise Today," *New York Herald Tribune*, July 1937, folder 2, box 36, RC.

67 Roche to Morgenthau, Feb. 14, 1938, Roche file, box 241, Morgenthau Papers.

68 Documents, 1938, folder 5, box 37, RC.

69 List of attendees: *The Nation's Health*, 106–114. Inviting opponents: I. S. Falk to Mr. Perrott, June 9, 1938, folder 5, box 37, RC. Leftists on the roster: Klein, *For All These Rights*, 144–145.

70 Weather and air conditioning: Dr. Ellen Potter, *Proceedings of the National Health Conference*, July 18–20, 1938 (Washington, DC, 1938), 73.

71 Roche's introductory remarks, *Proceedings of the National Health Conference*, 1.

72 *The Nation's Health*, 5–8. See also Roche to Miss Dorothy Kahn, June 22, 1938, Roche correspondence folder, box 5, CCHWA.

73 West's remarks: folder 4, box 37, RC. For the shape of the conference and every contribution, see *Proceedings of the National Health Conference*.

74 See, for instance, testimony of Dr. Morris Fishbein and Rev. Alphonse M. Schwitalla, *Proceedings of the National Health Conference*, 117–119. See also "Hospitals Back National Health Plans," *Washington Post*, Nov. 23, 1938, 15.

75 *The Nation's Health*, 64–65.

76 Ibid., 63–64.

77 Green testimony, *Proceedings of the National Health Conference*, 13–14.

78 Roche's closing remarks, *The Nation's Health*, 81–82.

79 Alice Hamilton to Roche, Aug. 3, 1938, folder 2, box 38, RC.

80 Mary Dublin to Roche, July 29, 1938, folder 2, box 38, RC.

81 Dr. Frederic Besley to Roche, July 23, 1938, folder 2, box 38, RC.

82 Dr. John Peters to Roche, July 23, 1938, folder 2, box 38, RC.

83 Robert Neff to G. St. J. Perrott, Aug. 2, 1938, Health Conference folder, box 11, CCHWA.

84 Charles Taussig to Roche, Aug. 17, 1938, folder 2, box 38, RC.

85 Emma Puschner to Roche, July 26, 1938, folder 2, box 38, RC.

86 Statement of Mrs. J. K. Pettengill, president of the National Congress of Parents and Teachers, *The Nation's Health*, 73.

87 "Majority of US Voters Favor Group Health Insurance," *Washington Post*, June 12, 1938, folder 5, box 38, RC.

88 Clippings in folder 1, box 38, RC. Analysis of 141 editorials on the conference: box 9, CCHWA. Invitations to speak: Roche correspondence folder, box 5 and documents in box 9 and box 10, CCHWA. Roche's speeches: folder 4, box 38, RC.

89 Requests for publications: J. C. Leukhardt to Roche, Feb. 24, 1939, Roche correspondence folder, box 5, CCHWA.

90 Klein, *For All These Rights*, 150–161.

91 Roche, "Statement before the Subcommittee of Senate Committee on Education and Labor," May 4, 1939, folder 1, box 8, RC. Arthur Altmeyer, "The National Health Conference and the Future of Public Health," American Public Health Association, Oct. 1938; Falk, address to Catholic Charities, Oct. 7, 1938, folder 1, box 39, RC. G. St. J. Perrott to Members of the Interdepartmental and Technical Committees, Dec. 1, 1938; George Bowles to Roche, Oct. 1938; folder 4, box 39, RC.

92 Roche, "Statement before the Subcommittee of Senate Committee on Education and Labor," May 4, 1939, folder 1, box 8, RC.

93   Roche to Roosevelt, Regarding the National Health Plan, [late 1938], folder 2, box 38; Roche to Roosevelt, Dec. 14, 1938, folder 4, box 39, RC. Roche's summary of proposals: Roche, "Statement before Subcommittee of Senate Committee on Education and Labor," May 4, 1939, folder 1, box 8, RC.

94   Roosevelt, "Health Security Message from the President," 76th Congress, First Session, Document #120, House of Representatives, Jan. 23, 1939, folder 5, box 38, RC. Martha May Eliot to Roche, Dec. 28, 1939, folder 4, box 39, RC.

95   Roche to Read Lewis, Dec. 26, 1938, RLP.

96   Isidore Falk to Roche, Dec. 20, 1938, folder 3[?], box 38, RC.

97   Senate Bill 1620, 76th Congress, First Session, Feb. 28, 1939, folder 1, box 40, RC.

98   Isidore Falk to Harold Ickes, Jan. 5, 1939; Jan. 14, 1939, folder 4, box 39, RC. Isidore Falk to Roche, Jan. 5, 1939, Roche correspondence folder, box 5, CCHWA.

99   Roche testimony, *Hearings before a Subcommittee of the Senate Committee on Education and Labor*, 76th Congress, First Session, S. 1620, part 1 (Washington, DC, 1939), 117–130.

100   Roche to Roosevelt, May 4, 1939, folder 4, box 39, RC.

CHAPTER 12   UNMOORED DURING WARTIME, 1939–1945

1   "Denver's Dynamic Josephine Roche Takes Treasury Post," *Washington Post*, Dec. 1934, folder 6, box 35, RC.

2   Roche to Read Lewis, Jan. 29, 1939, RLP.

3   Lea was employed by Roche at least as early as 1933: Mildred Lea to Dr. J. P. McDonough, Aug. 29, 1933, file 444, box 22, RMF Records, Special Collections, Denver Public Library. Other information: William E. Owens, interview by author, Ellicott City, MD, May 26, 2005.

4   Owens interview.

5   Roche to Read Lewis, Jan. 29, 1939, RLP.

6   Roche and F. C. Springer to Bondholders of the Rocky Mountain Fuel Company, Jan. 15, 1939, folder 2, box 20, RC.

7   Roche and Springer to Wilbur Newton, Feb. 29, 1944, folder 10, box 20, RC.

8   Roche to Mr. Henry Cottigan, Mar. 11, 1939, folder 11, box 7; Roche to the Bondholders of the Rocky Mountain Fuel Company, Jan. 15, 1939, folder 2, box 20, RC.

9   James S. Olson, *Saving Capitalism: The Reconstruction Finance Corporation and the New Deal, 1933–1940* (Princeton, NJ, 1988), 14, 16, 30, 42–44.

10   Roche and Springer to Wilbur Newton, Feb. 29, 1944, folder 10, box 20; "Million in UMW Funds Invested in Mining Firms," *St. Louis Post-Dispatch*, Nov. 1, 1942, folder 4, box 17, RC.

11   Roche and F. C. Springer to Bondholders of the Rocky Mountain Fuel Company, Feb. 1, 1939, with enclosure, folder 4, box 17; Roche and Springer to Wilbur Newton, Feb. 29, 1944, folder 10, box 20, RC.

12   Roche and Springer to Wilbur Newton, Feb. 29, 1944, folder 10, box 20, RC.

13   "Josephine Roche Reported Offered Welfare Post," *Washington Post*, June 14, 1939, 1. "Woman Likely U.S. Welfare Chief," *Los Angeles Examiner*, June 14, 1939, folder 1, box 44, RC.

14   Franklin Delano Roosevelt, *Reorganization Plan No. I*, 1939, www.ssa.gov/history/pdf/fdr.pdf, accessed Aug. 13, 2009.

15   John L. Lewis to FDR, May 25, 1939, box 9, Official File 285c, Franklin Delano Roosevelt Papers, FDRL (hereafter FDR Papers). Lucy Mason to Eleanor Roosevelt, May 11, 1939, reel 62, Lucy Mason Papers, Operation Dixie: The CIO Organizing Committee, Library of Congress, Washington, DC. Stephen B. Gibbons to Henry Morgenthau, July 5, 1939, box 107, Henry Morgenthau Papers, FDRL.

16   "Josephine Roche Reported Offered Welfare Post," *Washington Post*, June 14, 1939, 1. See also Ernest K. Lindley, "High Posts Vacant," *Washington Post*, July 10, 1939, 7.

17   Documents on Paul McNutt, file 2836, President's Personal File, FDR Papers. July 15, 1939, and July 24, 1939, Harold Ickes Diary, Harold Ickes Papers, Library of Congress, Washington, DC.

18   July 15, 1939, Ickes Diary.

19   Phone call, Lowell Mellett and Henry Morgenthau, July 10, 1939, 2:40 pm, book 202, Morgenthau Diaries, FDRL. See also July 15, 1939, and July 24, 1939, Ickes Diary.

20   Robyn Muncy, "Women, Gender, and Politics in the New Deal Government: Josephine Roche and the Federal Security Agency," *Journal of Women's History* 21 (Fall 2009): 60–83.

21   June 17, 1939, Ickes Diary.

22   Ira Katznelson, *Fear Itself: The New Deal and the Origins of Our Time* (New York, 2013), 300–305.

23   Transcript of meeting, Morgenthau and FDR, July 11, 1939, box 518, Morgenthau Papers. Almost identical conversation with Harold Ickes: July 14, 1939, Ickes Diary.

24   "American Legion," *Encyclopedia of American History*, http://www.digitalhistory .uh.edu/encyclopedia/encyclopedia.cfm, accessed Mar. 2, 2007.

25   July 15, 1939, Ickes Diary.

26   July 24, 1939, Ickes Diary.

27   Roche, quoted in NCL Bulletin, late 1938 or early 1939, reel 6, NCLR.

28   Mary Dublin to Roche, Aug. 2, 1939, frame 216, reel 33, NCLR.

29   Minutes, Board of Directors meeting, Sept. 26, 1939, frame 451, reel 2; Mary Dublin to Roche, Oct. 19, 1939, frame 212, reel 33, NCLR.

30   Landon R. Y. Storrs, *Civilizing Capitalism: The National Consumers' League, Women's Activism, and Labor Standards in the New Deal Era* (Chapel Hill, NC, 2000), 207–227.

31   Report of the General Secretary, Nov. 21, 1938–Jan. 12, 1939, frame 421, reel 2, NCLR.

32   Minutes, Board of Directors meeting, Sept. 12, 1939, frame 448, reel 2, NCLR.

33   Ibid.

34   Dublin to Roche, Aug. 2, 1939, frame 216, reel 33, NCLR.

35   Minutes, Board of Directors meeting, Sept. 12, 1939, frame 448, reel 2, NCLR.

36   Minutes, Board of Directors meeting, Nov. 9, 1939, frame 454, reel 2, NCLR.

37   Roche, "Industrial Justice—A Bulwark to Democracy," address before the Consumers League, Oct. 10, 1939, frame 201, reel 33, NCLR.

38   "McNutt Displaced as Health Leader," *New York Times*, Dec. 22, 1939, 1; "Roosevelt Plans to Build Hospitals for Needy Regions," *New York Times*, Dec. 23, 1939, 1.

39   Desire to undercut McNutt: Dec. 6, Dec. 10, and Dec. 24, 1939, Ickes Diary. McNutt's desire to head the campaign for the health bill: "Reminder for General Watson," Nov. 9, 1939, Federal Security Agency folder, Official File 3700, FDR Papers.

40   "Reminder for General Watson," Nov. 9, 1939, Federal Security Agency folder, Official File 3700, FDR Papers.

41   Minutes, Board of Directors meeting, Sept. 12, 1939, frame 448, reel 2, NCLR. Memo, EMW to Mr. Kannee, Sept. 25, 1939, Interdepartmental Committee folder, box 1, Official File 1731, FDR Papers.

42   *Legislative Low-Down*, Jan. 17, 1940, National Legislative Committee, 1940 folder, League of Women Shoppers Records, Arthur and Elizabeth Schlesinger Library on the

History of Women, Radcliffe Institute for Advanced Study, Harvard University, Cambridge, MA.

43   Roche to FDR, Dec. 20, 1939, Interdepartmental Committee folder, box 1, Official File 1731, FDR Papers.

44   Mary Switzer to Roche, Jan. 2, 1940, folder 634, box 61, Mary Elizabeth Switzer Papers, Arthur and Elizabeth Schlesinger Library on the History of Women, Radcliffe Institute for Advanced Study, Harvard University, Cambridge, MA. FDR to Roche, July 19, 1940, folder 4, box 39, RC.

45   Charles W. Hurd, "Josephine Roche Returns to Guide a Health Program," *New York Times*, Feb. 11, 1940, VAO.

46   Loan application, Feb. 1940, file 452, box 25, RMF Records, Denver Public Library, Denver, CO.

47   Lauchlin Currie to the President, Mar. 18, 1940, with President's reply dated Mar. 30, 1940, Interdepartmental Committee folder, box 1, Official File 1731, FDR Papers.

48   Kathleen McLaughlin, "Women Politicians Swamping Capital," *New York Times*, May 2, 1940, 23.

49   Ibid.

50   Josephine Roche, "What Do Women Want in the 1940 Democratic Platform," May 4, 1940, National Institute of Government Speeches, box 119, Papers of the Women's Division of the Democratic National Committee, FDRL.

51   Dorothy McAllister to Roche, July 12, 1940, and Roche to McAllister, July 12, 1940, Mrs. McAllister folder, box 76, Women's Division Papers. For broadcast, see "Today's Radio Highlights," *Washington Post*, July 13, 1940, 20.

52   "Women Report Out 14 Planks to Democrats," *Washington Post*, July 14, 1940, 2. Kathleen McLaughlin, "Equal Rights Plea Hit by First Lady," *New York Times*, July 16, 1940, 5. Dorothy McAllister to Eleanor Roosevelt, July 30, 1940, McAllister folder, box 721, Anna Eleanor Roosevelt Papers, FDRL (hereafter ER Papers).

53   Progressive women and the ERA: Nancy Cott, *The Grounding of Modern Feminism* (New Haven, CT, 1987); Cynthia Harrison, *On Account of Sex: The Politics of Women's Issues, 1945–1968* (Berkeley, CA, 1988); Kathryn Kish Sklar, "Who Won the Debate over the Equal Rights Amendment in the 1920s?" *Women & Social Movements in the United States, 1600–2000* (online serial) 4, no. 1 (2000), http://web.ebscohost.com, accessed Sept. 26, 2011; Dorothy Sue Cobble, *The Other Women's Movement: Workplace Justice and Social Rights in Modern America* (Princeton, NJ, 2004), esp. 60–68.

54   Press release by Mrs. Thomas McAllister, July 15, and news briefs, July 14, National Democratic Convention, Publicity (1), box 112; Mrs. May Thompson Evans to Molly Dewson, July 26, 1940, Molly Dewson folder, box 113, Women's Division Papers. See also Dorothy McAllister to Roche, July 12, 1940, and Roche to McAllister, July 12, 1940, Mrs. McAllister folder, box 76, Women's Division Papers. Kathleen McLaughlin, "Women, Hastily Named to Resolutions Committee, Speak Minds Freely," *New York Times*, July 18, 1940, 5. "Women Democrats at Odds on Plank," *New York Times*, July 9, 1940, 15.

55   Roche to Mrs. Thomas McAllister, June 6, 1940, Mrs. McAllister folder, box 76, Women's Division Papers. Dorothy McAllister to ER, July 30, 1940, McAllister folder, box 721, ER Papers.

56   Roche to Dorothy McAllister, Sept. 18, 1940, McAllister folder, box 76, Women's Division Papers. Speeches: Roche to Dublin, Sept. 19, 1940, frame 193, reel 33, NCLR.

57   Lorena Hickok to ER, Sept. 7, 1940, box 8, Lorena Hickok Papers, FDRL.

58   Roche's Daily Appointments Books, folder 1, box 43, RC.

59 Roche to Dorothy McAllister, Sept. 18, 1940, McAllister folder, box 76, Women's Division Papers.

60 Roche to Mrs. Thomas McAllister, Sept. 26, 1940, McAllister folder, box 76, Women's Division Papers.

61 Molly Dewson to Roche, Sept. 26, 1940, Molly Dewson folder, box 113, Women's Division Papers.

62 Dorothy McAllister to ER, Sept. 28, 1940, McAllister folder, box 721, ER Papers.

63 John Fisher, "Lewis Strives to Save Union's Funds He Lent," *Chicago Sunday Tribune*, Sept. 29, 1940; John Fisher, "Josephine Roche Seeks U.S. Loan to Pay Off Lewis," *Denver Post*, Sept. 29, 1940, folder 4, box 17, RC.

64 FDR to John L. Lewis, Oct. 18, 1940, file 5640, President's Personal File, FDR Papers.

65 Roche's Daily Appointment Books, folder 1, box 43, RC.

66 Roche to McAllister, Oct. 11, 1940, McAllister folder, box 76, Women's Division Papers.

67 Lorena Hickok to ER, Oct. 15, 1940, box 8, Hickok Papers.

68 Dorothy McAllister to Roche, Oct. 18, 1940, McAllister folder, box 76, Women's Division Papers.

69 Melvyn Dubofsky and Warren Van Tine, *John L. Lewis: A Biography* (New York, 1977), 355.

70 FDR to John L. Lewis, Oct. 18, 1940, file 5640, President's Personal File, FDR Papers.

71 Roche to McAllister, Oct. 21, 1940, Mrs. Thomas McAllister folder, box 76, Women's Division Papers.

72 Minutes, Board of Directors meeting, Reconstruction Finance Corporation, Oct. 23, 1940, vol. 485, entry 3, Records of the Reconstruction Finance Corporation, RG 234, NARA.

73 Roche's Daily Appointment Books, folder 1, box 43, RC.

74 Dubofsky and Van Tine, *John L. Lewis*, 357.

75 Handwritten note by McAllister, attached to a telegram from Mildred Lea to Mrs. Thomas McAllister, Oct. 30, 1940, McAllister folder, box 76, Women's Division Papers.

76 Mrs. Lowell Hobart Jr. to Dorothy McAllister, Nov. 3, 1940, McAllister folder, box 721, ER Papers. "Consumers League President to Be Guest of Honor Here," *Cincinnati Post*, Oct. 2, 1940, VAO.

77 Mrs. Lowell Hobart Jr. to Dorothy McAllister, Nov. 3, 1940, McAllister folder, box 721, ER Papers.

78 Daily appointment books shows she dined at the White House on May 15, 1941, folder 1, box 43, RC.

79 "Miss Roche Champions Lewis Acts," *Denver Post*, Apr. 12, 1950, folder 4, box 53, RC.

80 Roche to Read Lewis, Apr. 16, 1914, RLP.

81 Owens interview. Roche to Molly Dewson, Feb. 6, 1956, Roche file, box 3, Mary Dewson Papers, FDRL.

82 Minutes, Board of Directors meeting, Nov. 7, 1940, frame 479, reel 2, NCLR. "Josephine Roche Cites U.S. Peril," *San Francisco Examiner*, Nov. 25, 1940; "Woman Industrialist Will Address Forum," *Elizabeth, New Jersey Journal*, Dec. 7, 1940, VAO. "First Lady Asks Ceiling on Profits," *Washington Post*, Dec. 16, 1940, 15.

83 Mary to Miss Roche, Dec. 19, 1940, folder 14, box 2, RC.

84 Roche, "Our Stake in Industrial Democracy," Dec. 7, 1940, folder 4, box 8, RC. "Josephine Roche Cites U.S. Peril," *San Francisco Examiner*, Nov. 25, 1940, VAO.

85   Roche, "Our Stake in Industrial Democracy," Dec. 7, 1940, folder 4, box 8, RC.

86   Roche, "Labor Standards and Democracy," address before the National Consumers' League, Jan. 11, 1941, New York City, folder 1, box 8, RC.

87   First quote: Roche, "Youth on Today's Frontier," address before the National Educa- tion Association, 1941; second quote: Roche, "Saving the United States for Democ- racy," address before the Inland Empire Education Association, Apr. 11, 1941, folder 4, box 8, RC.

88   Roche to Hon. Jonathan Daniels, Apr. 3, 1942, folder 14, box 2, RC.

89   Daily Appointment Calendars, folder 2, box 43, RC.

90   Roche and Springer to Wilbur Newton, Feb. 29, 1944, folder 10, box 20; Daily Ap- pointment Books, folder 2, box 43, RC.

91   Roche to Pearl S. Buck, Sept. 17, 1942, folder 4, box 2, RC.

92   Nelson Lichtenstein, *State of the Union: A Century of American Labor* (Princeton, NJ, 2002), 100–103.

93   Robert H. Zieger, *John L. Lewis: Labor Leader* (Boston, 1988), 136.

94   Roche to Elizabeth Magee, May 7, 1943, frame 180, reel 33, NCLR.

95   Roche to E. Worth Higgins, May 6, 1943, frame 180, reel 33, NCLR.

96   Zieger, *John L. Lewis*, 114, 118, 132–147; Dubofsky and Van Tine, *John L. Lewis*, 417, 424–440.

97   Roche to Harold Ickes, Aug. 23, 1943; Albert L. Vogl to Office of Price Administra- tion, Oct. 5, 1943, folder 9, box 20, RC.

98   Roche and Springer to Newton, Feb. 29, 1944, folder 10, box 20, RC.

99   Ibid.

100   Ibid.

101   New caution: Roche to Elizabeth Magee, July 25, 1945, frame 158, reel 33, NCLR.

102   "Notice in the District Court of the U.S. for the District of Colorado in the Matter of RMFC, Debtor," July 10, 1944, folder 5, box 21, RC.

103   Roche to Mary van Kleeck, May 3, 1944, folder 16, box 28, MKP.

104   Roche to Mary van Kleeck, July 15, 1944, folder 16, box 28, MKP. Roche to Wilbur Newton, June 26, 1944, folder 10, box 20, RC.

105   Roche saw van Kleeck early on: Magee to Roche, May 6, 1944, frame 168, reel 33, NCLR.

106   Minutes, Board of Directors meeting, June 9, 1944, and Ballot of the NCL, 1944– 1945, both in frame 531, reel 2, NCLR. Full employment: Minutes, Board of Direc- tors meeting, May 22, 1945, frame 540, reel 2, NCLR.

107   Roche to Elizabeth Magee, July 25, 1944, frame 158, reel 33, NCLR. Roche to Wil- bur Newton, Oct. 20, 1944, folder 10, box 20, RC.

108   "New Unity Urged for Citizens of U.S.," *New York Times*, June 13, 1940, 16.

109   Common Council of American Unity (CCAU), "Mission Statement," *Common Ground*, Autumn 1940, inside front cover.

110   Colston and Leigh materials, folder 4, box 8, RC.

111   Minutes, Board of Directors meeting, Oct. 9, 1944, frame 534, reel 2, NCLR. CCAU's advocacy: see "Short Summary of Last Year's Activities," Notices and Agendas, 1944– 1945 folder, box 67, IRSA.

112   Roche to Hon. Jonathan Daniels, Assistant Director, Office of Civilian Defense, Apr. 3, 1942, folder 14, box 2, RC.

113   "Short Summary of Last Year's Activities," Notices and Agendas, 1944–1945 folder, box 67, IRSA. M. Margaret Anderson, "Get the Evacuees Out!" *Common Ground*, Summer 1943, 65–66.

114   "Display Ad," *New York Times*, Sept. 28, 1942, 9.

115   *Time Magazine*, Aug. 6, 1945, folder 6, box 21, RC.

116 Ibid.

117 "CF and I Goes into Hands of Receiver," *Rocky Mountain News*, Aug. 2, 1933, folder 7, box 17, RC.

118 Gerald R. Armstrong, telephone interview by author, Sept. 12, 2008.

CHAPTER 13   BECOMING A COLD WAR LIBERAL, 1945–1948

1 Paul Kellogg to Whom It May Concern, Sept. 12, 1945; HHC Prestige to HE Stebbins, Dec. 31, 1945; RB Shipley to Mr. Ambassador, Aug. 13, 1945; Mary van Kleeck to Whom It May Concern, Sept. 6, 1945, folder 2, box 44, RC.

2 See correspondence in folder 2, box 44, and folder 4, box 45, RC.

3 Roche to Mary van Kleeck, Feb. 17, 1946, folder 16, box 28, MKP.

4 Roche, "By Their French Bootstraps," *Survey Graphic*, Dec. 1945, 476, 494, folder 2, box 45, RC.

5 Ibid.

6 Ibid. H.H.C. Prestige to H. E. Stebbins, Dec. 31, 1945, folder 2, box 44, RC.

7 Roche, "Difficulties in French Coal Mining," *New York Herald Tribune*, Feb. 19,1946, folder 6, box 45; Roche, "By Their French Bootstraps."

8 Roche to Mary van Kleeck, Feb. 17, 1946, folder 16, box 28, MKP.

9 Negotiations between miners and the Coal Board did not begin until 1947 after Roche had completed her assignments. If she had studied the British coal industry a decade later, she might well have come to different conclusions. Kenneth O.Morgan, *Labour in Power 1945–1951* (Oxford, UK, 1984), 96–106. W. Kenneth Gratwick, "Labor Relations in Nationalized Industries with Particular Reference to the Coal Mining Industry," *Law and Contemporary Problems* 16 (Autumn 1951): 652–669; Sir Norman Chester, *The Nationalisation of British Industry, 1945–1951* (London, 1975), 747–803.

10 Sam Lusky, "Josephine Roche Praises France's Fight to Rebuild," *Rocky Mountain News*, Apr. 3, 1946, folder 6, box 45, RC.

11 Roche, "Productivity and Related Conditions in British Coal Mines during Pre-War Decade and Present Period," 1946, folder 16, box 28, MKP. See also Roche, "Britain's Coal: An Economic Issue," *New York Herald Tribune*, Jan. 15, 1946, and "British Coal—And Human Needs," *New York Herald Tribune*, Jan. 19, 1946, folder 6, box 45; "Coal—Touchstone of England's Recovery," *Survey Graphic*, Nov. 1946, and "Boys of the British Coal Pits," *Survey Graphic*, July 1946, folder 2, box 45, RC.

12 Roche to Mary van Kleeck, July 11, 1946, folder 16, box 28, MKP. See also "Final Decree in Matter of RMF Petitioner for Reorganization under Chapter 10," Mar. 1, 1946, folder 2, box 22, RC.

13 "Labor Rights Essential to Democracy," *Labor's Monthly Survey* (June 1946), folder 1, box 53, RC. For the oft-told UMW story, see, for instance, Melvyn Dubofsky and Warren Van Tine, *John L. Lewis: A Biography* (New York, 1977), 454–461.

14 National Bituminous Coal Wage Agreement of 1947, file 8, box 65, RC. Unsettled law: Beth Stevens, "Blurring the Boundaries: How the Federal Government Has Influenced Welfare Benefits in the Private Sector," in *The Politics of Social Policy in the United States*, ed. Margaret Weir, Anna Shola Orloff, and Theda Skocpol (Princeton, NJ, 1988), 141; Jacob S. Hacker, *The Divided Welfare State: The Battle over Public and Private Social Benefits in the United States* (New York, 2002), 129–132.

15 Unofficial consultation: Roche to Mrs. Esther Harlan, Sept. 8, 1952, folder 3, box 3, RC. Official hire: John L. Lewis to Mrs. Francis Fitzgerald, Nov. 22, 1947, folder 6, box 34, UMW Archives.

16 Roche to John L. Lewis, Nov. 24, 1947, folder 6, box 34, UMW Archives.
17 Much of this is captured in, for instance, Dorothy Sue Cobble, *The Other Women's Movement: Workplace Justice and Social Rights in Modern America* (Princeton, NJ, 2004), and Kim Phillips-Fein, *Invisible Hands: The Businessmen's Crusade against the New Deal* (New York, 2009).
18 Roche to John L. Lewis, Mar. 29, 1948, folder 6, box 34, UMW Archives.
19 John L. Lewis to Roche, Mar. 30, 1948, folder 6, box 34, UMW Archives.
20 Roche to John L. Lewis, Mar. 29, 1948, folder 6, box 34, UMW Archives.
21 William L. Laurence, "Health Assembly Sets Goals for U.S.," *New York Times*, May 4, 1948, 8.
22 *Official Report by the National Health Assembly* (New York, 1949), 216. Historians have argued over this point. Nelson Lichtenstein, "From Corporatism to Collective Bargaining: Organized Labor and the Eclipse of Social Democracy in the Postwar Era," in *Rise and Fall of the New Deal Order, 1930–1980*, ed. Steve Fraser and Gary Gerstle (Princeton, NJ, 1989), 122–152; Beth Stevens, "Labor Unions, Employee Benefits, and the Privatization of the American Welfare State," *Journal of Policy History* 2, no. 3 (1990): 232–260; Marie Gottschalk, "The Elusive Goal of Universal Health Care in the U.S.: Organized Labor and the Institutional Straightjacket of the Private Welfare State," *Journal of Policy History* 11, no. 4 (1999): 367–398; Alan Derickson, "Health Security for All? Social Unionism and Universal Health Insurance, 1935–1958," *Journal of American History* 80 (March 1994): 1333–1356; Nelson Lichtenstein, *State of the Union: A Century of American Labor* (Princeton, NJ, 2002), 123–127. Kevin Boyle, *The UAW and the Heyday of American Liberalism, 1945–1968* (Ithaca, NY, 1995), 1–9. Jennifer Klein, *For All These Rights: Business, Labor, and the Shaping of America's Public-Private Welfare State* (Princeton, NJ, 2003), 204–206.
23 Paul Starr, *The Social Transformation of American Medicine* (New York, 1982), 284–285.
24 Apr. 28, 1948: According to Roche's testimony before the Committee on Banking and Currency in the U.S. Senate on Aug. 1, 1949, folder 5, box 53, RC.
25 "Josephine Roche Appointed Miners' Pension Director," *Rocky Mountain News*, Apr. 29, 1948, folder 4, box 53, RC.
26 Landon R. Y. Storrs, *The Second Red Scare and the Unmaking of the New Deal Left* (Princeton, NJ, 2013). Doug Rossinow, *Visions of Progress: The Left-Liberal Tradition in America* (Philadelphia, 2008), 195–232.
27 Storrs, *Second Red Scare*.
28 Ellen Schrecker, *Many Are the Crimes: McCarthyism in America* (Princeton, NJ, 1998). Storrs, *Second Red Scare*.
29 Storrs, *Second Red Scare*, 52–53, 321, nn. 94 and 95, 229.
30 Landon R. Y. Storrs, *Civilizing Capitalism: The National Consumers' League, Women's Activism, and Labor Standards in the New Deal Era* (Chapel Hill, NC, 2000), n. 26, 349–350.
31 See van Kleeck's FBI file in folder 7, box 14, MKP.
32 Roche to the Ambassador of the Union of Soviet Socialist Republics and Madam Troyanovsky, Jan. 11, 1937, and Jan. 26, 1937, folder 7, box 34, RC.
33 Roche to Mrs. Elsie Elfenbein, Mar. 30, 1946; Norman Thomas to Roche, Apr. 10, 1946; Roche to Norman Thomas, Oct. 23, 1946; New Bulletin, Post War World Council, folder 15, box 6, RC.
34 Alan Derickson, "The House of Falk: The Paranoid Style in American Health Politics," *American Journal of Public Health* 87 (Nov. 1997): 1836–1843.
35 Schrecker, *Many Are the Crimes*, 190–200.

36 Gilbert J. Gall, *Pursuing Justice: Lee Pressman, the New Deal and the CIO* (Albany, 1999), chapter 8. Pressman's memory of introduction: Lee Pressman, "The Reminiscences of Lee Pressman," transcript of interview conducted by D. F. Shaughnessy, 1956–1958, Oral History Program, Columbia University, 25–26, microfiche edition.

37 Landon R. Y. Storrs, "Red Scare Politics and the Suppression of Popular Front Feminism: The Loyalty Investigation of Mary Dublin Keyserling," *Journal of American History* 90 (Sept. 2003): 491–524.

38 Transcript, Before the Loyalty Board, Department of Commerce, in the Matter of Mrs. Mary Dublin Keyserling, Aug. 24, 1948, entry #1001, NND 968093, box A170, Mary Dublin Keyserling, Oversize Personnel Security Investigation Case Files, 1928–1982, Civil Service Commission/Office of Federal Investigations, RG 478, Records of the Office of Personnel Management, NARA.

39 "New Group Plans Battle on Prices," *New York Times*, Jan. 18, 1947, 12.

40 Other evidence: Read Lewis, "Combating Anti-American Propaganda Abroad through U.S. Foreign Language Press and Nationality Groups," 1947, Notices and Agendas, 1946–1947 folder; Read Lewis to Board, Dec. 2, 1947, Notices and Agendas, 1946–1947 folder; Minutes, Board of Directors meeting, Nov. 24, 1948, Notices and Agendas, 1948 folder; "Brief Report of Activities for the Week Ending Oct. 29, 1949," 1949 folder, box 67, IRSA. W. Colston Leigh, brochure, "Josephine Roche," 1944–1946, folder 2, box 8, RC.

41 "UMW Welfare Fund Director Knows Her Job," *New York Herald Tribune*, June 13, 1948, folder 4, box 53, RC.

42 "In Goldfish Bowl," *Business Week*, May 22, 1948, folder 4, box 53, RC.

43 Roche testimony before the Committee on Banking and Currency in the U.S. Senate, Aug. 1, 1949, folder 5, box 53, RC.

44 For many other examples, see Storrs, *Second Red Scare*.

45 "Treasury Department Press Release," Jan. 12, 1935, folder 3, box 36, RC.

46 Narrowed parameters of the critique of racial injustice: Mary L. Dudziak, *Cold War Civil Rights: Race and the Image of American Democracy* (Princeton, NJ, 2000), 11–13; Penny M. Von Eschen, *Race against Empire: Black Americans and Anticolonialism, 1937–1957* (Ithaca, NY, 1997), 112–121; Carol Anderson, *Eyes off the Prize: The United Nations and the African American Struggle for Human Rights, 1944–1955* (New York, 2003), 5–7; Patricia Sullivan, *Days of Hope: Race and Democracy in the New Deal Era* (Chapel Hill, NC, 1996), 220–275. Split between consumers and labor: Meg Jacobs, *Pocketbook Politics: Economic Citizenship in Twentieth-Century America* (Princeton, NJ, 2005), 10–11.

CHAPTER 14   CREATING "NEW VALUES, NEW REALITIES" IN THE COALFIELDS, 1948–1956

1 Roche's remarks at the UMW convention, Oct. 8, 1956, Cincinnati, Ohio, folder 2, box 49, RC.

2 Roche to Martha Eliot, Sept. 1951, folder 170, box 12, Martha May Eliot Papers, Arthur and Elizabeth Schlesinger Library on the History of Women, Radcliffe Institute for Advanced Study, Harvard University, Cambridge, MA. Beyer: May 13 and May 14, 1965, spiral notebook, box 46, RC.

3 Oscar Chapman called Roche "one of the most brilliant people, man or woman, that I ever worked with." in Oscar L. Chapman, Oral History Transcript, Feb. 2, 1973, Washington, DC, by Jerry Hess for the Truman Library, www.trumanlibrary.org/oralhist /chapman15.htm, accessed Feb. 15, 2014.

4 For example, "Memo to File," Feb. 20, [1949], folder 7; Roche to Lewis, Nov. 9, 1949, folder 7; conference notes, Oscar Chapman, Sept. 28, 1951, folder 8; Roche to Lewis, Feb. 1952, folder 7; phone conference notes, Mar. 2, 1953, folder 9; Roche to Lewis, Oct. 5, 1951, folder 7, box 63, RC.

5 Fund, annual report, 1951, folder 2, box 52, RC.

6 A. H. Raskin, "New Medical Plan Set Up for Miners," *New York Times*, Oct. 7, 1948, 25.

7 *Digest of the Medical Survey of the Bituminous Coal Industry Made in 1946–47 by the U.S. Government*, folder 2, box 53, RC.

8 "Labor Rights Essential to Democracy," *Labor's Monthly Survey*, 1946, reprint, box 53, folder 1, RC.

9 Fund, annual report, 1959, folder 2, box 52, RC.

10 Roche, "Chronology of the U.M.W.A. Welfare and Retirement Fund, Covering the Period between 1945 and April 26, 1951," appendix B, Fund, annual report, 1951, folder 2, box 52, RC (hereafter "Chronology").

11 "Pension Service Claim Manual," "Instructions to Districts in Regard to Pensions," "Rules and Regulations Governing the Disability Benefits of the UMWA Welfare and Retirement Fund," box 2, Administrative File, FA. "Chronology."

12 Roche, "Progress Report for Trustees," Nov. 10, 1948, box 1, Board of Trustees Correspondence, Director's File, FA.

13 Ibid.

14 Ibid. Roche's testimony before the Senate Banking and Currency Committee, Aug. 1949, folder 5, box 53; Ruth Q. Sun, "Mine Workers Served by Unique Health Plan," *GP*, May 1953, folder 9, box 63, RC.

15 Quotes are from Roche's testimony before the Senate Banking and Currency Committee, Aug. 1949, folder 5, box 53, RC.

16 Roche to All Services, Nov. 22, 1948; Nov. 10, 1948; Oct. 26, 1948; Dec. 11, 1948; Apr. 13, 1949, Administration folder, box 34, Subject Files, Executive Medical Officer File, FA. Sundays: Roche to Read Lewis, Nov. 20, 1950, RLP.

17 William E. Owens, interview by author, Ellicott City, MD, May 26, 2005.

18 Towers, Perrin, Forster, and Crosby, "Final Report," Mar. 12, 1948, box 1, Actuary and Insurance Company Data, Director's File, FA.

19 Roche to Lewis, Nov. 18, 1948, box 2, Actuary and Insurance Company Data, Director's File, FA.

20 Ibid.

21 Roche to Lewis, Aug. 8, 1949, box 1, Board of Trustees Correspondence, Director's File, FA.

22 Roche, Memo, no date, box 2, Actuary and Insurance Company Data, Director's File, FA.

23 Alice Kessler-Harris, *In Pursuit of Equity: Women, Men, and the Quest for Economic Citizenship in 20th-Century America* (New York, 2001), 142, 149.

24 Roche to Lewis, Aug. 8, 1949, box 1, Board of Trustees Correspondence, Director's File, FA.

25 Kim Phillips-Fein, *Invisible Hands: The Businessmen's Crusade against the New Deal* (New York, 2009), chapter 1.

26 Roche to Lewis, Aug. 8, 1949, and all attachments, box 1, Board of Trustees Correspondence, Director's File, FA.

27 Roche to Lewis, Nov. 19, 1948, box 2, Actuary and Insurance Company Data, Director's File, FA.

28 Roche to Lewis, Mar. 30, 1949, box 1, Board of Trustees Correspondence, Director's File, FA.

29 Conference notes, Meeting with Area Medical Directors, Jan. 27, 1958, folder 2, box 55, RC.

30 Styles Bridges to Roche, Nov. 8, 1949, and attachment, box 1, Board of Trustees Correspondence, Director's File, FA. Roche to Lewis, May 20, 1948; Roche to Lewis, Feb. 28, 1949, box 1, Board of Trustees Correspondence, Director's File, FA.

31 Lewis's note on "Tribute of Recognition to Josephine Roche from the American Labor Health Association," June 17, 1958, folder 1, box 10, RC.

32 Evelyn Peyton Gordon, gossip column, *Washington Daily News*, Oct. 6, 1955, folder 4, box 53, RC.

33 Patterns of conferring are evident in Mildred Lea's spiral notebooks, box 46, RC.

34 A. H. Raskin, "UMW Fund Grants $2,000,000 Weekly," *New York Times*, Mar. 29, 1949, 28.

35 Ibid.

36 A. H. Raskin, "Pensions Handicap Job Shifts in War," *New York Times*, July 3, 1950, 6. Lewis to Roche, Dec. 22, 1949, and Jan. 25, 1950, and all attachments, box 1, Board of Trustees Correspondence, Director's File, FA. See also "Chronology."

37 "Chronology."

38 Styles Bridges to Ezra Van Horn, Nov. 7, 1949; Truman Johnson to Trustees, Nov. 3, 1949, box 1, Board of Trustees Correspondence, Director's File, FA.

39 Truman Johnson to Trustees, Nov. 3, 1949; Roche to Lewis, Dec. 5, 1949; Statement by Charles Dawson, Dec. 19, 1949; Lewis to Roche, Dec. 22, 1949; Board of Trustees Correspondence, Director's File, FA. "Chronology."

40 A. H. Raskin, "Pensions Handicap Job Shifts in War." Lewis to Roche, Dec. 22, 1949, and Jan. 25, 1950, and all attachments, box 1, Board of Trustees Correspondence, Director's File, FA. "Chronology."

41 Memos, Roche to Lewis, Feb. 20, 1950, and Feb. 24, 1950, folder 7, box 63, RC.

42 Sam Stavisky, "Prosecution Was Deliberately Weak, Taft Says, Asking Inquiry," *Washington Post*, Mar. 3, 1950, 1ff.

43 Memos, Roche to Lewis, Feb. 20, 1950, and Feb. 24, 1950, folder 7, box 63, RC. "Chronology." Melvyn Dubofsky and Warren Van Tine, *John L. Lewis: A Biography* (New York, 1977), 488–489.

44 "Chronology." Public's view of Roche: "Main Points in New Soft Coal Wage Contract," *Washington Post*, Mar. 6, 1950, 1; "UMW's Welfare Fund Administrative Autocracy," *Washington Post*, Sept. 9, 1950, 9.

45 "Chronology." See also Dubofsky and Van Tine, *John L. Lewis*, 489.

46 Barbara Ellen Smith, *Digging Our Own Graves: Coal Miners and the Struggle over Black Lung Disease* (Philadelphia, 1987), 59.

47 "Supplement to Chronology," Jan. 11, 1960, folder 3, box 51, RC.

48 Roche to Lewis, Apr. 19, 1950; May 6, 1950; May 26, 1950; Aug. 8, 1950, with attachments; Oct. 3, 1950, with attachments; May 3, 1951, box 1, Board of Trustees Correspondence, Director's File, FA. List of correspondence from Charles Owen to Roche as of May 31, 1950, box 6, Board of Trustees Correspondence, Director's File, FA.

49 Charles Owen to Roche and Lewis, June 16, 1950; Charles Owen to Lewis, Aug. 2, 1950; Charles Owen to Val Mitch, July 24, 1950; Charles Owen to Lewis, Dec. 17, 1950; Roche to Lewis, May 8, 1951, box 6, Board of Trustees Correspondence, Director's File, FA.

50 "Chronology."

51 "Meeting of District Presidents," May 2, 1950, folder 5, box 34, UMW Archives.

52 Ibid.

53 "Chronology." "Supplement to Chronology," Jan. 11, 1960, folder 3, box 51, RC.

54   Fund, annual report, 1951, folder 2, box 52; press release, Jan. 21, 1954, folder 9, box 63, RC.

55   Roche to Read Lewis, Nov. 20, 1950, RLP. Letters of resignation, folder 4, box 22, RC.

56   Roche to "Lube," Sept. 19, 1958, folder 5, box 64, RC.

57   Trends: Spiral notebooks kept by Mildred Lea, box 46, RC.

58   1952 and June 1959, spiral notebooks, box 46, RC. Roche to Mrs. Bruce Baird, Aug. 22, 1967, folder 1, box 65, RC. List of addresses in box 8, Board of Trustees Correspondence, Director's File, FA.

59   Dubofsky and Van Tine, *John L. Lewis*, 498–501, 494–495. Richard P. Mulcahy, *A Social Contract for the Coal Fields: The Rise and Fall of the United Mine Workers of America Welfare and Retirement Fund* (Knoxville, TN, 2000), 33–36, 57.

60   Dubofsky and Van Tine, *John L. Lewis*, 489–513.

61   "Supplement to Chronology," Jan. 11, 1960, folder 3, box 51, RC. "UMW Pyramid Nickels into a Billion," *Washington Post*, Sept. 4, 1955, E1. Robert J. Myers, "Further Experience of the UMWA Welfare and Retirement Fund," *Industrial and Labor Relations Review* 14 (July 1961): 556–562 confirms that the fund was one of the largest private benefit plans in the United States in 1960–1961.

62   "Report of the Third Conference on Medical Care in the Bituminous Coal Mine Area," Oct. 23–24, 1954, folder 1, box 53, RC (hereafter "Report of the Third Conference"). A. H. Raskin, "Pensions Handicap Job Shifts in War," *New York Times*, July 3, 1950, 6. Lower infant and maternal mortality rates: Fund, annual report, 1952, folder 2, box 52, RC.

63   "Supplement to Chronology," Jan. 11, 1960, folder 3, box 51, RC.

64   Fund, annual report, 1951, folder 2, box 52, RC.

65   "Statement by Officers of the Medical Service of the UMW Welfare and Retirement Fund Concerning Necessity of Additional Hospital Facilities in Coal Mining Areas," Oct. 8, 1951, folder 2, box 65, RC. See also Harry M. Caudill, *Night Comes to the Cumberlands: A Biography of a Depressed Area* (Boston, 1962), 294.

66   "Statement by Officers of the Medical Service of the UMW Welfare and Retirement Fund Concerning Necessity of Additional Hospital Facilities in Coal Mining Areas," Oct. 8, 1951, folder 2, box 65, RC. "Report of the Third Conference."

67   Appendectomies: Warren Draper, "The Medical Care Program of the UMWA Welfare and Retirement Fund," New England Hospital Assembly, Boston, MA, Mar. 25, 1958, folder 2, box 53, RC. Tonsillectomies: "Supplement to Chronology," Jan. 11, 1960, folder 3, box 51, RC.

68   "Report of the Third Conference."

69   Fund, annual report, 1954, folder 2, box 52, RC.

70   Smith, *Digging Our Own Graves*, 25–30, 63. Alan Derickson, *Black Lung: Anatomy of a Public Health Disaster* (Ithaca, NY, 1998), 112–142.

71   "Report of the Third Conference."

72   "Labor's War with the Doctors," *Business Week*, 1958, folder 1, box 64, RC.

73   Progressive Era developments: Paul Starr, *The Social Transformation of American Medicine* (New York, 1982), 194–196, 213, 247–248, 265.

74   Minutes of Committee on Medical Care, Nov. 20, 1937, n.f., box 43, Records of the Interdepartmental Committee to Coordinate Health and Welfare Activities, FDRL. Michael Davis to Isidore Falk, June 29, 1938, folder 2269, box 157; Michael Davis documents in folder 2250, box 156; Michael Davis to Isidore Falk, Dec. 17, 1938, folder 2270, box 157, Isidore Falk Papers, Manuscripts and Archives, Sterling Memorial Library, Yale University, New Haven, CT. Roche to Mary Dublin, July 18, 1939, frame 217, reel 33; Minutes, Board of Directors meeting, May 9, 1939, frame 445, reel 2; Minutes, Board of Directors meeting, Sept. 12, 1939, reel 2, Records of the National

Consumers League, microfilm, Manuscript Reading Room, Library of Congress, Washington, DC. Roche folder, box 71, Michael Davis Collection, New York Academy of Medicine Library, Archives and Manuscripts, New York City, New York. Warren Draper to Area Medical Administrators, June 10, 1954, box 31, Subject files, Executive Medical Officer File, FA.

75 Starr, *Social Transformation of American Medicine*, 111, 318.

76 Ibid., 285.

77 Ibid., 306.

78 "Report of the Third Conference."

79 "Report of the Third Conference."

80 "Statement by Officers of the Medical Service of the UMWA Welfare and Retirement Fund Concerning Necessity of Additional Hospital Facilities in Coal Mining Areas," Oct. 8, 1951; Statement presented to Trustees by Roche, Oct. 10, 1951, folder 2, box 65, RC.

81 "Supplement to Chronology," Jan. 11, 1960, folder 3, box 51; "John Lewis's 250-Mile Chain of Hospitals," *U.S. News and World Report*, Oct. 7, 1955, folder 1, box 53, RC.

82 Houses: Dec. 27, 1955, spiral notebook, box 46, RC.

83 Worries about competing for workers: "John Lewis's 250-Mile Chain of Hospitals," *U.S. News and World Report*, Oct. 7, 1955, folder 1, box 53, RC; Nate Haseltine, "Ten Hospitals for Miners Are Dedicated by Lewis," *Washington Post*, June 3, 1956, A1.

84 Roche dovetailed her programs wherever possible with public programs. Warren Draper to Area Medical Administrators, Mar. 1, 1951, box 31, and Draper to Area Medical Administrators, Mar. 12, 1956, box 29, Subject Files, Executive Medical Officer File, FA.

85 Roche to Lewis, Apr. 6, 1953, box 10, UMWA Correspondence, Director's File, FA. Murray Kempton, "Hobby's Lobby," *New York Post*, Apr. 1, 1953, 38.

86 Documents in box 10, UMWA Correspondence, Director's File, FA. Roche's remarks at UMWA convention, Oct. 5, 1960, Cincinnati, Ohio, folder 3, box 49, RC.

87 Warren Draper to Area Medical Administrators, Sept. 11, 1952, box 29, Subject Files, Executive Medical Officer File, FA.

88 Speeches, Dedication of Miners' Memorial Hospitals, June 2, 1956, folder 2, box 53, RC.

89 Ira Wolfert, "The Miners' Fund: A Tribute to Good Management," *Reader's Digest*, Sept. 1956, reprint, folder 1, box 53, RC; Howard A. Rusk, "Hospitals for Miners," *New York Times*, June 3, 1956, 78. "Glassiest hospital": Haseltine, "Ten Hospitals for Miners Are Dedicated by Lewis," A1.

90 Fund, annual report, 1959, folder 2, box 52, RC.

91 "Supplement to Chronology," Jan. 11, 1960, folder 3, box 51, RC.

92 Wolfert, "The Miners' Fund: A Tribute to Good Management"; Howard A. Rusk, "Hospitals for Miners," *New York Times*, June 3, 1956, 77.

93 Haseltine, "Ten Hospitals for Miners Are Dedicated by Lewis."

94 "Supplement to Chronology," Jan. 11, 1960, folder 3, box 51, RC. See also Robert J. Myers, "Further Experience of the UMWA Welfare and Retirement Fund," *Industrial and Labor Relations Review* 14 (July 1961): 556–562.

95 "Supplement to Chronology," Jan. 11, 1960, folder 3, box 51, RC.

96 Senate Subcommittee on Welfare and Pension Funds, *Final Report on Welfare and Pension Plans*, 1956, folder 3, box 54, RC.

97 Dr. Hugh Leavell to Roche, Sept. 26, 1958, folder 5, box 64, RC.

98 "Tribute of Recognition to Josephine Roche from the American Labor Health Association for Her Work at the UMW's Welfare and Retirement Fund," June 17, 1958, folder 1, box 10, RC.

99   Roche to Mr. P. R., Jan. 12, 1959, and attachment, box 11, UMWA Correspondence, Director's File, FA. USIA: Lewis to Roche, Sept. 15, 1959, folder 1, box 65, RC. Visitors from Mexico and Europe: spiral notebooks, July 1952, July 1956, Sept. 1956, box 46, RC.

100   "Labor's War with the Doctors," *Business Week*, 1958, folder 1, box 64, RC.

101   Wolfert, "The Miners' Fund: A Tribute to Good Management."

102   Sun, "Mine Workers Served by Unique Health Plan."

103   Ivana Krajcinovic, *From Company Doctors to Managed Care: The United Mine Workers' Noble Experiment* (Ithaca, NY, 1997), 173–175.

104   Fund, annual report, 1955, folder 2, box 52, RC.

105   Wolfert, "The Miners' Fund: A Tribute to Good Management"; Sun, "Mine Workers Served by Unique Health Plan."

106   Wolfert, "The Miners' Fund: A Tribute to Good Management"; Sun, "Mine Workers Served by Unique Health Plan," RC. Senate Subcommittee on Welfare and Pension Funds, *Final Report on Welfare and Pension Plans*, 1956, folder 3, box 54, RC.

107   Arthur Altmeyer to Roche, Mar. 18, 1952, folder 4, box 1, RC.

108   Office of public information: Charles Owen to Lewis, Dec. 17, 1950, box 6, Board of Trustees Correspondence, Director's File, FA. PR expert: "George Creel, Josephine Roche," *Rocky Mountain News*, Apr. 29, 1949, folder 4, box 53, RC. Letters in folder 7, box 63, RC. "Deeply moving": Ben M. Cherrington to Roche, Sept. 9, 1966, folder 4, box 2, RC.

109   Roche to Lewis, June 11, 1951, folder 7, box 63, RC.

110   Fund, annual reports from the 1950s, folder 2, box 52, RC.

111   Multiple drafts: Roche to Lewis, Sept. 14, 1951, folder 8, box 63, RC. Widespread circulation: Fund, annual report, 1955, folder 2, box 52, RC, and correspondence in folder 5, box 64, RC. Finest photographers: See photos by Fred Maroon, folder 24, box 2, Robert Kaplan Papers, Manuscripts and Archives, Sterling Memorial Library, Yale University, New Haven, CT.

112   Ellen Schrecker, *Many Are the Crimes: McCarthyism in America* (Princeton, NJ, 1998), 264–265.

113   Notes on conferences, Dec. 20, 1956, folder 2, box 55, RC.

114   "Supplement to Chronology," Jan. 11, 1960, folder 3, box 51, RC.

CHAPTER 15   DEMOCRATIC DENIALS AND DISSENT AT THE MINERS' WELFARE FUND, 1957–1963

1   Wallace Croatman, "Is Labor Through with Private Medicine?" *Medical Economics* (Oct. 1957): 175.

2   See, for instance, Fund, annual report, 1959, folder 2, box 52, RC.

3   See, for instance, "Statement of John L. Lewis before the Subcommittee on Welfare and Pension Funds of the U.S. Senate on Labor and Public Welfare," Nov. 28, 1955, folder 8, box 51, RC.

4   Ivana Krajcinovic, *From Company Doctors to Managed Care: The United Mine Workers' Noble Experiment* (Ithaca, NY, 1997), 79.

5   Conference notes, Conference of Area Administrators, Dec. 20, 1956, folder 2, box 55, RC.

6   Allen Koplin to Dr. Joseph Collings, Sept. 29, 1952, box 29, Subject Files, Executive Medical Officer File, FA. Conference notes, Apr. 2, 1957, Mar. 27, 1957, folder 2; conference notes, July 12, 1962, folder 3, box 55, RC.

7   Fund, annual report, 1968, folder 3, box 52, RC.

8 "Papers and Proceedings of the First National Conference on Labor Health Services," Mayflower Hotel, June 16–17, 1958, folder 4, box 54, RC. On some of these experiments and the AFL-CIO's financial support, see Wallace Croatman, "Is Labor Through with Private Medicine?" *Medical Economics* (Oct. 1957): 174–196. Conference notes, Oct. 30, 1956, folder 2, box 55, RC.

9 May 26, 1959, spiral notebook, box 46, RC.

10 Democratic Advisory Committee, News Release, Apr. 4, 1960, folder 10, box 2, MSS 400, Arthur Altmeyer Collection, State Historical Society of Wisconsin, copies in SSA.

11 Roche speech, *Daily Minutes of the 43rd Consecutive Constitutional Convention of the UMWA,* Oct. 5, 1960, Cincinnati, Ohio, 8, folder 3, box 49, RC. Democratic Advisory Council, News Release, May 12, 1960, folder 10, box 2, MSS 400, Arthur Altmeyer Collection.

12 "Background on Medicare, 1957–1962," bound volumes, SSA.

13 Conference notes, May 6, 1960, and May 10, 1960, folder 2, box 55, RC.

14 Ibid. A complete collection of proposals is in "Background on Medicare, 1957–1962," vols. 1 and 2, SSA. Evidence of Roche's continuing participation is in June 10, June 29, and Aug. 16, 1960, spiral notebook, box 46, RC. "Democratic Party Platform of 1960," Political Party Platforms, The American Presidency Project, University of California, Santa Barbara, http://www.presidency.ucsb.edu/ws/index.php?pid=29602#axzz1wBa1Bh3v, accessed Feb. 15, 2014.

15 See, for instance, Mar. 18, May 7, May 21, 1952, and entries throughout 1958, spiral notebooks, box 46, RC. See Roche's addresses to conventions of the UMW in, for instance, 1952, folder 1, box 49, and 1964, folder 3, box 50, RC.

16 Roche to Mrs. D. C., Dec. 6, 1956, box 2, Director's Correspondence, Director's File, FA.

17 Roche speech, *Daily Minutes of the 43rd Consecutive Constitutional Convention of the UMWA,* Oct. 5, 1956, Cincinnati, Ohio, 9, folder 3, box 49, RC.

18 List of staff at the Miners' Memorial Hospitals in Fund, annual report, 1959, folder 2, box 52, RC. Most importantly, see Albert Deutsch, ms on the fund's health system, 78–79h, folder 23, box 2, Robert Kaplan Papers, Manuscripts and Archives, Sterling Library, Yale University, New Haven, CT.

19 Officers of Local Union 4346 to Henry Schmidt, Oct. 20, 1959, Schmidt folders, box 8, Board of Trustees Correspondence, Director's File, FA.

20 Ibid.

21 Roche to the Officers of Local Union 4346, Oct. 26, 1959, Schmidt folders, box 8, Board of Trustees Correspondence, Director's File, FA.

22 Hospitals flooded in 1957 were Pikeville, Williamson, and Hazard Memorial Hospitals. "Supplement to Chronology," Jan. 11, 1960, folder 3, box 51, RC.

23 See, for example, spiral notebooks for Apr. 14, 1958–Sept. 19, 1958, and Jan. 22, 1957–July 3, 1957, box 46, RC.

24 June 5, 1957, and Feb. 10, 1959, spiral notebooks, box 46, RC.

25 William E. Owens, interview by author, May 26, 2005, Ellicott City, MD. Entries in spiral notebooks throughout the 1950s show Roche helping Bill gain admission to colleges. See spiral notebooks, box 46, RC. Feb. 19, 1957, and Feb. 21, 1957, spiral notebooks, box 46, RC.

26 For instance, Aug. 25, 1965, spiral notebooks, box 46, RC. For descriptions of Garfinkel's, see "The Metropolist," *Washington Post*, Aug. 21, 2008, B3.

27 Owens interview.

28 Melvyn Dubofsky and Warren Van Tine, *John L. Lewis: A Biography* (New York, 1977), 494–496.

29 Sept. 25, 1958, spiral notebook, box 46, RC.

30 Conference notes, Feb. 25, 1959, folder 2, box 55, RC.

31 Conference notes, Apr. 13, 1960, folder 2, box 55, RC.

32 Fund, annual report, 1959, folder 2, box 52, RC.

33 See, for instance, Mar. 23, 1959, and Apr. 6, 1959, spiral notebook, box 46, RC.

34 "Supplement to Chronology," Jan. 11, 1960, folder 3, box 51, RC.

35 Conference notes, Apr. 13, 1960, folder 2, box 55, RC.

36 Ibid. Richard P. Mulcahy, *A Social Contract for the Coalfields: The Rise and Fall of the United Mine Workers of America Welfare and Retirement Fund* (Knoxville, TN, 2000), 129–130.

37 Conference notes, Apr. 13, 1960, folder 2, box 55, RC. For a parallel story in anthracite coal, see Thomas Dublin and Walter Licht, *The Face of Decline: The Pennsylvania Anthracite Region in the Twentieth Century* (Ithaca, NY, 2005).

38 Conference notes, May 4, 1960, folder 2, box 55, RC.

39 July 1, July 6, July 28, and July 29, 1960, spiral notebook, box 46, RC. *Proceedings of the 43rd Consecutive Constitutional Convention of the UMWA,* vol. 2, Oct. 4–11, 1960, Cincinnati, OH, 34–35, folder 3, box 49, RC.

40 Roche to Lewis, Nov. 21, 1960, Lewis folders, box 1, Board of Trustees Correspondence, Director's File, FA.

41 "Supplement to Chronology," Jan. 11, 1960, folder 3, box 51, RC.

42 For sense of falling behind, see Jock Yablonski quoted in Trevor Armbrister, *Act of Vengeance: The Yablonski Murders and Their Solution* (New York, 1975), 145.

43 Fund, annual report, 1961, folder 3, box 52, RC.

44 See, for instance, Committee for Miners, "Eastern Kentucky Background Sheet," [late 1963 or early 1964], Committee for Miners folder, box 9, Subject Files, 1961–1965, Records of the Office of the Administrator, ARA Records, RG 378, NARA (hereafter ARA Records).

45 Conference notes, Feb. 24, 1960, folder 2, box 55, RC.

46 Conference notes, July 31, 1962, folder 3, box 55; conference notes, Nov. 7, 1962, folder 1, box 56, RC. Harry M. Caudill, *Night Comes to the Cumberlands: A Biography of a Depressed Area* (Boston, 1962), 327. See also Lewis v. Coleman, 257 F. *Supp.* 38 (1966), Civ. A. No. 709, United States District Court S.D. West Virginia Bluefield Division, July 25, 1966.

47 Conference notes, Aug. 24, 1962, folder 1, box 56, RC.

48 Conference notes, Aug. 2, 1962, folder 1, box 56, RC. Against legal counsel: conference notes, Aug. 24, 1962, folder 1, box 56, RC.

49 Conference notes, Aug. 13, 1962, folder 1, box 56, RC.

50 Conference notes, Aug. 15, 16, and 24, 1962, folder 1, box 56, RC.

51 Committee for Miners, "Eastern Kentucky Background Sheet," [late Dec. 1963 or early Jan. 1964], Committee for Miners folder, box 9, Subject Files, 1961–1965, Records of the Office of the Administrator, ARA Records.

52 See, for example, conference notes, Nov. 6, 1962, folder 1, box 56, RC. For the miners' feelings: Kate Black, "The Roving Picket Movement and the Appalachian Committee for Full Employment, 1959–1965: A Narrative," *Journal of the Appalachian Studies Association* 2 (1990): 114.

53 Conference notes, Nov. 6, 1962, folder 1, box 56, RC.

54 The failure to uncover Roche's knowledge began with *Blankenship v. Boyle* in 1971. See Decision of Judge Gerhard Gesell in the case, Apr. 28, 1971, 14, http://www.lexis nexis.com.proxy-um.researchport.umd.edu/hottopics/lnacademic/?, accessed Feb. 15, 2014. Dubofsky and Van Tine, *John L. Lewis,* 519; Mulcahy, *Social Contract for the Coal Fields,* 133–134; Ivana Krajcinovic, *From Company Doctors to Managed Care,*

154; Caudill, *Night Comes to the Cumberlands*, 328; Brit Hume, *Death and the Mines: Rebellion and Murder in the United Mine Workers* (New York, 1971), 32–33.

55 The exception is Mulcahy, *Social Contract for the Coal Fields.*

56 Norman Walker, "John L. Lewis Proudly Cites Benefits of Welfare Fund to His Mine Workers," *News-Sentinel*, Knoxville, TN, Sept. 25, 1955, VAO.

57 Conference notes, Nov. 6, 1962, and Nov. 7, 1962, folder 1, box 56, RC.

58 See, for instance, conference notes, Sept. 5, Sept. 21, and Sept. 27, 1962, folder 1, box 56, RC.

59 Roche to Lewis, Nov. 14, 1960; conference notes, Aug. 20, 1963; memo of evening telephone conference between Lewis and Roche, Sept. 19, 1963, West Kentucky Coal Company folder, box 3, UMWA Correspondence, Director's File, FA. When Roche and the fund were taken to court in 1971, this episode was uncovered, and Judge Gerhard Gesell actually did not hold Roche's and Lewis's behavior to be unlawful because they ultimately got the royalties paid. Decision of Judge Gerhard Gesell in *Blankenship v. Boyle*, 14, http://www.lexisnexis.com.proxy-um.researchport.umd.edu /hottopics/lnacademic/?, accessed Feb. 15, 2014.

60 For instance, spiral notebooks documenting the last six months of 1957 and summer of 1958, box 46, RC. Specific entries possibly referring to sham contracts: July 31, 1957; Dec. 10, 1957; June 4, 1958; July 17, 1958, box 46, RC.

61 Conference notes, Feb. 4, 1959, and Mar. 2, 1962, folder 2, box 55; Nov. 13, 1956, spiral notebook, box 46, RC. Clipping, *KAGP Journal*, Jan. 1963, Appalachian Regional Hospitals Background Material—1962–1963, Special Session 1963 folder, Appalachian Regional Hospitals File, Office of the Commissioner, Department of Finance, Commonwealth of Kentucky, Department for Libraries and Archives, Frankfort, Kentucky.

62 "Supplement to Chronology," Jan. 11, 1960, folder 3, box 51, RC. Julius Duscha, "Miners Fight for Last 'Possession,'" *Washington Post*, Jan. 20, 1963, E1.

63 Homer Bigart, "Aid Drive Pushed for Appalachia," *New York Times*, Nov. 19, 1963, 16. Draft of argument for supporting hospitals, June 2, 1963, Appalachian Regional Hospitals Background Material, 1962–1963, Special Session 1963 folder, Appalachian Regional Hospitals File, Office of the Commissioner, Department of Finance, Commonwealth of Kentucky, Department for Libraries and Archives, Frankfort, Kentucky.

64 Julius Duscha, "Miners Fight for Last 'Possession,'" *Washington Post*, Jan. 20, 1963, E1. Statistics since 1957: Caudill, *Night Comes to the Cumberlands*, 267.

65 Kate Black, "The Roving Picket Movement," 116. Violence: Homer Bigart, "Aid Drive Pushed for Appalachia," *New York Times*, Nov. 19, 1963, 16ff. Marjorie Kester, "The Miners' Memorial Hospitals in Eastern KY," Apr. 19, 1963, Regional Hospital Corporation folder, box 5, Office of the Assistant Administrator for Area Operations, Mixed Subject and Programs Files, 1961–1963, ARA Records. Committee for Miners, "Eastern Kentucky Background Sheet" and "The Miners' Movement Background Details," [late Dec. 1963 or early Jan. 1964], Committee for Miners folder, box 9, Subject Files, 1961–1965, Records of the Office of the Administrator, ARA Records.

66 "A Splendid and Christian Act of Mercy," *Presbyterian Life*, Aug. 1, 1963, clipping, and Julius Duscha, "U.S. Set to Help Church Save UMW Hospitals," *Washington Post*, Apr. 27, 1963, clipping, Miners Memorial Hospitals folder, box 9, Subject Files, 1961–1965, Records of the Office of the Administrator, ARA Records. "Most precious asset": Caudill, *Night Comes to the Cumberlands*, 393–394.

67 Quoted in Julius Duscha, "Miners Fight for Last 'Possession,'" *Washington Post*, Jan. 20, 1963, E1.

68 Committee for Miners, "The Miner's Movement Background Details," n.d., Committee for Miners folder, Subject Files, 1961–1965, Records of the Office of the Administrator, ARA Records. Robyn Muncy, "Coal-Fired Reforms," *Journal of American History* 96 (June 2009): 72–98.

69 Julius Duscha, "Miners Fight for Last 'Possession,' " *Washington Post*, Jan. 20, 1963, E1.

70 See, for instance, Letter, July 1964, Kentucky folder, box 15, Subject Files, 1961–1965, Records of the Office of the Administrator, ARA Records.

71 Committee for Miners, press release, Nov. 18, 1963, Committee for Miners folder, Subject Files, 1961–1965, Records of the Office of the Administrator, ARA Records.

72 Committee for Miners, "The Miners' Movement Background Details," n.d., Committee for Miners folder, box 9, Subject Files, 1961–1965, Records of the Office of the Administrator, ARA Records.

73 "Committee for Miners," Feb. 1964, Committee for Miners folder, box 9, Subject Files, 1961–1965, Records of the Office of the Administrator, ARA Records.

74 Fund, annual report, 1963, folder 3, box 52, RC. Robert Barrie to Roche, Feb. 1, 1963, Appalachian Regional Hospitals Miscellaneous Information folder, Appalachian Regional Hospitals File, Office of the Commissioner, Department of Finance, Commonwealth of Kentucky, Department of Libraries and Archives, Frankfort, Kentucky. Muncy, "Coal-Fired Reforms," 72–98.

75 Michael Harrington, *The Other America: Poverty in the United States* (New York, 1962), 57–58. Julius Duscha, "Can Life Begin at 40 for a Nation's Jobless?" *Washington Post*, June 18, 1961, E3.

76 Quotation is from "Justification for ARA Assistance for Purchase of UMW Hospitals," [1963], Regional Hospital Corporation folder, box 5, Mixed Subject and Programs Files, 1961–1963, Records of the Office of Assistant Administrator for Area Operations, ARA Records.

77 "Statement by the President," [early 1963], Miners' Memorial Hospitals folder, box 9, Subject Files, 1961–1965, Records of the Office of the Administrator, ARA Records.

78 Conference notes, July 23, 1963, folder 2, box 56; conference notes, Mar. 15, 1965, and Apr. 14, 1965, folder 3, box 56; Apr. 1, 1965, Apr. 14, 1965, June 8, 1965, and June 18, 1965, spiral notebook, box 46, RC. "Recommendation to the Administrator," June 19, 1963, Regional Hospital Corporation folder, box 5, Records of the Office of Assistant Administrator for Area Operations, Mixed Subject and Programs Files, 1961–1963, ARA Records. Additional evidence of Roche's toughness in negotiations: Memo, Dr. E. D. Rosenfeld to Rev. Kenneth Neigh, Apr. 12, 1963, expandable folder titled Appalachian Regional Hospitals Miscellaneous Information, Appalachian Regional Hospitals File, Office of the Commissioner, Department of Finance, Commonwealth of Kentucky, Frankfort, Kentucky. Conference minutes, Apr. 14, 1965, 2:00 pm, folder 3, box 56, RC. Karl Klicka to Felix Joyner, Oct. 22, 1965, Appalachian Regional Hospitals Correspondence File, Office of the Commissioner, Department of Finance, Commonwealth of Kentucky, Department for Libraries and Archives, Frankfort, Kentucky. See also documents in expandable folder titled Appalachian Regional Hospitals Miscellaneous Information, and folder titled Appalachian Regional Hospitals Background Material, 1962–1963, Special Session 1963, both in Office of the Commissioner, Department of Finance, Commonwealth of Kentucky, Department for Libraries and Archives, Frankfort, Kentucky. Conference notes, July 23, 1963, folder 2, box 56; conference notes, Mar. 15, 1965, and Apr. 14, 1965, folder 3, box 56; Apr. 1, Apr. 14, June 8, and June 18, 1965, spiral notebook, box 46, RC. Annual reports of ARA, 1963 and 1964, box 13, Publications and Reports Relating to Development, Records of the Office of Area Development, ARA Records.

79 John Whisman to Gordon Reckord, Feb. 15, 1963, Miners Memorial Hospitals file, box 9, Subject Files, 1961–1965, Records of the Office of the Administrator, ARA Records.

80 Marjorie Kester to William Batt, Williams, and Metz, Sept. 24, 1963; "A Splendid Act of Christian Mercy," Aug. 1, 1963, *Presbyterian Life*, clipping, Miners Memorial Hospitals file, box 9, Subject Files, 1961–1965, Records of the Office of the Administrator, ARA Records.

81 Jennifer Klein, *For All These Rights: Business, Labor, and the Shaping of America's Public-Private Welfare State* (Princeton, NJ, 2003), 7, 15. In fact, historians have generally argued that one explanation for the paltriness of the welfare state in America has been the strength of competing private sector security schemes, especially health and retirement benefits provided by employers. Roche's work suggests that the reverse was true as well: private sector provision of Social Security benefits sometimes generated demand for more expansive public programs.

For current understandings of the public/private welfare regime, see for example, Jill Quadagno, *The Transformation of Old Age Security: Class and Politics in the American Welfare State* (Chicago, 1988), 2–3, 77, 171, 185–186; Beth Stevens, "Labor Unions, Employee Benefits, and the Privatization of the American Welfare State," *Journal of Policy History* 2 (1990): 232–260; Alan Derickson, "Health Security for All? Social Unionism and Universal Health Insurance, 1935–1958," *Journal of American History* 80 (March 1994): 1333–1356; Kevin Boyle, *The UAW and the Heyday of American Liberalism, 1945–1968* (Ithaca, NY, 1995); Marie Gottschalk, "Elusive Goal of Universal Health Care in the U.S.: Organized Labor and the Institutional Straight Jacket of the Private Welfare State," *Journal of Policy History* 11 (1999): 371–372; Nelson Lichtenstein, *State of the Union: A Century of American Labor* (Princeton, NJ, 2002), 117–126; Jacob S. Hacker, *The Divided Welfare State: The Battle over Public and Private Social Benefits in the United States* (New York, 2002), xiii.

CHAPTER 16   CHALLENGED AND REDEEMED BY THE NEW PROGRESSIVISM, 1960–1972

1 William E. Owens, author interview, Ellicott City, MD, May 26, 2005.

2 Nov. 27, 1964, and Dec. 26–31, 1964, spiral notebook, box 46, RC.

3 Roche to Read Lewis, May 11, 1962, and Feb. 10, 1965, RLP. For instance, Mar. 8, 1965; May 13, 1965; May 14, 1965; May 29, 1959; and June 20, 1958, spiral notebooks, box 46, RC. Correspondence re annual reports, folders 1 and 5, box 65, RC. Owens interview.

4 For instance, Jan. and Feb. 1965, Aug. 1965, spiral notebooks, box 46, RC.

5 Owens interview. For instance, Aug. 14, 1964; Aug.–Oct. 1964; and Feb. 24, 1965, spiral notebooks, box 46, RC. Will: May 7, 1965, spiral notebook, box 46, RC. Last Will and Testament of Josephine Roche, July 18, 1972, Montgomery County Register of Wills, Rockville, MD. Glasses: photos by Earl Dotter, 1972, in author's possession.

6 *Congressional Record*, 87th Congress, Second Session, Feb. 7, 1962, 2010–2015. Robyn Muncy, "Coal-Fired Reforms: Social Citizenship, Dissident Miners, and the Great Society," *Journal of American History* 96 (June 2009): 94–95.

7 Eye on Congress: Nov. 18, 1964; Nov. 20, 1964; Nov. 30, 1964; Dec. 1, 1964; Dec. 3, 1964; Dec. 16, 1964; Jan. 29, 1965; Feb. 3, 1965; May 18, 1965; and virtually every day of Oct. 1965, spiral notebooks, box 46, RC. Actuary: Conference minutes, Dec. 8, 1964, folder 3, box 56, RC.

8 Conference notes, Dec. 22, 1964, box 2, Administrative File, Director's File, FA. Jan. 12, 1965, spiral notebook, box 46, RC.

9 Dec. 22, 1964; Dec. 30–31, 1964; and Jan. 4, 1965, spiral notebooks, box 46, RC.

10 Sept. 2, 1965, spiral notebook, box 46; Fund, annual report, 1967, folder 3, box 52, RC.

11 Roche's speech, *Proceedings of the 45th Consecutive Constitutional Convention of the UMWA*, Denver, Colorado, Sept. 4–13, 1968, vol. I, 323–327, folder 1, box 51, RC.

12 "State of the Union," Jan. 9, 1964, *New York Times*, 1ff. Miners' plight: Muncy, "Coal-Fired Reforms," 93.

13 Innovations: Frances Fox Piven and Richard A. Cloward, "The Politics of the Great Society"; Edward Berkowitz, "Medicare: The Great Society's Enduring National Health Insurance Program"; and Hugh Graham, "The Great Society's Civil Rights Legacy," in *The Great Society and the High Tide of Liberalism*, ed. Sidney M. Milkis and Jerome M. Mileur (Boston, 2005), 253–269, 320–350, 365–386.

14 Lyndon B. Johnson, *Special Message to Congress*, Mar. 16, 1964, *Internet Modern History Sourcebook*, http://www.fordham.edu/halsall/mod/1964johnson-warpoverty .html, accessed Feb. 15, 2014. Johnson and New Deal: William E. Leuchtenburg, "Lyndon Johnson in the Shadow of Franklin Roosevelt," in Milkis and Mileur, eds., *Great Society and the High Tide of Liberalism*, 185–213. Milkis's introduction to the volume and Mileur's conclusion analyze continuity and change in the Great Society. Origins of Job Corps in New Deal: Eileen Boris, "Contested Rights: The Great Society between Home and Work," in Milkis and Mileur, eds., *Great Society and the High Tide of Liberalism*, 115–144, esp. 122.

15 Attachments to Opal Gooden, notes on meeting with VISTA Director Velma Linford, Nov. 24, 1964, box 29, Subject Files, Executive Medical Officer File, FA.

16 "Transcript of President's News Conference on Foreign and Domestic Matters," *New York Times*, Apr. 26, 1964, 64. Muncy, "Coal-Fired Reforms."

17 "Transcript of President's News Conference on Foreign and Domestic Matters," *New York Times*, Apr. 26, 1964, 64. Muncy, "Coal-Fired Reforms."

18 Leuchtenburg, "Lyndon Johnson in the Shadow of Franklin Roosevelt," in Milkis and Mileur, eds., *Great Society and the High Tide of Liberalism*, 185–213.

19 Lyndon B. Johnson, Remarks at the University of Michigan, May 22, 1964, *Public Papers of the Presidents of the United States*, Lyndon B. Johnson, book I (Washington, DC, 1963–1964), 704–707, in The American Presidency Project, University of California, Santa Barbara, http://www.presidency.ucsb.edu/ws/?pid=26262, accessed Feb. 15, 2014.

20 Underlined article: "Social Security Is 33 Years Old," *Washington Post*, Aug. 15, 1968, A3, folder 10, box 7, RC.

21 Arthur Altmeyer, "Social Security and the Human Touch," address to the Social Security Administration, Aug. 14, 1968, http://www.ssa.gov/history/altm7.html, accessed Feb. 5, 2014.

22 "State of the Union," Jan. 9, 1964, *New York Times*, 1ff. U.S. Department of Health, Education, and Welfare, *Medicare—Social Security Amendments of 1965* (Washington, DC, 1965), box 42, Subject Files, Executive Medical Officer File, FA.

23 U.S. Department of Health, Education and Welfare, *Medicare—Social Security Amendments of 1965* (Washington, DC, 1965), box 42, Subject Files, Executive Medical Officer, FA.

24 Wilbur Cohen to Roche, Mar. 13, 1968, folder 10, box 7, RC.

25 Ben Cherrington to Roche, Sept. 9, 1966, folder 1, box 65, RC.

26 Senator Wayne Morse, "Tribute to Josephine Roche," *Congressional Record—Senate—*Oct. 13, 1965, 25884–25885, Josephine Roche File, Revolving File, SSA.

27 Wilbur Cohen, Acting Secretary of HEW to Roche, Mar. 13, 1968, folder 10, box 7, RC.

28 June 3–7, 1965, spiral notebook, box 46, RC.

29 Memo to File, Mar. 23, 1964, Josephine Roche File, Revolving File, SSA.

30 Roche to Alice Hamilton, Nov. 23, 1964, folder 14, box 3, RC.

31 Roche to Read Lewis, Jan. 1956, RLP.

32 Roche to Read Lewis, May 11, 1962; Feb. 10, 1965, RLP.

33 Mrs. Richard Borden (Radcliffe) to Roche, Feb. 1955, folder 1, box 6; James E. O'Neill (FDRL) to Roche, Feb. 22, 1971, folder 10, box 7, RC.

34 Roche speech, *Proceedings of the 45th Consecutive Constitutional Convention of the UMWA*, Denver, Colorado, Sept. 4–13, 1968, vol. I, 323–327, folder 1, box 51, RC.

35 July 29, 1965; July 30, 1965; Aug. 4, 17, and 18, 1965, spiral notebooks, box 46, RC.

36 Aug. 17, 1965; Sept. 2, 1965; Sept. 10, 1965; Nov. 3, 1965; Nov. 8–9, 1965, spiral notebooks, box 46, RC. Conference notes, Oct. 20, 1965, and Apr. 12, 1966, folder 3, box 56, RC. Roche to UMWA District and Local Union Officers, June 21, 1966; Roche to Widows Over 65, Dec. 20, 1965; and loads of correspondence in box 2, Administrative File, Director's File, FA.

37 Oct. 22, 1965; Nov. 9, 1965; and Nov. 29, 1965, spiral notebooks, box 46, RC.

38 Resolution 347 from Local Union 9111, Waltonville, Illinois, *Proceedings of the 44th Consecutive Constitutional Convention of the UMWA*, Bal Harbour, FL, Sept. 1–11, 1964, vol. II, 62, 80–81, 97, folder 3, box 50, RC.

39 *Proceedings of the 44th Consecutive Constitutional Convention of the UMWA*, Bal Harbour, FL, Sept. 1–11, 1964, vol. II, 81, folder 3, box 50; Roche's speech, *Proceedings of the 45th Consecutive Constitutional Convention of the UMWA*, Denver, CO, Sept. 4–13, 1968, vol. I, 327, folder 1, box 51, RC.

40 *Proceedings of the 44th Consecutive Constitutional Convention of the UMWA*, Bal Harbour, FL, Sept. 1–11, 1964, vol. I, 240–241, folder 3, box 50, RC.

41 Nov. 29, 1965, spiral notebook, box 46, RC.

42 Fund, annual report, 1967, folder 3, box 52, RC.

43 Senate Subcommittee Hearing, Mar. 17, 1970, "Stenographic Transcript of Hearings before Subcommittee on Labor, Committee on Labor and Public Welfare," folder 8, box 58, RC.

44 Robert C. Maynard, "Miners' Suit Says UMW Misuses Fund," *Washington Post*, Aug. 5, 1969, A1.

45 "New Riots Catch Police Short," *Washington Post*, Apr. 6, 1968, A14; Ward Just, "The City Besieged: A Study in Ironies and Contrasts," *Washington Post*, A14; Willard Clopton, "Curfew Imposed as Roving Bands Plunder and Burn," *Washington Post*, Apr. 6, 1968, A1ff; Robert Asher and Martin Weil, "City's Diary of Violence Goes on without Let Up," *Washington Post*, Apr. 7, 1968, A10; Hobart Rowan and S. Oliver Goodman, "Stores, Hotels Reel from Riot Impact," *Washington Post*, Apr. 7, 1968, D1.

46 Joseph Alsop, "Officials Are Split on Need for Federal Riot Legislation," *Washington Post*, Jan. 12, 1968, A17.

47 Owens interview.

48 L. F. Cornwell to Costigan, July 8, 1914, folder 2, box 7, ECP.

49 Ben A. Franklin, "Hope Is Dim for 78 Caught in Mine Fire," *New York Times*, Nov. 22, 1968, 1ff; Robert Levey, "Hope Slim for 78 Trapped Miners," *Washington Post*, Nov. 21, 1968, A1; Nick von Hoffman, "TV: Pressures and Possibilities," *Washington Post*, Mar. 31, 1969, B1.

50 Trevor Armbrister, *Act of Vengeance: The Yablonski Murders and Their Solution* (New York, 1975), 35–62; Brit Hume, *Death and the Mines: Rebellion and Murder in the United Mine Workers* (New York, 1971), 3–17; Daniel Edelman, author interview,

Washington, DC, Sept. 5, 2008; Richard P. Mulcahy, *A Social Contract for the Coal Fields: The Rise and Fall of the United Mine Workers of America Welfare and Retirement Fund* (Knoxville, TN, 2000), 148–149.

51 Ben A. Franklin, "New Drive Begun for Coal Mine Safety Reform," *New York Times*, Nov. 26, 1968, 32.

52 Ben A. Franklin, "Mine Safety Failures Conceded at Capital Parley on Hazards," *New York Times*, Dec. 13, 1968, 24.

53 Dr. Lorin Kerr's testimony at *Coal Mine Health and Safety: Hearings . . . on H.R. 4047*, the House of Representatives' General Subcommittee on Labor, 91st Congress, 1st Session (Washington, DC, 1969), 309–328.

54 Barbara Ellen Smith, *Digging Our Own Graves: Coal Miners and the Struggle over Black Lung Disease* (Philadelphia, 1987), 28–29, 101–135.

55 Daniel M. Fox and Judith F. Stone, "Black Lung: Miners' Militancy and Medical Uncertainty, 1968–1982," *Bulletin of the History of Medicine* 54 (1980): 43–63, esp. 56.

56 Armbrister, *Act of Vengeance*, 4, 68–69.

57 Hume, *Death and the Mines*, 51.

58 Ben A. Franklin, "Hope Is Dim for 78 Caught in Mine Fire," *New York Times*, Nov. 22, 1968, 1ff, quotation at 50.

59 Fox and Stone, "Black Lung," 53; Armbrister, *Act of Vengeance*, 49; Mulcahy, *A Social Contract for the Coal Fields*, 148.

60 Fund, annual report, 1968, folder 3, box 52, RC.

61 Hank Burchard, "Miners Rally to Promote Black Lung Legislation," *Washington Post*, Jan. 27, 1969, C1; Hank Burchard, "Who Speaks for U.S. Coal Miners?" *Washington Post*, Mar. 2, 1969, 2; Leonard Downie Jr., "Loans to Coal Mine Owners by UMW Bank Hit by Nader," *Washington Post*, Mar. 21, 1969, A2; "Nader Charges Miners' Union with Nepotism and Corruption," *New York Times*, Apr. 28, 1969, 23. Articles on Nader, folder 4, box 57, RC.

62 Use of OEO monies: Fox and Stone, "Black Lung," 52–53. VISTA: "All Mining Ceases in Raleigh County," *Beckley Post Herald*, July 23, 1970, folder 2, box 61, RC. Earl Dotter, author interview, Silver Spring, MD, June 23, 2006. Hume, *Death and the Mines*, 104–106.

63 "Union Fund Inquiry Urged," *New York Times*, Apr. 7, 1969, 10.

64 Thomas W. Lippman, "Union Told It Can't Withhold Pension for Nonunion Work," *Washington Post*, Apr. 25, 1969, C4. "Nader Charges Miners' Union with Nepotism and Corruption," *New York Times*, Apr. 28, 1969, 23.

65 Interoffice correspondence, Harold Ward to Miss Roche, Apr. 11, 1969, folder 4, box 57, RC.

66 Roche, "A Statement by the United Mine Workers of America Welfare and Retirement Fund," Apr. 18, 1969, folder 4, box 57, RC.

67 *Proceedings of the 44th Consecutive Constitutional Convention of the UMWA*, Bal Harbour, FL, Sept. 1–11, 1964, vol. II, 60, 63, file 3, box 50, RC.

68 Roche, "A Statement by the United Mine Workers of America Welfare and Retirement Fund," Apr. 18, 1969, folder 4, box 57, RC.

69 Frank C. Porter, "UMW Aide to Run against His Chief," *Washington Post*, May 30, 1969, A12. Ben A. Franklin, "Board Member Opposes Boyle for Presidency of Mine Union," *New York Times*, May 30, 1969, 9.

70 Trevor Armbrister, "Coal-Black Shame of the UMW," *Reader's Digest*, Oct. 1970, 135–140.

71 Armbrister, *Act of Vengeance*, 74.

72 "John L. Lewis Dies," *New York Times*, June 12, 1969, 1.

73 See, for instance, documents in folder 2, box 63, RC.

74 "Stenographic Transcript of Hearing before the Subcommittee on Labor of the Committee on Labor and Public Welfare," United States Senate, vol. 3, UMW Election, Washington, DC, Mar. 17, 1970, folder 8, box 58, RC.

75 John Owens to Roche, June 23, 1969, box 8, Board of Trustees Correspondence, Director's File, FA.

76 Stenographic transcript, Senate Subcommittee Hearing, Mar. 17, 1970, folder 8, box 58, RC.

77 Press release, June 24, 1969, box 8, Board of Trustees Correspondence, Director's File, FA.

78 Stenographic transcript, Senate Subcommittee Hearing, Mar. 17, 1970, folder 8, box 58, RC.

79 Mulcahy, *A Social Contract for the Coal Fields*, 154–157; Frank C. Porter, "Ex-Management Aide of UMW Fund Accused: Minutes Are Read," *Washington Post*, Mar. 21, 1970, A2.

80 Stenographic transcript, Senate Subcommittee Hearing, Mar. 17, 1970, folder 8, box 58, RC.

81 See, for instance, W. A. Boyle to Roche, Oct. 24, 1969; Roche to Boyle, Oct. 1969; Boyle to Roche, Oct. 10, 1969; Boyle to Roche, July 29, 1970, and Nov. 25, 1970, box 8, Board of Trustees Correspondence, Director's File, FA.

82 Hume, *Death and the Mines*, 236–241.

83 Armbrister, *Act of Vengeance*, esp. 180, 186–189, 193, 210, 234.

84 Ethel Altmeyer to Roche, Jan. 1, 1970, folder 10, box 7, RC.

85 Robert C. Maynard, "Miners' Suit Says UMW Misuses Fund," *Washington Post*, Aug. 5, 1969, A1ff.

86 Hume, *Death and the Mines*, 250; Armbrister, *Act of Vengeance*, 201.

87 Armbrister, *Act of Vengeance*, 209–212, 233, 239, 241, 251.

88 See photo accompanying Frank C. Porter, "Veteran UMW Trustee Denies Giving Boyle Proxy," *Washington Post*, Mar. 18, 1970, A2.

89 Cane: E-mail message, Clarice Feldman to Robyn Muncy, Feb. 28, 2011, in author's possession.

90 Stenographic transcript, Senate Subcommittee Hearing, Mar. 17, 1970, folder 8, box 58, RC.

91 Ibid.

92 Mulcahy, *A Social Contract for the Coal Fields*, 157. Clippings in folder 1, box 58, and letters in folder 6, box 63, RC.

93 "Denver's Dynamic Josephine Roche Takes Treasury Post," *Washington Post*, Dec. 1934, folder 6, box 35, RC.

94 "Ask Arnold Miller," *UMW Journal*, Aug. 1, 1972, 20, in Earl Dotter's private collection of union newspapers, Silver Spring, MD.

95 Kenneth Yablonski to Welly Hopkins, Oct. 13, 1970; Roche to Kenneth Yablonski, Oct. 20, 1970; Roche to Boyle and C. W. Davis, Oct. 20, 1970, box 8, Board of Trustees Correspondence, Director's File, FA.

96 See, for instance, "All Mining Ceases in Raleigh County," *Beckley Post Herald*, July 23, 1970, and other articles underlined by Roche in folder 2, box 61, RC. Roger Petterson, "Pensioners Close 16 Mines in Dispute with UMW Union," *Washington Post*, July 14, 1970, A4; "Wildcat Coal Strike Idles 150 Mines," *Washington Post*, July 23, 1970, 9; "UMW Rebellion Erupts in Wildcat Strikes," *Washington Post*, Aug. 10, 1970, A3.

97 "Pensioners Group Sets Sunday Meet," *Dominion News*, Sept. 5, 1970, folder 5, box 61, RC. "UMW Rebellion Erupts in Wildcat Strikes," *Washington Post*, Aug. 10, 1970, A3.

98 Trevor Armbrister to Roche, June 16, 1970, folder 10, box 61, RC.

99 Trevor Armbrister, "Coal-Black Shame of the UMW," *Reader's Digest*, Oct. 1970, 135–140. Roche named as source of this quotation: "Retired Miners and Widows Win Benefits They Earned," *Miner's Voice*, Winter 1973, 4, in Earl Dotter's private collection of union newspapers, Silver Spring, MD.

100 Available at http://www.childrensdefense.org/about-us/our-history/washington -research-project.html, accessed Mar. 7, 2011. "The New Public Interest Lawyers," *Yale Law Journal* 79 (May 1970): 1069–1152. The legal team moved from the Washington Research Project to Arnold and Porter before the case went to court. E-mail message, Ruth Greenspan Bell to Robyn Muncy, Dec. 1, 2012, in author's possession.

101 See, for instance, "Current Developments Section," clipping, Feb. 5, 1971, folder 4, box 59, and Judge Gerhard Gesell, "Memorandum Opinion," Apr. 28, 1971, folder 6, box 59, RC.

102 Quotation is from trial transcript, 957–960, quoted in Judge Gerhard Gesell, "Memorandum Opinion," Apr. 28, 1971, folder 6, box 59, RC.

103 Quoted in Judge Gesell's "Memorandum Opinion," Apr. 28, 1971, folder 6, box 59, RC.

104 George Lardner Jr., "UMW Fund Chief Criticizes Hoarding," *Washington Post*, Feb. 9, 1971, A3; Judge Gerhard Gesell, "Memorandum Opinion," Apr. 28, 1971, folder 6, box 59, RC.

105 Gesell, "Memorandum Opinion," Apr. 28, 1971, folder 6, box 59, RC.

106 Dec. 24, 1958; Dec. 29–31, 1958, spiral notebooks, box 46, RC. Mulcahy, *A Social Contract for the Coal Fields*, 158–159; Gesell, "Memorandum Opinion," Apr. 28, 1971, folder 6, box 59, RC.

107 Gesell, "Memorandum Opinion," Apr. 28, 1971, folder 6, box 59, RC.

108 Investments: box 8, Board of Trustees Correspondence, Director's File, FA.

109 Gesell, "Memorandum Opinion," Apr. 28, 1971, folder 6, box 59, RC.

110 Taft quotation in Gesell, "Memorandum Opinion," Apr. 28, 1971, folder 6, box 59, RC.

111 Gesell, "Memorandum Opinion," Apr. 28, 1971, folder 6, box 59, RC.

112 For instance, Roche to Boyle and Davis, June 9, 1971, box 8, Board of Trustees Correspondence, Director's File, FA.

113 Memo to All Employees of the UMWA Welfare and Retirement Fund from Edward Carey and C. W. Davis, July 15, 1971, box 8, Board of Trustees Correspondence, Director's File, FA.

114 Armbrister, *Act of Vengeance*, 274–327.

115 Files bulging with articles are in boxes 60 and 61, RC.

116 Mulcahy, *A Social Contract for the Coal Fields*, 164.

117 Roche, public statement, in "Close Associate of John L. Lewis Endorses Miller-Trbovich-Patrick," *UMW Journal*, Nov. 15, 1972, 28.

118 Roche's statement was sent out by the AP wire. "Josephine Roche Is Supporting Miller," *Harlan Daily Enterprise*, Nov. 22, 1972, and *Baltimore Sun*, Nov. 25, 1972, A18. Washington reporters: Nicholas von Hoffman, "One More Battle," *Washington Post*, Nov. 24, 1972, B1. This piece was reprinted in other newspapers. See, for instance, *Toledo Blade*, Nov. 25, 1972, 9, and *Chicago Tribune*, Nov. 27, 1972, 22.

119 Michelle Clark, Interview with Josephine Roche, *CBS Morning News*, Dec. 1, 1972, WTOP TV, Washington, DC, folder 14, box 88, Miners for Democracy Records, Walter P. Reuther Labor Library, Wayne State University, Detroit, MI.

120 Earl Dotter, telephone interview with author, April 26, 2006.

121 Photograph taken by Earl Dotter in Nov. 1972 and published with "Retired Miners and Widows Win Benefits They Earned," *Miner's Voice*, Winter 1973, 4.

122 E-mail message, Clarice Feldman to Robyn Muncy, Feb. 25, 2011, in author's possession.

123 Stenographic transcript, Senate Subcommittee Hearing, Mar. 17, 1970, folder 8, box 58, RC. Nicholas von Hoffman, "One More Battle," *Washington Post*, Nov. 24, 1972, B1.

124 Clark, Interview with Josephine Roche, Dec. 1, 1972, Miners for Democracy Records, Walter P. Reuther Labor Library, Wayne State University, Detroit, MI.

125 Ibid.

CHAPTER 17   ONLY TEN MINUTES LEFT? EPILOGUE AND ASSESSMENT

1 Nicholas von Hoffman, "One More Battle," *Washington Post*, Nov. 24, 1972, B1.

2 Trevor Armbrister, *Act of Vengeance: The Yablonski Murders and Their Solution* (New York, 1975), 333–334. "IEB Report," *UMW Journal*, Feb. 1, 1973, 2–9, in Earl Dotter's private collection of union newspapers, Silver Spring, MD. Richard P. Mulcahy, *A Social Contract for the Coal Fields: The Rise and Fall of the United Mine Workers of America Welfare and Retirement Fund* (Knoxville, TN, 2000), 166.

3 Mulcahy, *A Social Contract for the Coal Fields*, 166–181. Ivana Krajcinovic, *From Company Doctors to Managed Care: The United Mine Workers' Noble Experiment* (Ithaca, NY, 1997), 166–175.

4 Mulcahy, *A Social Contract for the Coal Fields*, 166–181; Krajcinovic, *From Company Doctors to Managed Care*, 166–175.

5 Statistics: http://www.bls.gov/news.release/union2.nr0.htm, accessed Feb. 15, 2014. Judith Stein, *Pivotal Decade: How the United States Traded Factories for Finance in the Seventies* (New Haven, CT, 2010); Jefferson Cowie, *Stayin' Alive: The 1970s and the Last Days of the Working Class* (New York, 2010); Nelson Lichtenstein and Elizabeth Tandy Shermer, eds., *The Right and Labor in America: Politics, Ideology, and Imagination* (Philadelphia, 2012).

6 William Owens, interview with author, Ellicott City, MD, May 26, 2005. Certificate of Death, Josephine Roche, State of Maryland, Maryland State Archives, Annapolis.

7 See, for instance, Werner Bamberger, "Josephine Roche Dead at 89: Treasury and U.M.W. Official," *New York Times*, July 31, 1976, VAO; Jean R. Hailey, "Josephine Roche Dies: Miners' Advocate," *Washington Post*, July 31, 1976, E4.

8 She was not alone in this. Daniel Horowitz, *Betty Friedan and the Making of* The Feminine Mystique: *The American Left, the Cold War, and Modern Feminism* (Amherst, MA, 1998); Landon R. Y. Storrs, *The Second Red Scare and the Unmaking of the New Deal Left* (Princeton, NJ, 2013).

9 Bruce Lambert, "Judge Gerhard Gesell Dies at 82," *New York Times*, Feb. 21, 1993, http://www.nytimes.com/1993/02/21/us/judge-gerhard-gesell-dies-at-82-oversaw-big-cases.html, accessed Feb. 15, 2014.

10 Gesell, "Memorandum Opinion," Apr. 28, 1971, folder 6, box 59, RC.

11 "UMW Fund Chief Criticizes Hoarding," *Washington Post*, Feb. 9, 1971, A3.

12 Decision of Judge Gerhard Gesell in *Blankenship v. Boyle*, Apr. 28, 1971, 17, http://www.lexisnexis.com.proxy-um.researchport.umd.edu/hottopics/lnacademic/?, accessed Feb. 15, 2014.

13 Joseph E. Finley, *The Corrupt Kingdom: The Rise and Fall of the United Mine Workers* (New York, 1972), 36, 162–163, 188, 198, 219. Brit Hume, *Death and the Mines: Rebellion and Murder in the United Mine Workers* (New York, 1971), 35. For these quotations, I thank Angela Cavalucci, my research assistant at the Woodrow Wilson International Center for Scholars in 2007–2008. Such important and deeply valuable later works as Melvyn Dubofsky and Warren Van Tine, *John L. Lewis: A Biography* (New York, 1977) relied on these works and inadvertently perpetuated the version of Roche as a rubberstamp of Lewis's.

14   The history of the FLIS is documented in IRSA.

15   Available at http://www.arh.org, accessed July 5, 2013.

16   Bonnie Lefkowitz, *Community Health Centers: A Movement and the People Who Made It Happen* (New Brunswick, NJ, 2007). Robert Politzer, Ashley Schempf, Barbara Starfield, and Shi Leiyu, "The Future Role of Health Centers in Improving National Health," *Journal of Public Health Policy* 24 (2003): 296–306; Craig Tanio, "Innovations at Miami Practice Show Promise for Treating High-Risk Medicare Patients," *Health Affairs* 32 (June 2013): 1078–1082. Elisabeth Rosenthal, "Apprehensive, Many Doctors Shift to Jobs With Salaries," *New York Times*, Feb. 14, 2014, A14.

17   Gerald R. Armstrong, telephone interview with author, Sept. 12, 2008. Daniel Edelman, interview with author, Washington, DC, Sept. 5, 2008.

18   Available at http://www.bouldercounty.org/family/housing/pages/aspinwall.aspx and http://www.openstreetmap.org/browse/way/143178371/history, accessed July 5, 2013.

19   Roche, "Grace Abbott," reprinted from the *Welfare Bulletin*, Feb. 1940, folder 2, box 1, RC.

SELECT PRIMARY SOURCES

**ARTHUR AND ELIZABETH SCHLESINGER LIBRARY
ON THE HISTORY OF WOMEN IN AMERICA**
RADCLIFFE INSTITUTE FOR ADVANCED STUDY
HARVARD UNIVERSITY, CAMBRIDGE, MASSACHUSETTS

League of Women Shoppers Records
Martha May Eliot Papers
Mary Anderson Papers
Mary Elizabeth Drier Papers
Mary Elizabeth Switzer Papers
Mary Simkhovitch Papers

AURARIA LIBRARY
DENVER, COLORADO

John A. Carroll Papers

BANCROFT LIBRARY
UNIVERSITY OF CALIFORNIA AT BERKELEY

Sidney Coe Howard Papers

COMMONWEALTH OF KENTUCKY
DEPARTMENT FOR LIBRARIES AND ARCHIVES, FRANKFORT, KENTUCKY

Appalachian Regional Hospitals File, Office of the Commissioner, Department of
Finance Records

DENVER PUBLIC LIBRARY
WESTERN HISTORY COLLECTION, DENVER, COLORADO

Rocky Mountain Fuel Collection

FRANKLIN D. ROOSEVELT PRESIDENTIAL LIBRARY
HYDE PARK, NEW YORK

Anna Eleanor Roosevelt Papers
Aubrey Williams Papers
Franklin Delano Roosevelt Papers
Henry Morgenthau Jr. Diaries
Henry Morgenthau Jr. Papers
Lorena Hickok Papers
Lowell Mellett Papers
Mary Dewson Papers
Papers of the Women's Division of the National Democratic Committee
Records of the Interdepartmental Committee to Coordinate Health and Welfare Activities

HOOVER INSTITUTION
LIBRARY AND ARCHIVES, STANFORD UNIVERSITY
STANFORD, CALIFORNIA

Commission for Relief in Belgium (1914–1930) Records

HOUGHTON LIBRARY
HARVARD UNIVERSITY, CAMBRIDGE, MASSACHUSETTS

Theodore Roosevelt Collection—Progressive Party Papers

HUNTINGTON LIBRARY
SAN MARINO, CALIFORNIA

Sonya Levien Papers

IMMIGRATION HISTORY RESEARCH CENTER
UNIVERSITY OF MINNESOTA, MINNEAPOLIS

Records of the Immigration and Refugee Services of America

LIBRARY OF CONGRESS
WASHINGTON, DC

Benjamin Barr Lindsey Papers
Harold Ickes Papers
National Association for the Advancement of Colored People Collection
Records of the National Consumers' League
Samuel Gompers Letterbooks

NATIONAL ARCHIVES AND RECORDS ADMINISTRATION
BALTIMORE, MARYLAND

Arthur Altmeyer Collection, State Historical Society of Wisconsin, copies in Social Security Administration

Records of the Social Security Administration, RG 47
   Records of the Committee on Economic Security
   Roche File, Revolving File

NATIONAL ARCHIVES AND RECORDS ADMINISTRATION
COLLEGE PARK, MARYLAND

Records of the Area Redevelopment Administration, RG 378
Records of the Children's Bureau, RG 102
Records of the Committee on Public Information, RG 63
Records of the Department of the Treasury; Central Files of the Office of the Secretary, Assistant Secretaries, RG 56
Records of the National Reconstruction Finance Corporation, RG 234
Records of the National Recovery Administration, RG 9
Records of the Office of Personnel Management, RG 478

NEW YORK ACADEMY OF MEDICINE LIBRARY
NEW YORK

Michael Davis Collection

NORLIN LIBRARY
ARCHIVES, UNIVERSITY OF COLORADO, BOULDER
Colorado Labor Advocate
Colorado State Federation of Labor Papers
Edward P. Costigan Papers
Josephine Aspinwall Roche Collection
Records of the Rocky Mountain Fuel Company

PENNSYLVANIA STATE UNIVERSITY LIBRARIES
HISTORICAL COLLECTIONS AND LABOR ARCHIVES, STATE COLLEGE

United Mine Workers of America Archives

PRIVATE COLLECTION

Read Lewis Papers

SMITH COLLEGE LIBRARIES
SOPHIA SMITH COLLECTION, SMITH COLLEGE, NORTHAMPTON, MASSACHUSETTS

Mary van Kleeck Papers

STERLING MEMORIAL LIBRARY
MANUSCRIPTS AND ARCHIVES, YALE UNIVERSITY, NEW HAVEN, CONNECTICUT

Isidore S. Falk Papers
Robert Kaplan Papers

THOMPSON LIBRARY
SPECIAL COLLECTIONS, VASSAR COLLEGE, POUGHKEEPSIE, NEW YORK

Biographical Files
Vassar College Catalogs
Vassarion
Vassar Miscellany

VASSAR COLLEGE ALUMNAE OFFICE
POUGHKEEPSIE, NEW YORK

Josephine Roche File

WALTER P. REUTHER LABOR LIBRARY
WAYNE STATE UNIVERSITY, DETROIT, MICHIGAN

Miners for Democracy Records

WEST VIRGINIA UNIVERSITY LIBRARIES
WEST VIRGINIA AND REGIONAL HISTORY COLLECTION
WEST VIRGINIA UNIVERSITY, MORGANTOWN

United Mine Workers of America Health and Retirement Fund Archives

INDEX